INTO U
D0269018

Warfare and the Third World

Warfare and the Third World

Robert E. Harkavy and Stephanie G. Neuman

palgrave

WARFARE AND THE THIRD WORLD

Copyright © Robert E. Harkavy and Stephanie G. Neuman, 2001. All rights reserved. No part of this book may be used or reproduced in any manner what-soever without written permission except in the case of brief quotations embodied in critical articles or reviews.

First published 2001 by
PALGRAVE™
175 Fifth Avenue, New York, NY 10010 and
Houndmills, Basingstoke, Hampshire, England RG21 6XS.
Companies and representatives throughout the world.

Palgrave is the new global publishing imprint of St. Martin's Press LLC Scholarly and Reference Division and Palgrave Publishers Ltd (formerly Macmillan Press Ltd).

ISBN 0-312-24009-0 (cloth)
ISBN 0-312-24012-0 (paper)

Design by Westchester Book Composition, Danbury, CT 06810 USA

First Edition: September 2001
10 9 8 7 6 5 4 3 2 1

Printed in the United States of America.

CONTENTS

ACKNOWLEDGMENTS

The authors are indebted to a number of institutions and people without whom this book could not have been written. We cannot possibly thank individually all our colleagues and students who contributed to it. All we can do here is identify and thank those most closely involved.

This book has been a long time in the making. Both authors acknowledge with gratitude the generous support of the U.S. Institute of Peace and the Bradley Foundation. We are especially grateful to our then program officer at Bradley, Hillel Fradkin, for his enduring confidence that this book would be completed. Robert Harkavy also received research grants in connection with sabbatical leave years from the Alexander von Humboldt Foundation in Germany and the Earhart Foundation. During that time he received extensive administrative support from the Institute of Political Science, Christian-Albrechts-University, Kiel, Germany, directed by the late Professor Werner Kaltefleiter. Additional administrative support was granted to Robert Harkavy by Penn State University's Institute for Policy Research and Evaluation (IPRE) (director, Professor Irwin Feller) and its Department of Political Science.

The bulk of the manuscript was typed by Tammi Aumiller, who performed at her usual high level of organization and efficiency. Additional secretarial assistance was provided by Michelle Aungst and Angela Narehood of Penn State's IPRE. A number of Penn State undergraduates, too numerous to name individually, contributed research assistance over a number of years, for extra credits.

Stephanie Neuman wishes to acknowledge her debt to the Institute of War and Peace Studies, Columbia University, which provided the rich environment and efficient administrative support that made the writing of this book possible. Over the years a number of graduate and undergraduate students assisted her in various associated research tasks. Deserving of special mention are: Christopher Sandersfeld, Marius Hentea, and Sulakshini Fernando, all of whom struggled to create useful databases from incomplete, often incoherent data; Tim Liston, who somehow managed to keep her on schedule during hectic research trips; and Heather Kulp, who tirelessly carried out the detailed repairs needed to ready the manuscript for publication. Boris Nevelev, too, then a researcher at the Stockholm International Peace Research Institute (SIPRI), voluntarily and generously took time away from his own work to photocopy material collected from the SIPRI files. The willingness of these young colleagues to help, their good cheer, enthusiasm, and intelligence made their collaboration on this project a real pleasure.

Stephanie Neuman's personal debts extend also to those colleagues who graciously consented to read parts of the manuscript before it went to print. Margaretha Sollenberg, Uppsala Conflict Data Project in Sweden, kindly offered clarification and suggestions regarding the war data in this book. Daniel Gallik, Bureau of Verification and Compliance, U.S. Department of State, patiently helped us to better understand published arms transfer data. A special thanks, too, to Dr. David Gold, Rutgers University; Jack Snyder, Columbia University; and Major Isaiah Wilson, United States Military Academy, for their useful comments and suggestions. It is difficult to find the right words to thank all these busy people for the gift of their time.

Finally, we wish to thank our editor, Karen Wolny, for her encouragement and flexibility, qualities not always found in an editor. We were fortunate to benefit from her good editorial judgment and guidance.

We are very grateful for all the assistance we received. Needless to say, all who helped did not necessarily agree with everything in this book. We alone take responsibility for what we have written.

LIST OF ACRONYMS

ACDA	Arms Control and Disarmament Agency
AFV	armored fighting vehicles
APC	armored personnel carrier
ASW	anti-submarine warfare
ATGM	anti-tank guided missile
ATGW	anti-tank guided weapon
AWACS	airborne warning and control system
CENTO	Central Treaty Organization
CINC	commander in chief
CINCPAC	commander in chief, Pacific
COIN	counterinsurgency
CORDS	civil operations and revolutionary development support
COW	Correlates of War Project
CSIS	Center for Strategic and International Studies
DTAP	Democracy Transition Assistance Program
DSP	Defense Support Program
ECOMOG	ECOWAS Monitoring Group
ECOWAS	Economic Community of West African States
EO	Executive Outcomes
EOKA	National Organization of Cypriot Fighters
EU	European Union
FBS	forward-based systems
FLIR	forward-looking infrared
FLOT	forward line of troops
GLCM	ground launch cruise missile
GPS	global positioning systems
GWAPS	Gulf War Air Power Survey
HOT	high-subsonic optically teleguided
IAF	Israeli air force
ICRC	International Committee of the Red Cross
IDF	Israeli Defense Force
IFF	identification friend or foe
IGO	intergovernmental organization

IISS	International Institute for Strategic Studies
IPRE	Institute for Policy Research and Evaluation
IR	international relations
ISTAR	intelligence, surveillance, target acquisition and reconnaissance
LANTIRN	low altitude navigation and targeting infrared for night
LDC	less developed countries
LIC	low-intensity conflict
LRMP	Long Range Management Program
MACV	Military Assistance Command, Vietnam
MAD	mutually assured destruction
MFN	most favored nation
MIC	medium-intensity conflict
MILEX	military expenditure
MORH	Ministry of Defense, Croatia (Ministarstvo obrane Republike Hrvatske)
MPRI	Military Professional Resources, Inc.
MTR	military-technical revolution
NCO	non-commissioned officer
NGO	nongovernmental organization
OMG	operational maneuver group
OPEC	Organization of Petroleum Exporting Countries
PGM	precision-guided munition
PLA	People's Liberation Army
PMC	private military company
PSYOP	psychological operations
R & D	research and development
RMA	revolution in military affairs
RPG	rocket-propelled grenade
RPV	remotely piloted vehicle
SAM	surface to air missile
SAS	Special Air Service
SBS	Special Boat Service
SEALS	Sea, Air, Land Forces
SEATO	Southeast Asia Treaty Organization
SES	socioeconomic status
SIPRI	Stockholm International Peace Research Institute
TEL	transporter-erector-launcher
TOW	tube launched, optically tracked, wire guided missile
UNHCR	UN High Commissioner for Refugees
UNOSOM	United Nations Operations in Somalia
UNPROFOR	UN Protection Forces
UNSC	UN Security Council
UNTAC	United Nations Transitional Authority in Cambodia
WEU	Western European Union
WMD	weapons of mass destruction
WMEAT	World Military Expenditures and Arms Transfers

INTRODUCTION

One of the curiosities associated with modern scholarship on war is the yawning gap between what has come to be known as "conflict studies," a field dominated largely by international relations specialists in political science departments, and military history. The practitioners of these two fields, both devoted to the study of war, work in vastly separate worlds. Most political scientists in this area know little military history, nor much about military tactics and weapons, all the more so in the case of younger scholars, most of whom have never served in the armed forces. Military historians, on the other hand, seldom interest themselves in the theoretical aspects of "conflict studies," now largely given over to quantitative methods and formal modeling.

To some extent, this interdisciplinary chasm results from the fact that political scientists and historians in this field tend to focus on different aspects of war. It may be argued that the study of war breaks down into four discrete subject areas: the causes of war, the patterns of war, the conduct of war, and the remedies for war. Under "causes," there is the prolific theoretical and quantitative literature devoted to multivariate analysis involving such independent variables as polarity, polarization, and economic growth rates, as well as the more discursive albeit conceptual work of scholars such as Van Evera and Blainey. Regarding patterns, the Stockholm International Peace Research Institute (SIPRI), the Correlates of War (COW) Project, and others have dwelled on basic methodological questions and statistical trends pertaining to the frequency of wars, their regional breakdowns, casualties, and duration, leading some to draw an analogy with the medical field of epidemiology. Under the heading of "remedies" fall broad fields such as international organization, international law, arms control and disarmament, mediation and arbitration, peacekeeping and peacemaking, and conflict resolution, each of which may be subjected to varying degrees of theorizing and quantification.

Rarely if ever do political scientists venture into the area of the conduct of wars, i.e., how the wars are fought, with what weapons and tactics, and with what result in terms of who, militarily speaking, wins or loses. That has long been the domain of military historians, and remains so even in the current era in which many such historians have strained to remove themselves from the traditional focus on war-fighting in the direction of war-related social history.

What that means is that the contemporary study of the conduct of war is left without much of a conceptual base, much less any serious theory and/or quantification. The sole exception here is the developing tendency, within the relevant U.S. government agencies such as the Pentagon and the service-related war colleges, to utilize a "levels of analysis" format which, while subject to variations, is centered on the spectrum from grand strategy to strategy to operations to tactics, i.e., a spectrum running from the macro to the micro. On the one end, grand strategy pertains to the broadest possible perspective on warfare, its politics and diplomacy, as seen from the perspective of the nation's top executive and command structure. On the other end of the spectrum, the tactical level is concerned with how an infantry platoon takes a hill or fords a stream, or how combat pilots dogfight high in the sky. In between are the (variously defined) strategic, operational, and grand tactical levels. By the 1990s, almost all wars, whether or not they involved the U.S., were subjected to detailed, routine analysis at all of these levels by intelligence and military officials tasked with divining "lessons learned" by way of preparation for future wars. This use of macro-to-micro levels of analysis parallels the similar use of "levels" by international relations theorists dealing with the causes of war at the individual, nation-state, and international systems levels of analysis, sometimes elaborated upon (as is the case for the military "levels") to allow for additional "group" and "alliance" levels.

Meanwhile, contemporary scholars have grown accustomed to classifying wars along a spectrum running from all-out conventional warfare, to more limited conventional warfare, to various types of low-intensity conflict (LIC) under the varied headings of revolutionary, insurgency, guerilla, civil, internal, and ethnic warfare, as well as coups and border frictions. These wars have now also habitually come to be measured and classified according to their magnitude (size of contending forces), severity (casualties), and duration (length of time), which data also ramify into questions of what is or is not to be counted as a war, or conflict, or "militarized dispute." In recent years, there has been a marked shift away from conventional and toward various forms of LIC, mostly ethnic conflict, leading many scholars to assume, rightly or wrongly, that this has become a permanent trend. Hence, studies of 1990s ethnic conflict (more their causes, patterns, and remedies, less their conduct) have come to dominate current security and conflict studies.

Some fifteen years ago, the authors of this book co-edited two volumes on the "lessons of recent wars," focusing somewhat asymmetrically on conventional wars in the wake of a spate of them in the 1960s, 1970s, and 1980s, but devoting some attention as well to then contemporaneous LICs. It was remarked upon that the various "case study" chapters on wars provided a certain unevenness, with some authors (usually professional political scientists) more comfortable at the grand strategy level, while others (usually military officers) were relatively more comfortable with the operational and/or tactical levels. This was natural and expected as well as dismaying. Having taken note of this problem, the authors have here assayed a more explicit recognition of this problem by organizing our book along the lines of a matrix, which on one axis deals with the levels of analysis (grand strategy, strategy, operations, and tactics), and on the other axis with the spectrum of war/conflict running from large-scale conventional to various types of LIC. This allows us to focus, in a conscious, explicit way, on the various facets of warfare, such as the tactical aspects of small-scale ethnic wars, or the grand strategic features of large-scale conventional wars.

This is not an easy framework to "operationalize." The "data," for instance, for the war-fighting aspects of ethnic wars are scarce and hard to come by. But, our conceptual outline is fairly easy to apply to the realm of tactics, operations, and doctrines in conventional wars. It is also applicable to important subjects such as geography and culture, so that one might move easily between strategic and tactical geography, and strategic and tactical cultures. In some of the areas we have addressed, although critical to the conduct of war—such as arms resupply, security assistance, or outside intervention—our framework is less relevant. Despite these conceptual problems, it is hoped that this book will be a modest step toward a conceptual analysis of the conduct of modern warfare and, in the process, serve to bridge the heretofore separated worlds of military history and conflict studies.

CHAPTER 1

The Study of Warfare in the Third World

It is a much belabored but accurate truism, bordering upon cliché, that most writings on trends in international affairs (and related theories of international relations) are heavily reflective of their immediate historical context, that is, of recent events. And, ipso facto, most predictions about the future are merely extrapolations from present trends. Surprises, discontinuities, sudden upheavals, and cyclical movements are much harder to anticipate.

For instance, earlier in the 1970s, the rise to power of OPEC and the associated fears about an impending relative shift of economic power from North to South gave rise to a vast literature on interdependence, dependency, and scarcity, some of it verging upon hysteria with its doomsday predictions about an eventual total collapse of the world's economy and environment.[1] In the early 1980s, American anxiety about seemingly growing Soviet military power ("SDI-ski," Soviet naval expansion into the Third World, the possibility of a sudden Soviet blitzkrieg into Western Europe, Spetsnaz attacks on continental U.S. installations) formed the basis of a huge, anxious national security literature, as well as the eerily parallel fictional scenarios of authors Tom Clancy, General John Hackett, and others.[2]

Similarly, during the late 1970s and early-to-mid-1980s, the bunched-up breakout of several major wars in the Third World—China vs. Vietnam, Ethiopia vs. Somalia in the "Horn War," Lebanon, Afghanistan, the Falkland Islands, Iran vs. Iraq—gave rise to a new vogue of military "lessons learned" writings, representing also a resurgent interest in the long-dormant study of military history.[3] There was indeed a renewed interest in the *conduct* as well as the causes of wars—battle histories.[4]

Indeed, some scholars saw these wars as perhaps heralding the onset of what would be a proliferation of major interstate wars in the Third World—a "post-post-colonial period" that might become reminiscent of the Europe of earlier centuries.[5] And, too, coupled with the then seemingly interminable standoff in Central Europe between NATO and the Warsaw Pact, these wars were carefully monitored for military "lessons," which might then be used to gauge the relative military power of the two dominant blocs. Here, indeed, numerous analysts were to remind us of the manner in which the Spanish Civil War (obviously) and the Soviet-Japanese War of the late 1930s (much less obviously) had provided clues to the forthcoming conduct of World War II.[6] Similarly, much had been written about the failures of European military staffs; because they paid insufficient heed to what might (with the aid of hindsight) have been the lessons of the 1905 Russo-Japanese War, the Anglo-Dutch Boer War, or even the much earlier U.S. Civil War, military planning was ill-suited for the war that eventually became known as World War I.[7]

Certain seemingly obvious and salient lessons were divined from the experiences of the several aforementioned recent Third World wars. Or, at least, certain disparate but remarkable images had emerged from most if not all of them, whether or not they provided "true" lessons under closer scrutiny. The Iran-Iraq War, for instance, reminded many people of World War I, a murderous, defensive attrition war in which huge casualties were absorbed for small gains along a long, stationary front, during intermittent "final" offensives. But that war also saw some other, old and new, technological lessons: the introduction of gas warfare on a large scale for the first time since 1918; the use of surface-to-surface missiles for terroristic bombardment of cities in a manner reminiscent of the German V-1 and V-2 attacks on Britain; the development (on the Iraqi side) of mobile defenses, artillery on barges, and barriers for interdicting paratroopers. There was also the imagery of religious fanaticism, of human wave assaults, that in turn spawned new interest in the cultural determinants of war-fighting, particularly as they applied to the capacity for absorbing punishment.

The Falklands War, suffused somewhat with the imagery of comic opera, its lethality notwithstanding, provided numerous "instant" military lessons. They had to do with the value of attack submarines for driving surface ships from the seas, the new importance of aircraft-borne antiship missiles, the renewed value of long-range conventional bombing afforded by tanker refueling, the value of VSTOL (Vertical Short Take-off and Landing) aircraft in distant power-projection operations where large carriers were not available, and the use of readily convertible civilian transport ships. They also had to do with the comparative value of a highly motivated professional army, providing a seeming counterlesson to that provided simultaneously by Israeli conscripts and reserves in Lebanon.

The 1982 war in Lebanon, deemed by some analysts to be the harbinger of a truly new form of modern warfare, saw the advent of the electronic battlefield: ECM (Electronic Countermeasures) and ECCM (Electronic Counter-Countermeasures), highly sophisticated command and control, battle management aircraft, more sophisticated artillery fire direction, the use of drones or remotely piloted vehicles (RPVs) for battlefield surveillance, sophisticated combined arms operations for knocking out surface-to-air missile sites, and modern tanks (but also reactive tank armor).[8] But on a more traditional level, there were also the more mundane lessons having to do with the relationship of terrain to armored warfare and, indeed, regarding the wisdom (or lack of it) of punitive, preemptive wars with ill-defined strategic goals or "exit strategies."

Afghanistan too provided lessons, some of them eerily repetitive of those learned from the earlier American experience in Vietnam. Those had to do with the fundamental difficulties of conducting counterinsurgency (COIN) operations in a large theater involving rugged terrain, against determined foes. They also had to do with the possible crucial role of the introduction of a single weapons system, in this case the Stinger surface-to-air missile, which rendered Soviet aircraft and helicopters highly vulnerable to unacceptable losses. In a broader sense, there were the lessons (also repetitive of Vietnam) of what happens to a modern army trained and equipped to fight a big armored slugfest in Europe, when called upon to deal with a nasty low-intensity conflict against a dispersed and elusive foe—which requires tenacious light-infantry forces.[9] As with the U.S. experience in Vietnam, there were other broader political lessons, i.e., dilemmas about the practical uses of deliberate brutality and intimidation and about the perils of ratcheting up and down the ladder of escalation in situations whose basic reality is not easily captured by game theory or "rational" models of conflict. It came to be recognized that American (and Soviet) decisionmakers had largely ignored the factor of comparative pain thresholds.

In the Horn, too, there were lessons, howsoever arguable. One was the impact that suddenly can be brought to bear on a Third World war fought by relatively poor nations by introducing a limited numbers of forces ("volunteers" or "proxies") from larger or more developed states. There were also geography lessons such as the futility of a preventive war started by a smaller nation against a larger foe where factors of terrain and distance preclude a definitive, early knockout blow. The China-Vietnam War provided the imagery of a short but very intense war fought mostly by massed infantry, which resulted in huge casualties in the space of only a few weeks. Indeed that war impelled some analysts to question the value of one nation trying to teach another a "lesson" without actually attempting to achieve a "victory."[10]

The second Gulf War spawned a virtual cottage industry of analyses of lessons learned, albeit with often conflicting conclusions.[11] Some saw that war as finally vindicating the earlier air power theorists who had predicted the potential decisiveness of strategic air power.[12] The important nexus of air and space control to the facts of terrain and weather was underscored, and indeed the U.S.-led coalition had a huge advantage in marrying its hi-tech systems to a war on flat desert terrain. The value of a highly trained professional army was indicated, along with advanced simulations in training. Above all, the continued viability of fighting a static defensive war in fixed positions against a more flexible, mobile, hi-tech force was brought into question, even to the point where traditional Clausewitzian nostrums about mass and concentration of forces were brought into question.[13]

Contrary to the expectations earlier cited, i.e., those of the advent of a historical epoch witnessing more widespread conventional warfare in the Third World, the turn of the decade in 1990 saw a dramatically altered historical context. That can be discussed at two interlocking levels; that of the broader international system featuring the rivalry of the major powers, and that of the frequency and nature of warfare in the Third World.

The broader global context, of course, first saw perestroika, glasnost, detente, the drawdown of military forces on both sides of the Central European divide, the destruction of the Berlin Wall, German reunification, the Romanian revolution, the destruction of communism throughout Eastern Europe, Soviet problems in Azerbaijan and in the Baltic; in sum, the dramatic, effective collapse of communism after forty-five years of postwar Cold War. It also saw the rise of Japanese and other Asian nations' economic power, the advent of a more unified and powerful Western Europe presumably en route to some form of complete integration and beyond, and Tiananmen Square.

As the 1990s progressed, there was a newer focus on the rise of Chinese economic and military power,[14] perhaps yet to rival the U.S. Europe after Maastricht progressed toward unification via the EU, WEU (Western European Union), the Euro, etc., while Russia seemed slowly, fitfully to move toward democratization and a market economy. India too was a rising power, with its huge population adjacent to the Persian Gulf oil resources. Central Asia had become a major factor in the energy markets and hence, a strategic prize. Increasingly, weapons of mass destruction and their delivery systems came to be seen as the major emerging security problem of the turn of the century. Generally speaking, there was enormous ambiguity and fluidity about the nature of, or definition of, the newly emerging international system. Various analysts focused on one or another combination of (1) a three-bloc geoeconomic competition between a Japan-led Asia, a U.S.-led Americas bloc, and an EU-headed European bloc; (2) a balance-of-power revisited traditional system featuring five or six poles—U.S., China, Japan, Russia, Europe, maybe India; (3) a U.S.-led unipolar system; (4) a clash of civilizations; or (5) an incipient U.S.-China bipolar confrontation. What any of these, singly or in combination, would entail for the pattern of warfare in the world, was a wide-open question.[15] Presumably, warfighting or the conduct of war would be much more affected by technological changes in weaponry than by macropolitical shifts.

The 1980s and 1990s had actually seen a lengthy evolution of a "dominant paradigm" or scholarly "group think" as applied to the nature of modern warfare. And indeed, as had been borne out in so many situations in the past, the scholarly zeitgeist at any given point appeared—if only unconsciously and rarely articulated—a reflection of ongoing current events, then confidently extrapolated to the future, sometimes in the form of teleological or even messianic projections that posited a permanent or perpetual "outcome" of sorts.

In the early 1980s, there had been a resurgence of interest in the conduct (as contrasted with the causes) of warfare, indeed, then even hinting at a convergence or rapprochement between the then hitherto oddly separated academic worlds of military history, security studies, and conflict studies (the latter two normally emanating from political science departments).[16] That appears to have resulted largely as a backwash from the interest in conventional warfare spawned by the cluster of wars in the Falklands, Lebanon, the Iran-Iraq border, Afghanistan, the China-Vietnam border, and the African Horn as well as by the previous (1967 and 1973) Middle Eastern and (1965 and 1971) India-Pakistan wars. Perhaps, too, the conservative intellectual counterrevolution that accompanied the administrations of Reagan and Thatcher penetrated somewhat into academia, at least to the extent of legitimizing, somewhat, scholarly efforts that appeared as a counterweight or complement to "peace studies."

There was a vogue of "lessons learned" studies as exemplified by the massive three-volume study by Anthony Cordesman and Abraham Wagner, covering all or most of the aforementioned wars.[17] In a related vein, the study of the international arms trade occupied the attention of many scholars, particularly spurred on by the massive transfers of weapons to both sides of the Iran-Iraq War.[18] Some political scientists appeared to discover the works of the most prominent contemporaneous military historians: John Keegan, Martin van Creveld, Paul Kennedy, Brian Bond, et al.[19] There was also a renewed interest in the history of seapower, which in turn came to be related to some of the voguish trends in international relations theory, i.e., long-cycle theory and the theory of hegemonic stability.[20] Clausewitz too underwent a major revival, if only mostly in the military journals and among the devotees of Harry Summers' analyses of the U.S. debacle in Vietnam.[21] No one expected the Cold War to end. And, some scholars, in viewing the seemingly significant outbreak of conventional wars in the Third World, predicted more of the same, maybe even a long-term period of frequent warfare at the conventional level reminiscent of Europe of the seventeenth and eighteenth centuries.[22]

Even before the end of the Cold War created an entirely new zeitgeist there had been some demurrers. Writing toward the end of the 1980s just before the crack-up of the USSR, John Mueller posited the "obsolescence of major war."[23] His thesis was different from that long propounded by Kenneth Waltz, who had seen the advent of nuclear MAD (mutual assured destruction) in a bipolar context as militating toward stability (ditto for prospective nuclear pairings in regional contexts).[24] Mueller actually downplayed the role of nuclear weapons in the "long peace," averring that such a peace would probably have been sustained in their absence. Rather, Mueller saw a long trend going back over two or three centuries in which major warfare had become increasingly obsolete, the seeming lessons of World War I and World War II notwithstanding. He said that his

> book develops a third explanation: The long peace since World War II is less a product of recent weaponry than the culmination of a substantial historical process. For the last two or three centuries major war—war among developed countries—has gradually moved toward terminal disrepute because of its perceived repulsiveness and futility.[25]

As noted, Mueller downplayed the role of nuclear weapons in this development. He stressed the economic side of it but really focused on a kind of cultural evolution whereby warfare, like slavery and dueling before it, was becoming unfashionable, obsolete, undesirable, maybe even ridiculous, i.e., an anachronism. Like slavery, Mueller saw warfare becoming first controversial, then peculiar, and then obsolete, with first some countries, like Holland, Sweden, and Switzerland, opting out of the "war system," and then later others.[26] At some point in some places, warfare would come to be seen as repulsive, immoral, and uncivilized.

Mueller hence turned on its head the famous statement by Clausewitz that "war is nothing but a duel on a larger scale," saying that "like dueling, it could become unfashionable and then obsolete."[27] He traced this trend throughout the twentieth century, focusing (and this becomes an important part of the intellectual skein leading into the 1990s) solely on the "developed world." Hence, the wars in Afghanistan, Lebanon, et al., were not yet then seen as existing or incipient anachronisms.

Then the Cold War ended, Germany (and Europe) reunited, but also shortly thereafter, there was the Gulf War. Those quick sequential events appear to have caused a somewhat curious bifurcation in the emerging zeitgeist, as it applied to perspectives on the causes, patterns, and conduct of war. First, as per Mueller, the peaceful ending of the Cold War, or the "long peace,"[28] seemed to reinforce the views of Mueller and others about the growing anachronization of warfare. Retrospectively, Mueller sees little evidence that the U.S. and USSR ever came even close to blows, the various crises—Cuba, Berlin, the Middle East, Hungary, Czechoslovakia, Afghanistan, etc.—notwithstanding.[29] He, unlike Waltz and others, sees nuclear weapons as having been largely irrelevant to the creation of the "long peace."

After the end of the Cold War, there was a considerable reduction in the number and magnitude of conflicts in the Third World. After the Gulf War, the next six to seven years saw no conventional conflicts, though a number of other low-intensity conflicts (Sudan, Kurdistan, Algeria, Chechnya, Cambodia, Sri Lanka, Liberia, Sudan, Rwanda-Congo) did involve massive casualties. Generally speaking, however, many analysts were inclined to attribute the drop in the number and severity of conflicts to the end of the Cold War—the declining role of ideological rivalries,[30] the cessation of the superpowers' "pushing" of arms sales to their respective clients, and, related to this, the fact that so many Third World states moved away from Marxism toward democracy and the market economy, resulting in a drop in one of the major contributing factors to Third World conflict, i.e., insurgencies by Marxist groups backed by the USSR, China, and Cuba. Likewise, the U.S. was no longer supporting "Reagan Doctrine" insurgencies against Marxist incumbent regimes. Militating in the opposite direction, perhaps, the superpowers no longer either explicitly or tacitly cooperated in tamping down Third World conflicts so as to reduce the danger of escalation, heretofore referred to as "catalytic warfare." In the early 1990s, there were a priori "predictive" arguments about what would or should be the impact of the end of the Cold War on the number and severity of Third World conflicts. As the century drew to a close, the arguments on behalf of a reduction in conflict seemed to be winning, at least for the time being.[31]

But the end of the Cold War spawned something much bigger in terms of a scholarly zeitgeist, involving for the most part an extrapolation of Mueller's (heretofore somewhat obscure) thesis about the obsolescence of war. It came to involve a number of strands of thought or speculation under the umbrella of "endism," defined by Samuel Huntington as "all bad things are coming to an end." Fukuyama's "end of history" theme posited an end to ideological conflict and the "war system" and the victory of capitalism, democracy, and liberal values.[32] That victory was, as per Mueller, deemed permanent and likely irreversible. Military historians such as Brian Bond and John Keegan heralded the belated death of Clausewitz's influence, deemed to have been distorted by *fin de siècle* militarists and social Darwinists and to have achieved an unnaturally prolonged life because of Hitler and Stalin.[33] War would no longer usually be a "continuation of politics by other means," nor would decisive battles be the hallmarks of political history, nor would military victories be valuable, cost-effective or sustainable.

Whereas Mueller had posited the obsolescence of "major" war (i.e., hegemonic wars among the major powers), the advocates of endism foresaw the end of warfare generally within the industrialized world and/or among democracies. Wildavsky and Singer saw a coming bifurcation between "zones of peace"[34] (North America plus Europe plus the Asian democracies plus the Antipodes) and "zones of turmoil," the latter encompassing the bulk of the old Third World, which was not anytime soon going to become democratic or wealthy. That view pretty much agreed with that of the "democratic peace"[35] as well as with writers such as Paul Kennedy and Robert Kaplan who were prophesizing a terrifying future of overpopulation, environmental disaster, ethnic conflict, famines—i.e., chaos—for the zones of turmoil, particularly in Africa, Latin America, and parts of the Middle East and Central Asia.[36]

Van Creveld, in his widely read *The Transformation of Warfare,* carried these themes to a kind of ultimate conclusion.[37] He too felt that the age of warfare had ended in the developed world, indeed, spoke of the "end of strategy." He saw the military structures of the large powers—U.S., Russia in particular—as having become virtual anachronisms, wholly unsuited to a world evolving toward the lurid prognostications of Robert Kaplan. Clausewitz was dead and gone. Unlike Mueller, Creveld saw nuclear proliferation as abetting these trends, as a stabilizing force, whereby not only would nuclear war be unlikely even in the major conflict pairings such as Iraq-Iran, Arab-Israel, and India-Pakistan, but also that the deterrent effect of these weapons would drastically reduce the probabilities of conventional war, even where long-term serial conflicts and primordial hatreds were involved.[38]

John Keegan, in the conclusion of his magisterial *A History of Warfare,* provides some interesting twists to the zeitgeist of endism and obsolescence of warfare. He focuses on the triumph, during the twentieth century, of a so-called "Western way of warfare," defined in the context of the Clausewitzian dictum to the effect that warfare was a continuation of politics. His overall emphasis is on the (comparative) cultural nexus of warfare,[39] whereby he sees Clausewitzism as having imposed upon the West—hence, also, elsewhere—an ideological or moral ethos of total warfare emphasizing a face-to-face style (taken from the Greeks), married to modern technology. According to him the triumph of the Western way of warfare was delusive in that it had proved irresistible against other cultures, but brought disaster when turned in on itself in the world wars. According to Keegan, nuclear weapons were a "logical culmination of the technological trend in the Western way of warfare, and the ultimate denial of the proposition that war was, or might be, a continuation of politics by other means."[40] Keegan (not, it should be noted, a theoretically inclined political scientist) makes no mention of the possible impact of the "democratic peace." In saying that "politics must continue, war must not," he merely makes a prescriptive statement.[41] One senses that he does agree with Mueller that warfare will now become a cultural anachronism. And he pays little attention to the future portrayed by Kaplan and others of interminable, brutal LIC in the Third World "zones of turmoil." Indeed, by reversal, he sees the West as having much to learn from "alternative military cultures, not only that of the Orient but of the primitive world also," a reference to the possibilities of "intellectual restraint and even of symbolic ritual that needs to be rediscovered."[42]

In the face of the zeitgeist of endism there have, of course, been some doubts, skepticism, even alternative, opposing views, just as the majority mood of idealism in the 1920s had been balanced off in part by a minority intellectual current of geopolitical theory.[43] Fukuyama himself, by now somewhat of a godfather of endism (curiously, he was a Cold War neoconservative and Reagan administration political appointee), allows for the possibility of cyclicality. He worries that the romanticism and heroic myths associated with warfare may bubble along under the surface, perhaps to rise later on if the Kantian peace should produce mass boredom and hence another bout of military romanticism such as what occurred at the turn of the last century.[44] Endism may not, in this view, necessarily be permanent. On a less exalted philosophical plane, some political analysts look to the inevitable revival of big-power rivalries in a multipolar or revived bipolar system, with a security rivalry dimension. That might or might not eventuate in warfare—new Cold Wars are possible. Hence, Bernstein and Munro have recently warned of a coming conflict with China.[45] Others worry about Russia and Japan, some see an inevitable rivalry between the U.S. and a united Europe psychologically driven by a revisionist form of collective Gaullism. Then, of course, there is the "clash of civilizations" thesis that centrally posits a coming conflict between the West and Islam or between the West and an alliance between Islam and China.

On another track, recent years have seen the development—mostly in professional military journals—of a vast literature heralding the advent of a military-technical revolution (MTR) or revolution in military affairs (RMA). That literature was inspired by the U.S. technological tour de force in the Gulf War, following upon the Israelis' demonstration of various new hi-tech weapons and associated tactics in the 1982 war with Syria. Following the Gulf War, numerous military analysts heralded what was deemed the latest in a long series of RMAs (one in the 1930s with the combined developments of tactical airpower, armor, aircraft carriers, radar, submarines; one more recently with nuclear weapons and long-range ballistic missiles). Centrally, that involved the main elements of, according to William Perry, intelligence sensors, defense suppression systems and precision-guided subsystems for "smart" (now, increasingly "brilliant") weapons, developments foreshadowed in the 1970s by advances in microelectronics and computers and by associated developments in systems management and tactics.[46] Admiral Owens, popularizer of the now widely used concept "system of systems," pointed similarly to three categories of requirements: intelligence, command and control, and precision force.[47] Other analysts saw a slightly altered trilogy of sensors (reconnaissance, surveillance, and target acquisition), fusion (C³I), and precision-guided munitions. The genesis of these developments was in NATO's search for an "offset strategy" to combat the Soviets' numerical advantage in Central Europe, which came to fruition with the AirLand Battle 2000 doctrine that hinged on effective use of intelligence sensors, stealth aircraft, and PGMs (precision guided munitions) geared to interdicting Soviet rear and support echelons well behind the forward line of troops (FLOT). But as evidenced in the Gulf War—and in the RMA literature that was spawned in its aftermath— a number of related themes came to the fore: the prediction that future warfare would be characterized by lethality and dispersion, precision of fire, the irrelevance and vulnerability of massed forces, and invisibility; and the blurring of the heretofore familiar and seemingly durable categories of the strategic, operational, and tactical levels of warfare, as well as the blurring of the traditional service functions corresponding to the land, sea, and air realms.[48] In the vast literature that emerged in the mid-1990s, numerous writers predicted a future battlefield on which the importance of now traditional weapons platforms (tanks, aircraft, warships, submarines) would be diminished. The large and complex would give way to the small and the many, with battlefields literally crawling with millions of sensors, emitters, miniprojectiles, and microbats, in a "soldierless battlefield."[49] Needless to say, those who studied RMA/MTR did not so automatically accept the assumptions about the "obsolescence of warfare."

Another aspect of the burgeoning RMA/MTR literature involved the attempts by analysts to divine what would be the rate of diffusion of the new technologies (and their integration into viable systems) first to major powers other than the U.S., and then down the international military pecking order to middle-range "regional" powers and others. Some saw the U.S. maintaining a huge technological lead for a long time to come, which in itself would be emblematic of a long-time U.S. unipolar dominance, at least in the security area. Others such as Andrew Krepinevich (main historian of RMAs) saw diffusion as inevitable as it had been in previous revolutions.[50] Some analysts developed a whole new typology of "peer competitors" or "niche powers" to describe various levels of diffusion.[51] The juxtaposition of RMA diffusion and nuclear proliferation was sensed as important, but remained a bit of an unexplored subject.

Of course, defense planners in the Pentagon and elsewhere must and will plan for future wars, indeed deal routinely with worst-case scenarios. And Kaplan's remarks about Pentagon sources[52] suggesting Creveld's book as required reading point to a certain convergence of views between "endists" and military staffs about the future of warfare being mostly if not entirely in the realm of LIC in the developing world, i.e., mostly ethnic, tribal, and religious warfare of the sort now ongoing in several African countries.

But it is worth noting that there is not *total* agreement on this point. The Pentagon, while moving ahead with its MTR technologies (whether or not at the expense of current readiness is much argued over), deals extensively with several key regional warfare scenarios, involving Iran, Iraq, the two combined,

North Korea, and Taiwan. Libya, Algeria, a possible postrevolutionary[53] Islamic Turkey or Egypt are also major foci of analysis, gaming, and scenario writing. Iran or Iraq conjure up images of a Desert Storm II. On the other hand, many analysts see little hope that Iraq or Iran could improve upon the former's performance in Desert Storm I, and see such regional nations working on so-called "asymmetric strategies" to combat the vaunted U.S.[54] MTR military machine: terrorism and megaterrorism, camouflage and concealment, some countering MTR developments to raise the costs of a possible U.S. intervention. Some analysts have noted, however, the widely publicized strictures of Indian General Sundarji who, when asked to provide the main lessons of the Gulf War, stated that regional nations should not tangle with the U.S. unless they have nuclear weapons.[55]

Despite the views of Creveld and others, some analysts still see the possibilities for large-scale conventional warfare in the three major dyadic conflict pairings in the Greater Middle East: Arab-Israel, Iraq-Iran, and India-Pakistan, as well as on the Korean peninsula. And the history of the Falklands War in 1982 serves as a pointed reminder that wars can erupt in highly unexpected places for very unanticipated reasons. Indeed, some recent press reports have indicated that the Israeli military has become increasingly concerned about the prospects for a renewal of warfare (this even before the seeming collapse of the "peace process" in the fall of 2000). And in each of these pairings, there appears the virtual inevitability of possession of weapons of mass destruction on both sides, raising the specter of escalation from conventional warfare. The U.S. military, meanwhile, has become increasingly concerned about the prospect of having to conduct a Desert Storm redux against a foe armed with nuclear weapons that could be targeted on neighboring states and/or U.S. forces or installations.

The possibilities for such conflicts does not entirely contradict the assumptions, strictures, or zeitgeist of endism. None of the above possibilities would pit democracies against each other. Still, Mueller's thesis about the obsolescence of warfare and Creveld's about its transformation amount virtually to predictions that such conflicts are becoming increasingly less likely or thinkable, either because of shifting cultural norms or because of the specter of nuclear or biological megadeath. Whether endism's secular projection or, on the other hand, other analysts' concession to cyclicality will prevail can only be answered much later with the aid of additional hindsight.

Indeed, the Third World in the late 1980s and first half of the 1990s had witnessed the surprising outbreak of what some pundits deemed a "peace epidemic," contradicting widespread expectations that the preceding "war epidemic" of the previous decade was a harbinger of still more to come. This peace epidemic applied, as noted, at least to the major conventional wars and some unconventional ones as well.[56] The long Iran-Iraq War with its huge casualties and immense economic costs—and also the use of chemical weapons—drew to a close. No major Arab-Israeli war has yet followed that of 1982, not yet. The Falklands and China-Vietnam Wars were not, for the moment, renewed despite the absence of definitive peace agreements. And the Soviet withdrawal from Afghanistan reduced the intensity (and visibility) of that war, which devolved into a nasty civil war pitting first an incumbent Soviet-backed Marxist regime against a splintered array of Islamic guerilla groups and then a war among the latter. But by 1999 there were no ongoing intensive Third World conventional interstate wars (that between Ethiopia and Eritrea emerged as an exception), though as we shall note, there were still numerous, nasty intrastate conflicts, some with a high level of mortality.

On the other hand, the peace epidemic notwithstanding, the turn of the decade saw the continuation of numerous Third World low-intensity conflicts, running the gamut from civil wars to large- and small-scale insurgencies of various intensities. Indeed, mirroring that new reality, the Pentagon, facing massive budget cuts and the possible large-scale withdrawal of U.S. forces from Western Europe, began to refocus its attention on Third World low-intensity warfare, including terrorism and the narcotics trade, as well as on "traditional" counterinsurgency against radical revolutionary movements deemed (at least earlier) beholden to Moscow.

Some standard compendia of contemporary conflict, such as the (formerly) annual book published by Australian John Laffin, *The World in Conflict,*[57] or the annual review contributed by a group of researchers at Sweden's Uppsala University to the SIPRI, *Armaments Yearbook,* had listed and discussed as many as thirty-five to forty still ongoing low-intensity conflicts as of the advent of the 1990s, but a lower number, near thirty, as of 1998–99. One might argue over whether one or another conflict might deserve inclusion in the data (battle-death data were sufficiently vague so as to render definitions precarious), but almost unmistakably, the global total of conflicts had trended downward since the end of the Gulf War, whether causally related or not.

Earlier, most such conflicts had taken place in what was then defined, albeit loosely, as the Third World, a category that by default included everything outside of the first and second worlds, respectively comprising the U.S.-led "Western world" and the Soviet bloc, or that part of it in Eastern Europe and Mongolia. As it happened, even before the end of the Cold War the term "Third World" had become less and less meaningful because of the differential rates of economic growth that saw the rise of East and Southeast Asia to the level of economic powerhouse, contrasted with the opposite experience of much of Africa and Latin America. But up to the end of the Cold War, most conflicts were outside the first and second worlds, with the exceptions, on the periphery of Europe, of Northern Ireland (where some thirty-two hundred deaths had resulted between 1969 and 1987), occasional flare-ups between Greece and Turkey over Cyprus, some incidences of terrorism involving the Basques in Spain and France, and the ongoing low-level conflict in Yugoslavia's Kosovo Province involving Albania. Above all, there was a solid wall between the southern borders of the old USSR and the conflict-prone regions to its south, even if that wall was somewhat breached by cross-border activities in both directions toward the end of the long Soviet-Afghan War.

After 1990, of course, the former distinction between first and second worlds on the one hand and the Third World on the other (as it applied to zones of conflict) completely dissolved. The fall of Eastern European communism reopened numerous long-dormant but simmering conflicts in Bosnia, Slovakia, Macedonia, the Albania-Serbia border, and Moldova and resulted in new border problems, irredentisms, and ethnic conclaves—Kaliningrad, the Baltics, Slovakia—that might yet fester into LICs.[58] That was likewise true for the Caucasus and Central Asia, where the collapse of the USSR engendered numerous ethnic conflicts—Chechnya, Nagorno-Karabakh, Georgia, and Tajikistan, among others. Although the term "Third World conflicts" persists, it is as a descriptor of wars fought beyond the borders of the U.S. and Western Europe.

However, after the Gulf War, the nostrums of some academic analysts about the "obsolescence of war" or the "transformation of warfare" appeared at least for the time being to be borne out. By 1999 there were no ongoing conventional wars (nor had there been any for some six years), and there was a reduced but still significant number of ongoing low-intensity conflicts, running the gamut of ethnic conflicts and civil wars based on one or another of various factors, i.e., ideology, race, ethnicity, religion.

In the Middle East, the Iran-Iraq War, with its huge casualties, had ended by 1988. The Arabs and Israel had not experienced a major conventional war since 1982 in Lebanon (though by 1997, there were some signs of increasing preparations for a new round). There had been the Palestinian *Intifada* (some eight hundred fatalities) and the continuing conflicts in Kurdistan involving Turkey, Iran, and Iraq. In Lebanon, the seemingly interminable multisided civil war (which since 1975 had caused some two hundred thousand deaths, dwarfing the statistics from the West Bank and Gaza), had abated or ended, leaving Syria de facto in control of Lebanon. Syria vs. the Christians, Christians vs. Druse, Amal vs. the PLO, had been among the various internecine conflicts, the high casualties for which largely were the results of continuing artillery bombardments, long a major battlefield killer. And, indeed, the earlier Syrian suppression of Sunni Muslim militants in the city of Hama earlier was reported to have resulted in between six thousand and twenty-five thousand deaths within just a few days, also the result of massive artillery bombardments.

But the Middle East still remained a cauldron. There was the interminable terrorism and reprisals involving the Israelis, Palestinians, Hamas, Islamic Jihad, etc., some of it spilling over into Lebanon, with a major upsurge in late 2000. In Egypt, the government fought a long-simmering miniwar against Islamic extremists who, notably, had targeted Egypt's Coptic minority. Algeria saw a continuing Islamic extremist terrorist campaign which, with its reprisals, had by 1999 caused some hundred thousand deaths. Algeria also had to cope with an ethnic separatist movement by the Riff people, a long-standing issue. The Kurds—badly split among themselves—continued to fight on in northern Iraq, eastern Turkey, and in Iran. Iran harbored Baluchi and Azeri ethnic dissidents as well as Kurds; Iraq had its problems with the Shi'a minority in its southern marshlands as well as with the Kurds. Iran and the UAE squabbled over control of islands in the Persian Gulf; Shi'a minorities in Bahrain and elsewhere linked to Iran provided grist for newer conflicts. There were several border disputes on the Arabian Peninsula: Saudi Arabia–Kuwait, Oman–Saudi Arabia.

The Soviets were long gone from Afghanistan. But in the early 1990s there was a complex, multisided conflict involving several Islamic factions that had fallen out after the victory over Moscow and the (briefly in control) Najibollah regime, which had been left in control after the Soviets' withdrawal. In the mid-1990s, the fundamentalist Taliban forces, backed by Pakistan in part on the basis of ethnic consanguinity, made a bid to take over the country, capturing Kabul and most other major Afghan cities.

Perhaps the biggest upsurge in low-intensity conflict was in the Caucasus and Central Asia in the wake of the breakup of the Soviet Union and the coming to independence of a host of newly independent states, as well as ethnic conflict in Russia. By 2000 the lengthy conflict in Chechnya was quiescent but simmering after a deal that apparently had given Chechnya considerable autonomy. Georgia earlier had seen two internal wars, in Abkhazia along the coast and inland in South Ossetia. Armenia had fought Azerbaijan over Nagorno-Karabakh, a situation still basically unresolved and latently violent. In Central Asia, there were several flashpoints, most notably in Tajikistan where Islamic elements related to forces in Afghanistan had skirmished with the remnants of the old Soviet regime—an ethnic and ideological conflict.

Most startling in historical perspective was the recrudescence of ancient conflicts within Europe with the fall of the Soviet empire and the disintegration of ex-Yugoslavia, prompting scholars such as John Mearsheimer to wax seminostalgic on behalf of the old, rigid bipolar stability.[59] Up to 1990, conflict within Europe—for a long time—had been restricted to a few nagging insurgencies or irredentisms—Northern Ireland, the Basque areas of Spain and France, minor flare-ups within Belgium. But after the end of the Cold War, there were, of course, the grisly events in ex-Yugoslavia (Bosnia-Herzegovina, Croatia versus Serbia over Slavonia and the Krajina, Kosovo, etc.). A latently explosive situation existed in Macedonia, and there was a brief minicivil war in Albania with some regional dimensions. Tensions resurfaced between Hungary and Romania, Hungary and Slovakia, Bulgaria and Turkey, and within each of the Baltic states with their large Russian ethnic minorities. Violence flared in Moldova, reawakening echoes of earlier tensions between ethnic Russians and Romanians, with the former temporarily creating a rump trans-Dniester republic. By 2000, most or all of these conflicts had been tamped down but all—particularly Bosnia and Kosovo—remained latently explosive.

In Asia, the still ongoing Sri Lankan conflict seemed often confusing, what with an odd juxtaposition of Tamil and Sinhalese guerilla insurgencies juxtaposed for a while to a (now ended) Indian occupation. That war was still raging in 2000, with total estimated mortalities perhaps having reached seventy thousand. The casualties were rather high, including those incurred by the Indian army. India and Pakistan, meanwhile, both had internal conflicts (Sikhs and Baluchis), and in addition, the long simmering problems in Kashmir appeared again in the mid-1990s to be at a flashpoint, including threats by India of a major war if Islamic insurgency in Kashmir should escalate. Negotiations have been held, but to little avail.

Burma, too, has seen continuing internal conflict composing some fourteen contending groups (but primarily involving the Karen National Union) and with over a thousand annual resultant deaths. Thailand and Laos too had continuing internal, low-level conflicts. Those in the Philippines, involving both communist and Islamic guerillas, were somewhat larger and more intense, having caused more than fifty thousand deaths since 1970, but by the mid-1990s running at a low level. In East Timor, meanwhile, a long-standing insurgency by Fretilin guerillas had virtually been suppressed by the central government in Jakarta, leading to foreign intervention by peace keepers. The result: perhaps more than 200,000 deaths out of an earlier total population of some 650,000, constituting a massive civilian massacre approaching genocidal proportions.

In Cambodia, by 1989–90, there had resurfaced a major war, centrally pitting the long incumbent regime backed by Hanoi against the resurgent former regime, the Khmer Rouge under Pol Pot. The latter, by 1990, was making a serious comeback, threatening the new regime's control of some major cities and involving traditional conventional warfare now almost unique to the entire Third World. In the early 1990s there appeared a successful peace agreement, but warfare broke out again, and only by 1997 did the Khmer Rouge forces appear to be exhausted.

Africa too saw continued low-intensity warfare in several places. In Ethiopia, following the interminable civil war pitting the Addis Ababa regime headed by Colonel Mengistu against regional-ethnic insurgencies in Eritrea and in Tigre Province, there was continued skirmishing along the Somali border with ethnics in the Ogaden region earlier contested for in the 1977–78 war. The Tigrean rebels had, by 1990, achieved considerable success, moving the conflict closer to Addis Ababa; meanwhile the Eritreans had captured the crucial port city of Massawa. Since 1970, some forty-five thousand military and some fifty thousand civilian deaths had resulted from these conflicts, which finally ended with the granting of independence to Eritrea and the defeat of the Mengistu forces. Later, in 1998-2000, fighting flared between Ethiopia and Eritrea.

The north vs. south war in Sudan, meanwhile, had incurred perhaps more deaths than any other recent conflict in the world with the exceptions of the Iran-Iraq and Cambodian wars. Some 220,000 deaths were reported, many from starvation and one-sided massacres of civilians. In early 1990, the war was reported to have escalated with the surrounding of government troops in the southern city of Juba. That war continued unabated through the 1990s, with the central government seemingly unable to achieve a knockout blow.

Elsewhere in Africa, the war in Angola between the MPLA-based Luanda government and Jonas Savimbi's UNITA forces came to a negotiated end with withdrawals of Cuban and South African forces but flared anew between 1998 and 2000. Negotiations between Savimbi and Luanda produced a tentative peace periodically interrupted by fighting. Elsewhere, lethal low-level internal conflict continued in war-weary Uganda, but ended in the mid-1990s. The same was true for tribal conflict in Zimbabwe. But in Western Sahara, it appeared that the long-lasting war pitting the Moroccans against the Polisario was indeed winding down as Polisario military actions appeared to ebb, partly the result of a reduction of external Libyan and Algerian support. Finally, the late 1980s saw some skirmishing and mutual suppression of transborder, ethnotribal refugees by bordering Senegal and Mauritania in a situation that periodically threatened to result in war between these two nations. Then in the 1990s, there was the rather major multi-sided insurgency war in Liberia, which began to involve other West African nations.

In the mid-1990s, there was the gruesome civil war in Rwanda between the Tutsi and the Hutus, resulting in a genocidal massacre of the former. Burundi, too, saw major conflict between these ethnic groups. And Tutsi forces were instrumental in the long offensive across Zaire that eventually overthrew long-time dictator Mobutu, with extensive civilian massacres en route. Further north, tribal warfare continued in Somalia in the wake of the ill-fated U.S.-led peace-making operation. There was turmoil in Sierra Leone and Guinea-Bissau, a bloody coup in Congo-Brazzaville, unrest off and on in Nigeria, and a multi-sided civil war in the Democratic Republic of Congo involving outside inter-vention by several nations on each side. Large portions of sub-Sahara Africa appeared on the brink of chaos with the failure of governments to build nations and maintain control over national territories.

Latin America, too, long a relatively peaceful region by Third World standards, has seen its share of warfare, mostly low-intensity conflict. At the end of the 1980s, the insurgencies in Nicaragua, El Salvador, and Guatemala continued. But with the withdrawal of U.S. support for the Honduras-based Contras, and then the election of Violeta Chamorro, the leftist insurgency in El Salvador con-tributed most of the continuing bloodshed. By the mid-1990s, all of these con-flicts, which had produced massive casualties, had more or less died down. Elsewhere, there was the deadly and expanding rebellion by the Shining Path guerillas in Peru, who by 1990 had succeeded in controlling some rural regions and in posing a threat to urban centers as well, and who remained a threatening force thereafter. The complex civil conflict in Colombia, meanwhile, involved an interrelated mix of Marxist revolutionary activities and paramilitary narco-terrorism, a situation that had gradually been internationalized to include extensive involvement of the U.S. as well as of mercenaries from Israel and elsewhere. And there was a new insurgency in southern Mexico, with ethnic as well as eco-nomic class implications.

In summary, the turn of the century witnessed a paucity of conventional wars, and a plethora of low-intensity, mostly ethnic, wars. Whether these trends would continue into the future was anyone's guess.

Types of War

The extensive literature on warfare offers a rich menu of classification in terms of the manner in which wars are fought and the scope of the conflict, as opposed to the cause. Only to some extent does this involve matters of semantics, that is, of varying choices of adjectives preceding the word "war," such as "limited" or "low intensity." Otherwise, the differences reflect the changing mix of wars around the world, which in turn reflect new political trends and an evolving international system now comprising some 190 nations. The vast outpouring of writings on LIC during the 1980s and 1990s inspired some analysts to devise subcategories within that rubric, providing new layers of fine distinctions between different types of conflict.

There are any number of criteria that, in various combinations, can be utilized to define different types of wars. Some authors utilize criteria such as magnitude (numbers of combatants involved), severity (number of battle-connected deaths), and the duration or length of war. The Iran-Iraq War, from 1980 to 1988, would have scored highly on all of these counts, as an eight-year conflict involving millions of combatants, hundreds of thousands of battle deaths, and high ratios of battlefield attrition. On the other hand, some wars, such as the 1967 Arab-Israeli War or the China-Vietnam War of 1979, have been short, intense, and of great magnitude, but the shortness of the wars has restricted battlefield deaths (severity) to fairly low numbers in absolute terms. Some wars, such as those still ongoing in Sri Lanka and southern Sudan, have been extremely high in severity and duration, but of minor magnitude and intensity, i.e., involving slow but large-scale attrition (mostly of civilians) with few major battles and negligible use of modern, advanced weaponry. The combinations are almost endless, and we shall return to these concepts while distinguishing these wars by still other criteria.

The most standard two-way breakdown of wars has long been that of "conventional" and "unconventional." The former conjures up the imagery of what we long were used to thinking of as *war*—large-scale, all-out slugfests between large formations among major or at least medium powers with a definable and moving (rapidly or slowly) "front." Here one assumes the large-scale use of the most modern, state-of-the-art weapons. One assumes as well a definable start and finish to war, if not necessarily declarations of war and treaties of peace. Such wars—the two world wars, the several Arab-Israeli and India-Pakistan wars—are easy to follow from day to day in the newspapers. Their progress will be charted and highlighted by flags and symbols and unit designations, and the movement of the "front" tells who is winning and losing at given points, the "tides of war." The wars are expected to be of high magnitude, and very intense—their duration will greatly vary, as witness the contrast between the 1967 (six days) and 1973 (twenty-two days) Arab-Israeli wars, and the ground phase of Desert Storm (a hundred hours) and the Iran-Iraq War (eight years plus).

Finally, conventional wars, depending upon the nature of the combatants, are those in which the most advanced state-of-the-art weapons are utilized; it is in a sense the most advanced form of combat. Hence, it is here where we seek to divine the most up-to-date lessons of modern warfare, involving the relationship between weapons, tactics, and strategies.

A subset of "standard" conventional war is what we have come to call a "limited" conventional war. In some essential respects, limited wars may not differ from the aforementioned "standard" conventional wars. The latter connotes a certain total war emphasis, regarding the utilization of most or all available weapons and the extension of the war to whatever geographical limits are perceived useful or rational by one or more of the combatants. Limited war, on the other hand, usually refers to one in which there are limitations either on the use of a full range of weapons or on the geographical scope of action utilized by either side. In the latter sense, this may not so much be a matter of formalized rules of engagement based on actual negotiations as it may be one of tacit "rules," mutually if warily observed. Keegan discusses this in the context of comparative cultural norms that feed into rules of engagement.[60]

The Korean War seems to have inspired a great amount of interest in limited conventional war, coming as it did after a world war that had seen few limits, with the possible exception of the abjuring of the use of poison gas by all concerned. And indeed, the conventional warfare itself, fought for three years across the narrow Korean waist, and up and down the peninsula, was anything but limited as measured by use of conventional firepower. But it was limited in a geographical sense—the U.S. denied itself the option of bombing the communist "sanctuaries" in Manchuria, and the Chinese and North Koreans denied themselves the (arguable) option of bombing U.S. ports, airfields, and logistical facilities in Japan. In addition, the U.S. did not use nuclear weapons, though the threat of such use was apparently part of the diplomacy of the war's termination.

Other major wars—maybe in some sense all of them—have had some limits, either geographical or involving the use of weapons or certain operations. That is true even of the Arab-Israeli wars. Those have seen certain limits imposed on the bombing of cities, with the Arabs presumably having been deterred by the high potential costs of such exchanges. And, in 1973, perhaps in part due to a recognition of American sensibilities, the Israelis eschewed use of Jordanian and/or Lebanese territory for what might have been more promising avenues of approach toward Damascus. In 1982, the Israelis fought Syria in Lebanon, but both sides carefully avoided spreading the war to the Golan Heights or to each others' cities.

In China's attack on Vietnam in 1979, meanwhile, there were three weeks of very intense conventional ground fighting. But it had all the earmarks of a very large-scale punitive raid, and China denied itself the option of a deeper penetration into the Red River Valley or beyond—albeit somewhat under the duress of a countervailing implicit Soviet threat to invade Manchuria so as to relieve the pressure on Vietnam.

The Falklands War also saw some limitations, again, in the form of geographical demarcations. The British did not attack the Argentinian mainland, though they could, presumably, have bombed Argentinian cities or at least ports and airfields involved in supporting operations toward the Falklands. Likewise, after the sinking of the Argentinian cruiser *Belgrano,* the Royal Navy did not further pursue the Argentinians' surface navy back to its home ports, as it presumably could have.

Wars may also be limited or unlimited in terms of a spectrum of war aims or what a victor may find acceptable as an outcome if a range of options is indeed available. The U.S. insisted on unconditional surrender by Germany and Japan in 1945 (though allowing the retention of the emperor in the latter case). Israel allowed a thoroughly beaten Egypt off the hook in 1967 and 1973, but in both cases external pressures were involved. But numerous writers have noted a long-term trend as one moves from the European "classical system of diplomacy" to the twentieth century, from wars of limited territorial gains for the victor to wars of annihilation.[61] Hence the generalizations about modern "total warfare" and an associated "American way of war." New international norms in the late twentieth century may have reversed these trends.

Not all conventional wars are interstate wars, just as not all interstate wars are conventional. This is a source of some confusion, as witness the difference between the conflict typologies presented by Bloomfield and Leiss, and by Sarkesian in Table 1.1.

The Chinese civil war in the late 1940s (or the Russian civil wars following the Bolshevik revolution) was a very large-scale conventional war evolving, according to classical Maoist doctrine, from a guerilla phase to large-unit operations. And, indeed, the phase of the Cambodian civil war preceding the truce—pitting the resurgent Khmer Rouge against the incumbent regime backed by Hanoi—had the military character of conventional warfare, i.e., large-unit formations and demarcated, fixed, or moving battlefronts. The Sri Lankan conflict also has sometimes had the character of a conventional war in recent years.

On the other hand, some interstate conflicts have had the character of unconventional wars. The Libya–Chad war or the periodic eruptions between Somalia

Table 1.1 Typologies of Warfare[62]

	Full Spectrum
Bloomfield and Leiss:	Conventional interstate
	Internal with significant external involvement
	Primarily internal
	Colonial
Sarkesian:	Conventional: limited to major
	Nuclear: limited to major
	Unconventional: special operations
	terror and counterterror
	low-intensity conflict
	revolutionary and counterrevolutionary
	noncombat: shows of force
	Low Intensity
Shultz:	Insurgency
	Anticommunist resistance movements
	Revolutions without guerilla warfare
	International terrorism
	State-supported insurgency and terrorism
	State-inspired subversion
	International narcotics
Evans:	Insurrection
	Guerilla warfare
	Terrorism
	Border friction
	Coups

and Ethiopia since 1978, or between Belize and Guatemala, have had the character of "border frictions." Another example would be that of the periodic skirmishing along the Thailand-Cambodia or India-Pakistan borders. Some wars between sovereign nations have, almost by necessity, had the character of unconventional wars just because of the absence of modern military units and equipment: for instance, the war between Mali and Upper Volta (now Burkina Faso), or the troubles between Tanzania and Uganda, or to a lesser degree the brief border war between Peru and Ecuador.

If the distinction between all-out (but rarely total) conventional and limited conventional warfare involves some restraints on weapons or demarcations of legitimate zones of combat, the division between either end of the conventional spectrum and what we have come to call low-intensity conflict is a sharp one. But, as we shall see, even that is not always the case.

In recent years there has been a profusion of writing on low-intensity or unconventional warfare. It was sparked by the American experience in Vietnam, perhaps later by the Soviet experience in Afghanistan and by the West's growing problems in combating terrorism; nowadays this category accounts for most wars. Depending upon the author, one can rely upon a considerable mix of classifications or typologies dealing with various aspects of this end of the conflict spectrum. To some degree, the differences are merely semantic; otherwise, there may be serious disagreements about the bases for classifying wars or conflicts of a lower intensity than those conflicts called "limited conventional." Ernest Evans, in a book characteristically entitled *Wars without Splendor* (hence vividly conveying the earlier U.S. military view of these wars as "dirty" and unheroic as well as vague and indefinable), divides low-level conflicts into five types: insurrection, guerilla warfare, terrorism, border friction, and coups.[63] Some analysts would prefer to deal only with the first two in studies devoted to war *qua* war. Evans's table (Table 1.2) depicts this classification, including the related breakdown of "type of low-intensity operation called for."

Sam Sarkesian, another prolific writer on low-intensity warfare, has a similar breakdown.[64] He first breaks conventional warfare down into "limited" and "major" categories, echoing our previous remarks but underscoring the point that "limited" can mean merely "small" as well as denoting limitations on weapons use or zones of conflict, whereas major wars (as in Korea) can have the latter limitations but still be of great intensity and magnitude. Otherwise, under the heading of unconventional (roughly coterminous with Evans's and others' use of LIC) he utilizes the categories of revolutionary, counterrevolutionary, special operations, and terrorism. Still other analysts tend to move back and forth between the terminology of "guerilla warfare" and "insurgency/counterinsurgency." At the higher end of this spectrum, some writers have come to use the category of MIC (medium-intensity conflict).

Schultz (see Table 1.1) has a broad spectrum, ranging from "revolutionary-insurgency" through anticommunist resistance movements, terrorism, covert aggression, coups, revolutions without guerillas, state-sponsored coups and terrorism to narcotics.[65]

By now one can begin to sense the core of the problem of definition and

Table 1.2   Low-Level Conflict and Low-Intensity Operations

Types of Low-Level Conflict	Nature of Conflict	Cause of Conflict	Type of Low-Intensity Operation Called For
Insurrection	Mass Uprising	Desire by revolutionaries to overthrow the government	Counter-Insurgency; Aiding Insurgents; Peace-Keeping
Guerrilla Warfare	Hit and run attacks culminating in a final offensive	Desire by revolutionaries to overthrow the government	Counter-Insurgency; Aiding Insurgents; Peace-Keeping
Terrorism	Incidents of violence designed to inflict costs	Desire by revolutionaries to overthrow the government	Counter-Insurgency; Aiding Insurgents; Peace-Keeping
Border Friction	Incidents of violence along a border	Hostility between nations or groups	Peace-Keeping
Coups	Armed Forces overthrow the government	Desire by revolutionaries to overthrow the government	Aiding Insurgents; Reversing Coup

Source: Ernest Evans, *Wars Without Splendor: The U.S. Military and Low Level Conflict* (New York: Greenwood Press, 1987), p. 20.

classification. On the one hand, there is the point that unconventional (or guerilla or insurgency) warfare is primarily distinguished by the manner in which the combatants fight. Wars are fought by small units using hit-and-run tactics, stealth, intermittent attacks, and ambushes. There is an unmistakably dominant imagery of jungle ambushes or quick nocturnal raids in the desert or from mountain hideaways. No large tank divisions nor extensive use of heavy artillery, no hint of large-scale battles of attrition. And the maps and newspapers depicting these wars do not indicate moving battlefronts from day to day nor convey any sense of clearly demarcated areas of respective territorial control.

But in the case of civil wars, one can have either conventional or unconventional modes of fighting. The recent conflict between the former Sandinista regime in Nicaragua and its opponents, the Contras, was on an unconventional level—jungle ambushes, firefights between patrols, incidents of urban sabotage. The same had been true for civil wars in Guatemala and El Salvador. But the Chinese civil war in the late 1940s was, at least in its latter stages, a large-scale conventional war on the same scale as that between Japan and China on the latter's soil.

Some interstate wars have been fought on a nearly unconventional level, perhaps because of the relatively unsophisticated nature of the combatants or the

Table 1.3   The Correlates of War Project's Two Typologies of War

Traditional Typology	Expanded Typology
I. International Wars	I. Inter-State Wars (Type I)
A. Interstate Wars	
B. Extra-systemic Wars	
1) Imperial	
2) Colonial	
II. Civil Wars	II. Extra-State Wars (with some formerly extra-systemic now transferred to civil)
	A. Conflict with Colony (Type 2)
	B. State vs. Non-State (Type 3)
III. Intra-State Wars	A. Civil Wars
	1. For central control (Type 4)
	2. Local issues (Type 5)
	B. Inter-Communal (In development) (Type 6)

Source: Meredith Sarkeus, Frank Wagman and J. David Singer, "Interstate, Intra-State and Extra-State War: A New Typology," unpublished paper.

extreme difficulties imposed by the terrain and logistics. One example was the 1980s war between Libya and Chad, which saw the Chadian soldiers using Toyota pickup trucks as effective desert fighting vehicles.

Unconventional (or low-intensity or insurgency) warfare within nation-states—i.e., intrastate wars or internal wars—can take any number of forms, some sliding into the "lower" end of the spectrum in the form of terrorism, coups, or merely sporadic outbursts of chaotic or random violence. This involves such variables as ideology, religion, race, ethnicity, social class, as they largely define what is at stake, i.e., who is fighting whom over what issues or territories.

Numerous earlier unconventional wars had involved insurgencies by Marxist revolutionaries against incumbent colonial regimes or those that evolved from colonial rule. That is what usually comes to mind when we speak of "revolutionary" war. (In military terms, we shall later return to the distinction between Maoist and *foco* insurgency strategies.) The models here are many and familiar: Algeria, Vietnam, the Philippines in two separate phases, Malaya, Rhodesia, Peru, Guinea-Bissau, Mozambique (earlier under Portuguese rule), Cambodia (under Sihanouk), the 1960 Cuban revolution. In one form or another, these usually involved support by Moscow and/or Beijing for leftist guerillas struggling to usurp a colonial regime or one tied to the West, such as Batista's Cuba or Magsaysay's Philippines.

In the 1980s, however, the tide turned, with the virtual collapse of communism in its home base and the simultaneous difficulties faced by beleaguered Marxist Third World governments. Here we had "counterrevolutionary wars," or those conducted against Marxist-based regimes by Western-backed forces. Many of these received extensive U.S. support under the Reagan Doctrine, a latter-day throwback to the old "roll-back" policies of the 1950s: the Mujahideen groups in Afghanistan, RENAMO in Mozambique, Jonas Savimbi's UNITA in Angola, and the Nicaraguan Contras. Not all anti-Marxist insurgencies were U.S.-backed, however, as witness the Eritrean and Tigrean insurgencies against the Ethiopian Marxist Mengistu regime—here, the insurgents themselves were self-professed Marxists, but with support in nearby Arab states based on Islamic or ethnolinguistic solidarity.

Some unconventional or guerilla wars are, primarily, civil wars between different ethnic, racial, or religious groups within a country, usually with one or another group in control of the government and the others acting in effect as insurgents. Some of these conflicts, additionally, may have an ideological component, if only as a subsidiary theme. The complex conflict between Tamil and Sinhalese ethnic groups in Sri Lanka (both sides have fielded antigovernment guerillas and terrorists and both sides have fought Indian interventionist troops) has fit this model, centrally pitting a Sinhalese majority-based regime against minority Tamil (Hindu) insurgents. The conflict in the Sudan has pitted a Muslim-based northern government against animistic and Christian southern insurgents—here there is a clear geographic demarcation between the contending sides. The earlier lengthy civil war in Uganda was fought for the most part along tribal lines; so too that in Angola, but there with a strong "ideological" component that correlated with the contending Cold War antagonisms, e.g., UNITA was backed by the U.S. and white South Africa, and the then incumbent Luanda regime by Cuba and the USSR. The earlier conflicts in Zimbabwe likewise contained a mix of tribal and ideological elements. More recently, however, African conflicts in places such as Rwanda, Congo, and Liberia have been absent an ideological component and are largely tribal and ethnic.

In Nicaragua an essentially ideological conflict also contained ethnic or tribal elements (Sandinistas vs. Miskito Indians); that in neighboring El Salvador ran more clearly along ideological or economic-class lines. In Peru also, what on the surface had appeared to be an ideological civil war—incumbent regime vs. "leftist" guerillas—had contained a strong element of traditional conflict between Spanish-based urban elites and Indian tribal groups from the inland mountainous areas.

Some of the Middle Eastern conflicts have seen complex mixes of ideological, ethnolinguistic, and religious fault lines. The huge Iran-Iraq War, mostly involving rival national states, nevertheless also involved the problem of a Shi'a minority within Iraq, an Arab ethnic enclave in beleaguered Khuzistan, and various Kurdish groups (some pro-Iran, some pro-Iraq, some leftist and Moscow-leaning) with mixed national and ideological attachments. The seemingly interminable Lebanese internal conflict had witnessed a crazy and confusing mix of religious, linguistic, ethnic, and ideological alliances that shifted from one phase of the war to the next. In the latter part of the war, rival Christian groups battled against each other, as had rival Shi'a Muslim groups attached to Syria and Iran (there had also been the complex alignments of more than one Druze faction, with the majority Jumblatt wing normally aligned with Syria). Afghanistan's war also had earlier seen a complex mix of ideological (pro- and anti-Soviet), religious (fundamentalist Islam versus others), and nationalist and/or tribal considerations after the Soviet withdrawal. That then became a complex mix of tribal, ethnic, and religious desiderata, pitting rival Islamic groups against each other, some with external backing in Pakistan and Iran. In Western Sahara, the "native" Polisario guerillas were deemed "radical" in view of their ties with Libya and Algeria, and were pitted against a "moderate," pro-Western Moroccan government.

Cambodia also saw a complex mix of conflict fault lines, though the primary basis of conflict appeared to be ideological in nature, or as reflecting external alignments variously with China, Vietnam, or the U.S. But there were also regional divisions and some ideological lines of conflict even after the end of the Cold War.

In a manner somewhat spanning or summarizing these various conflict fault lines, the SIPRI group of researchers responsible for its annual yearbook chapter on "major armed conflicts" (defined as requiring a thousand or more battle-related deaths) came up with a new, disarmingly simple classification: redefining war and/or conflict as "a contested incompatibility" that involved a distinction between wars over territory and those over government. Hence,

> An incompatibility concerning government is at hand when the warring parties have a stated general incompatible position concerning the type of political system or change of the central government or its composition. An incompatibility concerning territory is at hand when the warring parties have a stated general incompatible position concerning control of territory (inter-state conflict), secession or autonomy (intra-state conflict).[66]

In this scheme, most if not all interstate wars or contested incompatibilities are fought over territory. Of course, some such wars involve internal "fifth columns" or ethnic groups hoping to be freed by external attacks—Iraqi Shi'a groups may have hoped that a victorious Iran would have installed a government in Baghdad more to their liking, as did the Mukti Bahinis in East Bengal as war between India and Pakistan approached in 1971. Some intrastate wars can easily be classified on one or another side of the divide. The Marxist rebellions in

Algeria, Nicaragua, El Salvador, and the Philippines were clearly wars over control of the government. But many others—Bosnia, Sudan, Eritrea, Chechnya—involve mixes of incompatibilities—government and territory—even if one or the other is largely predominant. Wars centered on ideology are more likely to be wars over government, while ethnic or tribal wars—particularly if secessionist movements are involved—are more likely to involve territorial incompatibilities. But that is still complex and arguable. The Rwandan ethnic conflict was largely a war over government in a nation where the Hutus and Tutsis live cheek by jowl. The Sudanese war is largely one over autonomy or possible secession—the southern non-Islamic groups hardly contemplate ruling the country from Khartoum. Hence, there appears to have been a shift since the Cold War, to a predominance of conflict over territory.

One interesting question is how one may define many of the current LICs along a spectrum from all-out to limited warfare. In a sense, this involves a paradox of sorts. Almost by definition, LICs rank low according to two of the three criteria used by many scholars to measure wars: magnitude and severity, maybe more likely so in the former case. But it is worth noting again that many LICs—Rwanda, Angola, Mozambique, the Central American conflicts—have involved far higher casualties than all of the major conventional wars, Iran-Iraq excepted and Afghanistan (a mixed conventional and guerilla war) partly excepted. Further, it would appear that many of these LICs have—more so than their conventional counterparts—been fought without very many limits, be they geographic or pertaining to the use of weapons, killing of civilians and prisoners. By their very nature, ethnic, religious, tribal, and also ideological conflicts in the Third World, howsoever limited in the sense of the absence of high-performance aircraft and armored systems, nonetheless tend to be fought out on a brutal, unlimited basis. Hence, the huge casualties caused mostly by small arms and other handheld weapons, plus starvation and disease.

Generally speaking, by the late 1990s, the overall locus of conflict seemed to have shifted away from ideological considerations, as the Cold War structures faded and with them the superpowers' alignments with putative ideological bedfellows. Expanding in its stead were numerous festering racial, religious, and tribal wars, overall amounting to a return to a familiar historical norm.

The Levels of Analysis

In recent years, perhaps the most significant and pronounced advance in the analysis of wars (and of defense planning), has been that of the growing use of what now familiarly is called "levels of analysis." This by now almost ritually used framework of analysis has perhaps been inspired in part by the institutionalization of "lessons learned" exercises within the U.S. military establishment and elsewhere in the aftermath of the wars of the 1980s, followed by the Gulf War. It has further been inspired by the U.S. Army's resurgence of interest in the "operational arts" in the wake of the Vietnam debacle and in the context of efforts at dealing with the presumed counterpart Soviet attention to such "arts" as were embodied in the earlier feared Operational Maneuver Group (OMG) in Central Europe.[67] During the late 1980s, a mere perusal of *Parameters,* the journal of the U.S. Army War College, would have revealed a near obsession with the "operational arts."

As it happens, "levels of analysis" has long been familiar in another related context: to students of international relations theory, dating back some forty years to the seminal conceptualizations of J. David Singer.[68] There, it was recognized that no single "image" or angle of vision could suffice to describe or explain what, theoretically, was important to theorizing (or categorizing) in international relations. So, levels of analyses schemes were devised to provide multiple foci for analysis or, if you will, angles of vision or "images." Most commonly, this involved the "international system," "nation state," and "individual" levels of analysis as utilized, for instance, by Kenneth Waltz to examine alternative explanations for the causes of war. Still other analysts, for instance Patrick Morgan, preferred a more elaborate breakdown of "levels." He chose to utilize five of them:

1. International politics is ultimately created by *individuals* interacting; thus we must focus on the behavior of key individuals—presidents, foreign ministers, leading advisors, and the like.
2. International politics is created primarily by *small groups*—cabinets, National Security Council, Politburo—and by organizations, bureaucracies, departments, agencies; thus the focus must be on small-group and organization behavior.
3. International politics is dominated by the actions of *nation-states;* our concern must be with individuals, groups, organizations, institutions, and their processes only as they bear on nations' international actions. We must study foreign policy-making by the nation as a unit.
4. Nations don't act alone. International politics is interaction that falls into *patterns and clusters;* thus the thing to study is the cluster—the regional grouping, alliances, trade and investment groups, ideological blocs, voting blocs in the U.N., and the like.
5. Nations and their interactions constitute *a system.* This system and its changes over time determine actors' behavior, that is, environment determines behavior. Thus we must study this system and generalize about it as a whole.[69]

In a further related vein, writers such as Paul Viotti and Mark Kauppi have used such alternative frameworks as the "realist," "pluralist," and "globalist" images of international relations, in part encompassing "levels of analysis,"[70] but also further introducing a political-ideological dimension to the classification of international relations theories. Our later chapter 6 on the cultural aspects of war will reveal still another level of analysis scheme.

Likewise, analysts of warfare have learned that inevitably, various levels of analysis must be utilized if they are to avoid the mixing of apples and oranges or, rather, the juxtaposing or confusing of related but distinct ways of analyzing military affairs. There is nothing entirely new about such levels, in the simplest sense. For perhaps centuries, military writers have distinguished between strategy and tactics as the poles of macro and micro levels of analysis. The terms were used unselfconsciously, rarely rigorously defined, always implicitly understood in the broadest sense, i.e., respectively, "big think" and "how to take the next hill," macro to micro.

But in recent years, again, perhaps because of the more widespread institutionalization of "lessons learned" and perhaps also as a spin-off from the compulsive theorizing and construction of typologies so endemic to American social science academia, the use of levels has become more refined, more elaborated, more regularized and ritualistic. Such had been the case for the "levels of analysis" utilized for international relations theory: it was every person for his own mix of levels. Well, almost: there was indeed a central core of considerable convergence.

Most analysis converged upon an at best three-way division of the strategic, operational, and tactical levels. Some added a fourth, the "grand strategic," at the macro end of the spectrum. Others, such as Edward Luttwak, utilized a "technical" level at the micro end.[71] Still others utilized the concept of "grand tactics" as fitting between the operational and tactical levels, although some treated "grand tactics" and "operations" as largely synonymous.[72] In a major three-volume work on the "military effectiveness" of many major powers during several intervals dating back to World War I, Allan Millett and Williamson Murray utilized a "political" level of analysis as preceding "strategy" on the macro end of the spectrum.[73] For the sake of comprehensiveness, let us look at all of these, but with an eye to what would most be appropriate to a comparative study of contemporary warfare.

The Grand Strategic Level

In many respects, the grand strategic level of analysis is the easiest to define. Simply stated, it is that level that overarches all others. Thus, according to Luttwak:

> The entire conduct of warfare and peacetime preparation for war are in turn subordinate expressions of national struggles that unfold at the highest level of grand strategy, where all that is military happens within the much broader context of domestic governance, international politics, economic activity, and their ancillaries. Because ultimate ends and basic means are both manifest only at the level of **grand strategy,** the resource limits of military action are defined at that level, and so is its true meaning: even a most successful conquest is only a provisional result that can be overturned by the diplomatic intervention of more powerful states or even repudiated by domestic political decision; by contrast, even a major military debacle can be redeemed by the political transformations it engenders, or undone by the newfound allies that weakness can attract in the usual workings of the balance of power. . . .

If we recall the earlier image of strategy as a sort of multilevel edifice, with floors set in motion by the waves and counter waves of action and reaction, we would find that its highest level is very much more spacious than those below it, in a way that no feasible architecture would allow. For at the level of grand strategy, the interactions of the lower, military levels, their synergisms or contradictions, yield final results within the broad setting of international politics, in further interaction with the nonmilitary transactions of states: the formal exchanges of diplomacy, the public communications of propaganda, secret operations, the perceptions of others formed by intelligence official and unofficial, and all economic transactions of more than purely private significance. On this disproportionate top floor, therefore, the **net** outcome of the technical, tactical, operational, and theater-strategic emerges in continuous interaction with all those dealings between states that are affected by, and in turn affect, what is done or not done militarily within any one state. [Emphasis in original.][74]

John Collins focuses upon the distinction between military strategy and grand strategy:

"Military strategy" and "grand strategy" are interrelated, but are by no means synonymous. Military strategy is predicated on physical violence or the threat of violence. It seeks victory through force of arms. Grand strategy, if successful, alleviates any need for violence. Equally important, it looks beyond victory toward a lasting peace. Military strategy is mainly the province of generals. Grand strategy is mainly the purview of statesmen. Grand strategy **controls** military strategy, which is only one of its elements.

Grand strategy, which embraces such niceties as bluff, negotiation, economic skulduggery, and psychological warfare, debunks the belief—widely held since Clausewitz's day—that strategy simply is "the use of engagements to attain the object of war." On the contrary, it cleaves closely to Liddell Hart's conclusion that "the true aim **is not so much to seek battle as to seek a strategic situation so advantageous that if it does not of itself produce the division, its continuation by a battle is sure to achieve this.**" [Emphasis in original.][75]

Otherwise, it might be noted that the grand strategic level is that dealt with by the "National Command Authority," that is, by the apex of a government, be it a president and his closest aides, or the Politburo, or whatever would elsewhere be equivalent. Regarding the military aspects of a global war fought by a superpower, such a grand strategy clearly would involve allocations of efforts in a multitheater context.

The Political Level

Millett and Murray, focusing upon military effectiveness, utilize a "political" rather than grand strategic level "above" that of a strategic level. What they have in mind, however, relates mostly to the *preparations* for war, that is, to defense planning, rather than the broadest politico-military considerations involved in conducting an ongoing war. Stated another way, the key consideration at the political level is the securing of resources necessary to the conduct of war, that is, it involves budgets and force structures. Hence, according to Millett and Murray:

> For a military organization to act strategically, operationally, or tactically, it must consistently secure the resources required to maintain, expand, and reconstruct itself. Almost always, this requires the military to obtain the cooperation of the national elite. Hence, the effort to obtain resources for military activity and the proficiency in acquiring those resources constitute political effectiveness. Resources consist of reliable access to financial support, a sufficient military-industrial base, a sufficient quality and quality of manpower, and control over the conversion of those resources into military capabilities.[76]

As noted, this "political" level of analysis is utilized by Millett and Murray both for peacetime and wartime situations, which may or may not be wholly distinct from what Luttwak and others have in mind when referring to a grand strategic level. But grand strategy, whether in peace or war, relates wholly to strategy vis-à-vis or against an external opponent. The political level, contrariwise, appears virtually to pit the military authorities, if only in a less deadly rivalry, against the rest of society in a struggle over resources. It has to do with internal extraction of resources, albeit still in a somewhat zero sum situation, given the overall finite amounts of available resources.

The Strategic Level

Some writers treat the "strategic level" as the "highest" level of analysis, while others utilize it as a second rung beneath the overarching one of grand strategy. With the latter usage, the distinction usually resides in the division between an all-encompassing politico-military-economic focus and one which is—to the extent possible—more narrowly military.

Luttwak utilizes the notion of "theater strategy" under that of grand strategy. Here he refers to "the broader interaction of the armed forces as a whole within the entire theater of warfare . . . it is at this level of *theater strategy* that the consequences of single operations are felt in the overall conduct of offense and defense—those overriding military purposes that scarcely figure at the operational level." Further,

> The logic of strategy at the theater level governs the relationship between military strength and territory, and we can understand much of it in visual terms, seeing deployments and movements in a bird's eye view, or perhaps one should say in a satellite overview. Of course, strategy has a spatial aspect at the lower levels also, but at the tactical level it is the detailed

nature of the terrain that matters, and at the operational level geography merely provides the shifting backdrop of combat encounters that could be much the same in other settings as well.

At the theater level, however, it is some specific territory that is the very object of contention. It may be as large as a subcontinent or as small as an island, but unless that theater of war is marked off by political boundaries, it must be sufficiently separated from other theaters by important geographic barriers or sheer distance to be defensible or vulnerable on its own. Whether it amounts to a province, an entire country, or even a vast regional grouping of countries, a theater of war must form a self-contained military whole rather than just one part of a whole.[77]

Collins, meanwhile, subsumes "military strategy" under "grand strategy," indeed avers that military strategy is predicated on violence or its threat, seeking victory through force of arms, while "grand strategy, if successful, alleviates any need for violence."[78] (In that sense it is seen as closely related not only to diplomacy, but also to deterrence.) Collins, relying upon Rear Admiral J.C. Wylie, goes on to identify two elemental strategies, which he entitles "sequential" and "cumulative." Hence,

> Sequential strategies, as he describes them, comprise successive steps, each contingent on the one preceding, that lead to the final objective. Efforts to undermine the enemy's morale, isolate him from allies, deny him external supply, and destroy his internal lines of communication before invading his homeland would be a typical sequential strategy.
>
> Cumulative strategies conversely constitute a collection of individual, random actions that eventually create crushing results. Strategic bombardment and naval campaigns against enemy shipping are prime examples. The Soviets used cumulative techniques in a different vein in the 1940s when, one by one, they incarcerated nine countries behind the Iron Curtain. No single loss seemed shattering to the Free World, but suddenly it seemed the Kremlin dominated all of Eastern Europe.[79]

In the context of military effectiveness, Millett and Murray define the strategic level somewhat in the manner that others define "grand strategy" and "strategy." Hence, "strategic activity consists of plans specifying time, geography, vision, and objectives and the execution of those plans."[80] Subsumed within the definition are the analysis and selection of strategic objectives and the linkage of those objectives to national goals through the mechanism of campaign or contingency plans.

If the grand strategic level is pegged at that of the national command authority, the strategic level is pegged between there and the theater. Perhaps for the U.S., the strategic level could be said to be the responsibility of the Joint Chiefs of Staff and the secretary of defense, extending downward to the regional, theater "CINCs" (commander in chiefs).

The Operational Level

As noted, this level has received by far the most attention in recent U.S. military publications, if only because its importance appears to have been "rediscovered" by the U.S. military in the 1980s. Formally speaking, the U.S. military locates it—in the context of military command structure—at the level of "corps and above" or "echelons above corps." And further, most writings focused on this level tend to dwell, self-consciously, on the concept of the "operational arts."[81]

Luttwak reflects the view of the U.S. military, which rues the past underestimation of the operational level as follows, further amounting to an American nod of respect toward Germany and Russia on this score. Further, in defining the operational level:

> [e]vents at the operational level can be very large in scale, but never autonomous; they are governed in turn by the broader interaction of the armed forces as whole within the entire theater of warfare, just as battles are merely parts of campaigns. It is at this higher level of **theater strategy** that the consequences of single operations are felt in the overall conduct of offense and defense—those overriding military purposes that scarcely figure at the operational level, in which a bombing campaign might be launched by defenders while the aggressor is preoccupied with air defense, and which an attack can serve to better defend a front while holding operations on some sectors often figure in offensive warfare.[82]

We shall return to this later, but it is at this, the operational level, that Luttwak and others discuss the historically contrasting modes of fighting called "attrition" and "maneuver" (others use the terminology of offense and defense, or firepower, maneuver, and protection as basic alternating modes of analysis).[83]

Millett and Murray define the operational level in the context of military effectiveness as follows:

> The operational level of military activity refers to the analysis, selection, and development of institutional concepts or doctrines for employing major forces to achieve strategic objectives within a theater of war. Operational military activity involves the analysis, planning, preparation, and conduct of the various facets of a specific campaign. Within the scope of operational matters lie the disposition and marshaling of military units, the selection of theater objectives, the arrangement of logistical support, and the direction of ground, air, and sea forces. A combination of military concerns shape these operational-level decisions: the mission, the nature of the enemy, and his probable objectives, terrain, logistics, the available allied and national forces, and the time available for mission accomplishment.[84]

A review of the U.S. Army's journal *Parameters* in recent years reveals a spate of articles in which the operational level is further defined, not without some disagreements or alternative views. To some degree the differences are merely semantic, and virtually all use as a starting point the U.S. Army's 1982 edition of FM100–5, *Operations,* as amended somewhat by the 1986 edition. Ronald D'Amura explains the semantic confusion as follows:

> The 1982 edition of FM100–5, *Operations,* defines the operational level of war as that level where available military resources are employed to attain strategic goals within a theater of war. Here, the operational level is closely associated with the theory of larger-unit formations and the planning and conduct of campaigns. In the 1986 edition of the same field manual, the term "operational art" replaces "operational level," but the definition remains essentially the same. In this latest version, operational art still focuses on the attainment of strategic objectives through the design and conduct of campaigns. Gone, however, is the explicit connection with large formations—an apparent recognition that relatively small forces, such as those involved in the Grenada operation, can fight at the operational level. . . . In any event, the operational level of war and operational art are interchangeable terms used to describe warfare that achieves strategic aims.[85]

In a related vein, Dwight Adams and Clayton Newell insist upon the distinction between "theater of war" and "theater of operations" (the former, in the Vietnam context, would have been commanded by commander in chief, Pacific [CINCPAC] in Honolulu, the latter from Military Assistance Command, Vietnam [MACV] in Saigon). Wishing to move away from the habit of defining the operational level in terms of the sheer size of forces involved, the authors prefer to define it in terms of the conduct of campaigns within theaters of operations, i.e., war zones. Hence, and thus in consensus with the 1986 edition of FM100–5, they aver that "the operational art concerns the design, organization, and conduct of major operations and campaigns, while stipulating that no particular echelon of command is solely or uniquely involved."[86] This definition can then accommodate rather small campaigns by major maritime powers such as the U.S., Britain, or Japan, as for instance the Japanese campaign to capture Singapore in 1941 (involving three divisions of troops) or Wellington's Peninsular campaign in Spain in 1809. Hence, in tying the operational level to campaigns, one can be talking about "echelons above corps," but in some circumstances—perhaps decisive ones—we can be talking about much smaller forces if responsible for a theaterwide campaign.

The Tactical Level

In some respects, the tactical level may be the most difficult to define, for it may subsume several layers of activity. Some formal U.S. Army definitions subsume within it all operations at the division level or below. But at the division level (requiring a division command to coordinate the efforts of several brigades or battalions) this amounts really to what some would refer to as "grand tactics." At the other end of the tactical spectrum, one could be referring to infantry squad formations (or platoon formations) or to ways of assaulting a heavily defended hilltop bunker or to ways of conducting a squad-sized nighttime reconnaissance patrol.

Historical examples, particularly regarding innovations, abound. One thinks, for instance, of the successful "storm" tactics devised by German infantry toward the end of World War I or, on defense, the flexible tactics devised by the Germans to lure offensive Allied forces into "killing grounds" after a small advance. American use of flamethrowers against Japanese pillboxes on fortified atolls would be another example. Further back, one might point to the tactical innovations devised during the American Civil War for the infantry, featuring "rushes" and the use of cover to replace the older reliance on disciplined, massed formations, which had been rendered obsolete by the advent of automatic weapons as well as the more efficient use of single-shot rifles.

Millett and Murray, in the context of military effectiveness, define the tactical level as follows:

> The tactical level of military activity refers to the specific techniques used by combat units to fight engagements in order to secure operational objectives. Tactical activity involves the movement of forces on the battlefield against the enemy, the provision of destructive fire upon enemy forces or targets, and the arrangement of logistical support directly applicable to engagements.[87]

They go on to cite as examples such tactical problems as nonevasive flying of bombers by U.S. pilots in World War II, the use of wingmen in fighter combat, the U.S. Marines' use of flamethrowers against Japanese bunkers.

Luttwak, defining the core of the tactical level from a somewhat different perspective, focuses on the "intangibles of skill, leadership, morale, discipline, and unit cohesion."[88] He does that in order to demonstrate "why military-balance estimates formed at the technical level alone are so systematically misleading: in presenting lists of weapons side by side, they offer comparisons of attractive precision that exclude the greater part of the whole." Stated another way, it is the intangibles of tactics, qualitative distinctions that, along with mere fortune, i.e., chance and possibility, often determine the outcomes of battle in a manner overriding or even contradicting what would appear dictated by numerically based orders of battle. Partly that involves skill, partly "friction" or chance.

But in a longer perspective, it must be remembered that tactical innovations are driven by new weapons developments, if only often at a different pace, as such innovations are absorbed by rival or contemporaneous armies utilizing the same or similar weapons types. Hence, the introduction of PGMs drove new antiarmor tactics by Egyptian infantrymen in the 1973 war, in turn engendering new tactics by the Israelis for suppressing such infantry, which required more extensive use of the artillery arm that heretofore had been underutilized by the Israelis. Or, in 1982, the Israelis were able to introduce entirely new tactics devised for suppressing surface-to-air missiles, but based on emerging technologies, i.e., antiradiation missiles (both air-to-surface and surface-to-surface), remotely piloted vehicles, battle-management aircraft, and improved artillery-fire direction.

The Technical Level

Luttwak, almost alone among military analysts, appends a "technical" level to the by now standard breakdown of strategic, operational, and tactical levels. That is an apt analytical innovation which allows circumvention of what long had been a rather confusing juxtaposition of different forms of analysis as applied to what earlier had been commonly accepted as falling under "tactics."[89]

As it is, a perusal of some of the Pentagon's recent "lessons learned" exercises, such as those dealing with the Falklands War, would reveal a combining of what Luttwak separates out as the technical and tactical levels. We have defined the latter. The former has to do with the comparative efficacy of specific weapons systems.[90] Sometimes this may have to do with an individual weapons system, i.e., the performance of Britain's Harrier jump jets or Argentina's French-supplied Exocet missiles in the Falklands War (but such analysis can as easily apply to combat gear or to logistical systems.)

Just as often, such an analysis will apply to pairings of contending weapons systems or classes of weapons. One can seek lessons in a given war from the standoff involving tanks vs. antitank weapons, tactical aircraft vs. SAMs, tanks vs. armored personnel carriers, aircraft-mounted antiship missiles vs. fleet air defenses. Or such analysis can be attempted at the more specific level of stand-offs between specific weapons systems, i.e., Merkava tank vs. Sagger antitank missile, SAM-6 vs. low-flying Kfirs or Skyhawks, Roland SAMs vs. low-flying Mirages, T-72s vs. M-60s, F-117s vs. multilayered air defense systems. Narrowly speaking, and making allowances for the tactical capabilities of the forces involved, lessons of this sort are often used as guides for weapons acquisitions, force planning, and also training, or at least to make the relevant political, budgetary arguments.

The Merging or Blurring of Levels of War

In the immediate aftermath of the burgeoning use of levels of analysis in the 1980s brought on by the efforts to divine lessons from the several major wars of that period, there was a curious reversal, involving a paradox of sorts. That involved a new assertion on the part of some military analysts that the previously discrete and well-demarcated strategic, operational, and tactical levels were now becoming blurred, maybe en route to extinction. As it happens, there were some precursors to this perceived change. In the early 1980s there had been discussions along these lines in connection with the U.S. AirLand battle 2000 doctrine that envisaged extending the battlefield far to the rear to involve Soviet rear echelons. Then in the context of the strategic nuclear arms control negotiations of the 1970s and 1980s, there were the disputes about what were strategic, theater, and tactical weapons. These categories had long been defined primarily in terms of ranges, but in the 1980s U.S. employment of Pershing II and GLCM missiles

in Western Europe, in addition to its FBS (forward-based-systems) aircraft, provided the definitional dilemma of weapons of theater range being able to attack
the foe's homeland strategically.

But it was the U.S. conduct of the Gulf War, followed upon by the explosion
of writings about RMA/MTR that really focused attention on the blurring of
levels. Indeed, this projected development, along with the projected blurring of
the previously distinct roles of the traditional service components—army, navy,
air force—became a major focus of the MTR literature. Hence, according to
MacGregor, writing in the immediate aftermath of the Gulf War:

> The analysis suggests that in the future, the technologically altered battle-
> field dimensions of time and space will merge the three levels of war into
> a single new structure for the integration of complex air-land-sea combat
> operations. Linked to this greater scope for directing joint simultaneous
> offensive operations is the emerging capability to immediately convert tac-
> tical success on the battlefield into decisive strategic results.[91]

MacGregor traces what he sees as the gradual blurring of the strategic, operational, and tactical levels over almost two centuries, perceiving watersheds with
Napoleon's Ulm campaign in 1805, the German blitzkrieg against France in
1940, and the American-led Operation Desert Storm in 1991. Regarding the
latter, MacGregor states the following:

> What changed in 1991 was the sudden availability of precise deep-strike
> delivery systems on land and aboard ships and aircraft, combined with a
> vast inventory of lethal conventional munitions and long-range aircraft
> which could be guided by target-acquisition instruments to enemy targets
> under near constant surveillance. Equally important for the ultimate out-
> come was the decisive American overmatch in the direct-fire battle and
> the integration of tactical and strategic systems to support the tactical fight.
>
> To a much greater extent than ever before, the theater commander was
> technologically positioned to influence action on the battlefield by direct-
> ing global military resources to the points in time and space he regarded as
> critical to the campaign's success. For the Iraqi enemy, whose air defenses
> failed and whose intelligence-collection capability was either destroyed or
> deceived, the deep, close and rear battles were compressed into one seam-
> less, continuous fight. From the vantage point of the Iraqi command struc-
> ture, the categories of American capabilities and weapon systems directed
> against Iraqi forces in terms of their strategic, operational, or tactical points
> of origin were indistinguishable.[92]

And summing it up:

> The form of warfare collapses the three levels of war, so to speak, by enlist-
> ing the *tactics* of fire and movement directly on behalf of the strategic goal.

The new structure of warfare integrates and synchronizes redundant, multi-service warfighting systems in simultaneous attacks on the enemy throughout his entire depth and in the space above him as well. All of this means that in future conflict the three levels of war, as separate and distinct loci of command and functional responsibilities, will be spaced and timed out of existence.[93]

It was further noted that the identification of certain weapons systems normally defined as "tactical" or "strategic" had also become blurred in Desert Storm. Long-range "strategic" bombers from the Cold War context, such as the B-52s and F-111s, were used for tactical purposes on the immediate battlefield, while fighter-attack aircraft such as the F-15s and F-117s were used for "strategic" purposes, i.e., knocking out Iraqi infrastructure far behind the front lines. Similar blurrings occurred with respect to missile systems.

Of course, those strictures about the blurring of levels of analysis are meant primarily to point to the future of hi-tech conventional warfare, as well as to the lessons provided by Desert Storm. The focus upon the simultaneity of assaults at the forward battlefield and well behind it may still not change some basic, enduring components of "level" having to do with micro and macro operations and aims. The thesis about the blurring of levels hinges greatly on interpretations derived from the increasing importance of standoff weapons to dominate the battlespace. Much less does it dwell on the uses of various other new weapons. Later, if "fire ant" and "pop up" warfare should indeed come to pass with battlefields loaded with small sensors backed up by long-range shooters (and absent large platforms such as tanks), there will presumably be tactical considerations for the use of these new weapons. These considerations would not yet appear applicable to conventional warfare where the now vaunted U.S. MTR machine is not involved, less still to the myriad LICs that now form the central focus of conflict studies.

A Matrix: Types of War and Levels of Analysis

Heretofore, in numerous analyses and whatever the specifics of terminology, "levels of analysis" has been devoted almost entirely to "traditional" interstate warfare. Not accidentally, Luttwak's major work was pegged almost entirely to the Central European balance involving NATO and the Warsaw Treaty Organization. The same is true for the Millett and Murray work, which deals with the fighting of, and the preparations for, the two major world wars of this century.

But as we have seen, most recent wars have fallen toward the end of the scale away from conventional interstate warfare, somewhere along the spectrum of low-intensity warfare running from major guerilla wars to terrorism and coups. Generally speaking, there is no reason why the standard levels of analysis can not apply to the more intense end of the LIC spectrum, i.e., to large-scale unconventional, guerilla or civil warfare. Indeed, it can easily be applied at all levels, albeit on a more microcosmic scale. Concepts such as *foco* and Maoist modes of revolutionary warfare are easily recognizable as the heart of the operational level of guerilla warfare. At the lower level of LIC (coups, border friction, terrorism), the direct applicability of much of the levels of analysis, to one degree or another, fades away. Or does it?

There are, however, some obvious and salient differences in the applicability of levels of analysis, in comparing conventional and unconventional or low-intensity warfare. One has already been noted, that of scale. If in conventional warfare the operational level is defined (maybe somewhat arbitrarily) as "above the level of corps," a different scale clearly would be appropriate to divide unconventional operations from tactics. Grand strategy, on the other hand, is grand strategy at any level, but where unconventional warfare is involved, the strategies may be conducted by entities other than recognized national governments or their "command authorities." At the operational level, meanwhile, such central concepts as maneuver vs. attrition may clearly be less applicable to the analysis of unconventional wars.

There is, however, one major conceptual divide here between the conventional and unconventional. In the former, strategies, operations, and tactics are normally mutually symmetrical; that is, we are dealing with similar forces both of which can play either on offense or defense, much like a football team (or if one side is altogether dominant, the weaker side still normally utilizes conventional operations and tactics).

But in most guerilla warfare (or at least in SIPRI terminology, wars over government), there is usually an incumbent regime that utilizes counterinsurgency tactics against a revolutionary or insurrectionary force that utilizes insurgency tactics. And they don't switch roles during the war as so often is the case in conventional wars when or if the tide of the battle turns. Here, there are commonly discussed insurgency tactics and strategies (hit and run, *foco,* Maoist rural insurgency), and there are counterinsurgency strategies and tactics (fortified hamlets, spreading oil blotches, search and destroy), but they remain distinct. Unconventional warfare, then, is often a game played between two altogether different types of teams and, as it happens, more often to a definitive conclusion.

The Disciplines and the Study of the Conduct of War

Closely related to the levels of analysis problem as applied to the study of war are the varying perspectives provided by various disciplines. But only in part can these varying perspectives or angles of vision be organized along a "macro-to-micro spectrum" correlated with levels of analysis.

This is not entirely a new subject. Long ago, in Quincy Wright's enduring and classic study of war, he devoted a chapter to "the social disciplines and war," which catalogued and discussed the contributions provided by a variety of disciplines.[94] But the primary focus there was on the causes of war.

Wright's analysis ran along the following lines—keep in mind that this reflected the breakdown of academic disciplines as of a half century ago:[95]

Table 1.4

Disciplines Related to Social Science	Pure Social Sciences
History	Anthropology
Geography	Sociology
Biology	Philosophy and Ethics★
Psychology★	

Practical Social Disciplines	Applied Social Sciences
Theology and Religion★	Economics
Jurisprudence★	Political Science
Military Science	
Diplomacy	
Statistics	
Population	
Technology	
Social Psychology	
International Relations	

Several of the disciplines, cited by asterisk, make contributions almost solely in connection with the causes of war; hence, for our purposes, they are not centrally relevant. However, there might even here be a demurrer or two—the strictly religious basis of the "Islamic way of war" is an example. All of the other disciplines are, however, relevant, and some contribute at more than one level of analysis. Historians, specifically military historians, can write of strategy, operations, or tactics, though they are more likely to be comfortable at the "higher" end of the spectrum. The same is true for geographers, whose interests may range from grand strategy (geopolitics) to tactical geography (terrain, topography). Psychologists and sociologists can dwell on the prior misperceptions of military leaders planning wars or campaigns, or on the psychological and sociological problems of small units or individuals (battle fatigue, group cohesion, leadership, morale, etc.). Economists, in assessing the costs of war, and the preparation for it, are most likely to dwell on the trade-offs in connection with non-defense expenditures or on the long-term effects upon national economies of high defense budgets. That pertains to the grand strategic or strategic level. Demographers are likewise apt to contribute at a strategic level, dealing with the changing basis of national power as it is rooted in population changes, or on the demographic basis of comparable national pain thresholds, that is, who can take what kind of casualties.

Political scientists (usually meaning specialists in international relations or security studies) are most likely to be found studying grand strategy and strategy. It is their métier and, like most social scientists, they may be woefully ignorant of weapons technology or of the operational and tactical aspects of warfare. The latter tend to be the domains of specialists in military science, either serving officers (or retired ones) or the handful of military historians who have developed a real working knowledge of the military arts. Specialists in technology—scientists or engineers—can provide useful knowledge on the nuts and bolts of military systems, as for instance in comparing rival aircrafts' electronic countermeasures capability or aerodynamic characteristics. Specialists in diplomacy (either professional diplomats or international relations specialists), meanwhile, are likely to contribute on the diplomacy of war initiation and war termination, or on the political interactions and reciprocal leverage of dependent fighting nations and their big-power patrons.

Again, at the risk of belaboring the point, many studies of wars (or of comparisons of them) suffer from a tendency to focus solely on one or another level of analysis or one or another disciplinary perspective. A fully effective analysis of several levels will, as a matter of course, depend on the contributions of several disciplines.

The Literature on Warfare: A Classification

In the course of our inquiries on recent warfare, we have come to learn something about what is available—and not available—in the relevant literature. As a general statement, there appears less and less information and analysis available as one moves from the level of grand strategy to that of tactics; and less and less available as one moves from conventional warfare to the "lower" end of the LIC scale. There are, of course, occasional exceptions.

Overall, there would appear to be about nine distinct types of information and of military analysis, as follows, and with some examples. The following list may not be exhaustive, and there are, of course, gray areas spanning two or more categories.

1. Detailed battle histories

Pioneered in modern times by John Keegan and Paul Fussell, and explicitly intended by them to act as a corrective for the traditional and often romanticized "drums and bugles" military historians, this involves a vivid and detailed "insider's" or participant's account (or as Keegan has done for battles far back in the mists of history, equivalent reconstructions).[96] In this type of work, the reader is provided a real "feel" for the war; its sounds, sights, and smells, its blood and gore, its bravery and cowardice. In the process, a good portrayal may be rendered of the comparative cultural aspects of warfare, for instance, of the relationships between officers and enlisted men or degrees of unit cohesion. In the recent past, the books on the Falklands War authored by Colonel Nick Vaux (serving officer)[97] and Max Hastings (accompanying journalist) from the British side have constituted some excellent related examples, albeit at a somewhat broader level. So too, Avigdor Kahalani's work on armored warfare in the 1973 war.[98] Among the numerous accounts of the Gulf War, perhaps Rick Atkinson's *Crusade* and *The General's War* by Michael Gordon and Bernard Trainor are most representative of this genre.[99]

2. Standard military histories

These are the (essentially chronological and descriptive) histories of wars involving detailed posthoc reconstructions of campaigns or battles, though not usually with the bird's eye tactical level of detail provided in a "battle history," á la Keegan. The focus here tends to be at the level of operations or grand tactics. Journalists often can provide rather quick studies of this sort on the basis of some visits to the war zone (maybe only posthoc) and/or some briefings by participants, usually meaning higher level commanders. The numerous works by Edgar O'Ballance, including one on the Iran-Iraq War, are good examples, as were the earlier works by Winston Churchill III and Randolph Churchill[100] and of S. L. A. Marshall[101] on the 1967 Middle Eastern war and 1956 Suez War, or that by Ze'ev Schiff and Ehud Ya'ari on the 1982 Israeli invasion of Lebanon.[102] Very few if any of the recent LICs have received this sort of treatment.

3. Primarily political/diplomatic histories

These are works focusing on the politics surrounding the origins of wars and intrawar diplomacy—also the diplomacy of war termination. Often written by academic political scientists, these works tend to be pegged at the level of grand strategy. The works by Itamar Rabinovich and Walter Laqueur on the 1982 and 1973 Middle Eastern wars, respectively, constitute some good examples,[103] along with several works on Afghanistan such as that by J. Bruce Amstutz, *Afghanistan,* and Rosanne Klass, *Afghanistan: The Great Game Revisited.*[104] Another excellent recent example is Nayan Chanda's *Brother Enemy: The War after the War,*[105] which covers the Cambodian conflict up to 1979. Oftentimes, general coverages of a war from front to back will have some introductory chapters on its origins or proximate causes.

4. Analytical works on military effectiveness

These are works explicitly intended to gauge military effectiveness, i.e., to measure comparatively the efficacy of contending forces in one or more wars. The focus can be at several levels, such as the aforementioned works by Allen Millett and Williamson Murray ranging across the political, strategic, operational, and tactical levels.[106] There is no effort to provide a history or chronology here, and "effectiveness" tends to be illustrated by example as well as comprehensively assessed.

Millett and Murray examine military effectiveness on a nation-by-nation basis from an ant's eye perspective and eschew more than rudimentary use of numbers except, for instance, to deal with military budgets at the political level. Trevor Dupuy, on the other hand, analyzes military effectiveness mostly on the operational or tactical levels, with extensive use of quantification.[107] Rather than providing an ant's eye view from one side, he examines specific pairings in battles, i.e., the Israelis versus the Egyptians at the Chinese Farm in 1973, or the Germans versus the French at Sedan in 1940. Within that framework, he produces battle analyses involving a variety of factors—manpower, environmental variables, terrain, weather, seasons, mobility, and surprise—and moves from there to comparative measures of combat effectiveness, on a per capita basis, amounting at the bottom line to a comparative qualitative assessment of various armies.

Though existing in considerable contrast to one another, the respective analyses of military effectiveness by Millett and Murray and by Dupuy can be marvelously complementary as applied to given wars or to battles within them. The former is more about who wins wars (which includes their politics); the latter is more about who wins given battles and who has, on a per capita basis, a better fighting army, i.e., a qualitatively superior one, ultimate outcomes notwithstanding.

5. Compendia, anthologies on conventional war or LICs or both, utilizing a comparative framework

These are compendia, sometimes single-authored, more likely containing individual chapters for various wars authored by specialists and edited within a roughly comparative framework. The earlier Harkavy and Neuman volumes on lessons of wars in the Third World, comprising both conventional and unconventional conflicts, is one recent example.[108] Another, this time involving only guerilla warfare and with a single author, is the *War of the Flea* by Robert Taber, which covers numerous countries.[109] Another example is the comparative analysis of low-intensity conflicts edited by David Charters and Maurice Tugwell.[110] In all of these, the emphasis is more on war-fighting and less on the contextual politics of given wars. One typical problem is the tendency for different authors to focus on different levels of analysis, sometimes a matter of disciplinary perspective, sometimes resulting from a paucity of available information.

6. Comprehensive, interpretive military histories

These works tend to take a long-term panoramic view of many centuries of military history, dealt with according to a rough sequential chronology and often involving sections on key topics such as technology and logistics. A good recent example is Hew Strachan's *European Armies and the Conduct of War*, which begins with "The Age of Marlborough and Frederick" and ends with modern nuclear strategy, stopping along the way for a look at eighteenth-century tactics, Napoleon, Jomini, Clausewitz, the trench warfare of World War I and the blitzkriegs of World War II.[111] Similarly one could point to the classic work by Edward Earle on the strategists of recent centuries, a roughly chronological study of strategy as seen from the perspective of various military commanders and strategists.[112] Of course, there are also the massive comprehensive military histories—spanning many centuries and focusing on campaigns and battles—associated particularly with J. F. C. Fuller.[113] The latter's second volume alone moves from the Armada campaign of 1588 to Waterloo (1814) in some 550 pages of erudite detail, mostly at the operational and strategic levels, some at the tactical level.

By their very nature, the various contributions of this genre can tell us little directly about contemporary warfare in the developing world. But they can provide invaluable background and a "feel" for the ceaseless interplay, over the centuries, of weapons, tactics, operations, and generalship, and an additional feel for the role of imponderables, luck, and "friction." One is at least impelled thereby to ponder the question of whether "the more things change, the more they remain the same."

7. Brief reviews of current conflicts, with data

Several recent works, some in the form of annual offerings, provide perhaps the first point of departure for the study of contemporary conflicts. These can provide a year-by-year review of the fighting and associated diplomacy and a run-down of basic data: casualties, equipment attrition, costs, number of combatants involved, duration of conflict—altogether, an abbreviated encyclopedia of modern warfare. Most prominent here is the annual chapter in SIPRI's *Armaments Yearbook* put together by a group of peace researchers at the University of Uppsala in Sweden, and John Laffin's *The World in Conflict*.[114] The latter provides several pages each on some thirty-five to fifty ongoing conflicts. More detailed and going back over most of the conflicts since 1945 is Patrick Brogan's *The Fighting Never Stopped: A Comprehensive Guide to World Conflicts Since 1945*.[115] This book is organized by region, providing analyses both of the relevant political and military dimensions, but with a minimum of tactical-level battlefield analysis. Still more detailed and utilizing contemporary materials, war by war and region by region, is James Dunnigan and Austin Bay's *A Quick and Dirty Guide to War*, first published in 1984, later updated.[116] Stronger on the geographic and cultural aspects of warfare than some of the other aforementioned works, it still can provide little detail on tactics and operations.

Otherwise one could cite the various ambitious efforts at events data analysis covering the dimensions of conflict, both past and present, as is more notably represented by the Singer and Small Correlates of War (COW) Project. That and others by Francis Beer, Ned Lebow, Robert Butterworth[117] provide data mostly related to the sheer dimensions and causes of war, a macroquantitative perspective removed from the tactical conduct of war but important particularly to the study of its global and regional patterns. That in turn can provide a guide to the epidemiology of modern conflict and to its resolution.

8. Functional categories of war dimensions

Some works have focused on specific "functional" dimensions of warfare other than strategy and tactics: on logistics, command, economics, geography, etc. Within those rubrics, there is usually a roughly chronological treatment, often over a long span of history or of a comparative nature as applied to contemporary warfare. In the former category are the books on the history of command and logistics by the Israeli historian Martin van Creveld; in the latter the works of Patrick O'Sullivan on military geography.[118] By their nature, these works can be useful mostly for providing frameworks of analysis for comparative studies of recent wars.

9. The press, journals, magazines

Much of the available information on the conduct of modern war must be gleaned from the daily press, abetted by some materials in magazines and journals devoted to military affairs. The overall result, however, is considerable unevenness, particularly when it comes to the more obscure (even if sometimes very deadly) low-intensity conflicts. One can search almost in vain for an eye-witness description of the fighting in southern Sudan (which has killed more than one million) or in Sri Lanka. Reporting of the recent Liberian civil war has been better. Descriptions, if they exist at all, can be found only in the classified reports routinely assembled by intelligence agencies, in the case of the U.S., the Defense Intelligence Agency (or in classified studies done in the war colleges of the major nations).

The press is, however, quite useful when it comes to chronicling the major conventional wars such as those in the Falklands, Lebanon, Iran vs. Iraq, etc. But even in the latter case, by far the most deadly conflict of the recent era, the reportage was uneven. There would be detailed battle reports, particularly when the *New York Times'* Drew Middleton made one of his periodic trips to the battlefront. But in between his and others' trips there would often be huge gaps in the reporting of the war, even at times when fighting was intense, involving major offensives.

Otherwise, some magazines such as *Harper's* can be useful for occasional pieces by journalists or other writers accompanying forces on one or another side of the war—such articles appeared periodically to describe what the respective wars looked like from the side of the Afghan Mujahideen, the Guatemalan insurgents, the Ethiopians or the Eritrean guerillas, or contenders in the Liberian civil war, or the Colombian FARC and ELN.[119] These efforts, similar to those provided by Max Hastings for the entirety of the Falklands War, could give one a "feel" for the combat, if only on the basis of one long mountain or jungle patrol, or a week-long campaign. Some seemed to combine on-the-ground military analysis with something akin to a travelogue. Some have had a strong literary cast and have even provided a forum for novelists and academic literary critics interested in modern warfare and its accompanying horrors in the poor lands of the Third World.

Otherwise, the best sources of information on developing world wars, sometimes including those of the lower-intensity variety, are some of the weekly or monthly defense journals, some of which routinely review recent war happenings in a kind of ongoing tour d' horizon. Among the best of these sources are *Jane's Defense Weekly,* the *International Defense Review,* and *Defense and Diplomacy.* A comprehensive compilation of items from these journals provides the best available portrait of contemporary Third World warfare, including the provision of arms to combatants by the major powers.

One major problem regarding the various sources for the study of Third World wars is that they tend to be one-sided, asymmetric, involving only what is reported from the "pro-West" side or that of the good guys. This is the case for numbers 1 and 9 above, i.e. detailed battle histories, for war correspondents and Western defense journals. We have participants' accounts of the British assault on the Falklands but nothing in the way of an insider's account of how it looked from the side of the Argentinian army. Likewise, we have no picture of the Lebanon war from the Syrian side—what it looked like, for instance, from the perspective of a SAM-site radar operator in the Bekaa Valley. The Iran-Iraq reportage tended mostly to be from the Iraqi side, if only because access to the

Iranian side was more limited. We have little in the way of reports of what the Afghan war looked like from the perspective of a Soviet "grunt."

Summary

We have here proposed and adumbrated a loose "matrix" of sorts for the analysis of recent wars in the Third World. On one axis is a spectrum running from all-out conventional interstate wars to various forms of "low-low intensity" conflicts, not all of which qualify for data sets requiring a thousand battle-related deaths. On the other axis is a level of analysis continuum spanning the grand strategic, strategic, operational, grand tactical, tactical, and technical levels of warfare. Such a matrix can be applied to the actual fighting of various wars (strategies and tactics), but also to their geographical and cultural dimensions. As such, the matrix will form a rough template for much of the remaining material in this book.

Table 1.5   MATRIX: Study of Modern Warfare

Type of War	Grand Strategy	Levels of Military Analysis:		
		Strategy (or Theater Strategy)	Operations (or Grand Tactics)	Tactics (and Weapons Technology)
Conventional Interstate (all-out)				
Limited Conventional Interstate				
*Hi-Low Intensity				
*Medium-Low Intensity				
*Low-Low Intensity				

*These categories subsume what is normally put under the rubric of guerilla, insurgency, revolutionary, and ethnopolitical warfare, plus coups, insurrections, border frictions, etc.

CHAPTER 2

How Wars Start: Capabilities, War Aims, Perceptions

Generally speaking, or historically speaking, wars have begun for any number of reasons or as a result of a variety of possible sequences. Some have begun almost suddenly, erupting like a summer storm with little warning and with few prior expectations. Others have been the culmination of lengthy rivalries and feuds, involving arms races and serial crises. Some have begun definitively on a given day, with the opening of full-scale hostilities, while others have escalated slowly from a minor skirmish to all-out battle, sometimes involving an interregnum often characterized as "phony war." Some wars have been premeditated; others have involved crises escalating out of control, constituting wars that "nobody wanted." The variety is mixed and nearly endless.

There is, of course, a massive, prolific literature on the causes and correlates of war; it is now virtually enshrined as a subdiscipline of international relations under "conflict studies." That literature was inaugurated more than fifty years ago by Quincy Wright's seminal multivolume study, which formed the basis for so much subsequent work.[1] Nowadays, conflict studies or the study of the causes of war range across the board from macrostatistical analyses and formal modeling involving a plethora of variables and hypotheses to more traditional historical and discursive works such as those by Geoffrey Blainey and Stephen Van Evera.[2] Oftentimes the hypotheses suggested in the latter lead to more empirical work in the former category.

Some of this literature is pegged at an almost metaphysical level, involving a search for generic causes. Hence there are contributions by biologists and psychologists on the innate warlikeness of homo sapiens, instinct theories of aggression, intraspecies conflict, the functional nature of warfare for the improvement of the species, psychological explanations involving the phenomena of projection and displacement, frustration-aggression theory, social learning theory, etc. These are sometimes referred to as "microlevel" explanations, i.e., those deriving from individual human psychological and biological factors.[3]

Writers such as Kenneth Waltz have elaborated more complex schema, utilizing the "levels of analysis" approach. Therein, one can come at the question of the causes of wars from several different angles, only one of which involves explanations at the level of the individual.[4] There is a nation-state level, by which the explanations for war may be seen as derived from the nature of regimes (democratic states may be less warlike than totalitarian ones) or from the situation of certain nation-states, such as those harboring deep feelings of irredentism or revenge in relation to past wars. Then there is the systems level, where war is explained as more or less endemic and unsolvable because of the so-called "security dilemma": the lack of an overarching authority and the anarchy of an unregulated contest among major powers, which inevitably leads to war because of reciprocal, reinforcing fears and insecurities. In some minds, explanations at that level lead to calls for world government.

The Proximate Causes of War

In this study of recent Third World wars, we are less interested in theoretical or metaphysical arguments about their causes and in macrostatistical analyses that attempt to establish general hypotheses about the causes of war. Rather, we seek to compare and generalize about their proximate causes. That does not, however, remove us entirely from the literature on "large" causes. Some writers, Dougherty and Pfaltzgraff for instance, have laid out a number of macrolevel explanations, some of which have practical implications, that is, can be used to compare some of our recent wars.[5] Mostly this involves linkage politics (the linkage between domestic politics and foreign policy) and arms races. There is the very old generalization that says that nations commit aggression in order to distract public opinion from internal political or economic problems. War is thus seen as a safety valve or as a salvation for a particular ruling regime. Argentina in 1982, Egypt in 1967, and Iraq in 1980 have been characterized in those terms. Then there are the macrolevel explanations deriving from the dynamics of arms races, in turn ramifying into the linked concepts of preventive war and preemption. Here, wars are seen largely as a function of shifting balances of power, where one nation in a situation of rivalry with another sees a window of opportunity or senses a time or period in which its chances for winning a war will be maximized or an opportunity that may never again come.

One other historical datum bears mention here and that involves formal declarations of war. In the classical system of European diplomacy, such declarations were the norm, and they obviously remained in play for both of the world wars, each of which involved numerous combatants and phased declarations. In the contemporary world, that is, in the former Third World where most of our recent conflicts have taken place, formal declarations have been neglected. That is somewhat paradoxical in view of the growing role of the UN, much talk about the development of norms of international law, and the increase in the number of democratic states that, so one would think, would be inclined toward democratic processes that would require such declarations. For the U.S., of course, in the cases of Vietnam, Grenada, Panama, and Iraq, there has been the ongoing political struggle between Congress and the executive branch over war-making powers, which in the latter case came down to a congressional enabling resolution but no formal declaration of war.

Blainey's work offers pro and con analyses, rooted in historical examples, of some seven or eight general explanations for the onset of war. One has to do with high expectations and excessive optimism (usually on both sides) and what came to be known in the literature on the origins of World War I as the "short war illusion."[6] This explanation is connected in complex ways to rational-choice models that dwell on perceptions of gains and losses, winning and losing, in a probabilistic way. Another explanation has to do with the role of third parties, alliances, neutrals—the expectations of how these actors and factors will play out in the eventuality of actual war. Still another explanation, euphemistically called a "death watch" by Blainey, focuses on the level of key individuals and expectations of their demise and possible replacements,[7] a thesis with a contemporary ring in an era of Saddam Hussein and Hafez-al-Assad.

Like many other theorists before and since, Blainey focuses on the relationship of civil strife (unrest, revolutions, ethnic and racial conflict) to international war, and perceptions of same on the "other side" of a conflict. He refers to "scapegoat wars"; others prefer the psychological terminology of "displacement."[8] On the reverse side, some nations are seen as obsessed with strengthening internal unity so as to be positioned for prosecution of a successful war.

Blainey also discusses "war chests," the theory that nations blessed with a surfeit of resources may be tempted or impelled toward starting wars.[9] Others, in a related vein, have focused on various "economic moods," or points on economic cycles; aggression may be more or less likely when economic recoveries are underway or in the phase of a prosperous plateau. On a more macrostatistical basis, some scholars have looked at the long-cycle relationship between Kondratieff waves (innovations) or phases of global economic expansion or contraction in relation to the outbreak of wars.[10] Still others have looked at the relationship of economic growth rates or levels of economic development in connection with the propensity to initiate wars.

Blainey and others have also observed what he refers to as the "calendar of war,"—the role of the seasons and weather in prompting the outbreak of war.[11] The same kind of analysis has been assayed for civil strife, and the latter in turn can be related, as noted, to the initiation of major wars. The latter are more likely to be inaugurated in the spring and summer, though Blainey also analyzes the phenomenon of so-called "autumn wars," perhaps historically related to the end of the harvest season. Those matters would, presumably, vary greatly if one were dealing with wars outside the temperate zones of the northern hemisphere.

Finally, and closer to the concerns of many political scientists who deal with the combination of system structure and rational-choice models, Blainey looks at war in the context of comparative power measurements. Centrally, that involves the hoary problem of whether wars are more likely triggered by power balances or imbalances or transitions in one direction or another.[12] Here war is seen as often a dispute about the measurement of power, and the outcome as a ratifier of one or another view. Somebody is making rational choices, someone else is not. Blainey also looks carefully at the question of the sometimes "accidental" nature of warfare (escalation from a minor incident), be it over Jenkin's ear or something larger.[13]

Still another thesis regarding the initiation of war, according to Van Evera, has to do with cumulative resources. Hence, according to him, "a resource is cumulative if its possession helps its possessor to protect or acquire other resources."[14] Such cumulativity can involve either or both territory (military bases and strategic depth) or raw material resources, and are all the more germane to the temptation for aggression if located close to the borders of contending states.

Contemporary political scientists have attempted to analyze still other possible causes of war or to establish hypotheses in that connection. Some have dwelled upon so-called "lateral pressures," involving the combination of demographic pressures, economic growth and resource shortages, demonstrated, for instance, in nineteenth-century Europe or pre–World War II Japan.[15] There are hypotheses ranging across the structure of the system (bipolar versus multipolar primarily), the degree of "system uncertainty," the spectrum from risk acceptance to risk aversion on the part of decisionmakers (normally viewed as a unitary actor), trends in the balance of power and arms races between "challenger" and "challenged" states, the role of previous diplomatic defeats, stand-downs and confrontations, power transitions and uneven growth, the role of third party states in disputes (as causing uncertainty), and the role of nuclear weapons, among others.

Mostly these various hypotheses and theories have been applied by contemporary political scientists to major power wars or at least to conventional wars in the recent past. Just what applicability they might have in a Third World context, say to wars between Ethiopia and Somalia or in Afghanistan, is perhaps a difficult problem. Also problematic is the question of their applicability to wars further along the conflict spectrum toward limited warfare or various types of low-intensity conflict. Finally, there is the question of whether, in view of the current zeitgeist about war as represented by Mueller, Creveld, Keegan et al., plus all the devotees of "endism" and the "democratic peace," the massive literature on conflict and war is in the process of being rendered time-bound or even as a (albeit lengthy) historical anachronism.[16]

Of course a whole new set of theories and hypotheses may have been developed to serve as explanations for internal wars, "wars of the third kind" in Holsti's terminology.[17] He has proffered a typology ranging from local to regional to systemic sources of such wars. Mostly, he and others are convinced of the internal generation of such wars, having to do with "weak states" that lack either or both vertical and horizontal legitimacy. Holsti discusses the dynamics of "weak" or "frail" states along a spectrum, noting that there is often considerable shifting along a spectrum as legitimacy waxes and wanes.[18]

But there may also be external sources, current or historical. Some writers dwell on deep structural forces such as the legacies of imperialism or colonialism. Others dwell upon regional or big-power interventions; in the latter cases that begs questions as to whether bloodshed began internally followed by external intervention or whether the latter created opportunities for the former.

Other regional and/or international factors commonly discussed as generating conflict are arms transfers, global ethnic networks (Jews, Chinese, Irish, Muslims, Sikhs), contagion, and superpower competition. Still others stress systemic factors rooted in political economy, i.e., economic dependency structures left over from the colonial period. As stated by Holsti:

> For dependency theorists, for example, communal and other forms of group conflict against the state are explained by the historical class-formation process that occurred under the umbrella of imperialism. Groups and communities were set against each other for reasons of both political control and resource exploitation. The world imperialist system continues to create economic and other conditions that force communal and other groups to fight for limited resources, sometimes resulting in war between them.[19]

The dependency literature dwells on the importance of "comprador" elites in Third World countries, on essentially exploitative relationships between center and peripheries. It is a model that leaves little room for pride and nationalism, which has in some cases—Mexico, Burma, South Korea—led to highly restrictive mercantilist and exclusionist policies directed at the industrial-core countries.

Finally, Holsti subdivides the world (echoes of Wildavsky and Singer) into zones of war, no-war zones, zones of peace, and at the end of a spectrum, pluralistic security communities à la Karl Deutsch.[20] According to this scheme, Africa, some of the former Soviet republics, the Middle East, Central America, South Asia, and the Balkans are zones of war characterized by aggregated clusters of weak or failed states. Southeast Asia and East Asia (perhaps) are said to have graduated to a no-war zone, the Caribbean and South Pacific to a zone of peace, and North America, the Antipodes, and Western Europe to the status of pluralistic security communities. There is no total assurance of permanence in any of these categories.

In the case of so many conventional conflicts, as noted, it is feasible to attempt analysis of proximate causes of war, albeit in arguable ways. The 1967 war started with the closure of the Straits of Tiran by Egypt, but may have been rooted in the latter's fear of Israeli nuclear weapons.[21] The Iran-Iraq War may have originated as a classic "window of opportunity war." But in many cases of internal war or LIC, it is impossible to pinpoint the origin of the conflict, which escalates over a long period of time.

The Proximate Causes of War: Case Studies

Most of the macrostatistical analyses of the causes of war pay scant attention to the kinds of things that are picked up in case studies of individual wars, that is, their proximate causes. Often this involves very arguable matters, as both sides will blame the other for the start of wars. And even in cases that have been exhaustively examined—World Wars I and II, the several Arab-Israeli wars—various scholars will differ, sometimes profoundly, on the attribution of causes or origins. Hence, the debate over Fritz Fischer's *Griff Nach der Weltmacht* for World War I, or the disputes over Hugh Trevor-Roper's interpretation of the origins of World War II, or the differing attribution of economic versus psychological factors in the case of the latter.[22] Scholars still debate the "causes" of the 1967 war, some blaming the Arabs and some the Israelis.

In an almost anecdotal way, one can connect up some of the myriad, previously enumerated theses with the proximate causes of some recent conventional wars. Regarding personalities, Saddam Hussein's grandiose but somewhat irrational ambitions clearly fed into the origins both of the Iran-Iraq and Gulf Wars (the former was commonly referred to as Saddam's Quaddesiya in remembrance of an earlier Arab victory over the Persians in 637 A.D.).[23] Syria's involvement in wars with Israel has often been tied to Assad's alleged need to produce a personal victory before his demise.

There are numerous cases where linkage politics—the impact of internal domestic problems and foreign policy—appears to have been at least one contributing cause to war. This involves war as a safety valve, whereby nations commit aggression in order to distract public opinion from internal political or economic problems. Argentina in 1982, Egypt in 1967, and Iraq in 1980 have been characterized in those terms. So too has Iraq in 1990 when that regime, burdened with debts from the previous war with Iran, made a move to capture the lucrative Kuwaiti oilfields and in the process to eliminate debts owed Kuwait. In 1980, however, Iraq might have been characterized as a "war chest" case, a nation bloated with oil revenues, looking for a purpose to put them to.

In other cases, nations may have begun wars because they sensed the possibility of taking advantage of civil unrest in a rival state. Iraq in 1980 banked on the cleavages in Iran's society—and its professional military—as weakening Teheran's military posture. India, in 1971, took advantage of the breakaway movement in East Bengal paced by the Mukti Bahini guerilla movement. Somalia in 1977 took advantage of Ethiopia's having to combat secessionist movements in Eritrea and Tigre Province.

The seasons and weather have obviously played a role in the onset of some of these wars. Iraq attacked Iran in late summer in 1980 at a time it still had several months in which to conduct an offensive before the rains arrived. India's onslaught against Pakistan's East Bengal in December 1971 was timed to achieve a quick victory before the onset of the monsoons. Syria banked on inclement, rainy autumn weather to prevent the Israeli air force from playing its usual role in October 1973. China attacked Vietnam in December 1979, knowing that winter weather in Siberia and Manchuria would limit the possibilities for Soviet involvement on behalf of Hanoi.

The role of third parties has occasionally been important in some of these cases. In 1979 China took advantage of Vietnam's being tied down in Cambodia even as it had to worry about the prospect of reactive Soviet involvement. Iraq, in attacking Kuwait in 1990, could not easily predict the nature of the coalition that would form in reaction to that venture; earlier, in attacking Iran, it had had to deal with hostility, short of military intervention, from Syria. Israel invaded

Lebanon in 1982 not knowing exactly whether Syria would become a party to the conflict.

In these "regional" contexts as contrasted with the big-power conflicts that are the focus of most academic analysis, uncertainty about external third party arms resupply is a major item of calculation. In 1973 Egypt and Syria could not be sure whether Israel would be resupplied by the U.S. Iraq in 1980 could not easily predict whether Iran could find spare parts and replacements for its U.S.-origin weapons inventory after being cut off by Washington. The Chinese in 1979 could not easily predict whether Moscow would mount a resupply operation on behalf of Vietnam, nor could Somalia predict the extent of Soviet weapons support to Ethiopia in 1977–78.[24]

Blainey and Van Evera's theses about the tendency toward excessive optimism, either on one or both sides of conflicts (with respect both to the prospects for victory and the costs), is borne out in several cases of recent conventional wars and may be more the rule than the exception. Iraq seems to have misjudged on the side of excessive optimism both in 1980 and 1990, in the former case clearly laboring under a "short-war illusion." The Soviets, in invading Afghanistan, obviously no more anticipated the forthcoming quagmire than did the U.S. in Vietnam. Israel's effort to knock out the PLO in 1982 in Lebanon, and to install a more favorable regime in Beirut, also proved excessively optimistic, not to mention the overall costs in blood and treasure. Likewise Somalia in 1977 overrated its chances to defeat Ethiopia and capture the Ogaden even with the former's burdensome internal problems. In 1973, Egypt and Syria may in a way have achieved their war aims even while suffering a military defeat, in that a political process was set in motion that led to Israeli withdrawal from the Sinai. Of all the wars we have covered, perhaps only India in 1971 appears to have achieved its war aims. Israel's victory in 1967 now seems somewhat more ambiguous. Britain in the Falklands and China in its "lesson" for Vietnam in 1979 both appear also to have accomplished what they set out to do, albeit the lingering uncertainty about the long-run implications. In these Third World contexts, there is considerable uncertainty as to the validity of Brian Bond's anti-Clausewitzian thesis about the meaninglessness of military victory.[25] It appears applicable in the Israeli case, inapplicable in the Indian case, more ambiguous for Iraq, China, and Ethiopia in their recent wars. We shall return to this in discussing war aims.

The question of cumulativity has come up in several cases of our wars. Israel's acquisition of valuable strategic depth in Sinai, the West Bank, and the Golan Heights is one example. Iraq's attempt to add Iran's Khuzistan oil fields to its already large oil reserves in 1980 is another, as is Iraq's effort to take over Kuwait's oil fields in 1990–91. Somalia's effort to take over the Ogaden region in 1977 might also fall into this category in terms of reversing the strategic depth relationship between it and Ethiopia. India, in taking East Bengal (Bangladesh) in 1971, cut Pakistan's population in about half, magnifying its already huge advantage in numbers (but that may have been not so much premeditated as a matter of being dragged into a war by the Mukhti Bahini insurgency and the resultant refugee problem).

"Lateral pressures" are not easily conjoined to any of our recent Third World conflicts; they seem more connected to some recent historical cases involving major powers, or to whole regions such as Europe in the nineteenth century.[26] In the future, however, India could be a classic case with its combination of population growth, now rapidly expanding economy, the absence of resources, particularly energy, and its proximity to the major oil and gas reserves in the Persian Gulf and Central Asia.

Likewise, many of the theories, macrostatistical and otherwise, used to explain the causes of large-scale conventional wars, would appear to be largely inapplicable to LICs. Rational-choice models and game theory are difficult to apply in situations where there are no identifiable decision points at the outsets of conflicts. Many LICs are also difficult to analyze in terms of contending unitary actors. Lateral pressures, war chests, displacement, balance of power, nuclear weapons, uncertainties over the role of third parties and alliances (system uncertainty) all appear to be of minimal relevance. The intellectual baggage of the "democratic peace" seems also inapplicable; rather one deals with the chaotic world described by Robert Kaplan and others, featuring famine, ethnic and tribal violence, overpopulation, environmental degradation, and numerous instances where the writ of central governments does not extend far beyond the capital city, if that far.[27]

There are, indeed, other areas of theoretical concern that infringe upon questions of the causes and origins of LICs. Some scholars look at income distribution (rather, extreme maldistribution) within states as a primary cause of civil wars, i.e., wars over government.[28] In a related vein, others stress the role of the maldistribution of land. Ethnic, tribal, and racial conflicts are, of course, primordial. Many of the current ones have their roots in the distant past: Serbs versus Muslims in the Balkans, Russians versus Muslims in Central Asia, Hindus and Buddhists in South Asia, myriad African tribal divisions only thinly papered over by fragile and often artificial new nations. There are ongoing theoretical arguments about how or whether such conflicts could ever come to an end. Often, of course, ethnic conflicts are juxtaposed to economic maldistribution fault lines, as evidenced even in the developed world in situations such as Belgium and Canada's Quebec. One might speculate that conflict is reduced if there are separate core areas that can absorb rural emigration, as was the case for Switzerland with its separate urban complexes of Zurich-Basel-Bern on the one hand, and Geneva-Lausanne on the other. By contrast, Montreal and Brussels involved the economic dominance of one language group over another, a recipe for trouble. Numerous equivalent situations exist throughout the developing world, in Sri Lanka, Pakistan, Iran, and elsewhere. In Peru, for instance, a largely Westernized elite dominates commercial life in Lima, spawning constant conflict with Indian-mestizo peoples in the upland mountain regions and elsewhere in the countryside. Mexico may become another such case.

Capabilities and Power: How the War Rivals Match Up

Apropos the above discussion of the dynamics of arms races and power balances, it is surprising just how little attention has been paid to applying measurements of capabilities and comparisons of power to the initiation of war. For these are central to the questions of why wars start when they do. Presumably, nations only start wars they think they can win or otherwise bring to an advantageous conclusion, though as noted above there are numerous historical cases where both sides of a conflict manage to be optimistic about victory. That brings us to the question of perceptions of relative, contending power.

Numerous tracts have been devoted to measurements and comparisons of national power, most notably in recent years those of Klaus Knorr and Ray Cline.[29] And in all cases, there is the recognition of the value of indicative, objective measurements, tempered by the further recognition that subjective or unmeasurable factors are also involved.

Several major problems arise in comparing the power of nations. First, there is the matter of power-in-being versus potential power. In a quick war, one that allows little time for mobilization of economic or industrial assets, the contending forces may have to rely on what recently has been dubbed by Pentagon pundits as, "come as you are" capabilities. That is, you fight with the forces in being at the war's outset, not having time to further mobilize reserves and other resources. On the other hand, a lengthy, initially inconclusive war will allow for the underlying factors of economic potential to come into play. In World War II, initially more highly mobilized Japan and Germany were eventually overwhelmed by the huge U.S. war buildup based on a far superior gross national product. Ditto the eventual, inherent, advantage of the North over the South in the American Civil War and the U.S.-led coalition ranged against Saddam Hussein after five months' buildup. Such factors do, or should, as we shall see, loom large in the calculations of nations contemplating the initiation of a war.

Generally speaking, potential power and power-in-being can be subjected to some very simple measurements, usually valid in general terms, but subject to caution where marginal determinations of superiority or inferiority are involved. But it should be emphasized that there are real limits to effective quantification of comparative power capabilities.

The most commonly used composite measure of national power is that of gross national product (GNP). This provides a rough measure of the overall size of a nation's economy. GNP is, of course, a product of two factors: per capita GNP and population, representing, in the case of per capita GNP, measurement of a nation's average level of socioeconomic development[30] (its standard of living, which will usually also correlate with scientific and technological development; hence the quality of military personnel in a modern military environment), and, in the case of population, the basis for the size of its military forces (with strong ramifications for its capacity to sustain high casualties). It can further be seen that a given GNP can result from different mixes of population and per capita GNP, so that two nations with equivalent GNPs, but with large differences in their components, may have roughly equivalent overall power, but of different types. Egypt and Israel, for instance, have similar GNPs, reflecting the former's huge population advantage balanced by the latter's much higher level of socioeconomic development.

The foregoing pertains largely to potential power, that is, to latent, underlying factors that can be brought to bear in a mobilization or long military buildup. In a long war, most combatants will try to maximize their war efforts, and that can involve, as it did during World War II, nations putting around half their economies into military activity.

Other measures may be used as indicators of power-in-being. These will be all the more important in quick or sudden wars not allowing for mobilization of potential resources, i.e., the "come as you are" wars. Military expenditures are the best measure, given accurate data, which are not always easily available or subject to easy interpretation (U.S. intelligence analysts argued for years about Soviet military expenditures over a wide span of disagreement). There are also various questions about the meaning of different mixes or profiles of military expenditure (MILEX), i.e., readiness versus research and development, manpower versus equipment, "tooth and tail" (actual forces versus support elements), distributions between the services and in some cases between strategic and conventional forces. But it is a first good cut at a measure of extant power.

Another measure, more difficult to quantify with a bottom-line conclusion, is order of battle. There, one can compare numbers of army divisions, surface warships, tanks, combat aircraft, various types of missiles, to produce various types of force ratios. There are problems here too. Relatively speaking, there are "real" armies and "hollow" armies, depending on readiness, training, maintenance, ability to utilize complicated equipment. Particularly in the developing world, equipment orders of battle can be very deceptive because of poorly trained third-line forces that inflate actual force estimates, or high percentages of non-operational equipment (the Iranian and Somali air forces in recent wars are good examples). This is often encapsulated in the arms-trade literature by the term "absorption." And, indeed, there is no better example than the vast overinflation of Iraqi military capabilities by the U.S. press (and perhaps some of its intelligence analysts) before Operation Desert Storm, based upon taking too seriously the nominal numbers of Iraqi divisions and accompanying numbers of tanks, artillery pieces, etc.[31] A recent book by Anthony Cordesman has attempted to sort out the "paper" versus "real" orders of battle of both Iran and Iraq in the post–Gulf War period.[32]

The ratio of military expenditures to GNP (taking into account the practical difficulties in measuring both) is a frequently used measurement, as a good gauge of the extent to which a nation is translating its power potential into actual power-in-being. These ratios can vary widely. Numerous nations not under serious threat (much of Latin America, for instance, and much of Europe), usually run ratios of 2 to 3 percent. Nations engaged in major wars, such as those in World War II, can sustain MILEX/GNP ratios up around 50 percent. Those sorely threatened by regional foes will, even in the absence of ongoing conflict, carry ratios up around 30 to 35 percent, as have Israel and some other Middle Eastern states at various times in the recent past. These ratios, incidentally, will normally correlate with some related measures, for instance the proportion of the population under arms and relative per capita military expenditures.

Utilization of the foregoing classes of data, available on an annual basis from such sources as the U.S. Arms Control and Disarmament Agency (ACDA), the International Institute for Strategic Studies (IISS), and SIPRI[33] provides one avenue to the comparison of military power between contending developing nations, based mostly on "objective," i.e., quantifiable factors (the geographical factors of terrain and weather are also "objective" factors, albeit essentially non-quantifiable). Another methodology was earlier provided by Ray Cline, though with not dissimilar relative conclusions. Cline used population data and land area to compile a consolidated ranklist of what he called "critical mass" (this produced a three-way first-place tie between the USSR, U.S., and China, followed by India, Brazil, Indonesia, Canada, Mexico, and Argentina—Japan was eleventh, France sixteenth, West Germany nineteenth). He then fed in some economic variables ("command" versus "free enterprise" economies, GNP, energy production, nonfuel minerals, steel and aluminum production, trade, etc.) and came up with relative rankings of economic capability.[34] He then combined the critical mass and economic capability rankings for a consolidated ranklist. The five leaders, from the top, were the U.S., USSR, China, Japan, and West Germany (curiously, he ranked Canada ahead of both the U.K. and France).

However, Cline and other academic analysts who have conjured up schemes for assessing relative military power (most notably Klaus Knorr and A. F. K. Organski) are well aware that there are a number of subjective (nonquantifiable) factors that can serve to modify or alter the "objective" comparisons, surely at the margin and sometimes even in reversing what would appear to be clear disparities. In a subsequent chapter we shall discuss in this context the panoply of factors encompassed by military geography that affect defensive and offensive capabilities: size for strategic depth, location of key cities and industrial centers in relation to borders, topographical or water barriers, cover, weather, seasons. Hence Spanish defensive power has long been "multiplied" by the Pyrenees barrier (ditto for Switzerland's Alps); Polish and Belgian vulnerability underscored by the absence of such barriers; the two oceans have aided U.S. defensive capabilities but paradoxically made it more difficult for the U.S. to project power overseas.[35]

There are numerous other subjective variables feeding into measurements of comparative power. Cline covers manpower quality, weapon effectiveness, infrastructure and logistic support, and organizational quality in discussing conventional force balances. It should be noted, however, that several if not all of these factors will correlate with or are a direct result of what goes into per capita GNP—a good general measure of average socioeconomic status and closely related to educational levels.

In a more general sense, Cline and others discuss the factors of national will and morale, level of national integration, strength of national leadership, and the perceived relevance of national strategy to national interest. Others, such as Hans Morgenthau, have stressed nations' diplomatic skills as, in effect, constituting a key component of national power.[36] In this regard, the failures of German diplomacy in 1914 and 1940, and that of Iraq in 1990 (both created overwhelming counter-coalitions) is worth noting. And in recent years the resurgence of interest in national character or, rather, strategic cultures has added yet another dimension.

One needs not seek far afield to cite some obvious examples of how some of these factors have affected national power, both as pertains to recent cases in the developing world and to some other familiar situations. Some have pointed out that the remarkable military performances of Japan and Germany in World War II, the ultimate outcomes notwithstanding, were a result of high levels of national will and integration. On the other hand, Germany, both as pertains to World War I and World War II, had a poor record of diplomacy, in both cases resulting in its having to fight against hopeless numerical odds with its qualitatively superior army. Israel's advantage regarding will, morale, and national integration has often been cited (it has, however, done poorly in the broader diplomatic context). Its enemies are often cited as examples to the contrary and also as examples of why the standard quantitative measures of national power (GNP, MILEX, etc.) are not easily applied to the Arab-Israeli equation. In 1982 Argentina was another example where subjective factors appear totally to have overridden seemingly objective ones, involving among other things poor leadership on the Argentine side and Britain's availing itself of crucial help from the U.S.

Further, it must be pointed out that most developing nations are mostly if not totally dependent on major power suppliers for their weaponry. Hence, in examining Cline's cited factor of weapon effectiveness, there is a strong link to these nations' diplomacy, that is, it underscores the importance for developing states of the diplomacy of arms acquisitions. Pakistan had a much tougher time against India in 1971 than in 1965 largely because it lost its American arms pipeline and was forced into critical reliance on inferior Chinese weapons. Dependent Argentina had a tough time sustaining its forces with weapons and other military gear during the Falklands War because its diplomacy could not match British leverage in the U.S. and Europe. We shall return to these matters in more detail in this and subsequent chapters.

Table 2.1 shows comparisons of the most crucial power variables, organized according to the rival antagonists of recent wars. As previously noted, such measurements can be nothing more than roughly indicative of overall power balances, both as applies to latent and to actualized power. But the numbers do tell us some things, not only by way of predicting ultimate outcomes, but about why the wars began.

The relationship between India and Pakistan is shown as one of great asymmetry, as measured by GNP, population, and military expenditure, not at all modified by per capita GNP (and these gaps were widened after 1971 when East Bengal was split off from Pakistan to form Bangladesh). By 1971, Pakistan ran a relatively higher MILEX/GNP ratio, but that could not begin to compensate for an overwhelming asymmetry in the sizes of the two nations' populations and economy. Israel, meanwhile, is seen as vastly outnumbered in population, but able to compensate by higher per capita GNP and MILEX/GNP scores, generally speaking a high level of constant alert and mobilization (the figures for armed forces do not take into account Israel's efficient reserve mobilization system). But the data clearly show the facts of the Arabs' higher latent power in a

Table 2.1　Power Capabilities: Comparisons of Warring Nations

	GNP (mil $)	GNP percap $ percap	Population (Thousands)	MILEX (mil $)	MILEX/ GNP %	Armed Forces (Thousands)	AF per 1,000 popul
India vs.	36,895	74	501,600	1,400	3.8	1,000	2.76
Pakistan	13,450	60	117,000	485	3.6	279	2.90
(1965)							
India vs.	55,777	130	562,000	1,944	3.6	1,560	2.78
Pakistan	7,159	69.5	135,000	456	6.4	404	2.99
(1971)							
Israel	4,001	2,338	2,700	644	16.1	75	27.70
Egypt	4,377	224	30,900	292	6.7	220	7.12
Syria	2,039	568	5,700	313	15.4	80	14.10
Jordan	685	537	2,000	80	11.7	60	29.70
(1967)							
Israel	9,873	3,216	3,300	3,740	37.9	130	39.63
Egypt	7,383	248	35,400	1,140	15.5	390	11.02
Syria	3.923	677	6,900	589	15.0	115	16.67
(1973)							
Israel	25,220	7,693	3,900	5,418	21.5	205	53.1
Syria	20,410	2,583	9,300	3,224	15.8	300	32.3
(1982)							
China	47,100	465	1,012,000	44,500	9.4	4,500	4.4
Vietnam	NA	NA	53,700	NA	23NA	650	12.5
(1979)							
Ethiopia	3,137	120	26,100	178	8.7	225	7.5
Somalia	1.040	366	3,300	33	3.2	53	16.1
(1978)							
U.K.	474,996	8,482	56,000	24,169	5.1	334	6.0
Argentina	54.637	1,864	29,300	1,902	3.5	175	6.0
(1982)							
Iraq	39,747	3,533	13,100	8,629	21.7	350	26.7
Iran	92.179	2,766	38,800	6,737	7.3	305	7.9
(1980)							
Libya	29,310	8,084	3,600	5,225	17.8	90	24.8
(1984)							
Chad	636	139	4,400	12	1.9	16	3.6
(1985)							
U.S.	4,520,000	18,570	243,800	296,200	6.5	2,279	9.3
(1987)							
Iraq	54,350	3,331	17,000	16,710	30.7	788	53.0
(1985)							
Ethiopia	6,140	108	57,100	117	1.9	117	1.8
(1987)							
Eritrea	830	223	3,700	65	7.8	55	14.8
(1987)							

Source:U.S. Arms Control and Disarmament Agency, *World Military Expenditures and Arms Transfers, annual,* 1966–1999, Washington, D.C., U.S.G.P.O.

lengthy crisis or mobilization; hence, Israel's "preemptive imperative." Also it is noteworthy that by the time of the 1982 Lebanon war, in terms of both latent and mobilized power Syria alone was beginning to catch up, banking on an almost 3:1 population ratio. The importance for Israel of maintaining the Camp David Accords with Egypt is vividly highlighted.

There is, of course, a vast disparity of power between China and Vietnam. In more subjective terms, this gap was modified by the locale of the 1979 war (near Hanoi's power center and in what for China is a remote border area), by Vietnam's experience in previous wars, which had produced a battle-hardened army, and by Soviet backing of Hanoi, which forced Beijing to contemplate a two-front war. But it is clear that Vietnam could do little in an all-out war with China other than fight a defensive war of attrition. The prospect of that might deter such an eventuality.

In the case of Ethiopia and Somalia in 1977–78—rival nations that had fought before—there was also a seemingly large disparity in power as measured by the basic facts of population and GNP. That gap was bridged, however, by several factors: Ethiopia's internal ethnic and ideological divisions involving several then ongoing insurrections in the Eritrea, Tigre, and Ogaden regions, Somalia's more than doubly favorable per capita GNP figure, and the diplomacy of the arms trade, which saw Ethiopia in 1977 cut off from its traditional U.S. source of arms after the overthrow of King Haile Selassie. It was therefore not as far out of the question as it appeared that smaller Somalia attacked larger Ethiopia in 1977.

The U.K. is a major power (and a nuclear power) with a vaunted maritime tradition (also a vaunted tradition of fielding excellent if small land armies from Leuthen to Waterloo to El Alamein). It has a huge advantage over Argentina in all objective power measurement categories, including those of per capita GNP and MILEX/GNP. If fighting on neutral ground or a level playing field, no contest! As we shall see, Argentina banked on the compensatory factor of strategic geography: the huge power-over-distance gradient faced by the British in fighting a war thousands of miles from home with a lengthy logistics line, and an unfavorable climate.

Iraq and Iran are an interesting case here. By most measures, in 1980—and in the light of all prior estimates and expectations—Iran was the stronger nation. It was long considered as such under the Shah up to 1979, even to the extent that Soviet power was seen as deterring stronger Iran from attacking weaker Iraq. Iran had a much larger GNP based on a huge population advantage, modified by a marginal difference in per capita GNP between the two OPEC oil powers. Iraq, however, was more highly mobilized. But by 1980 Iran's loss of its main external supplier of arms, the U.S., and the disintegration of its military forces in the postrevolutionary chaos of the early Khomeini period, allowed Iraq to think it was temporarily stronger and to gamble on a war.

Libya appears to have a large advantage over Chad in terms of objective factors. Despite a slight disadvantage in population, its oil revenues translate into a huge advantage in GNP, per capita GNP, military expenditures, and the ratio of the latter to GNP. In this war, however, fought along the remote Chad-Libya border in the desert Aouzon Strip and in the Tibesti Mountains, both sides (neither technologically competent) labored under extreme difficulties in projecting power far from their effective centers of power. Chad had critical outside support, mostly from France but also from the U.S. The result was, effectively, a standoff.

Regarding Ethiopia and Eritrea, the former has a huge advantage in population and a significantly higher GNP, but Eritrea's much higher per capita GNP and MILEX/GNP ratio has served somewhat to rectify the overall disparities.

Little need be said regarding power variables comparing Iraq with the U.S.-led coalition that fought in Desert Storm. Iraq's very high level of mobilization, featuring a 30 percent ratio of MILEX to GNP, could not come close to compensating for the huge disparities it faced in numbers, wealth, and technological sophistication vis-à-vis the opposing coalition. Iraq banked largely on military geography, i.e., the power-over-distance gradient faced by foes requiring a massive strategic airlift. It also banked on being able to fight a successful stationary defensive war, as it had against Iran, and thereby to present the U.S.-led coalition with the prospect of unacceptable casualties, with the U.S. experience in Vietnam in mind. With time not urgent, that turned out not to be a problem (Iraq allowed the coalition a five-month *sitzkrieg)*.

War Aims and War Openings

We may now move to connect the basic information on power measurements to the linked questions of war aims and the different ways wars may begin. This is no easy task. Even for those past wars that have been the subject of massive analyses, including primary sources, there are still disputes among scholars about the war aims of major participants. One thinks about the big debate engendered by Fritz Fischer's work, *Griff Nach der Weltmacht,* over whether Germany had used the crisis in 1914 to carry out a long-planned conquest of neighboring areas,[37] or that about just what Japanese strategists had in mind when they overrode the doubts of those such as Admiral Yamamoto, who wondered out loud what the eventual strategic logic of a Pearl Harbor would be if the U.S. did not then immediately quit and concede the Central Pacific and East Asia to Japan.[38] There are still endless arguments in American journals about why the U.S. fought in Vietnam, i.e., what were or ought to have been its war aims.

Many of the wars we are examining here are recent, and for the most part, we do not yet, if we ever will, have access to government documents or memoirs detailing the decisionmaking process leading to war. We can only guess, or infer from certain actions, just why Iraq attacked Iran when it did in 1980, or why China assaulted Vietnam in 1979. The general answers in some cases may be fairly obvious. More difficult to ascertain are war aims and perceptions of the likely course of the war, i.e., what scenarios would play out and with what consequences. What, for instance, were Saddam Hussein's perceptions about the possibilities of a favorable outcome in 1990? Sixty percent? Forty percent? Were such calculations consciously made?

Indeed, in many cases, it is even a serious point of argument as to who was the aggressor, largely but not entirely a matter of finger-pointing by one or the other side of the conflict. For this reason, as often noted, the basis of the League of Nations' or United Nations' collective security mechanisms has often been problematic, even aside from the problem of the will of member states to stop or punish aggression.

In 1967, for instance, Israel struck first, justifying itself in "legal" terms on the basis that the Egyptian closing of the Straits of Tiran was a *casus bellis*. In reality, of course, it preempted an anxious Egyptian and Syrian military mobilization for purely military reasons, having long adhered to a military doctrine that required carrying the war immediately on to the foe's territory. Iraqis and Iranians argue about who was the aggressor in 1980; while most observers blame Iraq, the Iraqis point to Iranian efforts at subverting the Baghdad regime and some prior military skirmishing, along with the "justness" of some territorial arrangements in the Shatt al Arab area. India overran East Bengal and established Bangladesh in 1971, hence permanently tilting the South Asian military balance further in its favor. India claimed it had no choice because the Pakistani army was not only slaughtering East Bengalis, but creating an unmanageable flood of refugees in India's West Bengal. Somalia attacked Ethiopia in 1977, but claims it did so to rescue Somali ethnics in Ogaden Province who were suffering at the hands of the Ethiopian army. The 1973 Arab-Israeli war has its arguments as well, as does the 1982 war, justified by Israel on the basis of an assassination in London and years of rocket attacks on its northern settlements along the Lebanese border.

Several key issues seem to be at the core of the question of war aims. On one level, we can talk about a spectrum of war aims running from the essentially unlimited to much more limited expectations about what could or will be gained. Some wars—one thinks of Rome's assault on Carthage—have been initiated to completely annihilate the enemy. Germany's attacks on Poland and the USSR in 1939 and 1941 certainly had such an aim in mind, begging some questions about intent regarding wholesale massacres of citizens versus "merely" reducing them to slavery (before the battle of Moscow in 1941, Hitler apparently gave orders to have Moscow transformed into a large lake!).

Toward the other end of the spectrum, war aims are more modest, more limited, but hence, perhaps more complex or obscure. In some cases—Egypt in 1973 or Iraq in 1980 or perhaps Somalia in 1977—one might think in terms of a "seize and hold" strategy (Japan in 1941 also clearly had such ends in mind). Here, the attacking nation conducts a strategic offense followed by tactical defense, banking on its enemy not wishing to pay the price entailed in rolling things back to the original status quo ante. That is, one chews off some territory, digs in, and hopes that it can be ended there, with the long-run implications largely ignored. In 1990, in a variant of such a strategy, Saddam Hussein apparently calculated he could get away with a fait accompli in taking all of Kuwait, or at least its main oil fields.

Even here, as regards the status quo ante, there are different types, depending upon earlier such status quo antes. In 1973 Egypt was trying to gain back a part of the Sinai peninsula it had lost in 1967. Iraq in 1980 was trying to "recover" an area of Iran in Khuzistan largely populated by Arab peoples. Argentina, certainly not aiming to attack Britain itself, claimed it was trying to reassert control over the once Argentinian Malvinas Islands.[39] Hence many of these war openings have a form of revisionism in mind, rectification or revenge for past losses, reversals of the outcomes of old wars. But new revisionisms are created. Indeed, several of our conflict pairings—Arabs vs. Israel, India vs. Pakistan, Somalia vs. Ethiopia, Iran vs. Iraq—involve longtime serial wars or conflicts, in the case of Iran-Iraq going back a millennium or more to earlier Persian-Arab rivalries. Even long periods of peace among these contending forces can be viewed merely as extended truces or breathing periods, such as had been the case for Germany and France between the seventeenth and twentieth centuries.

The Chinese assault on Vietnam presents another type of war opening or war aim, that of "teaching a lesson," without any apparent aim at holding territory seized.[40] Such lessons may, of course, be expensive for the teacher as well as the putative pupil. On a more practical note, of course, China in 1979 was trying to create a new front for Vietnam after the latter had invaded China's ally in Southeast Asia, Cambodia. And, indeed, one partial parallel to this case may be that of Israel's incursion into Lebanon in 1982. It was for the most part a large-scale punitive raid, not intended to acquire new territory (though maybe a buffer zone occupied by friendly Lebanese forces), but also with the aim of creating new political "facts" in Beirut.

In a related vein, some wars may have as their primary intent that of bringing external attention to what one side sees as an untenable or unacceptable situation. It is a way of dragging others into a conflict. Egypt in 1973 clearly hoped to seize and hold territory, but also hoped to frighten the major powers, particularly the U.S., into taking diplomatic steps, into breaking what had become an impasse. For that reason, the U.S. seemed to signal it would have been satisfied with a limited Egyptian victory (also deemed useful to salve Egyptian pride), which could lead to a more comprehensive and durable political solution. Syria nowadays is often thought pondering another such venture to alter the political status quo in connection with the Golan Heights.

One thing stands out in relating the types of war openings to war aims, and that is the extent to which the seize-and-hold strategy is the weapon of the weak, as defined by "objective" power measurements. Vastly outmanned Somalia hoped to sever Ogaden from Ethiopia and then hold on (just what calculations were made about what Ethiopia would do later if it resolved its other problems in the north were not clear). Iraq hoped to take the Khuzistan oil fields, make some border adjustments further north, and consolidate its hold over the Shatt al Arab estuary; here too, its perceptions about how to deal with an eventually restored Iranian power are not clear. Egypt looked to take a chunk of Sinai and then rely on big-power pressures and diplomacy to forestall an Israeli counterattack. Argentina, of course, banked on Britain's conceding of the Falklands and South Georgia as too costly to retake. Earlier, Japan had hoped to capture the entire central Pacific island domain, and banked on the U.S. conceding that in the face of what would have been a costly and bloody effort to reverse the new status quo. It is striking that in all these cases, the seize-and-hold strategy failed, save perhaps in the case of Egypt in the longer run political sense, after the military disaster of 1973, which brought the Israeli army to the west bank of the Suez Canal.

The issue of long-term premeditation of war openings as contrasted with "accidental" wars or those that emerged as a result of escalating crises is an important but daunting one. There is much that is arguable. Depending upon the source, one can see arguments that both Israel and Egypt wanted a war around 1967—both sides thought they could win—and both used the Straits of Tiran crisis to escalate matters toward all-out war. (Charles de Gaulle on behalf of France used this pretext to reorient French policy toward a more pro-Arab orientation, and accused Israel of having waited eagerly for the opportunity that arose in 1967).[41] Some analysts see Gamal Nasser as having deliberately provoked a crisis so as to conduct a preventive war at a time the Arabs realized that Israel was about to go beyond the nuclear threshold.[42] It is clear that President Sadat had laid plans for an offensive war at least a year before the 1973 war took place and, indeed, it started with a surprise attack (Arab terrorists conducted diversionary operations against Soviet Jewish refugees in Eastern Europe right before the war started so as to create a "signal-to-noise" effect). Regarding the 1982 Israeli incursion into Lebanon, there are arguments over whether Israel used the pretext of an assassination of an Israeli diplomat to do something it had long wanted to do, or whether its patience finally snapped and it was compelled to teach the PLO and Syria a "lesson."

There are likewise arguments over the degree of long-term premeditation that went into the Iraqi attack on Iran in 1980, Somalia's assault in 1977, and the Argentinian invasion of the Falklands in 1982. The timing of the latter is somewhat obscure, aside from the weather factor, which dictated a military operation right before the onset of the foul and brutal South Atlantic winter. Some analyses have the Argentinian military junta responding to internal economic problems, but Argentina had then been in an almost constant economic crisis for a long time.

Going back to our "objective" data, it is clear that the related but very distinct concepts of preventive war and preemption are germane to several of these cases. That requires some initial consideration of these concepts which, erroneously, are sometimes used interchangeably or synonymously.

Preventive war relates to long-term premeditation and to the perception of changing power balances. Country A is in a stronger position than its rival, Country B, but fears that the military balance is shifting inexorably in B's favor. Such a shift could involve long-term demographic factors, as witness the rivalry between Germany and France in the nineteenth century. Or it could involve differential rates of industrialization. It could reflect a temporary advantage in arms acquisitions, where one side's diplomacy was more successful but also deemed to be of only temporary advantage. Or it could involve temporary political conditions in one country, so that a subset of preventive war might be something we can call a "window of opportunity" war (or "window war" for short).

Preemption on the other hand involves crisis conditions, often a crisis emerging from accidental factors not foreseen by anyone, as was the case for the assassination at Sarajevo which triggered off World War I. Essentially what is normally involved is a decision by one party, usually that which is weakest in terms of latent or mobilizeable power, to strike first, after it has concluded that war is wholly inevitable and that the only remaining valid question is who gets to strike the first blow. It follows that such preemptive action is more likely when there appears to be a strong advantage to getting in the first blow (in the related nuclear context, this is habitually discussed in terms of crisis stability, i.e., the nuclear balance is said to be stable if both sides have assured second-strike capability, and hence no significant advantage inheres to the side that strikes first). On the reverse side, a country that contemplates preemption may also have to calculate that in doing so, it may lose the "moral high ground," that is, may be labeled an aggressor even if not largely responsible for the crisis that engendered the temptation to preempt. This is what explained Israel's eschewing of preemption in 1973 after it had belatedly learned of an impending assault—the Israeli leaders ruefully spoke of being able to preempt only in every other war so as not to offend American sensibilities and endanger their most crucial political relationship and source of weapons.[43]

The 1956 Israeli assault on Egypt in collaboration with France and Britain was a classic case of preventive war, it being thought in Tel Aviv that massive Soviet arms shipments to Egypt and Syria were dramatically and permanently shifting the military balance away from Israel. Indeed, numerous analysts of German war aims in 1914, such as Barbara Tuchman, have seen the German operationalization of the Schlieffen Plan as a preventive war fought to establish German hegemony in Europe before Russia was able to actualize its latent power (the economic reforms initiated in Russia in 1912 were thought to have put Russia on the road to more rapid industrialization).[44]

Perhaps another good earlier example would be Japan's attack on Pearl Harbor in 1941, though in a case somewhat reversed from 1914. Germany in 1914 was very conscious of long-term power trends, particularly as regards Russia, working to its disfavor. Japan, in 1941, saw itself as temporarily more mobilized and ready than the U.S., but feared the results of a U.S. military buildup already underway because of the crises in both Europe and Asia. Ironically, as we now know, Japan's power in relative economic terms was rising *more* rapidly than that of the U.S., so that later analyses of the period at the beginning of World War II might be inclined to see Japan's thrust for power as having been premature.

None of the recent Third World wars constitutes as pure a case of prevention. One partial exception, at least in terms of perceptions never really actualized, was Pakistan. The latter had long held a qualitative edge over India to counterbalance a massive asymmetry in population and GNP, based largely on its being a recipient of U.S. weapons as part of its role in the Central Treaty Organization (CENTO) and Southeast Asia Treaty Organization (SEATO) alliances. Those weapons were embargoed and cut off during and after the 1965 war, forcing Pakistan to turn to China. But the U.S. arsenal remained operational for many years and Pakistan managed to acquire spare parts and some secondhand U.S. weapons from third-country sources such as West Germany and Jordan, with tacit approval from Washington. Meanwhile, Pakistani planners appear to have taken the Israeli blitzkrieg victory in 1967 as a model (all the more ironic in light of Pakistan's long-held hostility to Israel) for a possible quick preemptive assault against India, it not being quite clear just how such a victory could have been sustained and consolidated.[45] Such an action would really have been a preventive war to forestall or at least delay India's increasing advantage based on "objective" factors. Somewhat more obscure is the question of how Pakistan might have prevailed after the initial period of the war, against an enemy with great strategic depth and a much bigger population.

More common of late has been the "window" type of war opening, again, where an objectively weaker power sees its rival temporarily disadvantaged and reckons it has a chance to win an unexpected victory, and with it the spoils. Both Somalia in 1977 and Iraq in 1980 tried to take advantage of postrevolutionary situations in which their respective rivals had been cut off from their customary U.S. source of weapons and forced to look for other suppliers as well as sources for spare parts and replacements for U.S. weapons in their inventories. In both cases, it was presumably recognized that restoration of Iranian and Ethiopian power was inevitable and hence ominous, but the gambles were taken and lost. In 1990, Iraq may have taken advantage of what it thought was another "window," that of the U.S. political support it had achieved during its war with Iran.

As noted, Israel's successful attack in 1967 was the clearest case of pure preemption; also a case in point regarding Van Evera's and others' "offense-defense theory," regarding the role of advantage to the offensive in conducting first strikes.[46] Indeed, it was important in that case in particular because of Israel's reliance on mobile armored tactics and, hence, on control of the air in open desert terrain with clear skies. Israel's destruction of Syria's SAM installations in 1982 was another case of preemption, even if the action was taken only after Israel had launched a ground attack into southern Lebanon against the PLO. Argentina's taking of the Falklands and of South Georgia in 1982 had somewhat the character of a preemptive attack. But there was no prior crisis nor Argentinian fear of a British attack, nor was Argentina able to attack and destroy any really significant part of Britain's war capabilities, as Israel had done to Egypt in 1967. Actually, the mutual efforts of the Indian and Pakistani air forces at interdicting each others' airfields in 1971, at the time the war widened to the western front, had some of the characteristics of a preemptive situation.

Further, in complex, ironic ways, the U.S.-led coalition effort against Iraq may now be looked at in the context of preventive war. Not that Iraq threatened to rival U.S. power! But to the extent that the U.S. went to war in part so as to deal with Baghdad's growing nuclear capabilities, it might in a sense be perceived as a preventive war. Such an aim was not openly articulated by the Bush administration, which preferred to stress the aim of restoring the territorial status quo ante in Kuwait. Doubly ironic was the extent to which the U.S. underestimated Iraq's nuclear program and its abjuring of further military operations, i.e., a march on Baghdad, which presumably would have allowed for complete on-the-ground destruction of Iraq's nuclear infrastructure.

Low-Intensity Wars: Relative Capabilities and War Aims

In assessing the relative power weights of contending—or prospectively contending—nations or coalitions, there is at least a fairly decent objective basis for comparison, notwithstanding the complications of such subjective considerations as geography, morale, and other "human" or qualitative factors, political cohesion, etc. Economic data, i.e., GNP numbers, population, military expenditures, orders of battle, and weapons acquisitions can give us a pretty good feel for how nation X stacks up against nation Y. At the margin, when the numbers are fairly close, then subjective factors will tell us who is likely to prevail. When the objective factors indicate a wide gulf in power potential, predictions will usually easily follow with occasional exceptions such as the example provided by the case of Israel.

But for low-intensity conflicts, one is faced with an entirely different context for analysis. Indeed, at the outset and by contrast with conventional wars, one is faced with many different types of wars that defy easy comparison, not to mention predictions about outcome.

To begin with, comparisons of overall economic weight and of average levels of socioeconomic development, i.e., GNP and per capita GNP data, are here either not relevant or not available. We cannot, for instance, easily make such a comparison, say, for Eritrea (before independence) versus the central Ethiopian government or for the Contras versus the Sandinistas in Nicaragua (indeed, the economic output of regions containing rebel forces is presumably incorporated within that of the central government for statistical purposes). Hypothetically, such an analysis would appear more valid in the case of regional civil wars such as those in Ethiopia and Sudan, but the data are simply not available.

In one sense, GNP, GNP per capita, or related data may be important. In a general sense, they might tell us something about the capacity of a central government to mobilize its economy and military forces for a counterinsurgency operation. In a general sense, a nation's size or its state of development may be crucial to explaining its capacity for maintaining internal control. But, obviously, many other factors are involved.

Regarding classical guerilla or insurgency wars, there is or long has been a tendency for analysts to focus on numerical force ratios between central government counterinsurgency forces and the insurgents. Depending again upon such factors as terrain and size of theater there is still a rule of thumb generalization which says that an incumbent government requires at least a 10:1 force ratio in order to prevail. Indeed, that ratio was often cited by critics of the U.S. Vietnam War policy, who saw the U.S. and the South Vietnam government attempting to win a counterinsurgency war with a far less favorable ratio, while recognizing that increasing the number of U.S. forces so as to achieve such a ratio was not politically feasible.

But then too, and in some contrast to conventional wars, the force ratios between insurgency and counterinsurgency forces in a guerilla war will often depend on the dynamics or the momentum of the war itself. Indeed, from the perspective of the insurgents, picking up such momentum on the basis of initial victories or a perceived change in the correlation of forces, is what the war is all about. That, indeed, is the classic strategy of phases embedded in the insurgency strategy associated with Mao, Giap, or Guevara. From little acorns oak trees grow! And from small insurgencies, eventually come main-force battles between large conventional armies, once the tide has turned. Sometimes!

So if we are to ask about force ratios or comparisons of power variables in guerilla wars, we must first ask when, in what phase of the war, and with what direction of momentum, forward or backwards.

That, however, pertains only to certain types of LICs, i.e., those of an insurgency against a central government predominantly on ideological grounds, i.e., a Marxist insurgency against a pro-Western incumbent regime or, per the Reagan Doctrine, its reverse. In other cases involving regionally based ethnic or tribal wars, the kinds of numerical balances utilized to study conventional wars may be relatively more valid. But then, so many wars (Mozambique, Angola, Sri Lanka, etc.) fit in between, almost defying any kind of objective or empirical analysis. But, nonetheless, we can learn some things from the basic numbers, taken with obvious caution. Or, alternatively, one may raise some questions.

First, regarding that type of war pitting radical, i.e., self-styled Marxist revolutionary forces against pro-Western or more traditional incumbent regimes, it is clear that in the period immediately preceding the end of the Cold War, these insurgencies had in no case succeeded in overthrowing the latter—no repeats of earlier successes such as those in Algeria, Vietnam, Nicaragua, Ethiopia. And in few of those situations—with the exceptions of the Philippines and El Salvador and perhaps Western Sahara—had radical insurgents achieved the hoped for but only indicative 1:10 force ratio. In Turkey (Kurdish PKK), Israel (PLO), Morocco, South Africa (ANC), Colombia (FARC and ELN), Guatemala (URNG), and Peru (Shining Path), insurgents have fought at well below that ratio. Not coincidentally, in the cases of the Philippines (NPA plus the Moro Liberation Front in Mindanao) and El Salvador (FMLN), war casualties have been very high; indeed, in the case of El Salvador, cumulative mortalities dwarfed the figures for forces in being. But in some of the cases involving ratios of more than 10:1, insurgents have been more than a mere annoyance. The Polisario seemed near victory, but then lost its momentum and has since been amenable to negotiations. Shining Path in Peru, with meager forces, once dominated large sections of that country's uplands and was a force inside Lima. The Tamil Tigers in Sri Lanka have caused real havoc in that nation's capital and elsewhere. The Colombian and (earlier) Guatemalan governments have been sorely beset by insurgencies favored by very difficult terrain.

Interestingly, in all four of the anticommunist insurgencies associated with the Reagan Doctrine, insurgents had achieved better than the 1:10 force ratio. In each of these conflicts, casualties had been high, reaching grisly proportions in Afghanistan and Mozambique. Varying by degree (more so in Afghanistan, but with an electoral outcome in Nicaragua not entirely based on military factors in Nicaragua), these insurgencies of the 1980s were successful. Here too, other factors, i.e., geography and external support, counted a lot.

Force ratios are a bit more difficult to interpret in the cases of ethnic or religious civil wars, which nonetheless are characterized by an incumbent regime associated with one or another group. Whereas some of these conflicts have been fundamentally two-sided (Sri Lanka, Sudan), others (Lebanon, Ethiopia, Uganda), have been multisided wars of far greater complexity. And some (Syria in Lebanon, India in Sri Lanka, Congo) have seen the insertion of external armies into civil wars, either to protect one side or suppress another, to prop up a regime, or to constitute a somewhat uninvited presence with its own agenda, i.e., territorial aggrandizement. The combinations are many.

In Lebanon in earlier years, some forty thousand well-armed Syrian troops had imposed some order on a conflict involving some ten or eleven private armies or ethnically or ideologically based fighting groups ranging in size from twenty thousand down to a few hundred. Here, force ratios would require interpretation amidst a maze of shifting coalition politics wherein Syria had successfully played the ancient strategy of "divide and conquer." In Sri Lanka, in a very confusing situation, a large Indian pacification force had to withdraw after ending up as an enemy of the very coreligionists (Tamils) they were sent to protect. The Tamil guerillas have, however, maintained a strong fight against the central government, up until very recently.

Ethiopia's Marxist regime, fielding near a half-million troops, was ultimately defeated by much smaller Eritrean and Tigrean forces which were better organized and possessed of higher morale. Note that here as well as in Lebanon, both vicious communal wars, casualties were staggeringly high.

The Cambodian multisided war in its earlier phases pitted four large main forces against each other—here there was an ideological civil war that ended in stalemate. In Sudan, the southern forces have fielded almost as large a force as the government, with the resulting stalemate. Uganda's government maintained control with a very favorable force ratio; that in Liberia collapsed after losing its numerical advantage. In some of these conflicts, particularly in Sudan, casualties have been enormous, up at the levels of major conventional wars elsewhere. They had also been large in East Timor, where the Indonesian government had maintained a huge force ratio advantage.

But for the most part, quantitative analysis of force ratios in these numerous, diverse cases remains very hazy and imprecise. It is not easy to know in the case of insurgents just what is the proportion of frontline "fighters" to auxiliaries, adherents, and local support people. Likewise, it is difficult to measure what proportion of a government's forces (say Turkey in its Kurdish region or Sudan in the Upper Nile) are actually engaged in a counterinsurgency operation.

War Aims and War Openings: LIC

Paradoxically, by comparison with conventional wars, ascertaining the war aims of low-intensity conflicts or analyzing the origins of the latter is both more simple and more difficult. It is simple in the sense that the war aims may be less ambiguous. In conventional warfare, all-out defeat of an opponent (a war of annihilation) is only sometimes sought—more frequent aims are limited territorial objectives, overthrowing an opponent's government, or "teaching a lesson." In numerous LICs, the aims are total in the sense that most revolutionary wars are zero sum, with the revolutionaries aiming at the overthrow of a government (and often the complete destruction of its leadership), and with the incumbent government aiming at the complete suppression of a revolution. Or, so it often seems. The reality provided by our numerous recent cases is actually somewhat more complex.

In those wars described as revolutionary or counterrevolutionary (Marxist-oriented and later anti-Marxist), the war aims of combatants were usually total. In numerous earlier cases—Algeria, Vietnam, China, Cuba, Ethiopia, Iraq (1958)—during the postwar era of decolonization, defeated incumbent regimes were entirely destroyed, their leaderships either killed or forced into permanent exile (hence they were all "wars over government," from the standard SIPRI typology). But more recently, the case of Angola (with a strong regional-ethnic component) and maybe that of Cambodia have provided dénouements involving negotiated coalition solutions as a result of stalemated wars (the Angolan war has now flared anew). El Salvador may provide another such example. Numerous ideologically based insurgent wars—Guatemala (earlier), the Luzon component of the Philippines conflict—have continued on interminably, where although insurgent forces undoubtedly have sought total victory, in fact they were engaged as a seemingly endless and perpetual nuisance or, more optimistically from their viewpoint, a pinprick.

This can be stated in another way with the standard SIPRI typology of wars over government versus wars over territory in mind. Those in the former category tend to be zero-sum, with the prospect of total victory on one side or the other. Those in the latter category allow for other possibilities, i.e., federal solutions, the breakup of nations and creation of new ones. The current war in Afghanistan appears to be zero-sum. Those in Sudan and Bosnia have allowed for the possibility of new political and geographical demarcations.

In the other major type of LIC, that described in one way or another as ethnic civil war with a greater or lesser degree of regional demarcation, war aims often involve autonomy or independence, i.e., the breaking up of a nation state or a more devoluted federal solution. The Kurds, southern Sudanese, East Timorese, Punjabis, Tamils, and others all have independence or autonomy in mind. Of course, in many cases around the former Third World, as had earlier and is now again the case in Eastern Europe, the ideal of self-determination runs up against the facts of interspersed populations, sometimes mostly within urban centers, sometimes involving patterns of enclaves not easily amenable to territorial demarcation, even with the best of intentions. But not always! Sudan and Kurdistan could be demarcated, so too eastern Timor. In Burma, Liberia, Sri Lanka, Liberia, Uganda, Rwanda, and elsewhere tribal or ethnic insurgencies have little hope of producing viable new nation-states with easily defined borders. But the insurgencies are fought nevertheless, often where greater autonomy, or a change of regime, or the mere hope of reducing repression are the goals.

Unlike in the case of conventional wars, concepts such as preemption and preventive war are not useful in explaining the origins of these wars. They do not usually begin suddenly or have as their basis a strategic calculation involving the timing of an initial assault where an opponent is temporarily weakened or thought inevitably to be growing stronger over the long run. Indeed, it is often difficult to pinpoint the beginnings of many LICs or to point to a seminal event or watershed that launched a low-level conflict to a more significant or visible level. Many LICs have been fought over long periods, sometimes for decades. Some have escalated or deescalated very gradually; others have gone through sine-wave phases of greater and lesser activity, sometimes just flaring up periodically after long periods of relative quiescence. There are as many patterns as there are wars. There are some rough equivalents to 6 June 1967 or the less well known but equivalently determinable starting points of numerous conventional wars. But not many.

Some people would date the origins of the Cuban revolution to the breakout by Castro and his colleagues from the Moncada Prison. In Angola, there were the rather sudden mutual preemptive attacks by Cuba and South Africa, which signaled a broader and more deadly war. The 1979 Tanzanian invasion of Uganda, which deposed Idi Amin, ushered in a long internal guerilla war that killed well over a hundred thousand people. The 1986–87 phase of the Chadian conflict was inaugurated by a sudden attack by the Libyans and allied Goukouni (Chad) forces over the "Red Line" in northern Chad. The Soviet involvement in Afghanistan began with the lightning Spetsnaz assault on Kabul in 1979, and the installation as Soviet puppet leader of Babrak Karmal after the killing of Hafizullah Amin. In December 1978, Vietnam invaded Cambodia and completed the occupation of most of the country by 7 January 1979. In Sri Lanka, there was a major escalation of the conflict in 1982–83, after years of simmering troubles featuring riots, robberies, and murders. The most deadly period of the Lebanese civil war was inaugurated in 1975 by the Phalange massacre of twenty-five Palestinians at Kataib, by the end of that year, everyone including the Syrians had been sucked into a deadly, multisided civil war. In Yemen in 1986, there was a major coup and rebellion which caused some thirteen thousand deaths and signaled the beginnings of what was to become a Soviet withdrawal. The Turkish invasion of Cyprus in 1974 culminated a series of events begun by the sudden overthrow of President Makarios in a coup led by "Ethniki Organosis Kyrion Agoniston's", or National Organization of Cypriot Fighters's (EOKA's) Nikos Sampson. In El Salvador, a long-festering insurgency was sharply escalated after the Sandinista takeover of neighboring Nicaragua. Serious recent violence in Liberia and Sierra Leone was triggered by coups. The genocidal massacre of some five hundred thousand Tutsis by Hutus set off a long conflict that has spilled over from Rwanda to Burundi and then Congo, where Tutsi forces led the successful overthrow of the Mobutu regime, preceding the ongoing multisided civil war.

But in numerous other cases, it is difficult if not impossible to identify the beginnings of what is today an ongoing conflict. Some are perpetually festering ethnic, religious, or racial conflicts with origins going back decades if not centuries, often fought out in the form of periodic explosions of major violence bracketing long periods of low-level conflict. That in Burundi involving the Tutsis and Hutus has taken that form, punctuated by major massacres in 1972 and 1988. The war between Eritrea and Ethiopia had been grinding along for thirty years before the recent dénouement, back even before Haile Selassie's formal annexation of ex-Italian Eritrea. RENAMO was set up in 1976 in Mozambique only a year or so after that nation's independence, and its war against the government in Maputo gradually escalated over the subsequent fifteen years. SWAPO's revolt in Namibia began in 1966, but was only expanded to a significant level some ten to twelve years later. Burma's endless insurgencies—Karen, Kachin, and Shan ethnic groups, communists, and Muslim separatists—date back to the immediate aftermath of World War II. Bangladesh has had a long-festering internal problem with its Buddhist tribal people of Tibetan origins who feel threatened by encroaching Muslim Bengalis. In India, the various insurgencies involving Sikhs, Ghurkas, Mizos, and in the Nagaland all go way back without any seminal events. The same is true for Baluchistan within Pakistan, and the Mindanao Moro in the Philippines, not to mention the Kurds in Iraq, Iran, and Turkey. Guatemala's leftist insurgency dates all the way back to the 1940s, way before Arbenz's assumption of power in 1950 and the 1954 CIA-inspired coup, which followed Guatemala's acquisition of arms from Czechoslovakia.

In short, it is not easy to generalize about war openings or war aims when it comes to LICs in the Third World. The key words are interminability, fuzziness, sporadic, and escalation, but the patterns are endlessly varied. With the end of the Cold War and the (at least for the moment) tamping down of conventional conflict in the Third World, these somewhat vague and indefinable conflicts may now come to occupy center stage in the study of contemporary warfare. This phenomenon has recently been demonstrated, not only in the Third World, but by events in Croatia, Georgia, Kosovo, Chechnya, and between Armenia and Azerbaijan in Nagorno-Karabakh, among others.

CHAPTER 3

Military Geography

Introduction

Until very recently, and particularly in the United States, the field of military geography has remained mostly stunted and neglected. Indeed, in reviewing the massive compilations of newspaper articles, magazine and journal articles (including particularly those from the specialized military journals produced by the war colleges and services), and full-length books on Third World warfare, one may only rarely obtain a detailed, vivid picture, a "feel," for what is happening on the ground. Maps are not usually provided, and when they are, they are usually on a full-country or regional scale, "flat" maps devoid of attention to terrain or vegetation, providing little more than the location of cities, major rivers, and national boundaries. One obtains therefrom little sense of the relevant topography, particularly as pertains to the tactical or operational levels of warfare. The military implications of the weather and the seasons are noted only sporadically, cursorily. With much greater frequency, reporters and academic military analysts focus on weapons (and the arms trade by which they are acquired), in a manner almost ignoring *their* important relationship to the terrain and the weather. One gets technological determinism in a geographical vacuum. Or at least that *was* the case before the massive attention paid to the 1990–91 U.S. buildup in the Persian Gulf area and the actual war in 1991, which focused attention on the terrain and weather aspects of warfare in a manner not before seen.

There are several reasons for this long-time neglect. First, it was an apparent correlate of the languishing of the academic discipline of geography at many universities during the whole postwar period. Indeed, one could see this clearly in an annual publication entitled *Geography*, intended as a general introductory reader for university students.[1] Therein are some forty contributions running the gambit from historical and methodological surveys to the environment (rising sea levels, global warming trends, acid rain, ozone, Amazon fires, disappearing rain forests), agriculture (the "Green Revolution"), geographic patterns of influenza and AIDS, water, regional geography and cultural regionalization, patterns of urbanization and suburbanization, demographic trends and transnational migration, developing core regions in the Third World, transportation and gridlock, computer-mapping and remote-sensing satellites as applied to crop management and disasters. Summing up, the foci are the environment, demographics, new mapping technology, and settlement patterns. There is absolutely nothing on military or security issues. And there is therefore no hint that matters of tactical and operational military geography in places such as the Iraq-Kuwait or the Iran-Iraq borders or Lebanon might affect some of the larger issues of foreign affairs, indeed might heavily impact upon matters such as energy supplies, human migrations, and the environment, as well as upon the causes of and conduct of war.

Military geography has also apparently suffered from its (inherently) non-quantifiable or subjective basis, its sheer complexity. Tanks and planes can be counted; so too GNPs, defense expenditures, dead bodies, and prisoners. In an age of (real or pseudo) empiricism abetted by the alleged "managerialism" of the U.S. military (the bane of the U.S. "military reform" movement), the geographic aspects of warfare have come to be seen as a kind of "ringer," a rather indigestible exogenous factor, one usually relegated to parentheses, afterthoughts, and explanatory footnotes. It is therefore ignored in most of the academic work in "conflict studies."

There are still other reasons for this neglect of military geography. One might agree that the tactical aspects of the subject are simply too esoteric, too *military* for academic analysts not prone to seeing the broader ramifications. It is a subject they can't see and don't know. There is also a curious, somewhat inexplicable cultural aspect to this—a surprisingly large part of the literature of military geography has been published in Britain and Germany, to a lesser degree in Israel. The literature in the U.S. seemed to have peaked during World War II then declined, though some of the press reportage during the Gulf War may have served as a corrective, as does the unique very recent work of John Collins.[2]

There is a parallel here with the dominance by scholars in those countries of the field of military history as well. Finally, it is possible that, paradoxically, the study of military geography has been stunted by the fact of the dominant focus on Northern and Central European military affairs, an arena so much alike in terrain and climate (and settlement patterns and road networks) to the U.S. Midwest and eastern seaboard so as to preclude interest in the much different arenas elsewhere. Maybe!

The very recent past has, however, seen some increased interest in military geography, only in part spurred by the experience of the Gulf War. Preceding that war, the geography department at West Point produced a massive and very useful bibliography on the subject—the bibliography's outline format is itself useful as a checklist for all of the various subdisciplines of military geography.[3]

Britain's Hugh Faringdon has contributed a unique work on the strategic geography of NATO and the Warsaw Pact.[4] Patrick O'Sullivan, a transplanted Irishman in Florida, has contributed one general book on military geography at the various levels of analysis (macro to micro), and some pioneering work on the geography of guerilla warfare.[5] Julian Minghi and Roger Kasperson have also worked in this area, as has the Israeli Arnon Sofer.[6]

The three-volume set by Cordesman and Wagner on the lessons of recent Third World wars is auspicious for its attention to military geographic matters, such as the Soviets' ultimately futile counterinsurgency efforts in Afghanistan.[7] Going back to our comments in chapter one on the different genres of military writings on the Third World, some more than others pay attention to terrain and weather, if only in the interstices of more broadly gauged analyses. The battle histories by serving officers and on-the-spot journalists do usually try to provide some picture of what it all looks like on the ground. The realistic, reconstructed battle histories of John Keegan pay meticulous attention to terrain—not accidentally, too, Keegan and Wheatcroft's *Zones of Conflict* is a uniquely geographically oriented projection of possible future battlegrounds in the Third World.[8]

Finally, in 1997 there appeared the comprehensive, formidable primer on military geography by John Collins that fills a hitherto conspicuous void in the literature. That book appeared after the Gulf War, some of the coverage of which did pay attention to the vital importance of terrain and weather as did the subsequent MTR literature that dwelled heavily on the question of whether the results of the Gulf War were at least in part due to highly anomalous (and not likely repeatable) geographic factors.

What Is Involved: A Quick, Derivative Survey of Military Geography

Probably the best place to start in surveying the boundaries and subdivisions of military geography is the massive, recently published four-volume bibliography compiled by the geography department at the U.S. Military Academy. Some portions of that survey are more relevant than others to a study of the military geography of Third World wars.

One can, therefore, filter out large areas of inquiry, as demarcated by space, time, and technological detail. The by now huge literature on geopolitics and geopolitical theory can be roped off, perhaps with the partial exception of those works devoted to interpreting the causes and conduct of some recent wars as a function of distance from the superpowers themselves or of location in relation to superpower interests. Also some types of terrain and related military operations have not been particularly relevant to recent conflicts in the former Third World and in the new conflict zones created by the collapse of the USSR and Yugoslavia. Arctic operations would fit that exception, though one notes by way of mitigation that India and Pakistan have fought over glaciers in Kashmir, and that India and China, and the USSR and the Afghan Mujahideen have fought in the snowy Himalayas and the Hindu Kush range in northern Afghanistan. The West Point bibliography has extensive entries involving amphibious operations and, hence, the characteristics of coasts and beaches, reflective of considerable U.S. experience in this area during World War II, in the Pacific, and in North Africa, Italy, Normandy, and southern France. Such activities are largely absent from recent conflicts, but one notes the exceptions of the British landing in the

Falklands in 1982, roughly simultaneous but smaller-scale Israeli amphibious operations in Lebanon in 1982, and a small Indian amphibious operation on the East Bengal coast in 1971 (also U.S. planning in 1990 for amphibious operations in Kuwait which turned out to be a feint). Otherwise, however, some recent wars have seen extensive riverine amphibious operations: Iraq and Iran back and forth along the Karun River and in the marshlands along the Tigris-Euphrates estuary; India's operations en route to the capture of Dacca in 1971.

There are, of course, some very technical areas of military geography that, while ultimately relevant to the study of our wars, may be a bit too arcane and beyond the purview of this work and mostly of interest to military engineers and cartographers. The West Point bibliography has, for instance, extensive sections on new cartographic technologies, mapmaking topographical surveys, remote and aerial sensing, hydrology, geomorphology, geophysics, soil science, and the medical aspects of military geography. Yes, they are relevant. Soil science can tell us whether certain types of soil in certain seasons or weather can support armored operations, and there are obviously numerous esoteric medical problems involved in the extremes of terrain and weather: frostbite, heat stroke, leeches, poisonous snakes, trenchfoot, and much more. But the emphasis here will, of necessity, be on terrain, vegetation, weather, and seasons, as these factors affect fighting, logistics, and strategy, primarily at the operational and tactical levels.

What types of terrain then, what weather, what seasons? Perhaps somewhat ironically, just because the American military had so long had its main focus on Central Europe, with terrain and climate quite similar to what exists in the old core areas of the U.S., some "normal" types of Third World terrain are treated in the West Point scheme as "special operations." In larger armies, that further translates into special purpose troop units and equipment, such as mountain divisions or ski troops. The "special" terrain conditions are, nonetheless, more or less self-explanatory: arctic, desert, jungle, swamp, forest, mountain, amphibious, urban, river operations (riverine terrain). Weather is hot or cold; dry or wet; clear, cloudy or hazy; windy or calm; stable or subject to rapid change; all further subject to the vicissitudes of the seasons. The West Point bibliography (and also Collins, approximately) provides a breakdown of terrain as seen in Table 3.1.

Patrick O'Sullivan, in his recent signal contributions to military geography, has provided a classification of terrain, as applied to a number of recent wars. Hence, according to him,

> For the soldier the landscape presents openings and pitfalls for attack and defense. Hills, plains, rivers, forests, plough land, roads, and buildings resolve into observation and firing platforms, killing grounds, protection, hiding, commanding points, and lines of movement. Along with the lie of the land and its human occupation, the weather and its seasonal changes affect the ease of moving, seeing, and fighting. A snow-covered plain is a different proposition from summer fields. The rainy and dry periods of the monsoon still dictate the maneuvering of armies.

The two principal aspects of a geographic setting that bear on tactics are how far one can see and shoot, and how easy the land is to travel over. The characteristic length of sight line in an area depends on the ruggedness of the land, the vegetation, the weather, and the human additions to the scenery, like hedges, crops and buildings. Whether the going is good in a landscape, whether men and vehicles can move easily, depends on the pattern of water courses, the slopes, the firmness of the ground, the thickness of the vegetation, the types and spacing of fences, the variety of crops, and most importantly, the density of the road network.[9]

O'Sullivan further provides a simple chart arranged along two axes, so as to depict the landscapes of the Third World in a way that captures "the tactically most significant elements of the environment: ruggedness and rainfall."[10] Ruggedness is shown as increasing from plains to mountains on one axis, and rainfall increasing from desert to rainforest conditions on the other. He then goes on to discuss various recent theaters of war, both conventional and unconventional, in the light of terrain and weather factors, noting that they "range from the heated wetness of Central America to the harsh dryness of Afghanistan to the cool darkness of the Falklands."[11] As he and others have noted, there are two major modifiers here: the seasons (varying more the further the theater from the equator) and patterns of human settlements and densities (most recent Third World wars have been fought largely away from population centers, with the exceptions of Abadan and Khorramshahr in 1980, Beirut in 1982, and Kuwait City in 1991).

Table 3.1 TERRAIN TYPES

Shore Zones	islands
	reefs and atolls
Unique Terrain	volcanoes
	mountains
	glaciers
	caves
	landslides
	lava flows
Wetlands	rivers and streams
	floodplains
	marshes, swamps, and bogs
Vegetation	forests
	savannah
	deserts
	rainforests and jungles
	taiga and tundra
Soils	trafficability (various)
	permafrost
	mud

Source: Patrick O'Sullivan, "The Geography of Wars in the Third World," in Stephanie G. Neuman and Robert E. Harkavy, eds., *The Lessons of Recent Wars in the Third World: Comparative Dimensions,* vol. 2 (Lexington, MA: Deds., C. Heath, 1987), p. 51.

Collins offers an elaborate typology of terrain under "land forms." He has a basic three-way division between "high ground" (mountains, hills, hummocks, cliffs, bluffs), "relatively level land" (plains, plateaus, mesa tops, butte tops), and "depressions" (valleys, basins, canyons, gorges, ravines, caverns, caves, craters).[12]

There have been somewhat more elaborate attempts at classifying combinations of terrain and weather. Or, rather, there have been efforts at approaching the subject from a different angle or starting point. In 1949, Colonel H. M. Forde, writing for *Military Review* in the near-aftermath of America's global World War II effort, looked at some eight major types of military geography, involving various mixes of landforms (relief or topography), drainage, surface materials, vegetation and climate and weather.[13] And, indeed, he looked at some of the causal connections between these factors—some types of landforms tend to cause certain kinds of weather and vice versa. He then identified the following group of terrain/climate types, even while recognizing their indistinct boundaries: (1) the drylands, (2) the tropical forest lands, (3) the Mediterranean scrub forest lands, (4) the midlatitude mixed forest lands, (5) the grasslands, (6) the boreal forest lands, (7) the polar lands, and (8) the mountain lands.

These were in turn analyzed in terms of the obvious military criteria, i.e., their amenability to rapid troop movements, logistics, the use of tactical airpower, the seasonal consistency of military operations. And, for each of the "types," global maps were utilized to show what portions of the earth they corresponded to. On that basis, one could perhaps elaborate on O'Sullivan's more simple classification of Third World wars as they have been conducted in certain combined types of terrain and weather.

Some of these broad "types" of geographical regions are, for the most part, not represented in the areas where the recent wars have been fought. The "Mid-Latitude Mixed Forest Lands," for instance, are represented in parts of Europe (including the USSR), North America, Australia, China, and Korea, but almost nowhere in the developing world save small segments of Brazil, Chile, and South Africa. The Boreal Forest category (taiga and Mediterranean scrub forest) also applies mostly to the USSR, North America, and Australia, but also some parts of Lebanon, Turkey, and North Africa. The "Polar Lands" are . . . the "Polar Lands"! That leaves five major types represented where recent wars have been fought: drylands (deserts), tropical forest lands (jungle), grasslands (savannahs), Mediterranean scrub forest lands, and mountains.

O'Sullivan goes beyond the aforementioned "strategic," a.k.a., "environmental" factors to look at a host of critical requirements or criteria at the tactical levels of warfare. He discusses points of observation, avenues of approach, obstacles, fields of fire, cover and concealment, and key terrain.[14] Clearly, these are the "stuff" of modern armies' military training manuals as well as of numerous commentaries in professional military journals, often characterized by the acronym OCOKA.[15]

There is one exception, however, and that has to do with those cases where a war, or perhaps an important battle, has critically been determined by a terrain feature, by the presence or absence of an avenue of approach, of cover and concealment, by a key piece of terrain. Are there, in other words, equivalents to the role that can—and has—been played in football games by a close referee's call, by a fumble, where a game's or a war's outcome has turned on an event at the margin? That requires detailed analysis. In the Middle East, for instance, one recalls Israel's legendary turning of the Latrun salient in 1948 by the use of an obscure wadi, or Israel's advance across the "impassable" dunes at Abu Agheila in 1967, or its surprise crossing of Suez in 1973 after the Battle of the Chinese Farm. Britain's capture of key mountaintops in 1982 before Ft. Stanley also comes to mind, though there was really only one possible ultimate outcome. Were there key terrain elements that helped turn the Horn war around in 1977? Could one find a key terrain issue at the Fao peninsula in 1986? Or, contrariwise (in contrast to earlier European history), are there no longer key battles, skirmishes upon which the fortunes of nations turn?

Matching up these types of military environments with the numerous recent conflicts in the developing world is in some cases simple, but in others much less so. For as we shall later point out, many of these wars have been fought out in two or more of these environments, in separate theaters of operations, though one may have been the main theater. The conflicts in Afghanistan and Peru, for instance, have largely been fought in remote mountainous areas, but to a lesser degree, respectively, in desert areas and in urban habitats. Vietnam, Burma, Cambodia, the Philippines, and the several countries of Central America have all seen extensive fighting in tropical forest lands (but there has been fighting in the mountains of the latter). In the drylands category, there have been the wars in Western Sahara, Chad, and on the Sinai (but also the Rann of Kutch along the southern part of the India-Pakistan frontier, and the western part of Afghanistan). Grasslands or savannahs have been the scene of combat in Zimbabwe, Mozambique, and Sudan, among others; the Mediterranean scrub forests have hosted conflicts on Cyprus and in Lebanon. The category of "midlatitude mixed forest lands," mostly inapplicable to the developing world, nevertheless does best describe the main area of fighting between China and Vietnam in 1979, perhaps also some of the low-intensity combat arenas in the Caucasus and Central Asia.

Most introductory discussions of military geography deal mostly with the dualism of terrain and weather, with the former assumed to pertain largely to geography, to landforms or relief; that is, in O'Sullivan's terminology, to various forms of "ruggedness." Collins utilizes the additional criteria of vegetation, clearly related to and correlated with terrain and weather. But some analysts pay attention to another critical dimension, that of geological characteristics. And that does not necessarily or always follow from the dominant facts of topography. Thus, according to Major James E. Wilson, Jr.,

> From a topographic map, a soldier with an "eye for the ground" can evaluate quite nicely a given piece of terrain in terms of observation, fields of fire, cover, etc. In such an evaluation the familiar dimensions of distance and relief are employed. The careful, questioning individual wants to know more: How "tankable" is the ground off the roads? How easy is digging-in going to be along that ridge? What particular area does the enemy control

where extensive underground works might exist? Such questions involve another dimension—the subsurface or "fourth dimension" in terrain. This "fourth dimension" is an adjunct to terrain intelligence. It is obtained by an analysis of scientific formation (geology, geography, soils, engineering, etc).[16]

One point stands out here, particularly with reference to the traditionally easy assumptions about terrain types. And that is that under seemingly obvious, generic headings such as "desert," "jungle," or "mountainous" terrain, various soil conditions may obtain, with differing military implications. Deserts can be like much of the northern Sahara, made up of grainy sand. But they can also be of the type seen in Iran and Afghanistan; dry, rocky terrain made very difficult for walking or the movement of vehicles. Hence, according to an article by André Gimond,

> The common concept of the desert is that of a sea of sand extending beyond the range of vision, dune after dune under a burning and blinding sun. In places the desert does conform to this description, but uniformity of characteristics could hardly be expected in an expanse as great as the Sahara. On the contrary, one finds considerable variety of soils and climates. Alongside the sandy plains are mountainous deserts with barren rocks sculptured by wind erosion. These mountains are cut by wild canyons obstructed by boulders. There are also depressions filled with brackish mud and flat, stony, hard-surfaced areas stretching in vast plains, broken with sandy areas. In these desolate regions, the underground water in places approaches the surface, producing oases. Along the borders of the desert, moreover, are semi-desert zones with intermittent stretches covered with vegetation.[17]

This point was dramatized in the recent Gulf War. Despite all the talk during the long buildup about the difficulties of fighting in the desert, the coalition forces were able to mount a rapid armored movement well to the west of Kuwait, moving north and east to the Euphrates Valley at As Samawah and An Nasiryah. Clearly, the desert terrain in this part of southern Iraq was quite firm and suitable for the movement of armored forces, more so, for instance, than much of the Sinai Desert or the Libyan Desert.

Terrain and Weather, Ruggedness and Cover

The bulk of the literature on contemporary warfare provides some very common and widely accepted broad generalizations about the ramifications, comparatively speaking, of contrasting terrains and weather, or of various combinations of the two factors. To some extent, these generalizations need to be addressed on the nether sides of the divide between conventional and unconventional warfare, with a nod to the gray areas between them and some circumstances where that divide is rather blurred, as for example with the Lebanon war of 1982 or with Vietnam.

On the conventional side, flat and dry terrain (but not necessarily desert terrain) is deemed favorable for mobility, for offensive maneuver warfare featuring deep penetration and encirclement by armor, indeed, conjuring up the familiar images of Guderian, Patton, Sharon, and other legendary tank commanders. (Northern Europe, for instance is also considered "good tank country.") Contrariwise, wet *and* rugged terrain (or just rugged terrain with cover or with craggy defiles) is considered unfavorable for rapid offensive movement, for mechanized warfare. Flat jungle terrain, or that dominated by rivers, swamps, or marshes are said to provide equally tough going for large mechanized conventional forces. These are crude generalizations, of course, and any given theater of war does have terrain and weather specifics, idiosyncrasies, sometimes manmade features (the *bocage* in Normandy was tough for Allied armored forces in 1944, despite the overall flat nature of the terrain.)

Regarding unconventional or guerilla warfare, there are similar sets of common generalizations verging upon cliché. Areas with lots of cover, i.e., jungle canopy or rainforests and rugged terrain, are good for hiding guerillas, for providing bases, hideouts, and arms caches that are difficult to find on the ground and difficult to see from the air. Such terrain—all the more so if combined with rainy weather and habitual cloud cover—renders airpower (including the use of attack helicopters) virtually useless. Altogether, such terrain conditions tend to raise the ratios of counterinsurgency forces to insurgents required for victory for the former, and vice versa, also making more likely a more protracted, interminable, stalemated conflict that, more often than not, will be to the political detriment of an incumbent regime on the defensive. The opposite likewise holds true, i.e., flat and coverless terrain, particularly if combined with clear weather, will be advantageous to counterinsurgency operations, allowing technological advantage to come into play, particularly as pertains to airpower. Again, these are ideal-type cases, or hypothetical pure cases. The history of real-world conflict, on the other hand, often provides surprises, or at least more complex conditions that may defy such easy generalizations.

One problem with the easy generalizations, and with such simple matrices as provided by O'Sullivan and others, is that the theaters of many areas, perhaps even most wars, provide a complex mix of terrain and weather, rendered all the more complex if the wars last long enough to span the various seasons. And there are many more "complexities." There is, of course, the question of just how human settlement patterns and road networks are juxtaposed to terrain features, going beyond the simple and obvious generalization that inhospitable terrain and climate will normally correlate with low densities of population. In regard to terrain, there are such questions as the location of borders and major cities in relation to major terrain features such as mountains and rivers, with ramifications for such questions as the in-depth defense provided or not provided some nations, or the relationship of guerilla hideouts to major core areas. The relationships of lines of mountain ranges to axes of advances and to key core areas is also crucial, as is the relationship of terrain features to the size of nations and battle areas. What all this adds up to, obviously, is the requirement that military geography be put in specific context for specific wars. What further is implied is that there are very severe limits on really comparative analysis here. Each war, each nation is, of course, *sui generis,* in terms of its military geography. Generalizations can be ventured only with caution.

Some examples will serve to illustrate the importance of context. Take for example the matter of mixes of terrain for given nations and wars. The Iran-Iraq frontier is mountainous in the north, with the Zagros range making offensives by either side very difficult. In the south, however, there are some areas favorable to offensive warfare, though much of the Tigris-Euphrates frontier features rivers, marshes, and flood plains whose amenability to mechanized warfare and movement of troops will vary greatly by the season. Vietnam, of course, saw fighting in greatly varying terrains and weather, from the jungles of the Comau Peninsula to the northern mountainous highlands, from the urban sprawl of Saigon to the coastal plains further north. The conflict in Afghanistan, in its various phases, has been fought in snow-covered mountains, in cities, and on rough, hardscrabble deserts. The Spanish Sahara war has been fought on sandy desert but also in dry, rugged, terrain featuring wadis good for shielding guerilla fighters. Central America has mountain highlands, and coastal jungles and swamps. The Arabs and Israelis, in 1973, fought on the flat, sandy deserts and dry mountain passes of Sinai, on the rugged plateaus and "tels" of the Golan Heights, on the snowy slopes of Mount Hermon; India and Pakistan have fought in the mountainous regions of Kashmir and on the salt flats and marshes of the Rann of Kutch and in the Rajasthan Desert. Numerous insurgencies—Cyprus, Cuba, etc., have been fought, variously, in mountains, cities, and forests. Generally speaking, the smaller the theater of war, the more specific the terrain, but even this generalization has been belied in Lebanon, Sri Lanka, and elsewhere. The U.S, obviously, had to fight in all kinds of terrain and climate in World War II. At the other end of the scale, the terrain in the Falklands was relatively more consistent.

Concerning the relationship *between* ruggedness and cover, there are various combinations of them. In the U.S., for instance, there are rugged mountains in Nevada and New Mexico largely devoid of cover, while the eastern Appalachians—in a wetter climate—provide heavy forest cover; also less elevated and less rugged mountains. The mountains of Afghanistan have little cover; those of Lebanon and the China-Vietnam border much more; those of Central America more still. None of these mountainous areas would provide good tank country, but those that are covered make aerial surveillance and interdiction very difficult, and vice versa. Likewise, the Falklands terrain is relatively flat and wet—the Rann of Kutch and some areas of the Iran-Iraq border are flat and dry. And, again, all are inherently *sui generis.*

Regarding cover, some obvious lessons emerged from the recent Gulf War. Primarily that involved the lesson that control of the air over the battlefield is magnified in importance where there is little cover, few places in which to conceal men and equipment. But further, the new U.S. night-fighting technology—mostly involving infrared systems that allow for locating tanks and other targets at night—still further amplified the advantage in an area lacking cover to that side that controls the air. Indeed, some battle reports claimed the U.S. Air Force was able to target precisely even deeply revetted Iraqi tanks and artillery during the night.[18] Whether or to what extent such new technology can now produce greater "visibility" in areas of light or even denser cover is not here known.

The contextual placement of major terrain features and borders can be important. The fact of the Hindu Kush's relationship to the Soviet-Afghan border is an example. The distance of Teheran and Addis Ababa from the borders with Iraq and Somalia respectively, largely explained the failures of the latter in obtaining decisive victories at the outset of their wars. Pakistan's extreme vulnerability to an Indian offensive against its major population centers is obvious. One could as easily point to Israel's vulnerability (but also the reciprocal vulnerability of Amman and Damascus) or the defensive depth provided in such disparate cases as Luanda and Johannesburg, Tripoli and N'djamena. These factors in turn, as we shall see, have ramifications for the critical areas of preemptive offensives and preventive wars.

As has often been pointed out, the contextual geography of insurgency wars can be very telling, and that involves a certain paradox. Guerillas need sanctuaries, bases in rugged or covered terrains, far from the striking power of incumbent, counterinsurgency forces. But, to acquire momentum and gain public support, they need to demonstrate that they can strike at the major core areas of incumbent regimes.

Otherwise, in this connection, it is important to point out that some commonly accepted generalizations about the impact of terrain on the viability of some weapons and tactics may not necessarily always obtain. For instance, Vietnam was often said to have shown that tanks are not particularly useful in jungle warfare. But at Guadalcanal and elsewhere in the Pacific during World War II, the U.S. was able to make effective use of armor in jungle conditions, albeit in slowly moving offensive operations where the opposition lacked effective anti-tank weapons and where close infantry support was necessary. (Some tanks were used as flamethrower carriers for close-in support). Similarly, Israel in 1967 was able to use tanks in some desert areas thought almost impervious to the movement of vehicles. Thus, there are exceptions to many such generalizations. In the summer of 1990, the reports on the fighting in Cambodia indicated that the Khmer Rouge forces were conducting successful *offensive* operations, were taking territory, during the rainy season against a more mobile, mechanized incumbent regime's army. So, contrary to commonly accepted myth, not all wars grind to a halt during inclement weather, nor result in lengthy stalemates.

The Geography of Recent Conventional Wars in the Third World: Key Criteria

Over the past couple of decades, there were some eight wars that could have been described as "traditional conventional," as measured, variously, by magnitude (numbers of forces involved), intensity (casualties, materiel attrition), duration, use of large-unit formations and major weapons systems (armored divisions, massed artillery, extensive use of combat aircraft), and the identifiability of a definable moving battle front, i.e., a "forward line of troops" (FLOT) for both sides. In this category have been the 1971 India-Pakistan war, the Arab-Israeli war of 1973, the "Horn War" of 1977–78, the China-Vietnam war in 1979, Iraq vs. Iran (1980–1988), Lebanon in 1982, the Falklands War of 1982, the Gulf War, the final stages of the Vietnam agony, and the recent Ethiopia-Eritrea war. In a gray area in between "conventional" and "unconventional" warfare have been the contests in Afghanistan, Chad (Libya vs. Chad), the Angolan civil war (particularly as pertains to the main-force battles between South African and Cuban troops), Tanzania's 1979 invasion of Uganda, and the recent civil war in Cambodia. Otherwise, in the developing world, one could point to the quick preemptive use of conventional forces by the U.S. in Grenada and Panama, and to Iraq's invasion of Kuwait, each involving brief conflicts of low intensity.

Concerning the military geography of these conflicts, spanning somewhat their strategic and tactical levels, a number of major, general questions stand out as they might provide a basis for comparison or for broad generalizations. But the wars have come in all shapes and sizes, and one could as easily focus on the uniqueness of their generalized circumstances as those circumstances contributed to victory or defeat, stalemate or movement, long wars and short ones. Caveats aside, some main criteria are as follows:

- The general size of the battle theater (whether defined as the combined square mileage of the combatants' territories or, more narrowly, the square mileage of the battle arena); also, the shape of nations or theaters involved.
- The length or frontal width of frontiers or of the forward lines of battle (the latter could vary during the course of a war). But, more narrowly, one could speak of an "effective" length of battlefront, as some wars are fought along only a portion of the frontiers of contending forces, perhaps because of impossible terrain, particularly as it pertains to extended offensive operations.
- The depth provided either side by the geography of the war, i.e., the relationship of the frontiers to capital cities, core areas, industrial heartlands, key resources, agricultural breadbaskets, weapons-producing centers; this is a two-way relationship, i.e., the distance of the battle lines from the nation's core area is also important as it pertains to power projection.
- The ethnography of the battle area, particularly where multiethnic or multicultural societies are involved.
- Overall patterns of human settlement and road networks, i.e., is the war fought mostly in populated or unpopulated areas?
- The role of topography or terrain, i.e., the ruggedness or flatness of terrain and also rivers—how many, running with or against the grain of the axis of advance and retreat of contending forces.
- Weather and seasons, obviously of particular importance in the latter case in the event of protracted wars, i.e., those of more than a few months' duration.

- Cover-from jungles to plains to forests, etc., how much foliage, how dense and high, how passable or impassable, to what degree allowing for observation from overhead.
- Key military terrain features—mountain tops, road junctions, mountain passes, river crossings, etc. . . . in relation to each other and to the geography of the war.
- For either or both combatants (or more), is it a one-front or one-theater war . . . or two? How many "moving fronts?"
- How many distinct types of relevant terrain, weather patterns, etc.?
- The location of conflicts; specifically in relation to the superpowers or other major powers in the context of arms resupply operations, interventions, coercive diplomacy, etc.

There are other criteria too, beyond the scope of this study. Collins, for instance, notes the importance of location of water supplies and of materials useful for construction purposes.[19]

Size of Theater and Length of FLOT

As noted, the sheer scale—the size of the theater—of the various conventional wars we are dealing with varies immensely. On one end was the large-scale Iran-Iraq War between two very sizeable nations, fought, however, mostly all along their mutual frontiers as well as involving long-range bombardment of each other's cities and oil installations and some naval action as well. China and Vietnam are large nations too, the former relatively much larger, but their brief, intense war was strictly limited to their frontier area, and with little activity in the air. At the other end of the spectrum, the Falklands War was fought by two large nations in a tiny theater; that in Lebanon also in a surprisingly small space; that between large Ethiopia and Somalia along only a small portion of their very lengthy frontier. We shall note, as has Collins, that large size can be advantageous or disadvantageous to a combatant nation; large size provides a lot of strategic depth, but also, depending upon its shape, it can involve vulnerability to widely dispersed, omnidirectional attacks.[20]

The lengths of the battle lines (mostly coinciding with frontiers or lines closely parallel to them) of our wars varies greatly. But the "frontal width" of these wars does not necessarily coincide with their magnitude or intensity, as respectively measuring the sizes of forces involved and the human and materiel losses.

On the one end are the Iraq-Iran and India-Pakistan wars, both fought along frontiers about 730 miles long (of course in 1971 much of the fighting in the latter was along India's three-sided frontier with East Bengal, now Bangladesh, which has some 800 additional miles of frontier). The fighting in the Iran-Iraq War was heavily concentrated for eight years on the extreme southern end of the line in the Shatt Al Arab estuary between Abadan/Khorramshahr and Basra and to the north in the marshlands west of Susangird and Ahwaz. But there were other areas of frequent fighting—west of Dehloran, near Mehran only some seventy miles from Baghdad, near Khaneqin and Quasr-e-Shirin, also some seventy miles from Iraq's capital, and in Kurdish-populated areas around Panjwin in the mountains east of Kirkuk and Mosul. In between these areas there was little fighting, certainly no major offensives by either side, because of difficult terrain: rugged mountains in the north and marshlands in the south along the Tigris and Shatt Al Arab. Hence, the frequent comparison with World War I, with its endless and (literally) continuous trenches and fortifications from the English Channel to the Swiss border, is only partly correct.

The India-Pakistan border is also nearly eight hundred miles long, but the fighting in 1965 and 1971 tended to be concentrated in only a small portion of that front: in the areas north and south of the Lahore-Amritsar axis, particularly around Sialkot and Chhamb and in the Rann of Kutch marshlands east of Karachi and Hyderabad. There was only some limited fighting in the huge part of the frontier between the Thar and Great Indian deserts, involving an Indian advance, and in the high mountains between Jammu and Kashmir. As in the case of Iran and Iraq, the large armies of two large nations were involved.

The Ethiopia-Somalia frontier is actually some nine hundred miles long and, here too fighting was concentrated along only a small fraction of this frontier: mostly along the crucial axis between Hargeisa and Dire Dawa near the cities of Jijiga and Harar (potentially, at least, an invasion route toward Addis Ababa), and in some areas of the semiarid Ogaden where the fighting was more that of irregular, guerilla hit-and-run warfare. Likewise, the Ethiopia-Eritrea border is some six hundred miles long, but fighting between these countries in 1999 took place in only a small sector of the border.

Angola is some six hundred miles wide, east to west, having provided a long potential FLOT, either or both for the fighting between UNITA and the Angolan government, or at some points, between Cuban and South African intervention forces. This fighting (only in the latter case involving large conventional units) never did, however, involve a lengthy FLOT; rather, quick and mobile movements, perhaps more reminiscent of the American Civil War, with a major campaign centered near the town of Cuito Cuernevale. The subsequent war between UNITA and the incumbent Luanda government mostly assumed the character of a hit-and-run guerilla war, partly tribal as well as ideological in character.

The 1979 China-Vietnam war was fought along portions of a 450–mile frontier, with the fighting concentrated in the eastern sector north and east of Hanoi near the key town of Lang Son, but with several other points of Chinese invasion. But large-scale forces and battles were involved over a three-week period, and there was a "moving front" characteristic of a traditional conventional war.

The recent Gulf War presents an intermediate case. It first appeared that coalition forces would attempt to assault Kuwait across a relatively narrow 150–mile front comprising the Saudi-Kuwaiti border. But the coalition widened the front by moving numerous forces westward, so as to allow for attacking along a 300–mile front from the Persian Gulf westward almost to the Medina road which runs north to Najaf and Baghdad. As the western half of the front was virtually undefended, it allowed for a classic flanking and encirclement of the Iraqi army, in the manner of Cannae.

On the other hand, both of the well-publicized Lebanon and Falklands wars of 1982 were fought over a much narrower front. The Lebanon-Israel border is only some forty to fifty miles wide, east to west, and the width of the moving battlefront as Israeli forces struck north toward the Beirut-Damascus axis was only about forty miles at the widest (thirty miles from Beirut to the Syria border along the route to Damascus). Hence, the combat here was channeled into a rather constricted frontal width, even if fought by two large, modern armies. Likewise, the north-south distance along the main British line of advance toward the ultimate, conclusive objective of Ft. Stanley was only about thirty to forty miles. The British advanced rapidly in parallel columns, and there was no really continuous, fortified Argentinian defense line to block their paths. That was a small theater for a small war which, of course, saw decisive sea and air operations.

In between these extremes, there was the Sinai battlefield of 1967 and 1973. Relevant to the former, the Israeli frontier with Egyptian Sinai runs about one hundred twenty miles, with the larger distance from El Arish to the southern tip of Sinai amounting to some two hundred miles. But the 1967 war was fought along a much smaller line in the northern Sinai, maybe some eighty miles between El Arish and Nahkl. In 1973, the bulk of the war was fought along the Suez Canal between Port Said and Port Suez along a front about eighty miles long. The comparison with Iran-Iraq is clear, i.e., here was a much more condensed line of battle. With regard to a possible peace settlement, however, and with historical reference to the period 1948 to 1967, it is noted that tiny Israel then had very long borders because of its shape, rendering an all-aspects defense particularly challenging.

Strategic Depth

An important aspect of strategic military geography is that of the relationship of frontiers, FLOTS, or battle areas to the combatants' industrial core areas, capital cities, heartlands, or other key cities or centers of military production. Who could easily capture or overrun what with a quick preemptive attack or a feasible, methodical offensive? Conversely, there is the question of strategic depth— to what extent can a country withdraw within its own territories, absorb its opponent's initial offensive thrust, and eventually take advantage of that opponent's power-over-distance gradient problem, assuming that an offensive thrust becomes more difficult the further it must extend from its source of power? These are traditional staples of the military literature; illustrated, for instance, by the Germans' failure to knock out the Soviet Union in 1941–42, Japan's problems in trying to overrun China in the 1940s or, earlier, Napoleon's demise in the ill-fated attempt to conquer Russia.

How and to what extent do these traditional assumptions apply to modern warfare in the developing world? What are the implications regarding the perceptions that drive attempts at preemptive attacks intended to result in dramatic, conclusive victories? How important are the asymmetries involved in specific pairings of nations that have fought recent Third World wars?

Two good examples illustrating the advantages of strategic depth have been the Iranian and Ethiopian situations in 1980 and 1977 respectively. Iraq, then considered the weaker power in the Iran-Iraq pairing on the basis of population and/or GNP, launched an offensive, the central purpose of which was the seizing and holding of the Khuzistan oil region with its largely Arab population, with the hope that a truce or war termination could make that a "permanent" outcome. That strategy seemed, initially, a partial success. But there was little chance of a quick, fully decisive Iraqi victory because of Iran's vast strategic depth, further buttressed by the formidable barrier of the Zagros Mountains between the border and the major cities of the Iranian heartland. Teheran is more than three hundred miles from the border, Isfahan approximately 240 miles. The smaller cities of Kermanshah, Abadan, and Ahwaz were closer, but still not so easy to overrun with a quick offensive. As it turned out, only the area around Khorramshahr was easily subject to a quick "seize and hold" operation, with a more ambitious and longer reach offensive rendered difficult by Iraq's lack of a real offensive punch, which would have required both better coordination of combined arms tactics and better logistics.

On the reverse side, during the entire war Iraq remained highly vulnerable to an even modestly successful Iranian offensive, which despite enormous and costly efforts never succeeded. Baghdad is only some seventy miles from the Iranian frontier, Basra (heavily shelled during the war) only about ten miles. The major northern cities in the oil-rich Kurdish area, Kirkuk and Mosul, are also only some seventy and one hundred miles respectively from the frontier. Further, the main roads connecting these cities run parallel to and close to the frontier, providing other points of vulnerability. If Iran had not been so militarily weakened by its Islamic revolution, those could have been crucial factors. The asymmetries involved here are very marked.

An assessment of the question of strategic depth for the recent Gulf War is actually a bit complex. On the one hand, Iraq was faced with an only sixty-mile distance from the Saudi border to Kuwait City, seemingly the coalition's main war objective, at least as applied to its declaratory posture. Ironically, Baghdad's some 280–mile distance from the western end of the coalition's deployments appeared to provide considerable depth, but as it turned out that expanse was left largely undefended as Iraq concentrated its forces to defend Kuwait and Basra. On the reverse side, one could point out that important Saudi oil fields and loading points were only some 140 to 150 miles from the Kuwaiti border, vulnerable to an Iraqi drive if the latter had immediately carried on after the overrunning of Kuwait in August 1990. Postmortems after the war also noted that if Iraq had moved south of Kuwait in August, it would have been much more difficult for coalition forces to move and assemble their (ultimately) massive military forces. The Saudi capital at Riyadh, however, benefits from considerable strategic depth as well as difficult-to-traverse desert terrain.

The Ethiopia-Somalia situation bore some similarities to that of Iran-Iraq. There too an inherently weaker power (Somalia) attempted a preemptive offensive attack against a temporarily weakened stronger power (Ethiopia). But aside from the possibilities for "seize and hold" operations along the frontier (also taking advantage of ethnic Somali populations in the Ogaden), there was the problem for Somalia of Ethiopia's great strategic depth. The Ogaden has its vast reaches of plateau and semidesert leading west and north from Somalia toward the mountains and the Ethiopian Rift Valley, some four hundred to five hundred miles along a broad front. To a lesser degree this was also true of the main axis of the initial Somali attack running west from the staging area near Hargeisa toward Jijiga, Harar, Dire Dawa, and ultimately Addis Ababa. The latter is three hundred miles from the border, similar to Teheran's distance from the Iran-Iraq border. Dire Dawa at eighty miles and Harar at seventy ended up just beyond the penetrative thrust of the Somali offensive, which had the critical objective of cutting Ethiopia's lifeline to the sea, the rail line from Addis Ababa to Djibouti, which runs through Dire Dawa. If, after the war had turned to Ethiopia's favor, it had attacked east well into Somalia, it would have been only 40 miles to Hargeisa, 130 to Berbera, and east of the vast Ogaden some 200 miles to the capital of Mogadishu. Here there was also an asymmetry of strategic depth, but less so than was the case with Iran-Iraq, and with Somalia being relatively bereft of good defensive terrain between its border and its major cities.

The India-Pakistan standoff well illustrates the impact of asymmetries in strategic depth, as well as the "shape" of a nation or war theater. Pakistan is highly vulnerable to a quick, preemptive attack, or also to a more gradual, relentless one. Like Iraq but even more so, its main cities lay near the border, with critical road and rail communications running perilously close to and parallel to the frontier. Karachi is one hundred miles from the FLOT, Hyderabad eighty, Islamabad and Rawalpindi fifty, and Lahore only twenty. (Yet in 1965 and 1971 Pakistani forces managed to defend at or near the border against superior forces in short wars.) By contrast, Delhi is more than 200 miles from the frontier, Bombay more than 400, with Punjabi Amritsar more vulnerable only 20 miles away, Ahmadabad further at 120. These are critical factors in connection with the earlier well-publicized Pakistani ambition to imitate Israel in conducting a lightning preemptive strike toward Delhi, albeit over relatively favorable terrain for mechanized forces.[21] In 1971, with East Bengal then still belonging to Pakistan, Dacca's one-hundred-mile distance from the Indian frontier to the west, along with difficult riverine terrain, proved of insufficient defensive absorptive depth; it could not compensate for Pakistan's numerical inferiority, its impossible logistics problems, and its having simultaneously to fight an internal counterinsurgency war.

The Libya-Chad conflict has involved two nations, both of which have core areas far removed from the frontier. Tripoli is some 600 miles north, Ft. Lamy about 650 miles south. Not accidentally, the war was fought entirely in the vast uninhabited spaces in between the core areas, neither of which were remotely threatened by attack from ground forces, nor even from the air.

The China-Vietnam War provided still another example of this sort of strategic asymmetry. China, the larger nation and scarcely endangered by the threat of a Vietnamese offensive, has immense depth on its southern border (involving also rugged terrain), shielding its major southern population centers. Nanning, a provincial capital, is some 120 miles from the Vietnamese frontier. Vietnam, on the other hand, is far more vulnerable. Hanoi, Haiphong, and the surrounding core area of the Red River Valley are only some 75 to 80 miles from the border with China, much of it downhill through mountain valleys onto the flood plains. After three weeks of war, only a countervailing Soviet threat to China's northern border could have stopped the prospect of a serious Chinese incursion into the Red River Valley.

The Arab-Israel conflict has also illustrated the concept of strategic depth, albeit perhaps in some surprising, unexpected ways. Before 1967 it was common to speak of Israel's extreme lack of depth, along its borders with Egypt, Jordan, and Syria—from the West Bank, a Jordanian advance of only nine miles north of Tel Aviv could have cut Israel literally in half. Syria was in near proximity to the Galilee settlements, Egypt poised to strike quickly at Eilat, Beersheva, Ashdod, indeed, all of Israel. But Israel's preemptive assault in 1967 paradoxically was able to take advantage of interior lines, as so often described, allowing the small state to act like a "coiled spring." The dénouement gave Israel some 120 miles worth of strategic depth across the northern Sinai, then widely thought to be a strategic plus, a margin of badly needed safety. But Israel's defeats at the outset of the 1973 war along the Suez Canal proved again that the advantages of strategic depth are balanced off by the vulnerability resulting from long lines of communications, that is, a more challenging power-over-distance gradient. The 1967 capture of the Golan Heights, however, proved a critical positive depth factor for Israel in 1973. Then and again in 1982 Syria had to worry about the only thirty-mile distance from forward Israeli positions on Golan to its capital in Damascus, howsoever rendered difficult for an Israeli offensive by rugged terrain and the narrowness of the available front. Generally, both Israel and Syria labor under a precarious situation of shallow defensive depth vis-à-vis each other, which is why the Golan has remained such a contentious issue.[22] Amman, meanwhile, is only some thirty miles from the Jordan Valley; Jerusalem is equally close to the Jordanian frontier on the Jordan, albeit involving a more imposing defensive terrain rampart. Eilat and Aqaba, meanwhile, are contiguous mutual hostages. And in 1982 Beirut's fifty-five- or sixty-mile distance from Israel's northern frontier rendered it highly vulnerable to a quick armored strike, abetted somewhat by amphibious leapfrogging operations along the Mediterranean coast. Distances, generally speaking, are very short in the core Middle Eastern cockpit, producing in some cases hair-trigger strategic situations and obvious temptations for preemption.[23]

The Angolan war illustrated, by contrast, a situation of far more favorable mutual defensive depth. Luanda is more than 450 miles from the Namibian frontier, Benguela 300, Huambo 300, Lubango 140. Hence, a decisive South African thrust into the core Angolan area was rendered difficult, even on the basis of marked military superiority, all the more so after Namibian independence. Johannesburg was some 800 miles from the scenes of the fighting in Angola. In reverse, the vast depths (deserts, savannah) of southern Africa shielded the South African heartland around Johannesburg and Pretoria from any potential attack originating in Angola or Zimbabwe, perhaps less so from an attack that might have been staged through Botswana or Mozambique.

The more recent war between Ethiopia and Eritrea, fought entirely along the border between the two nations (the latter was earlier part of the former), also illustrates asymmetries of strategic depth. The two nations have a border running some 620 miles in length. Eritrea exists mostly as a long, narrow coastal strip some fifty miles wide along the Red Sea, broadening out and inland along the northwest frontier with Sudan. The narrow, coastal strip is mostly unpopulated rugged terrain. Its capital, Asmara, is only some seventy miles from the border and from the scene of recent fighting; its main port, Massawa, is another forty miles distant over the mountains on the Red Sea coast. Ethiopia's main advance during the war, through the Badami region of western Eritrea, brought its army some eighty miles west of Asmara at the captured provincial city of Barentsa. Ethiopia, meanwhile, has immense strategic depth in relation to the border with Eritrea. The capital, Addis Ababa, is some 440 miles from the frontier, as the crow flies; still further along the two main roads leading inland from Eritrea. The major city of Gondor is some 160 miles from the frontier. As it happens, Ethiopia, in successfully prosecuting the war in the late 1990s, evinced little desire to move further into the Eritrean coastal heartland. Most of the fighting took place along a 160–mile stretch of border running from central to western Eritrea, south and west of Asmara.

All by itself, of course, the Falklands War provided some entirely different lessons for strategic geography. There were no contiguous frontiers, no issues of related strategic depth. The key questions there had to do with long-range power projection, seemingly leaving the British with a severe disadvantage. But Britain's overwhelming naval superiority resulted in the main problem of power projection being that of Argentina's some four hundred-mile one-way aircraft trip from bases at Rio Gallego and Comodora Rivadavia in southern Patagonia. On the ground, the short fifty-mile trek from the landing place at San Carlos to Ft. Stanley left the Argentines little room for backing up and for absorbing the British offensive once the latter's landing force was in place and well protected and provided for by naval and air dominance.

Distance of War Theaters from Major Powers and Other Locational Factors in Relation to Arms Resupply and/or Intervention

Some of the recent regional conventional wars have illustrated the importance of location in relation to other major power noncombatants and big-power arms suppliers. These factors, by contrast to some others we have discussed here, are at the grand strategic or strategic levels of analysis. They are also highly idiosyncratic, involving maritime choke points, air overflight corridors, overland transport routes, etc.

Virtually all of the combatants in recent conventional wars have depended—varying with the length of the war—on external resupply of arms.[24] That has involved all manner of problems related to geographical location. Iraq, for instance, despite having its ports on the Persian Gulf destroyed or blockaded, could avail itself of access for arms supplies via Jordan's Aqaba. Israel in 1973 depended greatly on American use of the Portuguese base at Lajes in the Azores, but also on air access through and over the Gibraltar Straits between Spain and Morocco, neither of which would have allowed overflights for this purpose (it relied on resupply of arms from U.S. stocks in Germany through the same chokepoints). The USSR resupplied Vietnam in 1979, utilizing Indian airspace and perhaps staging points, and it overflew several nations in the Middle East in 1977–78 in resupplying Ethiopia during the Horn war. Argentina's great distance from the Middle East, meanwhile, made resupply from several potential sources very difficult and costly. Israel, in attempting to move arms to Iran during the Iran-Iraq War, required "illegal" and precarious overflights along the Soviet border.

Ethnography of Battle Areas or Borderlands

A number of the recent conventional regional wars have involved one or more multiethnic (or multireligious or multilingual) societies. That, of course, can take any of a number of forms, ranging from the "melting pot" model of the U.S. to other models where ethnic or religious groups are sharply demarcated by regions, perhaps even involving federal governmental structures or other arrangements allowing for degrees of autonomy. In turn, such factors can have profound military implications, particularly if populations along a border or in regions involved in major fighting contain populations related by blood or otherwise linked to the opposing side of the war, or dissident or disaffected populations ripe for rebellion or secessionist movements.

Iraq, for example, counted on support from the Arab populations of oil-rich Khuzistan Province, indeed hoped to end up in control of that region, which could be justified on a consensual "popular" basis. Iran, meanwhile, banked on support from disaffected Kurdish peoples along the northern end of the Iran-Iraq frontier, and from the very large Shi'a religious groups within Iraq thought vulnerable to the enticements of the Ayatollah Khomeini's Islamic fundamentalism (they remained loyal to Iraq during its war with Iran but revolted in Basra and elsewhere after the debacle in 1991). Somalia, in attacking Ethiopia in 1977, counted on extensive support (and received it) from the Somali population of the desertlike Ogaden Province, some of it nomadic. Additionally, Somalia's war plans (involving an attack on a far more numerous foe) banked on Addis Ababa's strength being sapped by then ongoing, full-scale insurgencies in Eritrea and Tigre province, albeit not directly linked to nor supported by Somalia.

There are, of course, numerous other relevant examples: the tribal breakdown in Angola, the role of Shi'a populations in southern Lebanon (first almost welcoming Israeli forces in 1982, then later bitter foes of Israel, in part because of the impact of the 1979 Iranian Revolution); India's Sikh problem in the strategic Punjab border region (also the ethnolinguistic divisions within and throughout Pakistan). On the other hand, the China-Vietnam and Falklands Wars were essentially bereft of these problems, despite Vietnam's containing a substantial Chinese minority (much of which earlier had fled or been driven out at the end of the Vietnam War), and the fact of the small British population in Ft. Stanley temporarily under Argentine occupation.

Patterns of Human Settlement, Road Networks

As pointed out by O'Sullivan and others, most of the recent wars in the Third World have been fought in empty spaces (varying, however, by topography) and in areas often not served by extensive road or rail networks even remotely comparable to Central Europe or North America.[25] The latter factor has been cited as one reason for the relative absence of long-distance, offensive maneuver warfare. The former factor has also meant, with a few exceptions (Israel in Tyre, Sidon, and Beirut; Iraq in Khorramshar and Abadan) that there has been little in the way of house-to-house urban warfare à la Stalingrad, Warsaw, or Berlin. But that may be changing, perhaps mostly with respect to low-intensity conflict.

Of course, the mere prospect of urban warfare, with its high casualties, may present a deterrent. The casualty figures for the Germans and Soviets in the final battle for Berlin in 1945 were simply staggering. Israel was reluctant to enter Beirut in 1982 for these very reasons, given its high sensitivity to casualties. In 1991 the U.S.-led coalition eschewed a final knockout of Saddam Hussein in part because of fears of massive casualties if Baghdad had had to be stormed in block-by-block urban warfare.

But again, most of our wars have been fought away from settled areas. The images are familiar: the stark deserts of Sinai, the rocky plateaus and tels of Golan, the Bekaa Valley (sparsely settled farmland), the rugged hills and valleys of Vietnam's borderlands near China, the cold, treeless bogs and hills of East Falkland Island, the empty wastes of the Ogaden, the marshlands and foothills of the Iran-Iraq border excepting the Shatt Al Arab area and some of the smaller towns interspersed all along the border further north.

Some of these wars, just because of the scarcity of good roads, have focused great importance on control over some roads and road junctions. Iraq's failure to capture the important road junctions of Ahwaz and Dizful has often been noted as a key failure at the outset of the war. Israel's offensive in 1967 focused attention on several key road junctions or roads in central Sinai, at Abu Agheila, Bir Lahfan, El Arish, Bir Gifgafa, and Bir El Thomada. Somalia's assault on Ethiopia likewise involved critical importance for several roads and junctions; specifically, the road between Jijiga and Harar over the mountainous Kara Marda Pass and the key rail junction at Dire Dawa. Israel made critical use of several roads leading north through the Lebanon valleys in 1982. China's assault in 1979 on Vietnam was concentrated along two roads leading out of South China toward Hanoi, particularly that leading over the "Friendship Pass." At the end of the Gulf War, Iraq found its road connections between Basra and Baghdad highly vulnerable to coalition flanking movements that severed its critical road communications. These factors are underscored in many cases by the combination of

large distances, the mechanization of armies, logistical requirements for ammunition and other materiel, and the vulnerability of road transport to attack from
the air. Few if any of these wars have included long-distance power projection
by dismounted infantry—China's attack on Vietnam in 1979 may have been a
partial exception, as too on a much smaller scale the forty-mile advance across
East Falkland by British soldiers and marines.

Mountains and Rivers: With or Across the Line of Advance

We have previously commented on the importance of—or lack of—mountainous terrain or riverine terrain (or the existence of one or more critical large
river) as constituting critical issues of military terrain. Hence, to repeat, there are
the familiar old generalizations about mountains providing barriers favoring the
defense and rivers too providing formidable defensive barriers. The historical
importance, in Europe, of the Rhine, Elbe, and Danube, and of the Alps,
Carpathians, and Pyrenees, needs no further elaboration here.[26] Similar factors
operate in the developing world. But the exact location of these barriers, and
their relation to potential axes of advance for offensive operations, does warrant
closer scrutiny.

In Iran and in Ethiopia, significant mountain ranges more or less parallel to
the borders (in any event, astride possible avenues of advance toward capital
cities or otherwise important core areas) have been critical terrain features.

Near the Iran-Iraq border, but back some distance on the Iranian side, the
Zagros Mountains form a defensive glacis protecting Iran, at least along northern
sections of the border, from Iraqi attack. But the mountains also make an Iranian
offensive against Iraq more difficult. Likewise, a Somali assault toward Addis
Ababa and the Rift Valley must surmount two ranges of mountains nearly perpendicular to an otherwise preferred line of advance (the mountains run southwest to northeast).

In the Israeli-Arab context, however, there is a mix of situations. The mountains of Lebanon, running north-south, ran parallel to the Israeli line of advance
in 1982 (but across the grain of any Syrian advance toward Beirut). But along
both sides of the Jordan Valley, north-south mountains block an advance either
toward Jerusalem or the Jordanian heartland, while in Sinai also, the north-south
mountain line in the west (crossed by the strategic Mitla and Ghidi passes) first
acted as a barrier to Israeli forces in 1967, then potentially as a barrier to a further Egyptian advance into central Sinai in 1973. In the China-Vietnam border
area, there was a complex mix of mountains running both parallel and perpendicular to the Chinese line of advance. In the Falklands, the low mountains
tended somewhat to run in a line east to west, paralleling the British line of
advance. But because of the small number of forces involved and the somewhat
scattered, nonlinear nature of the heights or line of mountains, the Argentinians
were not easily able to use the mountain lines to construct an organized line of
defense.

But, keep in mind, there are mountains and then there are mountains! Those in western Sinai and in the Falklands are only fifteen hundred to two thousand feet high, really just enlarged hills, by stricter standards of what constitutes mountains. Those along the Ethiopia-Somalia border are much higher and more rugged, around nine thousand to eleven thousand feet, almost precluding fighting by large units in the contested areas around Harar and Jijiga (those in front of Addis Ababa go up about thirteen thousand to fourteen thousand feet). Those of Kashmir are higher still, up around fifteen thousand feet. The spine running along the center of Lebanon's north-south mountains has about a four-thousand- to six-thousand-foot elevation. These measurements must, however, be taken somewhat with a measure of caution. Height above sea level cannot fully act as an indicator of ruggedness or of the steepness of inclines, i.e., the relief factor. And mountains of a given height may vary according to tree cover, extent of rockiness, soil, i.e., all that adds up to tractability for vehicles, cover for defensive forces, and visibility from the air.

The direction of rivers (assuming their importance to a given war) in relation to axes of advance or the positions of contending forces may be very important. That is nothing new, of course, and certainly not relegated to the study of wars in the developing world. Histories of World War II will immediately reveal the importance at various times of the Rhine, Seine, Danube, Meuse, Dnieper, Vistula, Arno, Irrawaddy, Yangtze, and many other rivers.

Some major rivers have prominently figured in recent Third World conventional wars. The Shatt Al Arab, from the confluence of the Tigris and Euphrates Rivers at Al Qurnah southeast to Basra, Khorramshahr, Abadan, Khosrowabad, Al Faw, and hence the Persian Gulf, largely defined the major battle areas of the war, forming a major barrier to advance in both directions.[27] Its tributary, the Karun River, coming first from the east and then from the north, was also a major barrier to be crossed by both sides' forces. The seasons and state of flood levels were crucial at various times. Minor rivers further north did not figure in the fighting, nor did the Tigris from Baghdad to Al Qurnah which, in the event of an Iranian march west, could have been a major barrier to Iran's cutting of the critical Baghdad to Basra highway.

Israel's advance north into Lebanon in 1982 required moving across several east-west river barriers—the Litani, Zahrani, Awwali, and Damur Rivers.[28] None proved to be a major obstacle, whether or not due to the absence of organized PLO defensive lines. After the war, the rivers would provide some obvious natural lines of demarcation for the several stages of the Israeli withdrawal. Some small northward flowing streams in the Bekaa Valley did not importantly figure in the fighting.

India's multipronged attack against Pakistan's East Bengal in 1971 required crossing of numerous north-south rivers leading to the mouths of the Ganges. Indeed, its main thrust from north of Calcutta to Jessore and on to Dacca required several river crossings even before that of the huge one produced by the confluence of the Brahmaputra and Ganges rivers. India's well-trained forces, well equipped with bridging equipment, amphibious vehicles, ferries, and helicopters, were not much hindered in the process; there were few lengthy pauses of the kind the U.S. and Soviet armies undertook before major river crossings in

1944 and 1945.[29] No such problems existed for India in the tougher fighting in the west in 1965 and 1971, but if India were ever to attempt to invade Karachi, a crossing of the major Indus River would be required.

Rivers were not at all a factor in several recent conventional wars: Chad, Ethiopia-Somalia, the Falklands. In China's incursion into Vietnam in 1979, the Chinese army attacked downhill along some river valleys leading out of the mountains toward the Red River Valley, but none acted as serious barriers across the grain of the Chinese line of attack. Whether or not, if necessary, Vietnam could have used the Red River as a barrier to an assault on Hanoi is hard to say—probably the Chinese could have attacked along the valley from the northwest.

Mountains and rivers running perpendicular to the main line of advance of large forces are the two things that come first to mind in considering defensive, terrain barriers. But there are others, at least potentially. The swamps and marshlands of the southern Iran-Iraq border area provided good defensive terrain for both sides, particularly during rainy seasons.[30] Large desert areas along the India-Pakistan border are so forbidding as to have precluded more than limited fighting over large areas of the border both in 1965 and 1971. The desert has also made for formidable barriers to offensive action on Sinai. In 1956 and 1967 even the rapid Israeli advances were largely restricted to a small number of roads, though in 1967 Israeli tank forces surprised the Egyptians with flanking moves across the sands near Abu Agheila and along some dry wadis leading south and west from that key junction. The deserts in northern Chad have likewise channeled combat in the Libya-Chad war into a few roads and otherwise passable areas.

The soggy bogs of the Falklands provide still another example of terrain that renders offensive movement difficult. The highly professional British army overcame this terrain largely with small units of well-trained infantry and by use of light-combat vehicles that could traverse the tricky, boggy terrain.

The Military Geography of Two-Front Conventional War

We have previously noted that in some conventional wars there may be vast differences in the terrain of an extended battle area, sometimes amounting to entirely different theaters as pertains to terrain and weather. For example, we have cited the wholly different environments provided by the northern and southern regions of the Iran-Iraq border or that between India and Pakistan or along the extended lines of the Cambodian conflict. But these are all examples of one single, albeit sometimes lengthy, forward line of battle, usually defined largely by a lengthy border or mutual frontiers or the areas adjacent to (or lines parallel to) those borders.

Some wars, however, have involved some nations having to fight along two fronts, usually against two allied enemies (this is somewhat of a microcosm of the U.S. problem of having to fight in two entirely different theaters in World War II).

One earlier excellent example was that of Germany's having to fight simultaneously on two fronts in both of the world wars, the so-called eastern and western fronts. And, the geographic aspects of those two-front wars is critical to an understanding of German strategy and tactics, both on the offense (earlier) and the defense (later) during different phases of these wars. In 1914 the Germans counted on a rapid offensive through favorable terrain in Belgium and northern France being concluded before Russian armies could be mobilized for offensives through the lake region of East Prussia.[31]

There have been some examples of recent conventional wars fought on the terrain of two disconnected fronts: the Arab-Israel wars of 1967 and 1973, and the India-Pakistan war of 1971. And further, China in 1979 had to plan for the possibility of a two-front war against not only Vietnam but the USSR as well, which planning was closely hinged on the factors of terrain and weather. Ethiopia, while fighting Somalia, had to deal with serious secessionist wars in Eritrea and in Tigre Province. More recently there was extensive speculation about the possibility of Iraq having to fight a two-front war against the Gulf coalition in the south and against Turkey in the north—as it turned out, Turkey was able to abstain, but it did tie down some Iraqi forces.

In 1967 Israel, in planning a preemptive war strategy hinged on its (precariously) advantageous use of interior lines, had to decide whether its initial emphasis would be on the Egyptian front or the Syrian-Jordanian front, just as Germany (with its vaunted Schlieffen Plan) had had to decide on whether to try to knock out France first—or Russia. In both cases, geographical issues momentarily aside, the interior power was outnumbered but qualitatively superior, and had to go for a quick, decisive victory before its more numerous foes could mobilize for a lengthy two-front war of attrition. The issue then was whether first to attack the stronger of two opponents or the weaker. In both of these cases, the interior power struck first at the stronger opponent (France in Germany's case, Egypt in Israel's case), perhaps somewhat in defiance of what would appear a more logical, practical alternative, i.e., knocking out a weaker foe and *then* concentrating all one's forces on the stronger one (if the stronger side is successfully knocked out first, defeating the weaker side next becomes more or less automatic).[32]

In part, in these cases, the reasons were those of military geography—space, terrain, and weather. The Schlieffen Plan was based on the assumption of Russia's slow mobilization (projected at six weeks) in a vast area with poor transportation networks; also on the assumption that Russia's enormous defensive depth, even despite its obvious military weakness, virtually precluded a quick knockout, as Napoleon earlier had had to learn. On the western front, meanwhile, the French defensive barriers along the Vosges Mountains and Ardennes forest dictated an asymmetric "hinged door" offensive through the more suitable terrain (for offensive operations) of Belgium and northern France (in 1940 the Germans surprised France by attacking through the Ardennes, a more direct but difficult route). Germany further counted on being able to knock out Belgium and France before the full weight of British power could be brought into play. And Belgium's neutrality was violated in large measure because the German military planners thought they needed to attack through that nation's favorable terrain.

Israel, in 1967, chose to concentrate on Egypt first. That allowed Israel to take advantage of its strength—that of mobile, fast-moving warfare ("armored pace") in a larger theater, albeit one of tough desert terrain, dry wadis, and few roads. But Israel was ready for that, or so it was to prove in a quick four-day victory. On the Golan Heights, en route to Damascus, it faced a very narrow frontal zone, one featuring rugged mountain and plateau terrain very suitable for fixed fortifications in depth, and not at all amenable to mobile, armored operations. After defeating Egypt, Israel defeated the Syrian army on Golan, but eschewed a pursuit toward Damascus, both because of external political pressures and the realization that that would entail extensive casualties.

In the 1973 war, Israel was initially on the defensive, then later on the offensive on both fronts. Here too it had to decide on this allocation of emphasis, both first on defense and then on offense. It concentrated its early defensive efforts against Syria because of the danger to its settlements in the Galilee, if the Syrian army had been able to move down from the Golan Heights. The Sinai, on the other hand, provided extensive spatial depth for retreat and regrouping. When Israel moved to the offensive, however—and despite some back and forth uncertainty about which front to concentrate on—it again chose to make its major effort against Egypt, for many of the same reasons as in 1967, i.e., the extent to which the large, open desert theater allowed for mobile offensive warfare, in contrast to the axis from the Golan Heights toward Damascus.

In 1971 India, fighting an inherently weaker foe on two fronts from a position on interior lines (in this case the exact same foe), chose to conduct an offensive on the weaker side first. To a great extent this appears to have been based on political grounds (independence for Bangladesh and the subsequent division and weakening of Pakistan) and on the basis of Pakistan's military being far stronger in the Punjab than in Bengal, which was difficult to resupply during the war and where Pakistan also faced a strong internal insurgency from the Mukti Bahini forces aligned with India. In the latter arena, the Indian army fought through very difficult riverine terrain in a nevertheless fast-moving offensive, while in the Punjab it faced much tougher going against better-entrenched forces.

China in 1979 made favorable use of the seasons in the timing of its winter offensive against Vietnam. At the time, a Soviet counterthrust against the PLA along the Siberia-Manchurian border would have been greatly hampered by winter weather. China's willingness to end the fighting quickly after administering a "lesson" to Hanoi may have been based on the knowledge that a few months later conditions would be more favorable for a Soviet ground attack in the northern theater designed to take the pressure off Vietnam and to force a Chinese withdrawal.

Ethiopia, while staving off the Somali invasion in 1977, was simultaneously compelled to fight against secessionist forces in Eritrea and Tigre Province.[33] Though the Somali and Eritrean operations do not appear to have been coordinated, Ethiopia, though nominally possessed of an "interior lines" position, was compelled to fight two widely separated conflicts with a poor logistics system, hence very distinct from the superficially similar situation of India in 1971.

The Weather and the Seasons: Addendum

Earlier we had discussed the varied terrain conditions in the Third World as they are relevant to military operations. These, of course, correlate closely with climate and seasonal weather patterns, i.e., prevailing weather in large part determines the amount of cover. But there are some additional points that need be made about the latter, again, as it pertains to recent conventional wars in the Third World.

There are three important levels to this subject: (1) the overall prevailing or dominant climate patterns of a region; (2) the seasonal variations in climate; and (3) the vagaries of day-to-day changes in the weather. Regarding the linkage to military operations, the critical items are the impact on (a) ground terrain (particularly regarding mobility for tracked and wheeled vehicles), (b) cover—as pertains both to surveillance from the air and concealment from the ground as well, and (c) temperature, particularly the impact of the extremes of heat and cold on combat troops and their equipment.

This is a large subject, and we can do little here but provide some illustrations from our recent wars. One could as easily provide examples from the numerous articles about U.S. preparations for a desert war in the Gulf in 1990 which, among other things, have focused attention on the relationship between weather, terrain, strategy, tactics, and weapons to a degree not equaled in recent memory.

Concerning broad, general climactic considerations, we have already noted the military implications concerning the gross disparities between desert, tropical jungle, northern forest, etc., conditions. That leads to the obvious implications regarding cover, visibility, maneuverability, as sometimes or partly modified by seasons and day-to-day variations.[34] We have also noted that some wars—Iran vs. Iraq, Vietnam, the Arab-Israeli wars—have been fought in different climates and with correspondingly different terrain, even where the distances involved— say between Vietnam's Northern Highlands and the Camau Peninsula or between Sinai and Golan—are a matter of only several hundred to a thousand miles.

Generally speaking, however, the Gulf crisis did highlight the relationship between planning, training, and the prospects for combat in unexpected places. Numerous analyses pointed out that by 1990, the elite units of the U.S. Army and Marine Corps were mostly prepared for low-intensity combat in jungles or temperate forest climes, if not also for high-intensity conventional combat in Europe. Even those troops trained in California's Mojave Desert were said to be wholly unaccustomed, psychologically speaking, to the vastness of the empty spaces of the Saudi desert.

And, generally speaking, the issues of cover and visibility in this theater were not much subject to seasonal variations, save maybe for some seasonal variation in the frequency of desert sandstorms, most hazardous for helicopter operations, as with the U.S. experience with the abortive Iran hostage rescue operation. Also, Iraq was able to make use of the variations in cloud cover to utilize its mobile Scud launchers against Israel and Saudi Arabia.

Hence, at the end of 1990, the U.S. press was full of speculations about when would be the most propitious time for an all-out offensive against Iraq's occupation of Kuwait. Most military analysts pointed to January, when temperatures would be most reasonable and would allow for some three months of operations under favorable conditions before the late spring again brought unbearable heat. Other analyses also pointed to the variations of moonlight as critical to military operations—infrared notwithstanding, a full moon would provide some additional visibility for nighttime operations. As it turned out, of course, the coalition did not have to worry about long-term climactic conditions. And ironically, the opening of the ground war was fought in unusually rainy and muddy conditions.[35]

But in some recent Third World wars, wide swings in seasonal weather patterns have had a big impact on the planning as well as the execution of military operations. The British, in planning the Falklands invasion as the southern hemisphere's winter approached, realized that further delays would present their troops with very unfavorable winter conditions—cold, wind, etc. (they were lucky, just as Hitler's armies in Russia in the fall of 1941 were unlucky with an early advent of winter). Indeed, this was a problem in the late spring, perhaps particularly involving the problems of keeping infantry troops' feet warm and dry (a problem for both sides!). Helicopters ferrying troops and ship-to-shore operations would become much more difficult with extreme cold and gale-force winds (as they did at any rate for the preceding operations on South Georgia Island). By contrast, the inclement weather should have given an advantage to the side with better troop training and morale, which of course it did on the side of Britain's excellent volunteer elite forces. Then too inclement weather would provide some protection for the invading British fleet and for its amphibious operations, subject as they were to the threat of interdiction by aircraft based on the Argentine mainland.

In the Iran-Iraq War, the pace and scope of military operations varied tremendously according to the seasons. Offensive operations—such as the several efforts at a "final push" by the Iranian Pasdaran hordes—were timed for the dry seasons in the Shatt Al Arab estuary area, which would allow for better use of armor and which were less hindered by flooding of rivers and marshland areas. By spring, such operations became impossible, and this was then abetted by the summer heat. Operations further north along the Iran-Iraq border were less affected by such considerations, and those areas saw winter conditions on the northern mountains as a hindrance to mobile operations.[36]

There are numerous other examples from other Third World wars. The Israelis in 1967 attacked at a time of extreme heat in the Sinai (the attack was, however ad hoc as a response to the Straits of Tiran crisis), but used better troop training and equipment maintenance to their advantage (the cramped and unventilated Soviet tanks used by the Egyptians were claimed unsuited for the climate, because of the absence of sand filters needed for movement in the desert).

In the 1973 war, which was fought in October, the Israelis had to face the beginnings of wet and cold weather on the Golan Heights, also posing the problem of accompanying cloud cover, which could nullify their air superiority and ability to interdict ground forces with tactical aviation. The comings and goings of the monsoons in Southeast Asia had a major impact on operations in the Vietnam War and the subsequent conflicts in Cambodia. China's use of the winter weather along the Sino-Soviet frontier in early 1979 has been noted. If Ethiopia had wished to capitalize on its victory over Somalia in early 1978 by moving into Somalia proper, it would soon have faced that region's rainy season, which would have made it difficult to move mechanized forces in an area with few desert roads.[37] India, in attacking East Bengal in December 1971, was able to surmount riverine terrain outside the seasons of heavy rains.

At a more "micro" level, one can always point to examples where the day-to-day vagaries of the weather can have a big impact on specific military operations, albeit the difficulty of predicting to whose advantage. Eisenhower and the other allied commanders feared inclement weather would endanger the Normandy landing on 6 June 1944 (and, indeed, considered postponing it), but the weather provided cover for the landing against German aircraft operations and long-range artillery proved to be to the allies' advantage on balance, despite the impact of the rough water on the amphibious operations. The sudden idiosyncratic sandstorms helped wreck the U.S. helicopter hostage rescue attempt in Iran in 1980. Generally favorable weather did help the British landing at San Carlos in the Falklands, even as it allowed for some Argentine air attacks on the assembled fleet and beachhead. And more recently, cloudy weather over Iraq at the end of the first week of the air assault phase of the Gulf War hampered U.S. aircraft operations for several critical days. As noted, ironically, the initial phase of the ground war saw unusually wet conditions.

It is obvious from the foregoing that it is not always easy to predict which side will benefit, asymmetrically, from "good" or "bad" weather, or from the early or delayed advent of summer or winter weather, even if one can predict that such answers should be provided by asymmetries in training and equipment.

Back to Earlier Questions: Conventional Wars

The aforementioned set of geographic criteria or issue areas raises a host of basic questions involving their impact on the conduct of wars, as follows:

- What is the impact of the extent to which the wars are fought along a spectrum from wars of maneuver to wars of attrition? Otherwise stated, what is the effect upon the possibilities for quick, decisive outcomes, resulting either from preemptive war openings or, generally, from long-distance offensive operations?

- What is the relationship to the advantageous use of certain kinds of key weapons systems, i.e., attack aircraft, armor, heavy artillery, etc.? Nowadays, what is the amenability of a given theater (terrain, weather, etc.) to the use of the new MTR/RMA weapons and tactics?
- What is the impact on logistics lines running from core areas to the FLOT?
- What is the relationship between geography (weather, terrain) and the qualitative advantages deriving from higher quality personnel and superior capability for using sophisticated technological systems?
- What are the implications for training, for advantages accruing to better-trained forces?
- How did military geography affect initial perceptions about predicted war outcomes; specifically, regarding the perceptions of aggressors planning offensive operations, preemptive strikes, "seize and hold" operations?
- What is the relationship between military geography and arms acquisitions, i.e., how suitable are the weapons acquired from preferred suppliers for the specific terrain and weather involved, whether or not there were reasonably available alternatives?

The impact of terrain and weather on the extent to which conventional wars are fought as wars of maneuver, or of attrition, provides particularly vexing questions. To begin with, the very terms maneuver and attrition are relative ones—most wars inevitably involve patterns of movement and fighting that fit both categories. And, indeed, historians have sometimes disagreed about the basic characteristics of given wars according to these concepts or terminology. It was long the accepted wisdom that World War I was, after its initial phases, basically a war of attrition, and World War II one of maneuver brought about by the advent of the tank and tactical airpower. (Most such analyses see some generals at the outset of World War II having attempted to fight the previous war over again despite the changes in the technological basis for warfare). But some revisionist analyses were later to take a more mixed view and to see the conduct of World War II as also having been dominated by attrition warfare, albeit the outcome(s) that did not feature lengthy stalemates, with some exceptions in Russia in 1941–42, in Italy at the time of the battle over Monte Cassino, and in China's Hunan Province.[38]

Some similar disagreements have been voiced about characterizations of the 1973 Middle Eastern war. In its immediate aftermath, some analysts rushed to contrast the wars of 1967 and 1973 as having been, respectively, wars of maneuver and of attrition, the fundamental change said to have been brought about by the advent of new PGMs—precision-guided munitions—in the areas of antitank and surface-to-air missiles, which had rendered Israel's old offensive tactics an anachronism, at least temporarily.[39] But later and with the aid of hindsight, many of these analysts saw less of a fundamental shift in 1973; rather, they saw Israel's ultimately successful offensive operations in the Suez area as reaffirming the dominance of maneuver warfare.

One problem here is that geography is only one of several factors, though probably a major one, determining whether wars will be dominated by maneuver or attrition. The state of military technology, and the ability of soldiers to effectively utilize that technology, is one major factor—on that basis the advantage can rotate through phases favoring protection, mobility, firepower, etc., as outlined by Creveld.[40] Then the extent or absence of military balance between contending forces will obviously impact on whether a war is fought as one of movement or maneuver. Geography may modify, but will not eliminate, fundamental imbalances that may allow one side to roll over another, either by frontal or encircling offensives. That is, it may serve merely to raise or lower the ratios of offensive to defensive forces required for sustained offensive operations.

Along these lines, the record of our recent conventional wars presents a mixed and perhaps even confusing picture. Israel was able to fight a war of maneuver in 1967 and—subject to interpretation—again in 1973 despite tough, sandy desert terrain, while having advantage for its tactical airpower by the lack of vegetation and cover. The terrain, however, made it tougher on the Golan-Damascus axis in 1973. Iran and Iraq, fighting with many of the same weapons, fought a long war of attrition from 1980 to 1988, even despite terrain—at least on the southern front outside of the rainy seasons—deemed by many fairly suitable for mobile, mechanized operations. The reasons: the nature of the opposing armies, cultural proclivities, an inability to sustain long-range combined arms operations, and overly hierarchical command structures that do not allow for much initiative by low-level commanders.

Somalia, meanwhile, in 1977, was able to fight a war of movement, initially, even despite relatively difficult terrain in the area of the Kara Marda Pass (so was Ethiopia in 1978 after it and its Cuban and Soviet friends had seized the advantage). The Chad-Libya conflict was one of considerable movement on desert terrain despite the relatively unsophisticated level of abilities of the forces involved. China was able to achieve a relentless forward movement over difficult mountainous terrain in 1979; likewise the British forces in the Falklands. And in 1971, India, facing very difficult riverine terrain, was able to fight a war of offensive movement even against a well-trained and competent army, albeit one sorely outnumbered and suffering a marked logistical disadvantage. Again, geography can be only one of many contributing factors to an analysis of the reasons for relative degrees of maneuver and attrition warfare. Generally speaking, it is obvious that very competent and well-led armies, i.e., an India or an Israel, can more easily find ways to transcend tough terrain and weather. But other armies, utilizing the same weapons, can find factors of military geography highly daunting.

Some of the other questions here raised are even less subject to comparative generalizations. Either there are inadequate data or an absence of tangible criteria for judgment. One can merely raise some questions, provide some illustrations.

Take logistics, for instance. What was the role played by terrain and weather—in relation to available road networks—in Iranian logistics from its heartland to forward areas; or likewise for China in 1979 having to supply its armies through the rugged areas of southern China? How did these factors play out, regarding logistics, for Ethiopia and Somalia in 1977–78? One obvious relationship of logistics to geography has to do with the extent the latter allows for interdiction from the air of war supplies moving forward to the front. Primarily, that involves the issue of cover. The U.S. had a big problem interdicting North Vietnamese supply lines to the south because they often consisted of jungle trails and roads nearly invisible from above. Israel, it has long been assumed, would easily be able to interdict Iraqi supply or tank convoys moving across Jordan toward the West Bank because the roads are in open, desert terrain (this also assumes, of course, control of the air). In some wars, however, the absence of usable, effective air-power on either or both sides has precluded interdiction of supply routes even in the case of relatively open terrain or that where roads can be surveilled in wooded, mountainous terrain. China in 1979, Iran and Iraq from 1980 to 1988, Somalia and Ethiopia in 1977–78, all fit this description. Perhaps only Israel among the "regional" combatants has a capability that reflects the strategy of the U.S. AirLand Battle 2000 doctrine, i.e., a heavy reliance on long-range interdiction of enemy logistics and reserve forces, as so well exemplified in the Gulf War of 1991.[41]

Similarly, many questions could be raised about the use—or lack of it—of key weapons systems, as a function of terrain and weather. The British and Argentinians were, for instance, restricted from using heavy armor on the bogs of the Falklands in 1982. India made very good use of amphibious vehicles in East Bengal in 1971.[42] China apparently could not easily utilize armor in the mountainous terrain of northern Vietnam (where it might have had an equipment advantage), and had to rely largely on light infantry and more modest crew-served weapons. The Soviets could not easily use (indirect fire) field artillery against Mujahideen bastions in the Afghan mountains; rather, they had to rely on direct-fire anti-aircraft weapons as well as helicopters.[43]

The problem of training for specific terrain is an interesting one. Some of our protagonists have, of course, fought on familiar, home ground and in familiar weather. The Israeli and (some) Arab armies train for the desert; Chinese and Vietnamese armies probably need little acclimatization for operations in wooded, highlands areas. But some of the British forces that invaded the Falklands needed remedial training on the Scottish moors beforehand, while U.S. forces trained in the Mojave Desert needed additional acclimatization in the Saudi desert in 1990.[44] The Soviets used the Bulgarian mountains to train troops for combat in Afghanistan. In these situations there was ample time for training for an unexpected situation. The Argentinian army, on the other hand, seemed totally unprepared for combat in the wet bogs of the Falklands. Earlier, Egyptian forces, mostly drawn from the Nile delta, seemed poorly trained for combat on the deserts of Sinai. Many of these countries, of course, have special units for specific terrain, such as the Indian and Pakistani mountain troops.

Without access to classified files regarding military planning, it is difficult to say just how, in some cases, misapprehension of military geography factors has affected planning for offensive preemptive attacks, preventive wars, etc., either as a matter of broad strategic factors or narrower operational or tactical ones. Syria may have underestimated the difficulties of overcoming the rugged "tels" of the Golan in 1973 as Israel was mobilizing its forces while fighting a delaying action. China may have underestimated the difficulties presented for offensive operations toward the Red River Valley in 1979. Iraq seems surely to have overestimated its ability to conduct offensive operations across the Euphrates-Karun estuary and the nearby marshes in 1980. And Somalia may have underestimated the barriers presented by the mountains shielding Harar and Dire Dawa in hoping for a quick seize-and-hold operation in 1977.

The fit of various Third World nations' arms acquisitions to the military geography of their conflicts is an interesting topic. Most combatants, of course, have been completely or largely dependent for their arms from big power or "second tier" suppliers—Israel, India, Argentina, and South Africa were partial exceptions, through rarely when it came to the so-called "big ticket" items, i.e., high-performance aircraft (and their electronics and weapons), main battle tanks, helicopters, etc. And usually—though perhaps now much less so in an era beyond bipolar, ideological conflict—these nations do not have an open choice of arms supplier(s), as this is dictated by political alignment.

Aside from the fact that some weapons produced by major-power arms suppliers are too sophisticated for their clients (note the oft-stated problems of the South Vietnamese army with U.S. equipment) as pertains to operations and maintenance, some also make a poor fit to the terrain and climate. American and Soviet (and Western European) weapons systems have tended to be optimized for the (earlier) possibility of full-scale warfare in Central Europe. They often needed to be modified (or substituted for) if the big powers themselves were contemplating combat in the deserts of the Middle East, jungles of Southeast Asia, or boggy heaths of the Falklands.

But for developing nations, this can present problems. The Egyptians complained bitterly about the lack of sand filters on Soviet tanks after the 1973 war and about the cramped crew space of those tanks, which exacerbated the problems of crew fatigue in the desert weather. The Israelis have had to extensively modify U.S.-supplied aircraft for Middle East conditions, and have been able to build cheaper indigenous models in part because of the absence of a requirement for all-weather capability, which would be taken for granted in the European context. Numerous articles detailed the need for the U.S. to modify its maintenance of weapons on the Saudi-Kuwaiti border, for instance, more frequent dealing with tank sand filters and aircraft engines.[45] There was even a revival of interest in the manner in which Rommel's army in North Africa had innovated with equipment modifications, using trucks with giant blowers to cause dust storms and to simulate the approach of a tank formation.

Some developing nations have managed to innovate with weapons acquisitions so as better to adjust to specific terrain or weather conditions. The classic recent case is that of Chad's effective use of Toyota pickup trucks mounted with machine guns and cannons, which prevailed against Libya's Soviet-supplied heavy tanks, the latter lacking the requisite mobility in tough desert terrain.[46]

Airpower and Military Geography

There is a wide range in the decisiveness of the role played by airpower in the numerous recent conventional wars, both conventional and LIC. But all in all, there are some obvious generalizations to be made with respect to the relevant military geography.

The Gulf War was, according to many of its analysts, perhaps the first in which airpower had been largely decisive. It was commonly asserted in its aftermath that the flat, open, desert conditions in southern Iraq and Kuwait had magnified the superiority of U.S. technology over the Iraqis' Soviet-supplied military arsenal.[47] One side was blinded, the other could see, and there was no place to hide troops and armored equipment on a flat desert in generally clear weather. Once Iraq's defensive systems had been neutralized, a one-sided massacre from the air ensued.

In the Falklands War, the nexus between geography and airpower was crucial. Argentina failed, almost inexplicably, to establish air bases and aircraft deployments on the Falklands after their initial invasion, forcing them to attempt to attack the British invasion fleet from the Argentine mainland at a crucial penalty in terms of loiter time and the ratio between fuel and munitions. The British relied on carrier-based Harriers and helicopters for air support, as well as long-range V-bomber interdiction missions mounted from Ascension Island, a prime example of the importance of oceanic island basing points (the air base on Ascension was also crucial for logistics operations en route from the U.K. to the Falklands).[48] The Falklands terrain was relatively uncovered but the seasonal weather was poor, hampering the Argentine air force's ability to knock out the approaching British invasion armada.

In some of our recent conventional wars, airpower appears to have played a minimal role in relation to ground operations. China thus made only minimally effective use of tactical air power against Vietnam in 1979. The China-Vietnam border area is heavily covered, hence, difficult for the application of tactical airpower. Russian and Cuban piloted aircraft played a seemingly minimal role in Ethiopia's defeat of Somalia in 1978, excepting the extensive use of helicopters for ferrying troops in encirclement maneuvers. The Kara Marda Pass area should by contrast have been amenable to such operations, which were limited by the inherent capabilities and aircraft inventories of the combatants. Likewise, Libya appears only minimally to have utilized its large (in terms of inventory) air force against Chad in terrain and weather that presumably was nearly ideal for tactical airpower operations. But somewhat unexpectedly, Ethiopian tactical airpower appears to have played a significant role in the combat against Eritrea in the late 1990s, abetted by clear weather and relatively uncovered terrain.

Low Intensity Warfare: Military Geographic Considerations

Low-intensity warfare (subsuming the concepts of guerilla, revolutionary, insurgency, civil, ethnic, etc. warfare) presents a somewhat different set of issues, as they relate to military geography. Generally speaking, some of the major differences are as follows:

- The wars are generally fought with less sophisticated weapons (more on the insurgency side), featuring those associated with light infantry, and with a much lesser role for mechanized forces, airpower, and seapower.
- The wars are fought by less sophisticated forces, reflecting socioeconomic development levels and as measured by per capita GNP.
- The wars, if basically involving a guerilla insurgency against an incumbent regime, are asymmetric, involving the wholly different opposing strategies and tactics of insurgency and counterinsurgency, respectively.
- The wars do not involve an identifiable moving "front," but rather a much more fluid and chaotic pattern of conflict not easily represented on maps (which may or may not involve extensive regional areas of control by insurgents).

There are, of course, some areas of commonality between conventional and unconventional warfare, as they relate to issues of military geography. The dualism of attrition and maneuver is relevant to both, albeit in a somewhat different way. Also relevant are matters related to offensive initiative and its opposite on the defensive side, in the context of the momentum or "tides" of battle.

Generally speaking, the primary criteria for analysis of the importance of military geography (terrain and weather) as applied to low-intensity warfare are as follows:

- The size of the theater or nation involved as measured by square miles; in turn, the relationship of this factor to the ratio of forces between the insurgent and counterinsurgent sides.
- Cover, i.e., vegetation and visibility from the air, as it applies to hiding, reconnaissance, the opportunities for ambush, impediments to use of high-technology weapons, etc.
- Urbanization—proportion of population in urban areas, importance of large urban areas overall relative to the countryside, etc.
- Strategic depth—the spatial or distance relationships of urban or built-up areas to remote redoubt areas (mountains, forest, swamps, etc.), affecting the ability to strike or respond in *both* directions.

An initial caveat is in order here. The rubric of low-intensity warfare covers a spectrum of disparate types of wars, with varying degrees of commonality. One could be speaking of an asymmetric counterinsurgency war involving a major power such as the U.S. or the former USSR in Vietnam or Afghanistan or Chechnya. Or one could be dealing with a regional or tribal or ethnic civil war, as for instance recently witnessed in Lebanon, Sri Lanka, Peru, Uganda, Zimbabwe, Rwanda, Congo, Liberia. Or one can be dealing with counterinsurgency operations conducted by relatively unsophisticated developing-country regimes: Peru, Guatemala, Salvador, Angola, Mozambique, are recent examples. Or one could be talking about a sporadically fought frontier war between the forces of unsophisticated developing nations, for instance, Senegal vs. Mauritania, or

Uganda vs. Tanzania, or Honduras vs. Belize. These differing types of conflict will, needless to say, provide somewhat different problems for an analysis of their military geography.

One can state the importance of this in the context of military geography in another way. Most of the literature, as it applies to low-intensity conflict, is focused on the geographic component of counterinsurgency: what geographic factors render the latter more or less do-able. In reality, however, that literature is focused primarily, if not entirely, on "classical" COIN, i.e., anti-communist COIN as exemplified by the models of Malaya, the Philippines, Vietnam featuring Western-backed incumbent regimes (with or without actual U.S. or British or French participation) against Marxist revolutionary insurgents. The latter were assumed to mix with their own populations (see the classic metaphor of fish in water), that is, were physically indistinguishable from them in what were "wars over government." That differs greatly from the situations of ethnic or tribal civil wars, which feature regional demarcations between contending forces, visible physical differences, and a "front" to the war, its overall low-intensity nature notwithstanding.

And even in looking at the above-noted geographic variables, one can see a bewildering mix of considerations that defy any easy generalizations on the basis of raw data alone. There are large and small countries, but even in the case of large ones, the low-intensity conflicts may have been fought out in only a portion of them as was the case for Angola, Mozambique, Chad, and Sudan, among others. Population density figures too are subject to varying interpretations—a given figure on a national basis could reflect the facts of one large urban area surrounded by a relatively empty hinterland, or it could reflect a significant rural population spread out over a large area. And, of course, the factors of cover and ruggedness will vary greatly within given nations.

Size of Theater and Population Density: The Basic Geography of Counterinsurgency

As indicated in the accompanying table, the recent Third World low-intensity conflicts have been fought out in arenas that vary immensely in size and population density, ipso facto in combinations of these two factors as well as those of terrain (ruggedness, cover) and weather. In a sense then—all the more so if different types of wars are considered—geographic comparisons are difficult. Each situation is, to a degree, fundamentally unique. But some gross distinctions may be pointed out.

Regarding size, the range is immense. Sudan, Angola, Mozambique, Afghanistan, Colombia, Burma, Peru, Namibia, Chad, Zaire (Congo), and Western Sahara have areas between one hundred thousand and over nine hundred thousand square miles. At the other extreme, Lebanon, New Caledonia, Cyprus, Northern Ireland, and El Salvador have less than ten thousand square miles. In a medium range are Nicaragua, Sri Lanka, Bangladesh, South Vietnam, Colombia, Kashmir, and Liberia. Of course, in Afghanistan, Sudan, Chad, and some others, the low-intensity conflicts have been fought out in only some areas of their large expanses; for instance, in Sudan's south and Chad's north. In some of the larger countries, we have witnessed "classic" insurgencies by revolutionary forces against incumbent regimes—not surprisingly, COIN efforts in Peru (partly an urban insurgency) and Mozambique were long largely futile, as they had also been in the middle-range cases of South Vietnam and Nicaragua. But even in some smaller places such as Cyprus and Northern Ireland, COIN operations had still been difficult; indeed Cypriot General Grivas had widely been quoted as saying the British put too many forces into a COIN operation that was not at all successfully run.[49]

In some large theaters, low-intensity conflict has taken the form of ethnic or tribal civil war—in some senses, closer to the model of conventional war except for the sporadic and unsophisticated level of fighting. But the sides are geographically demarcated. Angola, Chad, and Sudan have fit this pattern very well; Namibia and Western Sahara less so.

But the data for overall area must also be examined in connection with the population factor, in turn leading to great differences in population density. Generally speaking, it is normally assumed, where classical counterinsurgency operations are involved, that a denser population produces greater problems for control and suppression. Indeed, to an extent, that is what the familiar force-ratio considerations (sometimes including whole populations) are all about.

Most of the low-intensity wars involving high population densities are in relatively small countries and vice versa. Bangladesh, Sri Lanka, El Salvador, Cyprus, and Northern Ireland have fit this pattern, and one notes that COIN operations in each have been largely unsuccessful. The same is true for Cambodia and South Vietnam, larger countries with still fairly high densities. More successful COIN operations have been conducted in large countries with low densities—Namibia, Western Sahara, Chad—but here, still another variable intrudes. That factor is terrain—cover (vegetation), ruggedness, weather, to which we now turn.

As regards the critical (for insurgency/COIN operations) dimension of vegetation and cover, the accompanying seventeen-way breakdown is offered by the *Hammond Atlas* (without reference to its military ramifications).[50] It is a variant of the breakdown offered earlier to describe different milieus for conventional warfare.

A complex juxtaposition of the factors of topography, rainfall, seasons, vegetation (cover), and population distribution is involved in describing any theater of low-intensity warfare. And, of course, most countries where such warfare has occurred (or the borders between two or more of them) will normally involve more than one dominant type of terrain or vegetation, sometimes several. And, indeed, many of these wars have been fought in several types of terrain or geographic regions. In Peru, Colombia, Liberia, Sri Lanka, and elsewhere fighting has occurred in urban areas as well as in remote wooded or mountainous areas. As noted, some LICs involve "fronts" between forces (ethnic, religious, etc.), which does at least produce a more specific geographic content to the war (Chad, Angola, Kashmir, for example). Others involve large-scale insurgencies throughout a country or in various parts if it (Sri Lanka, Mozambique, for example), which usually correlates with the relevance of multiple types of terrain, weather, vegetation, population density, etc. Hence, we can here merely illustrate some typical cases representing broad "types" of military geographic situations, and each case is largely unique. Generally speaking, however, scant vegetation, flat and open terrain, and low population density make insurgency operations difficult and COIN easy, and vice versa. Likewise, and particularly where unsophisticated armies are involved, dense vegetation, rugged terrain, and rainy or otherwise inclement weather will limit military operations, producing stalemate or a lack of movement

Northern Ireland is characterized by lakes and hills, heavy precipitation; it has broadleaf forest and some heath and moor in the northwest (but the IRA insurgency has also largely been relegated to urban areas). Sri Lanka has a mix of terrains—the southwest is tropical rainforest, the rest is tropical woodland and shrub, with mountains in the center of the island north of Kandy rising to some eighty-three hundred feet (but here too the Tamil-Sinhalese fighting has been in the cities as well as the boondocks). Sri Lanka also has radical seasonal variations, with two rainy seasons alternating with long spells of dry weather. Burma, site of several insurgencies, has vast tropical rainforests, but also tropical woodland and shrub—to the east of the Irrawaddy Valley and other related rivers are mountains, with the rugged Chin Hills in the east (here the fighting has mostly been outside the cities).

Bangladesh, scene of limited insurgencies since independence, is virtually all tropical rainforest, and has its cyclical monsoon patterns. Its topography is dominated by the deltas that drain the Ganges and Brahmaputra Rivers, making for highly compartmentalized and difficult terrain, but where also there is a high population density. Mindanao, scene of a seemingly endless Muslim rebellion against the central Filipino government, has mostly rugged, mountainous terrain running up to five thousand to six thousand feet with some river valleys. These are covered with tropical rainforest, making location of insurgents very difficult, all the more so as it is a large island. New Caledonia, also a good-sized island, has rugged mountains up to seventy-three hundred feet, also covered with tropical rainforest.

Some of the locales of low-intensity conflict involve desert or semidesert conditions, though within that rubric, the terrain can vary markedly. Much of Afghanistan is without extensive cover, but varying from the deserts of the southwest to the rugged mountains of the northeast. Western Sahara is real desert, but with broken and uneven terrain that does allow for some cover and concealment. Chad is mostly desert in the former zones of fighting in the north below the Libyan border and the Aouzou Strip, but the northern area also comprises the rugged albeit bald Tibesti Mountains, which rise up to over eleven thousand feet. Kurdistan is rugged but with limited vegetation, as are the uplands of Eritrea, though in the latter case there is a lusher area along the Red Sea coast.

Some of the nations where low-intensity conflicts have been fought involve radically diverse climate, terrain, and vegetation. Colombia has tropical rainforests along its coast, large urban areas, and high rugged mountains (Cordillera Central, West, and East) flanking the urban areas of Bogota and Cali. Peru's

Table 3.2 VEGETATION, COVER, WEATHER: A TYPOLOGY

1. needleleaf forest

2. broadleaf forest

3. mixed needleleaf and broadleaf forest

4. woodland and shrub (Mediterranean) } green midlatitude forest

5. short grass (steppe)

6. tall grass (prairie)

7. tropical rainforest (selva) } midlatitude grassland

8. light tropical rainforest (tropical semideciduous) → desert and desert shrub

9. tropical woodland and shrub (thorn forest)

10. tropical grassland and shrub (savanna)

11. wooded savanna } tropical forest

12. desert and desert shrub

13. river valley and oasis } tropical grassland

14. heath and moor →

15. tundra and alpine →

16. unclassified highlands →

17. permanent ice cover →

coastal areas give way gradually to the high Andes—Shining Path's rebellion has been fought out in the shantytowns around Lima but also in the elevated Upper Huallaga Valley. Lebanon's earlier civil wars were fought out in the streets of Beirut and Sidon, in the valleys, the mountains, and along the coastal plains of the Mediterranean. In Central America, the contras fought the Sandinistas in jungles and in upland tropical woodlands; Guatemala's insurgency has been fought out in the forested mountains, and in lowland tropical jungles. Angola's war in its southwest was fought in relatively level wooded savannahs and shrub-lands, and in the more elevated areas of Cunene and Cuando Cubango.

We shall return to some of these matters later in discussing the doctrines, strategies, and tactics of insurgency and counterinsurgency, as they have been applied to numerous, varied developing world locales.

Few of the recent LICs have seen the effective use of tactical airpower, indeed, none of the conflicts in Sub-Sahara Africa or Central America. Some tactical use of airpower was apparently evidenced in the brief Yemen civil war where the terrain and weather were ideal for such operations. The Russians made extensive use of airpower in Chechnya, so too the Sri Lankan government in its civil war, where the terrain and cover offer easy concealment to the rebel Tamil forces. Morocco earlier made effective use of helicopters in desert COIN operations in Western Sahara. And some civil wars have seen sporadic terror bombing of civilians by government air forces, as was recently reported in the case of southern Sudan.[51] In Afghanistan in 1997, it was reported that both the Taliban Islamic army and its opponents were making some use of airpower, for tactical purposes and to terrify civilians.[52] Mostly, technological considerations limit the use of airpower in these LICs, whatever the nature of the terrain.

Technological Change and the Military Geography of Recent Wars

It goes without saying that the impact of military geography (terrain, topography, etc.) on the conduct of war is not static or fixed for all time, but rather is subject to technological change. Such change is important in altering the impact of geography all along the spectrum from grand strategy to operations to tactics. This is a large subject, and we can here only make some major points and cite some salient examples.

At the grand strategic level, the main point has to do with the annihilation of the distance factor by evolving technology. Planes and ships (particularly with the aid of in-air and at-sea refueling) have longer ranges and can move much faster. In 1941–42, the U.S. had to ferry tactical aircraft to British forces fighting in Egypt using staging points in various Caribbean islands, British Guyana, northeast Brazil, and West, Central, and East Africa. By 1973, the U.S., with the aid of aerial refueling, could mount an airlift for Israel with the use of only one staging point in the Azores Islands, and could fly many air transport flights direct from Delaware to Tel Aviv. In 1990–91, U.S. B-52 bombers based in Louisiana were able to fly round-trip bombing missions in Iraq without intermediate landing points. Likewise, carrier battle groups provide the U.S. the ability to strike almost anywhere in the world without the use of forward bases. Not only the U.S. has such long-range strike capability, as witness the British V-bomber attacks on Falkland Islands airstrips from a base on faraway Ascension Island, or Israel's conduct of the Entebbe raid with the aid of tanker refueling and Kenyan bases.

Technological change has also served to enhance the ability of various war combatants to overcome the limits of geography at the operational and tactical levels. As evidenced by the U.S. in Vietnam, the Soviets/Russians in Afghanistan and Chechnya, Israel in Lebanon, and the Cubans/Ethiopians on the Somali border with Ethiopia, helicopters (developed after World War II) have become critical for ferrying troops and material as surrogates for long-range artillery with "nap of the earth" pop-up tactics, and for vertical envelopment operations in rugged, near-impassable terrain. The various tracked and wheeled vehicles used by U.S. forces in conducting their "Hail Mary" left-hook offensive around

Iraq's defensive forces demonstrated an advanced ability to traverse desert terrain. American aircraft using advanced Forward Looking Infrared (FLIR) technology were able to "plink" Iraqi tanks buried in the sand, using the heat signatures of rapidly cooling tank hulls. Indian forces attacking into East Bengal across difficult riverine terrain made effective use not only of helicopters but advanced bridging equipment and barges to maintain an offensive pace even in the face of river barriers. These are but a few of numerous possible examples.

But technological change does not always militate in the direction of allowing for effective offensives. Many developing nation combatants, such as Iran and Iraq, Somalia and Ethiopia, China and Vietnam, have demonstrated real problems in conducting combined arms offensives in difficult terrain. Here, as with Iraq in 1980, geographic barriers have retained their importance, so too even for Israel in attempting a rapid offensive through the rugged Lebanon mountains in 1982.

But it was the U.S. performance in the Gulf War in 1990–91 that convinced many analysts that newer technologies—satellite reconnaissance, optical and electronic surveillance systems, precision sensor-shooter systems, had transcended geography, involving both factors of distance and the masking of military equipment by terrain. Space systems were at the heart of such assumed revolutionary change.

The emerging vast "lessons learned" literature on Operation Desert Shield/ Desert Storm is making the point that the use of space systems in that war has marked a turning point in the history of warfare. In a wider sense, that involves various aspects of communications, targeting, reconnaissance, warning, navigation, weather—according to one source, "the use of space systems transformed the performance of every critical military function," and it involved strategic, operational, and tactical levels of decisionmaking.

In a narrower sense, germane to the subject of this chapter, the new space systems may also have altered some assumptions about military geography. But there is a paradox here. On the one hand, the amazing new capabilities of reconnaissance satellites were most effectively used in Kuwait and Iraq just because of the nature of the open, relatively flat, desert terrain. For the Iraqis, there was no place to hide either stationary or moving targets. And as Iraq had no comparable space capability, there was a tremendous asymmetry in intelligence capabilities, wherein the U.S.-led coalition was able to move a huge army westward some 150 miles without detection (this also depended on the Soviets not providing satellite information to Iraq). Many postmortems of the war declared that the topography and weather were almost perfectly suited to U.S. high-tech capabilities, indeed, that such an advantage would not be repeated in a theater involving more rugged terrain, more cover, more inclement weather (the periodically foul weather in Iraq did make location of Scud missile sites somewhat more problematic).[53]

But some of the new technologies did appear to point to the transcending of traditional geographic facts. Infrared capabilities on satellites now allow for tracking the movement of vehicles at night and in foul weather. New radar satellites, such as the Lacrosse system with synthetic aperture radar, can pierce cloud cover and can detect items buried ten feet or more underground and pinpoint missiles and other equipment hidden in trenches and bunkers.

These capabilities now belong more or less solely to the U.S. and its allies, less so to other extant space powers such as the USSR and China. But in the future there will be new entrants to the space game—India, Israel, Brazil, later maybe a host of developing world nations or combinations of them. This will then become a major consideration in future wars, involving indigenous satellite technology, technology transfer, or the actual reliance on big-power satellite capabilities during wars. Further, the major powers—and some lesser ones—may begin to apply these technologies so as better to "see" and to pursue counterinsurgency operations even in rugged and covered terrain. With today's space technology, the U.S., for instance, might have been able to conduct a much more effective COIN operation in Vietnam. (Not only in the Gulf War, but also in Bosnia, satellite reconnaissance and targeting was very important.) But then too, nations or groups subject to such satellite monitoring will work to improve capabilities for cover and concealment, all the more easily pursued if they have had access to big-power satellite capabilities, as did Iraq during its war with Iran, which preceded the Desert Storm episode.

Table 3.3   THE THEATERS OF LOW INTENSITY WARS: SIZE AND DENSITY

Country	Area in Square Miles	Estimated Population	Population Per Square Mile
Afghanistan	250,000	19,530,000	78
Angola	481,353	6,090,000	13
Cambodia	69,898	8,215,000	118
Cyprus	3,572	625,000	175
El Salvador	8,260	4,152,000	503
Guatemala	42,042	5,920,000	141
East Timor	5,745	714,847	124
Eritrea	36,185	3,500,000	97
Kashmir-Jammu	86,024	6,400,000	74
Liberia	43,000	1,730,000	40
Mozambique	302,329	9,380,000	31
Nicaragua	50,200	2,185,000	44
Northern Ireland	5,463	1,545,000	283
Peru	496,224	16,080,000	32
Rhodesia	150,804	6,405,000	42
Sri Lanka	25,332	14,250,000	562
Western Sahara	102,700	122,000	1.2
Uganda	91,134	11,705,000	128
South Vietnam	67,108	21,265,000	317
Bangladesh	55,126	77,650,000	1,408
Burma	261,790	31,415,000	120
Chad	495,800	2,700,000	54
Colombia	439,737	21,960,000	50
Kurdistan	n.a.	n.a.	n.a.

**Table 3.3 THE THEATERS OF LOW INTENSITY WARS:
SIZE AND DENSITY (continued)**

Country	Area in Square Miles	Estimated Population	Population Per Square Mile
Lebanon	4,015	3,485,000	868
New Caledonia	7,358	138,000	19
Mindanao	38,291	10,905,000	285
Namibia	317,827	870,000	2.7
Sudan	967,499	14,790,000	15
Rwanda	10,169	7,164,994	705
Zaire	905,000	44,061,000	49

Source: Data derived from several standard atlases and encyclopedias.

CHAPTER 4

How the Conventional Wars Are Fought:
Strategies, Doctrines, Tactics, Weapons

Having discussed the manner in which the wars have begun (war aims and openings); their geographical settings; and the basic power capabilities of the various contenders, we may now look at how the wars have actually been fought. This concerns strategies, weapons, and tactics as well as leadership, morale, and other "human factors." For a basic outline, we return to the matrix or guide set forth in our opening chapter, which crossreferenced types of wars—all-out conventional, limited conventional, insurgency or guerilla warfare, low-intensity conflicts, etc.—to the various levels of analysis, running from the broader aspects of grand strategy to small-unit tactics and use of weaponry.

Several caveats are in order at the outset. First, that there is a dearth of information at some levels, as earlier reported for some of our wars, particularly those in the low-intensity category or those conventional wars where access for Western reporters and academics both to the battlefields and to battle records was limited. The China-Vietnam, Ethiopia-Somalia, and Ethiopia-Eritrea wars are good examples of the latter where, unavoidably, one must rely on little more than their contemporaneous news reports or a scattering of postwar reconstructions by military writers. Next, our information is skewed not only in comparing the wars, but as pertains to the levels of analysis. At the grand strategic or strategic levels, the most basic and necessary information is available, if only by inference from what happened in the absence of the opening of military and political archives that might reveal cabinet discussions or those among the hierarchies of military general staffs. At the tactical level, however, information is much scarcer. There have been no diaries or memoirs available to Western scholars written by Somali or Vietnamese war participants that might give us a "feel" for the fighting on the ground equivalent to what has been provided, for example, by British or American participants in the Falklands or Gulf Wars. But enough is known to allow for some analysis and comparison, for the painting of a broad brush.

One further caution is provided. For the sake of clarity and organization, we have chosen to compare our wars according to our levels of analysis, as earlier outlined. But, obviously, these levels are not entirely discrete nor easily demarcated, nor can they easily be discussed in isolation. Expectations about the validity of certain tactics or the efficacy of certain weapons obviously is a component of grand strategy. And to the extent that the balance of forces is determined somewhat by alliance politics (grand strategy level), that too may determine whether certain operations or tactics will prevail, or even where and when they can be attempted. The Gulf War spawned commentaries about the blurring, particularly as pertains to air warfare, of the strategic and tactical levels.[1] Up and down the scale of "levels," one sees in reality a seamless web of interlocking cause and effect, of complex interaction. Summing it all up is not easy, and that is why the analysis of warfare, an always tremendous and complex undertaking, is so difficult.

Grand Strategy in Modern Conventional Warfare

The recent writings of Paul Kennedy, Edward Luttwak, and others have provided us with a wealth of definitions of grand strategy, all of which roughly converge on the same main points. Hence, Kennedy quotes the military strategist Edward Mead Earle as follows:

> "The highest type of strategy—sometimes called grand strategy—is that which so integrates the policies and armaments of the nation that the resort to war is either rendered unnecessary or is undertaken with the maximum chance of victory." By such a definition, Earle massively extended the realm of enquiry about "grand strategy" to encompass national policies in peacetime as well as in wartime. But perhaps even that was not as radical in its implications as the argument advanced by the military writer Sir Basil Liddell Hart in his book *Strategy,* where he proposed that since "the object in war is to obtain a better peace—even if only from your own point of view—. . . it is essential to conduct war with constant regard to the peace you desire."[2]

Or, further, quoting from Liddell Hart:

> Grand Strategy should both calculate and develop the economic resources and manpower of nations in order to sustain the fighting services. Also the moral resources—for to foster the peoples' willing spirit is often as important as to possess the more concrete forms of power. Grand Strategy, too, should regulate the distribution of power between the several services, and between the services and industry. Moreover, fighting power is but one of the instruments of grand strategy—which should take account of and apply the power of financial pressure, of diplomatic pressure, of commercial pressure, and, not least of ethical pressure, to weaken the opponent's will. . . . It should not only combine the various instruments, but so regu-

late their use as to avoid damage to the future state of peace—for its security and prosperity.[3]

Several key points, according to Kennedy, emerge from a review of the literature on grand strategy. First, that true grand strategy is concerned with peace as much as war. Second, that it is about the balancing of ends and means, i.e., is about costs, of all sorts, political as well as economic. Third, such a broad definition directs our attention to the critical importance of husbanding and managing national resources, to the vital role of diplomacy (gaining allies, winning the support of neutrals, subtracting enemies), to issues of national morale and political culture. At the bottom line, according to Kennedy, "the crux of grand strategy lies therefore in *policy,* that is, in the capacity of the nation's leaders to bring together all of the elements, both military and nonmilitary, for the preservation and enhancement of the nation's long-term (that is, in wartime and peacetime) best interests."[4] More or less, this amounts to the same thing as what we usually mean when we speak of a nation's national security policy or even foreign policy, albeit with an unmistakable military emphasis. That, in turn, implies a threatening environment, and ever-dangerous military as well as economic struggle where basic values, i.e., survival, power, and status, are involved.

Most writings on grand strategy have, for better or worse, dwelled upon the strategies of the most powerful nations of a given era. Luttwak and others have focused on U.S. and Soviet grand strategies in the Cold War context; indeed, the more disaggregated notion of "competitive strategies" had become a vital concept within the walls of the Pentagon by the late 1980s.[5] Kennedy's edited volume had three chapters on British grand strategy in various periods (the War of the Spanish Succession, World War I, and World War II), one each on the Roman Empire, Imperial Spain, Germany, and France around World War I, and the U.S. and USSR during the Cold War and looking beyond it. Millett and Murray, utilizing different terminology, also analyzed the grand strategies (or "political level" of strategy) of several key nations during or before the two World Wars and after.[6] Indeed, one can reasonably ask whether such a magisterial concept as grand strategy can be deemed applicable to Argentina in the early 1980s, or to Ethiopia at the end of the Haile Selassie era or to the Iraq of Saddam Hussein. Logically, yes, if one concedes that the constraints of less-than-superpower status lend themselves, nevertheless, to analysis on such a broad level. Indeed, for smaller countries contemplating or actually fighting a war, alliance politics becomes *more* important. They are less autonomous and more constrained than the superpowers.

The habitual use of the concept of grand strategy *only* with reference to the major powers brings us to another critical point, one easily seen in the Kennedy work. That has to do with types of grand strategies or, stated another way, with comparisons of the situations of major powers contemplating or fighting wars or struggling for survival. Or, rather than labeling types, we should look at what general considerations form the basis or "bottom line" for grand strategy. This is simultaneously banal and very complex. It may also vary in different epochs.

Nations large and small can have different basic goals or motivations, "bottom lines" if you will. Some look to expand their power and enhance their prestige, often by acquiring new territories or colonies. Others look merely to retain what power they have or to consolidate it. Some look merely to increasing their average wealth (per capita income), though this too can often involve military considerations, as witness the political rivalries swirling about the politics of the Persian Gulf in recent years. Some nations wish merely to be left alone in peace. It is an open question as to whether the latter goal is easier or harder for a small nation or a large one, as, for instance, witness the historical complexities of U.S. foreign policy surrounding the issue of isolationism, or for Swedish or Swiss armed neutrality.

Some writers have even claimed that in recent centuries, major nations' primary goals have changed from or evolved through mercantilist economics to territorial aggrandizement to industrial growth.[7] Recently, the now renowned conservative writer Francis Fukuyama has trumpeted an "end to history," which, among other things, may involve a cessation of the tradition of warfare long thought ineradicable from human affairs by all but far-out idealists.[8]

That brings us back to our grand strategy "types" or "situations." Kennedy's work, for instance, sees Ancient Rome, Spain in the early eighteenth century, and Britain more recently (maybe also the U.S. today) all as cases of grand strategies driven by the requirement to defend empire or to maintain, as long as possible, a preeminent power position doomed inevitably to withering and decline.[9] Germany before both world wars was, of course, a nation with a grand strategy keyed to nascent, growing power—something made altogether clear in the strident, militarist writings of various German military experts. France, on the other hand, was by the turn of the century a declined power sorely and permanently outnumbered by its major rival, meaning that the focus of its grand strategy must necessarily have had to focus on diplomacy and alignments as "force multipliers."

Several themes or variables seem to stand out in classifying the "situations" that drive grand strategies. Power is in absolute terms great, medium, or small in magnitude, and either rising or falling (or feared or perceived as such) in relative terms. A nation is threatened or not threatened to various degrees, is ambitious or not in varying degrees. On a psychological dimension, a nation may or may not be revisionist, i.e., driven by past defeats or humiliations, whether or not visited upon it by a superior force. In various degrees, a nation may or may not be autonomous, or may require alignments for its security. Large or small, sheer survival may or may not be at stake. The combinations are myriad.

One other point, germane to an analysis of Third World grand strategies, has to do with "rational" decisionmaking and the (very arguable) use of realpolitik models to interpret foreign policies and the workings of the international system or, less ambitiously, its various regional subsystems. Implicitly, largely, writers such as Kennedy and Luttwak work from such a model, though obviously aware of its limitations. Its main ingredients are power and national interest as the coins of international relations, the playing of the balance of power game, the endless rise and fall of nations, whether or not rendered inevitable by such quasiautomatic mechanisms as "imperial overstretch." They may or may not carry it so far as is done in the purist realms of realpolitik, where domestic politics and the ideological bases for foreign policies are said to count for little or even nothing. And indeed, Kennedy's work does look at the competing grand strategies of the U.S. and USSR as having some ideological dimension in what, nonetheless, is still a clash of rival nationalisms or traditional nation-states.

But what about the grand strategies of medium powers or smaller developing states in these respects, or, at another level, what about the workings of regional subsystems or power balances? Steven David, in a seminal piece on the application of the realist framework to the Third World, has concluded that it is largely inapplicable, not only because some strategies there (Iran, Libya) are obviously largely driven by ideology, even to the point of near irrationality in conventional Western terms. He also concludes that the foreign policies (and by logical extension, grand strategies) of numerous Third World states are largely driven by domestic considerations, specifically, those having to do with ruling elites' requirements for maintaining power.[10] Indeed, some might argue that such considerations have not always been absent from the strategies of major, contending European states. But, if true, it adds a whole new dimension to the analysis of grand strategy.

One more point bears mention here by way of introduction, one that emerges from the Kennedy volume. Some analyses of grand strategy involve very long-term considerations of survival or retention (or augmentation) of power—sometimes viewed on a scale of decades—even in the absence of imminence of major war, or what could decisively alter a nation's position. Rome and Imperial Spain were so viewed, as was U.S. grand strategy as viewed by George Modelski in the context of "long cycles" and "watchful waiting" (the antidote to "imperial overstretch.")[11] But in other cases, grand strategies have been gauged in the context of expected and imminent and/or ongoing wars, so that one can refer to the German or French grand strategies guiding decisions and actions before and during World War I.

But such considerations may be viewed differently in the context of some of our smaller or limited wars in the developing worlds. For Germany or France in 1914 or 1940, the world war was *the* war, the obvious central focus of a grand strategy. But for Britain in 1982, the Falklands War would be seen as just one aspect to be fitted within a broader discussion of grand strategy, and indeed, because that war was wholly unanticipated, its grand strategic aspects would have to be viewed solely with respect to the conduct of the war. The same could partially be said for the USSR in Afghanistan, though here, one could question whether Soviet decisions there had a grander design in mind, be it expansive (access to areas adjacent to the Persian Gulf) or defensive, i.e., concern over Islamic fundamentalism in Soviet Central Asia. Similar questions could be raised about the grand strategic aspects of the American conduct of the 1991 Gulf War, which, in a broader sense, was a mere subset of U.S. grand strategy. However, for Israel or Syria in 1973 or 1982, or for Ethiopia and Somalia in 1977–78, short "local" wars were roughly congruent to or wholly germane to the broader outlines of grand strategy.

Such considerations may determine whether a nation will go all-out in the conduct of certain wars. The U.S. in Vietnam and the USSR in Afghanistan pulled out of disastrous small wars just because "grand strategic" stakes were not involved (later analyses of the reasons for the collapse of the USSR may, retrospectively, have altered this perception). China too in 1979 could view its war with Vietnam as merely a punitive raid just because ultimates were not at stake. For Pakistan, Israel, Ethiopia, Iran, and Iraq, ultimates were, or could have been, at stake.

Some Snapshots: Grand Strategies in Third World Wars

The difficulties inherent in attempting to deal with the grand strategy level for developing wars are well illustrated in the case of the Falklands War. In a way, one might say that on both sides, the U.K. and Argentina, strategy was driven by the psychology of decline, by prestige factors. For that reason, and despite its deadly nature, the Falklands War was widely viewed as an atavism, a throwback to an earlier colonial period, or even as slightly comic.

The Argentina of 1982—as long before and ever since—was the inheritor of a civilization that a generation before boasted a standard of living equal to that of most of Western or Northern Europe. In the intervening years, its standard of living had—in a relative sense—declined dramatically, and remained at the level of a poor developing nation. During that whole time the nation had gone through endless political turmoil, alternating between Peronism and military rule, wracked by endless inflation and unmanageable urbanization. A once proud nation had gone to seed. Ironically, its one long-held strategic threat, that from regional rival Brazil, had declined in importance as the two nations had moved from an adversarial situation to one more readily defined as mutual wariness and increasing cooperation. There was an intermittent territorial dispute with Chile, some occasional hassles over dams and rivers with northern neighbors. One major piece on Argentinian security policy, published early in 1982, barely mentioned and did not dwell upon the Falklands/Malvinas problem.[12] The war situation, which arose in 1982, came on suddenly. Argentina itself obviously had not prepared well for it; indeed, one must almost infer from the planning for the war that the Argentine military did not really anticipate a British response. Otherwise, Argentina might have readied itself with attention to acquiring planes with sufficient ranges to loiter over the Falklands, or might have planned to build airfields on the islands after its capture so as to interdict a British fleet and invasion force, or might have planned to train and provision an army to fight in the cold and wet conditions of an early South Atlantic winter. For Argentina, grand strategy seems to have consisted of little more than a policy of prestige or revisionism, one devoted to bolstering national honor to compensate for unresolvable internal problems. It was a classic case of a nation projecting internal problems outward against external enemies, otherwise almost devoid of strategic sense.[13]

For Britain, on the other hand, the Falklands were but a minor, marginal matter. That nation's grand strategy had long been defined as that of a declined former imperial power that became part of an American-led alliance structure directed against the Soviet Union. A small nuclear force provided minimum deterrence and also the prestige of near great power status. The empire was long gone and little regretted, save a few remnants, some of them strategically important, such as Diego Garcia, Ascension, Belize (then), Bermuda. Britain's policy in the Falklands was justified on the grounds of self-determination for the island's inhabitants, and the repulsing of unprovoked aggression was seen as operating within the law. But in reality, Britain's response could be explained as one based on honor and prestige, as well as an opportunity for a Conservative government to enhance its political prospects by identifying itself with nationalism and the upholding of national honor. It was a great opportunity to flex muscles, to "stand tall" again. For neither the U.K. nor Argentina was survival at stake nor, as it happened, critical national interests, so long as the war was limited to the area around the Falklands themselves (some analyses pointed to the threat of British nuclear-armed submarines if the war had widened; if a British landing force and fleet had been destroyed, forcing Britain into escalation against the Argentinian mainland, it could have raised the stakes at least on the Argentinian side). On both sides, the war reflected the grand strategies of nations dealing with decline, perhaps more in a psychological than a real strategic sense, then rationalized on the basis of moral principle.

By contrast, the eight-year war between Iran and Iraq can more easily be discussed in terms of rival grand strategies, even if the condition of rationality is here sorely tested. Indeed, the grand strategies of the two nations involved could be seen as mirror images of each other.[14] Both were nascent OPEC regional oil powers, both ambitious on the basis of new-found wealth and leverage, but also both heavily affected by the humiliations of subordination to the former colonial powers of the West. Iraq, in addition, shared the collective humiliation of the Arab world brought about by several defeats by Israel. In broadest terms, both Iran and Iraq sought to become *the* preeminent regional power astride the crucial Persian Gulf oil fields. That rivalry, more or less zero sum and further propelled by long-held historical animosities between Arabs and Persians, was what the war was about, beyond the narrow territorial issues of control or sharing of control over the Shatt al Arab, some islands in the Persian Gulf, and some issues of national or religious self-determination involving Arab populations in Iran's Khuzistan Province and large Shi'ia Muslim populations within Iraq.

Iran under the Shah up to the 1979 revolution had played its regional hand more or less according to traditional balance of power rules. It relied on American protection against the Soviet menace to the north, and it banked on its large, mostly U.S.-supplied arms arsenal and its much larger population to cow Iraq into regional subordination. Indeed, it was Iraq which feared Iranian aggression and utilized the USSR as a counter-balance. The Gulf States such as Kuwait and Saudi Arabia viewed both Iraq's and Iran's regional ambitions warily, played them off against each other, but leaned toward the Iraqi side mostly on the basis of Arab consanguinity and solidarity. But indeed, during the 1970s, the Shah had abandoned the Kurds and had come to a (conciliatory) agreement with Iraq over the disputed areas of the Shatt al Arab because he feared a war that could result in the mutual destruction of valuable oil-producing installations. Iran's grand strategy up to 1979 was pretty much one attached to the status quo, but with larger ambitions and the desire for higher status, perhaps later to involve nuclear weapons. On an almost covert basis, Iran also maintained a quasialliance with Israel to balance off the westward Arab threat, more or less mirroring Israel's "strategy of the periphery," which featured the Iranian links as well as others with the Kurds and Ethiopians on the outer fringes of the Arab world.

By 1979, of course, everything had changed. The advent of the Khomeini regime brought with it a change in grand strategy, as traditional balance of power considerations gave way to a highly ideological strategy that, in the eyes of outsiders, appeared to contain some rather irrational elements, or at least impractical ones from the standpoint of power politics. In a way, it was a grand strategy reminiscent of early Bolshevik Russia, another case where ideology came to transcend balance of power considerations. It featured a self-inflicted pariah status—in this case ironically involving the loss of the U.S. arms supply and resupply relationship—coupled with a messianic foreign policy hinged on Islamic fundamentalist unity. Specifically, that entailed banking on internal subversion by Iraq's large Shi'a minority, and links to other Shi'a groups in Lebanon and around the Gulf. In time, alliances with Libya and Syria would also become important (to outflank Iraq and to provide sources of Soviet-bloc weaponry) as well as an at least somewhat friendly relationship with Pakistan; indeed, these alignments plus the periodic resort to covert arms acquisitions from Israel and the U.S. represented a certain schizophrenia whereby a fanatical ideological posture sometimes gave way to realpolitik considerations.

Before the war, Iran's grand strategy consisted mostly of consolidating its revolution but also of exporting it next door to Iraq and beyond. Destroying Israel and restoring Jerusalem to Islamic status was also part of this strategy, at least on a rhetorical level. As the war unfolded over eight years, however, Iran's grand strategy became complex and ambiguous, and shifting. It relied on its population advantage finally to overwhelm Iraq and force a favorable decision, involving the overthrow of Saddam Hussein in Baghdad. But the need for arms—including, critically, spare parts for its predominantly U.S.-origin arsenal—forced a curious and tortuous diplomacy involving the U.S., USSR, China, both Koreas, Israel, Syria, and Libya, all as sources of arms at various points despite the absence of ideological bedfellowship, and in a few cases despite open enmity. It was, in short, the grand strategy of a revolutionary power with expansive ambitions, tempered by the realities of dependence. By 1988, as the war turned against Iran (Iraq's successful use of chemical weapons and interdiction of cities with Scuds were crucial) a note of desperation and weariness crept in, which led resignedly to a ceasefire and fragile peace.

Several years later, however, Iraq's complete defeat in the Gulf War would appear, as of 1992, to have rekindled Iran's older ambitions for regional—Gulf—hegemony, which was reflected in a new arms buildup and also in a revved-up nuclear program intended to match that underway in Iraq. By this time, in 1992, the former USSR could no longer act as a counterweight to Iran on behalf of Iraq. The U.S., meanwhile, conducted a strategy of "dual containment" vis-à-vis Iran and Iraq, a strategy mostly not shared by its European allies.

Iraq's grand strategy could be seen in several stages, with roots going back to the 1950s when, even then, Iraq aspired to replace Egypt as the leader of the Arab world and of pan-Arabism.[15] But up to the 1980 watershed, its role had been muted, as witness its minor contributions to the Arab cause in 1967 and 1973. Mostly, Iraq had been a quasisatellite of Moscow, relying on Soviet arms and protection against what was assumed to have been the Shah of Iran's superior power. In the 1970s, however, Iraq had somewhat settled its territorial differences with Iran and, as part of the bargain, got a green light from Iran and the U.S. to deal severely with its Kurdish problem.

But Saddam Hussein had larger ambitions, and the 1979 revolution in Iran opened up a big window of opportunity. Heavily armed and oil-rich Iraq decided on a gamble, that of attacking temporarily weakened Iran with the hope of taking full control of the Shatt al Arab plus Iran's oil-rich (and Arabic-speaking) Khuzistan Province. If that could be done in a preemptive assault, it was hoped that Iran would sue for peace and accept permanently a new status quo that, among other things, would result in Iraqi hegemony in the Gulf region.

It is not clear just why Iraq, perhaps similar to Japan in 1941 at the time of Pearl Harbor, assumed its rival would so easily quit (or if it did quit, would not resume hostilities when better prepared). Or did Saddam Hussein bank on a larger victory, which would allow for a "magnanimous" pullback that would still involve retention of Khuzistan and some other border areas? After the war turned into an attrition stalemate, one asymmetrically disadvantageous to less populous Iraq, the latter's grand strategy appeared to become more defensive, banking on Iran accepting a stalemate and the status quo ante, also banking on U.S. fears of an Iranian victory—as that could impact on the entire region—to result in critical albeit quiet assistance, which indeed was forthcoming.

Perhaps almost as a surprise to itself, Iraq was on the verge of a major victory in 1988; indeed, it was widely acclaimed the victor of the first Gulf War. This greatly raised its status in the Arab world, including among the Gulf oil states that had lavishly funded Iraq's long defense against Iran. But victory led to arrogance and hubris, and only some three years later, to Iraq's invasion of Kuwait and its subsequent defeat. Here again, Iraq's preemptive grand strategy—the expectation of a quick victory and uncontested fait accompli—proved an inaccurate perception. One major question that later emerged along with the facts of Iraq's surprisingly advanced nuclear weapons program, was just why Iraq invaded Kuwait in 1990 when it was only a few years short of a nuclear deterrent, which, later on, might have been used to consolidate its gains in the Gulf as a result of the "seize and hold" strategy. Obviously, the Iraqi leadership did not anticipate a strong U.S. response, nor the adherence of some Arab states to the U.S.-led alliance, which served to "legitimize" U.S. actions, nor the magnitude of the Soviet political changes and overall demise, which removed the Soviet factor as a deterrent to U.S. actions in the Gulf area. It was a classic case of a bungled grand strategy, based on serious political miscalculations. But as of the turn of the century, Saddam was still alive, and so were his nuclear, chemical, and biological weapons programs.

Israel and Its Arab Foes: Grand Strategy

Discussion of Israeli and Syrian grand strategies, as they applied to the Lebanon war is highly complicated. Perhaps more fruitfully, one might move back a decade or two to provide a larger perspective. On the Arab side, one can to a degree look at an overall, combined Arab grand strategy, but one must also disaggregate to the level of the strategies of individual Arab states, there obviously being only limited congruence among Egypt, Syria, Jordan, Lebanon, Saudi Arabia, et al., with the exception of the overriding central goal, if one accepts it as valid, of the elimination of Israel. Israel's grand strategy, on the other hand, is a pure case of survival at the bottom line, maybe uniquely so, given greater force in a psychological as well as a practical sense by the background of the Holocaust.[16]

One can discuss the rival Israeli and Arab grand strategies according to several criteria: time frame and historical momentum, alliances or alignments, and military doctrine at the broadest levels. Regarding time perspectives, there is an interesting paradox revolving around the question of whose side time is on. Familiarly, we think of time as the Arab's ally, their banking on the inevitability that a huge and growing population advantage and oil wealth would finally translate into ultimate conventional military superiority, after the skills level of average Arab soldiers could be raised a bit above the admittedly dismal historical norm. Indeed, the advent of "fire and forget" hi-tech weapons and the supposed new-found advantage to the defensive side in warfare in 1973 were thought (temporarily) to have hastened the day of Arab ascendance.[17] Then too, as has often been remarked, the Arabs can afford to lose many wars, but Israel cannot afford to lose even once, which was thought to involve a probabilistic advantage factor to the Arab side.

But, paradoxically, some have claimed that the advent of nuclear weapons first in Israel and then later, presumably, on the Arab side, would freeze in permanently a situation of strategic stalemate, a balance of terror similar to that which long existed between the superpowers. The Arabs themselves have long worried about that, about "the sands running out" on their chances of final victory once Israel possessed nuclear arms, though subsequent Arab acquisition of such weapons could introduce a counterdeterrent that might reopen the possibility of an overwhelming Arab victory without nuclear weapons being used.[18] Still, it is not clear as to whose side time is on, a question now altered by the collapse of the Soviet Union and massive new emigration of Soviet Jews to Israel, among other things.

Israel's alignment strategy has, of course, long centered around the U.S. tie (more strongly since 1967) involving arms supplies, arms resupply during wars if that should be necessary as it was in 1973, diplomatic support, and ultimately, if required, military intervention if conventional defeat on the battlefield loomed. Prior to 1967, beginning around 1955, Israel had leaned heavily on its French connection, particularly when Paris's foreign policy was in the hands of strong friends such as Guy Mollet and Pierre Mendes-France. Since then, France and the remainder of the European Union have been at best neutral, mostly Arableaning, so that one major problem for Israeli diplomacy has been that of fending off unwanted pressures from Western Europe and also the latter's pressures on Washington to tilt in a more pro-Arab direction. The Soviet Union, of course, was long a very anti-Israeli force, running the gamut from U.N. diplomacy to arms transfers and (particularly in 1973) arms resupply, to outright intervention (1969–70 in the Suez Canal war of attrition), and counterdeterrence of Israel's nuclear deterrent force. More recently, however, there have been some indications that during the 1980s Israel had quietly managed to keep its lines to Moscow open, involving a trade-off of intelligence assistance for a more forthcoming Soviet policy on Jewish emigration. By 1992, however, the remnants of the Soviet Union had come to play a much reduced role in the Middle East, at least for the time being.

Otherwise, one could also point to Israel's "strategy of the peripheries" aimed at reducing its regional isolation and pariah status. Israel had long sought to establish security ties with enemies of its enemies, to force Arab confrontation states to concentrate more on a "second front."[19] Israel's long-term and mostly covert ties with the Shah's Iran (but also, covertly, with Khomeini's Iran during the Iran-Iraq War) involved arms trade, missile tests, military training, intelligence cooperation, oil sales, etc., and long diverted Iraq's attention eastward. Israel also assisted the Kurd rebellion within Iraq, Ethiopia (both under Emperor Haile Selassie and Marxist Mengistu Haile Mariam) against Islamic and pro-Arab Somalia, and the black Dinka tribe rebellion in southern Sudan. The Ethiopia tie also resulted in covert basing access for Israeli ships and overflight rights for its aircraft, in addition to arms transfers. Idi Amin's Uganda during the earlier part of Amin's reign was still another example.

Specifically, the 1982 war was also an example of Israel's playing its "periphery" card.[20] In this case, it banked on a seemingly rational linkage with Lebanon's beleaguered Christian minority, hoping thereby to diminish or eliminate the influence both of the PLO and Syria in Lebanon, and then subsequently to deal with Jordan over the West Bank from a strengthened position. The strategy failed, for reasons much argued over: the fecklessness and treachery of Israel's putative Maronite allies; U.S. counterpressures, which forced an Israeli withdrawal; Syria's then-successful diplomacy and strategy of attrition via terrorism and sporadic military action. Israel ended up disillusioned with its Maronite card.

Arab alignment strategy vis-à-vis Israel has in most respects involved some simple and obvious goals and policies. The Soviet Union was looked upon by the left-leaning states as an ally, arms provider and protector, albeit with periodic diplomatic impasses (Egypt under Sadat, Iraq during the early part of the first Gulf War). Western Europe, despite the legacy of the Holocaust, has been kept better than neutral by OPEC oil pressures, export markets, etc., as reflected in heavy and (relative to Israel) asymmetric arms supplies, and diplomatic pressures, particularly during wars. (Other than France from 1955 to 1968, Germany has been an occasional exception, albeit quietly, as regards weapons technology and allowance of use of German bases for arms resupply in 1973.). Some EU countries, such as Spain, Portugal, and particularly Greece under Andreas Papandreou,

have been radically pro-Arab in orientation, reflected even in almost open support for Arab terrorists. Otherwise, Arab states have worked hard to produce
"even-handedness" in Washington via economic pressures and utilizing the consistently pro-Arab bias of the U.S. State Department and Defense Department
bureaucracies.[21] Arab pressures have also been exerted to cut off Israeli arms sales
to the developing world in places such as Sri Lanka, Thailand, Taiwan, and all
over Latin America, so as to thwart Israel's effort at reaching some degree of
weapons-producing independence by amortizing costs through exports.

All in all most notable as it applied to the 1982 war was the pressure exerted
in Washington by Saudi Arabia, Jordan, and the Gulf States to abort Israel's victory over the PLO and Syria. There have been endless arguments since about
whether those pressures aborted a possible Israeli storming of Beirut relative to
other inhibiting factors, i.e., the Israeli government's sensitivity to casualties in
an urban warfare environment.

One can also contrast some broad military doctrines on either side here. For
Israel, this involves the strategy of preemption in connection with a doctrine that
requires carrying wars immediately outside its own borders.[22] The rationales
here are obvious and in no need of repeating, i.e., the lack of strategic depth, vulnerability of its populations located close to Arab borders, and above all, the need
to strike quickly and decisively in response to a crisis so as to take advantage of a
rapid mobilization system before more numerous foes can fully mobilize and
deploy and move into position larger forces. Such a doctrine, however, often
puts pressure on Israeli diplomacy, particularly with the U.S., with regard to who
is blamed for initiating actual hostilities (the so-called "moral high ground"),
resulting, as in 1973, in alternating Israeli propensities to eschew their wanted
doctrine so as not to offend others' sensibilities.

The Arabs' broad military doctrine, as it applies to Israel, is perhaps a bit more
ambiguous but still clear.[23] As noted, it involves a belief in the inevitability of
final victory through superior numbers. That in turn dictates, to the extent it
can be made possible, a doctrine of attrition warfare. Israel, the Arabs realize,
cannot sustain high casualties nor lengthy wars that cost a lot of money. Israel
thus looks for quick victories; the Arabs are happy with stalemates or even less-
than-decisive defeats that significantly bleed its opponent, though the psychological humiliation of continuous defeats militates to the contrary. The Arabs
also know that they can gamble on wars, for if defeat looms, the major powers
and the U.N. will abort Israeli victories and pressure the latter to withdraw to
prior frontiers, as was done in 1956, 1967, 1973, and 1982. More problematic is
the Arabs' striving for the capability to wage an all-out "final" offensive, in connection with the ever-looming problem of Israel's nuclear deterrent.

China vs. Vietnam: Grand Strategies

The China-Vietnam War in 1979 can be placed within the context of grand
strategies on either side, though in retrospect it can be seen that both nations'
broader political aims were then undergoing a period of flux that continues on
to the present.[24]

China, by 1979, had more or less "quasialigned" itself with the U.S. in the lengthy wake of the Shanghai communiqué. Its relations with Moscow were poor, and it played its America card just as in reverse America was playing its China card within the complex triangular relationship then existing among the major powers. But more traditional aims also played a role. China had long thought itself a natural hegemon in Southeast Asia, was concerned about Vietnam's expansion into Laos and Cambodia, and also about mistreatment of Chinese ethnics in Vietnam after the U.S. withdrawal. By 1979 it had come to fear encirclement by Soviet and Vietnam power, to the extent it had come to rely on the U.S. as a counterweight. Still, it also sought to maintain legitimacy for its Third World revolutionary credentials. It also sought to protect its friend in Cambodia and to outflank Vietnam with political relationships within the Association of South East Asian Nations (ASEAN) grouping. But overall, in 1979, its aim was to discredit and humiliate Hanoi by "teaching it a lesson," which also required keeping Soviet power at bay, utilizing the U.S. counterpresence.[25]

Vietnam's grand strategy was mostly a mirror image. It sought to dominate Laos and Cambodia and to cow Thailand as well, but required Soviet pressure on China's northern frontier to keep Beijing at bay or to limit the extent of its military options. It also banked on U.S. reluctance to become involved in the region only a few years after its humiliating withdrawal at the end of the Vietnam War.

By contrast to Israel in Lebanon or Britain in the Falklands, neither China nor Vietnam unduly feared an attrition war. Both were historically accustomed to taking casualties in long wars, and both were well insulated from public pressures on this score, even aside from the weight of the prevailing cultural attitudes toward protracted conflict.

Ethiopia vs. Somalia: Grand Strategies

Ethiopia's long-held grand strategy, one ultimately to be rendered futile, involved the need to hold together a polyglot, diverse and rebellious African empire, while fending off threats from neighbors that, while smaller and weaker, nevertheless had ties to dissident elements within Ethiopia and the associated desire to see the latter dismembered and thus permanently weakened.[26] As the Selassie monarchy was replaced by a Marxist dictatorship, an already complex mix of ideological and ethnoreligious factors was radically transformed, so that Ethiopia was caught flat-footed in the midst of a difficult transition.

Under Selassie, Ethiopia had banked on its ties with the U.S. to assure weapons supplies and diplomatic support (in exchange for granting the U.S. access to important bases, particularly the communications and intelligence complex at Kagnew) against both the Eritrean rebels and Somalia, both of which were backed by the USSR and the radical Arab states linked to Moscow. Israel also was a valued ally whose interests were congruent with Addis Ababa and who also had ancient ties of consanguinity. After Mengistu took power, however, and after a tortuous transition period, Ethiopia came to rely on help from Cuba and the USSR, still maintained ties to Israel, but also received help from some radical Arab states such as Libya and South Yemen. It was a curious and complex security diplomacy, and where the holding together of a polygot territorial state was very much at stake.

Later, in the late 1990s and beyond the millennium, Ethiopia's grand strategy was bound up with its continuing problem with Eritrea after the latter had gained independence. There were remnant problems of border territories, perhaps also Ethiopia's humiliation over a prior defeat. In the period of 1998–2000, Ethiopia's (successful) strategy consisted of consolidating its control over disputed border areas, while reestablishing a position of dominance over Eritrea, a goal made easier by Ethiopia's no longer having to dissipate its strengths against Somalia and its formerly rebellious Tigre Province.

Somalia's grand strategy was similar to that of Iraq vis-à-vis Iran. It looked to a "window of opportunity," to utilize temporary Ethiopian weakness so as to carve off the Ogaden region of Ethiopia populated by Somali ethnics. Like Iraq in 1980 or Japan in 1941, it banked on its larger rival accepting a fait accompli, particularly as Ethiopia was otherwise heavily engaged in its secessionist civil war in Eritrea. When Somalia lost its Soviet connection because Moscow preferred ties with larger Ethiopia, it turned to the U.S. and its European NATO allies, which in turn were under pressure from Arab friends such as Saudi Arabia to come to Somalia's assistance. The lukewarm U.S. response came to constitute a serious flaw in this grand strategy, juxtaposed to that of the failure to figure out how to hang on to the Ogaden if Ethiopia were able to turn its full attention to getting it back. Like Iraq in 1980, Somalia was taking a big gamble, playing with a weak hand.

India vs. Pakistan–1971: Grand Strategies

The face-off between India and Pakistan had always, since 1947, involved a vast quantitative asymmetry of population and size. But basically, where Pakistan's grand strategy involved survival and utilization of alignments to rectify the objective facts of weakness, India's involved a thrust toward a more solid and finalized regional hegemony that required trumping Pakistan's counterbalancing alignments.[27]

In 1965 Pakistan had fought India to a virtual standstill in a brief war, three years after the latter had suffered a humiliating defeat against China in the Himalayas.[28] Afterwards, India underwent a major defense buildup featuring both arms imports and indigenous production, and meanwhile Pakistan lost its U.S. arms connection and was forced to turn to China. By 1971 Pakistan faced a rising rebellion in Bangladesh which threatened to split its nation into two parts.

Retrospectively, it is hard to divine a grand strategy that guided Pakistan in 1971 just because it faced a near-hopeless or no-win situation. It could no longer both deploy and sustain large forces in East Bengal and also defend West Pakistan against a larger Indian army. Its strategy thus was very constrained, though some analyses point to the fantasy of an Israeli-like preemptive offensive to defeat India in the West, or a move to sever India from Kashmir in compensation for loss of East Bengal. But in reality, by 1971, Pakistan, its former qualitative edge no longer sufficient to outweigh its quantitative disadvantage, held only the hope of rescue by China or the U.S. China, however, was unable to help over the snowbound Himalayas during the winter, and the U.S., winding down its Vietnam debacle, could contribute only a "tilt" in the form of a mere political gesture—a meaningless fleet movement amidst what was largely a land war on a large subcontinent. Afterwards, Pakistan, its population halved and now unable to present India with a two-front threat, would move further toward reliance on a nuclear deterrent, the ultimate deterrent of the weak.

India's grand strategy was both simple and complex.[29] Simply stated, it wished to dismember Pakistan, thereby permanently unhinging the South Asian balance of power away from a real balance. But it had also to worry about China, nuclear-armed China, and to some extent about the U.S. Like Vietnam, it banked on the USSR to keep China occupied, if necessary by intervention, though it was noteworthy that Moscow had not actively intervened in 1962. By 1971, however, India held all the cards, what with an internal rebellion inside Bangladesh and with Pakistan no longer able to bank on the U.S. arms pipeline. Some were to claim that India actually fomented or instigated the 1971 crisis. On the downside, India had then to reckon that a dismembered and frightened Pakistan would no doubt turn to nuclear weapons as a last-resort deterrence, curiously, here too somewhat in imitation of Israel's response to (potential) quantitative conventional inferiority based on the realities of demography.

Grand Strategy, and the Missing Link

We have compared the grand strategies of a number of nations involved in recent Third World wars, according to war aims, goals, alignments, and according to basic situational types, such as decline or ascent of power, relative weakness and strength in regional balances. There is here, however, one missing link, and that has to do with what some writers have incorporated within a so-called "political level" of analysis, but which others would put under the label of "defense planning." More specifically, that has to do with the juxtaposition of warfare scenarios to defense budgets, force structures, and weapons acquisitions. In a variety of other places, it is equivalent to what is done in the U.S. now by the Pentagon's PA & E office (Program Analysis and Evaluation). Some writers, such as Millett and Murray, prefer to address this aspect of the "political level," in a comparative sense, according to how effectively various regimes are able to "extract" resources from their nations' overall output for defense purposes, a matter of budgetary allocations and also fiscal policy as it applies to defense planning.

If this is done on an evaluative basis, there may be serious problems regarding the relationship of the long and short run. The former Soviet government did a terrific job of extracting resources, with a somewhat baneful final ending. The U.S. government too has been effective in this sense, and some earlier had claimed that this had hurt America's long-term economic growth vis-à-vis Japan and Germany, perhaps ultimately with serious implications for its military power, i.e., the familiar theme of "imperial overstretch." Israel has long had a high ratio of MILEX to GNP, no doubt unavoidable, but that has hurt its economic growth with an ultimate impact on military expenditures themselves. But timing may be important here. Stalin is said to have foreseen World War II and thus pushed the Soviet Union into forced draft industrialization and military production, which, whatever the long-run effects, was a rational preparation for an upcoming war. Japan, on the other hand, with the aid of hindsight, now appears to have made its big bid for world military power, in the 1940s, too early—a few decades before it would achieve global financial and technological power.

Otherwise, with more specific reference to the grand strategies of nations involved in recent wars, it must be said that an analysis of the juxtaposition of scenarios and war plans is not easily done. We don't have access now to the files and the minutes of high-level meetings nor to classified research materials. That may one day be available in some cases, but not now. But even a cursory review of the conduct of some recent wars raises some interesting questions, particularly, as pertains to war scenarios and defense planning.

Argentina, for instance, seems to have done little to prepare itself for the Malvinas war, all the more odd as it was itself the aggressor in a premeditated way, though perhaps with only hasty premeditation. Yet, such a war as did take place should have been a standard "base case" scenario within Argentinian military planning circles. Yet it failed to acquire aircraft (or tankers) with sufficient loiter time over the islands, not to mention the absence of planning for building airfields *on* the Falklands after invading them. The absence of effective antisubmarine capability and even of warm winter clothing for troops to be sent to the Falklands in winter weather (timing the war for the onset of winter was otherwise a smart move) were other obvious lacunae, as was that of insufficient training of soldiers to fight on the relevant terrain.[30]

Britain, on the other hand, seems to have done little actual planning for a Falklands war. Its defense planning and scenario focus was, of course, on Central Europe and perhaps the Middle East.[31] Yet the capabilities it displayed in 1982 seem most of all to be a monument to flexibility in defense planning, with the very intelligent integration of systems that had other primary tasks. Old V-bombers built for nuclear missions over the USSR were used for conventional bombing of airfields in the Falklands, banking on the critical availability of a base on Ascension Island. Short take-off Harriers based on small carriers were very effective in the Falklands arena, while numerous civilian ships were quickly reprogrammed for military convoy work, based on planning for a major war which would have required enhanced sealift in the Atlantic. Otherwise, of course, where there were gaps in British capabilities (satellite reconnaissance, inventories of some weapons such as air-to-air missiles), the U.S. was willing to help out.

There are numerous other examples. Vietnam's defense planning had focused for years on the U.S. and on fighting within Cambodia, and not on what would be required to stop a massive Chinese infantry attack, i.e., a lot of field artillery and some airpower, and perhaps some fixed fortifications. China, meanwhile, had a massive conscript army obviously designed to fight a defensive war of attrition and absorption against the USSR, which would concede large casualties. It obviously was not prepared for an offensive war to the south, which would require better logistics, including transportation nets and more effective use of airpower. Its performance, albeit the achievement of a limited victory, frightened the Chinese leadership into extensive reforms in the direction of a smaller but higher-quality and better-led army.

Iran, of course, must presumably have done extensive planning for an offensive war against Iraq, which was, after all, by far the most likely war scenario visible to Iranian planners for decades. But the war came after a revolution that destroyed most of Iran's professional officer corps and also the link to Iran's major supplier of arms and spare parts, so that all prior planning was rendered "inoperative." Indeed, the loss of former military elites even meant that their replacements could not deal with the system of inventories of spare parts already on hand for such basic weapons platforms as tanks and aircraft.

Somalia, which presumably also would have planned for a long time a war against its long-time rival—and which conducted a premeditated war, which normally implies extensive, exhaustive planning—still seemed lacking in some basic weapons requirements. When it had to go on the defensive against the mix of Cuban and Ethiopian forces, it seemed to lack surface-to-air and antitank missiles and interceptor aircraft needed to deal with the opponents' helicopters and tanks used to such great effect in the early part of 1978. The USSR, too, fought a war unprepared in Afghanistan. Like the U.S. before it in Vietnam, it used weapons and formations intended for Central Europe in a manner wholly inappropriate for a counterinsurgency operation in rugged terrain. Its planning problem was with appropriate doctrines, tactics, and training, to some extent involving weapons acquisitions. Pakistan, meanwhile, in contemplating an obvious two-front war with India, seems not at all to have dealt with the need for effective naval (or air) forces to break a blockade, and its air forces were wholly inadequate for working the problem of air superiority over the battlefield. In this case, however, one was dealing with a relatively weak power that probably was unable to plan for a war that, basically, it did not want and could not easily have avoided.

Theater Strategies, the Operational Level, and the Operational Arts

At the extremes of our spectrum of levels, there is little ambiguity over definitions or boundaries. Most writers know grand strategy when they see it (even if they call it only strategy), and everyone seems to agree on what tactics are all about, i.e., face-to-face combat on the ground, up front, weapon against weapon. But in the middle, forming the boundaries of what by various writers is called strategy, theater strategy, or operations is very much up in the air. Mostly, it is a matter of choice, of semantics. But often, the problem arises from the fact that wars are fought on wholly different scales, as measured by the size of the battle theater, the numbers of theaters, numbers of combatants. There is on the one end Iran versus Iraq along an eight-hundred-mile border involving nearly a million troops, and on the other end a much smaller scale for conventional combat in the Falklands or northern Chad.

Let us rely then on two primary sources, among the many available, to lay out what is involved or at issue, namely, the U.S. Army's Field Manual 100–5, *Operations*,[32] and the aforementioned modern classic by Edward Luttwak, *Strategy: The Logic of War and Peace*.[33] Secondly, we may also lean on several articles published in recent years in the U.S. Army War College journal, *Parameters*, which has had a continuing focus on the operational arts, deemed something in need of conceptual revival in the wake of the Vietnam debacle and also in response to (unfounded?) anxieties in the U.S. Army establishment about Soviet professional attention to operational arts and the use of operational maneuver groups, anxieties now obviously muted after the fundamental upheavals of 1990–91.[34]

FM 100–5 actually does not deal with a level of grand strategy, preferring to subsume it under "military strategy," but where the focus of the latter is on "the art and science of employing the armed forces of a nation or alliance to secure policy objectives by the application or threat of force."[35] More specifically, military strategy is said to "set the fundamental conditions of operations in war or to deter war . . . and to establish goals in theaters of war and theaters of operations."[36] Luttwak on the other hand places the level of "theater strategy" between those of grand strategy and operations, saying "a theater of war must form a self-contained military whole."[37] It could amount to a province, an entire country, or even a vast regional grouping of countries.

FM 100–5 discusses operational art as dealing with "the employment of military forces to attain strategic goals in a theater of war or theater of operations through the design, organization and conduct of campaigns and major operations."[38] The key here is the campaign, which is "a series of joint actions designed to obtain a strategic objective in a theater of war."[39] It refers further to the possibility of simultaneous campaigns when the theater of war contains more than one theater of operations and of sequential campaigns in a simple theater.[40] Major operations (the coordinated actions of large forces in a single phase of a campaign or in a critical battle) are said to decide the course of campaigns. Whereas the operational level deals with campaigns, the tactical level, to be discussed next, deals with the battles and engagements, the former consisting of a series of the latter. Fundamentally, the operational art is said to involve decisions about when and where to fight and whether to accept or decline battle. Further, the essence of operational art is claimed to involve the identification of the enemy's operational center of gravity—his source of strength or balance—and the concentration of superior combat power against that point to achieve a decisive success, a point we still return to.[41]

Luttwak, more or less on the same page when it comes to defining the operational level, refers to "the struggle of directing minds," expressed in conceptual methods of action (blitzkrieg, defense in depth, "strategic" air bombardment, layered naval defense), the ongoing command of the forces involved, and the "actual adventures and misadventures of those forces."[42] But most of all, he focuses on the prevailing "style of war" in a given setting, more specifically, the placing of it on a spectrum of attrition and maneuver, that now traditional staple of military analysis.

This dualism of attrition and relational maneuver, sometimes involving other parallel terminology such as that used by Liddell-Hart in discussing indirect and direct approaches, has become the core of much of modern military analysis.[43] It can involve policy advocacy, i.e., an assertion that one or the other is a preferable way to fight for a given nation. Or the terms can be used to describe the basic nature of given wars along a spectrum, so that World War I or the Iran-Iraq Wars were obviously stationary attrition slugfests, whereas the recent Gulf War, or the Israeli blitzkrieg of 1967 or the equally effective Indian blitzkrieg in East Bengal in 1971 could easily be defined as wars of relational maneuver, whatever the expectations or plans of generals beforehand. That's just the way it played out! Many wars, as we shall see, are not so easily described at one or another end of this spectrum, may involve mixes or an overall status in between or wholly distinct places or theaters of operations where both types of warfare are in evidence.

Attrition war is one described by the use of brute force, with Luttwak referring to it as "a war waged by industrial methods."[44] The side that has superior firepower and material strength—note our previous data for comparative power—uses its advantage to wear down the other side, where there can be no cheap victory and where roughly symmetrical but heavy losses will favor the side that, in a quantitative sense, can best afford to take the losses. Grant before Richmond can be added to the above examples. With relational maneuver, instead of trying to destroy the enemy physically, wearing him down, the goal is to "incapacitate by systemic disruption."[45] One avoids the enemy's strength, and attempts to achieve selective superiority against the enemy's weakness, be it physical or psychological, technical or organizational. It is the strategy of the weak, numerically speaking, but when there is qualitative or intellectual superiority, perhaps only a temporary or surprise strategy. It is also a high-risk strategy that, if it fails, can be catastrophic, whereas attrition warfare is said to be "full cost but of low risk," a blunt instrument.

We shall later attempt to apply this duality to our recent Third World wars. But one caution intrudes. The duality is easy to explicate, particularly at the extremes, that is, with obvious cases such as World War I versus Israel's classic victories of 1956 or 1967. In many cases, however, defining a policy or a war itself according to the duality of attrition or relational maneuver is not so simple a matter. It must be viewed from both sides, from the offensive and defensive ends, to the extent that is consistent in a given war.

For the reader of FM 100–5, there are numerous other checklists or concepts that are useful for comparing recent wars, beyond their intended use for pedagogical purposes in training U.S. and other career officers. It is not, furthermore, as most U.S. military training manuals used to be, a dry or primitive or overly simplistic "how to" manual. In its more recent editions, published by TRADOC, the Army's Training and Doctrine Command, it is a lively and well-illustrated work, one which is chock full of interesting maps and historical examples and surprisingly devoid of nationalistic bias or provincialism.[46] Let us look at some of these checklists or comparative criteria before applying them to our recent wars.

One has to do with what are called the "dynamics of combat power." Subsumed under that heading are "maneuver," "firepower," "protection," and "leadership," which immediately rings a bell in connection with Luttwak's dualism of attrition and relational maneuver, and with some interesting analysis by the Israeli military historian, Martin van Creveld.[47] The latter, trying to divine lessons from the Israeli experience in 1973 (he saw it as an attempt at relational maneuver in Sinai gone awry because of advances in defensive weaponry, e.g., surface-to-air missiles [SAMs] and antitank guided missiles [ATGMs], went back into history and theorized that the whole long skein of military historical development involved an endless rhythm whereby the dominance in weaponry alternated advantage between maneuver, firepower, and protection. Therefore, supplementing Luttwak, he saw the possibilities for "relational maneuver," as depending on the prevailing state of the art weaponry as giving an advantage to maneuver. That had been the case from 1940 up to the Israeli victory in 1967, which was described (and lamented) as the "last battle of World War II." The chances for fighting wars of relational maneuver depended somewhat on the state of weaponry and also on the ability of certain nations to use such weapons to maximum effect. Relational maneuver, then, was not always necessarily a possible choice, as the Germans were said to have learned, to their chagrin, in the summer of 1914 in France.

Under "AirLand Battle 2000 doctrine," FM 100–5 discusses four basic tenets said to determine success in battle: initiative, agility, depth, and synchronization.[48] These all relate, in one way or another, to the dualism of attrition and relational maneuver. Agility is defined as the ability of friendly forces to act faster than the enemy—it is clearly critical to indirect maneuver operations. Synchronization—the arrangement of battlefield activities in time, space and purpose to produce maximum relative combat power at the decisive point—has to do critically with combined arms operations (naval, air, land), the successful or unsuccessful conduct of which is one thing that distinguishes developing world military forces, particularly when it comes to wars of maneuver. Synchronization also refers to the three-way comparison of close operations (at the battlefield with committed elements), deep operations (interdiction behind the enemy's front of reserve forces and logistics), and rear operations (your own support and reserve forces). Ability to deal effectively, in particular with deep and rear operations, is one more criterion separating out the relatively more and less capable of the developing world armies.

Regarding offensive operations, both the army's manuals and some sources in the academic literature deal with the "classical maneuvers of warfare," which, needless to say, has been at the heart of the military historical analyses familiar to readers of Liddell-Hart, Fuller et al. Such maneuvers—and their defensive counterparts—form the core of analyses that discuss the alternation of advantage between offense and defense throughout history, in turn as a function of endless new weapons developments. Such analyses are also made vivid and interesting to

American readers who may be reminded of the parallel development of football tactics and operations that also see perpetual innovation and concomitant changes in dominant offensive and defensive maneuvers.

The army's official manuals discuss five such standard maneuvers: envelopment, the turning movement, infiltration, penetration, and frontal attack.[49] It is noted that "while frequently used in combination, each attacks the enemy in a different way, and each poses different challenges to the attacking commander." It can also be said, with some caution, that whereas envelopment and turning movements—where large formations are involved—fit the criteria of relational maneuver as laid out by Luttwak, the frontal attacks are associated with an attrition style of operation. Penetration fits the latter somewhat, while infiltration may better belong to a relational maneuver style, it being understood that this is not just a matter of preferred "style," but also a matter of what is feasible in given circumstances. Penetration is, of course, most closely associated with modern armored blitzkrieg operations, so that there is an element of speed involved—the Israelis call it "armored pace"—as well as the standard spatial relationships. All of these forms of maneuver can be conducted either on a rather small scale, perhaps best described as at the tactical level, or on a much larger scale covering an entire theater of war, constituting microcosm and macrocosm.

These are somewhat arbitrarily chosen styles of maneuver, and they are not necessarily exhaustive. The British military historian David Chandler has outlined seven such maneuver styles, some of which are congruent with those offered by FM 100–5. They are: penetration of the center, envelopment of a single flank, envelopment of both flanks, attack in oblique order, the feigned withdrawal, attack from a defensive position, and the indirect approach.[50] Here, the envelopment of a single flank appears to subsume two of FM 100–5's categories—envelopment and the turning movement. Infiltration is not included, while two styles are included that appear based on turning initially defensive operations into offensive ones, that is, they are styles of counterattack.[51] Chandler's oblique order is not represented in the U.S. Army's array of maneuvers.

Quite probably the differences between Chandler and FM 100–5 are explained in part because the former is more historically oriented, while the latter is, after all, a primer for officers being prepared for modern combat. Chandler finds historical examples for all of his maneuver styles, but for the attack in oblique order, for instance, his examples are drawn entirely from the period of 1757 to 1812, spanning the careers of Frederick the Great, Napoleon, and Wellington.[52] It is not entirely clear whether it could be applied in a modern context, particularly where mechanized forces are involved. Likewise not clear is whether FM 100–5's category of infiltration would have many examples from the premodern period, as it is obviously inspired by such recent examples as Korea and Vietnam, and perhaps by some Soviet operations during World War II.

All of these maneuvers, incidentally, as applied both to the present and past, seem to assume large combat formations drawn up in a line against each other over a substantial front. No doubt, these assumptions held in the cases of the two recent Gulf Wars. It is, however, questionable as to whether such styles could be applied to much more fluid battlefield conditions where armies are more dispersed and not so ranged against each other in a linear way, for instance in the Falklands or along the Chad-Libya border. But no matter. They can still form the point of departure for the comparison of operational styles and also for a closer look at modern applications of Luttwak's dualism of attrition and relational maneuver.

Still one other related dual concept is discussed in FM 100–5, one which is closely related to the above-discussed operational maneuvers. It has to do with the classical distinction between movements on interior and exterior lines.[53] FM 100–5 discusses this more in the context of logistics, whereas Chandler sees it as contrasting situations presented to armies contemplating offensive operations. Again, there is a question of scale here. Such concepts can be applied to a simple battle. They can also be applied to the overall geopolitical relationships between contending nations, for instance regarding the advantages of interior lines that have inhered to the situations both of Israel and India vis-à-vis regional opponents.

According to Chandler, interior lines are said to be preferable in that they give the opportunity to divide superior opponents by faster concentrations, and that of achieving local superiority of force against one sector of a divided opponent. Contrariwise, exterior lines are said to provide advantages in giving an opportunity for envelopment if sufficient strength is available, and also a better opportunity at achieving total victory.[54] We shall return to this.

Though so many military histories concentrate on offensive maneuvers (that is what, after all, produces victories), there are as well alternative defensive patterns. And as is noted by FM 100–5, while they may take a variety of (not always discrete) forms, can be divided into two categories:

Mobile defenses—these focus on the destruction of the attacking force by permitting the enemy to advance into a position which exposes him to counterattack and envelopment by a mobile reserve.

Area defenses—these focus on the retention of terrain by absorbing the enemy into an interlocked series of positions from which he can be destroyed largely by fire.[55]

The army's manual goes on to note that each of these patterns, seemingly representing ideal types at the extremes, actually employ both static and dynamic elements, and that defending commanders will often utilize both patterns. Hence, "typically, defending commanders will combine both patterns, using static elements to delay, canalize, attrit, and ultimately halt the attacker, and dynamic elements—spoiling attacks and counterattacks—to strike and destroy his committed forces."[56] It goes on to say that "the balance among these elements will depend on the unit's mission, composition, mobility, and relative combat power, and on the character of the battlefield."[57] That is, geography is important and so is the size and nature of the combatants. The Gulf War is one thing, the Falklands another. But our sample of recent Third World wars does comprise some interesting cases both of mobile and area defenses, such as the felicitous use of both types by Iraq in the first Gulf War, and the mobile defenses used by Israel on the Golan Heights in 1973 and by Vietnam against China in 1979.

Further, FM 100–5 notes that defenses are organized into five complementary elements: security force operations forward, defensive operations in the main battle area, reserve operations in support of the main defensive efforts, deep operations in the area forward of the battle lines, and one's own rear operations. All of these elements can, to the extent information is available, form the basis for comparative analysis.[58]

FM 100–5 also provides a typology for retrograde operations, that is, movement to the rear or away from the enemy, which they note can be either forced or voluntary. Under that rubric they discuss delays, withdrawals, and retirements (a force not in active combat with the enemy conducts a movement to the rear). There are some good examples of these maneuvers in our recent wars, for instance, the Israeli delaying tactics on both fronts at the outset of the 1973 war, or the initial withdrawals of the Ethiopian army in the summer of 1977. Clearly, such maneuvers are extensions of defensive maneuvers or result when the latter has failed or is deemed impossible or imprudent.

Further criteria for comparative analysis may be provided by the various attempts by military authorities or historians to establish broad "principals of war." Those utilized by FM 100–5 are said to be slight revisions of principles formulated by British Major General (and historian) J. F. C. Fuller and developed during World War I. But they are also similar to principles laid down by Clausewitz and amended by his numerous admirers and followers. They are at a level of generality that allows a lot of room for argument over applications and over interpretations of historical examples pro and con, that is, successful and unsuccessful efforts at applying them. And some are not so easily illustrated by examples from our recent wars. But they do provide some additional bases for comparison, or some criteria for evaluation of the operational performances of contemporary armies that have seen combat.

Nine principles are advanced, as follows:

1. **objective**—direct every military operation toward a clearly defined, decisive, and attainable objective (this principle clearly has its most crucial application at the level of grand strategy as note, for instance, the U.S. experience in Vietnam)
2. **offensive**—seize, retain, and exploit the initiative (but note some military theorists, to the contrary, trumpet the superiority of the defense)
3. **mass**—concentrate combat power at the decisive place and time (note the relation to the previous discussion of the enemy's center of gravity)
4. **economy of force**—allocate minimum essential combat power to secondary efforts (note this too is applicable at various levels, but perhaps particularly at that of grand strategy)
5. **maneuver**—place the enemy in a position of disadvantage through the flexible application of combat power
6. **unity of command**—for every objective, ensure unity of effort under one responsible commander

7. **security**—never permit the enemy to acquire an unexpected advantage
8. **surprise**—strike the enemy at a time or place, or in a manner for which he is unprepared
9. **simplicity**—prepare clear, uncomplicated plans and clear, concise orders to ensure thorough understanding

In relation to the previously discussed offensive and defensive maneuvers, and in the light of what reasonably is known of the histories of some of the recent Third World wars, those principles most amenable to comparative analysis are the objective, offensive, mass, maneuver, and surprise.[59] We shall return to these.

Finally, and in relation to the above, FM 100–5 discusses three other concepts said to be central to an understanding of operational art, to the design and conduct of major operations.[60] These are the center of gravity, the lines of operation, and the culminating point. The first, center of gravity, relates to the principle of mass, and refers to those sources of strength or balance, what Clausewitz defined as "the hub of all power and movement, on which everything depends."[61] This can be a mass of the enemy force, a vital command center, a boundary between major combat formations, a line of communication, but may also be something more abstract, i.e., the psychological state of a key enemy commander or (see the U.S. experience in Vietnam) even a nation's popular and political support of the war.

The second, lines of operation, refers to the previously mentioned distinction between interior and exterior lines of operation. Interior lines can benefit a weaker force by allowing it to shift the main effort laterally more rapidly than the enemy. On the other hand, a force is said to be operating on exterior lines when its operations converge on the enemy, and this requires a stronger force but one which offers the opportunity to encircle and annihilate a weaker opponent.[62]

Third, there is the concept of "culminating points," a point in an offensive operation where the strength of the attacker no longer exceeds that of the defender and beyond which continued offensive operations risk overextension, counterattack, and defeat. Hence, the art of attack at all levels is to achieve decisive objectives before the culminating point is reached. FM 100–5 cites a number of historical examples, among them Rommel's drive into Egypt culminating at El Alamein, the Japanese drive from Burma into India culminating at Imphal-Kohima, and the German counteroffensive into the Ardennes culminating at the Battle of the Bulge.[63] Probably, the German defeat at the Marne in 1914 represented an effort at overextension beyond a culminating point. We can cite some clear examples from recent Third World wars, such as the culmination of the Iraqi advance in 1980 into Iran before Dezful, or the culmination of the Somali attack into Ethiopia before Harar and Dire Dawa. We shall expand on these themes.

Case Studies—Military Strategy and
Operational Arts in Third World Conventional Wars

The foregoing discussion has provided a large number of criteria by which the Third World wars of the last twenty years or so can be compared. Needless to say, a complete evaluation of eight or nine such wars—greatly varying among them according to magnitude and duration—would be beyond the space limitations of this work and, in addition, information from public sources is in some cases less than sufficient. But we can proceed to illustrate, highlight some salient points, and make some broad-brush comparisons. Mostly, we shall focus on what military historians consider to be the real core of such comparative analysis, that is, on the alternating advantages and disadvantages—or successes and failures—of offensive and defensive operations, and comparisons of wars that, by contrast, evidence marked tendencies either to movement and maneuver, or to lack of movement and of attrition.

We shall consider these wars in approximate chronological order (but note the Iran-Iraq War from 1980 to 1988 brackets some much shorter wars in between, i.e., those in the Falklands, Lebanon, and Chad). This will allow us somewhat (again the variations in scale and duration intruding) to gauge the extent to which lessons have been cumulative or even if they have explicitly been applied on the basis of past experiences, whether nearby or far afield.

India-Pakistan (1971)

First off, as noted in our discussion of grand strategy, this was a war that for months before the onset of full-scale hostilities had involved a gradual escalation from the Mukti Bahini insurgency within East Pakistan (East Bengal). By the time what was to become a three-week full-scale war had begun, both sides had had considerable time to prepare. India had a great opportunity to mortally wound its rival; Pakistan was more or less trapped in a no-win situation, all the more so as India wisely awaited the full onset of winter in the Himalayas in early December so as virtually to preclude a Chinese intervention, Pakistan's only hope, with that in turn begging the question of a possible countering Soviet intervention.[64]

By November and into early December Pakistan was gradually being sucked into a major counterinsurgency operation and simultaneously India launched several major incursions into East Bengal (called defensive actions in response to alleged Pakistani shelling) in the form of probing operations, most notably in the area of Hilli in northwest East Bengal.[65] That involved a reinforced infantry brigade and a regiment of tanks. But by early December India had mobilized some two hundred thousand troops (nine divisions) all around the 1,350–mile border, against a far smaller Pakistani force of some seventy-two thousand men (four divisions).[66] The onset of winter had allowed India to redeploy some of the seven to eight mountain divisions it normally deployed along the Chinese border. Meanwhile, India's numerical advantage in troops was matched by a proportionate advantage in tanks, artillery, and combat aircraft, with the qualitative advantage held by Pakistan in the somewhat equal 1965 war having been erased because of Pakistan's loss of its U.S. weapons source and because India had greatly strengthened its arms inventories.

Pakistan was then in a strategic bind. It could not easily defend East Bengal, particularly as Indian air and naval superiority (promising a blockade) would preclude significant reinforcement or logistics support, unlikely in any event because Pakistan could not afford to weaken its more critical western front. With the advantage of numbers, India had the further advantage of an interior lines position (often, otherwise, a counterbalancing advantage of the weaker side), but where the distances involved made this a less flexible situation for moving troops between fronts than Israel had had in 1967 (the comparison with Germany in two world wars might have been more apt, but the latter had a far more effective internal transportation system, one designed in part with two-front war in mind). Pakistan was thus left, as noted, with a rather hopeless defensive strategy in East Bengal, counting on mobile defense, phased withdrawals, and the hope that enough attrition of Indian forces could perhaps bring about a halt in hostilities. (Palit claims Pakistan's defensive scheme was more rigid than this and, hence, failed.) [67] In the west, it counted on a much better prepared linear defense of its key areas in the Punjab and in front of Karachi, combined with the possibility of capturing the Vale of Kashmir or attacking Jammu in trying to cut the road from the Indian Punjab to Kashmir, which would isolate Indian forces in Kashmir and Ladakh. Hence, Pakistan's unavoidable mobile defensive strategy in the east was balanced by an offensive maneuver strategy, to the extent possible, in the west. [68]

India, meanwhile, sought a major decision, one which would override the stalemate of 1965 fought almost entirely in the west. Its strategy was to fight a holding operation in the west while overwhelming Pakistani forces in the east on the basis of substantial superiority in land, air, and sea forces. Having accomplished that, it would then have the option of turning the full force of its 828,000–man army toward the west for a major thrust into west Pakistan. [69] Even if the latter was avoided, or if only a limited incursion were assayed (limited territorial gains or perhaps a large-scale "punitive raid"), India would have changed the balance of power in the subcontinent forever. It was a strategy that worked to perfection and was conducted in rapid fashion, making it the one example outside the Israeli wars and the U.S. Gulf War offensive that could be called a textbook case of successful conduct of an offensive war.

On an operational level, and referring back to our discussion of "styles of maneuver," India can be said in East Bengal to have fought a war of movement and maneuver, but one that was at the same time a widely spread frontal assault all along the East Bengal periphery. Reports from the early phases of the war had Indian troops attacking on some nine axes all along a three-sided front, though later, four major thrusts were identified. [70] But because Pakistan's seventy-thousand-man army was thinly stretched out (and in part due to the nature of the riverine terrain, which dictated strong-point defenses in places like Jessore), India was able to leapfrog and bypass Pakistani strong points, forcing continuing withdrawals from all directions back toward the Pakistani core at Dacca.

The Indians pushed their foe into an ever-shrinking circle around Dacca. India made effective use of infantry, armor, and airpower, and particularly of bridging equipment and helicopters for establishing bridgeheads across numerous rivers.[71] Overall, its operational maneuvers could be described as combining frontal assault with multiple penetrations and infiltration (the latter aided by the indigenous guerillas), allowing for a surprising—given the terrain—war of maneuver, which covered more than a hundred miles a day at some points. It was all over in a couple of weeks, a thoroughly successful Indian campaign.

Pakistan largely failed to operationalize a counterbalancing offensive in the west, where it had two armored divisions and eleven infantry divisions comprising over two hundred thousand troops. Some Pakistani forces penetrated some fifteen miles into the western Rajasthan Desert, but were repelled shortly thereafter. An attack by two Pakistani brigades at Chhamb, in the crucial Punjab theater, supported by Chinese-origin T-59 tanks, was repulsed.[72] But India simultaneously pushed into West Pakistan at Sialkot to protect the trunk road that leads from New Delhi to Srinagar, capital of Kashmir. After a week of war, Pakistan had launched some five assaults in an effort to cross the shallow, sandy Munnewar Tawi River, hoping to sever the critical Indian road eight miles eastward so as to cut off Indian troops in Kashmir. (They had crossed the river and almost but not quite reached the road in 1965.)

By the end of the war, India was beginning to move in the west. It thrust into West Pakistan in the Shakargosh area south of Sialkot in the Punjab, but also captured vast desert areas east of the Pakistani city of Hyderabad, in turn beginning to threaten Karachi.[73] Mostly, the war in the west was a somewhat stationary attrition slugfest reminiscent of 1965, but by the end it appeared India was on the verge of transitioning to a war of movement both in the north and south. If Pakistan had banked on an offensive strategy in the west, it had come to a very quick culminating point near Chhamb.

India, meanwhile, had scored high on several of the principles of warfare: objective (it had erased East Bengal and permanently changed the balance of power), offensive, mass, and maneuver. Pakistan's only chance to repeat the 1965 stalemate had been that of achieving a defensive war of attrition on both fronts. But by 1971 India's strength in combined arms operations—airpower and armor, in particular—did not allow for this, nor did the vast size of the battle theaters and the terrain, which made it difficult for an outnumbered army such as that of Pakistan to canalize operations into a narrower area where the advantages of defensive warfare could be brought into play.

Ethiopia vs. Somalia (1977)

We discussed this war at the level of grand strategy as an example of a "window of opportunity" war, one in which Somalia hoped to benefit from the temporary weakness of a larger and more powerful enemy to make territorial gains it hoped it could somehow hold on to, permanently. What then was its operational strategy to implement its broader aims, keeping in mind that on both sides in this war, one is talking about relatively primitive armies (both nations have very low per capita GNPs) highly dependent on outside assistance for arms, training, and (as it turned out for Ethiopia) the insertion of proxy forces ultimately crucial to the war's outcome? This was a war fought almost entirely on the ground, with naval forces effectively nonexistent (even though both sides have lengthy adjoining coast lines and the mutual prospect of interdicting external supplies) and air forces so ineffective that even though both sides had modern jet combat aircraft, they were never more than a minor factor in the prosecution of the war. (Actually, both sides lost a substantial part of their operational air assets early on in the war.)[74]

Somalia's operational strategy at the outset clearly had two related dimensions. First, utilizing a combination of Somali regular forces and irregulars from the Western Ogaden Liberation Front (Somali ethnics within Ethiopia), there was an effort to quickly overrun the huge, sparsely populated, and largely undefended Ogaden desert area, an area about six hundred miles wide by four hundred miles long. Essentially this involved overwhelming small Ethiopian frontier garrisons in small towns (Gode, Kahri Dehar, Dagabure, Werdere).[75] These Somali gains could be maintained only if the Ethiopian army were occupied elsewhere to defend more critical areas.

The second and more critical part of the Somali operational strategy consisted of a concentrated advance on a rather narrow front along an axis running west from the Somali city of Hargeisa in the direction of the Ethiopian heartland (the Rift Valley and the capital, Addis Ababa). This involved, crucially, first the capture of the Ethiopian border town of Jijiga, and then an advance over a key mountain pass in an attempt to capture the critical urban centers of Dire Dawa and Harar. The latter move also entailed in the process an effort at cutting the key rail line which runs from Addis Ababa to its outlet on the Red Sea in neighboring Djibouti.[76] If this could have been accomplished, it could have resulted in a total Ethiopian defeat (still, however, leaving the possibility of an Ethiopian counterattack after regrouping back toward the capital), perhaps forcing the Mengistu regime into a ceasefire agreement that would cede the Ogaden to Somalia in exchange for a Somali withdrawal from Dire Dawa and Harar. But, despite initial success, Somalia never did get quite that far. Jijiga was taken, the Kara Marda Pass crossed, the key rail line interrupted, but the offensive then stalled in front of Dire Dawa and Harar, while Addis Ababa was never directly threatened. If Somalia were the stronger nation, in a fundamental and durable sense, it might then have used its "seize and hold" position to force a ceasefire and an advantageous (territorially) conclusion, still begging the question of later Ethiopian revisionist drives, particularly if the latter could be relieved of its other "fronts" in Eritrea and Tigre Province.[77]

On offensive, at least up to the Harar-Dire Dawa line, Somalia was able to fight a war of maneuver. That was also true in Ogaden. It was an indirect approach in the classical Liddell-Hart sense, whereas the attack from Jijiga toward Dire Dawa over the mountains, in terms of operational style, could be described as a penetration of the center—indeed, Somalia's main problem appears to have been that the rugged mountain terrain precluded flanking maneuvers.[78] It seems to have been weak in defining its objective (could it have contemplated taking Addis Ababa, or was cutting the rail line enough?) and succeeded credibly in dealing with the principle of mass, concentrating power on one critical decisive area.

On defense, whether or not as a result of a deliberate operational strategy, Ethiopia was successful in conducting a mobile defense, trading space for time, conserving its forces for a later counterattack, and above all avoiding a disastrous battlefield defeat and/or decisive attrition of its forces. Inherently stronger and availed of more reliable outside support, it had merely to play for time.

Several months later, in February, fully armed by the Soviets and utilizing Cuban proxy troops as well as Soviet military advisors, Ethiopia launched its major counterattack. Its prospects were favored by Somalia's failure during a four-month lull to acquire a major arms supplier after having lost Moscow, though it got support from friendly Arab governments.

Ethiopia counterattacked along two axes, east from Harar toward Jijiga (reversing Somalia's earlier offensive thrust), and north from Dire Dawa toward Djibouti.[79] The first of these axes also put the Ethiopian army on an axis toward the important Somali city of Hargeisa which had been used as a marshaling center for the August Somali offensive. Ethiopia this time made extensive use of heavy armor and of Soviet attack aircraft, mostly MIG-21, MIG-23, and SU-7 planes. And at the outset of its offensive, it concentrated on reopening the rail line from Dire Dawa to Djibouti.

The main thrust of the Ethiopian offensive was along the sixty-mile stretch of twisting mountain road from Harar to Jijiga. After more than a month of fighting, Jijiga fell to Ethiopian troops on 5 March 1978. Critical here, according to some reports, was the Russo-Cuban use of "vertical envelopment" in moving some seventy tanks over the mountains by helicopters.[80] This caused Somali withdrawal from the Jijiga area and back into Somalia, at which time Ethiopia abjured an attack across the open plains toward Hargeisa and Berbera.

Similar to Somalia's earlier offensive along the same axis, Ethiopia relied on straightahead penetration and a slow attrition forward offense, at least for a few weeks. The vertical envelopment by heliborne tanks is the modern equivalent of a flanking maneuver, overcoming Somalia's reliance on fixed fortifications in the mountains and a slow retreat intended to produce sufficient attrition. But there was no use of the vast available spaces for classic envelopment maneuvers which, again, was precluded by the nature of the mountainous terrain which kept both armies largely road-bound, on one major axis.[81]

China-Vietnam (1979)

Some eighteen months after the Somali army moved over the Kara Marda Pass, China invaded Vietnam in what was to become an intense three-week conflict involving hundreds of thousands of troops. This was a good example of grand strategy driving operations, in that China's war aim—really that of a strong punitive raid to make a point in connection with Vietnam's drive into Cambodia—did not, apparently, involve the aspiration to retain captured territory (that would, at any rate, have run the risk of bringing the Soviets actively into the conflict). Whereas Somalia (and Iraq in 1980 and perhaps Israel in 1982) contemplated "seize and hold," China appears to have contemplated "seize and withdraw," recognizing as they obviously did that an attempt at territorial aggrandizement might well have brought the Soviets into the fray in a more active way.

This war, of course, was on a much larger scale than that in the Horn, involving hundreds of thousands of troops. And it was fought by tougher and better-trained armies. But the Chinese Army had seen little combat since Korea (excepting the brief mountain war with India in 1962 and a few skirmishes in Tibet and along the Ussuri River), while the Vietnamese had fought almost continuously for more than a generation and were widely regarded as the best light infantry in the world. But against China in 1979, Hanoi fought largely with reservists and second-line forces as the cream of its army, 100,000 to 175,000 men, was deeply engaged in Cambodia.[82]

Some of the press reportage about the Chinese operational strategy was ambiguous and contradictory. In part, that resulted from the fact that at the outset, Beijing's aims were not clear, so that the basic outline of what it was up to with its three-week offensive unfolded only gradually as the war proceeded.

For instance, the *New York Times* reported at the war's outset,

> The most likely avenue for a Chinese thrust would be from Pingsiang on the frontier down the highway and railroad toward Lang Son and the road to Hanoi. This is the area where the strongest Vietnamese forces are likely to be deployed.
>
> [. . .]
>
> Chinese infantry tactics, as they have developed since the Korean War, emphasize thrusts of high speed against single objectives rather than broad mass attacks. It is probable, therefore, that a major drive toward Lang Son would be accompanied by other thrusts farther south along the coastal plain and at least one holding operation in the north directed on Cao Bang or Ha Giang, 15 miles from the frontier.[83]

The same analysis also predicted that "swift and successful operations" would depend on air support, and talked about the Chinese having moved about 150 MIG-17, MIG-19, and MIG-21 planes into bases immediately behind the front, utilizing ten airfields within 125 miles of the Vietnam frontier.

But only a week or so later, as Chinese troops poured across the border, Drew Middleton, in an article headlined "A Classic Military Operation," expressed a wholly different view of Chinese operations, one seemingly derived from an interpretation of Chinese military history. A parallel was drawn to the assault over the Himalayas against India in 1962. Hence, "The Chinese invasion of Vietnam followed, at the outset, the classic pattern of attacks over a wide front—with the defender left guessing about the principle axis of advance."[84]

He noted that the main thrust might be in the far northwest in the Lao Cai area, intended to cut the main rail line running from Yunnan Province to Hanoi. But then,

A second attack, in the Lang Son area, northeast of the capital, also appeared to be gaining momentum. But it was possible that one or both of these might prove to be holding operations and that the main thrust along the front of about 480 miles might come from elsewhere, possibly along the coast.[85]

After a week or two of fighting, and after the Chinese had moved forward in two major spurts interspersed with pauses for renewal, the main lines of Chinese operational strategy became clearer.[86] Basically, it involved strong thrusts by infantry accompanied by armor—and backed by a lot of artillery—along the two axes toward Lao Cai and Lang Son. The two other road approaches through the mountains toward Hanoi-via Lai Chau and the Route 2 west of Lang Son—were relatively ignored. After three weeks of warfare, during which Lao Cai was captured early on, the main focus of the Chinese offensive came to be the capture of Lang Son, increasingly seen as a symbolic, if not militarily vital, objective.[87] In the process, the Chinese also practiced scorched-earth tactics, destroying communications networks, industrial enterprises, and utilities.

A later analysis by Middleton, focused on why the Chinese came to attach such importance to one provincial capital, emphasized the Chinese wish to draw Vietnamese main forces into battle.[88] The Chinese, he said, "need not emphasize territorial advantages. Lang Son was important to the Chinese, analysts believe, only because the development of an attack toward it would probably attract strong Vietnamese forces to the town's defense."[89] This emphasis, then, was rooted in Mao Tse-Tung's dictum on the aim of war: "destroy the effective strength of the enemy rather than hold lands or cities."[90] The Vietnamese, outnumbered, were seen as preferring to avoid a major battle under unfavorable conditions, but were drawn into the defense of Lang Son because it was a major city but, paradoxically, perhaps also because they thought they might seriously bloody the Chinese army. After heavy fighting, the Chinese did capture Long San, then called for a ceasefire and retired, claiming victory.

On defense, Vietnam played a "bend but don't break" game, retreating, causing attrition, hoping for Soviet intervention. They had to defend at all points, worried up to the end of the fighting that the Chinese might decide to move on Hanoi. Curiously, neither side made much use of available airpower. It was a classic war of infantry and artillery, and some limited use of armor in largely forbidding, wooded, mountainous terrain. In terms of the offensive categories laid out by Chandler, China's offensive was an effort at penetration at the center, a frontal onslaught emphasizing mass.

On the Chinese side, high marks could be given regarding the "objective." Paradoxically, this involved "teaching a lesson" by taking some territory, causing damage, and then withdrawing.[91] The element of surprise was lacking, but it didn't matter, as the Chinese were willing to take casualties and were not look-ing for an ultimate "victory." But they paid a big price in casualties and perhaps also in prestige.

Lebanon (1982): Operational Strategy

The Israeli invasion of Lebanon in 1982 was, paradoxically, a classic case of a bril-liantly executed military victory, but, because of the lack of clearly defined or well-thought-out objectives, a political failure, verging upon disaster. On the other side, the war may actually have been a political victory for the PLO, and a military defeat for Syria, though in the latter case somewhat of a "moral vic-tory" just because some elements of its forces performed better than expected. Or so hindsight tells us. Many years afterwards, it is still a controversial war, sub-ject to conflicting, angrily polemical interpretations.

On the operational side, for Israel, it is a difficult war to analyze just because of the extent to which its confusing overall strategy dictated the details of oper-ations, and because the military under Ariel Sharon had to fight what was almost a covertly designed operation relative even to Israel's own political leadership. As such, one has to see it as a well-thought-out (up to a point) overall plan which needed to be operationalized piecemeal but also hurriedly, seriatim, in a climate of strong internal and external (Reagan administration) political pressures.

As has ably been portrayed in two excellent political military analyses of the war—by Richard Gabriel and jointly by Ze'ev Schiff and Ehud Ya'ari—the Israelis contemplated three different war plans in the month preceding the war, whose final trigger was the shooting of the Israeli ambassador in London by ter-rorists.[92] This, of course, is at the grand strategic level, but in this case in particu-lar it dictated the basic plans at the operational level. The first plan called for an invasion of Lebanon to destroy the PLO in the south and stop artillery and ter-rorist attacks on Israeli border settlements, to be fought only against the PLO, and not at all against Syria. This would be an expanded version of the 1978 Operation Litani, and would carry the Israeli army as far as the Awali River, forty kilometers north of the border at Rosh Hanikra. Similar to China's offen-sive in 1979, it would be a large-scale punitive and preemptive raid.[93] And indeed this plan remained Israel's "declaratory policy," vis-à-vis Washington and its own people, even after the invasion had been launched.

A second plan also called for hitting the PLO but not Syria, but allowed for the Israel Defense Forces (IDF) going as far north as Beirut, with the Christian Phalange being relied upon to destroy the PLO inside Beirut (later this fantasy would be the nemesis of Israel's strategy).[94] A forty-kilometer limit would here also be used as a declaratory posture, but this time as measured from Metula, Israel's northernmost border town, allowing for a line drawn eastward from Beirut along the Beirut to Damascus highway.

A third plan, Operation "Big Pines," was more ambitious still.[95] It involved a war against both the PLO and Syria, the capture of Beirut by Phalangists and the IDF, the driving of the PLO from Lebanon, and the installation of a regime friendly to Israel in Beirut. This plan was favored by Defense Minister Sharon and some high-ranking military leaders including Chief of Staff General Rafael Eitan, but had to be introduced piecemeal, ad hoc, and almost stealthily as the war unfolded. That had major and damaging implications for Israeli operational planning. In particular, just because little a priori planning or training for such an operation could be conducted (particularly important regarding the pace of reserve mobilization, emplacement of forces, the jumping-off time of the operation on the first day), Israeli operations later fell somewhat behind schedule and exhibited less of the precision and coordination familiar to earlier operations.[96] Added to that, Israel was fighting in what for it was not very suitable terrain (its forces are configured and armed more for mobile warfare in Sinai), and in addition it may somewhat have underestimated the fighting ability and will both of the PLO and Syria, no doubt because of the typically poor performance of Arab armies in the past.[97]

Syria, meanwhile, mostly tried to stay out of the war. But pride and the Assad regime's political requirements for retaining power dictated something better than open avoidance of a challenge, so that Syria was forced to respond, and was sucked into the war. But it too was not really ready, so that its operational planning appears to have consisted of little other than ad hoc measures geared to making Israel (as always highly sensitive to even minimal casualties) pay for its adventure. On the PLO side, there was also confusion over operational planning. Like the Syrians, they had little hope of anything but a futile, attrition defense that would make the Israelis pay for a victory. But whereas some PLO leaders anticipated only something at the level of Israel's first plan, some, such as Arafat lieutenant Abu Iyad, sensed that Israel would come to Beirut and seek a conclusive victory over the PLO.[98] That would dictate a mobile defense moving gradually back toward Beirut, but also an urban guerilla defense which, if successful, could constitute a "mini-Stalingrad" which, whatever the ultimate outcome, might constitute a severe blow to Israel.

Several factors dictated Israel's operational strategy in the context of the gradually unfolding and somewhat covert overall plan. There was nothing new about them—they were altogether consistent with Israel's long-time military doctrine of "strategic defense/tactical offense," which emphasizes quick preemptive strikes geared to carrying the war immediately into the enemy's territories. In Lebanon, in 1982, the emphasis was on speed (in part to preempt U.S. diplomatic action, as usual), avoidance of casualties (always a paramount concern), trapping of the PLO and administering, as far as possible, a decimating and overwhelming defeat, and also administering a defeat to Syria, which would render the latter less able to make war on Israel for a number of years. In the end, Israel had only partial success in all these dimensions, less than it had hoped for.

The Israeli "Operation Peace for Galilee" basically was conducted along three axes, with the major part of the operation, up to the siege of Beirut, being conducted in six days, beginning on June 5.[99] First, there was a major thrust along the coastal highway via Tyre, Sidon, and Damour toward Beirut, which was intended to destroy much of the PLO presence in Lebanon, which was largely based on refugee camps in the Tyre and Sidon areas as well as further north in the Beirut area. Here the Israeli mechanized infantry forces had a large advan-

tage in men and equipment, and there was little chance for the PLO to do anything but give the Israelis a bit of a bloody nose: administer casualties to a force
very sensitive even to a score or two of deaths.

The Israelis, on the other hand, labored under the difficulties inherent in the
nature of the geography. They had to move along a narrow coastal highway,
flanked by the sea and by citrus groves, which are ideal for guerilla ambushes, in
turn flanked by rugged mountainous foothills. To minimize casualties and to
maximize trapping of guerillas, they conducted a large-scale amphibious landing
south of Damour near the mouth of the Awali River, intended to block fleeing
PLO fighters and to act as a springboard for a quick assault on Beirut.[100] They
anticipated a quick (two-day) hook-up of the main force with the landing force,
but PLO resistance, particularly near Sidon, slowed the pace of the planned
operation. Otherwise, moving from the border up toward Damour, the IDF
strategy was to bypass strong points such as refugee camps and urban areas,
leapfrogging forward, hoping that the bypassed strong points would then be easily reduced and prone to surrender. As it happened, PLO resistance was surprisingly strong, particularly at Ein Hilweh outside Sidon (as it had been earlier for
the Syrian army) and the Israelis (who were careful about killing unarmed civilians) had to take greater than expected casualties.[101] Finally, although the IDF
captured massive stores of military equipment, far more than could be used by
the some fifteen thousand PLO fighters in south Lebanon, they were unable to
trap the bulk of the PLO fighters, many of whom slipped through their lines
into the Beirut area or into areas controlled by the Syrian army.

A second axis for the Israeli offensive was along Lebanon's central spine,
straight north from the border past the Beaufort Castle, the road junction at
Nabatiya, past the Litani and Zaharani Rivers, via the critical town of Jezzine,
and on through the Shouf Mountains and the villages of Ain Zhalta and Ain
Dara to the midpoint of the Beirut-Damascus highway between Bhamdoun and
Chtaura.[102]

This operation had several purposes. First, it allowed a strong, mobile Israeli
armored force to quickly move across the Litani, bypassing Beaufort Castle and
then to move west from Nabatiya to link up with the forces moving up the
coastal road, so as to form a pincers around the PLO forces south of Sidon. Following immediately on the heels of those forces, other armored units raced
north to Jezzine and further, encountering heavy resistance. Their ultimate
objective was to cut the Beirut-Damascus highway, thereby either trapping Syrian forces trying to flee back into Syria, or precipitating such a movement with
the purpose of driving the Syrians out of Lebanon.[103]

A third Israeli line of operations, springing out of upper Galilee just southwest of Mount Hermon, was directed against the Syrian army. It began a couple
of days after the other operations, after the Syrians had been drawn into combat
in the area of Jezzine, and after the major operation that saw elimination of the
nineteen Syrian surface-to-air (SAM) batteries in the Bekaa Valley and the
destruction of some ninety Syrian aircraft, which resulted in complete Israeli
control of the air. It had the purpose of driving the Syrians out of the Bekaa Valley in the area south of the Beirut-Damascus highway.[104]

This operation was conducted along several axes: along the mountain line to the west of Bekaa, around both sides of Lake Karoun, and further to the east along the foothills of the mountains along the axis running from Marjayoun to Hasbaiya to Rachaiya. This axis also acted as a blocking force to the south of the Syrian main forces as the IDF raced north to cut the main highway, presenting it with the specter of encirclement against the mountains if the Syrian flank should be turned further north.[105] Slower than anticipated, with more than expected resistance from unexpectedly courageous Syrian forces, the Israelis did succeed in overrunning most of the southern Bekaa in a few days. At the end of the operation, they were only twenty five kilometers from Damascus.

In the next phase of the war, one which lasted much longer than the Six Day War of movement, which had captured all of southern Lebanon, the Israelis were faced with the dilemma of what do with Beirut. Should they overrun it or should they try to persuade the Christian Phalange to do the job for them, or (as ultimately happened) should they seek a diplomatic resolution that would result in the evacuation of PLO forces (at least temporarily) from Lebanon?[106]

Since 1982 there have been extensive arguments over what Israel might or should have done at the gates of Beirut, with military and political dimensions. There was first the long-held Israeli tenet of not moving armies into large Arab cities, a matter of symbolic as well as practical importance. There was pressure from Washington. And there was a fear of extensive casualties if the IDF were forced into block-by-block fighting in urban areas, mostly by snipers. The IDF is not, for the most part, trained or equipped for urban warfare.

After the war, some Israeli commentators were to wonder whether the IDF could have taken Beirut at acceptable cost if it had moved in quickly around June 12, before the PLO fighters had had time to build fortifications and organize a defense. Israel relied on heavy artillery and air bombardments to weaken the resolve of its foes and to soften up its defenses. But it did not work—time was on the PLO's side, as it turned out.

Operationally, both the PLO and Syrian forces fought from well-thought-out and rational defense plans. Having no chance at a victory in conventional terms, they were forced to rely on a mobile defense and gradual withdrawal, but emphasizing attrition and the taking of casualties from a foe known to have a low pain threshold. The emphasis was on ambushes along roads, in citrus groves, and from mountain defiles, making heavy use of rocket-propelled grenades (RPG), automatic weapons, and helicopters firing high-subsonic optically teleguided (HOT) missiles. In that they succeeded—Israel suffered greater casualties in Lebanon than its political situation would permit. The ultimate, ironic result may have been to increase the level of Syrian and PLO deterrence threat to another such Israeli invasion of Lebanon.

Regarding types of operations, Israel did succeed in a classic penetration maneuver from its central axis with subsequent envelopments to both flanks in the rear, enveloping the PLO south of Sidon, and Syrian units in the Bekaa Valley south of Lake Karoun. In terms of basic principles, Israel obviously had major problems regarding its objectives, in large part a function of internal political disarray but also because of the limitations on its freedom of action imposed

by external political pressures. To some extent, it was not fully able to operationalize what is usually one of its strengths—concentration of force—because
of the somewhat hurried, haphazard, and improvised nature of its buildup and
initial assault. It had needed more time for initial plans and preparations though,
of course, a longer buildup interval might also have reduced what it achieved by
way of strategic surprise.

The Falklands: Operational Strategy

Despite the small scale and short duration (of the actual combat phase) of this
war, it is in some respects more complex in its operational aspects than some of
the larger conventional wars. That is because in some senses the Falklands War,
more than the others (the Gulf War being an exception), involved combined air,
naval, and ground operations, the effective coordination of which was critical to
the British success and the Argentine failure.

After Argentina had secured the Falklands (and South Georgia), Britain was
faced with the seemingly impossible task of retaking the islands at the end of an
eight thousand-mile logistics line, and with the onset of an habitually bitter
South Atlantic winter looming. Argentina, clearly the weaker military power in
an overall sense, had the advantage of much closer geographic proximity to the
war zone, some four hundred to five hundred miles, though it too had to operate in inclement weather out of naval and air bases located in the relatively
inhospitable southern part of the country. Between it (and its first-leg staging
area in Gibraltar) and the Falklands, Britain was availed of one major and irreplaceable strategic asset in small Ascension Island, a British possession whose
main air base at Wideawake Field had long been shared with the U.S. Without
Ascension as a staging and training base (also a launching point for bombers and
their tankers), the already difficult operation would have been nigh impossible to
mount all the way from the U.K.[107]

The main operational issue all along—perhaps paralleled in some senses with
the precedent of the Normandy invasion or U.S. Pacific operations in Iwo Jima
and Okinawa—was that of whether Britain could seize and hold a beachhead on
the Falklands. For Argentina, the main issue was, by contrast, whether it could
block Britain from establishing a defensible beachhead which would then be
used as a springboard for recapturing the Falklands. On both sides, all energies
focused on that point, as it was recognized that once a substantial British presence was so established, victory would automatically follow.

With that central criterion in mind, Britain moved rapidly to establish naval
and air superiority around and over the Falklands. This involved first the sinking
of the Argentine cruiser *Belgrano* by a British nuclear attack submarine, which in
turn caused the remainder of the Argentine surface navy to head for port, out of
harm's way.[108] Afterwards, the British enforced a two-hundred-mile exclusion
zone around the Falklands, which effectively ended any surface naval threat to
the British armada steaming toward the Falklands. Otherwise Argentine conventional diesel subs were to remain a threat to the British naval armada all the way
through the war, but were kept at bay by various countermeasures.

Achieving air superiority over and around the Falklands was a more difficult matter for Britain. Indeed, Argentina appeared to have a major advantage with bases only four hundred miles away for its considerable force of Mirage fighters (upgraded Israeli versions), Super Etendard naval attack craft (armed with Exocet missiles), aging Skyhawk fighter bombers, and indigenously built but smaller Pucara light attack aircraft. A major failing for Argentina was its inability to construct a major air base on the islands themselves on which to base Mirages and Skyhawks which, because of insufficient operational radii, could otherwise loiter only briefly over the British fleet or, ultimately, a landing place and beachhead.[109] Britain's Vulcan bombers (originally part of its strategic nuclear-strike force), based on Ascension and availed of critical tanker refueling, repeatedly pounded the Port Stanley airstrip, which (along with smaller strips) was never able to accommodate aircraft other than the lightweight Pucara and some Hercules transports flying resupply operations from the mainland. When Britain's small carriers arrived in the battle area, their Harrier VSTOL "jump jets" were able to establish nearly unchallenged air superiority over the Falklands—they were technologically better as air superiority fighters than anything the Argentines possessed, and once in the area, had a basing and loiter-time advantage over Argentine aircraft forced to fly over four hundred miles from mainland home bases.[110] That technological superiority was enhanced by acquisition of U.S.-supplied AIM-9L Sidewinder missiles during the war, one of numerous instances of quietly supplied U.S. assistance to Britain in the face of difficult diplomatic cross-pressures, involving relations with the remainder of Latin America.[111]

Hence, in summary, during the first month of the conflict, but before an actual landing, Britain was able to overcome, indeed reverse, the seeming disadvantages imposed by the disparities in geographic proximity to the battle area by several interrelated operations: use of submarines to achieve total superiority on the ocean's surface, use of reconfigured former nuclear bombers designed for deterrence against the USSR to prevent Argentina's establishment of a serious combat aircraft presence on the Falklands, and use of small carriers to launch Harrier fighters which could establish air superiority in the prospective main battle area.

One other operational advantage was established by Britain. By May 1, a month after the crisis had unfolded, it had put ashore by helicopter several SAS (Special Air Service) and SBS (Special Boat Service) units for purposes of reconnaissance, intelligence, and sabotage. Like the Iraqis years later, the Argentines were gradually blinded during this war, while their British foes were availed of a full view of the area of operations, further afforded by apparent U.S. assistance with overhead satellite reconnaissance. The SAS and SBS units would be particularly useful in choosing and monitoring possible sites for the all-critical main landing point.

Indeed, the choice of a landing point was the single most critical British decision of the war, and it was the subject of considerable debate within the higher British war councils. Some advocated a landing at the ultimate objective, Fort Stanley. Others advocated a sudden, direct commando attack on the town, intended to decapitate the Argentine high command on the islands and to produce a swift victory. According to the *London Times'* "Insight" team, the following three options were considered, with pros and cons, the last of which was chosen.

1. To establish a base at Ascension Island, mount a series of selective raids on the Falklands, then, when reinforcements were ready, launch a major operation to establish a bridgehead. The principal advantage of this was that it gave the landing forces time—for intelligence gathering, training, and establishing naval and air superiority around the islands. It would not guarantee quick results.

2. To sail south to the exclusion zone, remain at sea, mount selective raids, then establish a bridgehead. Again, this offered time and had the advantage of maintaining limited security for the naval force against air attack while still offering some overt military action. But it meant the main land force's having to spend more time at sea in bad weather, when the risk from enemy air attack was still considerable.

3. To establish a bridgehead on the islands as soon as the ships arrived from Ascension. It would be politically attractive because it was fast and it would maintain momentum. But it allowed only minimum time for intelligence-gathering and for special forces operations on the islands, and no time at all to establish naval and air superiority. It also placed the land forces ashore at great risk. It had always been the least favored alternative of them all.[112]

The landing at San Carlos was, of course, hugely successful.[113] It was not strongly opposed on land (a larger Argentinian effort with artillery registered on the beachhead could have altered the outcome if better intelligence and follow-up had been achieved). Otherwise, the Argentine Air Force did mount a major assault on the invasion fleet during the operation at San Carlos Bay, which was ultimately unsuccessful but which did knock out several Royal Navy ships and disrupt the landing operation somewhat.

Once a beachhead was established, some three thousand elite British soldiers, marines, and commandos were faced with a march along a forty-mile axis toward Fort Stanley over inhospitable mountains and boggy terrain against a land force some four times its size but obviously at a major disadvantage in terms of weapons, leadership, training, and morale. That was the reverse of the traditionally assumed requirement for a 4:1 favorable ratio on behalf of the side on the offensive.

The British land advance across West Falklands Island was, in operational terms, a rather fluid but aggressive effort, one featuring bold, rapid actions, leapfrogging forward on land, by helicopter, and by amphibious craft. It was more a war of maneuver than one of attrition, at least up to the final assault on Fort Stanley and its environs. But en route, the British force conducted one major head-to-head battle at Goose Green, there also in the face of seemingly imposing odds as measured by force ratios. That battle was fought not so much because Goose Green was a major obstacle on the route to the final objective (it could easily have been bypassed), but because the British wished, in a psychological sense, to establish battlefield dominance and to put fear and a sense of resignation into their foes.[114] Afterwards, the war's ultimate conclusion was no longer in doubt. After a number of skilled leapfrogging moves that put the British in a ring around Fort Stanley, the latter was finally taken in a classic straightforward infantry shock action, featuring small arms and bayonets. The nature of the terrain and the location of Fort Stanley allowed for little other than a straight-ahead assault with pressure on all points across a front.

On defense, the Argentines conducted a rather confused and futile operational strategy. They first failed to do the one thing that might have turned the tide, which would have been a determined defense of the beachhead or a determined effort at destroying it (by artillery and infantry assaults) before it became established and the full British force and its equipment were ashore. Afterwards, with a comprehensive linear defense up and down the island ruled out by the insufficiency of forces (only some twelve thousand total), the Argentines assayed a somewhat mobile withdrawal strategy, relying on defense of fortified strong points (Goose Green, Mount Harriet, etc.) between San Carlos and Fort Stanley, apparently hoping to win by attrition on the basis of fielding a larger force. That strategy failed, as the Argentines rapidly lost much higher than a 4:1 ratio of forces by surrender and mortality, and as the balance of logistics and air support progressively worsened.

Yet for Argentina, despite its disadvantages in training and morale, it was a war that might have been won by better skill or luck on several operational dimensions. Better use of airpower against the British fleet (an airfield on the Falklands or better use of antiship missiles) or of submarines could have turned the tide. A more effective or rapid response to the San Carlos landing could also have turned the tide, particularly if artillery could have been brought to bear on the beachhead. Or a more serious effort at moving manpower and materiel to the islands could have been conclusive—Argentina had a full month to raise its army well above the level of the some twelve thousand troops that ultimately fought on the Falklands.

Iran and Iraq: Operational Strategies

Discussing the operational side of the Iran-Iraq War in summary terms is no easy matter. Relative to others, it was a very long, drawn-out war, one that went through a number of more or less discernible phases. More so than some of the other recent wars, it had interrelated operational developments on the ground, at sea, and in the air (planes and missiles), though the first-named predominated by far. Cordesman and Wagner, in a major work, devoted chapters on aspects of the operational side of the war: the "C³I and Battle Management," "Combined Arms and the Land-War," "The Air and Missile Wars," and "The Tanker War and the Lessons of Naval Combat." There was diversity of terrain and climate along a thirteen-hundred-kilometer front, and further it was a war that was internationalized to a degree that makes it hard to discuss in isolation.[115]

Somewhat paradoxically, on the other hand, this war lends itself to simple overall characterization, to a kind of "typing" along the familiar spectrum running from wars of maneuver to those of attrition. Simply stated, this was about as close as one could come to a case of pure attrition war, and it is an unassailable cliché, one repeated by numerous commentators, that this war was an eerie replay of World War I, with its protracted stalemate, its stationery slugfest fought again and again over the same terrain and in the same places, its long lines of fixed fortifications stretching over hundreds of miles, its periodic resort by either side to one last "final offensive," indeed, the use of poison gas as well, not altogether a coincidence, but rather a function of the type and duration of the war.

Even the nature of the beginning and of the end of the war bore an uncanny resemblance to World War I. In both, the initial aggressor (which in both cases claimed it was forced into a preemptive attack by the stronger side) fought according to a long-held and often-rehearsed strategy, one intended to produce a quick and total victory or at least a "seize and hold" victory translatable into a favorable peace agreement.[116] And in both, one side finally and somewhat suddenly and unexpectedly collapsed from exhaustion after itself having had the initiative (and having expected a victory) for much of the war.[117]

One major question here is just why this war so long maintained the character of a stationery attrition contest. In other contexts, including World War I (and perhaps also the Virginia end of the U.S. Civil War), military historians have been prone to a form of military technological determinism. They claimed that the extant state of the art of weaponry in general, or the existence of a (temporary) dominance of one or another type of weapon, had created a stalemate. For World War I this meant new automatic weapons, massed and accurate artillery, and barbed wire before the advent of effective tank and tactical aircraft technology.

But for the Iran-Iraq War such a simple technological determinism is not easy to swallow. For, indeed, most of the same weapons were used—on both sides—in the 1973 and 1982 Middle Eastern wars and the India-Pakistan contest of 1971 (the 1973 war was hastily characterized by some as a defensive attrition war even despite the Israelis' successful prosecution of a mobile offensive after less than three weeks). Therefore, the Iran-Iraq War cautions us to take into account the subjective "human factors"—training, leadership, "absorption" of technology, the intellectual capacity to conduct combined arms operations, etc.

Iraq planned for a short war. According to Cordesman and Wagner (in turn based on documents captured by Iran from Iraqi prisoners of war), this involved the aspiration of taking Khorramshahr, Abadan, Ahwaz, Dezful, Masjid e-Suleiman, and some of the key oil centers in Khuzistan in ten to fourteen days.[118] It also envisaged the taking of territory in several salients further north, near Mehran, Quasr e-Shirin, and Panjwin, which in combination could have provided additional protection against an Iranian counterattack toward Baghdad and the Kurdish-area oil regions in the triangle Kirkuk, Irbil, Mosul.[119] But the main thrust was in the south, involving attack by three armored and two mechanized divisions along a broad front from Khorramshahr to Musian. This involved the aim of capturing Khorramshahr and then Abadan, and also crossing the Kharkeh River to engage Dezful and the road from there to Ahwaz, which, if severed, would have cut off all Iranian land communications between the Iranian core area and the oil regions of Khuzistan. Iraq counted on Iran being disorganized and unprepared in this postrevolutionary period.

Iraq succeeded only to a degree. Khorramshahr was captured after a fierce struggle, but Abadan proved a tougher nut to crack. And although Iraqi armored units managed to move through and beyond Susangerd, they failed to take the critical command center at Dezful. They crossed the Karun River, but also failed to take Ahwaz, the administrative center for Iran's oil industry. Further north, Iran's main success was the taking of a three-hundred-kilometer square area near Panjwin, adjacent to the Iranian town of Marivan, which helped to secure Iraq's control of Kurdistan and to aid the anti-Iranian Kurds in that area.[120]

The military literature on this war is endlessly concentrated on the limited nature of Iraq's victories in 1980, despite a seemingly massive advantage in deployed forces, the element of surprise, and in usable weaponry backed up by available resupply sources in both the East and West blocs. Several reasons, which span the operational and tactical levels of analysis, are usually advanced. In brief, this crucially involves first the failure to coordinate a combined arms offensive utilizing aircraft, various elements of the land forces, and command and control; and second, connected to the above, an overall excessive caution and lack of boldness and panache.[121] Iraq blew what might have been an opportunity for a quick, decisive victory, begging the question of how it could have concluded the war successfully without extending an offensive into the Iranian core areas or destroying the bulk of the Iranian Army itself.

The lack of combined arms coordination is cited by analysts of the war at several levels. Armor was used without proper support from infantry and artillery or (later) used reflexively in stationery defensive positions or as a substitute for artillery. In the attacks on Khorramshahr and Abadan, there was an overreliance on reducing the garrisons by artillery fire and armor rather than utilization of the infantry operations needed for urban warfare. Generally, in the critical zone of the war near Ahwaz and Dezful, and also at Abadan, Iraqi armor moved too slowly, moving into hull-down positions and waiting for forward areas to be cleared by artillery. There were not enough quick armored dashes either to penetrate or to encircle Iranian forces.[122] Further, Iraq made wholly insufficient use of tactical airpower in connection with ground operations.[123]

A main question is whether Iraq might, at the war's outset before the battle lines hardened, have utilized another and more successful operational strategy. This has to do with relative emphasis between areas along the battle line. Could Iraq, by concentrating more on one place, perhaps at Ahwaz or maybe further north, have achieved a critical breakthrough rather than diffusing its efforts in launching attacks at several points along the frontier? We will never know.

In a second phase of the war in 1981–82, Iran regained virtually all of the territory it had lost in Iraq's initial assault in 1980—salients at Quasr e-Shirin, across the Kharkeh River toward Dezful, another toward Ahwaz west of the Karun River, and the city of Khorramshahr. With little use of air support or offensive use of tanks (and with a disastrous use of tanks near Susangerd), Iran's mixed force of regular troops and Pasdaran irregulars succeeded with massive infantry wave assaults in pushing Iraq back to the original border lines in most areas, including the recapture of Khorramshahr. This offensive culminated in major Iranian victories in the period March to May, 1982.[124] Both sides incurred huge casualties in a campaign that still saw some motion before the war became bogged down in an endless stalemated slaughter. Iraq, on the defensive, had not yet learned the more mobile defensive tactics that would become more effective in subsequent years. And the nature of the Iranian offensives, minimizing the roles of armor and tactical air support, made it impossible for Iran to achieve decisive breakthroughs that might have resulted in a quicker end to the war. Iran's cumbersome offensives in 1981–82, effective only to the extent of a costly recapturing of lost territories, were a mirror image of Iraq's in 1980, whereby decisive victories could not be achieved because of lack of coordination of armies and branches, and particularly the absence of effective armored spearhead forces.

From June 1982 to March 1984, Iran was usually on the offensive, utilizing massive infantry wave assaults, banking on a more or less symmetrical attrition that would favor the more numerous Iranian forces.[125] But the gains were modest, even if Iran did penetrate into Iraq at a few points. During this period, Iraq resorted to elaborate fixed fortifications—massive earth berms, cleared "fire zones" in front of them, and extensive use of mortars, heavy artillery barrages, minefields, and flooding of some lowlands. The war hardened into a replica of World War I or of the phases of the American Civil War when the North fought an attrition campaign against Richmond. And while Iran made some advances, it did little more than return the lines of engagement to the prewar status quo ante.

These offensives involved efforts at breaking the Iraqi defensives all along the frontier battle line, particularly involving the first seven Operation Wal Fajr offensives, and a huge effort in February-March 1984 involving five hundred thousand troops in the area of the Haweizeh Marshes. One major success for Iran was the capture of the strategic Majnoon Island in February 1984.[126]

From 1984 to 1986, the war settled into a grinding, near-stationery war of attrition. Actually, for the first two years, Iran was mostly on the offensive, but conducted only a few really major offensives. Iraq, on the defensive, escalated its tanker war, trying to take away Iran's major source of income. But beginning in early 1986 and continuing on into 1987, Iran launched a series of what it hoped would be war-ending "final offensives." As in World War I, this involved a continuous shifting of pressures at different points on the forward line of battle, probing for a weak spot where a decisive, culminating offensive could be mounted.[127]

The Iraqis opened 1986 with a surprise attack, largely successful, on the Iranian positions on Majnoon Island. But the following weeks saw the massive Iranian Wal Fajr 8 and 9 assaults primarily against Basra, the Fao peninsula, and Majnoon Island in the south, but also involving a diversionary attack against Sulaimaneyeh, much further north in Kurdish territory. The Iranians took Fao, which was a major victory.[128] But in May 1986, the Iraqis took Mehran, which victory was reversed the next month by Iran's Operation Karbala 1.

For the remainder of 1986 and into 1987, Iran battered away with its Operation Karbala series, alternating emphasis between various sectors of the front, culminating in 1986 with Karbala 4, a major attack in the south at Umm Rasas. Despite a massive effort, Iran was repulsed with huge casualties.[129]

Early 1987 saw the Karbala 8 and 9 offensives by Iran, which in some respects marked the end of Iran's multiyear efforts to win the war with ever new, final offensives featuring straight-ahead meat grinder tactics reminiscent of World War I.[130] In those offensives, Iran, at the cost of huge casualties, both in absolute and relative terms, succeeded only in limited tactical victories such as that temporarily achieved at Fao. Iraq countered with massive firepower, the mobility of its reserves, some advantage in tactical airpower, and (as we now know is omitted in early war histories) U.S. satellite reconnaissance that could spotlight and inform Iraq of Teheran's preparations for new offensives. According to one source, Iran may have lost fifty thousand men between December 1986 and April 1987, making a total for the war up to that point of six hundred thousand to seven hundred thousand killed and twice that number wounded.[131]

Just as in the first World War, the interminable standstill on the front lines led to efforts at "indirect strategies"—note the failed British operation at Gallipoli and German air and naval attacks on England's east-coast cities. In the Iran-Iraq War, that involved missile and aircraft attacks on cities (the "war of the cities") and the "tanker war" in which both sides attacked tanker traffic coming into and going out of the Persian Gulf.[132] The battle of the cities was mostly to Iraq's advantage, owing to its more numerous and more accurate modified Scuds, and that became a factor in lowering Iranian morale toward the close of the war, albeit of limited military significance.

In the tanker wars, Iraq worked at hitting the critical Iranian Kharg Island facility and its tanker "shuttle" to larger tankers out in the Gulf, intermittently disrupting Iran's oil exports, which were critical to its foreign reserve situation and hence to its prosecution of the war.[133] Iran, meanwhile, attacked tankers going to and from Kuwait, leading to Western and Soviet "reflagging" operations and to a large Western (U.S., France, U.K., Italy) naval presence in the Gulf that increasingly came to confront and thwart Iranian efforts, contributing to Teheran's deepening diplomatic isolation. Iran's mining efforts in the Gulf and the Western response with convoys and counter-mine activities were critical.[134] For short periods, both sides attempted all-out oil warfare, limited by the absence of maritime patrol craft, better capability in combat aircraft, and associated C^3I systems.

By late 1987, and into early 1988, Iran went through still another shift in emphasis in its land offensive strategy, now concentrating more on the northern front. Indeed, even at the juncture of 1987–88, Iran still seemed to have the strategic initiative, and there were few hints of the virtual collapse that was to come in mid-1988. According to Cordesman and Wagner, three sets of factors shaped the final phase of the war and led to Iraq's victory: changes in Iraq's forces and its methods of warfare; a diminution of Iran's ability to prosecute the war due to the cumulative impact of its huge losses and its mismanagement of the war; and as noted, the Western naval presence in the Gulf and Iran's diplomatic isolation.[135]

While Iran moved forces to the north and concentrated on limited offensives in the mountainous areas where it did not face the kinds of dense barrier defenses that had stalled it in the southern region, improved Iraqi forces began to prepare for offensive operations. It built a bigger army (up to almost one million men), built more air bases and acquired more modern combat aircraft, created elite naval infantry units that could conduct aggressive infiltration and assault operations, and turned to the extensive battlefield use of chemical weapons. All of these preparations were eased by the downscaling of previously almost unremitting Iranian offensives that had been conducted up through mid-1987. Above all, Iraq improved its capabilities in combined arms operations, a capability sorely lacking in the failed offensives at the war's outset. Not only did it upgrade its road network, but it built up to fifteen hundred tank transporters so as to allow rapid movement of armored forces from one sector of the front to another: rapid movement along interior lines that Iran could not match even when on the defensive.[136]

Somewhat ironically both the land and air wars remained relatively quiet at the beginning of 1988, giving few hints of the impending dénouement. Mostly, Iran achieved a few limited successes in the mountainous northern areas, while Iraq's air force concentrated on dams, bridges, and refineries, as well as Kharg Island. Iraq revved up the "war of the cities" with newer variants of the Scud, featuring the terror-producing effects of loud bangs and broken windows. These attacks caused large numbers of civilians to flee Teheran by March 1988, a major contributing factor to the subsequent end of the war.[137]

Iran continued its limited offensives in the mountainous north, but at the cost of weakening its forces in the south. But Iraq began to take some of these areas back, now using chemical weapons on Iranian forces as well as on civilians in nearby Kurdish towns. But then in March and April 1988 came the beginning of the end.[138]

Using a major deception operation—feinting to move troops to the north—Iraq built up large stockpiles near Basra and then launched its biggest offensive since 1980 against weakened Iranian forces, resulting in the retaking of Fao.[139] This operation involved amphibious forces and also extensive use of nonpersistent nerve gas to smash through Iranian lines, taking advantage of dry conditions and good weather. The Iranians collapsed, leaving huge amounts of armor and artillery on the battlefield. In May 1988 there was another major Iraqi attack south of Basra and on to Salamcheh, carrying forward to the eastern side of the Shatt al Arab, also featuring panic-causing nerve gas and erasing all of Iran's gains from 1987.

By June 1988 Iraq had conducted successful offensives further north at Mehran and also in the southern sector near the Majnoon Islands and the Hawizah Marshes, again with the critical use of nerve gas. In July there were further offensives in the central front, in which Iraq advanced forty kilometers into Iran and took Dehloran and some fifteen hundred square miles of Iranian territory, providing movement not seen in this war since its beginning phase in 1980. The Iranian forces were collapsing and, in effect, sued for peace under U.N. auspices.[140] Iraq declined to pursue what might have been a much bigger victory, probably because of its own exhaustion and because of Iran's great strategic depth, which might have created a quagmire even for a victorious Iraqi army. Iraq had won a war of attrition and exhaustion, partly by the introduction of new weaponry (gas) but also because of its favorable diplomatic situation, which granted better access to weapons and crucial intelligence assistance from the U.S.

Noteworthy in this long war—on both sides—was the utter absence of opportunity or ability to conduct a war of movement or maneuver along exterior lines (the "war of cities" and tanker wars represented indirect strategies in a broader sense). Both sides repeatedly attempted penetration operations, perhaps hoping at some point to create the possibilities for envelopment, but neither ever came close in eight long years of war. Iraq's road system and the (paradoxical) fact of its lesser strategic depth and closeness of the front to its core areas allowed it the advantageous use of interior lines that abetted by nerve gas, eventually provided it a belated victory.

The Gulf War: 1990–1991

Generally speaking, the key operational aspects of the Gulf War are so well known and familiar to the general public that only a brief review is here proffered. Few if any wars have received as much media attention to the operational details. In outline form, the war was prosecuted by the coalition in three phases: the five-month buildup of forces and materiel amidst extensive diplomatic negotiations; a one-month serial assault to destroy Iraq's infrastructure (command and communications, roads, bridges, headquarters, air defenses, etc.) and to soften up its forces on the battlefront and to "prepare" the battlefield; and a rapid hundred-hour ground assault featuring a "Hail Mary," large-scale envelopment movement by rapidly moving armored forces. It was a classic application of Liddell Hart's "indirect approach" and of war of movement.[141]

The operational-strategic aspects of the war can actually be discussed at the two levels of air and ground warfare that in this war, at least, were virtually sequential, i.e., the air phase of the war was used by the U.S.-led coalition to prepare for the ground phase.

The basic philosophy and operational strategy used by the U.S. and its allies during the air phase of Desert Storm involved five identifiable and somewhat discrete objectives, each with a list of targets. These objectives stressed military over civilian targets to the extent the latter could be separated out and left alone.

The first objective was to isolate and incapacitate the Iraqi regime itself, requiring attacks on command and control installations, power production facilities, bridges, telecommunications nodes, etc. The second target set was Iraq's air defense system: radars, surface-to-air missile sites, airfields, etc. Success in that would then give the coalition air supremacy and largely blind an Iraq that lacked satellites and depended on aircraft for reconnaissance. A third target set involved nuclear, chemical, and biological research, production, and storage facilities, the extent of which, as it subsequently was learned, was vastly underestimated up to and beyond the end of the war. The fourth target set involved Iraq's military production infrastructure and power projection capabilities: Scud missile production, launcher and storage facilities, short-term oil production and storage facilities, naval forces and port facilities. Only lastly, as the ground phase of the war approached, the fifth target set—the Iraqi army and its mechanized equipment—was softened up and attrited for the impending ground assault.[142]

These air operations were, of course, hugely successful, even despite unusually inclement weather for that region at that time of year, resulting in postmortem analyses that claimed that the old airpower theorists (Douhet, Billy Mitchell et al.) had been vindicated in their predictions about the dominance of air power in modern warfare (World War II, Korea, and Vietnam had seemingly not borne those projections out). Still, there were continuous debates about the extent to which this was the case (or would or could be in future wars) along with even more contentious debates about the efficacy of the U.S. Air Force's "smart" weapons vis-à-vis more traditional "dumb" iron bombs and nonstealthy aircraft, on a cost-effective basis.[143] Noteworthy was the minimal resistance offered by the Iraqi air force, a portion of which, quixotically, flew to the Iran with which it had less than three years before concluded a brutal eight-year war. Further noteworthy was the extent to which the coalition was able to coordinate and sequence aerial attacks involving huge numbers of aircraft and some thirty five thousand total combat sorties mounted from bases in Saudi Arabia, Turkey, the U.K., Louisiana, and aboard several aircraft carriers.[144] That involved the integrated and precise use of "tanker tracks" in Saudi Arabia, i.e., the marshaling and coordinating of strike aircraft overhead of Saudi Arabia en route to bombing missions.[145]

The operational side of the ground offensive has, as noted, received so much attention from the media and popular press as to be well imprinted in the minds of almost everyone. Basic to the coalition's operational strategy was the so-called "left look" or "Hail Mary" strategy (the latter reflective of American football jargon and hence not necessarily comprehensible elsewhere) that was often compared with the Carthaginian Hannibal's Cannae versus Rome (successful) or the younger Moltke's operationalization of the Schlieffen Plan (ultimately unsuccessful) as a classic example of an envelopment operation.

The "Hail Mary" operation was thus described in capsule form in the Pentagon's own posthoc study:

> The plan envisioned a supporting attack along the Kuwait-Saudi Arabian border by the I Marine Expeditionary Force (IMEF) and Arab Coalition Forces to hold most forward Iraqi divisions in place. Simultaneously, two Army Corps, augmented with French and UK divisions—more than 200,000 soldiers—would sweep west of the Iraqi defenses, strike deep into Iraq, cut Iraqi lines of communication and destroy Republican Guards forces in the KTO (Kuwait Theater of Operations).[146]

The ground attack followed thirty-eight days of aerial bombardment, the latter stages of which were largely devoted to preparing the battlefield for the ground forces as well as to completing the process of blinding Iraqi forces. The ground operation was completed in a hundred hours.

Before the ground operation, coalition forces had clandestinely repositioned from defense sectors in eastern Saudi Arabia to forward assembly areas farther west (the Soviets apparently did not provide Iraq with what could have been the necessary intelligence on this). The coalition moved the equivalent of seventeen divisions laterally hundreds of miles over a very limited road network, a move that continued twenty-four hours a day for two weeks under cover of the air campaign. Thousands of tons of supplies—water, food, fuel, ammunition, spare parts—had to be moved, undetected by the Iraqis.

The coalition also made use of related deception operations involving aggressive feints, demonstrations, and artillery raids in the direction of the Iraqi defenses nearest the Wadi Al-Batin, and combined arms raids, psychological operations (PSYOP) loudspeaker broadcasts, deceptive communications, dummy positions, etc. in the Al Wafrah area. These operations were complemented by the deception effort carried out by amphibious forces off Kuwait's coast, intended to create the expectation of an amphibious landing by the U.S. Marines. That further involved a well-publicized amphibious rehearsal in Oman and a raid on a small island off the Kuwait coast. These deception operations were critical to achieving both tactical and operational surprise and, ultimately, the ground offensive's success.[147]

Using the straight-ahead attack by the U.S. Marines and allied Arab forces directly north into Kuwait and to Kuwait City as a kind of anvil, the coalition's mechanized forces conducted a multiple-layered envelopment, stretching as far westward as As-Samawah (which the critical Basra-Baghdad highway straddled) and the crucial inner area north and west of Kuwait where the elite elements of Iraq's armored forces were encountered and destroyed, not without some bitter fighting albeit the lopsided outcome. The Pentagon's study estimated that in the process, 3847 tanks, 1450 armored personnel carriers, and 2917 artillery pieces were captured or destroyed in this operation.[148] The blinded and (by aerial attacks) demoralized Iraqi forces were unable to conduct an effective defense on the basis of interior lines and long-constructed fortifications, nor were they able to conduct an effective mobile defensive withdrawal that might at least have succeeded in what Iraq had thought was its primary deterrent to attack, namely, the imposing of high casualty rates.

Regarding the operational principles deemed relevant to the successful prosecution of this war, the Pentagon's own posthoc study lists four:

1. Initiative—to set or change the terms of battle by offensive action;
2. Agility—the ability of friendly forces to act mentally and physically faster than the enemy;
3. Depth—the extension of operations in space, time, and resources; and
4. Synchronization—the arrangement of battlefield activities in time, space, and purpose to produce maximum relative combat power at the decisive point.[149]

Ethiopia vs. Eritrea-2000

Though the reports rendered by press coverage were sparse concerning the operational details, somewhat of a picture emerges regarding the savage combat between Ethiopia and Eritrea in three phases between 1998 and 2000, culminating in the former's victory just past the millennium in the spring of 2000.

This war, fought along a central front south of the Eritrean capital of Asmara, and in the southwest corner of Eritrea (the Badame region), centered on a contest for the town of Zalambessa, in a semimountainous area.[150] Mostly, this involved a straight-ahead meat grinder offensive by the Ethiopians against fixed fortifications, involving some use of armor and tactical airpower (ex-Soviet MIG-29s), and taking advantage of a favorable ground-force ratio of about 350,000 versus 250,000 troops. The war culminated with the Ethiopians' capture of the strategic towns of Zalambessa and Omhajer. The Ethiopian operational strategy was somewhat reminiscent of Grant before Richmond, and both sides in World War I and the Iran-Iraq War. Like Iraq in 1988, Ethiopia did not press its victory much beyond the contested borders.

The Tactical Level of Modern Third World Conventional Warfare

To a striking degree, journalistic coverage and the more academic analyses of developing-world warfare tend to ignore tactics on the micro end. Specifically, that refers to formations, weapons, and the relative mix of different types of combat arms such as armor, artillery, and infantry. A good picture of what goes on at this level can best be derived from the (usually somewhat personal or autobiographical) accounts of participants at relatively low levels of command or by journalists accompanying forces. But there are only a few good examples of the latter genre; for instance, Nicholas Vaux's description of the British Marines' combat march across East Falkland Island to the final assault on Fort Stanley, or Avigdor Kahalani's detailed rendition of the tactics—and sight and sounds—of Israeli versus Syrian armored combat on the Golan Heights in 1973. Some journalistic work on the Gulf War was equally helpful. But generally speaking, tactics are ignored by comparison with the politics, grand strategies, and operational aspects of modern war, and military censorship may be only one reason.

This has not always been the case. Some comprehensive coverages of the entire panorama of military history (Marathon to the Mitla Pass), such as those by Lynn Montross or J. F. C. Fuller, can provide an adequate portrayal of the endless skein of development, the ebbs and flows of military tactics.[151] It is a vast subject, not easily reduced to generalizations or principles. But there is some wisdom that can be extracted, specifically for the purpose of shedding light on tactics in the modern world.

The tactical level here refers to small-unit operations or the "tactical systems" of substantial armies, i.e., how they fight. More specifically, that refers to formations or positioning (both on offense and defense, to the extent this distinction is not altogether muddied in practice); the use of various types of weapons and mounts for weapons, the introduction of new weapons systems by way of adaptation or to create surprise, and the mix of different types of combat forces, either within land armies (infantry, cavalry, etc.) or involving a distribution between, let us say, ground and naval forces.

In ancient times, most combat took the form of large set-piece battles, or a series of such battles culminating in a campaign or war. For the most part, this involved large armies (belonging to a nation or political entity such as an empire) endlessly marching, countermarching, or maneuvering up to a decisive contest. Usually there were no extended lines or comprehensively defended borders that defined the geographical relationship between rival forces. Most or many such set-piece battles were fought out on open terrain, with one or another combatant succeeding in a choice of the place of battle. But otherwise, there were also numerous sieges of cities and walled fortresses, so that the tactics of siege warfare acquired the status of a second major type of tactical operation, here with a much sharper distinction between offense and defense.

In simplifying what clearly is a highly complicated subject, it may be said that several factors—in complex interrelationships to each other—have served to determine tactical systems throughout history. These are geography and weather, the state of weapons technology, demographic factors (who outnumbers whom, or to what extent an individual state anticipates fighting either with or without a numerical advantage), and cultural factors, i.e., the extent to which tactical systems may be explained as expressions of cultural forms or attributes.

Geography clearly is critical, though, oddly, Montross claims that Greek tactical systems rarely allowed for taking advantage of rivers or mountains to protect a flank.[152] Open plains or deserts clearly lend themselves to cavalry (in ancient times) or armor (at present); while heavily forested terrain or mountains or both are more likely to correlate with an emphasis on infantry.

To some extent, tactical systems may—in a never-ending and cumulative sense—vary according to technological developments, though this may be more the case at present in an era of constant and rapid technological development (spurred by determined R&D programs everywhere) than in earlier periods, which saw very slow technological development spread over centuries (and, horizontally, relatively slow diffusion of weapons innovations). This factor can rarely be separated out from that of geography. Over the course of centuries, certain watersheds can be discerned where the development of new technologies has greatly and permanently altered tactical forms. Among others, Montross points to such determining watersheds as the development of siege technology such as catapults and rams by armies near the end of the reign of Alexander the Great; the development of stirrups for cavalry during the Dark Ages around the time of Charlemagne's Frankish Empire; the English development of the longbow against armored horsemen; Prussian and French development of effective mobile artillery in the eighteenth century, and, of course, the advent of the tank during World War I.[153]

Dramatic new technological developments in weaponry always require wholesale new developments in tactics and often lead to dramatic shifts in balances of military power as prior advantages are eliminated or reduced.

Numerous writers have chosen to discuss the relationship between weapons and tactics in terms of altering advantages between the offense and defense. Thus developments in artillery, automatic weapons, and barbed wire are claimed to have shifted the advantage to the defensive side at the outset of World War I, while by the outset of World War II, developments in armor and tactical air-power are said to have reclaimed the advantage for the offense, allowing for the German blitzkrieg tactics of the early 1940s.[154] A similar shift in reverse is said to have been augured by the advent of precision-guided antitank and antiaircraft weapons introduced by Syria and Egypt at the outset of the 1973 war.[155] Such examples could be multiplied throughout history, with the caveat that the relationship between offense and defense is often blurred—offensives often emerge from counterattacks.

Cultural factors have long been strong determinants of tactical systems. Breaking that down, one could point to such factors as the relative extent of democracy or social equality (or slavery) in given situations; the impact of dominant economic activities, be they agriculture, commerce, fishing, and propensities to warlike behavior, as traditional aspects of some cultures. Here, one could use as examples the Roman legion system as an expression of Roman culture, the horseback/archer tactics of the Scythians, Parthians, and Byzantines, the cavalry hordes of the Mongols. Montross refers to a "national frame of mind" which, for the Romans, emphasized "pride in bold and straightforward fighting," the Roman scorn for ruse and the stratagem and indirect approach.[156] Further for the Romans, he says, "subterfuge has always been held a token of weakness—an attitude which made the Roman mentalities peculiarly vulnerable to Hannibalic guile."[157] This is too big a subject to review here, but one point appears to stand out in relation to modern warfare: as we move toward the modern period, there appears less scope for cultural idiosyncracy or for specific tactical systems associated with a nation or empire.

The Greek hoplites, the Macedonian phalanxes, the Roman legions with their precisely enumerated formations and maniples, the Carthaginian elephant cavalry, the Mongol hordes, the medieval Swiss pikemen formations—all are associated with one specific culture or political entity, even if they may have been imitated by degree by friend or foe.

Nowadays it is relatively harder (but not always impossible) to associate tactical systems with one nation or culture. Stated another way, there is a tendency toward global convergence of tactical forms, again, as modified by technology and levels of advancement. No doubt this is largely a function of global communications and widespread intelligence capabilities, and the rapid and widespread dissemination of information and techniques. This is furthered by the facts of most nations' dependence on arms acquisitions from a few available sources, which in turn results in most nations being the recipients of military training and advice from a few sources. Numerous nations have U.S., Soviet, or French arms and training, so it is not surprising that there is a distinct lack of diversity in tactical systems. Technological uniformity, modified by the relative abilities of nations to absorb technology, results in extreme tactical uniformity.

Demography too plays a role in determining tactical systems associated with given nations. According to Montross, the ancient Greeks, small in population, had to rely upon phalanxes often with a depth of eight ranks, while the more numerous Egyptians "found it necessary to form masses of a hundred ranks and a hundred files."[158] For the Greeks, "sheer lack of population made it needful for them to develop superior skill and courage as compared to the bulky onslaughts of the East."[159] Generally speaking, Montross shows how in numerous historical situations, outnumbered nations—or those highly sensitive to casualties because of sparse populations—have had to rely on preemptive shock tactics so as to establish the "moral high ground," and to avoid attrition warfare, which naturally favors the more numerous side. Then and now, this has had important implications for tactics.

Montross stresses the relationship between morale, moral advantage, the momentum of battle, and tactics, noting that in innumerable historical battle circumstances, tactical advantage leads to rout, massacre, and lopsided victories, as one side perceives the contest lost and loses heart.[160]

But in relation to the present, most of all, military history divulges the constant importance, for analysis of tactical systems, of the endlessly changing mixes of forces, of allocations between combat arms, in response to ever-changing circumstances. Nowadays, as applied to land forces, we think of armor, artillery, and infantry, or also the trade-off between tactical airpower and land-based artillery and missile interdiction systems. That problem has changed surprisingly little since antiquity.

Keegan, in his history of warfare, describes in detail the tactics of the Assyrian army's charioteering force under Sennacherib, as well as the siege tactics involving battering rams, infantry attacks, mines, breaches, and siege engines.[161] Later, the wars between the Egyptians and Hittites are said to have involved what we now call combined arms tactics involving chariots and infantry.[162] The so-called "chariot system" of this period is said to have involved not only chariots, but the composite bow, the horse, and all its trappings.[163] Later, the Persian army at the time of Darius IIII was centered on a chariot nucleus, but included heavy cavalry forces and large numbers of Greek mercenary infantry.[164]

Montross, Keegan, and others portray the Greek reliance on shock infantry (spear and sword), the Macedonian emphasis on both heavy and light cavalry and siege warfare with ballista and catapults, the Roman legions' stress on infantry shock tactics as well as archers, chariots, and javelin men, the Carthaginians' mixed use of cavalry and infantry, the Byzantine stress on masses of horse archers, and the "tactical system" of the formidable Mongol hordes under Genghis Khan and his successors who roamed from China to Central Europe. Montross describes the Mongol tactical system as follows:

The touman of 10,000 may be considered a Mongol division, with the decimal system prevailing all the way down to the unit of ten horsemen. The bow, scimitar and lance were the principal weapons, though front-line troops carried lances equipped with a hook for dragging an adversary out of his saddle. Two sorts of bows were used: a light one for rapid-fire use on horseback, and a more powerful siege weapon reinforced with horn or steel. Likewise, the three different "calibres" of arrows served various tactical purposes.

Each trooper has his own tools, rations, and camp kettle, his extra clothing being packed in a watertight bag of sewn skins which could be inflated for crossing rivers. The armor consisted of tanned hide covered with overlapping plates. Both men and horses in the first two ranks were completely armored for shock attack, while the three rear ranks wore lighter equipment for missile and skirmishing tactics.

The Mongol tactical system was rigid in conception, had been designed to foresee any problem which might arise in the field. The officer had only to give the indicated command at the proper moment, his thinking having been done in advance for him by military scientists.

The entire system was built up around the natural fighting qualities of the individual warrior of the steppes. His virtues, it will be recalled, were mobility and hardihood; his vices, indiscipline and skulking.[165]

The Arab armies during their period of primacy made use both of camels and horses. Camels were available in large numbers and though high in endurance were relatively slow and awkward. Strategically, they allowed for the traversing of very difficult terrain and unexpected arrival on the battlefield, but were of little use at close quarters. Arab tactics then consisted of making an approach on camelback, and then transferring to horses for actual battle, i.e., camels were used mostly for logistics. Arab armies of this period also fought dismounted, armed with composite bows, utilizing defense terrain features.[166]

But in the Middle Ages, the English longbow reversed the thousand-year-long dominance of cavalry, just as gunpowder and the rise of mass armies would overwhelm the tradition of fortified castle strongholds.[167] Subsequent centuries would see other reversals, based on technological changes, but the problem of balancing mixes of forces between shock arms, mobility, missilery, and artillery would remain, with endless variations.

One good example (and it relates to the Iran-Iraq War) was that of the competitive efforts of Germany and its Western foes (Britain, France, U.S.) to develop tactics that might succeed in breaking the long stalemate of the trenches in France, over some four years worth of World War I. Endless massed infantry assaults, usually proceeded by massive artillery bombardments, had succeeded on both sides only in causing enormous casualties even for gains of only hundreds of yards. Defensive tactics were likewise uniform and constant, also causing enormous casualties on the defensive side in efforts to hold firm and lose no ground.[168]

Later in the war, the Germans produced altered offensive tactics, described as follows by Sheffield.

The willingness of the German army to adapt and change made it the most formidable fighting machine on the Western Front. In contrast to the Allies, it had encouraged the cultivation of a high level of initiative among junior commanders, precisely the qualities needed for effective application of "infiltration" tactics. Although Laffargue's ideas were not the only influence on German thinking, they did play an important role in the development of the successful infantry tactics of 1917–18. The infantry strength of each division was reduced, but its firepower was considerably augmented to include 50 mortars and 350 heavy machine guns. (The comparable British figures were 36 and 64.) "Storm" battalions were organized around assault teams armed with light machine guns, mortars, flame-throwers and light artillery pieces. These units had a dual purpose: of providing the cutting edge of infantry attacks (and counterattacking in defense positions) and of training other units in their techniques. As they demonstrated at Riga, Caporetto and Cambrai in 1917, and against the British Fifth Army on the Somme in March 1918, the Germans produced an infantry tactic that, although far from infallible, did on occasion succeed in combination with artillery in breaking the deadlock of trench warfare.

The result was the adoption of a policy of "elastic" defence in depth. In place of linear defences, a thinly held outpost zone of scattered defences, 500–1000 metres deep, would serve to canalize an attacking force, who would first have to pass through the German barrage. Then they would run into the "battle zone," which would be 2 km or more in depth. This consisted of a series of mutually supporting strongpoints capable of all-around defence, which were intended to continue to resist even if surrounded. If an attacker succeeded in fighting through this zone, he would face a further line of machine gun pits in front of the field artillery. The essence of this defence was the counterattack. Squads dedicated to this role were stationed in the defensive zones, and units of storm troops were positioned in the rear to sweep the enemy back. In the winter of 1916–17, the Germans constructed the Hindenburg Line on these principles, and flexible defence was also adopted by the French and British, although the Allies tended to station large numbers of troops in the forward zone, with unfortunate results. However, by 1918 the principle that defences should be held in depth was firmly established. It was a lesson that would have to be painfully relearnt, on a much larger scale, in 1939–45.[169]

Tactical Systems in Contemporary Third World Combat

As earlier indicated, published battle reports provide only some scant pictures of contemporary tactical systems, at least in the detail that would allow for distinguishing between them. And again, many are merely derived from big-power practices, sometimes to the detriment of the imitators, in inappropriate circumstances. But still, there are some salient examples of emphases in one direction or another, driven variously by the factors of geography, culture, demographic balances, and capability for technological absorption. Some illustrations may then be provided regarding the following (interrelated) factors: formations, varying mixes within a combined arms scheme, propensities to offensive and defensive tactics, and use of unusual or innovative weapons systems and/or tactics. That may still fall short of being able to define and illustrate a tactical "system" or "culture" for many or most of the recent Third World combatants. But it may allow us to examine some situations where failures have resulted from poor tactical systems or inappropriate mixes of combat arms types.

Tactics: Arab-Israeli Wars

Again, much of what now bears analysis involves nuance or emphasis, particularly as it involves the preferred mix of armor, infantry, and artillery. In 1967, the Israelis, after taking control of the air on the first day of the war, were able—actually in a near-repeat of the Sinai campaign of 1956—to sustain an offensive all the way across Sinai with almost sole use of armored shock tactics backed by tactical airpower. There was the constant resort to envelopment, the cutting off of Egyptian combat units from rear logistics sources, and racing to seize key road junctions and mountain passes. Retrospective histories dredged out the (ironic) memory of German General Heinz Guderian, and the 1967 war was called the "last battle of World War II." That was true, at least, on the Sinai front. Israel's uphill capture of the Golan Heights required a more normal mix of armor and infantry, the former paced by armored bulldozers to clear paths for tanks attacking uphill.[170]

After this contest, a lot of criticism was directed against Arab tactics against the Israeli blitzkrieg. To some extent the blame was laid at the feet of Arab commanders being too willing to imitate standard Soviet tactics, which may have been battle-proven in other contexts, in World War II. The Egyptian army was characterized as having over-relied on fixed fortifications, emphasizing linear infantry defense, massed artillery, and tanks used defensively fighting from fixed points, buried up to their turrets.[171] In a large theater such as Sinai, and against a foe good at devolving responsibility to tank company and platoon commanders (also good at finding tank routes across the desert dunes), the static Egyptian defenses proved hopelessly deficient. (Ironically, years later, similar Iraqi tactics against Iran were to prove successful, but then subsequently unsuccessful against U.S. and allied armored forces in the Gulf War.)

In 1973 the Israelis' overreliance on armor came a cropper at the outset of the Sinai battle with Egypt. Israel lost large numbers of tanks in trying to counterattack against infantry armed with antitank missiles—Saggers and RPGs. Afterwards, the lesson was drawn that greater attention to artillery was required to suppress infantry (and to keep their heads down), and likewise that larger numbers of infantry, mounted in armored personnel carriers (APCs) or armored fighting vehicles (AFVs), were required to accompany armored forces facing infantry armed with modern antitank missiles.[172]

Israel succeeded, as the 1973 Sinai war progressed, in reestablishing the dominance of its armored shock tactics and creating its favored war of maneuver, in part because its air force learned to deal with the Egyptian SAMs and was again able to clear the way for armored forces.

There is another irony here. Israel had to fight on the defensive, greatly outnumbered, for several days against invading Syria on the Golan Heights. Kahalani's description of that defense shows that this was done mostly by armored forces—with minimum use either of infantry, artillery, or supporting air power, the latter having been nullified by Syrian SAMs—operating both in fixed and mobile modes. At the outset, however, the Israeli tank forces made extensive use of preprepared, sheltered firing ramps with intersecting fields of fire.[173]

Ironically, in reporting on Israeli tank tactics in 1973 on the Golan, Kahalani reports on some serious technical deficiencies for Israel, which altered its normal preference for night-fighting. The Israelis were chronically short of illuminating shells (star shells launched by artillery) and did not have as effective infrared sighting systems as those possessed by Syria's Soviet-supplied tanks.[174]

In 1982, "lessons learned" reports on Israeli ground tactics during the Lebanon war also remarked on the overreliance upon armor and the deficient utilization of infantry screens and of artillery to suppress Syrian infantry. Despite the overall success of the campaign, Israeli armored forces were subject to numerous ambushes in mountainous Lebanese defiles, by infantry carrying handheld antitank weapons. Additionally, the Syrians had some success with helicopters hitting tanks with French-supplied MILAN missiles. Hence, according to chronicler Richard Gabriel:

> These conditions were a great disadvantage for the Israeli Defense Force. As we have noted, the IDF is configured in heavy-armored formations designed to make rapid advances supported by mobile infantry. But here the IDF was consistently short of infantry. Moreover, it had no strategy or experience in using infantry as a screen to cover an armored advance. The Syrians broke up their armored units into smaller units of two and three tanks, spreading them in defensive positions supported by infantry commando groups armed with antitank guns, rocket-propelled grenades, and antitank missiles. As the Israeli forces worked their way up narrow roads, they were met by the Syrians in ambush and heavy casualties were inflicted, and then the Syrians would withdraw to the next position or to the next bend in the road and repeat the process. In this way, the Israeli advance was considerably slowed down in the east and center zones.[175]

Israel's chronic shortage of infantry, in conjunction with the difficult terrain in Lebanon, was cause for extensive commentary. Hence, according to Gabriel:

> The tactical plan and the Israeli deployment of forces seemed generally sound. On closer analysis, however, it seems to have failed to take sufficient account of the terrain. The advances were much slower than expected, and, especially in the east, were far more costly in men and equipment than anticipated. The IDF had no experience in mountain warfare, and the tactics they brought to bear on this war—rapid advance, heavy-armor for-

mations, and mounted infantry—were more suitable for open terrain and desert warfare. Equally important was the fact that the IDF was chronically short of infantry. Because of the value the Israelis place on the life of each soldier, the IDF has never developed the use of infantry screens as protection for armor. A more effective way of advancing on mountain roads would have been to pattern their tactics after the mountain campaigns fought by the American and British forces in Italy. In these campaigns, infantry was deployed in front of the tanks. Deployed in this manner, infantrymen are less susceptible to being killed by tank fire and force the enemy to disclose its ambush position. If the enemy chose not to engage, then the infantry could engage tank units, to the tanks' great disadvantage. In addition, the commando units which the Syrians deployed with the tanks could have been brought under infantry attack without risking Israeli tanks. IDF tactics in Lebanon clearly reflected its past experience. The IDF was not adequately prepared to fight a mountain campaign and to deal with the kind of resistance that it met.[176]

The mountain warfare in Lebanon was not the only milieu in which Israel's traditional near-total reliance on the tank (a function itself of shortages of personnel and of sensitivity to casualties) was at issue. Its operations along the Mediterranean coast, leapfrogging and bypassing armed PLO camps, left it vulnerable to antitank and sniper attacks from the orange groves that line the coast and that channel advances along the coast road only a few miles from mountainous inclines. And once to Beirut, Israel relied heavily on artillery bombardments to reduce the Lebanese capital, reluctant to risk large casualties which were expected to result from house-to-house urban fighting for which the meager Israeli infantry forces were not well trained.

But weapons have historically driven tactics, and the changes between 1973 and 1982 were no exception. Israel's tanks were, by 1982, much better protected by their active and passive add-on laminated armor. Then, its U.S.-supplied tanks had been given better internal fire-fighting systems, lessening the mortality rates for the crews of stricken tanks, while its own indigenously produced Merkava tanks were designed to trade off mobility for crew protection through the location of their engines.[177]

But for Israel, the main tactical innovations after 1973—excepting tank armor and design—appear to have been in connection with reviving the power of its air force, which had been badly hampered in 1973 by the advent of newer air defense systems (SA-6, SA-3, SA-7, and also the Zilka ZSU) in Egypt and Syria. In 1982, the Israeli air force quickly knocked out the bulk of the Syrian SAM batteries, utilizing decoy drones (Scout and Mastif RPVs), E2C Hawkeye airborne warning and control systems (AWACs) and Boeing 707 ECM aircraft, antiradiation missiles, and perhaps surface-to-surface missiles. Thus according to Gabriel:

> The Bekaa missile raid was a textbook example of modern-day electronic warfare. The Israelis used remote-piloted vehicles (RPV) to a considerable

degree. RPVs are pilotless drone aircraft which can be used in various ways. The Israelis had both Mastif and the Scout RPVs designed and built in Israel. The RPVs were first flown over the battlefield, emitting dummy signals designed to confuse the missile-tracking radar into thinking real aircraft were attacking. That set the Syrians to tracking the RPVs. The Mastifs which were being tracked then relayed the tracking signals to another Scout RPV out of range of the missiles. The Scout picked up the signals and relayed them to E2C Hawkeye AWACS [Airborne Warning and Control System] aircraft orbiting off the coast. The Israelis used the RPVs to "excite" the electronic battlefield, and the data gathered were analyzed by the E2C Hawkeye AWACS aircraft and also by Boeing 707 ECM aircraft.

The Israelis then overflew the area, using Elta and other jamming radars to blind the missile-tracking radars. Data gathered from these operations were analyzed and relayed to air-force and ground artillery units. The ground artillery units which had been moved into position around Hasbaiya and Koukaba began to shell the missile batteries and radar locations that were in gun range to destroy them or to force them to move. At the same time, F-4 fighter-bombers and F-16s overflew the area, dropping flares and chaff to confuse and disorient the missile-tracking radars further. Behind the chaff and flares came the attacking aircraft homing in on the radar-tracking vans. Using laser target designators (smart bombs), they fired antiradiation missiles, both Israeli-made and U.S.-made Shrike missiles, and destroyed seventeen of the nineteen SAM missile batteries. SAM-8 and -9 mobile versions were better camouflaged and were able to move. But while they were being moved, they were unable to fire and were easily destroyed by conventional bombs dropped by F-16s on normal bombing runs. At least one SAM-8 was destroyed by an RPV configured with an ammunition payload.[178]

In addition, its air tactical superiority, now abetted by advanced AWACS-type aircraft, allowed for a large ratio of combat kills vis-à-vis the Syrian aircraft (about 90:1), most of which were knocked off while trying to gain altitude to enter the fray. The result was the resumption of Israel's previously held domination of the skies, which could then be utilized for a huge advantage in fighting on the ground.

Tactics: China vs. Vietnam

By contrast to the Arab-Israeli fighting, the war between China and Vietnam in 1979 was much more one dominated by infantry and saw much less use of tanks and of tactical airpower. This may have represented a lesser degree of technological sophistication on both sides, a correlate of a lower per capita GNP. But there is an obvious additional reason, namely, that both China and Vietnam, by dint of their populations, are less sensitive to casualties and far more willing to risk high casualties in massive, sustained infantry assaults. *New York Times* reportage on this war claimed that Chinese troops were accustomed to marching long distances and moving into battle without truck transport.[179] The Chinese army was said to have been weak in logistics and supply; hence, it was said to move ahead offensively in small bursts.[180] There were some references to combined arms offensives utilizing artillery and tanks,[181] but the following captures the essence of Chinese tactics:

> The war has been the infantry's fight. The principal support for the Chinese soldier has come not from tanks or aircraft, but from artillery, chiefly 122mm and 130mm guns. Chinese tactics have been elemental; short, fierce attacks for limited objectives, consolidation and careful preparation for the next advance.[182]

Another report states that Chinese tactics consisted of headlong rushes, preceded by heavy artillery barrages.[183] At a still more micro level, another report stated that "theirs is an infantry army, and tactics are tailored to take advantage of the superiority in numbers that they expect against an enemy."[184] Further, "the emphasis in training" is to get as close as possible to the enemy; "to embrace the enemy" as Chinese regimental commanders say.[185]

Still more reports had the Chinese eschewing the human-wave tactics they had favored in Korea and that later characterized Iranian assaults against Iraq.[186] Infiltration by small units, large-scale rushes, and extensive use of night fighting (favored both by China and Vietnam) were reported on. Chinese troops were said to have had fewer automatic weapons than the norm for a modern army, though one report states that "the decisive weapon so far has been the machine gun and its offspring, the automatic rifle."[187]

Neither China nor Vietnam made much use of tactical airpower. American officials at the time said that for the Vietnam side the planes were too valuable to be risked.[188] All in all, and by contrast to Arab–Israeli contests, it was an infantry-intensive war. And there were few if any "innovations" that would become entries in histories of tactical warfare.

Tactics: India vs. Pakistan

The contrast between the victorious Israeli and Chinese tactical systems would appear, on the surface, to be a function of geography (cover, mostly) and population (sensitivity to casualties). But such easy generalizations may be belied by reports on the Indian tactical system as they emerged from fighting both in East Bengal and on India's border with West Pakistan in 1971, just shortly before the 1973 Arab-Israeli war which saw use of many of the same weapons systems on both sides.

Along with Israel, India alone among the developing nations—with its vaunted officers corps rooted in the British tradition and its ethnic-based regimental system—appears to have been capable of conducting a sustained offensive over a broad front and with penetration in depth, making use of all of the relevant modern ground and air systems. In East Bengal, with a huge numerical advantage over an overmatched Pakistani force stretched thinly along a 1,350–mile border, there was felicitous combined use of tactical air power, mechanized formations, and artillery. Extensive artillery barrages were used at the outset of the fighting. Mechanized forces made rapid headway against dug-in Pakistani forces, utilizing country lanes to circumvent Pakistani bunkers astride main roads. India's air force destroyed most of Pakistan's aircraft either on the ground or in the air, allowing it then to cause havoc with fleeing Pakistani forces, particularly when the latter were forced to ford rivers. Indian forces avoided head-on direct battles, constantly bypassing Pakistani strongholds, forcing the latter to abandon fortified positions and to draw ever further back toward Dacca, harassed all the while by Mukti Bahini guerillas blowing up bridges to slow down the Indian advances. Most of all, in terrain not particularly suited for "armored pace"—it is described as soft and marshy, a lacework of shifting rivers and waterways—the Indian army managed rapid movement across waterways, utilizing a mix of ferries, helicopters, amphibious vehicles, and hastily erected prefabricated bridges. India clearly is strong in its engineering units.

Both India and Pakistan launched mixed armored-infantry assaults on the western front, in far more open and rugged terrain in the north, desert terrain in the south.[189] Pakistan's attack at Chhamb, for instance, where it was repulsed, was conducted by some forty-eight hundred men backed by forty-five Chinese T-59 tanks; a larger force was used in a nearby assault on Munawar Tait.[190] In the Rajasthan Desert, Pakistan attacked primarily with armored forces.[191] Both sides made extensive use of artillery and tactical airpower, with India having the advantage in the latter after knocking out much of the Pakistani Air Force in the air and on the ground. In more open but mountainous terrain, control of artillery observation points was important, analogous somewhat to Israeli-Syrian fighting on the Golan Heights.

India's utilization of naval and (for other purposes) air forces is also worth noting. Its navy blockaded and mined Pakistani ports in East Bengal, preventing either reinforcements for or withdrawal of Pakistan's trapped army.[192] Its navy was used to bombard the Chittagong and Karachi areas, while the Indian Air Force caused great destruction, particularly around Karachi, of railroad yards, oil storage facilities, and port facilities.[193] The war ended before these attrition tactics could count in military terms, but were presumably intended as a deterrent to Pakistani resumption of hostilities, again similar to Israeli actions against Syria. Technologically and tactically, it was a war fought nearly on the same level as the succeeding—two years later—Arab-Israeli war.

Tactics: Ethiopia vs. Somalia

The war between Ethiopia and Somalia in 1977–78, fought in two distinct phases—a Somali offensive phase in 1977 and an Ethiopian offensive phase in 1978—saw considerable use of modern weaponry, involving armor, artillery, and tactical air power. After Somali irregulars had cleared most of the Ogaden region of Ethiopian forces—quick attacks on isolated garrisons comprising a total of eight thousand troops, widely spread out, which abandoned equipment and fled—the bulk of the war was fought along a road leading up to and beyond Jijiga and over the Kara Marda Pass toward Harar and Dire Dawa.

On the offensive, Somali forces making limited use of armor and artillery, more use of bazookas, lured Ethiopian forces out of mountain fortifications onto the plains, and then surrounded them.[194] After a two-week siege, Ethiopian forces broke and ran in the face of an all-out offensive on 26 August 1977, abandoning some tanks, APCs, and artillery pieces.[195] Both sides made limited use of strafing runs by aircraft (Ethiopia using U.S.-supplied F-5s), and extensive use of mortars in mountainous terrain.[196]

In this fighting both sides employed about thirty thousand troops. After its defeat at Jijiga, Ethiopia's forces were able to regroup around Harar and withstand a siege along with extensive artillery shelling from nearby mountainsides.[197]

The next winter saw an Ethiopian counteroffensive, making extensive use of Cuban surrogate forces and Soviet officers. Cuban pilots flying MIG-21s and 23s made tactical airpower a factor in terrain with little cover, albeit with rugged ravines, etc. Ethiopian tanks and artillery now outgunned the retreating Somalis, who fell back step-by-step utilizing fortified mountain bunkers.[198]

Somali forces, however, first appeared able to hold a defensive line in rugged terrain along ridges and ravines some six miles north of the strategic Babile Gap, which was unsuitable for tanks. The Somali front was described as not an unbroken line that advances or recedes, but rather an ill-defined and porous alignment of isolated troops spread across the mountainous terrain.[199] But then, Soviet- and Cuban-led Ethiopian forces sprang a tactical surprise in the form of helicopters carrying some seventy tanks over the mountains into the Somali rear area. This was accompanied by extensive use of tactical airpower, some forty to sixty bombing runs a day.[200] This vertical envelopment tactic caused a collapse of the Somali defense, and a rout ensued with Somali forces withdrawing from their salient within Ethiopian borders.

Tactics: Iran vs. Iraq

The long and deadly Iran-Iraq War divulged a large number of "lessons," or at least, areas suitable for analysis and discussion on a tactical level. Most importantly, according to Cordesman and Wagner, and others, that war provided a good illustration of the strengths and limitations of developing-world armies (mostly limitations) and not the relative effectiveness of their weapons.[201] Lack of organization and training for modern war is said to have resulted in there being little impact of force ratios on the outcomes of battles.

There is consensus that the main lesson of the war—on the operational and tactical levels—was that neither side could consistently carry out combined arms operations, though Iraq improved sufficiently in this respect by 1987–88, so as to provide for a limited overall victory. But generally, neither side effectively blended armor, infantry, artillery, and helicopters, except when fighting from static defenses or in the initial assault phase of an offensive.[202]

At the war's outset, both sides squandered much of their large inventories of tanks and other armored vehicles, using them either without proper support from infantry and artillery in offensive operations, or inflexibly in static defense roles and as direct-fire artillery (the latter resulting from an inability to bring artillery into play in a more normal way).[203]

From the outset, Iran, with much of its armor not operational, had to utilize an infantry-heavy offensive strategy. Its massed infantry fought alone, taking huge casualties with only limited artillery support. Without armor or more artillery, Iran was unable to sustain offensives or any level of decisive results. Even later in the war, Iran could not exploit limited gains because of lack of armor, mobility, and also logistics support.[204]

That is not to say that neither side made extensive use of artillery. Far from it! Much of the time, this was primarily an artillery war, and acquisition of artillery shells was a key criterion in arms acquisitions. According to Cordesman and Wagner, there was, however, an asymmetry, whereby Iran was superior in target acquisition and shifting fires, and Iraq superior in massing artillery and achieving high rates of fire.[205]

Most offensive maneuver in this war was infantry maneuver rather than mechanized, though Iraq—particularly later in the war—successfully used mechanized maneuver defensively to shift its forces (presumably greatly aided by U.S. photo reconnaissance intelligence).[206] Hence, the fighting did often resemble World War I on the western front, whereby most of the limited gains all along the front resulted from the use of massed infantry, sustaining very high casualties.

Ironically, in the opening Iraqi offensive into Khuzistan, the latter made primary use of tanks and mechanized units without sufficient support by non-mechanized infantry units. And indeed, water barriers (the Karun and Euphrates Rivers) and defenses in urban areas made for difficult conditions for the Iraqi armored forces, i.e., they were inappropriate for urban warfare.[207]

In 1981–82 Iran did actually achieve some limited victories on the basis of massed infantry, not matched by relatively ineffective Iraqi infantry.[208] Later, Iraq developed more effective defensive infantry forces, and by 1987–88 it had developed its infantry into a more effective offensive combat arm.[209] Generally, Iraq relied for most of the conflict on static defenses, and rarely patrolled aggressively in mountains, marshes, and other rough terrain, much less offensively as a maneuver force in such terrain.

Iran, on the other hand, began the war with much less armor and artillery, and the disadvantage subsequently was magnified due to Iran's relatively greater difficulties with respect to external arms resupply. Hence, according to Cordesman and Wagner, "this lack of resupply and sustainability reinforced Iran's ideological emphasis on popular warfare and helped lead it to try to use its larger manpower base to create superior numbers of infantry as a substitute for weapons numbers and technology."[210] For years, it launched an almost endless series of infantry-dominated offensives (making some limited headway along a long front) with only limited armored and artillery support, logistical backup, or air support. Its Pasdaran forces conducted human-wave attacks. It made extensive—and sometimes effective—use of massive initial night attacks that "saturated Iraqi defenses and penetrated to the rear."[211] But Iran never developed the capability for long-range penetration, not even for limited exploitation of gains, nor for special forces groups that might have disrupted Iraq's rear defenses and echelons and its ability to maneuver defensive forces. And throughout, despite its numerical inferiority, Iraq had far superior weapons based on better sources of arms, good fixed defenses, air superiority (of limited relevance), and an advantage in armor and artillery.

Tank warfare had some impact on the Iran-Iraq War, but never in terms of the maneuver warfare demonstrated in the Arab-Israel wars (mostly by the latter) and the India-Pakistan wars. Tanks were rarely used effectively. In the initial Iraqi move on Abadan, tanks were used much too slowly, i.e., an absence of what elsewhere is called "armored pace."[212] Tanks were dug into hull-down positions and then waited for the preparation of the battlefield by massed artillery. Iraqi use of tanks as mobile artillery also resulted in excessive wear on tank barrels. In the Khuzistan cities, as noted, Iraqi tanks were unsuited for urban warfare and vulnerable to rocket-propelled grenade fire in built-up areas.[213]

The Iranians also consistently did poorly with armor and related tactics. As it happened, they expended most of their armor during the war's first year, afterwards having great difficulty acquiring resupply of tanks and other AFVs, resulting in terrific attrition of their armored forces.[214] (They did receive some Chinese T-59s and some Soviet-origin T-62s and T-72s from allied Libya and Syria). Early in the war at the critical battle of Susangerd in January 1981, Iranian armor was utilized without proper infantry support and was badly defeated.[215]

Regarding both Iran and Iraq, but pertaining to developing-world armored battles in general (Israel and India-Pakistan aside), tank fighting was characterized by lack of accuracy, lack of maneuver, and lack of long-range fire. According to Cordesman and Wagner, "tank warfare in the Gulf rarely took advantage of the more advanced features of modern tanks, including fire-control and range-finding equipment."[216]

Both sides in this war made extensive use of mines and barriers, more so than in any other recent conventional war, save the later Iraqi defensive efforts during Desert Storm.[217] Iran, on the defensive at the war's outset, made use of deliberate flooding to channel Iraqi forces along a few approach routes and used water barriers to block Iraq's attack on Abadan.[218] When Iraq subsequently went on the defensive, it made large-scale use of flooding, water barriers, fixed-barrier defenses and mines.[219] It created chains of fortifications linked by a vast network of roads that allowed for "mobile defenses." It also made use of earth barriers and artificial ridges in its rear areas to protect against aerial attack.[220] Cordesman and Wagner summarize the Iraqi defenses as follows.

> Mines and barriers have been as important as Iraq's superior weapons strength to maintaining Iraq's defense. Iraq also steadily improved its use of defensive lines and barriers as time went on. Iraq steadily expanded the length of its defenses along the front. It also created extensive concrete tank and anti-personnel barriers at the first defense line to improve on its former earth mound defenses. Iraq created several lines of barrier defenses

around key objectives like Basra as early as 1984, but it generally had relied on one strong line backed by extensive rear-area logistic and firepower support. Iraq's defeat in Faw [sic] in 1986 then led it to shift to defenses with several parallel road lines and with high capacity lines further in the rear. It also further improved an already high inventory of tanker transporters. After the Iranian attack on Basra in 1987, Iraq shifted from strong initial forward defense barriers to the extensive use of defense in depth. All of these improvements had a significant effect in allowing Iraq to counter Iran's human-wave assaults.[221]

Going the other way, Iran also made extensive use of minefields, and Iraq in turn had some success in adding mine ploughs to T-72s and mine rollers to some T-55s to aid attacks through Iranian minefields.[222]

Both sides made some use of attack helicopters to combat armor, but never on an effective scale. Iraq made some use of helicopters as forward artillery at the battlefront against advancing Iranian infantry.[223] Both sides also made use of ATGMs, with Iran having relied heavily on U.S.-origin tube-launched optically-tracked wire-guided missiles (TOWs) for interdiction not only of tanks, but more so of bunkers, urban and mountain defensive positions.[224]

To some extent, the Iran-Iraq War (like World War I) has been described essentially as an "artillery war." Iraq used massive artillery barrages against the major Khuzistan cities, with arguable results. Later, Iraq became more effective in using artillery against advancing Iranian infantry. By 1988, it had managed to develop some capability for artillery barrages in support of armor and infantry in offensive operations.[225] Iran was less effective in this area, though like Iraq, it found the "disruptive effect of random and mass artillery shelling to be useful." On both sides, artillery was said to be unresponsive to the needs of maneuver elements. Most of the effectiveness of artillery was said to be against exposed infantry out in the open during daylight operations. Generally, artillery (including multiple-rocket launchers) seems to have accounted for a high proportion of the war's casualties. Acquiring sufficient artillery ammunition was also an important consideration in both sides' efforts at arms acquisitions from abroad.

This was mostly a ground war, with the role of tactical airpower on both sides having been minimal, more minimal in the case of Iran, whose air force suffered irreplaceable losses early in the war, and could not easily acquire spare parts and replacement equipment.

Tactics: Gulf War

Perhaps no war has been subjected to more formal "lessons learned" analyses on all levels than Desert Shield/Desert Storm. The Pentagon's own massive official analysis—*Conduct of the Persian Gulf War*—is widely viewed as a "lessons learned" classic, preeminent within the genre.[226] Numerous other works, including during the early to mid-1990s much of the burgeoning literature on the Revolution in Military Affairs (RMA), have focused on that war's lessons.[227]

As regards the ground phase of the war, the tactical and technical (weapons systems) lessons can probably be broken down into two major categories, pertaining to the "straight-ahead" and the "maneuver" sectors of the war respectively. The frontal assault on Kuwait, primarily by the U.S. Marines but involving also some U.S. Army and allied (Arab) coalition forces, produced lessons with respect to fixed defensive positions, the breaching of minefields and other barriers, much of it a follow-on to the preceding Iran-Iraq War. But then, the rapid, mobile "left hook" or "Hail Mary" offensive around the western side of Kuwait produced a somewhat separate set of tactical lessons, pertaining to tank warfare, the use of attack helicopters, combined operations. Then the air war, primarily involving the coalition's deep interdiction attacks on Iraq's command and control infrastructure, weapons sites and depots, transportation networks, produced a different set of lessons.

Iraq, of course, following the hoary dictum to the effect that generals are always refighting the last war, planned a defensive, attrition war that if successful would cause unacceptably high American losses, it being assumed (rightly so) that the U.S. public had a low tolerance for casualties. The defensive tactics used against Iran for eight years—which had caused some one million casualties— were again put into play. Hence, according to the Pentagon's own official report:

> The Iraqis prepared for the expected assault into Kuwait in a manner that reflected the successes of their defensive strategy during the Iranian War. They constructed two major defensive belts in addition to extensive fortifications and obstacles along the coast. The first belt paralleled the border roughly five to 14 kilometers inside Kuwait and was composed of continuous minefields varying in width from 100 to 200 meters, with barbed wire, antitank ditches, berms, and oil filled trenches intended to cover key avenues of approach. Covering the first belt were Iraqi platoon and company-size strongpoints designed to provide early warning and delay any attack attempting to cut through.
>
> Obstacles and minefields mirrored those of the first belt. They were covered by an almost unbroken line of mutually supporting brigade-sized defensive positions composed of company trench lines and strongpoints. The minefields contained both antitank and antipersonnel mines.[228]

Although Iraq had some five months to prepare its defenses along the Kuwait-Saudi border, and had a rather compact sector to defend, these tactics were far less effective than on the Fao peninsula or the Hawizah Marshes north of Basra. The U.S. Marines and their allies broke the Iraqi defenses in short order and moved on to take Kuwait City. To some extent this was because of the previous relentless aerial bombardment, involving precision fires against defensive bunkers, dug-in tanks, artillery emplacements, and also the B-52 area bombings that sowed terror and reduced morale. Also the Iraqi troops were cut off from vital food and water supplies. But also the U.S. forces were better equipped and trained for frontal assaults even against such elaborate defenses. The Pentagon report claims that the Marines quickly succeeded in breaching the two main defensive belts, opening some twenty-six lanes through detailed preparations, including reconnaissance and mapping of obstacles, and extensive training and rehearsals.[229] Tanks, TOW-equipped Humvees, and heavy artillery did much of the work, along with Apache helicopters armed with laser-guided Hellfire missiles. Effective in the breaching operations were mine-clearing line charges and M-60 tanks with forked mine plows and rakes. Armored forces were able to get through berms, mines, and fire ditches. Hence, a more sophisticated army than the one fielded by Iran in 1985–86 quickly made mincemeat of what previously had appeared near-invincible defensive tactics and weapons. It was another example of the importance of combined arms tactics and their great advantage when deployed by a modern, sophisticated military force.

In the west, the coalition forces utilized wholly different offensive tactics appropriate to maneuver warfare, and where Iraq—in the absence of fixed fortifications—was forced to fight a delaying defensive retreat featuring tanks in hull-down, fixed-firing positions. The analogies here, if there were any, were with the rapid Israeli armored advances in 1956, 1967, and (after a hiatus of some 10 days) in 1973.

But the technologies here used were well in advance of anything available in 1973, and the tactics were accordingly also somewhat new. Now, rapid armored movements featured a combination of helicopters, tanks, and armored fighting vehicles (AFVs). Helicopters were used to move infantry and materiel well forward as well as to provide forward artillery, specifically for interdicting tanks. Tanks with infrared sights and improved ammunition now could hit targets at much greater distances and while on the move. AFVs carrying TOWs provided additional antitank capability. As noted by the Pentagon's report, U.S. technology had a big advantage in dust and darkness, and where tank, AFV, and helicopter crews working together could hit Iraqi tanks at thirty-five hundred meters before the Iraqis saw them. Modern artillery technology on the U.S. side was also important, as artillery crews located opposing artillery with fire-finder radars and returned up to six rounds of counterbattery fire for each incoming round. Precise tank gunnery, the use of automatic grenade-launcher fire from AFVs, overwhelming artillery and rocket fire, and long-range interdiction by attack helicopters amounted almost to a new form of warfare.[230]

Laser technology along with improved infrared technology provided major new tactical advantages. The laser-guided Hellfire missiles used by helicopters were aided in target designation by spotters with infantry units.[231] The tanks' thermal sights allowed for long-distance fire at "hot spots," at night and during sandstorms, and Iraqi tanks in fixed firing positions were quickly destroyed by thermal imaging equipment.[232] American tankers were provided a long-range view of Iraqi tanks and a great first-shot advantage. Helicopters used to attack tanks also greatly benefited from thermal imaging. In the big desert, Global Positioning Systems (GPS) were vital to maneuver forces in establishing their own locations and allowing for accurate navigation on land.[233]

Noteworthy in this war was the use of a very diverse array of artillery weapons: self-propelled howitzers, multiple-rocket launchers, and tactical missiles. The latter two types of systems provided great accuracy at surprisingly long distances. Apache helicopters, used for long-range artillery, were often guided by

JSTARs intelligence aircraft that could locate and track moving vehicles far from the front.[234]

There were numerous other tactical innovations and combinations, too numerous to mention. Battleships were used for supporting artillery.[235] In other supporting operations, Navy SEALs (sea, air, land forces) were used for reconnaissance and feints, while other Special Operations Forces moved about stealthily in dune buggies and were used for long-range interdiction (sometimes using laser designators to guide aerial weapons) and reconnaissance, including with respect to Iraq's mobile Scud missiles.[236] Left unanswered is the question of the extent to which this panoply of weapons and tactics might have fared against a more sophisticated opponent or perhaps also in more difficult terrain and inclement weather.

The pace of the rapid armored movements (abetted by tankers and other cross-country supporting vehicles) is worth commenting upon. Coalition armored forces moved between 200 and 370 kilometers in a hundred hours of high-speed offensive maneuver. One U.S. armored division moved more than three hundred tanks at night across two hundred kilometers without any breakdowns. As much as possible, tanks were moved forward in the theater by tank transporters so as to reduce wear and tear on treads.

Some analyses of the war also commented on the armored formations used by brigade-size units. Dunnigan and Bay comment on the "armored wedge" and "armored V" (reverse wedge) formations used by advancing U.S. armored brigades. Hence,

> The armored wedge is, in some ways, easier to control. The standard wedge formation has one battalion task force, usually a mechanized infantry battalion in Bradleys reinforced with tanks, leading the formation. Tank battalions follow on the flanks, ready to reinforce the mechanized battalion or envelop the enemy. A "reverse wedge" puts two battalion task forces in the front and one to the rear. This is used when combat is expected and more firepower is needed up front. Generally, a deployed armored or mechanized brigade moves in a nine-kilometer-long by nine-kilometer-wide box. The direct-support artillery battalion (twenty-four self-propelled howitzers) is "tucked" behind the lead battalion.[237]

Air Operations and Tactics

In the aftermath of the Gulf War, numerous analysts asserted, not without some rebuttal, that this war had been the first in which airpower had been altogether decisive, leaving the ground phase of Desert Storm to appear almost as a mop-up operation. It was routinely said, perhaps unarguably, that desert conditions in western and southern Iraq and Kuwait magnified the superiority of Western technology over Iraq's Soviet-supplied technology. Billy Mitchell, Giulio Douhet, Alexander de Seversky, Curtis LeMay, and Arthur "Bomber" Harris all appeared finally vindicated, almost a half-century beyond the Strategic Bombing Survey, which had concluded with skepticism about the decisiveness of strategic bombing in World War II, and twenty years after the failure of the U.S. Air Force to bomb North Vietnam and the Vietcong into submission, much less back into the Stone Age, as some American generals would have had it.

In recent decades, airpower has played a mixed role in several other conflicts in the greater Middle East (and in the recent Ethiopia-Eritrea war), with the extent of that role being largely determined by a combination of geographical and technological factors. With respect to the former, our standard generalizations hold water: airpower tended to be most efficacious in flat and uncovered terrain and in good weather but effective only when it was in the hands of technically proficient and well-armed air forces that could establish air control.

Israel's air force (IAF) was a crucial if not dominant factor in the wars of 1956, 1967, 1973, and 1982. (It was not a major factor in 1948.) In 1956 it was virtually unopposed, as was the Israeli army in Sinai. In 1967 there were the heralded preemptive strikes that quickly destroyed the bulk of the Egyptian, Syrian, and Jordanian air forces, abetted by clear weather, good intelligence, and the lack of proper dispersal and revetments for the several Arab air forces. Following the initial strikes, the IAF provided critical support for Israel's armored forces in their quick blitzkrieg. In 1973 the IAF was initially thwarted by newly introduced Soviet SAM systems, but after initial setbacks and heavy losses regained its usual dominance, which in turn allowed for victory on the ground. In 1982 the IAF, using new weapons and tactics (RPVs-remote-piloted vehicles), antiradiation missiles versus SAMs, battle management, electronic countermeasure-electronic countercounter measure (ECM-ECCM) aircraft, and down-looking radars) completely obliterated Syrian SAM installations in the Bekaa Valley, while the Israeli air force had a kill ratio versus the Syrians of something like 92:2. [238]

In the India-Pakistan wars, airpower was a relatively less decisive factor, although there was significant activity. Generally speaking, airpower was used primarily for the interdiction of the rival's airpower and to some degree for other strategic purposes—much less for tactical support by comparison with the Israeli case.[239] In 1965 Pakistan launched a preemptive strike and caught some Indian air bases by surprise; afterward there was considerable air-to-air combat in what was largely a land war. In 1971 Pakistan preempted again, but India had anticipated that and dispersed many of its aircraft to rear bases, illustrating in this case the advantage of strategic depth. Pakistan struck only some forward air bases, scoring no kills, and did not use its newly acquired French Mirages for deeper strikes against available targets in New Delhi and Lucknow. India responded by moving planes up to forward bases and then attacking some eight Pakistani airfields and radar stations. Pakistan had no such equivalent strategic depth and was highly vulnerable to strikes by Canberra bombers. After that, the Indian air force played a moderate tactical role in the main northern theater and a major one out in the desert in stalling a Pakistani armored attack in the Rajasthan sector. On a strategic level, the Indian air force did succeed in attacks against the Karachi port complex and against oil and gas storage facilities. Air reconnaissance over the Indian Ocean was also vital. But as in 1965, land warfare was dominant and that was dictated by the combination of mostly covered terrain and limited tactical bombing capacity.

The Iran-Iraq War saw a much more limited role for airpower even though much of the terrain (and the weather, depending upon the seasons and the sector of the contested frontier) was suitable for the use of airpower. Thus, according to Cordesman and Wagner, "air power had an important impact upon the war, but it never had the major strategic or tactical impact that the number and quality of the weapons on each side should have permitted"; further, "a variety of factors sharply limited the ability of fixed-wing aircraft to provide effective close air support, although helicopters were somewhat more successful."[240]

Both sides had some limited success against strategic economic targets. Iraq, for instance, using Soviet-supplied Tu-22 bombers, did extensive damage to Iranian automobile and steel plants near Teheran.[241] In some phases of the war Iraq caused a significant drop in Iranian oil exports by strikes against tankers, oil facilities, and Kharg Island. Iran had some success in attacking Iraqi oil facilities and power plants at the outset of the war, but Iraq had a virtual monopoly on strategic bombing after 1982. Both sides, despite the relatively open terrain, were unable to use fixed-wing aircraft effectively for close air support of their land forces. Iran, armed with Maverick missiles, could not use them against Iraqi tanks in the face of such factors as difficult terrain, poor visibility, and dust. Both were incapable of nighttime support operations.

On the other hand, mostly on the Iraqi side, helicopters were useful for close support operations. The Iraqis did learn to fly low, use pop-up tactics, and take advantage of terrain-masking. Both sides learned to use helicopters for moving across water barriers, for small tactical moves in mountain areas, and to fly around terrain barriers.

The Soviet experience in Afghanistan presented a mixed picture for the use of airpower. There was no air-to-air combat in Afghanistan nor, because the Soviets' foes were mostly bands of guerillas armed with light weapons, was there much need for strategic warfare or concern with industrial infrastructure, fuel storage sites, and airfields. But there was some terror bombing of Afghan villages.

The war saw extensive efforts by the Soviets to use both fixed-wing and rotary-wing aircraft for counterinsurgency measures, sometimes in support of large-scale and large-unit Soviet ground operations. Those operations were conducted in a variety of terrain and weather conditions, mostly in rugged mountains with limited cover but also on plains and in valleys and under desert conditions, and in weather ranging from hot dry summers to winter snows.[242] In the latter stages of the war, the Soviets had to contend with the U.S.-supplied Stinger SAM, at the time the world's most up-to-date man-portable air defense weapon.

The Soviets made extensive use of several different types of fixed-wing aircraft for close air support.[243] Their targets were mostly hardened mountain locations that controlled the heights and narrow ravines as well as villages and the creeks leading to them. Soviet ability to locate and hit targets in rough terrain apparently improved by 1984–86, particularly with the use of Su-25s and related

An-12 transports used as spotter planes and with the use of more advanced targeting and delivery technology, such as laser range finders, low-light television, infrared sensors, computers, and radar. Laser-guided bombs came to be effective against tunnels, cave mouths, and hard-to-reach strong points by about 1986. The Soviets also launched high-altitude attacks on area targets, including extensive use of "carpet bombing." Long-range navigation systems and electro-optical delivery systems were apparently somewhat successful at night and in poor weather. But overall, airpower was not finally decisive in this war as it would be in Desert Storm because of the guerilla nature of the war, notwithstanding the massive civilian casualties that resulted from the bombing.

On the broader and more strategic level one might point to some additional, essentially geographic, issues in relation to airpower. Strategic depth versus aircraft ranges and the tanker refueling capabilities of opponents is an obvious one. We have noted India's ability in 1971 to disperse its aircraft to the rear, out of range of the Pakistani air force, and Pakistan's inability to do the same. Israel was easily able to reach all of Egypt's, Syria's, and Jordan's airfields in 1967, and those in western Iraq, even without refueling, and again in 1973 with respect to Egypt and Syria (the distances were shorter than those faced by U.S. planes based in Saudi Arabia en route to Iraq in 1990–91). Iraq, of course, also flew many aircraft to Iranian sanctuaries of sorts. Israel is similarly vulnerable, but its preemptive strategy and stronger defenses, based mostly on airpower, have not yet brought this to the test. (There has been much speculation about the possibilities for Syria's use of chemical weapons on Israeli airfields.) This vulnerability is one of the main reasons for its reluctance to relinquish high ground in the West Bank and Golan that provides for early warning installations that cannot easily be replaced by airborne systems.

The Gulf War, both during the initial "air war" phase and then during the ground war phase, saw some interesting tactical innovations and lessons. At a more "micro" level shading into an operational level, the U.S. Gulf War Air Power Survey (GWAPS) presents some fascinating detail on how a series of "tanker tracks" was established across central and northern Saudi Arabia, so as to allow for coordinated refueling of complex "strike packages" typically combining F-16 fighter bombers, F-15 air superiority fighters, F-4G Wild Weasels for suppression of enemy air defenses, EF-111s for electronic warfare, and navy and marine EA-6Bs and F/A-18s, so that they could move across the frontier as a coordinated force that could jam radars, knock out SAM sites and airfields, fly combat air patrol against enemy aircraft, and attack targets.[244]

GWAPS and also the Pentagon's *Conduct of the Persian Gulf War* provide a wealth of materials and analysis concerning the more tactical aspects of the air phase of the war.[245] As there was only minimal air-to-air fighting (the bulk of Iraq's air force was quickly destroyed on the ground or fled to neighboring Iran), most of those lessons had to do with air-to-ground interdiction of Iraqi infrastructure, ground forces, and Scud missile launchers aimed at Israel and Saudi Arabia, particularly at night and in adverse weather conditions.

Critically, this war saw the introduction of a range of new or improved technologies that in turn drove tactical innovations. Particularly, this involved the increasing ability to bomb at night and in inclement weather. There was the development of ground-mapping and terrain-avoidance radars that made low altitude penetration of radar-controlled, ground-based defenses feasible. A-6s and F-111s penetrated at night at altitudes often below a thousand feet, utilizing terrain-masking to defeat Iraq's radars. Then, there were night-viewing devices able to identify point targets, buildings, vehicles; these were used on side-firing A-10 gunships. A pivotal development was the fusing of night-vision devices such as FLIR (forward-looking infrared) with laser-designated bombs.[246] This combination allowed accuracy in night bombing with real precision from high altitudes, if the targets could be identified by FLIR and targeted with laser designators. The F-111s developed the ability for "tank plinking at night," picking out the thermal images of tanks dug hull-down in sand, taking advantage of the differential cooling rates of steel and sand.[247]

The introduction of stealth aircraft was crucial—they accounted for a high percentage of hits on Iraqi infrastructure. Then there was the use not only of B-52s, based in the U.K., among other places, but also B-2s based at Barksdale Air Force Base in Louisiana, used not only for "strategic" bombing but for area terror-bombing of troops near the front lines. The attack aircraft used a mix of laser-guided and electro-optical weapons, as well as infrared guided weapons, in the former two cases somewhat dependent on the weather or daytime.[248]

In order to save pilots' lives, the USAF limited its vulnerability by conducting the bulk of its bombing raids at medium to high altitudes, after having knocked out the SAMs that are effective above medium altitudes. GWAPs reports that A-10 pilots using Rockeye bombs against tanks had to use shallower-than-desirable dive angles because of inclement weather.[249]

Finally, there were all of the aerial tactical problems involved in the "great Scud hunt," which proved a more difficult and more futile operation than might have been anticipated.[250] These operations, somewhat novel in historical perspective, were concentrated in the two main "Scud boxes" located in western and southern Iraq, where missiles were targeted, respectively, on Israel and Saudi Arabia. The Iraqis used effective tactics in hiding and moving the Scuds, which were fired from presurveyed launch positions and utilized transporter-erector-launchers (TELs). The launch areas were in rugged territory, and the TELs could be moved about rapidly and concealed in ravines, beneath highway underpasses and in culverts. The Pentagon's study claimed that within fifteen minutes after launch, the Scud launch crews could be anywhere within nine miles of the launch point. AWACS, DSP satellites, and JSTARS were used to locate mobile Scud launchers and their transporters. B-52s bombed suspected Scud sites day and night. During the day, A-10s and F-16s patrolled the area and were directed to potential launch sites; at night, LANTIRN-equipped F-16s and F-15Es, and FLIR-equipped A-6Es took up the task. Following Scud launches, attack aircraft were concentrated in the launch area to search for and attack Scud transporter vehicles. As more focused intelligence identified Scud boxes or specific launching areas, aircraft dropped CBU-89 area denial mines into suspected operating areas. Special Operations Forces on the ground, moving about in dune buggies, were also used to locate Scud firing sites. It remains to be seen whether tactics developed almost ad hoc in response to the Scud problem in 1991 will be refined or altered in the case of another such episode—perhaps to involve more deadly weapons.

Naval Warfare: Operations and Tactics

With the exception of the Falklands War, naval warfare and naval operations have not been crucial in the recent history of Third World warfare. As a matter of fact with the exception of India, all of the "regional" navies can be characterized as "white water" rather than "blue water"; that is, they are largely engaged in coastal defense and short-distance power projection operations. But in some of the recent wars there was a significant naval component, as exemplified by the massive U.S. logistical effort by sea in Desert Storm, the successful feint used by the United States in regard to a possible Marine amphibious landing in Kuwait, which tricked Iraq into positioning its defensive forces badly; the Iran-Iraq tanker battles during the 1980–88 war in which each side attempted to interfere with the other's logistics in the Persian Gulf (Iran to interdict supplies coming in via Saudi Arabia and Kuwait, and Iraq to interdict Iran's oil exports out); India's successful blockade both of Chittagong and Karachi in 1971 and its well-executed naval assault on the latter; and Israel's destruction of significant parts of the Egyptian and Syrian navies in 1973 and its successful, leapfrogging amphibious landings along the Lebanese coast in 1982. Then too there was the sinking of the Israeli destroyer *Eilat* by Egyptian Styx missiles after the 1967 war, often cited as marking the beginning of PGM warfare.

Submarines and ASW have so far played a fairly limited role in most of the recent wars and major Third World conflicts. The Iran-Iraq War and the several Arab-Israeli wars have seen little if any action by submarines or ASW units. In between major wars, the Israelis have apparently used submarines in some long-distance clandestine operations, such as the raid on Tunis against the PLO leadership there.

On the other hand, submarines did figure to some degree in the naval phase of the 1971 India-Pakistan War in the relatively shallow waters of the Arabian Sea and Bay of Bengal. India feared Pakistan's Midget and Chariot submarines, one of which sank an Indian ASW frigate, and a Pakistani submarine in the Bay of Bengal that was positioned to keep the Indian carrier *Vikrant* further south near the Andaman Islands, was sunk in Vizag harbor.[251] The recent Iranian purchase of a few Soviet diesel submarines has raised the question for the United States as to whether such vessels operating out of Bandar Abbas near the Strait of Hormuz could be effective against U.S. forces in the Persian Gulf. While the shallowness of the water would appear to render ASW detection difficult, the limited operating area for submarines in the face of the vaunted U.S. ASW capabilities would appear to render them highly vulnerable. Generally speaking, submarines are considered to be well suited for littoral warfare of the type anticipated in the greater Middle East.

There have been some instances of amphibious operations during these wars and contingency planning for much more. Israel used leapfrog operations reminiscent of U.S. operations in New Guinea and Italy during World War II in an attempt to bypass and trap the PLO forces fleeing north toward Beirut in the 1982 war. The tides and beaches appear not to have been impediments. In 1971 India, concerned that Pakistani troops were escaping from East Bengal via Cox's Bazar, landed a force there from a merchant ship.[252]

On a more macro or strategic level, some further generalizations can be made about the naval military environments of some of the recent conflicts. Generally this involves such factors as distance, contiguity, the spatial relationships between contending forces, the lengths of coastlines, the particularities of specific situations involving chokepoints, and the configurations of the key regional bodies of water, that is, the Mediterranean, Red, and Arabian Seas and the Persian Gulf.

Israel has a contiguous coastline with Egypt and Lebanon-Syria. Iran and Iraq have coastlines that face one another across the narrow Persian Gulf. India and Pakistan have a contiguous or continuous coastline along the Arabian Sea (they had another in the east up to 1971), as do China and Vietnam. Those are entirely different than the geographic relationships between, for example, the United States and Russia, the United States and China, or the United Kingdom and Argentina. Within the former group there are possibilities for quick, preemptive naval strikes at the outset of a conflict, in which one or another navy can be caught in or near port and immediately destroyed (airpower used to attack ships is also, ipso facto, close by). Israel rapidly knocked out a good part of the Syrian navy in 1973; India did likewise to Pakistan in 1971, particularly with its daring and effective naval attack on Karachi harbor. China, on the other hand, did little in 1979 to attack Vietnamese naval facilities and ships. Somalia and Ethiopia, with contiguous coastlines, made little if any use of naval forces.

Some nations have particularly narrow and vulnerable access to the sea and so are easily bottled up and blockaded. Iraq's hopeless position at Basra-Umm Qasr resulted in its navy being almost wholly inoperative during the Iran-Iraq War. Pakistan is also disadvantaged by having a short coastline, and in 1971 the not-much-larger Indian navy was easily able to block its access to Chittagong in the east and to Karachi in the west, though in the latter case the coastline is actually several hundred miles long and there is another decent port further west at Gwadar in Baluchistan that was coveted by both the USSR and the United States at various times during the Cold War. India by contrast has an immense 3,750–mile coastline with numerous excellent ports, and is thus in a situation of very favorable maritime strategic depth. Iran could position some naval units outside the Persian Gulf on a rather remote coastline but would be forced to operate largely within the Persian Gulf, where its naval units would be highly vulnerable to air and naval attacks from superior U.S. forces. Many regional naval powers must operate from a small number of good harbors: Israel from Haifa, Eilat, and Ashkelon (only the first being a good natural harbor); Egypt from Port Said and Alexandria; Syria from Tartus and Latakia; Vietnam from Haiphong and Camranh Bay. These navies are all highly vulnerable if an opponent achieves air superiority.[253]

With few exceptions, none of the Third World military powers involved in recent wars has made extensive use of outlying, perimeter bases as part of a broader power-projection strategy. India, which has often been discussed in this context in recent years, has access to its Andaman and Nicobar Islands in the Bay of Bengal, and the Lakshadweep Islands off its southwest coast (perhaps also to Maldives, an independent republic). With an expanding navy and the proclamation of two hundred-mile economic exclusion zones (within which it has valuable offshore mineral and oil deposits), it has an extended peripheral reach. Iran has been rumored to be seeking some naval access in Sudan, an ideological bedfellow, which would allow it to flank Saudi Arabia at sea, for whatever that is worth in the light of its naval capabilities. Israel has apparently had some access to Ethiopian islands in the Dahlak Archipelago at the southern end of the Red Sea for operations involving patrol boats near the Bab El Mandeb chokepoint, which controls access from Eilat to the Indian Ocean (Israel-South African ties had earlier been germane here). China has been rumored periodically to have acquired some naval access (and intelligence facilities) in Burma's Coco Islands, which would involve an outflanking of Vietnam and perhaps a potential threat to India.

Summary

It has become a virtual article of faith among many analysts that the era of interstate conventional warfare (dating back into the mists of history) is now passé, having been relegated to history's dustbin by new international norms and regimes, the Kantian peace, even by nuclear weapons. Ironically, this vogue of the "obsolescence of war" comes right after a previous period of some thirty years that had seen a rash of conventional wars—Arab-Israel, India-Pakistan, Iran-Iraq, the Falklands, Afghanistan, China-Vietnam, and Ethiopia-Somalia. The near dearth of conventional warfare in the 1990s (the Gulf War and Ethiopia-Eritrea as exceptions) seemed to underscore the point. But recent flare-ups between India and Pakistan, the potential for the "internationalization" of the second *Intifada,* and the powder keg straddling the Taiwan Straits has caused some commentators to wonder whether the beginning of the new century may yet see a resumption of large-scale conventional warfare. Surely, the major states of the conflict regions of the Middle East, South Asia, and the Far East continue to acquire weapons at a rate that corresponds with the prospects for warfare, and this fact should not simply be dismissed as worst-case-scenario mongering.

In this chapter, we have discussed and compared many of the conventional wars that have taken place over the past forty years or so, according to the loose levels of analysis framework outlined in the opening chapter. Hence, these numerous wars and their political contexts were compared at the grand strategic, operational, and tactical levels. Among the numerous major theses that emerge from such an analysis are:

- The difficulties in analyzing grand strategies for nations below the super- or major-power level, whose strategies pertain to regional and mostly contiguous rivalries, but in the larger context of big-power rivalries.

CHAPTER 5

Strategies, Operations, Tactics in Low-Intensity Conflict

As previously indicated, recent years have seen a great increase in the importance of internal wars or—viewed from a different angle—low-intensity conflicts, some of which have had interstate dimensions. As pointed out in a recent article by Steven David, internal wars have made up over 80 percent of the wars and casualties since the end of World War II, and that preponderance has become even more marked since the end of the Cold War (between 1989 and 1996 only five of ninety-six armed conflicts were between states, in 1993 and 1994 there were no interstate conflicts, and in 1995 there was just the brief border skirmish between Ecuador and Peru).[1] As David further states, "those interested in contemporary warfare are left little choice but to focus on internal war."[2]

That newer focus is obvious to anyone observing the mix of papers on conflict presented at recent meetings of the International Studies Association and other such scholarly conclaves. It contains the assumption, as previously noted, that major conventional warfare is becoming passé or obsolete; hence, the recently crystallized scholarly group-think on "the obsolescence of war," the "democratic peace," and "endism," whether or not restricted to relations between or among democracies. Indeed, in this vein, even the arms-trade literature has shifted accordingly, with its newer primary focus on the small-arms trade (previously deemed unmeasurable and vaguely peripheral and irrelevant), and the obvious assumption that most low-intensity wars are fought primarily with small arms, if not indeed caused or exacerbated by that trade.[3] In short, internal wars, whether over territory or government, have become the primary current focus of strategic and conflict studies.

Apropos the central thrust of this work—the conduct of war or war-fighting per se—there is another pertinent point to be made in relation to these trends. This has to do with the virtual absence of a literature on the nature of the actual fighting of contemporary low-intensity conflicts, in contrast not only with recent (though infrequent) conventional wars, but also with the low-intensity conflicts of the Cold War period.

As we have noted, there is at least a fairly significant "lessons learned" literature for recent conventional wars, as exemplified by the Cordesman and Wagner volumes on the Arab-Israeli, Iran-Iraq, Falklands, and Afghanistan wars, the prolific monograph literature on the Gulf War, the Los Alamos and Center for Strategic and International Studies (CSIS) studies of the lessons of the latter, etc., as previously cited. There is a degree of coherence in this literature to the extent much of it utilizes, explicitly or implicitly, a levels of analysis approach covering the familiar spectrum running from strategy to operations to tactics.

True, however, the conventional war literature on war-fighting is overshadowed, particularly within the political science profession, by the massive theoretical literature on the origins and causes of those wars.[4] In the current literature, inspired by the Correlates of War project, that involves mostly "large N" studies geared to testing a variety of hypotheses involving such theoretical concerns as balance of power, displacement, lateral pressures, polarity and polarization, status discrepancy, system structure, etc. But as earlier noted, and as analyzed by Holsti, these theoretical considerations are largely inapplicable to the LICs that dominate the statistics of contemporary conflict.[5]

Still more recently, in response to the caveats of Holsti and others, there have been efforts at laying out a spectrum of theoretical considerations involved in the causes of internal, primarily ethnic, wars. Earlier, that literature had focused on issues of identity, nationalism, social structure, and nation-building. With the end of the Cold War, a new literature emerged that uses neorealism in an attempt to make internal war understandable, focusing on the traditional concepts of anarchy, security dilemmas, balance of power, etc. Still others, such as Michael Brown, have focused on "bad leaders."[6] Still others focus on the collapse of domestic authority, ethnic hatreds, economic problems, repressive rule, issues underlying conflicts, the internal politics of each side, the military balance, the role played by third parties, inclusiveness of societies, the nature of (often only temporary) settlements, etc. In parallel and concurrently, scholars such as Chaim Kaufmann have written about competing views on cures for ethnic civil wars.[7] Kaufmann (with Bosnia in mind) derides the hopes of others for power-sharing arrangements, international conservatorship to rebuild states, and reconstruction of exclusive ethnic identities into wider, inclusive civic identities. Rather, he insists on the necessity of separation and population transfers to create ethnically homogeneous states at the cost of considerable temporary dislocation. These are arguable matters, but the point holds that there is now a dominant thrust in the literature toward identifying the causes, and then the cures, for internal, mostly ethnic, conflicts, as a follow-on to the long tradition of conflict studies as applied to interstate wars.

A perusal of this burgeoning literature reveals little about the actual conduct of those wars, their strategies, and tactics. There is little descriptive material, even less analysis. For descriptions of the actual fighting, one must rely on disparate press reports, scattered articles in publications such as *Jane's Defense Weekly,* and (as noted in chapter one) the occasional article in magazines such as *Harper's* or *Atlantic Monthly* authored by writers who have accompanied forces on the ground in places such as Afghanistan, Nicaragua, Eritrea, or El Salvador and can give the reader a "feel" for the sights and sounds of the war. There are no numbers, no empirical analyses. The one presumed preeminent repository of serious detailed military analysis and battle histories, that is, the U.S. Defense Intelligence Agency, is off-limits in the realm of classified materials, as would also be the case for other major nations' defense intelligence services. One exception in the recent "causes of war" literature applied to ethnic conflicts is Kaufmann's brief excursion into military strategy, in which he avers that "because of the decisiveness of territorial control, military strategy in ethnic wars is very different than in ideological conflicts," and that "unlike ideological insurgents, who often evade rather than risk battle, or a counterinsurgent government, which might forbear to attack rather than risk bombarding civilians, ethnic combatants must fight for every piece of land . . . by contrast, combatants in ethnic wars are much less free to decline unfavorable battles because they cannot afford to abandon any settlement to an enemy who is likely to 'cleanse' it by massacre, expulsion, destruction of homes, and possibly colonization."[8] Implied here is the idea that, in terms of the conduct rather than the causes of war, there is a sharp bifurcation between SIPRI's long-standing division of "wars of government" and "wars of territory," that they are wholly different types of war, strategically, operationally, and tactically. This point is, however, somewhat muddied by the fact that some internal wars—Peru, Lebanon, Nicaragua—may be complex mixes of "wars of government" and "wars of territory," albeit the fact that the bulk of internal wars are one or the other. We shall return to that.

Another exception is in Mary Kaldor's recent work, wherein she (after disposing of the LIC concept as anachronistic) points to the similarities between the fighting of modern ethnic wars, and some aspects of traditional counterinsurgency, i.e., the avoidance of battle and emphasis on territorial control through political control of populations and the central aim of sowing "fear and hatred."[9]

In addition, Kaldor makes the point that the very organizational structures of ethnic warfare "actors" is something new. Hence,

> In contrast to the vertical organized hierarchical units that were typical of "old wars," the units that fight these wars include a disparate range of different types of groups such as paramilitary units, local warlords, criminal gangs, police forces, mercenary groups and also regular armies including breakaway units of regular armies. In organizational terms, they are highly decentralized and they operate through a mixture of confrontation and cooperation even when on opposing sides. They make use of advanced technology even if it is not what we tend to call "high technology" (stealth bombers or cruise missiles, for example). In the last fifty years, there have been significant advances in lighter weapons-undetectable land mines, for example, or small arms which are light, accurate and easy to use so that they can even be operated by children. They also make use of modern communications—cell phones or computer links—in order to coordinate, mediate and negotiate among the disparate fighting units.[10]

The absence of an analytical literature on the fighting of modern LIC is all the more curious in that in broader historical context this has not at all always been the case. There is, or was indeed, a huge literature on guerilla warfare, revolutionary war, insurgency, and counterinsurgency, in the 1960s and 1970s, inspired by the conflicts in the Philippines, Greece, Malaya, and uppermost, Vietnam, not to mention a variety of earlier historical circumstances.

A review of this earlier literature reveals some interesting definitional or conceptual problems at a time before the term LIC had entered the consciousness and vocabulary of military analysts, and well before SIPRI's development of the fundamental distinction between wars over government and those over territory, which, sometimes in altered terminology, tends to define current typologies of LIC. Earlier, the definitional problems seemed to center on the (often confused or muddied) distinction between guerilla warfare on the one hand, and insurgent or revolutionary war on the other (the latter tellingly paralleled by the usage of counterinsurgent or counterrevolutionary warfare). Guerilla warfare, by one definition, was defined as "military and para-military operations conducted in enemy-held or hostile territory by irregular, predominately indigenous forces."[11] Hence, guerilla warfare really referred to how the war was fought rather than the nature or roles of combatants. Hence too, guerilla warfare might be evidenced in a general war, a struggle between two governments trying to destroy each other; in a limited war, i.e., armed conflict between governments where each is prepared to use only limited resources to secure a restricted or limited area; or in an insurgent war characterized by a struggle between an established government and an antigovernment force. In a general war, guerilla war might be resorted to by the weaker side as a last stand after it had largely been defeated, or might be used in a supporting role to regular forces as they were used by the Soviets in World War II. They might also be used in a supporting role in limited war, as were North Korean guerillas in the Korean War. In an insurgent war, guerillas may play a large role in the early phases when the insurgents are not yet strong enough to deploy large units of regular forces.

It is important to note that the concept of "guerilla" or "little war" goes way back to the role of Spanish irregulars fighting Napoleon's forces in the Peninsular War from 1808 to 1814 after France had defeated Spain's regular army. Inspired by that example, Clausewitz wrote about "people's war," identifying the crucial factors of mobility, dispersion, and speed of action with emphasis on the enemy's flanks and rear. He also noted a number of conditions under which a "people's war" might be effective, among them: the location of war in the country's interior, the absence of altogether decisive main-force battles, the broken and inaccessible nature of terrain.[12] Also, during the nineteenth century, French military theorists focused on guerilla warfare tactics and operations on the basis of France's interminable counterinsurgency struggles in North Africa.[13]

But beginning with Marx and Engels in the nineteenth century, and then on through a developmental skein running through Lenin, T. E. Lawrence, Mao Tse-Tung, Vo Nguyen Giap, Che Guevara, and Carlos Marighella, there developed by the middle of the Cold War what came to be viewed as the central corpus of theory and prescription regarding revolutionary war. On the military side, that still involved—at least in early stages—guerilla warfare as earlier defined, i.e., small-unit, dispersed, partisan warfare. But this skein of intellectual development focused on guerilla warfare only in the narrow sense of its application to insurgent war, that is, to revolutionary warfare.

Marx and Engels provided the theoretical foundation for communist revolutionary warfare, with their assertion of the inevitability of class-based revolutionary upheavals.[14] Lenin added the concept of leadership by "organization," saw that revolutionaries needed a party of a new type and "to create an organization of revolutionaries able to guarantee the energy, stability, and continuity of the political struggle."[15] The focus was on armed uprising and the establishment of a "dictatorship of workers and peasants." According to one source in summary, "Lenin's theories on organization, urban uprising, the use of propaganda, and worldwide revolution, combined with their practical application, led to a successful revolution in Russia and elsewhere and have had a major impact on the current strategies of guerilla warfare and insurgent war."[16]

T. E. Lawrence, a.k.a. "Lawrence of Arabia," may have been the first theorist on guerilla warfare. As Lenin had expanded on Clausewitz's ideas on the political aspects of insurgency war, so Lawrence expanded on Clausewitz's ideas on its military aspects. On the basis of his role as British advisor to Arab forces fighting Turkey in World War I, he summed up the following nine tenets of his wisdom in *Seven Pillars of Wisdom*.

1. Be superior at the critical point and moment of attack.
2. Attack enemy weaknesses.
3. Never defend; avoid contact except at your choosing.
4. Highly developed intelligence and counter-intelligence are of major importance.
5. High mobility is a must.
6. Psychological warfare must be employed. (Mass and individual—against enemy and friendly forces—local and international).
7. Emphasis for a small force must be on speed and time—not hitting power.
8. Tactics should be characterized by "tip and run"—no pushes, but strikes.
9. Surprise is the main element of guerilla tactics. Mobility, deceit and ambush are among its strongest weapons.[17]

Lawrence may have had a major impact on Churchill and on the use of guerilla warfare in World War II, and he expanded upon Clausewitz with his emphasis on the use of psychological warfare, offensive, initiative, mobility, the use of intelligence.[18]

Mao Tse-Tung combined elements of Clausewitz, Lenin, and Lawrence, and combined their political and military theories into a strategy that led to a successful revolution in China in the late 1940s and became a blueprint for many other insurgency wars during the Cold War. His theory was that of a protracted war, agrarian based, and carried out in military, political, psychological, and economic dimensions. He developed his famous three stages of revolutionary war: strategic defensive, strategic stalemate (preparation for the counteroffensive), and strategic counteroffensive.[19] He stressed four basic elements of his strategy: the organization of a party (from Lenin); mass support and a united front; a loyal, professional army; and rural revolutionary bases or strategic bases of operations, which ideally would be in rough terrain with poor communications and, if possible, in isolated border regions between jurisdictions.

A tactical base area was deemed of particular importance, with Mao's own base in northwest China during World War II set forth as an example. The characteristics of a good tactical base were:

1. Difficult terrain which is remote from modern transportation.
2. Land which is cultivable.
3. A friendly local population.
4. Climate hospitable to ill-clad guerillas.
5. Proximity to a foreign sanctuary, if possible.[20]

Mao stressed mobility, surprise, initiative, deception, and flexibility, here also inspired by Sun Tzu. "His forces divide into small groups and at the proper time concentrate to make quick defensive attacks on the enemy."[21] He didn't want his forces to become prematurely, decisively involved, hence the famous dictum: "the enemy advances, we retreat; the enemy camps, we harass; the enemy tires, we attack; the enemy retreats, we pursue." He explained a true guerilla as one that "swims like a fish through a sea of men."[22] In summary, he conjured up the following ten principles of guerilla or revolutionary warfare.

1. Attack dispersed, isolated enemy forces first; attack concentrated strong enemy forces later.
2. Take small and medium cities and extensive rural areas first; take big cities later.
3. Make wiping out of the enemy's effective strength our main objective; do not make holding or seizing a city or place our main objective.
4. In every battle, concentrate on absolutely superior forces, encircle the enemy forces completely, striving to wipe them out thoroughly and do not let any escape from the net.
5. Fight no battle unprepared, fight no battle you are not sure of winning.
6. Give full play in our style of fighting . . . outrage in battle, no fear in sacrifice, no fear of fatigue, and continue fighting.
7. Strive to wipe out the enemy when he is on the move.
8. With regard to attacking cities, resolutely seize all enemy fortified points and cities which are weakly defended.
9. Replenish our strength with all the arms and most of the personnel captured from the army.
10. Make good use of the intervals between campaigns to rest, train and consolidate our troops.[23]

When the enemy no longer has numerical superiority and weapons superiority, only then does Mao advocate moving into the final stage, and that is a stage of conventional warfare and all–out civil war. In that stage, the stress is on mobile warfare and concentration, culminating in a war of annihilation à la Clausewitz. This requires the availability of outside sources of heavy weapons, as was the case for the Chinese Red Army in the late 1940s. Later too, Lin Piao would expand Mao's revolutionary doctrine to include the whole world, utilizing by analogy the idea that the Third World was a big agrarian base that could be used to encircle and destroy the Western world.[24]

General Vo Nguyen Giap is commonly viewed as Mao's successor and protégé, and his strategy in Vietnam pretty much mirrored that of Mao's. He saw revolutionary war divided into three phases: a state of contention, a stage of equilibrium, and a stage of counteroffensive.[25] He had many of the same tactical principles as Mao, paying particular attention to the decisions to move from guerilla warfare to mobile conventional warfare. The general "counteroffensive" is distinguished by not only mobile warfare, but with some positional warfare and continued guerilla warfare which assumes a secondary role.[26] Decisive battles are engaged in only when victory seems certain (as was the case at Dienbienphu vis-à-vis the French and later in 1974 vis-à-vis South Vietnam after the U.S. withdrawal). Giap also added to Mao's theories the concept of a "general uprising," one that was operationalized with mixed results in 1968 at the time of the Tet Offensive.[27] On the whole, Giap's views on revolutionary warfare mirrored Mao's, but he added or emphasized some key elements and put them to practical use: the importance of the international situation, outside support, the proper mix of guerilla forces and regular forces, the critical decision to move from guerilla to mobile warfare, and the promotion of a general uprising.[28]

Still another important school of thought on insurgency warfare is associated with the names of Che Guevara and Regis Debray, particularly the former in his role of chief theorist for Fidel Castro. They too were students of Mao and Giap. Guevara wrote more on a tactical level, Debray more on a strategic and political level.[29] They, of course, dealt with a Latin American rather than Asian context, but together they developed an identifiable "Cuban revolutionary strategy." That strategy, perhaps somewhat developed post hoc by inference from the experience of the Cuban revolution (and it failed dismally later in Bolivia), is habitually referred to as "guerilla *foco*." That strategy is summarized in the following three elements.

1. Popular forces can win a war against an army.
2. One does not necessarily have to wait for a revolutionary situation to arise; it can be created.
3. In the underdeveloped countries of the Americas, rural areas are the best battlefield for revolution.[30]

This strategy stresses the military over the political, and is less patient or less inclined to wait for the development of requisite mass political conditions. Thus, according to Debray, "the principal stress must be laid on the development of guerilla warfare and not on the strengthening of existing parties or the creation of new parties."[31] The beginnings of revolutionary warfare must be developed by armed action, maybe by thirty to fifty armed men, the guerilla force, which not only conducts armed actions, but acts as a "political vanguard from which a real party can arise."[32] Political and military cadres are the same. But even with this emphasis on the armed nucleus, Guevara follows Mao in his emphasis on the rural peasantry, with the guerilla band as an armed nucleus of the rural masses. With Guevara, however, there was less emphasis on elaborate, remote base areas, more emphasis on mobility—"the guerilla lives on mobility, and the guerilla's knapsack is his base of support."[33] Only later were more permanent base areas established, for industry, supply, training, and hospital facilities. But generally, Guevara and Debray saw their revolutionary warfare going through phases similar to those foreseen by Mao and Giap, culminating in regular force conventional warfare (though this stage never really was needed or consummated in Cuba). Finally, Debray in particular put more emphasis on suburban warfare, on the effect guerillas could have on commercial and industrial life in cities.[34] But generally, Guevara was not a believer in urban warfare.[35] Also, guerilla *foco* was a failure in Bolivia, primarily because Guevara could not establish a base of peasant support there.

As it happens, however, the final skein of development of "Marxist" revolutionary warfare was a theory of urban insurgency, and it is associated with the Brazilian Carlos Marighella, who was killed in Sao Paulo in 1969 while leading an urban revolutionary movement, one that was also witnessed in Uruguay, among other places. (The earlier Algerian insurrection had had strong urban roots as well, albeit the lack of a "theory.") The failure of peasant rebellions in Latin America had caused some revolutionary theorists to shift their attention to urban insurgency, in line with increasing urbanization and associated despair in Latin America.[36] But actually, many theorists thought in terms of combining urban and rural insurgency, or using the former in support of the latter. Marighella stressed the central role of urban guerilla warfare. The basics are, however, the same as with Mao or Giap, involving small guerilla groups, establishing a logistical base, intelligence networks, etc., and featuring terrorist operations, sabotage, propaganda warfare, etc.[37] Marighella believed in very small group organization, revolutionary cells of four or five referred to as "firing groups," and in combinations, "firing teams."[38] He believed in decentralized control, groups operating on their own. The purpose was to wear out government forces, and cause the collapse of the government. Marighella did aver, however, that in the final stages of revolution rural guerillas would still play the decisive role in revolutionary war.[39] Urban insurgency groups were vital in inducing governmental retaliation against sabotage and terrorism, hence alienating the masses and causing them to revolt against the government. Generally speaking, many theorists of insurgency warfare earlier saw urban areas as unfavorable to insurgency. We shall return to that question in the current context.

In summary of this section, the overwhelmingly central focus on revolutionary or insurgency warfare during most of the Cold War was inspired by the reality of numerous wars pitting Soviet- and/or Chinese-backed insurgents against colonial regimes or against their more or less pro-Western postcolonial successors. The various Mao-Giap-Guevara-Marighella guerilla strategies (they differed according to region and revolutionary context, but also were fundamentally similar) were played out in numerous theaters: China, Vietnam, Cambodia, Malaya, the Philippines, Cuba, Brazil, Uruguay, Nicaragua, Guatemala, Algeria, Tunisia, South Yemen, Greece, Kenya, Rhodesia, Namibia. Many (Vietnam, Algeria et al.) were successful guerilla wars; others (the Philippines, Greece, Malaya) were not so successful. The successful ones tended, essentially, to follow the classic Mao-Giap stages, running from guerilla warfare to conventional mobile warfare (Cuba was an exception and the experience inspired the *foco* theory that subsequently fell flat in Bolivia). It is important to note, of course, that while we are here focused primarily on military affairs, politico-economic context varies throughout these cases: economic growth rates and distribution patterns, rates of urbanization, land distribution, effectiveness of government, corruption, mass alienation, relationship of incumbent regimes to colonial powers. These combined with military factors to produce outcomes, pro or con.

It is also worth noting that wars over territory, primarily ethnic warfare, were not altogether lacking during the Cold War period. That is, low-intensity conflict was not entirely defined by the broad model of Marxist-Leninist insurgency versus incumbent governments, as related to the Cold War. There were some ethnic conflicts largely removed from class-based revolutionary warfare, such as the Biafran war in Nigeria in the 1960s, tribal warfare in Kenya, the main stages of the Lebanon civil war in the 1970s, the lengthy Eritrean and Tigrean insurgencies against Ethiopian regimes under Haile Selassie and Mengistu, and the endless Karen insurgency in Burma and others in that country. It is important to note that some revolutionary wars that we would think of as fitting the classic Mao-Giap-Guevara model did actually have an important, indeed crucial, ethnolinguistic component. This was true of Malaya, of the early Kurdish insurgencies in Iraq and Iran, in Laos, and in some Latin American countries such as Peru, Bolivia, perhaps also in Central America, where seemingly class-based urban and rural rebellions often concerned the divide between elites of European and mixed origin, and native Indian tribes.

By the mid-1980s, the so-called U.S. Reagan Doctrine produced still another curious reversal. That doctrine involved an attempt by the U.S. to "roll back" the tide of communist-related takeovers in the Third World by supporting revolutions *against* Marxist-style regimes supported and armed by Moscow and often providing it basing access.[40] That "roll back" policy was supported in Afghanistan, Ethiopia, Angola, Mozambique, Cambodia, and Nicaragua. The literature reveals no efforts to compare the strategies and tactics of these insurgencies with the classic Mao-Giap model. Indeed, their main purpose, from the U.S. perspective, may have been to create havoc with Moscow, to inflict costs in blood and treasure. Some involved an ethnic component, as witness U.S. reliance on Pathan insurgents in Afghanistan, the Eritreans, tribal groups associated with Jonas Savimbi in Angola, and the Miskito Indians in Nicaragua. None of these cases evidenced, ultimately, a Maoist or Giapist third stage of mobile conventional warfare, though the insurgency in Afghanistan did force a Soviet withdrawal, but also led to fighting among the components of the victorious forces. But there is no "theorist" of Reagan Doctrine warfare, lest it be former CIA director William Casey in the context of a (largely unstated) peripheral attrition strategy vis-à-vis the USSR.

Counterinsurgency Doctrines and Strategies

Almost constituting a mirror image of the theories, doctrines, and strategies of revolutionary insurgency are their counterparts on the side of counterinsurgency. That came to constitute a fairly massive body of writings during the Cold War period, first greatly impelled by the central focus given it by President Kennedy in the early 1960s, and then subsequently by the U.S. experience in the Vietnam War and, in its aftermath, the endless postmortems, *mea culpa* autobiographies, and "lessons learned" tracts. The Kennedy administration, in response to Khrushchev's pronouncements about Soviet support for national liberation movements, made a near fetish out of counterinsurgency plans and doctrines, not only the military side of it, but also closely linked issues of Third World political and economic development.[41] The broader context of this comprised the "flexible response" doctrine (in lieu of the, by 1960, noncredible "massive retaliation" doctrine) whereby the U.S. and its allies intended to create strength all up and down the spectrum from guerilla to limited to conventional to nuclear warfare, in an attempt to achieve escalation dominance at all levels. That requirement came about in response to the Soviets' achievement of second-strike nuclear deterrence vis-à-vis the U.S. in the late 1950s, enshrining a situation of mutual assured destruction (MAD) for the remainder of the Cold War, in effect providing an umbrella for conventional and LIC warfare and provocations.[42]

As it happened, the Kennedy administration, no more than the British authorities in Malaya in the 1950s, did not really discover counterinsurgency or various doctrines or strategies in its pursuit. Whether they called it that or not, the French practiced counterinsurgency against the Spanish guerillas during the Peninsular War in the Napoleonic period. The Romans conducted a counterinsurgency campaign against the Jews at the time of Masada. No doubt there are countless other historical examples. But a review of the contemporary strategy literature, for instance the classic volume edited by Edward Earle on modern strategists, reveals that the French practice of *guerre Algerienne,* as it was pursued for more than a century in Algeria, Morocco, and elsewhere, beginning around 1830, constitutes a durable paradigm for the study of modern counterinsurgency. Indeed, in Jean Gottmann's chapter in the Earle volume on "Bugeaud, Gallieni, Lyautey: The Development of French Colonial Warfare,"[43] virtually all of the major themes of the 1960s through 1970s counterinsurgency literature are previewed or anticipated: comparative emphasis on military and political ("hearts and minds" civic action) factors; the viability of "local" forces in counterinsurgency; the need for mobile, quick-reaction forces rather than large-formation conventional forces suitable for major war in Europe; problems of large-space and rural-base areas; the problem of brutality and highly coercive methods alienating the populace; the usefulness of "strategic hamlet" strategies; and the strategy of weakening the insurgents by sowing internal discord and creating antagonisms between varied interests, groups, and leaders. Oddly, Gottmann sees French counterinsurgency strategies in the 1830s as having been modeled on ancient Roman strategies in the same area.[44]

As noted, the U.S. at the outset of the Kennedy administration evinced a strong interest in counterinsurgency, which was then considered the pivotal battleground of the future as it was surmised that the USSR was following the (older) Leninist and newer (Lin Piaoist) strategy of defeating the West by encircling it, and exhausting it by numerous revolutionary wars aided by Moscow and Beijing. There was a mood of pessimism and urgency. But also the examples of Greece, the Philippines (Huk rebellion in early 1950s) were thought to provide successful examples that, among other things, came to be thought of as possible models for Vietnam later in the 1960s. In Greece, the incumbent regime was thought of as having operationalized the old French "oil slick" method of counterinsurgency, gradually increasing the areas under government control, pushing the insurgency to the peripheries and border lands, while increasing public support and morale.[45] In the Philippines, the very successful political methods of the Magsaysay government (advised by the legendary CIA operative Col. Edward Lansdale), including land grants to surrendered insurgents, provided still another model focused on "hearts and minds." In Malaya there was the successful use of "strategic hamlets" used to provide ever-expanding areas of control but also to move elements of the population into protected areas (the British model here was aided by the ethnic bifurcation of Malaya).[46]

By contrast, Algeria and Cuba were viewed as counterinsurgency failures. The former did eventually constitute a real model for Vietnam, wherein excessive government brutality aided the insurgents, who swam like fish in the population, where the incumbent regime was unable to sustain a high level of attrition and also suffered serious domestic dissension at home, and where the latter never really did seem to grasp the psychological factors of nationalism, ethnicity, and race vis-à-vis Cold War ideological elements. In Cuba, as later in Vietnam, a hopelessly discredited and corrupt regime could not begin to sustain popular support nor conduct an effective counterinsurgency, and merely toppled of its own weight. Numerous other insurgencies merely proved that colonial powers were doomed in the face of anticolonialist, nationalist movements, and unable or unwilling to sustain lengthy, bloody, and ultimately futile colonial wars: Palestine, Cyprus, Aden, Kenya, Rhodesia, Indonesia, Namibia, Nicaragua were among the cases of failed counterinsurgency against (in reality or rhetoric) insurgents imbued with Marxist-Leninist strategies, values, and outside support.[47] Elsewhere, other than Greece, the Philippines, and Malaya, some other "leftist" insurgencies were defeated or contained by "pro-Western" incumbent regimes backed by the U.S., mostly in Latin America, in Guatemala, El Salvador, Venezuela, Uruguay, and Argentina, with some of the latter insurgencies having consisted mostly of urban terrorism.

The general emphasis and skein of development of U.S. counterinsurgency strategy and tactics leading up to and during the Vietnam War has been commented upon in many other places and needs only brief review here. The Kennedy administration early on, under the aegis of General Maxwell Taylor and others, stressed the political and economic developmental side of the problem, emphasizing civic action, i.e., the reorientation of military elites (particularly in Latin America) from external threats to internal insurgency threats (one result was a batch of military takeovers in Latin America).[48] In Vietnam, the U.S. first tried, for some four years, the "strategic hamlet" program—"forced resettlement of rural villagers into fortified compounds, linked together in an interdependent network—that was hoped eventually to squeeze the Vietcong into isolated jungle areas."[49] As pointed out by Charles Maechling, the idea was not novel, having been tried before with varying success by the Spaniards in the Cuban revolution of 1895–97, the British in the closing phases of the Boer War, the French in Indochina, and the British in Malaya.[50] As devised by Sir Robert Thompson, the hamlet network should have been expanded outward from one or more secure centers, i.e., "oil slick redux." It didn't work. Later, the U.S. turned to the strategy of "search and destroy" (using conventional tactics and weaponry to fight a counterinsurgency war and emphasizing "body counts"), where the emphasis was on destroying an unseen enemy rather than holding territory. This featured large-scale ground sweeps preceded by air and artillery bombardments and accompanied by helicopter landings on the enemy flanks and rear. The second prong of U.S. strategy, termed "pacification," was a plan to gradually bring the entire rural South Vietnamese population under the administrative control of Saigon, in contrast to the hamlet-by-hamlet approach. A vast "nonmilitary" advisory organization called Civil Operations and Revolutionary Development Support (CORDS) was set up to advise and train village defense militias and to reimpose central government administration.[51] This was supplemented by the notorious Operation Phoenix assassination program aimed at liquidating the Vietcong political apparatus in the villages. All of this failed because of the fecklessness of the South Vietnam regime and the failure of the U.S. to understand the basic facts of a nationalist-based insurgency.

Later, in the 1980s, the Soviet Union would try and fail in Afghanistan at another large-scale counterinsurgency effort, in the context of a U.S.-aided (also aided by Egypt, Saudi Arabia, Pakistan, and others) Reagan Doctrine insurgency against a Soviet-backed "Marxist" regime. The Soviets eschewed strategic hamlets, but like the U.S. in Vietnam, they strove mightily to utilize conventional warfare methods to eliminate the various Afghan Mujahideen groups.[52] The Soviets exercised a higher level of outright brutality in deadly search-and-destroy missions (featuring mechanized forces, helicopters, artillery, tactical airpower, and "scorched-earth" tactics) and emphasized the "hearts and minds" side of pacification less. But like the U.S., they could not cope with an enemy willing to sustain high casualties, forbidding albeit much different terrain, and outside sanctuaries and sources of arms and money. Later, the Soviets (Russians) would experience still another counterinsurgency fiasco in Chechnya, albeit on a much smaller scale, but with many of the same problems of trying to utilize a conventional army and conventional tactics against a determined guerilla force fighting on its home ground (in a second round, however, the Russians were more successful). The Soviet counterinsurgency "model" may also have come closer to what is now the basic paradigm of ethnic counterinsurgency: where an ethnic incumbent regime attempts to crush an ethnic (or religious, linguistic) insurgency. As evidenced earlier in Biafra and Iraq's Kurdish areas that normally involves brutal, scorched-earth tactics, large-scale starvation of civilians, and massacres—a model that would become more familiar in the predominantly ethnic conflicts of the 1990s.

By the late 1990s, the long-familiar paradigm of insurgency/counterinsurgency had all but disappeared, indeed, might be added to large-scale conventional warfare as one of the perceived anachronisms of the post–Cold War period. Mao, Giap, Marighella, Guevara, also Lansdale and Thompson, had become historical data related to the Cold War period. There remained perhaps only one case of a Marxist-inspired revolutionary war against a traditional incumbent regime backed by the U.S., that of the Sendero Luminoso/Tupac Amaru insurgency in Peru, and even that had a strong ethnic as well as class-ideological component. Perhaps the same might be said for the Kurdish PKK vis-à-vis Turkey, maybe also the Zapatista revolt in southern Mexico, although Marxist rhetoric and external connections were lacking in the latter case. Marxist-Leninism had more or less exited the global stage, the USSR was gone, China had ceased altogether to support developing world insurgencies, and Castro's Cuba was isolated, impotent, and altogether in a defensive mode.

A glance at the U.S. military's field manuals in this area reflected the new situation. Revolutionary insurgency was by now just one of many categories or problems subsumed under the general rubric of LIC, along with various other categories such as terrorism, drug trafficking, peacekeeping (peace enforcing, peace making, etc.), and the various subcategories of LIC along a spectrum (high-, medium- and low-intensity conflict).[53]

Interestingly, FM 100–20, *Military Operations in Low-Intensity Conflict,* does provide a simple typology of modern LIC, somewhat parallel to the SIPRI distinction between wars of government and wars of territory. It distinguishes between what it refers to as "mass-oriented insurgencies" (Chinese revolution, Vietcong, Shining Path) and "traditional" (Afghan Mujahideen, Ibos in Nigeria, Tamil Tigers in Sri Lanka), with the latter based on "very specific grievances," i.e., springing from tribal, racial, religious, linguistic, or other such identifiable groups.[54] The traditional type (most of it ethnic insurgency) is seen as comprising a range of activities running from strikes and street demonstrations to terrorism to guerilla warfare. The military publication also discusses a "critical cell pattern" of insurgency, one variant of which is the old Cuban *foco* model, i.e., a single armed cell which "emerges from hidden strongholds in an atmosphere of disintegrating legitimacy," and the other of which is "the co-opting of an essentially leaderless, mass popular revolution," of which the Sandinistas' takeover of the Nicaraguan revolution is said to have been a case in point, along with the Bolshevik revolution.[55] A final type is deemed a "subversive" pattern in which insurgents "penetrate the political structure to control it and use it for their own purposes."[56] The Nazi takeover in Germany in the 1930s is cited as an example of this pattern, obviously closer to what we think of as a coup or putsch.

FM 100–20 also contains a lengthy analysis of counterinsurgency, noteworthy (in relation to the Cold War period) for its deemphasis on violence and military operations. It stresses the integration of military and civilian programs, fore-stalling insurgency by correcting conditions that prompt violence. Four major elements are stressed: balanced development (political, social, and economic pro-grams), security (protecting the populace and providing a safe environment for development), neutralization (physical and psychological separation of insur-gents from the population), and mobilization of popular support for the govern-ment.[57]

That, of course, represents a model and strategy for COIN operations in which the U.S. is supporting a regime elsewhere. But the U.S. has gotten involved in only a few COIN operations of late, mostly in the area of peace-keeping (Bosnia, Somalia, Haiti, Macedonia), and has eschewed such involve-ment in most ethnic conflicts, that is, up to the Kosovo situation. What is more relevant in the 1990s are the counterinsurgency doctrines of established regimes battling ethnolinguistic insurgencies, to which we shall soon turn.

Ethnic Wars, Ethnicity, and Internal Wars

We have established that most contemporary wars are internal wars on the low-intensity end of the scale, with a few exceptions for cross-border LICs, and that most recent internal wars have been "ethnic conflicts," effectively, wars over ter-ritory by most definitions. Yet it is also important to note that there is a massive and growing literature on "ethnicity" and "ethnic conflict" that stresses the con-troversial and ambiguous nature of this subject as it applies even to the most basic definitions involved. That literature was recently summarized in an article by Victor T. LeVine, who also provided a "model ontology of ethnic conflict," its typical phases, which somewhat parallels the heretofore discussed phases of insurgency warfare à la Mao, Giap et al., and viewed from the angle of coun-terinsurgency doctrine, the Pentagon.[58]

LeVine states the obvious in noting the wide range of definitional and con-ceptual confusion when it comes to terms such as "ethnic" and "ethnicity," even noting that with respect to European conflicts, scholars have preferred the cate-gories of "nationalities" and "ethnonationalism." Related terms providing con-fusion are "race," "culture," or "socioculture," "minority status," and "majority status." LeVine notes, for instance, that ethnicity is also not immutable, that "group boundaries may shift as groups divide, merge, erode, aggregate, or redefine themselves over time," and that "when social nexuses change, the norms of 'ethnic identity' can change as well; so it is that minority groups not infrequently take on the cultural traits of their more powerful or higher status neighbors, or intermarry with them and thus literally assume new ethnic identities."[59] "Minority status" is seen also as problematic as a concept applied to a subculture, as "such definitions tend to deny ethnicity to the majority or to majority groups."[60] LeVine further reveals the problems with all of the various "termino-logical surrogates": nationality, tribe, ethnic, primal groups, nuclear community, "autochthony," and "indigeneity," noting that attempts to define self-referential groups often involve normative ideologies of ethnoracial pride, self-assertion, and sociopolitical separatism.[61] "Ethnonationalism" is said to produce its own problems—"nationalism is only one of many kinds of political assertion, and that not all 'ethnic' groups seek a 'national' or 'nationalist' solution to their existential problems."[62]

Some recent attempts at defining ethnic identity have resorted to typologies involving dimensions such as "primordial," "instrumental," and "socially constructed." And they have categorized what, variously, ethnic conflict is *over:* status differentials; inequities in resource allocation; caste relations; distinctions based on race in "ranked" systems; territorial disputes; boundary maintenance; competition for resources in an "unranked" one.

LeVine ends up conceding that "ethnicity" and "ethnic conflict" do not lend themselves to precise definitions, but that notwithstanding he provides a "propositional inventory" in an effort at clarification, involving such issues as: ethnicity is largely a cognitive phenomenon shaped reciprocally in the perceptions of both members and nonmembers of a group; the ostensible markers of ethnic identity are many and varied; ethnicity (also "community") is a group phenomenon; ethnicity can be evoked or arise endogenously as shared behavior and/or modes of consciousness within the group or in the interplay between exogenous (perceptions and actions of others) and endogenous (self-generated) referents; ethnicity varies as to scope, intensity, and salience; ethnicity also varies in both textual and operational complexity; ethnicity's operative content locates it at the larger end of relevant self- and group-referents; at one of its core configurations ethnicity involves kinship, real, fictive, or (more likely) imagined, and primordiality; and ethnic identities represent variables in that the contents, expressions, and boundaries of ethnicity can change.[63] In short, this is a difficult and complex subject, not given to easy generalization or categorizations. It is important to note this, even in a work devoted primarily to the *military* aspects of internal warfare.

LeVine, going beyond the (obligatory and necessary) addressing of conceptual and definitional problems, presents a "model category of ethnic conflict." He presents a model that outlines the typical "stages and paths" of ethnic conflict, even while recognizing the essential uniqueness of each conflict.[64] It is a three-stage model, as were those for revolutionary/ insurgency war as posited by Mao and Giap, and while there are some parallels, there are also important differences. The three stages are (1) an "incipient phase," (2) an "open phase," and (3) an "out of control phase."

The incipient phase is one in which "the parties begin to come forward onto the political arena and define the stakes involved and their respective positions in relation to each other and the stakes, and when the modalities of conflict involving the use of violence are still at manageable levels." In the open phase, "the parties are in active, visible contention both in the institutional part of the arena, and if matters have escalated beyond those precincts, in its noninstitutional or informed sectors." In the "out of control" phase, a hypothetical "point of no return" is reached, "at which point violence may have escalated beyond the ability of the domestic agents of resolution to affect the outcome, and/or the conflict has begun to threaten the peace, security, or vital interests of proximate and more distant neighbors." It is stressed that there is nothing preordained about a transition from the first to the second, or the second to the third phase—at each stage there can be a plateau, escalation, or deescalation.[65]

In looking at the LeVine model for the escalation of ethnic conflict by comparison with, variously, the parallel but distinct Mao/Giap/Guevara "models" for revolutionary insurgency, several main points stand out, perhaps obvious and banal, but worth stressing in relation to war-fighting. The first is that whereas Mao, Giap, and Guevara (albeit Marxist-Leninists all, hence given to notions of historical inevitability and automaticity) provided basically *prescriptive* models involving phases of insurgency warfare (how it should be done and in what circumstances), LeVine's model for phases of ethnic conflict is largely empirical, albeit without large N formal modeling. The latter is laying out a typical pattern, but is in no way trying to provide a blueprint for the successful conduct of an ethnic war. Hence, it is not a coincidence that whereas revolutionary/insurgency doctrines have spawned their opposite counterdoctrines (how to conduct counterinsurgency operations), the ethnic-conflict literature focuses on conflict resolution. The latter, mostly written by Western scholars, tends to be politically neutral and is avowedly ameliorative, eschewing for the most part the taking of sides.

A second difference has to do with the primordial nature of ethnic conflicts, and here there is a bit of a paradox with respect to LeVine's "incipient phase." Most if not all ethnic conflicts have deep historical roots—those in Bosnia and Kosovo, for instance, go back six hundred years or more—and the same is true for Armenia-Azerbaijan, Ireland, Greece-Turkey, and various tribal conflicts in Africa or the native-European/mestizo divide in Latin America. In a sense, all of the current ongoing conflicts have emerged from long-simmering incipient or latent phases. Many have involved serial conflicts that have come and gone over centuries, albeit as previously noted, the ever-shifting nature of ethnic-religious-tribal identities.

Next, as is stressed in Chaim Kaufmann's work, there is the decisiveness of territorial control in ethnic conflict, causing military strategy in such conflicts to be very different from that in ideological conflicts. Hence, according to him:

> Unlike ideological insurgents, who often evade rather than risk battle, or a counterinsurgent government, which might forbear to attack rather than risk bombarding civilians, ethnic combatants must fight for every piece of land. By contrast, combatants in ethnic wars are much less free to decline unfavorable battles because they cannot afford to abandon any settlement to an enemy who is likely to "cleanse" it by massacre, expulsion, destruction of homes, and possibly colonization. By the time a town can be retaken, its value will have been lost.
>
> In ethnic civil wars, military operations are decisive.[66] Attrition matters because the sides' mobilization pools are separate and can be depleted. Most important, since each side's mobilization base is limited to members of its own community in friendly-controlled territory, conquering the enemy's population centers reduces its mobilization base, while loss of friendly settlements reduces one's own. Military control of the entire territory at issue is tantamount to total victory.[67]

There is a curious paradox in relation to this point, by way of comparison with projections of the future of conventional warfare. Regarding the latter, there is now a common generalization in the literature on the "military-technical revolution" (MTR) or "revolution in military affairs" (RMA) that territory, or geography in general, has become *less* important. So it is asserted, future conventional warfare will feature all-out preemptive destruction of massed enemy forces subject to a rain of precision-guided munitions directed in real time by satellite reconnaissance and "fusion" with firing systems. The traditional emphasis on "mass" will be passé, and controlling critical terrain barriers and borders will also become less important. Future conventional warfare is seen in a way as hyper-Clausewitzian with its emphasis on hi-tech, "kesselschlact" (near total) destruction of enemy forces on the field of battle, after which territorial control may be assured virtually as an afterthought. But in modern ethnic warfare, territory and boundaries remain altogether important in what is often a zero-sum relationship.

Fighting Low-Intensity Wars of the 1990s: Key Criteria

The post–Cold War period of the 1990s, as we have noted, has been dominated (from the perspective of conflict studies) by myriad low-intensity conflicts, even if the overall number of global conflicts has decreased. There has been a near absence of conventional wars. Most of the LICs have been wars of territory (rather than wars of government); they have been ethnolinguistic, religious-tribal conflicts (those of conflicting identities) rather than conflicts over ideology or divisions of economic class or labor and capital. These trends have received a lot of attention from modern-conflict analysts. Much less attention has been paid to how those wars have been fought, and to doctrines associated with that warfighting. The insurgency/counterinsurgency literature of the Cold War period, that part of it devoted to how wars are fought and who has been successful or unsuccessful and why, has not at all been cloned or superseded by an equivalent corpus of analysis for ethnic wars.

The beginnings of such comparative analysis would appear to require attention to some of the following areas, some of which, of necessity, need to be discussed in combinations.

- The spatial nature of the conflicts, i.e., whether contending sides are sharply demarcated territorially or interspersed, obviously involving myriad, idiosyncratic patterns.
- The geography of LICs, i.e., size of war theater, terrain, weather, relationship to contiguous nations, etc., as these matters fit into traditional criteria for insurgency warfare à la Mao, i.e., remote base areas, cover and concealment, access to outside help.
- Levels of economic development, i.e., per capita income (involving both sides or multisides of conflict)—these wars are fought in relatively rich countries (Northern Ireland, ex-Yugoslavia) and very poor ones.

- Basic asymmetries in populations, forces, i.e., ethnic insurgencies by tiny outnumbered minorities vs. those by large minorities or even majorities.
- Social distance between contending forces, hatred, vengeance, historical grievances, etc.; relative tendencies toward "war without mercy," dehumanization of enemies, etc.
- Strategies and tactics specific to LICs and comparatively within this rubric.
- Levels of weaponry used, i.e., wars involving only small arms, and other LICs seeing use of tactical aircraft, armor, etc., on one or both sides;
- The location of given wars along a spectrum within the LIC rubric from high low-intensity to low low-intensity conflict to terrorism, coups, border frictions, etc.
- LIC as internal war vs. LIC as intrastate or cross-border war.

Grand Strategy and the "Objectives" of Internal Warfare

Looking at the Cold War history of revolutionary insurgency warfare, it is apparent that in most of the relevant and important cases one was dealing with all-or-nothing situations. Insurgencies—wars over government—tend either to be fully successful or ultimately unsuccessful, despite the often protracted nature of such conflicts, as evidenced in Vietnam, the Philippines, Algeria, etc. Almost always, if the insurgency is successful, the previous incumbent regime is wiped out (literally), or sent to reeducation camps (Vietnam), or forced into exile, perhaps to plot a counterrevolution. That is a common syndrome, evident throughout the skein of history that runs from the English revolutions in the seventeenth century, to the French Revolution in the 1790s, to the Bolshevik insurgency and on to the aforementioned Cold War cases. On the other hand, failed revolutions, where control over government and ideology are at stake (Malaya, Greece, the Philippines, Guatemala, Brazil), usually result in the complete extirpation of insurgency forces. But there are exceptions, such as the resurgence of a Filipino Marxist insurgency long after the defeat of the Huks in the 1950s. There are also occasional cases where what are basically wars over government end up in precarious, uneasy coalition situations, as may perhaps characterize (partly) Cambodia in recent years, or Angola after the departure of Cuban and South African forces (actually, the struggle in the latter between the Luanda-based MPLA and Jonas Savimbi's forces also has had a strong ethnic component).

Hence, the concept of grand strategy in relation to LIC may be much less relevant than for the cases of nation-states dealing with diplomacy and the prospect of conventional warfare, maybe in a way so simple as to obviate the need for extensive discussion. In ideologically based conflicts (wars over government), the grand strategy of the insurgents is, simply stated, that of overthrowing and taking over the government, whereas the incumbent government, fighting a counterinsurgency operation, has as its grand strategy that of eliminating the insurgency or, just occasionally, absorbing and coopting it. More or less, these are opposing, reciprocal zero–sum strategies.

Defining grand strategies in the context of ethnic wars is more complex and situational. For the most part, ethnic insurgents have the overall aim of greater autonomy, oftentimes the achievement of independence, but sometimes that of a looser federal solution. A majority-based regime in an ethnic conflict will normally have the overall aim of holding a country together, territorially, and not allowing for independence or greater autonomy on the part of insurgents. Both sides normally aim at maximization of territorial control. Sometimes, of course, annihilation in the form of genocide, or varying degrees of "ethnic cleansing" (which can involve mass murder and/or large-scale relocations) can be the grand strategy in an ethnic war, as recently demonstrated in Bosnia, Kosovo, and Rwanda, and in numerous earlier circumstances.

Vengeance, Hatred, Honor, Domination: Impact on War-Fighting

Only recently have some long-ignored aspects of international relations—generally falling under the heading of political psychology—been paid the attention they deserve. In line with the increasing attention paid to the cultural aspects of international relations (with regard to warfare, strategic, operational, and tactical cultures), some scholars have begun to study long-suppressed subjects such as revenge, honor, humiliation. Hence, Susan Jacoby and Thomas Scheff have written books on revenge (only a portion of which had to do with international affairs), Donald Kagan has highlighted the importance of "honor" (national and subnational) as a factor driving nations' behavior (a modification of realist and rational-choice models), and Jonathan Mercer has produced papers on the factor of hatred in world affairs.[68] Still other scholars have focused on the concept of irredentism, both with respect to territorial and psychological factors such as defeat and humiliation, while psychiatrists have recognized the concept of "narcissistic rage," normally applied to individuals suffering from humiliation and defeat, as applicable to national or subnational behavior.[69] Running throughout all of this is a basic conceptual problem: whether the terminological baggage long applied to individuals by clinical psychologists can be made useful for aggregates either at the national or subnational level (tribes, ethnic groups). That in turn devolves into tricky methodological and conceptual problems surrounding the concept of identity, i.e., the extent to which aggregates may collectively hate, be vengeful and humiliated.[70] Methodological problems notwithstanding, interest in such areas is burgeoning, particularly as it comes to be recognized that large N studies of the causes of war, utilizing a variety of variables (polarity, polarization, power rankings, etc.) may be inherently limited by their absence of attention to (not easily measured) "psychological variables."

The factors of humiliation and vengeance are particularly germane here. So many of the internal wars of recent years (as well as some conventional ones) have been propelled by historical traumas, past defeats and humiliations, histories of dominance of one group over another. Examples come easily to mind. The Serbs reference themselves to a long-ago defeat at the hands of Muslim Turks in Kosovo. The Hutus react to a long history of domination and humiliation by

Tutsis. Hindu Indians remember the centuries of defeat and humiliation by the Muslim Moghuls. The Khmer people in Cambodia look back on centuries of hateful relations with the Vietnamese. When Saddam Hussein attacked Iran in 1980, Iraqis spoke of "Saddam's Quaddasiya," in reference to a long-ago Arab victory over the Persians. The Arabs seethe over their defeats at the hands of Israel, particularly that in 1967, and Greek Cypriots seethe over their defeat by Turkey in 1974.[71] Armenians battling Turkic Azerbaijan remember the genocide during World War I. In Africa, there are countless pairings of rival tribes or ethnic groups whose hatreds, rivalries, and dominance patterns go way back into the mists of history.

Indeed, this subject of revenge and hatred has even ramified into current discussions of nuclear proliferation and deterrence. It has been noted that throughout the Cold War, a "war" basically hinged on an ideological divide, there was very little hatred between the American and Russian peoples who, indeed, seemed even to like each other and had no history of defeat, humiliation, or dominance (for that reason it is now observed that only *after* the Soviet "defeat" at the end of the Cold War did some Russians begin to hate Americans). And the two nations were geographically far apart, a helpful factor. As we move toward the seeming inevitability of three weapons of mass destruction (WMD) dyads in the Greater Middle East (India-Pakistan, Arabs-Israel, Iraq-Iran), numerous analysts worry about more dangerous situations caused by explosive combinations of deep historical hatreds, contiguity, and hence some serious questions about the rationality of behavior.

One subject that then surfaces here, with regard to internal (particularly ethnic) warfare, is the degree of hatred, humiliation, past dominance, and compulsion to vengeance involved. But at the same time, there is no available empirical evidence on this subject—it is a virtual black hole. John Dower, in his major work on the U.S.-Japan war in the 1940s, *War without Mercy,* did a remarkable job of portraying the social distance, reciprocal racism and hatred, and poisoned history of two peoples who, when they came to a war, fought without mercy, indeed ending with the use of atomic weapons.[72] They took few prisoners, just as the combatants in Bosnia-Herzegovina, Chechnya, and Rwanda have taken few prisoners. Dower's point is that in a war where deep hatreds are involved, the result will likely be massacres, ethnic cleansing, perhaps even genocide. Such outcomes are far less likely in wars over government, where the contending sides often derive from the same identity groups, by race, religion, language, or ethnicity. That is the case even if one can point out that at the close of some revolutionary wars the losers (usually just incumbent government elites) may be executed, as occurred in France in the 1790s, Russia in 1917–18, Vietnam in 1975. But ethnic wars are different, even if largely fought over territory.

As noted, there is no "data base" in this area which, at any rate, if it were to go beyond the merely anecdotal level, would require extensive survey research to tap feelings of hatred, vengeance, humiliation, racism. But indeed almost all of our current and recent ethnic conflicts appear to involve high levels of hatred and compulsions to vengeance, with the end result of brutality, massacres, and various forms of savagery. The Afghanistan civil war, fought now between

Uzbek and Pathan-based Islamic groups, has evidenced terrible brutality. The recent reignition of the Abkhazia-Georgia civil war (even with Russian troops interposed) is being described as another case of ethnic cleansing. Hundreds of thousands of people have apparently been massacred or have starved to death in southern Sudan. There were the grisly descriptions of tribal massacres in and around Monrovia during the Liberian civil conflict, not to mention the severing of hands in Sierra Leone. The Iraqi government mercilessly gassed Kurdish civilians in Halabja. Tutsis were massacred en masse by Hutus, in most cases wielding nothing more than hoes, axes, and knives. For these reasons too, ethnic wars rank high in "severity," i.e., casualties.

Spatial Nature of Conflicts: The Role of Geography

In an earlier chapter we discussed some aspects of the geography of LICs; in particular, we analyzed the role of the overall size of nations in which internal wars have been fought, as well as the terrain—cover, weather, seasons, topography, urbanization, road networks. These criteria have long been deemed important to the analysis of revolutionary wars and counterinsurgency (wars over government!). Hence, China's vast depth and primitive countryside allowed Mao's forces to establish secure base areas, the Vietnamese and Cambodian jungles made it extremely hard for U.S. and South Vietnamese counterinsurgency operations and for interdiction of supply routes running south from North Vietnam, the rugged and remote Escambray Mountains made for a good jumping-off point for Castro's *foco* insurgency. Relations with external, contiguous nations were also vital. Vietnam could easily be supplied by arms from China, while arms supply to the Philippines with its many islands was clearly harder.

But what about the key geographic aspects of ethnic conflicts or other internal wars characterized as wars over territory? Here too, the overall size of battle theater, terrain, border contiguity with possible sources of arms may be important. But there are other criteria as well, falling mostly within the categories of demography and patterns of urbanization in relation to geography.

The key questions have to do with how the contending forces are a priori geographically demarcated, in the context of Kaufmann's earlier noted remarks about the all-importance of territorial control. In turn, this relates to obvious questions of symmetry or asymmetry of the populations of the contending forces, i.e., to what extent is one talking about big majorities and small minorities.

One might introduce this subject by noting, somewhat hypothetically, what kinds of "ideal types" might exist at the extremes. One could be dealing with sharply demarcated ethnic or other identity groups, each firmly embedded in whole or nonfragmented territories wholly contiguous within themselves, and perhaps too with a firm long-term historical basis. At the other extreme, one could be dealing with a very interpenetrated ethnic or other identity group mix, maybe even involving peoples not easily distinguished from each other, at least until they speak. In between, of course, are myriad, unique circumstances (often involving more than two identity groups, maybe several) whereby groups are somewhat spatially demarcated, but with enclaves within enclaves, all manner of possibilities. Ex-Yugoslavia has, of course, illustrated some of the possibilities.

Urbanization has, of course, created new complexities. In some places (numerous African nations are examples) where once tribes or ethnic groups were clearly spatially demarcated in rural, sparsely populated domains, some groups may now have migrated heavily into burgeoning cities; although they may live within urban neighborhood enclaves, these are still cheek by jowl in a manner in which explosive historical animosities can be easily triggered. The recent urban warfare in Liberia and Sierra Leone appears to have followed this pattern; Beirut's multisided conflicts in the 1970s were an earlier example.

The impact of urbanization on ethnic conflict may be seen even in some situations among the more developed European and North American nations, particularly as they pertain to asymmetric and dangerous dominance patterns. In Canada, Montreal came to be the dominant core area in Quebec, comprised largely of an English-speaking economic elite and a French-speaking underclass or working class, with the two groups sharply separated by neighborhood. To no one's surprise, this has caused trouble. In Belgium, there was a sharp spatial demarcation between Walloons and Flamands, and in Brussels a Walloon economic elite was once dominant. In South Africa during the period of apartheid there was a sharp demarcation between Boer and English regions, but with both groups well represented in Johannesburg, the core city, whose large corporations were dominated by the English. In Switzerland, German and French urbanization into the core cities (Zurich, Bern, Basel for Germans, Geneva and Lausanne for French) paradoxically maintained a degree of ethnic separation whereby each group controlled a core area. Hence, conflict was muted. There is a need for fuller examination of such trends and patterns in a variety of other contexts: Indonesia, Burma, India, Pakistan, numerous African states that have one core area into which numerous identity groups migrate and vie for influence and political and economic dominance. The data are scarce, hence the paucity of analysis of ethnic conflict and internal war.

Of course the problem of interspersed or noncontiguous configurations of ethnic populations and territories is nothing new. At the close of World War I at the Paris Peace Conference, it was the aspiration of Woodrow Wilson and others to reorganize the nation-state map of Europe so as to accommodate as much as possible the hopes for self-determination of many peoples, and hence to reduce the problem of territorial irredentism. This was at a time when the phenomenon of nationalism was thought, potentially, to be a positive force, and when it was thought possible to give each "people" its piece of turf. That aspiration turned out to be a mirage, as the post–World War I peace process became mired in the problems of hard-to-disentangle ethnic groups in Hungary, Poland, Czechoslovakia, Turkey, Yugoslavia, et al. That problem has now been repeated and magnified in the 1990s all over the Caucasus, Central Asia, the Baltics, and sub-Saharan Africa. And some scholars, such as Kaufmann, see the only true solution in large-scale population transfers and complete demarcation of ethnic groups, as was somewhat successfully done in Turkey-Greece-Macedonia after World War I, and in India–Pakistan after World War II, in the latter case still with continuing large-scale violence.[73]

Indeed, still another determinant in the conduct of ethnic or other identity-group warfare is the extent to which rival groups can identify people as a member of one side or the other. One might think that Irish Protestants and Catholics would not be able to tell each other apart, but apparently they can, almost unerringly. One might think the same of Palestinian Arabs and Sephardic Jews who have emigrated from Arab lands, or of Serbs and Croats who share the same language as well as ethnicity, but are divided by religion. This subject too needs further research. Its military importance lies in that, unlike in insurgency wars (wars over government but largely between economic classes, i.e., elite vs. mass), insurgents cannot swim like fish in their own home waters, to borrow the Maoist dictum. On the contrary, they are in danger of being caught outside their own home waters.

Finally, in relation to the geography of ethnic conflict, there is the factor of symmetry or asymmetry of populations and armed forces, and this too takes many forms. The long-dominant Tutsis are a small minority in Rwanda and Burundi. The Kurds are vastly outnumbered in Turkey, Syria, Iraq, and Iran, albeit sharply demarcated and with an overall demarcated area often dubbed "Kurdistan." Kosovo is 90 percent Albanian. The Basques are a tiny minority in Spain, albeit with a well-demarcated and fairly large region. The same is true for the Zapatistas in southern Mexico, the "ethnics" in Timor within Indonesia, the Baluchis in Pakistan, even in the Punjab region in India, the Sikhs—a large ethnic minority with a venerated history as a warrior people, yet very outnumbered within India as a whole. So too the Riffs within Algeria and the Muslims on Mindanao Island in the Philippines.

These two factors have important implications for military strategies, on both sides. A small minority, even if sharply demarcated territorially, will not likely have the military wherewithal to win a major military victory in which it conquers its larger opponent, usually an incumbent government dominated by a majority group. Hence, in striving for independence or autonomy, it will probably fight mostly on the defensive, looking to cause enough casualties, economic costs and political problems so that the incumbent regime will at some point concede independence or a larger degree of autonomy. A majoritarian government fighting a small ethnic minority will need to take the offensive to suppress a conflict, hoping to inflict enough pain and damage so as to bring about capitulation. Its aim is to maintain the territorial integrity of the state. The earlier independence of Eritrea nicely illustrates many of these points, and it is interesting that that conflict has now restarted after not having fully been resolved.

In an attempt to sum up this section, we have drawn up a table that lays out, in an approximate way, the various types of situations in connection with internal warfare and those few LICs that can be defined at least in part, as interstate conflicts. At the risk of some (unavoidable) oversimplification, that involves a basic two-way matrix, with a spectrum describing degrees of demarcation and within-group contiguity on one axis, and a spectrum describing asymmetries of population size and military power on the other. Unfortunately, these two factors do not always correlate. The Tutsis have more power in Rwanda than their population might predict, likewise Serbs in Kosovo. Admittedly, this spectrum captures only two, if major, variables critical to defining ethnic conflict (or more broadly, LIC and/or internal war). Levels of per capita GNP (including the comparative aspects *between* groups) would have made an additional factor worth including. The role of external borders (neighboring states related by ethnicity to one or another group, military assistance, sanctuaries) also needs to be factored in, particularly as neighboring related powers will often play a large role in ethnic conflicts on behalf of their brethren, as Russia may do in the Baltic states, Moldova, and Kazakhstan, and as Serbia did in Bosnia. But the main problem is that of the absence of detailed maps for all of the many relevant situations of internal warfare that might detail the patterns of ethnic populations, including the neighborhoods of large cities ranging from Riga and Tallinn, to Alma Ata and Tashkent, to Amritsar, to Managua and Mexico City. We can here make classifications mostly on the basis of scattered, sometimes imprecise, estimates and "verbal maps."

With regard to war-fighting and war outcomes, some tentative conclusions may be drawn from the (merely indicative) data for asymmetries and demarcations. First, it is clear that where sharp demarcations exist and some rough symmetry in military capabilities, the result will often be that of independence for an ethnic group wanting autonomy, or short of that, some degree of real autonomy, either formalized or rendered de facto by military stalemate. Hence, the Eritreans fought Ethiopia on roughly even terms for many years, achieved formal independence, and until recently at least, were able to more than hold their own in a new (interstate) skirmish. Abkhazia has achieved de facto autonomy and has been strong enough to conduct "cleansing" operations against Georgians left on the nether-side of the ethnic divide. In Angola, there is an uneasy semitruce between balanced forces in the wake of a seeming peace agreement. Where power is roughly balanced in less clearly demarcated situations, a precarious stalemate may result, as in Ireland and Nagorno-Karabakh. Where there is sharp demarcation but less than overwhelming power asymmetries, the weaker side may achieve some autonomy via deterrence, i.e., avoid being overwhelmed, as has been the case for the southern Sudanese, the Iraqi Kurds, Tajik ethnics within Uzbekistan, Muslims in Kashmir (actually a majority, but facing the Indian Army), Biafrans and Yorubas in Nigeria. In many of these cases, the military capabilities of the majority-run state are too limited, particularly when it comes to logistics and sustained combined arms operations, to allow for a definitive military solution. But the previous Russian failure in Chechnya, since brutally corrected, shows how difficult this can be against a determined foe, even for a modern, advanced military machine.

Where there is a sharp spatial demarcation between identity groups but a marked asymmetry of power, i.e., where there is a small, outgunned minority unable to fend off the majority group and its entrenched government, massacres or brutal domination may occur, as they have in East Timor, Iraq's Kurdish and marsh Shi'ite areas, and earlier with the Miskito Indians vis-à-vis the Sandinistas. These factors may, however, sometimes be mitigated by geographic factors— remote mountains, jungles—that allow vastly outnumbered and outgunned minority insurgents to at least persevere and carry on, albeit with high casualties and a seemingly hopeless situation. That may characterize the Kurds in Turkey's eastern mountains, the Karens in Burma's eastern jungle, the Riffs in Algeria's mountains, and the Zapatistas in Mexico's rugged and primitive south. Some of the groups in this category conduct merely sporadic terrorist operations, with no real hope of moving to a "higher" level of military operations—the Basques in Spain would well illustrate this point.

LIC: Tactics, Operations, Weapons

As previously noted, there is little extant comprehensive analysis of the war-fighting aspects of modern LIC, indeed, few if any detailed case studies equivalent to those earlier conducted for the Philippines, Malaya, Greece, and of course

Table 5.1   Patterns of Ethnic Warfare

	Sharp Demarcation	Medium Demarcation	Weak Demarcation (i.e., Interpenetration)
Approx. Symmetry of Power and Population	Georgia (Abkhazia) Somalia (clans) Ethiopia (re. Eritrea) Angola	Azerbaijan (Nagorno-Karab.) Ireland	Liberia Lebanon (multisided)
Some Symmetry of Power and Population	Iraq (Kurds) Uzbekistan Philippines (Muslims) Afghanistan Nigeria Sudan Kashmir	Sri Lanka Kazakhstan Estonia, Latvia, Lithuania Peru (Indians) Kosovo Malaysia Canada (Quebec) South Africa Palestine Chechnya Syria (Alawis)	Rwanda New Caledonia Bosnia-Herz.
Marked Asymmetry of Power and Population	Turkey (Kurds) Iran (Kurds) India (Punjab, Assam, Nagaland) E. Timor Spain (Basques) Algeria (Riffs) Myanmar (Karens, etc.) Georgia (S. Ossetia)	Nicaragua (Miskitos) Mexico (Zapatistas) Bangladesh (JSSSB) Colombia	Egypt (Copts) Indonesia (Chinese)

Vietnam. That abets the absence of a more conceptual literature equivalent to the insurgency/counterinsurgency writings of the past generation. With the exception of SIPRI's annual compilation of information on certain aspects of contemporary LICs—classification of the war as over government or territory, force sizes involved, casualties, duration of conflict—there is also very little data. As earlier noted, the arms-transfer data in connection with these conflicts is likewise sparse. There is nothing at all equivalent to the structured "lessons learned" analyses of several earlier conventional wars provided by Cordesman and Wagner, O'Ballance, Dunnigan, and Bay. Such analytical exercises exist, presumably, on a classified basis within the secretive confines of U.S. Defense Intelligence Agency (DIA) and perhaps other major powers' military intelligence organizations.

What we have are fragmented press reports and occasional articles in the military journal literature, particularly *Jane's Defense Weekly, International Defense Review,* and as noted, an occasional piece in magazines such as *Harper's* or *Atlantic Monthly* by a writer invited to accompany one or another side of a conflict on a raid or patrol, or in a bivouac area.

On that basis, we get merely fragmented images and sporadic battle reports, but little on the operational or tactical details or on the effectiveness of specific weapons. We read of Chad's successful use of Toyota pickup trucks mounted with light weapons as a form of modern cavalry. We read of teenage Tamil Tigers, male and female, conducting suicide missions as human bombs against the Sri Lankan army. We read of large Abkhazian patrols conducting "cleansing" operations against Georgians near Sukhumi; of rival Taliban and other Afghan forces' rocket and artillery barrages in and around Kabul. Rival tribal and/or political groups are portrayed slugging it out in urban warfare in Monrovia, Brazzaville, and Freetown, while Islamic militants in Algeria massacre civilians (often by slashing their throats) and are themselves hunted down by the Algerian army. In Yemen, northern forces utilizing Soviet aircraft and tanks conduct a fairly extensive combined-arms operation against the south. In Peru, Shining Path guerillas bomb banks, power stations, and police stations, and take hostages. On the West Bank, Palestinians fight with stones and occasional human suicide bombs. In Zaire, in a previous phase of war, a mixed army of Rwandan Tutsis and native insurrectionists conduct a lengthy and successful offensive against the Mobutu regime over hundreds of miles of rough jungle terrain and primitive road networks. In southern Sudan, a rebel force under General Garang controls the countryside and some small towns, fighting an increasingly successful insurgent war against the northern-based regime in Khartoum.

How then to order or classify some of these wars? A start was made in earlier SIPRI and COW Project publications, as indicated, concerning the traditional categories of magnitude (size of forces), levels of casualties, and durations of war. Much greater attention needs to be paid to the types and numbers of weapons systems involved. Some of the following questions and criteria will be addressed, broken down by types of war: wars over government vs. those over territory, cross-border wars vs. internal ones.

- What size are the forces involved and what degree of symmetry or asymmetry?
- What level of sophistication are the forces involved, i.e., some rough estimate of per capita GNP or other correlative measures of SES (socioeconomic status)? What kinds of symmetries or asymmetries are there here?
- What level of weapons use can one ascertain, i.e., are tanks, armored equipment, artillery, and ships involved (on one side or both?), or merely small arms, crew-served weapons, mines, explosives?
- To what degree are large-unit forces involved on either side and to what extent is there an identifiable "front" demarcating the contending forces, as contrasted with chaotic patterns of raids, ambushes, bombings, more rightly associated with terrorism or the low end of the LIC spectrum?
- To what extent are external powers involved regarding arms supplies, cross-border sanctuaries, surrogate or "volunteer" forces, provision of intelligence data?
- What is the mix of military and civilian casualties, symmetric or asymmetric?

Perhaps the best starting point in looking at some of these interconnected issues is the question of the extent to which some of these wars have come closest to conventional wars, are "quasi-conventional," as measured by force sizes, the use of sophisticated "combined arms," and the existence of moving "fronts" and large-scale battles. Among the recent cases that have approximated this "model" are Sri Lanka, Afghanistan (after the Soviet withdrawal), Cambodia, Chad-Libya, Sudan, North Yemen–South Yemen, maybe Angola (there might be an argument for putting Ethiopia-Eritrea in this category). Even with this mix of cases, there are strong variations with regard to some of the key criteria listed above. The Chad-Libya conflict has had strong interstate dimensions, mixed with internal fault lines. The level of sophistication of forces—measured by per capita GNP and other measures of development—is probably much higher in Sri Lanka than in Sudan or Angola. But all of these situations have involved large-unit forces, sophisticated modern weapons such as jet combat aircraft and tanks, and the existence of a "moving front" demarcating large geographic areas controlled by contending forces. The ebbs and flows of the progress of the wars can be followed on a map. Some of these cases have involved a rough symmetry of force sizes and capabilities (Ethiopia-Eritrea, Cambodia, Chad-Libya, Angola), while the Sri Lankan conflict has involved a fundamental asymmetry of capabilities between an incumbent, ethnic-based regime and a rebellious ethnic majority, doomed to fighting as an embattled underdog.

Sri Lanka has seen an exceptionally long war between the central government and the Tamil Tigers, with an interregnum in which a hundred-thousand Indian forces were involved (and ended up, paradoxically, fighting against their Hindu brethren).[74] The Tigers have had a fairly extensive territorial home base, first in the Jaffna Peninsula in the north and along the 650–mile Tamil Nadu coastline, and in the Vanni jungle south of Jaffna. The government has fought a brutal counterinsurgency war with large-unit "search and destroy" operations, tactical airpower, and naval forces. The Tamil Tigers have fought pitched battles with infantry and some mechanized equipment, but also have specialized in terrorist attacks, suicide bombings, etc., which have often carried into the nation's capital in Colombo and the port of Trincomalee. Several years ago the Tigers managed to kill some fourteen hundred government soldiers in one battle at Mullaivie,[75] and they have also succeeded at shooting down transport aircraft with SAMs and sinking government patrol boats such as the Israel-supplied Dvora-class and the Shanghai-class from China.[76] Altogether, at least sixty-two thousand forces have died in this struggle.[77] The government now holds Jaffna and the Jaffna Peninsula, after an offensive in late 1995, and the war has shifted to the jungle south of there.[78] On the other hand, much of this war has also involved ethnic fighting more similar to Bosnia and India. The Tamils have conducted terrorist bombings, but Sinhalese mobs have burned Tamil businesses in Colombo. In its attempt to extirpate the Tigers in their redoubts, government forces have explicitly used a version of the Malay "defended village" concept called Forward Defense Line (FDL), a static bunker line to stop infiltration outside Tamil areas. On the other side, the Tamil Tigers have used "Black Sea Tiger" suicide squads to sink navy cargo ships, have employed micro-light aircraft for suicide attacks, and have held government forces at bay with arrays of minefields, booby traps, mortars, RPGs and the like.[79]

The recent phase of conflict in Afghanistan, pitting the Taliban against several rival, feuding remnant Islamic forces from the previous war with the USSR, has also somewhat had the character of low-level conventional warfare. The Taliban forces swept from an initial base area in the country's south and east to a dominant position including control of the capital, Kabul, and also the large cities of Herat and Kandahar. Their rapid advance was paced by a force of some twenty-five thousand troops organized as an army, with two hundred tanks, a dozen or so fighter aircraft, and several helicopters. Battles over Kabul featured air attacks and extensive rocket and artillery bombardments, which have caused extensive civilian, as well as military, casualties. The war now pits Taliban, controlling Kabul and much of the country, against General Doestam's Uzbek-based National Coalition of the North, which according to one report deploys leftover MIG-21s, cargo aircraft, and "endless ranks of Soviet-made tanks."[80] That war now involves a moving front, large units, and a sharp demarcation of ethnic areas. In the earlier phase of the successful Taliban takeover of much of Afghanistan, the war appears to have consisted of a series of offensives by mechanized, truck-transported soldiers, supported by some airpower and heavy artillery, moving from one major city to another, creating an ever-expanding base. On a smaller scale, it was a bit reminiscent of the communist takeover of China in the late 1940s.[81]

The lengthy internal war in Cambodia, now over with the collapse of the Khmer Rouge, had the character of a low-level conventional war. It featured large-unit forces, extensive use of armored equipment including tanks, and moving fronts and demarcated areas occupied by (even after the withdrawal of two-hundred thousand Vietnamese troops) the forces led by Hun Sen's remnant post-Vietnam regime, the Khmer Rouge, and the Sun Sen Group associated with former King Sihanouk.[82] These contending forces have fielded about forty thousand, twenty-four thousand and twenty thousand troops respectively. Earlier, the Khmer Rouge had expanded its domain, conducting large-unit operations with armored forces. More latterly, the Khmer Rouge had been reduced to a smaller guerilla force based in a few enclaves located along the Thai border, after which the war was largely fought by infantry units but also featured extensive artillery duels.[83] On the other hand, the use of airpower was scarcely in evidence—none of the contending forces had a viable air force, and the terrain was not much amenable to the effective use of tactical airpower.

The war between Chad and Libya, peaking with some heavy fighting in 1988, did at least briefly entail the character of a conventional interstate war. There was an earlier phase in 1983 that was primarily a civil war, but where Libya weighed in with air attacks by Soviet-supplied Tu-22 bombers and MIG-21s.[84] In this phase, France intervened against Libya-supplied rebels, involving seven hundred French marines, SAMs, and antitank weapons brought in from the Central African Republic.[85] France pulled out in 1984, and Libya, reneging on an agreement, kept six thousand troops in northern Chad, causing the previous antagonistic Chadian sides to coalesce against Libya. Chad at the time had little in the way of air defense. In 1987–88, combat involved some twelve thousand Libyan forces versus ten thousand Chadians, in which several thousand Libyans were killed and some $1.5 billion in Soviet-supplied weapons was destroyed or captured.[86] There was a major Chadian victory based on superior tactics and morale and aided by sandstorms. The main battle took place at Faya Largeau, where two thousand Chad troops defeated a four thousand-man mechanized Libyan force heavily supported by Soviet-origin aircraft. In the process, Chad captured the main Libyan air base at Wadi Doum, which was protected by five thousand troops. Many Libyans were taken prisoner. Chad made effective use of antitank missiles and machine guns and mobile attacks by forces mounted on Toyota pickup trucks against Libyan armored columns deploying T-55 tanks and APCs. There was no use of artillery or mortars in a victory characterized by speed and flanking tactics.

The long struggle in Sudan, basically involving an ethnic-based insurgency on the part of non-Islamic ethnic or tribal groups in that nation's southern section against an Islamic-based central government in Khartoum, actually involves a mix of conventional and low-intensity war-fighting characteristics. There is a sharp geographic demarcation between the Islamic and non-Islamic spheres (actually this complex conflict has also involved intertribal conflicts in the south), but with government control over the main towns, particularly Juba, and rebel control over most of the countryside. As measured by severity, this war has been one of the deadliest in modern times—some estimates claim more than a million military and civilian deaths, from fighting, massacres, and starvation.[87] Regarding magnitude, basically the war has pitted some sixty thousand government troops against anywhere from twelve thousand to forty thousand rebels.[88] But otherwise, regarding the weapons used, the war has escalated toward something with a conventional character. In October 1995 the rebels under General

Garang launched an offensive with heavy artillery, AAA, and tanks (rumored obtained from either or both Uganda and Ethiopia) that threatened Juba and took some other towns. No longer were the rebels merely a ragtag army; ironically the Islamic side apparently resorted to suicide attacks on Garang's tanks near Juba.[89] The rebels, by 1997, may have been supported by Ethiopian tanks and artillery, while the central government deployed four battalions along the Ethiopian border.

By 1998 the character of the war had been altered somewhat. First, it was reported that the shifting coalition led by John Garang had become more successful after a stalemate of some three years, even to the extent of opening up a new front in the northeast near Ethiopia/Eritrea. Some reports now had it that Garang might aspire to more than just independence or autonomy for the south. But Khartoum was said to have bought off some southern leaders and turned them loose on their own people. Then too, one source claimed that "another scourge is the Popular Defense Force Militia—Arab horsemen recruited as army civilians, who also raid southern villages, stealing cattle, shooting young men and kidnapping women and children."[90] Ironically, as Garang's forces upgraded to armored equipment and artillery, the Khartoum government had initiated tactics more reminiscent of Ghenghis Khan's Mongols, or the Confederate cavalry during the American Civil War.

The equally long Eritrean rebellion against Ethiopia, which resulted in Eritrean independence, also came to have somewhat of a semiconventional character. In the main phase of the war in 1987–88, the Mengistu regime used the whole complement of modern weaponry including tactical airpower, mostly acquired from the USSR, against Eritrean rebels armed largely with captured equipment. But they had a lot of that: 130 mm rockets, ZSU-23 AA guns, some T-55 tanks.[91] In one main battle in December 1987, the Eritreans killed or captured some eighteen thousand Ethiopian soldiers. By 1988, the Ethiopians pitted some 120,000 troops against 50,000 Eritrean and also 15,000 Tigrean rebels.[92] There were attacks and counterattacks, and an identifiable line of battle. The Ethiopians used scorched-earth tactics and starved civilians, but ultimately the rebels succeeded with a rolling offensive toward Addis Ababa against a demoralized government army, using captured T-54 and T-62 tanks and B-24 MRLs, much of it taken in a big battle earlier at Afabet in 1988.[93] This was a fairly extensive war as measured by magnitude, severity, and duration. There was heavy fighting around the port city of Massawa in 1990, involving some thirty thousand casualties, and then more heavy fighting at Keren.[94] The rebels ultimately won the war with a conventional offensive, a war fitting the classic Maoist pattern, all the more ironic as it entailed the defeat of an avowedly Marxist incumbent government. In 1998 fighting resumed between newly independent Eritrea and Ethiopia, this time featuring some border skirmishing and artillery duels but also bombing raids by both sides on the others' civilian areas near the border. Later came a larger war in 1999–2000.

The long Angola war also had some of the characteristics of a conventional war, both before and after the withdrawal of Cuban and South African forces, supporting respectively the MPLA government in Luanda and Savimbi's

UNITA (after the Abadolite Agreement, fifty thousand Cuban troops left Angola).[95] Even in the latter phase after the withdrawal, there was extensive use of tanks and MIGs on both sides, which were demarcated along a front between two large contending regions.[96] The government forces tried to get at Savimbi's headquarters, located for a long time at Jamba, convenient for getting supplies from South Africa; they used a forward MIG base at Mavinga for this purpose. The Savimbi forces tended to rely somewhat more on guerilla tactics, particularly the bombing of trains along the old Benguela railroad.[97]

Later, in 1997, the overthrow of the long incumbent Mobutu regime in Zaire also had somewhat the character of a conventional war. Insurgent Zairian forces, abetted by Rwandan Tutsi forces, conducted a lengthy offensive all across Zaire, utilizing mostly mechanized infantry, and succeeded in conquering the country and taking over the capital at Kinshasa.[98] Just afterwards, there was a war in Congo-Brazzaville which had some elements of conventional warfare but also had characteristics of an urban military coup. There were four months of fighting in Brazzaville, characterized by very destructive artillery duels that destroyed substantial parts of the city. The successful rebel forces, aided by Angola, used MIGs and tanks in this fighting.[99]

In late 1998, the second major phase of the ongoing Congo conflict also had some characteristics of an interstate conventional war. Here President Kabila, who had defeated the previous Mobutu regime, came under attack from his former allies, Rwanda's Tutsis and Uganda. But Angola and Zimbabwe aided Kabila with aircraft and tanks and, apparently, the ferrying of troops by transport aircraft between several major areas of fighting. The rebels took over much of the eastern part of the country, also the southwest area near the Angolan border, and launched attacks on the major cities—Kinshasa, Kisangani—before being repulsed.[100]

On the next tier down the scale toward the middle range of LICs are a number of wars fought on a smaller scale (severity, magnitude) than those previously discussed, and with less use or no use of larger weapons platforms such as modern combat aircraft, but where there is a moving front and spatial demarcation between combatants organized in large combat units. Abkhazia–Georgia, Azerbaijan–Nagorno-Karabakh, Tajikistan, and Bosnia all seem to have more or less fit that pattern. In all of these cases there has been relative symmetry between forces of roughly equal combat power.

The battles in Abkhazia have involved a mix of urban skirmishing, ethnic cleansing by small, organized armed bands, but also some small-unit battles, and those where there is a demarcation between contending sides, albeit also some pockets of Georgians within semiautonomous Abkhazia.[101] Further complicating matters has been the presence of some twenty-three thousand Russian troops located at forward bases, who have acted somewhat as an interposition force. In one major battle in 1993 involving an Abkhazian offensive toward the port city of Sukhumi, four hundred Abkhazians and eleven hundred Georgians were reported killed, Sukhumi was reported pounded by rockets, artillery, and even air bombardment by Abkhazian rebels trying to regain the city from Georgian troops who had captured it a year before. Later, in Abkhazia, half of whose population is Georgian, five hundred Georgian men were said to have attempted to recapture a province, involving small massacres and ethnic cleansing.[102] The nature of the fighting here, as measured by the size of the forces and the levels of weaponry involved (some use of rockets, artillery, tactical airpower, light armored equipment), resembles that in Bosnia, perhaps a bit lower on the scales of magnitude, severity, and duration.

Roughly the same levels and nature of combat took place in Nagorno-Karabakh in a conflict that ended, for the time being, in 1994 after seven years of fighting, during which Azerbaijan lost a fifth of its territory. (Whether Azerbaijan, now growing wealthy and increasingly possessed of political clout with the major powers, will accept this "conclusion" remains to be seen.[103]) But for the time being at least, Nagorno-Karabakh is, de facto, part of Armenia. Both sides in this fighting were availed of significant quantities of ex-Soviet military equipment left when the Russians withdrew in 1991. The Armenians had SAMs to combat the Azerbaijanian air force. The Russians helped the Armenians after first helping Azerbaijan; Turkey helped train the latter's army. Azerbaijan also benefited from extensive Ukrainian weapons shipments, including MIG-21s, Su-15s and 25s, and some 100 T-55 tanks.[104] Fighting took place in mountainous terrain involving large units and with a clear geographic demarcation between forces utilizing tactical airpower (mostly on the Azerbaijanian side), some tanks and APCs, and heavy artillery.

Somewhat similar was the nature of the combat in Tajikistan, where somewhat similar to Georgia, Russia has maintained some twenty-five thousand troops to support a postcommunist regime under pressure from Islamic rebels supported by Tajik sources in northern Afghanistan.[105] That war has resulted in some forty thousand deaths and up to eight-hundred thousand refugees.[106] The Tajik rebels have used helicopters and some armored equipment in a war characterized by some large-unit formations and a battle "front," but also involving bombings and other terrorist activity. The more familiar (to Western readers of the daily press) Bosnia conflict (and that between Serbia and Croatia) saw extensive use of heavy artillery, mortars, rockets, and only minimal use of airpower, but where generally speaking, there were large-unit formations and a very discernible "front" between contending forces. The resulting casualties, including those from massacres of civilians, was on a considerably higher scale than in Abkhazia, Nagorno-Karabakh or Tajikistan, reflecting the larger scale of the war, that is of its magnitude, i.e., size of forces involved.

The conflict in Somalia that brought on the ill-fated U.S. intervention may also be placed in this category, albeit the fighting occurred at a lesser degree of sophistication as pertains to weaponry. The contending Somalia forces based on clans had a definite geographic demarcation, and they were armed largely with automatic weapons and recoilless rifles and RPGs often mounted on vehicles. There was little if any use of armored equipment, heavy artillery or aircraft. The conflict appears to have been relatively symmetric.[107]

The recent conflict in Serbia's Kosovo Province has involved a degree of overall symmetry subsuming dual asymmetries, one on each side. On one side, the province is overwhelmingly Albanian ethnic, comprising some 90 percent of the population, and in this sense there is similarity to Iraq's Kurdistan, in that an incumbent regime is using overwhelming preponderance of advanced weapons in trying to control a breakaway province. But the Kosovo Liberation Army (KLA) also has the advantage of sharing a border with Albania, which is supportive in terms of arms shipments and providing sanctuary. The nature of the fighting was illustrated in the battle over the town of Orahovac in July 1998. There, Serbian police officers armed with AK-47s were besieged by KLA forces utilizing artillery and machine guns.[108] The Serb army also utilized heavy armor and helicopter gunships, and the KLA defended against this threat with hand-held antiaircraft missiles, presumably variants of the SAM-9. Ambushes and battles appear to have caused casualties in the hundreds. Later, near Orahovac, KLA rebels were reported moving "their white sandbagged positions and pickup trucks with heavy machine guns" south toward other towns.[109] Nearby, in Malishevo, a rebel stronghold, "rebel soldiers in full body armor and heavy weaponry scurried into cars that sped to the front lines."[110] The description of the fighting was reminiscent of Bosnia, perhaps Chechnya, perhaps also Lebanon early on, involving a mix of fairly sophisticated weapons, asymmetrically favoring government forces, but also utilization of civilian pickup trucks and cars for transport and mounting of weapons. Indeed, early on, the Serbian army made extensive use of heavy armor, something that was mostly lacking in the Bosnian Serb forces. As the fighting continued in late 1998, Serb forces appeared increasingly unimpeded in conducting sweeps of Albanian ethnic areas, burning villages, and driving refugees out with artillery fire, in somewhat of a scorched-earth policy.

The above ethnic conflicts, typically involving a breakaway ethnic group against an incumbent government, have as noted been characterized by a relative symmetry of forces, have ended or have continued on in a state of relative stalemate or standoff. In some other recent ethnic wars, there has been a much greater degree of asymmetry, involving a powerful government armed with an array of modern weapons against greatly outnumbered and outgunned ethnic minorities. The latter cannot contemplate a military victory but bank on causing enough casualties and other costs to gain themselves a begrudged independence, or degree of federalized autonomy, or a degree of de facto autonomy amidst an ongoing or intermittent conflict. Some such embattled minorities have managed to deploy some sophisticated arms, either acquired from abroad or captured. And in those conflicts, minorities have managed to retain control over significant ethnic enclaves, i.e., have a degree of geographic separation. Among the conflicts in this category: Chechnya; the Kurd's revolts in Iraq; Iran and Turkey; East Timor; and the West Bank (Kosovo may now be counted in this category).

In Chechnya, in the first round in 1996, the Russians used extensively tactical airpower and heavy armor units to combat an outgunned Chechnyan force compelled to rely mostly on small arms, mines, crew-served weapons, and some light artillery and mortars. But as is so often the case in such conflicts, a road-bound modern army suffered some defeats and heavy casualties in trying to deal with a determined albeit outgunned foe. The war was first fought largely in and around the capital at Grozny, then in the smaller towns and mountain foothills

south and east of the capital. Here, an outgunned ethnic force tried, perhaps successfully, to create just enough casualties so as to approach the pain threshold for
the dominant force and to induce domestic discontent among its citizens and
government.

In the second round of the Chechnya war, the Russians, having learned some
painful lessons, utilized altered tactics. This involved massive use of tactical airpower (including assault helicopters) and long-range artillery to gradually force
retreats of Chechnyan insurgents first from the country's northern plains, and
then from Grozny (the latter still turned out to be difficult to capture on the
ground with infantry using urban warfare tactics). Ironically, the Russians, who
had been willing to absorb truly massive casualties in World War II, seemed
almost as sensitive to casualties as the Israelis or Americans, no doubt an indicator of the shift toward a more modern polity and economy.[111]

Likewise, the long, interminable wars involving the Kurdish rebels against
Iraq and Turkey (to a lesser degree, Iran) have involved the massive firepower of
middle-range powers (airpower, heavy armor, etc.) pitted against outgunned and
outnumbered insurgents. Relative to Chechnya, however, this has involved
much larger spaces—the Kurds occupy the northern third or so of Iraq and a
large area in eastern Turkey. In northern Iraq, the government has benefited
from divisions within the Kurdish rebels and recently was able to align with one
against another tied to Iran. Both the Turkish and Iraqi armies have suffered
extensive casualties fighting the Kurds, who still fight on with limited weapons
capabilities, but with the advantage of large spaces and an ethnically separated
region within which they can operate. The Turkish Kurds (PKK) have benefited
from training camps in Syria-controlled Lebanon, and have resorted to terrorist
acts as well as small-unit operations. The Iraqi Kurds earlier benefited from Iranian and Israeli weapons support, after the Gulf War from the protection of Western forces. The fortunes of the Kurds in both countries appears to have waned in
recent years.

In East Timor, the Fretilin movement has fought a long ethnic guerilla war
against the overwhelming force of the Indonesian government, one that is
reputed to have cost the lives of some hundred thousand people on the island.
This conflict was characterized by terrorist and sporadic guerilla-force operations, with the East Timorese having been mostly subdued despite the difficulties
posed to the Indonesian forces of harsh jungle terrain and the logistics of fighting on a peripheral large island. But Fretilin still can be characterized as a military force of sorts, or was until the referendum that appears for the time-being to
have muffled violence.[112]

Still further along the spectrum are ethnic or other internal wars characterized by extreme asymmetries, where the insurgent force engages primarily in
terrorist or merely small-unit operations, and where the chances of their ultimate
success (defined as independence or autonomy) would appear to be minimal or
nonexistent. But in still other conflicts where terrorism or small-unit harassment
operations are the primary modus operandi, there may well be a chance of a positive political outcome from the insurgents' perspective. In the first category is
the ongoing conflict in Peru, perhaps also the more recent Zapatista rebellion in

southern Mexico, or the still ongoing rebellion in Colombia, or the sparse remnants of leftist rebellions in Guatemala and El Salvador, albeit in the latter case with a peace agreement of sorts and the beginnings of democratic elections.

In Peru, more than thirty-five thousand people have died in fighting over many years between the central government and the two revolutionary groups, Sendero Luminoso (Shining Path) and Tupac Amaru, themselves mutually antagonistic. As previously noted, this has generally been a war over government, but with an ethnic component, notwithstanding the fact that much of the Shining Path leadership is of European rather than of Amerindian background. To only some extent has there been a geographic demarcation between contending sides, with the guerillas able to operate in the countryside and having somewhat of a base in the Huallaga Valley. But mostly the insurgency has had the character of an earlier phase of a classic Maoist insurgency, featuring commando or terrorist acts—bombings, including car bombings (of power stations and American fast-food restaurants), bank robberies, kidnapping of business executives, hostage-taking (as in the major incident involving the Japanese Embassy in Lima), and ambushes of army and police patrols. These insurgent activities have taken place in Lima, provincial towns in the interior, and in the countryside. Mostly, this has involved automatic weapons, explosives, even machetes, and the government's COIN responses have been at the level of small units armed with infantry weapons.[113] Earlier, around 1994, Shining Path had succeeded with bombings of research institutes, banks, the knocking out of Lima's electricity, and numerous ambushes of police patrols. More recently, the Fujimori government's COIN operations have appeared increasingly successful, so that the insurgents no longer really concern themselves with controlling territory or ambushing army and police units, but rather with commando operations intended to destabilize the government.

In Mexico's Chiapas state, by contrast, the insurgency has been more limited, seemingly with no hope of overthrowing the central government—it is an ethnic insurgency but with overtones of class warfare. There are 1.2 million Chiapas Indians within a nation of ninety-seven million people.[114] Mostly this has involved limited action with small arms and small units, and the Mexican army has responded likewise with counterinsurgency actions by small infantry units. Recent reports indicate that the Mexican army has deployed twenty-five thousand soldiers backed by helicopters, and that those soldiers have surrounded rebel villages and set up hundreds of roadblocks. The Indians appear to have only about a thousand trained fighters, and ranchers have armed some anti-Indian paramilitary groups. More than a thousand Indians were killed despite a cease-fire that was called after twelve days of combat in 1994, after which the conflict simmered down. Generally speaking, whether because of the terrain or settlement patterns or the efficacy of Mexican forces, the Zapatistas seem less able to establish a viable rural base for an insurgency, relative to Shining Path in Peru. In neither Peru nor Mexico has airpower or armored equipment or artillery been engaged. That has likewise been the case in the ongoing, simmering conflict in Guatemala, with roots going back forty years, which also has both class-based and ethnic components. That insurgency has had somewhat of a geographic base in the mountains and along the Mexican border; in recent years the conflict has been dormant.

In some senses, the ongoing Islamic fundamentalist insurgency in Algeria has similarities to the Peruvian conflict, but in fundamental respects it is different. For one thing, there is much less of an asymmetry in forces—the Algerian fundamentalists have deep roots and widespread support, similar to Iran in the 1970s (indeed, they won a national election, the results of which were then voided by the government). And in the Algerian case, though the jury is still out, there would appear to be a substantial chance that ultimately the fundamentalists will prevail against a discredited government.[115] But even less than the insurgents in Peru, the Algerian insurgents have no real demarcated geographic base—this is, indeed, fully a war over government, with a religious rather than ethnic basis of conflict. The nature of the fighting has some similarities to Peru and maybe also to Sri Lanka, with bombings and ambushes, but also with grisly massacres of civilians in which large numbers of people have had their throats slit. The government's COIN operations have apparently featured mobile small-unit operations, and there has been no use on either side of airpower, armored equipment, or heavy artillery.[116] The fundamentalist insurgency in Egypt, meanwhile, has a somewhat similar character, except on a smaller scale and with a lesser base of popular support for the insurgents. Egypt's small Coptic minority has been a target of Islamic insurgents, introducing a religious-ethnic component to the conflict lacking in Algeria. In the latter country, however, the growing Riff rebellion, wholly separate from that by the fundamentalists, has an ethnolinguistic basis, and the Riffs do have a discrete geographic regional base in the mountains. That "revolt" has not yet taken on a marked military character.

Some of the more recent conflicts, particularly in sub-Saharan Africa, have largely involved urban fighting in connection with military coups, sometimes with an ethnic or tribal component. As previously cited, in the case of Congo-Brazzaville that involved large-scale combat with artillery and rockets and light armored equipment. In others, it has had the character of large-scale gang warfare except with heavy casualties, as has recently been the case in Liberia and in Sierra Leone, in both of which external peacekeeping forces have been involved.[117] Here too, fighting has been conducted more or less entirely with small arms and crew-served weapons—in Liberia, opposing groups have used M-16 and AK-47 rifles.[118]

The 1992 short war in Moldova, which cost between fifteen hundred and seventeen hundred battle deaths, was fought on approximately the same scale as in Abkhazia.[119] Here, there was a fairly clear geographic divide between ethnic Moldovans, related to Romania, and a more urbanized Russian and Ukrainian minority in the "Trans-Dniester Republic" seeking independence. The Russian side was availed of "volunteers," including Cossacks, led by General Lebed. Airpower was not used, but there was some use of tanks on the Moldovan side. Mostly, the war saw use of artillery, rockets, some ground-to-ground missiles, and extensive use of small infantry units and snipers. The conflict ended inconclusively, a military stalemate, leaving the "Trans-Dniester Republic" de facto an autonomous unit, albeit without formal external recognition. The parallel with Abkhazia is apparent.

In Asia, there have been two additional examples of long, drawn-out internal insurgencies characterized by asymmetry—in Burma and the Philippines. Burma has experienced about a dozen insurgencies, involving several ethnic groups: Karens, Kachins, Mons, and Shans in the east, Arakanese in the west, and also some Marxist-inspired insurgencies in the north and in ethnic areas.[120] Some of these insurgencies, similar to Colombia, have been related to the control of the drug trade. The fighting has been mostly sporadic and low level, fought with infantry weapons and mortars, primitive to the point that the Mon National Liberation Army was reported using bullock carts for ambulances. But the insurgencies endure.[121] Elsewhere in Asia, the Philippines have experienced two separate, long-term insurgencies that have flared and abated for decades, resulting in tens of thousands of mortalities, many of them civilians. On the southern island of Mindanao, the Islamic-based Moro National Liberation Front (MNLF) has conducted an ethnoreligious war intended to produce autonomy or independence. On the main island of Luzon and on several other islands including Negros, the leftist NPA (New Peoples Army) has fought another major insurgency, this one under the rubric of "war over government." The war in Mindanao has involved large-scale counterinsurgency operations featuring tactical aircraft and helicopters, but in forbidding, mountainous, jungle terrain. The insurgency in Luzon has featured hit-and-run tactics, bombings, assassinations, etc. by the NPA, fought by COIN operations but also civil, political, and economic efforts by the government. By the late 1990s, the latter conflict had largely petered out.[122]

The Role of External Forces in Internal Wars

In various internal wars, whether wars over government or wars over territory, there has been involvement by external forces: by major and noncontiguous powers, by contiguous regional nations, or by regional peacekeeping forces. This can take the form of direct intervention by external forces, the provision of sanctuaries where contiguity is involved, or arms transfers, or combinations of these factors. Let us look at the first of these two categories. (Arms transfers are covered in chapter 7.)

Numerous recent internal wars have seen direct involvement by external forces, variously involving ethno-religious-linguistic consanguinity or identification, or balance of power considerations or both. Russian troops have, for instance, been directly involved in Georgia-Abkhazia and Tajikistan, the latter of which is no longer contiguous to Russia. In the former case, Russian troops have acted primarily as an interposition force (at least in the more recent phase of conflict), whereas in Tajikistan they have supported the post-Soviet incumbent regime against Islamic fundamentalists backed by Tajik ethnic forces in northern Afghanistan. In short, both sides have had external support in this conflict.

In Lebanon, of course, Syrian troops have actively intervened, at various times for and against the Christian Maronite faction, while Israel earlier intervened on behalf of the latter and also earlier supported Shi'a factions in the south. The U.S. and other Western nations had, for a while, shielded the Kurds from the Baghdad government. Pakistan openly supports its coreligionists in Kashmir, though without direct Pakistani army involvement (this may have changed a bit lately). In an earlier phase of the Sri Lankan conflict, some hundred thousand Indian troops were engaged, first to help fellow Hindu Tamils, later in conflict with the latter. Ethiopia and Uganda have supported southern Sudanese forces with arms and sanctuary but not with direct involvement. Rwandan Tutsi forces intervened on a large scale to assist rebel forces that overthrew former Zairean President Mobutu, while Angolan government forces were directly involved in the urban civil war in Brazzaville. In the next phase of the Congo (formerly Zaire) war, the new incumbent Kabila regime was supported by interventions by Angola and Zimbabwe, while the new rebels were supported by Uganda and Rwanda. Nigerian forces have been directly engaged in internal conflicts in Liberia and Sierra Leone. Russian forces under General Lebed intervened in Moldova. South African forces intervened on behalf of Jonas Savimbi in Angola, Yugoslav government forces on behalf of Bosnian Serbs.

Other cases have involved the use of cross-border sanctuaries. Thailand was long a sanctuary and base for Cambodian Khmer Rouge forces. Pakistan long served as a sanctuary and base for Afghan forces fighting the USSR in the 1980s. Kurdish areas in northern Iraq have provided sanctuary for Turkish Kurd rebels who have been pursued inside Iraq by Turkish forces.[123] Albania has recently provided bases and sanctuaries for KLA rebels fighting in the Kosovo. Ireland has, de facto, acted as a sanctuary for the IRA. Indeed, many internal wars, mostly ethnic, have had cross-border implications. But there are also numerous exceptions: Peru, Mexico, Somalia, Algeria, Eritrea, Nagorno-Karabakh, Afghanistan (recent phase), Yemen, East Timor, Colombia, maybe Burma.

Smaller Conflicts

There are a number of additional internal conflicts, most of which have not attained the SIPRI threshold of a thousand combat-related deaths, which nonetheless are listed in some contemporary compendia of recent and ongoing conflicts. A number of these have been cited by David Keen in his recent study of "The Economic Functions of Violence in Civil Wars."[124] In most of these cases, the contemporary literature, or even the press, have revealed little if anything about the nature of conflict, assumed in all cases to have been fought out sporadically at the low end of the LIC spectrum, i.e., modest casualties, nothing beyond small-arms use, terrorist acts, and limited skirmishes. Among these have been the conflicts in Bangladesh, Burundi, the Central African Republic, Colombia, Comoros, Mali, Niger, Papua New Guinea, Senegal, and Uganda. These smaller conflicts have been concentrated in Africa, most with tribal-ethnic implications and characterized as "wars over territory." But that in Colombia, similar to the case of Peru, represents a more classic conflict over government, in the manner of a Cold War–era leftist insurgency.

In Colombia a narrowly ideological war has been in progress for forty years, recently involving three rebel groups—FARC, ELN and ELP—the first two of which have been more important and representing respectively a standard leftist position and a more extremist Castroite position. This war, which together with conflicts over drugs and other murders, took thirty thousand lives in 1997, has been fought mostly in the south and east of Colombia. Mostly it has involved small-unit combat and hit-and-run tactics in the rural hinterlands, though the government has employed tactical aircraft and attack helicopters to little avail in rugged terrain. In March 1998, an entire Colombian army battalion got wiped out in one battle, and there have been four major government defeats in the last year. This conflict, at its height, has rivaled that in Peru—interestingly, together they constitute a remnant of classic Marxist revolutionary warfare, albeit involving drugs.[125]

The conflict in Bangladesh has largely been an ethnic LIC, involving a non-Bengali and non-Islamic tribal minority in the Chittagong Hills Tracts, where the government has tried to move in Bengali Muslim settlers. The war has been fought at a low level in very tough jungle terrain, mostly involving small units and small arms, wherein the insurgents attack the settlers. The conflict has tied down a good portion of the Bangladesh army, while Dacca is suspicious of Indian involvement, even to the point of giving it a pro-Pakistani cast.[126]

Not to be ignored are two recent, major conflicts dating back to the Cold War era—in Western Sahara and Mozambique. These are now dormant, although there is still no comprehensive settlement in Western Sahara where the Polisario, in the 1970s supported by leftist Algerian and Libyan governments with Soviet weaponry, fought a lengthy and bloody insurgency against the Moroccan government. This was a war over territory, over the question of Western Saharan independence.[127] The Moroccan government was assisted by the U.S. with COIN military equipment. Famously, it built a very lengthy sand berm wall as the basis for its defense, backed by attack helicopters and tactical airpower that could be effective in open desert terrain. (The terrain in Western Sahara is rugged and craggy enough to allow for some hiding by guerillas, who mostly specialized in mobile commando tactics and fairly large-scale raids with light vehicles armed with automatic weapons and some light armored equipment). The phosphate deposits at Bu Craa were a major strategic prize in this conflict. Gradually, the Moroccans' defensive tactics, hinged on the fortified berm and aerial interdiction, seemed to prevail, leading to a formal ceasefire in 1991, much argument over possible referenda, but no final settlement. The UN is now involved, and a plebiscite will presumably be forthcoming.

In Mozambique, the RENAMO antigovernment forces fought a long insurgency with mixed tribal and ideological elements and where the rebels controlled large swathes of territory in the central Mozambican interior and along the border with Zimbabwe. The casualty figures for this war, mostly accounted for by village massacres, were huge, commonly estimated in the hundreds of thousands, rivaling Sudan, Rwanda, and Angola.[128] The war, which mirrored

Cold War politics (a Soviet-backed regime under siege from the more Western-oriented RENAMO), was ended by a general peace agreement in 1992 and is cited as a conflict that ended because of the end of the Cold War. But of course the main external involvement was from the former white South Africa, which backed RENAMO. The war was primarily ideological and regional in its basis, less so tribal or ethnic. FRELIMO came to power in 1975 after a long struggle against Portugal, and alienated traditional elites. It operated out of neighboring Tanzania, giving it a northern base, while South Africa supported RENAMO from the south, via a corridor into the country's central region, and was focused on keeping open a railway into Beira. There were some ethnic overtones to this conflict, but they were not central.

The secessionist movement on the part of the Bougainville Revolutionary Army (BRA), begun in the late 1980s, is partially ethnic in character (Papua New Guinea has a large number of tribes and languages), but mostly is explicable on the basis of regional economic interests and control of resources, specifically a copper mine on Bougainville. That conflict had been a low-level guerilla war, with forces on either side numbering in the hundreds. The casualties have been correspondingly modest. Recent peace negotiations sponsored by Australia and New Zealand may have been successful, and if so would allow for some autonomy for Bougainville. More recently, also in the southwest Pacific area, there was a coup in Fiji with strong ethnic overtones.[129] Likewise in the Solomon Islands, a coup involved fighting by the rival ethnic groups from Malaita Island and Guaklacanal.[130]

Back to Africa, there have been several other small low low-intensity conflicts that have emerged in recent years, usually with an ethnic or tribal component, but often involving other dimensions, perhaps economic or environmental. The central governments of both Mali and Niger have faced secessionist insurrections involving guerilla groups based on the Tuareg tribe (in Mali, the MFOA or Mouvéments et Fronts Unifiés de l'Azouadi; and in Niger, three Tuareg groups with the initials, FDR, CRA, and ORA). Uganda, after the reign of Idi Amin, saw a chaotic series of tribal and ethnic conflicts before a more stable regime asserted itself.[131]

In Mali, the desert-based Tuareg people have been dually pressured by desertification and government efforts to resettle them, but also by government efforts to resettle other farmers in northern Mali. The land available to the Tuareg has been reduced, and the Tuareg have sought autonomy, leading to guerilla attacks against the government. After the installation of President Konare, a peace agreement was achieved resulting in greater autonomy for the Tuaregs. There have subsequently been some scattered incidents involving attacks on military convoys. Similar problems have existed in Niger, where a ceasefire has been less effective after the government was overthrown in a military coup. There too at stake were preservation of the Tuareg heritage and land rights, spurred by an environmental crisis. That has caused sporadic low-level fighting with only modest casualties—a flow of refugees has also resulted.

In Senegal since the late 1970s there has been a cyclical, ongoing conflict involving a rebellion by the Mouvément des Forces Démocratiques de la Casamance (MFDC). This involves a secessionist rebellion by the Casamance region in southern Senegal south of the Gambia salient, which is Senegal's richest agricultural area but feels disadvantaged by the government's economic allocation policies which favor the northern region around Dakar. There are more casualties here than in Mali or Niger in a conflict that is not purely tribal or ethnic or religious—indeed, the Casamance region itself has numerous tribal groups. The rebellion has made little headway toward independence, but it hasn't been squelched. The MFDC is mostly a well-armed group of bandit guerillas, utilizing small arms, land mines, and RPG shoulder-fired rockets. The war has overflowed into Guinea-Bissau and Gambia, both of which have had to absorb refugees from the conflict in Casamance.

Also involving Senegal, this time on a cross-border basis but more explicitly involving tribal conflict, has been the intermittent border skirmish between Senegal and Mauritania. This evolved from a coup attempt in Mauritania in 1990 by Afro-Mauritanians related to co-ethnics in Senegal against a Berber-dominated regime in Mauritania. There were expulsions on both sides of the border, the severing of diplomatic relations, and a heavy flow of refugees both ways. Most of the violence involved killings of Afro-Mauritanians by Berbers within Mauritania.

The conflict in Burundi, featuring several armed groups pitted against the reigning government, largely mirrors the Hutu vs. Tutsi struggle in neighboring Rwanda, with the same deadly results. Since 1993, over 250,000 people have died in Burundi as a result of the war, a figure that dwarfs many other LICs. The government has recently been controlled by the Tutsis, the parliamentary opposition by elected Hutus, who represent some 85 percent of the population, roughly the same ratio as in Rwanda. The fighting, as in Rwanda, has consisted mostly of large-scale massacres by roving bands armed with small arms and machetes. There has recently been intermittent fighting amidst ongoing all-party peace talks under the auspices of former Tanzanian President Julius Nyerere, though there is not yet an agreement on the modalities of a ceasefire.

In the Central African Republic (CAR), recently there has been an LIC involving army rebels versus the government. The conflict has been ethnic in origin, involving a change of power whereby a new president, Ainge-Felix Patusse, a Sarce, replaced a defeated president, Andre Kolingba, a Yakoma. There were economic conflicts related to this changeover, and that triggered a series of three army mutinies in 1996 in which the bulk of the army, comprised of Yakomas, broke out of their barracks and installed themselves within the areas occupied by their co-ethnics in Bangui. Rockets (RPGs) and small arms were used in combat that killed several thousand people, also damaging the French Embassy. That combat involved a lot of raids into neighborhoods by both sides. Here, the casualties were higher than in nearby Niger and Mali. By early 1997, a Francophone summit and, subsequently, a six-nation African peacekeeping force, restored order and collected some arms from rebels. A UN peacekeeping operation is now being set up, supplementing French troops.

Summary

A review of current and recent LICs throughout the world presents a vast and complex panorama of wars of all shapes and sizes, large and small, of short and long duration. The conflicts have taken place in virtually all corners of the globe save North America: in Ireland, Bosnia, Moldova, and Kosovo; in Azerbaijan, Chechnya, Tajikistan, and Kurdistan; in Algeria, Western Sahara, Chad, Niger, and Mali; in Mozambique, Angola, the Comoros Islands, and Rwanda; in Sri Lanka, Kashmir, and the Chittagong Hills; in New Caledonia, East Timor, and Bougainville; in Colombia, Peru, Mexico, Guatemala, and many more.

As previously noted, the current academic literature has focused on the causes and patterns of these conflicts in terms of recent trends and on issues of war termination and conflict resolution. That literature has come to some general conclusions, as follows. First, that warfare in the modern world has become mostly a phenomenon of LIC, and that it is based on ethnic-religious-tribal divisions to the point where it is speculated that interstate conventional warfare may have become an anachronism (variously due to new "norms," the "democratic peace," the end of the Cold War, etc.). Second, that Europe and Central Asia are now major cockpits of new LICs, ending the Cold War period in which LICs were considered largely a "Third World" phenomenon. The overall number of LICs, however, does appear to have declined since the end of the Cold War, although whether or not there is a direct causal relationship here is arguable. But many of the remnant LICs—Sudan, Rwanda, Sri Lanka, Angola, Burundi—have been very deadly, involving mortalities in the six-figure range, howsoever ignored in the western press and academic literature. But then, academic theory aside, it is not entirely clear that the heyday of conventional interstate wars is gone. Finally, despite optimism over war termination and conflict resolution, many LICs appear to have extended lives and the prospect of reignition, as witness newer outbreaks in Cambodia, Angola, Eritrea, where long-simmering conflicts were considered resolved.

But the major focus here has been on the conduct of these wars' tactics, operations, strategies, and weapons. As noted, information and data are hard to come by, ipso facto generalizations, trends, "theories." But a few trends or generalizations appear to have emerged. First, there is a partial trend toward the merging of higher-end LICs with some aspects of conventional war, as in some conflicts—Bosnia, Sri Lanka, Yemen, Chad, Sudan, Angola—modern major weapons platforms have come into use in wars with definable "fronts" between contending sides. Second, however, there appears little correlation between the "magnitude" of conflict (sizes of forces, types of weapons used) and their "severity" (deaths). Many of the conflicts ranking low on magnitude have had huge levels of severity (military and civilian deaths): Sudan, Mozambique, Angola, Rwanda, Burundi, Zaire, Afghanistan (post-Soviet withdrawal) and the Central American conflicts. Large numbers of people obviously have been killed in village massacres, raids, etc., with the use of only small arms and handheld weapons, much less so with aircraft, tanks, and artillery. Hence, maybe as many as eight hundred thousand persons have died in Sudan, and only a few thousand in Palestine and Kashmir, the latter more highly publicized. Next, while we think of most of these wars as "civil" or "internal" wars, many of them have had external, inter-state, cross-border dimensions, as witness Cambodia, Sri Lanka, Abkhazia, Kosovo, Western Sahara, Sierra Leone, Tajikistan, Kashmir, Kurdistan, Eritrea, Congo, Angola, Senegal (Latin America here again represents an exception). Finally, while most of the current LICs are largely ethnic in nature, and only a few are ideological in the Cold War sense (mostly in Latin America, i.e., Peru, Colombia, Guatemala), a closer look at many of them reveals complex patterns of ethnic-tribal, regional, economic, and environmental roots, rendering the dis-tinction between "wars of government" and "wars over territory" a useful but sometimes crude and simplistic one.

For sure, the earlier theoretical constructs associated with insurgency and counterinsurgency doctrines (Marx, Mao, Giap, Guevara et al. and their COIN counterparts in the Pentagon) are now passé, of little use to a discussion of con-temporary LIC. The Cold War's passing removes that itself as a framework for analysis. Clausewitz too is passé in this context. And there is no emerging futur-istic paradigm equivalent to what is wrought by the advent of MTR/RMA and nuclear weapons for conventional warfare. Mostly, these myriad miniwars need to be examined case-by-case, as sui generis, even as in the aggregate they have come to define the state of modern warfare.

One area where knowledge remains scant in connection with LICs—all the more so the further one goes toward the lower end of it, i.e., small-scale ethnic conflict—is that of the role of arms transfers (or more broadly, weapons acquisi-tion) in relation to combat. This has only minimally been rectified by the grow-ing interest in small-arms transfers. There are some cases where the basic pattern of transfers is known, such as in the case of Bosnia and Yugoslavia where much was written about the (not well enforced) embargo, Serbia's transfers to Bosnian Serbs, ultimate U.S. assistance to Croatia. There, one could see the pattern of combat altered by weapons shipments. In some cases of LIC, battlefield capture of weapons has been crucial, as in the case of the Eritrean insurgency against the feckless Ethiopian army which abandoned huge inventories of Soviet-origin equipment, including main battle tanks. Where LICs have involved incumbent, established regimes battling insurgents in a (usually) asymmetric war, the sources and types of the regime's weapons (other than small arms) are usually well pub-licized: Iraq, Sri Lanka, Turkey, Algeria, Peru, Indonesia, India, Colombia are examples. But in the cases of low low-intensity wars, particularly those with symmetrical balances of forces (and where the level of severity is often high), the sources and types of weapons held in inventory are not easily visible to outside observers. What, for instance, are the sources and inventories of weapons of Peru's Shining Path, the Zapatistas, Colombia's FARC, south Senegal's Casamance insurgents, the Turkish PKK Kurds, the Chittagong Hills rebels in Bangladesh, East Timor's FRETILIN movement, the Abkhazians? In most of these cases, presumably, there is some mix of capture from government sources, private-trader activities, or perhaps (as with Kosovo's PLA or Nagorno-

CHAPTER 6

Culture and Warfare

When we read about recent wars in distant places we are often struck by how differently foreign armies perform and the surprising ways in which hostilities end or do not end. During the 1982 episode in the serial Lebanon war, for example, regular Palestinian fighters gave a generally poor performance on the battlefield, shying away from head-on clashes, surrendering quickly, and breaking down easily under interrogation. Only militia in the refugee camps—when defending their homes and their families—displayed tenacity and resistance. In contrast, the Israeli army displayed aggressiveness and innovation on the battlefield. It not only prevailed over the Palestinians but operationally, tactically, and logistically out-fought the Syrian air force and air defense system.

Similarly, in 1987, Chadian troops in Toyota trucks armed with antitank weapons successfully attacked the better-equipped Libyan army in Chad. Reportedly none of the Libyans fired a single shot in their own defense. In the battle over Wadi Doum a few days later, once the main defenses were breached the Libyans made no attempt to counterattack or continue fighting—although they enjoyed enormous weapons superiority. A mass Libyan attempt at escape was reported.[1]

The Iraqi and Iranian armies also exhibited diverse performances on the battlefield at different times between 1980 and 1988. Iran's surprising ability to endure eight years of war in spite of Iraq's technological superiority is contrasted by Iraq's lackluster military performance, particularly between spring 1981, when Iran launched several counteroffensives, and July 1982, when the war shifted from Iranian to Iraqi territory. Nevertheless, as the war progressed, the Iraqi army denied Iran its intended victories in southern Iraq and a cease-fire agreement was negotiated, with many analysts declaring that Iraq had won the war.

Again, in the 1991 Gulf War, the world puzzled over Iraq's war-fighting capabilities. While American commentators predicted fierce resistance from Saddam Hussein's troops and large coalition casualties, Iraqi soldiers surrendered in large numbers, inflicting little damage on their enemies.

How can these variations in performance be explained? Why do armies behave differently on the battlefield? Why are some armed forces more or less adept at war fighting, and under what circumstances?

In this chapter we look to cultural and psychological factors—sometimes referred to as "human" or "ideational" factors—for answers. Although there is no standard definition of culture, most social scientists refer to it as a complex system of psychocultural factors (such as shared beliefs, norms, customs, ideas, or attitudes) that human beings use to interpret the world around them (see discussion below [p. 240]). Here we will examine the contributions of various analytical schools of thought across disciplines in an effort to understand how culture affects the conduct and outcome of war.

The field of international relations (IR), our own discipline, has had a stormy love/hate relationship with the concept of culture. Once largely ignored by mainstream international relations theorists during the Cold War,[2] culture began making a cautious theoretical comeback in 1990 and has been a growth industry since.[3] Some academics and policy activists argue that since the end of the Cold War, culture has emerged as the predominant causal factor in international relations. Rejecting the dominant realist model as inadequate to explain state behavior, these analysts believe culture is now the primary engine driving world affairs. The current lively academic debate over the possibility of transforming human behavior hinges on the concept of culture and the ability of man to manipulate it. Proponents of the "transformative" nature of culture question the permanence of aggressive societal attitudes and behavior, suggesting that states can unlearn these impulses in their relations with other states. In their view, the norms, ideas, and identities that give rise to war can be altered to foster a more peaceful world.[4]

Although these arguments cry out for empirical confirmation, to date IR scholars writing about culture rarely conduct such research or suggest how it might be done.[5] As William Wohlforth observes about the field of international relations generally: "the gap between demand and supply of empirical research is predictable in a field that appears to reward theory development over testing."[6] The return of culture to international relations theory, with few exceptions, has been limited to the debate over the causes of conflict and how to end it. How culture affects the conduct and process of war remains a relatively unexplored question.

Universalists vs. Cultural Relativists: An Ongoing Controversy

In general, then, there is a paucity of empirical research on the relationship between culture and the conduct of war. What does exist in the field of international relations is largely theoretical, written by Western analysts who have focussed primarily on Western societies, and to a lesser extent on the former Soviet Union. Their work can be divided into two main schools of thought: the universalists, who do not believe that culture can explain differences in human behavior, and the cultural relativists, who do. This theoretical schism characterizes the work in other disciplines as well. Muddying the conceptual waters, however, are several intellectual streams that coexist within each school. For heuristic purposes they are presented here as separate and distinct intellectual subcategories even though there is much overlapping among them and individual scholars often subscribe to several of them simultaneously.

The Universalists

Universalists believe that general principles can explain human behavior. Their thinking is characterized by a search for explanations that are universally applicable. Patterns of behavior that do not fit these general principles or cannot be explained by them are considered deviant. To believe otherwise suggests that some cultures, and therefore some people, are superior or more equal than others, which is anathema to much Western thinking. Cultural differences imply inequalities; universally applicable principles do not. Since the end of World War II, these universalist principles have been based almost totally on American values and beliefs. As one writer observes: "For most of the postwar period Americans have aggressively promoted a kind of cultural universalism—in effect a U.S. global culture."[7] Particular cultures for universalists, if they are considered at all, are thought to be regressive factors hindering the inevitable march toward universal development and modernity.[8] As applied to the military, much of what is written about human behavior during wartime is based upon the assumption that soldiers, regardless of nationality or ethnicity, respond in like ways to conflict, whether at the strategic or tactical level. This formulation appears in several variations in the literature, as described below.

Modernization Theory

The proponents of this school assume that the process of modernization is more or less global. Once industrialization begins, a number of social and behavioral patterns occur, regardless of cultural context, which lead inexorably to modern democratic, industrial behavior.[9] There is a single, unilinear path of development, which culminates in a system that looks like a Western democracy. Based on their reconstruction of the Western experience, modernization theorists assume that the same sequences of development will occur elsewhere.[10] With regard to the military, it follows that observed differences on the battlefield are a function of underdevelopment. With time, less developed militaries will resemble those in the developed world in skill and effectiveness. As society develops, it produces better, more competent, effective soldiers. Time is the critical factor. Over time, all armies will come to resemble each other in the ways of war. As one study concludes:

> After reviewing various arguments about the relation between broader socio-economic modernization and modernization in the military, we concluded that an effective fighting force, capable of engaging a sophisticated adversary, is most likely to emerge out of a developing society. Only then will the skills and outlooks necessary to successfully prosecute a mod-

ern war be available. We considered, but ultimately, rejected, the alternative model, which posits the building of an advanced military capability in isolation from, or even as a precursor to, general development."[11]

Seth Carus's assessment of the Iraqi military's performance in 1980 illustrates this approach. He observes that the Iraqi military lacked the skilled personnel to operate advanced modern equipment or to perform the associated administrative functions necessary in modern warfare: movement of supplies, maintenance of equipment, provision of medical aid to wounded soldiers, procurement, strategic and operational planning, and finance. Commenting on this as a problem of modernization, he observes that "Much of the inactivity of the Iraqi military during its current war with Iran is probably nothing more than an inability to supply spare parts to combat units in an expeditious manner."[12]

The Rational-Actor Model
Unlike modernization theorists, those subscribing to the rational actor model do not attribute particular importance to time. They assume that policy, whether military or political, is determined by a means–end calculation. Military planners, regardless of culture, will attempt to maximize their gains and minimize their losses given the resources at their disposal. Failures in military planning or engagements are due to a lack of complete information or other assessment errors, or to objective factors such as relative military balance, geography, training, etc.

Brig. Gen. S. L. A. Marshall, for example, warned in his book *Men Against Fire: The Problem of Battle Command* (1947) that an infantry commander should know that "when he engages the enemy not more than one quarter of his men will ever strike a real blow. . . . I mean that 75 percent will not fire or will not persist in firing against the enemy and his works. These men may face danger but they will not fight."[13] General Marshall assumed that his observations of American riflemen during World War II applied to all modern soldiers. If commanders everywhere comprehend these tactical principles they will be less likely to fail.

States and their armies are members of a world of nations that respond in like ways to an accepted norm of rational behavior. When wars are lost the loss is attributable to errors of judgment on this means–end continuum. Miscalculation, to which all men may be found guilty, explains defeat in battle. Iraq's failure to quickly win the war against Iran in 1980, analysts of this school argue, was due to a mistaken assessment of the military balance—an overestimation of its own capabilities and an underestimation of Iran's.[14]

Learning Theory
A third subgroup of the universalist school draws upon learning theory to explain human behavior. Machiavelli, who wrote that "Good discipline and exercise will make good soldiers in any country, and the defects of nature may be supplied by art and industry—which in this case is more effective than nature itself."[15] might be considered their forebearer. His modern heirs, however, often

draw their inspiration from Skinnerian psychology. They suggest that training will elicit a certain type of learned response—and produce a generic type of military man regardless of cultural differences. A number of recent works have cited inadequate training as the cause of Third World militaries' poor performance.[16]

In addition, many defense analysts—often military planners themselves—believe that what armies learn from one another and from the war-fighting experience itself is critical to future performance. The concept of "arms races," for example, is grounded in this principle. When country A purchases a particular weapon system, its enemy, country B, will respond by searching for an antidote to it, which will, in turn, elicit a procurement response from country A. It is, then, the learning process that dictates what equipment armies buy for use on the battlefield.

How the weapons are used is also considered a form of "learned" behavior. Innumerable studies describe how military planners take great pains to "learn" from the strategies, tactics, and weapons used in recent wars. The concept of "lessons of war" is derived from the belief that learning about what transpired in the last war will help military planners prepare for the next one. The Gulf War is only the most recent example. One writer observed: "As the Gulf War winds down, defense analysts are busily sharpening their pencils. The war has created a unique opportunity to examine the performance of a wide variety of weapons, support systems, and procedures under combat conditions."[17] Canada's 1991 defense policy paper, which was to establish long-term planning for the Canadian armed forces, was delayed in order to give defense planners an opportunity to study the implications of the Gulf War. There are many new lessons about the future of warfare to be learned from that war, the Canadian defense minister declared.[18] Since the Gulf War ended, it has received close attention from military planners all over the world. The Los Alamos National Laboratory conducted a massive survey of the lessons learned from the perspectives of a variety of major and middle powers.[19] For most military planners and analysts, learning, not culture, determines military effectiveness.

Psychology and Psychoanalysis
Psychological explanations of human behavior, too, are founded on univeralist principles. An accepted behavioral norm exists, beyond which is deviant behavior, irrespective of ethnicity, nationality, or religious orientation. Most analysts and therapists share the belief that unconscious factors motivate warlike, aggressive human behavior which can be treated or ameliorated by various psychoanalytic or psychotherapeutic techniques. The underlying assumption is that the principles upon which the discipline is founded—although spawned and largely practiced in the West—are, nonetheless, universally valid.

As applied to the military, classical psychoanalysts are concerned primarily with the causes of aggression. War is considered a manifestation of mass pathological behavior, grounded in the inherent self-destructive instinct in humans—which Freud described as the death wish.[20]

More recently, others have focused on the behavior of military leaders and the conduct of soldiers under fire. One psychologist, for example, has attributed battlefield failures to psychologically crippled leaders. Norman Dixon argues that generals who fail share similar psychological traits. They are passive and courteous, obstinate and rigid, ambitious and insensitive. In general, according to Dixon, promotion within the military selects people with anal-retentive charac-teristics—those who are conformist, obey their superiors, and regard discipline and submission to authority as virtues. The soldier who reaches the top is likely to be unimaginative, inflexible, and lacking adventurousness—qualities that, in his view, explain leadership failure.[21]

But whether the examples given are drawn from the Western experience or not, this approach implicitly assumes that the psychological principles formulated in the West can explain human behavior generally across peoples, and culture.

Genetic/Biological Model
Based in large part on animal research, members of this school posit that humans are aggressive for biologically determined reasons. Some endocrinologists, eth-nologists, and physiologists link war to a genetic human predisposition.[22] They see aggression and conflict as a normal biological feature of human nature. One group of anthropologists, social psychologists, and philosophers view aggression as instinctive behavior, and war as a periodic manifestation of man's innate aggressive nature.[23] Others of this school believe war derives from the struggle for survival or as some have termed it, "inclusive fitness," the imperative driving living things to act to preserve genetic material identical with their own—namely, kin or related people—those who are genetically similar.[24] According to them, all successful societies have developed the social institutions necessary for engaging in warfare as a means of survival.

Recently, scientific attention has centered on the brain as the locus for aggression. Experiments on animals suggest that genetic patterning in certain sections of the brain, particularly the limbic system, may determine whether some of a species are more aggressive than others.[25] Autopsies on humans have led some social scientists to similar speculations. Dennis Sandol of George Mason University in a paper entitled "A Genetic Theory of Violent Conflict," delivered at the International Studies Association Conference, 30 March 1989 in London, presents this theory. He offers as an example, a twenty-five-year-old Texas man, Charles Whitman, who, after killing his wife and children in August 1966, climbed to the top of the University of Texas, Austin, tower and began shooting at people indiscriminately, leaving thirteen dead and many more wounded. An autopsy found a tumor pressing on the limbic part of Whitman's brain, which according to Sandol may explain his sudden and inexplicable aggressive behavior.[26]

Other current and related work is based on the assumption that aggression can be controlled chemically. Advocates of this view believe that if aggressive behavior is physiologically determined, then there is the potential for enhancing, neutralizing, or suppressing it with drugs, or even, perhaps, by genetic engineer-ing. For some, the implications of all this for a world without armed conflict is not unimaginable. For others, drugs to alter behavior represent yet another method of defeating the enemy on the battlefield. Calmative agents that lower aggression or cause sleepiness in enemy soldiers are thought to have valuable applications in situations ranging from urban terrorism to peacekeeping activities to conventional war.[27] Similarly, some biogenetists believe it is possible to create so-called chemically enhanced "super-soldiers." In the future "it may be possible to alter the performance and capabilities of a soldier by drug inducement or other types of manipulation . . . [that include] pills or the application of precise electromagnetic pulses that can be made to mitigate the effects of fear, lack of sleep as well as produce increased strength and aggression."[28] Ultimately, for these analysts, genetics, biology, and chemistry, trump psychocultural explanations of behavior.

These then are some of the main universalist tenets informing much of the literature on military performance. Overall, it reflects the notion that there are universal laws of human behavior that can be ascertained from the Western experience alone.[29] The militaries of the non-Western, less developed countries, when discussed at all, generally are treated as an extension of that experience. Concerned essentially with the causes of wars and how to stop them—universalists virtually ignore or reject the notion of culture as a factor affecting the conduct and outcome of war itself.

The Cultural Relativists

We turn next to cultural relativists, who stand in substantial tension with the universalist school. In eclipse during the late 1970s and early 1980s, cultural relativism began enjoying a conceptual comeback in the late 1980s.[30] Since then, it even has made inroads into an intensely universalist discipline—psychiatry—whose members are beginning to question the universality of their theories.[31] Psychiatrists treating Asian patients discovered that feelings of shame or unquestioning filial devotion labeled neurotic in Western psychoanalytic thought are accepted, even valued, norms of behavior in Eastern cultures. As a result, some have begun to ask whether Western psychoanalytic thinking has much to offer non-Western patients. One psychoanalyst, Arthur Kleinman, observed: "The ethnocentric arrogance of Western psychotherapy is being challenged head on by the growing recognition of the problems of treating non-Western immigrants."[32]

A similar reassessment is underway in biopolitics, a field that studies the biological origins of political behavior. These political scientists have concluded that some types of behavior are universal while others are culturally determined. Roger Masters, for example, writes: "Human behavior includes both hedonic ('positive' or pleasurable) and agonic ('negative' or competitive) dimensions, each of which has natural as well as cultural components."[33] But despite these tentative moves toward synthesis, most univeralists vehemently differ with cultural relativists over the roots of human behavior and vice versa.

The term "cultural relativist," like that of "universalist," subsumes a number of theoretical schools of thought. What these theorists hold in common is the belief that culture—variously defined—can explain diversity in human behavior. Their disagreements center on the "roots" of culture—whether cultural patterns are determined by history, ethnicity, genetics, or a myriad of other factors.

Although there is no consensus on exactly what culture is, most define it as some mixture of the beliefs, values, norms, habits, customs, attitudes, or ideas of a society which, through socialization, are passed down from generation to generation. It is the prism—the frame of reference—through which people view, interpret, and respond to the world around them.

Unlike past writings, which were generally discursive, normative treatises on the subject of culture and its impact on human behavior, often referred to as "national character," current research looks more systematically and empirically "at *patterns* of . . . beliefs and orientations; it tries to understand other societies on their own terms."[34]

Culture and the Military

Cultural relativists who apply this model to the military hold that members of the armed forces are part of a larger society and therefore reflect its character and predispositions.[35] Political and military decisionmakers may approach problems of war and security in some purely rational, interest-maximizing fashion, but it is done within the context of the norms and values of their particular culture. Rationality then, in this approach, is a relative concept. Means-ends calculations are culturally determined. What is rational for one society is not necessarily rational for another. Thus during World War II, Western military planners were unlikely to consider using kamikaze pilots to stop enemy warships, although in the Japanese circumstances the tactic apparently met some criteria of rationality. As Lucien Pye observes:

> Culture is unquestionably significant, in some undetermined degree, in shaping the aspirations and fears, the preferences and prejudices, the priorities and expectations of a people. . . . Culture is not a matter of the rule of the irrational as opposed to objective, rational behavior, for the very character of rational judgment varies with time and place. Common sense exists in all cultures, but it is not the same from culture to culture.[36]

Cultural relativists, then, challenge the universalist notion that behavior is determined by general categories of thinking, which are the same regardless of country or culture. Rather, they believe and seek to show that people in different societies think differently about security and the use of force and thus behave in culturally distinct ways militarily.

As a function of cultural relativism's revival, various kinds of military behavior are increasingly explained in terms of cultural differences. The most common are endurance, combat effectiveness, and military doctrine.

ENDURANCE Endurance—levels of acceptable pain or damage in combat—is one example. Because the concept of endurance is associated with the expected duration of a war and how hard the enemy will fight, assessments of it have been subject to close scrutiny in the literature—often in psychocultural terms.

Israel's military doctrine has been explained in terms of the "Holocaust Syndrome"—the view that every Jewish life is of value, and therefore great effort must be expended to save each soldier's life. Because the level of acceptable damage is so low, analysts argue, Israel necessarily adopted a short war strategy and the blitzkrieg tactics used during recent wars.[37] Even the design of the Merkava tank and the Lavi plane are thought to be technological extensions of these culturally determined patterns of military thought.

Culture also is believed to determine a combatant's calculus regarding his enemy's pain threshold. Often based on ethnocentric projections,[38] a combatant's assessment of how the enemy will respond may often be wrong with unintended military consequences for his army on the battlefield.

During World War II, for example, both Germany and the Allies were surprised by the Soviet Union's willingness to accept heavier casualties than the Western countries could contemplate sustaining—demonstrated by the way Soviet commanders cleared minefields simply by sending troops across them, rather than by slower and less costly technical means.[39]

Similarly, the Israelis were reported to be unprepared for the determined PLO resistance in the refugee camps during the Lebanon war. Based on past experience, the Israeli military viewed the Palestinian fighters as "artful dodgers, shying away from head-on clashes and, especially shrinking from contact with Israeli units. . . . Many of the fighters were in a hurry to surrender and, after taken prisoner, easily broke down under interrogation and readily informed on their comrades."[40] This negative view of the Palestinians' pain tolerance was reported to have been responsible for the Israeli army's disorganized response when the Palestinians did put up a determined fight in Rashidya, Burj Shimali, Ein Hilwe, and other camps.[41]

Whether accurate or not, assessments of the enemy's pain tolerance are believed to have important implications for the strategy and tactics of war. Various studies of the Vietnam War found that rising casualties had a critical impact on American public opinion and consequently on the ability of the U.S. to sustain its military effort. Although there are conflicting opinions about the validity of this finding,[42] apparently the North Vietnamese and other U.S. adversaries did operate on the assumption that military withdrawal would be the preferred U.S. policy as casualties rose and public support dwindled. During the Vietnam War, for example, Harrison Salisbury reported the statement of North Vietnam's Prime Minister Pham Van Dong that the U.S. would lose the war despite its military superiority because, lacking a high enough pain threshold or cost tolerance, it would abandon the fight before attaining its objectives.[43] According to Miroslav Nincic, similar expectations guided Saddam Hussein's actions before Operation Desert Storm and those of the Bosnia-Serb leader Radovan Karadjic during the early stages of the Bosnian conflict.[44]

Israel's perceived sensitivity to casualties, too, is reported to influence the strategy and tactics of its foes. Attributing Prime Minister Barak's unilateral withdrawal from Lebanon to the Israeli population's sensitivity to casualties, various Muslim leaders and commentators advised the Palestinians to adopt a strategy of violence which, they predicted, would lead to the liberation of the West Bank and Gaza too.[45] One commentator observed that the strategic target of the Hezbollah's guerilla tactics in Lebanon had been Israeli public opinion, not the military, "because an army can withstand losses in equipment and even in personnel as long as this does not influence public opinion. . . . [It was] the rise of a public opinion in Israel that started to exert pressure on the political leadership and demand an exit from this quagmire."[46] A former Iranian foreign affairs minister drew a like lesson: "The path to saving Palestine is not the path of compromising with the Zionist regime. Rather, it is the path of *jihad,* armed struggle, and the return to Islamic values, which is the only path the Palestinians can take to liberate themselves."[47] Hamas militants in the West Bank and Gaza also interpreted the success of the so-called "Hezbollah model" to mean that the Palestinians should cease negotiating and expel Israel through armed struggle.[48] To both Israeli and Arab observers, the "liberation" of Lebanon in May 2000 and the onset of Israeli-Palestine fighting the following September were intimately related events.[49]

COMBAT EFFECTIVENESS Like endurance, an army's combat effectiveness has also been attributed to a variety of cultural factors. Puzzlement over the indifferent performance of the Arab armies has generated a sizable literature on wars in the Middle East.[50] One military analyst, for example, ascribes Iraq's reluctance to press its advantage in 1980 after it had invaded Khuzistan to a consensual form of decisionmaking in Iraqi society that discourages overt disagreement among decisionmakers. This, he maintains, produced a false consensus that encouraged optimistic wishful thinking among Iraqi commanders about the capabilities of the Iranians.[51] Others regard the hierarchical structure of Iraqi society—reflected in its military organization—as a major factor inhibiting field officers from taking the initiative on the battlefield. According to some scholars, this also explains the generally cautious and hesitant battlefield behavior of the Iraqi troops and Arab armies generally.[52]

Kenneth Pollacks's exhaustive study of the military effectiveness of five Arab states—Egypt, Iraq, Jordan, Saudi Arabia, and Syria—between 1945 and 1991, supports these conclusions. Noting that throughout the postwar period, Arab militaries were incapable of effective maneuver warfare or effective mechanized warfare, he finds that "certain patterns of behavior fostered by the dominant Arab culture were the most important factors contributing to the limited military effectiveness of Arab armies and air forces from 1945–1991."[53] These cultural attributes include those that favored centralization of authority; discouraged initiative, flexibility, improvisation, and independence among subordinates; supported the manipulation of information to suit individual preferences; encouraged individuals to see knowledge as discrete, compartmentalized entities; and dissuaded individuals from undertaking manual labor or learning technical skills. On the battlefield, these cultural tendencies hampered the ability of Arab junior officers to assume active leadership, impeded the flow of accurate information throughout the command structure, and seriously reduced the ability of Arab militaries to conduct maneuver and mechanized warfare effectively.[54] Pollock concludes that Arab culture was the most important cause of Arab military ineffectiveness.[55]

MILITARY DOCTRINE: STRATEGY, OPERATIONS, AND TACTICS A number of scholars also explain the grand strategies, operational doctrines, and battlefield tactics of states in terms of culture. Those associated with this approach maintain that the basic ideas societies (or their elites) hold about the role of war, perceived threats, and the use of force explain, in some part, why particular states wage war in historically persistent ways. Some call this "strategic culture."[56]

While the term "strategic culture" is relatively new—coming into academic vogue in the late 1970s—respected scholars and military analysts speculated about the cultural origins of military doctrine well before then, whether they explicitly called it "strategic culture" or not. Dating back to Sun Tzu in the sixth century b.c., cultural explanations of doctrine have been offered at different levels of analysis—strategic, operational, and tactical—by scholars who may not self-consciously associate themselves with the approach.

At the strategic level, for example, Hew Strachan describes how the traditional "British [maritime] way of war" was resistant to change even under the pressure of the continental military crisis in World War I.[57] The huge commitment of infantry troops in 1914–18 did not alter Britain's dominant maritime strategy in the years following the war, despite the infantry experience of an entire generation of Britons.[58] Richard Pipes contrasted the way the U.S. and USSR thought about war and nuclear weapons in cultural terms.[59] Contending that the Soviets had a war-winning perspective regarding the Cold War and the strategic nuclear balance, he argued that Soviet strategic culture did not allow for permanently enshrined stable deterrence balances based on arms-control regimes. Ironically, Lincoln Bloomfield wrote about an "American way of war," which stressed total victory in the tradition of Clausewitz.[60]

Boorman, addressing the zeitgeist of guerilla war and protracted conflict in the 1960s, saw the Chinese strategic culture with its roots in Sun Tzu as more suited to protracted struggle and ambiguous outcomes than its Western counterparts; indeed, he saw the differences between the Chinese game of "go" and Western chess as reflective of these cultural differences.[61]

Other writers have concentrated on the operational level of warfare—using culture to explain a state's preference for attrition or maneuver warfare, static or forward defense. The Soviet Operational Maneuver Group, for example, feared by NATO planners in the 1980s for its ability to call-up large-scale mobile reserves, is cited as a legacy from the Mongols that was passed down through Russian history.[62] On the other hand, Arab preferences for static defenses and attrition warfare, their inability to conduct combined arms and extended offensive maneuver operations, as we have seen, have also been regarded as culturally based.[63]

The literature provides numerous historical examples of cultural preferences in tactical warfare as well. The ancient Greeks preferred infantry tactics, while the Persians utilized chariots, and the Byzantine armies favored cavalry-mounting archers.[64] Sometimes, nations or other political entities have appeared to eschew potentially effective weapons because of cultural constraints. Social norms, according to Larus, explain the ancient Hindu armies' persistent use of elephants in battle even after serial defeats by opponents on horseback demonstrated the elephants' ineffectiveness.[65] Cipolla characterizes the Ottoman Turks, who delegated the artillery function to slaves, as unable to use modern artillery because of cultural factors.[66]

Recent works on doctrine are methodologically more self-conscious as they strive for definitional clarity, rigorous empirical enquiry, and a "falsifiable" theory of how culture influences military and political actions.[67] Some of this research is discussed below in connection with other related culturalist approaches.

The examples cited above that link theory to behavior illustrate the general approach and thinking of cultural relativists, whether they consider themselves to be such or not. As theorists, they discriminate sharply among societies and find within them cultural explanations for military/political decisions and actions. Other theoretical approaches build on this general model. Presented below as distinct models, they all embrace the premise of culturally determined behavior but differ in how they explain the sources of culture itself.

Related Culturalist Approaches

HISTOCULTURAL SCHOOL Cultural and military diversity in this model derives from ancient historical experiences. Developed in the early history of a people and molded by centuries of common experiences, the religious, social, and ethical values of a society are thought to have persistent implications for the way a society thinks about, fights, and ends wars.

As we have seen, during the Cold War, analysts searching for cultural explanations of political/military behavior concentrated largely on the former Soviet Union and the U.S.[68] The few scholars interested in the non-Western world found themselves outside the academic mainstream and were often considered mavericks by those within it. Complaining that existing research was Eurocentric, noncomparative, and ahistorical, they turned to the early, precolonial literature and classic writings of non-Western countries for insight into their ways of war.[69]

Joel Larus's study of India covers the period of premodern Hindu India (c. 2500 b.c. to sixteenth century [1565 a.d. Battle of Talkota]) when Muslim forces defeated the last politically significant Hindu kingdom in southern India and dominated the subcontinent until the coming of the Europeans. Larus found the complex Hindu religio-caste social system to be an important factor explaining Hindu serial combat defeats and particularistic style of warfare.

One puzzle for him was India's historical rejection of naval power. Even though India sat astride the ancient world's major maritime trade route—between the Persian Gulf and Red Sea in the West and the South China Sea in the East—possessed a 3,750-mile coastline, and enjoyed abundant resources (such as teak, iron, copper, and hemp) for shipbuilding, unlike the Greeks, Romans, and other early Mediterranean people, the early Hindu kings consistently abjured all forms of naval activity. They produced neither a navy nor a class of overseas merchants that could have advanced India's power in the ancient and medieval world.

Larus finds the explanation for this in India's complex historical experience and social system. First, he believes the Central Asians who migrated into the peninsula over the centuries found the land so fertile that there was no incentive to go elsewhere. Without a need for further conquest, these early settlers became a land-based people engaged in hunting, herding, gathering, and later farming.

Not only was seafaring needless, according to Larus, but ancient Aryan/Brahman religious customs forbade it. Since isolation from unpure foreigners was mandatory for the orthodox, it was necessary for them to avoid sailing to remain pure. This prohibition was bolstered by innumerable other requirements regarding cleanliness that dictated their lives and behavior—particularly after the caste system was institutionalized in India. What Brahmans ate and drank had to be cooked by a Brahman; bathing three times a day was required; a Brahman's water could only be drawn from certain wells. Sea travel meant discontinuation of these rituals and possible exclusion from the caste social system. According to Larus, these were powerful disincentives to naval activity in ancient times. One can only speculate as to whether vestiges of these cultural constraints survived well into the twentieth century, inhibiting the establishment of a blue-water navy for over twenty years after Indian independence.

Joseph Rothschild also turns to histocultural factors to explain the conduct of Iran and Iraq during the Iran-Iraq War. He wonders whether Iraqi feelings of cultural inferiority in comparison to the rich Iranian civilization and heritage were responsible for Iraq's "clumsy ineptness in this conflict."[70] He suggests that the tenacity and self-confidence of the Iranian armed forces during the war might have been due to their "sense of being the heirs of a great, ancient, and continuous imperial civilization, compared with which Saddam Hussein's Iraq is but a peripheral upstart."[71] Awareness of a rich imperial heritage, he contends, can be a powerful psychocultural asset that is translatable into military prowess on the modern battlefield.[72]

Edward Boylan, too, finds in China's historical experience powerful and consistent influences on its military behavior. Analyzing China's ancient and modern works on defense strategy he finds common threads running through them from Sun Tzu to Mao Tse-Tung in the twentieth century.[73]

According to Boylan, China has exhibited a consistent preference for nonviolent strategies—the use of psychological methods over physical violence to overcome the enemy and achieve the desired political end. Throughout Chinese history, he claims, attacking the mind of the enemy has taken precedence over military force. Unlike the West where warfare is associated with hard fighting—in China, war has been an art requiring many skills—not the least deception and fooling or manipulating the enemy into making his own mistakes and defeating himself. The second historical thread Boylan detects is the Chinese preference for strategies of defense rather than offense and for wars of attrition rather than annihilation. The third is a predilection for cooptation rather than destruction of the enemy. Traditionally, he argues, China's rulers have insisted upon tribute from, rather than total defeat of, its enemies.

Boylan traces these preferences to China's unique and turbulent historical past. He maintains that China after the second century b.c. was not expansionist. Uninterested in acquiring new territory, defense became the strategy of choice. China conceived of itself as the center of the universe—a Great Power among lesser powers—a civilized society among "barbarians" to which deference was due.[74] China's policy of tribute and cooptation, according to Boylan, reflects this orientation. Furthermore, he asserts, constant civil war meant that the enemy China faced was often one it hoped to later rule and assimilate. Decimation or total defeat of the enemy was not only unnecessary but counterproductive. The Chinese partiality for victory through persuasion rather than force and for a strategy of attrition rather than annihilation, is therefore, according to Boylan, a product of its historical experiences which have been perpetuated in its defense policy today.

Other analysts concur. Harlan Jencks, for example, writes that China's attitude toward Vietnam in 1979 derived directly from China's traditional perception of itself as a Great Power. When Vietnam, historically a tributary, refused to withdraw its troops from Cambodia, China responded militarily on 17 February 1979, intent upon "teaching Vietnam a lesson." The political objective was to persuade Vietnam to withdraw, not to annihilate it. Although China did not immediately achieve its goal, it had reasserted its claim as a Great Power in Southeast Asia.[75]

Until recently, this image of China's "unique" strategic culture was the generally accepted one. Now a new generation of China specialists and scholars is challenging it. Analyzing the *Seven Military Classics* (*Wu Ching Chi'i Shu*) of ancient China and the Ming dynasty's foreign/military behavior, Johnston in his book *Cultural Realism* holds that there are not one but two Chinese strategic cultures. One is based on the Confucian-Mencian preferences (reflected in Sun Tzu's writing) for a foreign policy based on diplomacy and winning over one's foes through noncoercive means. When force is necessary, it should be applied defensively and minimally. The second cultural strand is derived from assumptions and preferences indistinguishable from those associated with Western realists. Johnston maintains that the ancient Chinese writers on strategy believed the best response to force was to meet it with force, preferably with offensive rather than defensive strategies.[76] It is this second paradigm, according to Johnston, that is dominant in Chinese history, whether the Chinese were faced with an ancient Mongol invasion or more modern threats.[77]

Arguing from a universalist perspective, Michael Handel, too, contends that the approaches of Sun Tzu and Clausewitz, the consummate realist, are not that different. He contends that the confusion arises because Sun Tzu and Clausewitz use different levels of analysis and therefore approach war from different perspectives. "While Sun Tzu is primarily concerned with the conduct of war on the highest strategic level, Clausewitz focuses on the lower strategic/operational levels."[78] Nevertheless, Handel finds substantial areas of accord: "Clausewitz would surely agree in principle that victory without fighting or bloodshed is desirable; but he also recognizes that this is rarely possible and proceeds forthwith to examine the more likely alternatives."[79] After carefully studying these two "opposing paradigms," he concludes that "the basic logic of strategy, like that of political behavior, is universal."[80]

MILITARY SUBCULTURE SCHOOL A somewhat different approach is taken by what we call the military subculture school. These analysts believe that it is the history of the military itself—its organizational values and attitudes—which explains military behavior. Although armed forces are members of a larger, overarching culture, they also constitute a distinct subculture within it. The strategic, operational, and tactical doctrines of specific armed forces are expressions of sustained institutional histories and a discrete set of values that in themselves shed light on how and why armies fight they way they do.[81] Yitzhak Klein, for example, limits his definition of strategic culture to:

> the set of attitudes and beliefs held within a military establishment concerning the political objective of war and the most effective strategy and operational method of achieving it.[82]

In this paradigm, military culture is seen as distinct, rather than a mere reflection of the larger society's culture. It is often considered to be derived less from historical experience than from recent events. Elizabeth Kier, for instance, argues that during the interwar years, British and French military doctrines were shaped by the organizational values of their armed forces. She maintains that it is the military's view of its world that constrains choices between offensive and defensive doctrine, not changes in the international balance of power, or a primordial military preference for offensive doctrines. She charges that both France and Britain adopted defensive military doctrines that were incapable of defeating Germany because the organizational culture of the respective armies made them incapable of imagining a mechanized and offensive battlefield.[83]

Jeffrey Legro, using a similar approach, explains why three types of warfare—submarine attacks against merchant ships, the bombing of nonmilitary targets, and the use of chemical weapons—were stigmatized prior to the outbreak of World War II yet, with the exception of chemical weapons, were found acceptable by war's end. Rejecting realist explanations, he contends that

> it was the organizational cultures of militaries that more significantly structured how states understood their situations, what types of capabilities they saw as important, and ultimately, how desirable it was to violate the norm or maintain mutual restraint.[84]

ETHNICITY The ethnicity model, on the other hand, holds that there is a sense of social bonding that attends membership in a particular group. This school is generally concerned with subcultural identities within a larger culture. These include particular religious, racial, or language groups as distinct from other neighboring peoples such as Sikhs, Pathans, and Bengalis who are also Indian,

Pakistani, or Bangladeshi in nationality; Sunni or Shi'ite Muslims who are also Saudi Arabian, Iraqi, Iranian, or Kuwaiti citizens. Historically, analysts applying this model to the military have hypothesized that the ethnic composition of armies influences military morale and hence combat performance.[85] Ethnically homogeneous armies are regarded as effective and reliable whereas multiethnic armies are not since elements within them may be unwilling to fight ethnically related groups. According to some observers, experience in recent wars offers support for this contention.[86]

The Soviet Union, for example, initially sent largely Central Asian troops to invade Afghanistan. Joseph Collins concluded that this decision, designed to facilitate movement and communication with the ethnically related local popu- lace, was a mistake. Low combat morale, unreliability, a high rate of defection, and an unwillingness to fight peoples perceived to be "brothers" characterized the Muslim Central Asian troops in the invading Soviet army. Collins cites the testimony of an Afghanistan resistance leader:

In the very beginning, when the Soviets first entered our country in 1979 . . . most of the soldiers were Soviet-Central Asians. . . . When these people realized that the only people they were fighting in Afghanistan were Afghans . . . then these Soviet Central Asians began helping us. They began leaving us packages with ammunition and weapons caches.[87]

Another report claimed that the changing ethnic balance of the Soviet army— 37 percent of Soviet draftees came from the seven Central Asian republics, many of whom did not speak Russian fluently—compromised its effectiveness as a fighting force.[88]

The multiethnic character of the military has caused problems for the Soviet government even within the confines of the Soviet Union. As ethnic fighting in the Caucasus intensified in the early 1990s, both Azerbaijani and Armenian sol- diers aided their respective people in obtaining automatic rifles, grenade launch- ers, antiaircraft rockets, and, reportedly, helicopters. Some officers and conscripts of both nationalities were reported to have removed the identifying insignias from their uniforms to go AWOL and join the conflict on the other side.[89]

The performance of other multiethnic armies in recent wars is also viewed as problematic. During the 1982 Lebanon war, Druse normally considered loyal to Israel and who serve in the Israeli Army, refused to fight their brother Druse in Lebanon. And when civil war broke out between East and West Pakistan, Ben- gali soldiers mutinied to join the Bengali separatists.

In practice, the multiethnic character of most Third World states and the shaky legitimacy of the ruling elite (often drawn from one particular ethnic group) has meant that the army, at least at the officer level, is recruited from a group (or groups) the ruling elite considers loyal—men who can be counted on to use their equipment for assigned missions against external enemies rather than attack the central government itself. The preferred ethnic group is often, but not always, the political and governmental elite's own. Syria's President Hafez al- Assad's reliance on Alawi officers and President Idi Amin's utilization of his

Muslim Nubian coethnics in Uganda are only two examples. Perhaps the most striking illustration, however, can be found in Iraq. According to Efraim Karsh, the issue of ethnicity and the consequent choice of incompetent military leaders was "the major reason for the failure of its war strategy" during the Iran-Iraq War. After gaining power by a military coup, the Ba'ath regime's desire to control the armed forces led to a situation where Sunni and Takriti affiliation were the most important criteria for military promotion.[90] Thus, it was not professional criteria but loyalty to the regime that determined military leadership in Iraq and according to Karsh, poor performance on the battlefield.

ETHNOCENTRISM The concept of ethnocentrism, the research province largely of anthropologists, is closely related to and often considered a component of the ethnicity model. It focuses on the feelings of centrality and superiority that are perceived to be a by-product of membership in a particular ethnic group. It is the "view of things in which one's own group is the center of everything, and all others are scaled and rated with reference to it."[91]

An example in the military sector would be the attitudes of Pakistanis. Reportedly they remain proud of their Aryan and Mogul heritage, which they believe gave them their martial qualities and are contemptuous of the former East Pakistanis' (now Bangladeshis) military capabilities and cultural heritage.[92] Examples of how ethnocentric attitudes are thought to affect military judgement and performance were discussed above.

THE BIOCULTURAL MODEL A related explanatory approach is the biocultural model. Like cultural relativism, this school emphasizes the particularistic differences among peoples. But it is "inheritance"—the source of culture itself—that explains variety in social and military behavior.

Pre–World War II adherents of this school believed that certain nations or peoples are naturally endowed with martial prowess, whereas others are not. In their view, ethnonational modes of warfare are inherited and therefore perpetuated from generation to generation.

For example, the colonial Indian Army was organized by the British on the principle of "martial races." According to one account, this principle itself grew out of Britain's respect for the peoples who had fought most vigorously against them.[93] Whatever the reason, the British chose Indian soldiers from ethnic groups thought to be endowed with particular warlike qualities. These were the Nepalese (Gurkas), Sikhs, and later the Muslim Punjabis. Southerners and Bengalis were considered to be "nonmartial races" because they were "short, lacking in toughness, overeducated, and politically inflammable."[94] This model was applied to recruitment in other British Asian and African colonies, and was adopted by the French, the Dutch, the Italians, and the Belgians who also sought "martial" qualities for their enlisted men.[95]

A variant of this concept is propounded by Professor Ewald Banse in his book *Raum Und Volk Im Weltkriege,* which was written to prepare the German leaders and people for World War II. One chapter, "The Psychological Geography of War," devoted to how to raise an efficient army, was reprinted in English in the

Pakistan Army Journal with a laudatory introduction. Banse rejects the theory that training can determine a country's capacity to fight, declaring that "any racially homogeneous unit is stronger than a racially heterogeneous one."[96] According to Banse, there are warlike races, nations, stocks and classes and there are pacific ones, and he sternly advised military commanders to judge his own and his enemy's troops according to these criteria.

More modern proponents of the biocultural model can be found among anthropologists who believe that warfare and the ability to fight aggressively derive from environmental factors that include the dietary preferences of particular peoples. Earlier anthropological research on the Aymara people in the Bolivian highland, who are reputed to be one of the most bellicose people in the region, led Ralph Bolton to conclude that hypoglycemia was the culprit. He maintains that hypoglycemia, caused by a protein poor, high-carbohydrate diet, has biological effects that in turn have the cultural consequence of rebelliousness and frequent warfare.[97]

Questions but No Answers

Causality

These, then, are some of the models and approaches analysts have used to explain the differential performance of men in battle. Some are compelling but, alas, raise more questions than they answer. It is still not certain, despite the claims of the cultural relativists, that the culture of a society provides a plausible, functional explanation for its political–military behavior. Even if we accept that culture plays a role, we do not know what proportion of military behavior it explains. How do we measure it against the myriad other factors at play? Can we be sure that what we observe on the battlefield is causally connected to culture, however conceived, and not to something else?

Rationality

Likewise, the issues raised by the rational-actor model are particularly perplexing. How do we know when behavior is prompted by universal laws of rationality or by particular cultural values? How do we recognize the difference when we see it? For example, was Argentina's initial underestimation of Great Britain's willingness to defend the Falklands a function of unique cultural factors that derive from a Germanic influence in Argentine society which sees the British as an effete people who will do almost anything to avoid a fight? Or was this misperception a product of rational decisionmaking based on the estimated value of the real estate and past British performance, e.g., the unwillingness of the British to use force versus Gandhi's nonviolence campaign in India?

Can an analyst from one country ever be sure that the military acts he or she attributes to the cultural eccentricities of another are not, in fact, rational behavior based on economic exigencies, internal politics, secret diplomacy, access to military technology, or a host of other factors a foreign analyst may not be aware of or fully comprehend?

Learning and Change

Another thorny question relates to the role of imitation and learning. How to explain changes in military performance over time? At what point do historical psychocultural influences give way to modern, worldwide, cultural influences? What role does learning play in the adoption of new methods and strategies of warfare? When do external international factors or new experiences provoke predictable change, overriding historical values and traditional norms of behavior—and why does it "kick in" when it does? History provides many examples of radical change in a people's warrior tradition. How to explain, for example, the historic reality that during the eighth century to the sixteenth century Arab armies specialized in blitzkrieg as they swept across the Arabian peninsula, North Africa into the Iberian peninsula, the Middle East through the Fertile Crescent into Iran and beyond as far as the Indian subcontinent and the Indonesian islands—yet during the twentieth century they have exhibited a cautious and indifferent military performance? Similarly, what explanation can be given for the transformation of the Jewish image from a pre–World War II passive, non-fighter to one of martial prowess and warrior status since then?[98]

The discussion above regarding India's aversion to naval activity is relevant in this context as well. As we have seen, India, which for thirty centuries did not become a naval power, is now (since the 1970s) aggressively acquiring a blue-water navy. Was this a lesson learned from the successful blockade of the Karachi port in 1971 or from the British ability to project naval power in the Falklands? If so, at what point did other cultural preferences fade in importance?

Similar questions are raised by India's historical approach to warfare. Throughout early Indian history, military strategy and tactics remained undeveloped. Hindu kings made no effort to defend the northwest passes through which invaders poured time and again. No policy of alliance was adopted, despite the humiliation of dozens of Hindu armies; no fortifications or walled cities were built to protect the population.[99] In sum, early Hindu military leaders did not seem to "learn." Even after independence, analagous strategic and tactical weaknesses were observed in the 1962 China/India border war.[100] But the situation has changed since the 1971 war on the subcontinent and India's intervention in the Sri Lankan conflict in 1987. India's strategic planning and the performance of the military was given better marks by the Western defense community, and India's doctrinal changes indicate that "learning" did indeed taken place. But when and why did change occur? Why did India imitate and adopt the strategies and techniques of other armies in the twentieth century but resisted doing so in its early history?

Some analysts believe that political centralization holds the answer. Keith Otterbein's cross-cultural study of fifty societies concludes that "as political communities evolve in terms of increasing centralization, the manner in which they wage war becomes more sophisticated."[101]

Thomas U. Berger, on the other hand, posits that it is major traumatic national events that precipitate change in culture, doctrine, and behavior. What, he asks, accounts for German and Japanese antimilitarism since the end of World II, given their past history? The answer to this question, he believes, can be found in the lessons each country learned from its troubled past.

> In both cases these lessons were shaped by the fierce political debates of the early postwar years, which took different routes in each country and provided the resulting antimilitary sentiments of each with decidedly distinct flavors.[102]

On the other hand, others maintain that a "culture of modernity" grounded in parochial Western values[103] has evolved in the late twentieth century to which elites, whatever their national origin, belong. Zartman and Berman in their work on negotiations conclude that "By now the world has established an international diplomatic culture that soon socializes its members into similar behavior. Even the Chinese have learned to play the U.N. game by its rules."[104] Military assistance is seen as yet another conduit for change. During the Cold War, Arab tactics were attributed to Soviet tutelage in connection with arms transfer and training programs.[105] More recently, private American "advisory" companies have been delegated the task of changing the way particular U.S. allies think about and fight wars-an overt attempt to alter the strategic culture of other countries. MPRI's role in Croatia, discussed in chapter seven, is only one of a growing number of examples.

If these analysts are correct, are we witnessing the gradual evolution of a universal culture? Are the military forces of the world and the populations they fight for being coopted into an international strategic culture? Or have the norms, values, and practices of individual societies withstood the kinds of pressures these analysts propose?

Levels of Change and Continuity

These questions raise other equally difficult puzzles since they imply that "culture" is not static but fluid, that it changes in response to events and circumstance. This notion challenges the assumption of cultural continuity and invariability that implicitly has been part of cultural relativist thinking in the past. But even if the idea that values, attitudes, and beliefs do change is accepted, we still do not know under what conditions they do so. Nor do we know whether "new" values displace traditional values completely or whether they meld to form a new but particularistic set of cultural norms. If a "culture of modernity," exists, what balance exists in the minds of men between its values and those of their own parochial cultures?

It is the broadness of the concept of culture itself that creates the difficulty. Clearly all people possess mental prisms that color and interpret the vast array of phenomena around them. But, as we have seen, there is little agreement as to the sources of culture or its impact on behavior. Nor has much attention been given to the variety and types of values and attitudes that influence and motivate human beings to act, even when they are part of the same social unit. Is it not possible that a constellation of values—global, national, subnational—all reside simultaneously in the human mind motivating it to respond differently under diverse circumstances? The idea of a "military" or "strategic" culture, for example, assumes that the armed forces of a state are unified. Yet the army, navy, or air force may each comprise different subcultures, and within the services, ethnic, occupational, social, religious, or regional subcultures may create further cleavages among them. The same may be said for the elites who plan for war and the population that must bear its costs. We still do not understand what variety or hierarchy of values exist in the human mind and which take precedence when. Are all values, attitudes, and beliefs equally relevant to all behavior, or do different sets of values govern responses in different situations? To assume consensus may distort the richness and complexity of any particular society, but to assume otherwise seriously complicates the task of parsimonious theory-building to explain and predict military behavior.

An added difficulty is the concept of war. It, too, is broadly defined and undifferentiated in the literature. Throughout history there have been many kinds of wars: interstate and civil; regional and global; wars fought on land, sea, or in the air; wars fought offensively and defensively. There have been conquests, invasions, sieges, massacres, raids, and mutinies. Yet there has been no attempt to test whether men's behavior in battle changes with context. We know, for example, that many Israeli soldiers who excelled during the Lebanon war, performed poorly on the West Bank during the *Intifada*. But if military response varies with circumstance, then the difficulty of finding causal connections between the two disaggregated concepts—culture and war—increases exponentially. Where do we look for causal connections among many subcultures and numerous types of military performance?

Thus far we have been discussing the impact of culture on war. However, the reverse has also been postulated. Anthropologists, for example, have found that war plays an important role in state formation and social change. The development of a military force, military strategy, and military equipment, they maintain, contributes to "social differentiation and political complexity."[106] Various political scientists, too, claim that warfare not only has independent effects on social institutions such as economic and administrative structures, and the relationship between citizens and state,[107] but on a society's values, attitudes, and beliefs as well.[108]

Yitzhak Klein, focusing on the military, suggests that the experience of war converts "the combatants themselves into independent factors conditioning each other's strategic environment."[109] Thus, he maintains, the way an enemy fights and plans for war conditions a combatant's strategic and tactical response.

Others have argued that not only the process of war but its outcome may have important cultural implications. Like Thomas Berger, Harry Eckstein points to the German experience as an example. West Germany emerged from World War II totally defeated and as a by-product had a democratic form of government imposed upon it. Over the last half century, through a process of sociocultural evolution, Eckstein maintains, German democracy became "increasingly enculturated."[110] He speculates that although pre–World War II attitudes and values may have affected the way the German military fought World War II, cultural change as an unanticipated consequence of that war may have important implications for the way Germans do or do not fight the next war.[111] Culture and war, then, as these theorists suggest, may function symbiotically, each serving at different times as an inhibitor of and catalyst for change in each other—acting as both independent and dependent variables. But, again, understanding that the process is complex does not provide answers as to when and how attitudes toward armed conflict and associated behaviors predictably change—or, for that matter, which set of attitudes are relevant when. There is little consensus in the literature to help us answer these questions.

Conclusion

The still sparse literature indicates that culture *matters* in some way that has yet to be precisely determined. The field of international relations and security studies is only beginning to subject culture to systematic empirical and theoretical attention. But as R. B. J. Walker observes, the term still performs a largely catch-all function:

> its multiple meanings providing a convenient label by which to identify a variety of themes left over after all the primary explanatory variables . . . have been dealt with.[112]

Concluding that culture *matters* is not to suggest that it can or will explain all variation in military behavior. Rather we would argue that until empirical research proves otherwise, it should be considered one of the critical variables that shape the process and outcome of war. Admittedly, at this stage of our knowledge, the conceptual, methodological, and theoretical obstacles seem insurmountable. Thus far it has not been possible to establish causality, if in fact it exists. Nevertheless, because the claim that culture and war are somehow related seems intuitively correct to so many analysts from so many disciplines, it is important that efforts to decipher the puzzle continue—in spite of the difficulties.

This discussion, then, has been intended as an intellectual exercise of consciousness-raising, to bring to the reader's attention the many approaches analysts use to explain the different ways wars are fought and end, and the major conceptual and methodological gaps that still remain. Based on existing evidence, that culture *matters* seems indisputable. How much it matters, in what context, under what conditions, has been more difficult to determine and, in the the end, may prove to be an insoluble, unanswerable puzzle.

CHAPTER 7

Security Assistance and Warfare

Since the end of World War II, security assistance patterns have reflected the shape and character of power relations among nations and states. As these have changed, so too has security assistance, particularly to combatants. Between 1969 and 1989, during the Cold War, the U.S. and Soviet Union together accounted for approximately two-thirds of global arms transfers, a robust indicator of their political and military dominance in the international system.[1] In comparison, their closest competitors, France and Great Britain, averaged between 4 and 6 percent of the total arms market. But by the 1990s—with the collapse of the Soviet Union and communist regimes in Eastern Europe, the changing regional balances, the rampant instability in Africa and parts of the former communist world—the structure of the arms market and the international system reflected a radical transformation of power relations taking place among states. The U.S. alone was now dominant in a contracted arms market, its closest competitors sharing a relatively smaller share of the arms trade.

However, the concept of security assistance as used here embraces more than the transfer of arms and military equipment. It includes a broad range of political, economic, and military acts, overt and covert, that directly or indirectly influence the conduct of war. So conceived, the global political hierarchy becomes less visible, the avenues of control less evident, and the ways of war less predictable.

This chapter analyzes the patterns of security assistance in recent wars, using them as empirical indicators of the structural changes taking place in the international system. As in the past, security assistance is used to protect and project the interests of those who give it. What has changed is the "how" not the "why" of these policies. Surveyed here are: the ways in which combatants obtain military supplies, training, services, and various other kinds of support, and from whom; and how security assistance has been used to influence the conduct and outcome of recent wars. Key organizing questions are: What forms of security assistance are provided to whom during combat? Who are the suppliers: regional neighbors, major powers, other states, or nonstate actors? In what ways has the supply of security assistance changed or remained the same since the end of World War II? What do the observed changes and continuities tell us about power relations within the international system and the conduct of war?

Security Assistance

A Definition

Security assistance traditionally has been associated with the arms trade. To date, much of the literature has used security assistance (sometimes termed military assistance) as a synonym for arms transfers and vice versa.[2] In this chapter, security assistance is defined more broadly to encompass any and all acts by external actors—states, international organizations, or nonstate entities—which intentionally or unintentionally influence the process or outcome of an armed conflict within or between states. Omitted from our definition are goods and services acquired by combatants domestically, such as the theft of arms from government depots, or coerced military service. Pillaging, abduction, hostage-taking, ransom, and blackmail by the combatants are also not included.[3] These domestic sources of supply can be important strategic assets (and are discussed below), but for the purposes of this study, the definition of security assistance is limited to aid originating outside the recognized territorial boundaries of the combatants or war zone.

The term, then, refers to a wide range of "friendly" or "hostile" acts by foreign actors, that directly or indirectly influence the capacity of one or more combatants to fight a war. These calculated acts, utilizing an array of economic, military, and diplomatic/political instruments, may be "overt" or "covert," with anticipated or unanticipated results. Frequently, as in the case of humanitarian assistance, an intended "neutral" act may favor one combatant over another, and have unintended consequences for a conflict. Often it is difficult to know whether these policy outcomes are "intended" or "unintended." For example, Operation Restore Hope, the U.S.-led and UN-authorized military intervention in Somalia, was allegedly a response to a November 1992 report by UN Special Envoy to Somalia Ismat Kittani which found that 70–80 percent of food deliveries to Somalia were lost or stolen. Operation Restore Hope was then created to establish "a secure environment for the delivery of humanitarian relief" (UN Resolution 794, 3 December 1992). But the UN bureaucracy and NGOs disputed the Kittani figure, arguing that it was used as a pretext for military intervention. A senior UN official bluntly stated: "This figure of 80 percent blasted about. That's crap. It was used by the U.S. to justify intervention-it did not come from the agencies."[4] To General Aideed, a southern Somali clan leader, Operation Restore Hope was not a humanitarian venture but a clear attempt to defeat him in the Somalian civil war by the U.S.

In fact, after much soul searching, some suppliers openly acknowledge that food aid *is* security assistance during war. The U.S. plan in 1999 to give food directly to the Sudan People's Liberation Army fighting the central government in Sudan was intended as an overt attempt to bolster the rebel side and isolate the government in a civil war. According to U.S. government officials, the food would allow the rebels to maintain or expand their positions in the parched, food deficit areas where they are fighting the northern army and government-backed militias and "where it is difficult to maintain a logistical line."[5] Thus food, objectively one of the most neutral kinds of humanitarian aid, during war, metamorphosizes into a form of security assistance.

Electronic and communication devices, too, neutral instruments during peacetime, have become important tools of warfare. CNN television broadcasters, for example, were accused of providing the Iraqis with useful information during the Kuwait war. In the former Yugoslavia, Milosevic used the electronic media extensively to spread his nationalist message in order to build domestic support within the Serb population. It is argued, however, that he lost the propaganda war—if not the Bosnia-Herzegovina and Kosovo wars themselves—when he underestimated the power of the electronic media to influence world public opinion.[6]

Although rarely mentioned in the literature as a military-related transfer, electronic and communication devices have been an integral part of military-support programs, especially those designed to destabilize foreign regimes. Computers, fax machines, tape recorders, cellular phones have proven to be powerful weapons of war, permitting combatants to communicate and coordinate with far-flung supporters and diverse fighting units. Fax machines and tape recorders, for example, served a critical function for Khomeini during the Iranian Revolution, allowing his supporters from different parts of the globe to communicate easily with each other and to subvert the Iranian government without the necessity of a physical presence in the country. In the U.S., the Reagan administration channeled communications equipment through various intermediaries to the Polish Solidarity Movement during the 1980s as part of an effort to "separate the Poles from the rest of the Warsaw Pact;"[7] and the Clinton administration, which made toppling President Saddam Hussein a major objective, allocated $2 million in 1998 for anti-Saddam radio broadcasts into Iraq, and sent computers, fax machines, and financial assistance to reunited opposition groups in 1999 for that purpose.[8]

In civil conflicts, both sides wage wars for the "hearts and minds" of the population with these tools. Even printing presses have been considered potentially lethal weapons. The African National Congress (ANC) in its war against apartheid, for example, urged international suppliers to refrain from selling a printing press to the South African Defense Force, arguing that such a sale would be in contravention of the arms embargo.[9]

In sum, security assistance, as we define it, is a multifaceted cluster of undertakings by foreign actors designed to provide or deny combatants the ability to deter, survive, or win a war.[10] For our purposes here, if an act helps one side or the other to pursue armed hostilities, whether intended or not, it is considered a form of security assistance. By broadening the definition in this way, some might argue that the distinction between security assistance and other kinds of support has been blurred, and that may be true. In some cases, it may be the deliberate intent of the supplier to do so. But during an ongoing armed conflict, if either the combatants or the donors believe the venture to be a form of security assistance, or if in hindsight it is judged to be so, it is considered to be security assistance here as well. Our definition of security assistance encompasses many acts that may be benign during peacetime but are regarded as forms of security assistance during armed conflict. It is our contention that any service or materiel rendered (or denied) by an external actor to a combatant inevitably benefits or disadvantages the military effort of one side or the other in war. Although often difficult to separate, wherever possible, we have focussed on the consequences of a particular act, rather than the supplier's stated intention.

A Typology

As we have discussed, security assistance during war can take many forms, some quite unlikely. In an attempt to bring some order out of chaos, we created a typology, dividing security assistance into three main categories: Diplomatic/Political; Economic; and Military. Each individual act may be overt or covert, hostile (to limit or deny the war aims of one or more of the combatants) or friendly (to assist one or more of the combatants to deter, survive, or win the war) or neutral or nonpartisan in intent. Listed below are the three categories of security assistance and selected examples of the ways in which each might influence an ongoing conflict. We do not pretend to comprehensiveness. There are surely other ingenious ways suppliers and recipients have found to support or subvert a war effort which we have inadvertently overlooked or simply do not know about.

Diplomatic/Political
Diplomatic/political assistance attempts to steer a conflict toward a particular outcome using nonmilitary and noneconomic tools of statecraft. These might include pronouncements of support or condemnation of a particular combatant; the provision or denial of sanctuary for political refugees or military personnel;[11] lobbying for sanctions or supplying political backing in international fora; enlarging or reducing a diplomatic presence, recalling an Ambassador, cutting back on staff, and/or closing an embassy; restricting or allowing landing rights; increasing, limiting, or suspending visa allocations; boycotting or encouraging cultural, athletic, academic, or scientific exchanges; aggressive propaganda programs, threats of punishment, promises of rewards; and other acts designed to undermine the political stability of the opponent.

Economic
Economic aid is another major form of security assistance. It includes loans, grants, rescheduling or forgiveness of debt, extending favorable terms of trade, civilian technical assistance, development projects, and a variety of humanitarian services. Economic aid to a combatant may also, however, consist of punishment directed toward its enemy. Here economic assistance takes on the character of economic warfare, such as implementing economic sanctions, partial or full trade

embargoes, asset seizures, investment restrictions, the withdrawal or denial of technical assistance, terminating development projects, denying or revoking humanitarian services; and other actions intended to weaken the economic welfare of an opposing belligerent.

Military

Military aid, most commonly associated with security assistance, is generally the most easily identifiable. These acts, emanating from the supplier's military sector, are intended to benefit or degrade the military infrastructure of the recipient. We have divided them into two categories, direct and indirect military aid, in order to distinguish between actions immediate to the battlefield, and those more ancillary to it.[12] Direct military aid, for example, involves a show of force and other recognized acts of war toward an adversary, such as the commitment of uniformed troops. It might also entail sending mercenary or voluntary combat forces, civilian or military employees to operate or repair equipment, assist in strategic or tactical planning, and logistics or intelligence-gathering. Military personnel participating in peacekeeping/peace-enforcing operations are included here as well,[13] since these activities, more often than not, are interpreted by one side or the other as partisan military intervention.[14] Historically, the United Nations has been reluctant to define the principles of peacekeeping and this has caused considerable terminological confusion and conceptual disarray.[15] As a result, over the years, a variety of terms have been created on an ad hoc basis to encompass the unanticipated military activities undertaken in the UN's name in the cause of peace. To date, the conceptual confusion persists, but to the contending parties these "peacekeeping" activities are interpreted as military operations that either benefit or disadvantage their own war effort. (See discussion below, on pages 297-298.) They are, therefore, included here as a form of direct military aid.

Indirect military assistance, on the other hand, does not involve physical intervention on the battlefield. These are ventures executed by the donor's military but often undertaken in situations where policymakers decide that direct military aid is politically, economically, or militarily ill-advised or unfeasible. However, indirect aid is also often used to supplement direct military interventions. When combat troops are committed, other forms of assistance generally follow. Indirect military aid, then, might include dispatching military equipment, technical assistance, or logistical support to a war zone; providing training or intelligence information; engaging in joint exercises; orchestrating the intervention of proxy forces; the transport of troops or materiel; providing sanctuaries or base facilities; or other measures to strengthen the military capability of the recipient.

Indirect military aid, however, may also be hostile acts, such as the suspension or denial of military goods and services; sanctions and embargoes on military items; the disruption of command, control, and communication systems; suspension of joint exercises; and a variety of other unfriendly military activities that are meant to dissuade or stop a belligerent from further action.

In sum, during peacetime each type of foreign aid may be used by suppliers to achieve a variety of political and economic goals. But during wartime, whether it is furnished openly or covertly, by private or government suppliers, any type of foreign aid becomes a form of security assistance that influences the fighting capabilities of the combatants. Since the end of World War II, as the concept of "total war" began to fade from our military lexicon, it was security assistance that assumed the character of "totality."[16] Suppliers, hoping to influence a war's outcome have used all available resources at their disposal, effectively erasing the distinction between foreign aid and security assistance. In today's world, "security assistance" to a combatant connotes an array of activities that transcends those traditionally associated with the military sector. Although diplomatic/political, economic, and military instruments were used to influence the conduct and outcome of wars in the past, changes in the international political structure, declining military budgets worldwide, and the reluctance of the major powers to expend human capital have increased their utility and use as tools of leverage in recent wars.

Types of Security Assistance and Their Frequency

The relative frequency of the different types of security assistance is difficult to measure and still harder to disaggregate. Governments and private organizations are not always eager to publicize the extent and type of their assistance to combatants and may go to great lengths to disguise it.[17] The collection, coding, and analysis of information about security assistance for this book was, therefore, a demanding, time-consuming, and often frustrating task . It involved an extensive search of the literature—scholarly publications, the media, the internet, fugitive works—from which we derived a database of security assistance acts during wars fought between 1991 and 1997. Generally, we used duplication of information as a criterion for inclusion. If the act was reported in more than one source, it was entered in the database. But given the nature of the data, we were not always able to find confirming evidence.[18] In those cases, we used our own judgment. If the circumstances appeared to be consistent with earlier reported supplier or recipient behavior, it was included. If the event seemed to be an isolated, unconfirmed incident, it was not. In sum, we tried to carefully assess the credibility of our data, using repetition and agreement among diverse sources as one criterion, and intuitive logic as another. Clearly, our methodology is not foolproof, and so we cannot vouch for the reliability of the database or for its completeness. We believe, however, that the information is valid enough to measure general trends and patterns of security assistance in recent wars, and we have used it for that purpose.

Table 7.1 below indicates the relative frequency of the different kinds of security assistance provided during forty-three wars waged between 1991 and 1997.[19] Indirect military aid was the most frequent form of security assistance across all wars (36 percent), with direct and indirect military aid together comprising over 50 percent of all security assistance.[20] Across regions, indirect military aid dominated as well, totaling approximately one-third of the security assistance supplied to combatants in Latin America, Asia, Europe, and the Middle East. Forty-four percent of Africa's security assistance was indirect military aid as

Table 7.1 SECURITY ASSISTANCE BY TYPE AND REGION
(Percent of Total Number of Acts) 1991–1997

REGION	No. Of Wars	Diplomatic/ Political	Economic	*Military Indirect*	*Military Direct*	Military Total
AFRICA	17	18%	18%	44%	20%	64%
AMERICAS	4	36%	23%	37%	4%	41%
ASIA	9	31%	31%	31%	7%	38%
CENTRAL ASIA	4	23%	25%	25%	27%	52%
EUROPE	4	24%	18%	33%	25%	58%
MIDDLE EAST	5	38%	23%	31%	8%	39%
TOTAL	*43*	*27%*	*22%*	36%	15%	*51%*

was 25 percent of Central Asia's. The major types of indirect military aid received were training, weapons, and financing for the military. Combatants in Central Asia, Europe, and Africa also received significant amounts of direct military aid, 27 percent, 25 percent, and 20 percent respectively. Only Middle Eastern forces received almost equal amounts of diplomatic and military support. Nevertheless, diplomatic/political and economic forms of assistance together constituted 49 percent of all security assistance delivered to combatants between 1991 and 1997.

Trends in Security Assistance

This section describes trends in security assistance to combatants in recent wars—who is providing what to whom, and how it is utilized. We have tried to trace developments that reflect change and continuities not only in security assistance and how wars are fought but in the structure of the international system as well.

The Changing Arms Market: The Analyst's Dilemma

Obtaining accurate quantitative and qualitative data for the arms trade and military aid generally has always been difficult. Since the end of the Cold War it has become even more so. Suppliers and recipients are finding ever more inventive ways to disguise what they are providing to whom.[21] This, unfortunately, seems to be a growing trend.

Small Arms and Light Weapons
A striking change in the post–Cold War arms market is the burgeoning trade in small arms.[22] It has been accompanied by a decline in sales of heavy weapons

such as tanks, armored vehicles, long-range artillery, aircraft, and surface war-ships, all traditionally associated with "war" in the twentieth century.[23] As the number of internal wars has increased, the demand for small and light weapons has risen—to such proportions that some conclude the arms trade has been rev-olutionized.[24] Anecdotal evidence suggests this may be true. UN officials claim that small arms were the only weapons used in forty-six of the forty-nine con-flicts waged since 1990.[25] In Africa, alone, according to a U.S. State Department report, state-to-state arms transfers during the Cold War involved primarily heavy weapons, such as jet fighters, helicopters, transport aircraft, and tanks. These systems then made up the largest portion of many African military budg-ets. With the end of the Cold War, these state-to-state transfers declined 94 per-cent, from $4,270 million in 1988 to $270 million in 1995.[26]

Of course, the use of major weapons has not become obsolete. Even in the post–Cold War period when sales of these items declined, some combatants relied upon them with lethal effect, such as the Serbian artillery in Bosnia, Russ-ian aircraft and artillery in Abkhazia, and U.S. aircraft in Kosovo. Even in Africa, major weapons remain popular. Angola, Botswana, Eritrea, Ethiopia, Nigeria, Rwanda, South Africa, Uganda, and Zimbabwe continue to obtain heavy weapons, although only Zimbabwe has been reported to have used them.[27] In the post–Cold War world, however, with the exception of Yugoslavia, these weapons have had a limited presence in recent conflicts. Small arms and light weapons have become the weapons of choice for most combatants.

But the actual size of world demand and how much it has grown is still largely unknown. No government or private agency keeps comprehensive track of this trade, and buyers and sellers are not interested in sharing such informa-tion.[28] The best guess of their annual value, according to the U.S. State Depart-ment, is probably hundreds of millions of dollars.[29]

The annual dollar values for all countries' "conventional" arms transfers is published by the U.S. Department of State, Bureau of Verification and Compli-ance in *World Military Expenditures and Arms Transfer (WMEAT)*.[30] The data include all "weapons of war, parts thereof, ammunition, support equipment, and other commodities designed for military use" that are exported and imported by the U.S. and other countries.[31] But the dollar values provided are not broken down into weapon types or services, frustrating any attempt to estimate the number and value of small arms and light weapons transferred.[32] The same is true for the publications of other U.S. government agencies.[33] Moreover, col-lecting data on this type of transfer is difficult even for U.S. government and intelligence agencies. As *WMEAT* cautions: "the latter estimates are based on U.S. Government sources, which may not be able to capture the full extent of small arms, spare and production parts and components, and defense services exported by those countries."[34] It is true that major weapons account for most of the dollar value of arms transfers and, as one analyst pointed out, including "the dollar value of small arms, light weapons and ammunition would change the reported country totals probably by less than one percentage point, if that."[35] But most weapons-related deaths in post–Cold War combat are caused not by modern major systems, but by small arms, mines, and light artillery.[36] To date, we know very little about the magnitude of the trade in weapons that equip most combatants in recent wars.

Technology Transfers, Services, Upgrades, and Components

Technology transfers, services, upgrades, and components present yet another analytical problem. The changing arms trade, once composed largely of major weapons systems, in the past ten to fifteen years has increasingly been characterized not just by small arms, but by a variety of dual-use items, technological know-how, components, defense industrial facilities, and a variety of military services including training, supply operations, construction, and other forms of technical assistance. As in the case of small arms, the number and value of these transfers are not documented anywhere, and what is included in the official country totals may not be accurate or complete. What we do know is that over the last decade, the number of major weapons transferred worldwide declined by nearly 60 percent, yet the dollar value of arms deliveries dropped only 44 percent. Since the cost of major weapons rose dramatically in the past twenty years, a sharper decrease in the dollar value of arms transferred might be expected. The relatively smaller decline suggests that other types of military items are making up the difference.[37] Although there is much anecdotal evidence to suggest buyers are relying on new technologies, components, and services to upgrade the capabilities of equipment already in inventory, there is little hard data to confirm this trend.

Other Types of War Materiel

Publicly available data sources also ignore a variety of maintenance and logistical support systems that frequently determine the ability of governments to continue fighting—items that are often provided by private contractors, such as foodstuffs, medical equipment, petroleum products, and other supplies as well as different kinds of humanitarian, economic, and diplomatic/political aid. Again, it is not possible to glean from current statistical compendia what proportion of security assistance is composed of these items. Nor is the extent to which they contribute to an individual combatant's comparative military capability well understood.[38]

Subnational Combatants

Even more discouraging is the lack of credible information about military aid to subnational combatants. U.S. and other publications shed little light on the issue. Official U.S. arms transfer data, for example, provide the dollar value of transfers to "countries" without distinction as to the recipient in those countries. But in civil wars, the government is only one of the recipients. Where do the transfers to the other nongovernment parties appear? Curiously, there is little agreement among U.S. government officials themselves on this question. Some claim that published U.S. arms import/export figures for foreign suppliers and recipients include all "knowable" transactions, including those to dissident groups.[39] Others disagree.[40] But for our purposes, it makes little difference, since the dollar values for these transfers cannot be separated out from the country totals. Hence information about military transfers to at least one-half the number of the combatants in recent wars is unavailable. Ironically, although almost all warfare since the end of the Cold War has involved subnational forces, detailed, accurate information about military transfers to these groups is unavailable.

Covert Illegal Arms Transfers

A closely related problem is finding data on "unofficial" illegal arms deliveries. Little is known about the size of these transactions, although they have played an important role in the arms trade since the end of World War II.[41] Here, too, there is disagreement among U.S. government analysts. One maintains that "U.S. export/import figures for foreign countries presumably include the estimated dollar value of these "covert" transfers when they are 'known.'" But another observed that if that was once true, it may no longer be so. "During the Cold War it was considered important to identify other suppliers' legal and illegal deliveries to foreign countries. We never got everything, but we got a lot. Today the intelligence agencies like to give the impression that they are getting most everything. But the arms trade statistics aren't as complete as they once were. The incentive is gone and I think most of the covert trade slips by unnoticed. Everyone is just too tied up with other things."[42] Add to this the proliferation of electronic communication and encryption devices[43] and the tendency of combatant buyers to use deception to hide their purchases, and the chances for comprehensiveness in the data are very slim.[44]

For our purposes, again, it matters little. Official information about the size and character of covert transactions, to all intents and purposes, is lost since it cannot be differentiated from the total dollar values attributed to the individual countries in U.S. data—whether it is or is not included. What is available on these illegal or "covert" transfers can be found in the publications of advocacy groups, nongovernment think tanks, research institutes, special government-sponsored reports, congressional testimony, academic journals, the media, and now the web. But this information is anecdotal and of unknown accuracy. A search of the literature yields only unofficial "guesstimates" of the size of the world covert arms market,[45] and little on the dollar value of covert transfers to subnational groups. Information on what military hardware is actually delivered is equally limited.

Arms transfer transparency was never complete, but as long as there were concerned government analysts working the issue during the Cold War, leaks and media reports made it possible for outsiders to occasionally view the covert market in action, as media reports on the Iran-Iraq War demonstrated. Today, these transactions are even less transparent.

Changing Procurement Strategies

All of this would be academic were it not for the changing nature of war and the response of much of the world to it. The Iran/Iraq War provided sobering lessons for many government defense planners. They watched the conflict evolve into a war of attrition fought on a low technological level, despite the modern weapons in inventory on both sides. The Iranian and Iraqi forces simply lacked the skills to maintain and operate the systems they had acquired from their industrialized suppliers. The 1990–1991 Gulf War demonstrated, on another level, the huge military technological gap between the developed and less developed world, and led some non-Western defense planners to conclude that current ways of fighting interstate wars would soon be outmoded.[46] Added to these concerns were the spiraling cost of advanced weapons, deteriorating world economic conditions, and diminished sources of grant aid and subsidized military assistance.

By the mid-1990s, many Third World governments had reevaluated their military doctrines in terms of their most likely security threat—ethnic conflict and insurgencies. In Malaysia, for example, Lt. Gen. Datuk Seri Othman Haron explained: "We are looking at re-emphasizing small operations and tactics using modern infantry equipment in accordance with our terrain and environment." He indicated the Malaysian armed forces could not go conventional, "Western style," with huge armored assets, massive artillery and high-technology missiles, partly because of cost limitations, but also due to technological and international political and environmental constraints.[47] Small and light arms were always the primary weapons used by subnational forces. In the new strategic environment, however, many Third World governments and their armies also have come to further appreciate their value.

Declining Transparency

What little we know about the arms trade is limited principally to large government-government deals that are difficult to keep secret or those that governments publicize for political reasons. Good intelligence on the growing trade in small arms, light weapons, components, other support technologies, and services is missing for both legal and illegal transfers. Official publications, once a passable source of data from which general trends could be derived, today tell us little about the changing patterns of resupply and procurement in most parts of the world. The data problems described here promise to grow in the future, as Western government officials, academics, researchers, and the media—in a reduced-threat environment—lose interest and turn their attention to other economic, political, and social problems. For researchers outside the government, recent increased transparency efforts to the contrary, the ability to oversee and report meaningfully on the who gets what in the arms trade has diminished radically. It is a disturbing trend.

Changes and Continuities in Security Assistance

Incomplete as they are, the data indicate both change and continuity in the post–Cold War arms trade. The most striking changes are its shrinking size and fading bipolar nature. Yet the character of the arms trade has remained as dramatically skewed as it was during the Cold War, reflecting the dominance of the most powerful players in the system—then the U.S. and the Soviet Union, now the U.S. alone.

Moreover, the data suggest that developing countries, no longer able to rely on subsidies from contending superpowers, are now adjusting their procurement practices to fit their pocketbooks. They are buying fewer major weapons and making do with less sophisticated equipment provided by an array of old and new suppliers.[48] Despite these changes, however, many governments still look to former suppliers for security assistance. Military inventories, operational methods, personal contacts, procurement, and transportation networks shift slowly, particularly in poorer, embattled countries where Cold War dependencies have tended to endure in the military sector.

What the official arms trade data do not reflect, however, are the rising number of alternative sources of security assistance and the revolution in information and communication technology that has propagated them. Once largely a government monopoly, security assistance is now provided by a complementary, intricate web of private and public entities. International (governmental) organizations (IGOs), nongovernmental organizations (NGOs), regulatory agencies, special interest groups, and even private individuals increasingly share that function with governments.[49] NGOs participate in the distribution of humanitarian assistance, often performing other public services as well. Transnational ethnic, religious, cultural, political, and criminal networks actively support combatants with men, materiel, funding, and political backing. A complex mesh of government, private, and transnational legal, semilegal, and illegal enterprises function as intermediaries, helping combatants find ever more creative sources of supply. The number and variety of these sources seems endless.[50]

Transnational linkages, especially during wartime, are not new. Historically, exiles in the diaspora have offered material and moral sustenance for besieged kinsman.[51] But since the end of World War II, as new communication and transportation technologies spread to ever larger publics, these and other transnational groups have multiplied—mutating into bigger, better-organized associations, with access to abundant resources. Legal and illegal enterprises all over the world are benefiting from the information explosion and the technologies associated with it. People, groups, organizations, and governments are now able to interact as closely as neighbors.

Yet in spite of these momentous developments, continuities persist. The sections below examine some of these continuities and changes in government and nongovernment security assistance programs.

Government Sources of Security Assistance

The Major Powers

From 1986 to 1990 world arms deliveries averaged $59 billion a year; by the 1991 to 1996 period they had fallen by 39 percent to an average of $36 billion a year. For the most part, as discussed above, these figures refer to government-to-government transfers.[52] Moreover, worldwide military spending had declined by about 30 percent since the mid-1980s,[53] and procurement orders fell nearly 40 percent.[54]

Associated with these changes, and a consequence of them, is the dominant role of the U.S. as a supplier. In contrast to the 1980s when each superpower captured approximately one-third of the arms trade, U.S. military transfers between 1991 and 1996 rose to 61 percent of the total, eclipsing other suppliers, while the Soviet/Russian share dropped to nine percent. To illustrate the magnitude of U.S. dominance, the next closest competitor during this period was the United Kingdom which exported 12 percent of the world's arms. (See Table 7.2.) The United States also spends almost two-thirds of the world's military research and development (R&D) dollars.[55] Consequently, the U.S. is the principal innovator of state-of the-art military technologies—a situation that creates significant dependency among other powers that want to incorporate these systems into their own inventories.[56] Unless there is a radical change in the military R&D spending of other industrialized countries, this situation promises to continue in the foreseeable future.

Since the collapse of the Soviet Union, Russian defense spending has fallen faster than that of other countries. In 1995 the Russian military received only 35 percent of what it needed to support research, development, and new purchases. By 1996 the Russian arms industry was exporting more than it produced for its own military.[57] During the Cold War, arms trade statistics reflected the estimated dollar value of Soviet exports, but the Soviet Union rarely realized a profit, since much of what was transferred, in the interests of foreign policy priorities, went to countries without the resources to pay for them. Today, with rare exception, that is no longer the case.[58] Traditional customers, such as Syria and India, now pay cash, as does China. Some customers, such as Malaysia, attracted by the low cost of Soviet technology, pay part of the bill with natural resources, in this case palm oil.[59] But not everything has changed. Russia is still a relatively large supplier of military equipment to areas of conflict, although it is now revenue not ideology that drives these sales.[60] Many warring parties in the Third World are fighting with Soviet-origin equipment and look to Russia (or other former communist bloc countries) for resupply. Between 1991 and 1996, Russia was the second largest exporter to combatants, delivering 21 percent of the world's arms transfers to them. Thus demand and supply are driving Russian military sales to combatants. As in the past, the dollar value of published U.S. arms transfers to belligerents is proportionately less (45 percent) than its exports to other more peaceful customers, although U.S. military aid to warring countries is still the world's largest. (See Table 7.2.) Curiously, while the world's arms trade system is no longer bipolar, transfers to combatants retain some of its bipolar character. Together the U.S. and Russia account for two-thirds of the military goods and services delivered to war zones—a percentage that approximated their share of the world's arms trade during the Cold War—and this may underestimate the value of their other unrecorded transfers to combatants in recent wars.

Other continuities, not reflected in statistics, have persisted too. The most arresting is the use of proxy suppliers. During the Cold War, both the U.S. and the Soviet Union used surrogates to intervene in regional wars. Examples include: Angola, where the Soviet Union used Cuban troops and weapons trans-

Table 7.2 ARMS DELIVERIES, 1991–1996 (in millions of current US$)
BY MAJOR SUPPLIER Percent Total Delivered to All Countries and to All Combatants

Suppliers (%)/ Combatants	Arms Deliveries Total $ value	US	UK	Russia	France	Germany	China	Other NATO	Other West European	Other East European	Other East Asia	Others	Undistributed by supplier
WORLD TOTALS (all countries)	**218,768**	60.6	12.36	9.13	4.42	3.34	2.33	2.17	1.48	1.41	.38	2.32	NA
WORLD TOTAL (all combatants)	**37,463**	45.27	2.1	21.28	1.57	4.83	7.66	3.05	1.09	4.4	1.24	5.76	1.69

Source: These figures are derived from Table III, *WMEAT* 1997 (for 1994–1996) and *WMEAT* 1993–1994 (for 1991–1993). The 1997 edition of WMEAT substantially revises U.S. arms-export figures upward using a new interim method to calculate U.S. commercial exports by assuming that "deliveries constitute a medial 50 percent of total [commercial] authorizations by country." See the article, "Revision of U.S. Arms Exports Data Series" on the U.S. Department of State website under WMEAT 1997 [http://www.state.gov/www/global/arms/bureauvc.html]. The then Arms Control and Disarmament Agency (ACDA) provided us with revised U.S. commercial export figures for 1991–1993 which have been incorporated into this table. The 1993–1994 edition of *WMEAT* does not have the revised figures. [Since the 1998 edition, *WMEAT* has been published by the U.S. Department of State Bureau of Verification and Compliance.]

fers from Eastern bloc countries to support the MPLA; and the Afghanistan and Iran-Iraq Wars, in which the United States was similarly involved.[61] Since the end of the Cold War, the use of surrogates has proliferated. The major powers, as well as middle and small states once proxies themselves, are now using this device to provide security assistance to warring friends and allies, and to distance themselves politically from them.

Regional Powers

Another trend, not clearly reflected in the statistical data but suggested by it, is the rising role of regional powers as suppliers of direct and indirect military aid to neighboring countries. In 1997, for example, regional states contributed regular troops in three of the African conflicts. Angola, Chad, Namibia, Rwanda, Uganda, and Zimbabwe were involved in the Democratic Republic of Congo (formerly Zaire). Guinea and Senegal sent troops to Guinea-Bissau, and the Economic Community of West African States Cease Fire Monitoring Group (ECOMOG) sent forces to Sierra Leone, mainly from Ghana and Nigeria.[62]

Indirect military aid from regional powers has been even more common. China, accounting for only two percent of the total arms trade, supplies almost eight percent of the world total to combatants, providing many of them with an alternate source for Soviet-era technologies. Most of that aid goes to Asia (See Appendix 2). China's military assistance just to warring Asian parties, for example, grew from 0.2 percent in 1985–89 to almost 13 percent in 1991–96.

WMEAT does not provide information about the recipients of arms from other regional powers, so generalizing about the rising role of regional powers based on the arms export behavior of one supplier is speculative at best. It is supported, however, by other circumstantial evidence. During the Cold War both superpowers commanded a significant political price for security assistance to combatants, such as bases or other territorial and political concessions.[63] Today, regional powers, such as China, may be echoing that behavior. In exchange for providing about 80 percent of the military aid to Myanmar[64] and Laos, China has greatly increased its intelligence-gathering capability by establishing signals intelligence stations on Myanmar's Great Coco Island[65] and in southern Laos, bordering Cambodia and Thailand.[66] China also provided 54 percent of the military goods and services delivered to Sri Lanka between 1991 and 1997, and furnished economic aid, trade benefits, and technical assistance as well.[67] In return, China has gained a strategically positioned ally in Sri Lanka, which also offers China steady diplomatic/political support in international fora.[68] In an environment freed from superpower rivalry, it may be that regional powers, like China, see enhanced opportunities to seek regional hegemony and are using security assistance as one way to do so.

Ethnic/Cultural Agendas

Other policy agendas have also driven the security assistance programs of many regional powers. During the Cold War, the conventional military buildup of most Third World countries was made possible by the availability of subsidized weaponry from the Soviet Union and the U.S. With the Cold War over, these subsidies evaporated, but new suppliers with different political priorities appeared to take their place. As the tide of subnationalism has swelled, governments with ethnic, religious, and cultural ties to regimes or insurgent groups in other countries are offering substantial political and material help.

Islamic military assistance to fellow Muslims apparently far exceeds that of other groups in amount and geographical reach. Iran appears to be the most active supplier. It is reported to have provided weapons to Islamic militants in Lebanon and the Sudan and to have sent truckloads of "humanitarian" relief supplies, and possibly guns, to Shi'ite forces in Afghanistan.[69] Sudan allegedly joined Iran in sending arms to Muslim fundamentalists in Egypt and Algeria and to Somali militants in Djibouti, Ethiopia, and Kenya. Training camps for Islamic fundamentalists are also believed to be operating in Sudan.[70] Antigovernment Muslim forces in Tajikistan reputedly received weapons and ammunition from Afghanistan, Pakistan, and Iran.[71] Moro (Moro Islamic Liberation Front) separatists in the Philippines are said to have received financial help from Saudi Arabia, arms from Pakistan and possibly from Malaysia and Afghanistan.[72] Embargoed Bosnian Muslim forces nevertheless received large amounts of military equipment from Iran, Malaysia, Pakistan, Sudan, and Islamic elements in Tunisia and Afghanistan. Analysts estimate that as much as $2 billion worth of arms was delivered to Bosnia in 1993 alone.[73] And India has charged Pakistan with not only materially supporting but also instigating (Muslim) Kashmiri insurgents.[74] In fact, the North West Frontier Province of Pakistan is believed to be a training ground for terrorists who have struck in such disparate areas as the Philippines, Central Asia, the Middle East, North Africa, and possibly the World Trade Center in New York.[75]

Muslim governments are not the only ones wielding security assistance to promote political goals. Israel, surrounded by hostile Arab neighbors, has routinely employed foreign aid as a means of breaking out of its regional isolation. Much of Israel's security assistance has gone to forces fighting Muslim adversaries (such as Serbia,[76] India,[77] Ethiopia, Christian forces in Lebanon and Sudan).[78] In the Middle East, it has been used to build alliances with non-Arab states, such as Iran and Turkey. Even the Kurds in Iraq have received Israeli aid.[79] During the Shah's reign, for example, Israel furnished the Iranian military with arms and cooperated in other ventures. During the Iran-Iraq War, covert Israeli aid to Iran continued. One Israeli defense industry spokesman observed: "Our interest was that this war would last forever. Israeli companies were willing to sell virtually anything."[80] For other Israeli policymakers, however, in spite of the change in regime, Iran remained an important potential non-Arab ally. Military assistance to Iran is rumored to have continued into the 1990s, well after the war had ended. Even though Jordan in 1994 became the second country, after Egypt, to sign a peace treaty with Israel, Israel still considers military cooperation with any Arab country cautiously. Only recently did Israel tentatively break its embargo on arms sales to Arab countries by agreeing to sell Jordan weapons although the policy allows for the sale of ammunition and light arms only.[81]

Security assistance has also gone to those governments offering Israel an important strategic advantage vis-à-vis its Arab adversaries. Israel's relationship with Ethiopia and Eritrea, countries with large Christian populations in the Muslim-dominated Horn of Africa, stems from comparable concerns. Intent upon keeping the Red Sea from becoming an "Arab Sea," and preventing an Arab blockade of its southern port of Eilat, Israel provided military support to Ethiopia during its war with Somalia, and is reported to have given military aid to both Eritrea and Ethiopia, in spite of their ongoing hostilities.[82] In exchange, Israel has been able to preserve its freedom of movement in the Red Sea, arrange the emigration of Ethiopian Jews to Israel[83] and establish a military presence on the strategically positioned Dahlak Islands in the Red Sea "to better monitor fundamentalist groups in Sudan and Iranian access to Sudan's Red Sea ports."[84]

Often it is difficult to tell from published accounts whether aid of this kind is provided by government agencies, officially or unofficially, or by proxy suppliers. Statements by the recipients themselves suggest that since the end of the Cold War this so-called "gray" market has grown.[85] Joseph Garang, the leader of the Sudanese People's Liberation Army (SPLA), for example, when asked who supplied his army with arms stated that most of his weapons had been captured from the opposition. "The other source, of course the arms are available in the international black market. It is actually no longer a black market. It is much grayer than it used to be especially after the Cold War [sic]."[86] Reports of Israeli aid to the Bosnian Serbs support his statement. Although Israeli government officials have staunchly denied government involvement in the delivery of Israeli-made light weapons and artillery shells to the Bosnian Serbs, insisting "it could only happen through some private channels," one anonymous foreign ministry official suggested: "because of anti-Semitic sentiments in (croat president) franjo tudjman's book and the hezbollah-iran help to the moslems, you may draw the conclusion where our sympathies lie [sic]."[87]

Palestinian groups have been equally guarded about the source of their aid and the motives of their suppliers. Dr. Khalid Mush'il, one of Hamas's central leaders, when asked about Hamas' funding and weapons sources, responded: "We receive donations from Muslim countries . . . from Europe and the United States also."[88] Whether he was referring to official government assistance, unofficial government aid, the largesse of nongovernment groups and individuals, or all three is uncertain. Persistent reports in the media suggest that Hamas receives support from the Iranian government, as well as fundamentalist groups in Egypt, Sudan, and Jordan, and sympathetic exiles in the United States and Europe.[89]

Since the end of the Cold War, whether officially sanctioned or not, ethnic/cultural interests have influenced the security assistance policies of many governments. Even the U.S. plan to directly aid Christian rebels in southern Sudan (the Sudan People's Liberation Army [SPLA]) was said to be prompted by the concerns of the administration, Congress, and church coalitions over the Sudanese government's persecution and enslavement of Christian southerners.[90] Culturally motivated security assistance policies, while not new, have become more prominent in the post–Cold War world as Cold War agendas have receded in importance.

Embargoes and Sanctions

In the twentieth century, governments have used multilateral and unilateral sanctions with greater frequency and impunity to influence the behavior of other state and nonstate actors, particularly during periods of crisis. As Robert Pape writes: "Military instruments are often thought to be the only effective means for achieving ambitious foreign policy goals like taking or defending territory, altering a state's military behavior, and changing a state's regime or internal political structure." He argues that sanctions are now viewed as an alternative to war to achieve these objectives.[91] From the perspective of the combatants, embargoes and sanctions have also come to be viewed as a powerful source of security assistance.

Sanctions range across an ever-widening spectrum of coercive political, military, and economic instruments fashioned to impose costs in whole or in part on the economy, to politically isolate an adversary, or to degrade its military capability. These measures may include, for example, arms embargoes, denial of military training and services, foreign assistance reductions and cut-offs, export and import limitations, asset blockages and freezes, tariff increases, import quota decreases, revocation of most-favored nation (MFN) trade status, withdrawal of diplomatic relations, visa denials, cancellation of air links, travel restrictions, prohibitions on credit, financing, and investment.[92] Rarely are they imposed in isolation but rather in a blended mixture of painful measures concocted to induce a target to change its behavior.[93] Oddly, the literature makes little distinction between instruments designed to inflict political or economic pain and those meant to degrade an adversary's combat capability. They are all tossed together in a melange termed "economic sanctions."

No comprehensive catalogue exists to document the number or kinds of sanctions actually applied by governments and to whom. Generally only the most dramatic measures become known, while the vast number of partial restrictions, administrative rulings, and prohibitions levied against an increasing number of actors, remain unpublicized. This is particularly true for the United States.

Much research attention has been devoted to the effectiveness of sanctions by academics, policy analysts, and business interests, although there is little agreement among them on that issue. They do agree, however, that a startling number of sanctions have been levied since the end of the Cold War. The evidence, incomplete as it is, indicates that beginning in 1945 and throughout the Cold War there was a very gradual rise in the use of unilateral and multilateral economic sanctions followed by a sharp increase thereafter. The most ambitious collection of data documenting economic sanctions from 1914 to 1989 establishes the following gradual progression: 1914 to 1945: twelve cases; 1946 to 1969: forty-one cases; and 1970 to 1989: fifty-five cases.[94] The database ends with 1989.

Even though there is less statistical data available, the dramatic growth in the number of embargoes and sanctions since 1989 is noted by many analysts.[95] Greater cooperation between the U.S. and the former Soviet Union and the diminished threat of a Soviet veto, the reluctance of Western powers to use force to resolve regional conflicts, and pressure from a media-connected public to "do something" about the violent wars graphically recorded on TV and in the press, are thought to have stimulated much of the increase.[96]

Margaret Doxey, for example, observes that UN-sponsored sanctions alone have risen at a rapid rate. Prior to the 1990 to 1991 Gulf War there were only two cases on record: mandatory sanctions against Rhodesia (now Zimbabwe), and a mandatory arms embargo against South Africa. Since then, between 1990 and 1998, seventeen UN resolutions imposing a wide variety of restrictions, some comprehensive and others partial, were passed sanctioning ten countries: Iraq (1990); Yugoslavia and the successor states (1992, 1993, 1994, 1998); Somalia (1992); Liberia (1992); Angola (1993, 1997, 1998); Rwanda (1994); Haiti (1993,1996); Sierra Leone (1997); Libya (1992, 1993); and Sudan (1996)[97]— notably all non-Western states.[98] A SIPRI study focusing on arms embargoes found that between 1994 and 1998 regional and international organizations levied a total of thirty-two partial or complete embargoes on arms transfers, military services, or other military-related transfers to twenty-four countries and subnational groups.[99] Again, all of the targets were non-Western and most were combatants in recent wars, although in some cases sanctions were imposed for other reasons.[100]

By far, however, the largest number of sanctions implemented since 1990 are unilateral, and of those the majority have been imposed by the United States. A 1997 National Association of Manufacturers report, finds that sixty-one U.S. laws and executive orders were enacted between 1994 and 1997 against thirty-five countries.[101] The President's Export Council survey established that more than seventy-five individual countries were subject to or threatened by one or more unilateral foreign policy sanctions under a total of more than forty separate legislative acts in 1997 alone.[102] Another private study found that the United States was the main initiator of sanctions globally, accounting for 70 percent of the cases. One-third were unilateral sanctions; most of the others were ad hoc coalitions.[103]

This growth trend may not continue. Many governments and groups, and the UN itself are questioning the efficacy of sanctions as a foreign policy instrument.[104] This is particularly true with regard to sanctions imposed in recent wars. Bitter charges of inequities and double standards,[105] terrible humanitarian costs to civilians, infringement of sovereignty, flawed enforcement and implementation practices have become louder and more numerous, setting off a rancorous debate within academic, activist, and policymaking circles.[106]

The case of the Bosnian war is only one of the examples cited. For our purposes, it illustrates the ways in which sanctions and embargoes have become important sources of security assistance to belligerents during conflict. The arms embargo levied by the UN covered all of the parties equally—not only Serbia and Montenegro, but Croatia and Bosnia once they were recognized as independent states. From the perspective of the Bosnian Muslims, the arms embargo was biased and illegal, because it deprived them of the ability to defend themselves against their better-armed adversaries.[107] It was, in their view and those of their allies, a form of military aid to their opponents. Muslim governments in particular were united in their desire to see the UN arms embargo on Bosnia lifted but strengthened against Bosnia's enemies.[108] Russia, on the other hand, supporting the Serbian position, declared "unacceptable" any activities violating the UN Security Council-imposed arms embargo against the former Yugoslavia.[109] When efforts to lift the UN embargo failed, it was simply circumvented, with the collusion of many powers that had voted for it.

Persistent reports of illegal violations by the UN, the U.S., and other sponsoring states regularly appeared in the media. Implementation of the embargo, according to these sources, was anything but equitable. It was charged, for example, that governments used the United Nations Protection Forces (UNPROFOR) as a "blind" to channel arms to the Bosnians. A Bangladeshi battalion was accused of handing over its entire stock of weapons and ammunition to General Abdic's Bosnian Muslim forces. Turkish troops operating with UNPROFOR were accused of providing the Bosnian Muslims with components for their military industries "brought into the region under [the Turkish] blanket UN clearance."[110] Malaysian peacekeeping units, "fully supported by the Malaysian government," reportedly were a major channel of arms as well as equipment and materiel for the military ammunition factory controlled by the Bosnian Muslims and were said to be orchestrating a vast support program for them.[111] Argentine peacekeepers stationed in Croatia between 1993 and 1995 allegedly supplied materiel to the Bosnians as well.[112]

Aside from UN peacekeeping troops on the ground, larger quantities of war materiel were shipped via Austria, Hungary, and Slovakia from a variety of countries, financed by Saudi Arabia and Iran.[113] Croatia, too, benefited from the leaky embargo. According to some accounts, it skimmed off 50–70 percent of the illegal supplies that moved through Croatia to Bosnia as a transit fee;[114] Croatia also received arms from Hungary and Romania, as well as 6,500 tons of weapons and ammunition from Argentina during the war (all non-Muslim countries!)[115]

The Bosnian war illustrates how "impartial" sanctions can inequitably affect the war-fighting capability of combatants. It is not an isolated case. In 1975, ten years after the 1965 India-Pakistan War, the U.S. announced it was ending its arms embargo against India and Pakistan. India responded with a vigorous protest, declaring Pakistan had aggressive intentions. Joseph J. Sisco, then U.S. undersecretary of state for political affairs countered that lifting the embargo was necessary to correct "a rather anomalous situation." Not only was India receiving weapons from the Soviet Union (while Pakistan was barred from U.S. deliveries), but it had its own defense industry, which Pakistan did not. The Pakistani ambassador, responding to the U.S. decision, declared: "it would at long last enable Pakistan to meet its legitimate and basic security requirements."[116]

Perceived as a way of limiting the military capabilities of their opponents, combatants and their supporters try to manipulate imposed sanctions to their advantage—seeking to avoid the negative consequences for themselves while insisting on strict adherence for their enemies. All sides in a war view embargoes as another form of security assistance, if they can be adroitly exploited to disadvantage their opponents. The India/Pakistan case is only one of many examples. In South Africa, during the violent struggle over apartheid, the ANC urged the

UN to maintain sanctions against the South African government in all fields, especially the arms embargo.[117] Sudan's rebel leaders admonished the international community to impose economic and military sanctions on the Sudanese government to force it to end hostilities. The Sudanese military responded with a threat to review the supply of UN-sponsored humanitarian aid to rebel-controlled areas in the south.[118] When the European Union lifted its eight-year arms embargo on Syria in 1994, Israel, warning of Syria's aggressive intentions, protested.[119] In Rwanda, after vanquishing the Hutus, the Tutsi-dominated government decried the newly imposed May 1994 Security Council arms embargo, contending that Rwanda's former government forces were rearming in camps outside Rwanda's borders in preparation for an invasion, while the new government remained defenseless under a UN embargo. "We cannot see why the international community denies Rwanda the right to protect its own border and the right to protect its own people," Rwanda's ambassador to the UN complained. "It looks like they are punishing the wrong side." The exiled Hutu forces, in turn, placed the blame for their defeat by the Tutsis on the UN embargo which no longer applied to them.[120] Belatedly, in June 1995, the UN extended the embargo to include the Hutu camps in neighboring countries.[121]

The 1992 UN arms embargo on Liberia was similarly greeted with charges of inequity emanating from all sides. After six years of civil war, the 1996 Abuja Agreement offered hope that peace had come to Liberia. The election of Charles Taylor as President in 1997 was another auspicious sign. But violence persisted as opposition rebel groups continued to operate in the country, and so the 1992 UN arms embargo on Liberia was not lifted. As in much of Africa, the unsettled conflict spilled over into neighboring countries. Since then, complaints about the embargo have been registered by all sides in the war. The Nigerian ambassador to the UN urged the Security Council to tighten the arms embargo on Liberia to stop the flow of weapons going to the rebels in Sierra Leone.[122] Liberia, on the other hand, claimed Guinea was supporting armed dissidents within Liberia and that "external forces" had attacked it with major loss of life.[123] Denouncing the outside support for the Liberian dissidents, President Taylor protested that the so-called "impartial" embargo was in fact discriminatory: "Under international law we have the right to defend our territory but our hands are tied." [124] This was seconded by a Liberian spokesman in New York: "The issue of the arms embargo . . . is a moral issue. We can't have a situation whereby a whole nation is defenceless because it cannot buy arms to defend itself. . . . After two years of a democratically elected government, we do not see any reason why the embargo should continue."[125]

In Bosnia-Herzegovina, too, the game of cat and mouse with embargoes has continued since the war. According to one analyst, the military balance had changed in favor of the Bosnian Muslims by 1997. Now that it had, he predicted, Bosnia, after years of evading international sanctions itself, will carefully monitor the Serbian side for violations of the Dayton agreement.[126]

The game is played with remarkable frequency and intensity because the stakes are so high. Combatants and their supporters view embargoes as a critical form of security assistance. As sanctions have proliferated, all sides have participated in the risky ploy of seeking avoidance for themselves and strict adherence for their enemies, hoping to turn sanctions and embargoes to their strategic advantage.

Embargoes, Sanctions, and Domestic Military Industries

Another, perhaps unanticipated, consequence of sanctions is the spread of indigenous military industries. Ironically, sanctions have enhanced the appeal of domestic arms production as an alternate source of supply for many governments, particularly those engaged in or threatened by conflict. During the Cold War, a self-sufficient defense industry was considered vital by states seeking some form of autonomy from U.S. and Soviet Union arms export controls. In the post–Cold War world, as the threat and use of sanctions has risen, so too has the number of arms industries as governments endeavor to reduce their dependence upon imported weapons and foreign suppliers. In the end, few states have been able to do so.[127]

Israel, for example, fighting serial wars against its Arab neighbors since 1948 and the target of sanctions and restrictions from its principal suppliers,[128] has focused on building an indigenous arms development and production capability to mitigate its dependence on foreign imports. Since 1949, with each embargo, indigenous efforts were expanded. By 1981, the Israeli arms industry, although still not self-sufficient, gave Israel an initial advantage over its neighbors. No potential Arab adversary had a comparable production capacity.[129] In a war, they were dependent on support from the United States, France, Britain, or the Soviet Union.

However, Israel's military industrial capabilities did little to mitigate the impact of U.S. embargoes and restrictions during the Gulf War. The United States, determined to keep Israel out of the war in order to retain Arab participation in the United States-led coalition, denied Israel access to "friend or foe" codes and other key operational intelligence that the Israelis needed to carry out retaliatory raids in response to Iraqi SCUD missile attacks. Without such information, Israel could not be certain its planes could distinguish coalition forces from Iraqi forces or that the allies would not mistake Israeli aircraft for the enemy's. As a result, Israel's long-standing policy of retaliation to attacks on Israel could not be carried out, prompting Prime Minister Shamir to explain afterwards that Israel "had no alternative other than to work within the framework of the [Bush] administration."[130]

Attempts by other combatants to achieve military autonomy through domestic arms production has been equally disappointing. India, for example, after independence faced a hostile security environment, fighting China over a distant border area in the Himalayas (1962) and Pakistan over Kashmir. After the 1965 war with Pakistan, India was also subject to a U.S. arms embargo. Determined to stay unaligned during the Cold War and yet meet these challenges, India adopted a short-term three-pronged strategy—the procurement of sophisticated conventional weapons; the establishment of a nuclear/space program; and the creation of an indigenous military production capability. The goal was to acquire self-sufficiency in the manufacture of weapons—that is, the technological capability to produce within India all its weapons needs—in the hope of eliminating its dependence on foreign imports in the future. By the 1980s, after twenty years of development, India had achieved self-sufficiency in arms production up through medium artillery, but dependence on imported advanced weapons and components continued. The goal of weapons autonomy, however, even if it was to be delayed, remained government policy.[131]

The U.S. embargo levied on both India and Pakistan in the 1960s, although ostensibly "even-handed," disadvantaged Pakistan considerably more than India. The policy had minor effect on India, since it depended little on the U. S. for arms, but had a devastating effect on Pakistan's forces that operated almost totally with American equipment. As one analyst observed, "The Pakistanis never forgot this incident and other nations took note."[132] Forced to seek alternate sources of supply, Pakistan turned to China. But China during the 1960s was able to provide only unsophisticated technology "largely confined to small arms and light weapons."[133] Like Israel, the Pakistani government, with few other procurement options, turned to indigenous production as its surest supply source. Although its efforts were less successful than Israel's, Pakistan's complex of fourteen small arms and ordnance factories by the late 1990s supplied almost 100 percent of the army's requirements[134] and it had developed capabilities in other areas as well. (See Table 7.3.)

South Africa, too, during the war over apartheid gradually found itself isolated from major weapons suppliers in the 1960s. The ARMSCOR (Armaments Development and Production Corporation), which had been established in 1947 to develop and manufacture weapons, remained relatively inactive during those early years since imported arms were readily available. Starting in the 1960s, however, in the wake of mounting embargoes, South Africa expanded its arms-production capacity, with the goal of achieving "self-sufficiency" in terms of its defense needs.[135] By the late 1980s, South Africa's military industries were producing much of the country's own defense equipment—artillery, small arms, armored vehicles, missiles, electronics, and communications equipment, but it still lagged behind in "such critical fields as aircraft, tanks, and avionics."[136] (See Table 7.3.)

The Islamic Republic of Iran followed a similar pattern. During the brutal Iran-Iraq War, the U.S. denied Iran components, spares, and parts for its Western-made, largely U.S. inventory. Iran, with few other options, responded by resurrecting the country's domestic arms-production potential initiated by the hated Shah in the 1970s, in addition to buying from the black and gray market for its immediate defense needs. By the end of the 1980s, Iran had an estimated 240 defense manufacturing sites, and some twelve thousand privately owned workshops engaged in research and production of military equipment. By the early 1990s, Iran not only had rocket systems in production but claimed to be self-sufficient in the manufacture of small-caliber ammunition, some types of artillery shells, and small arms.[137] (See Table 7.3.)

All of these producer states reached varying levels of manufacturing capability. Some reduced their dependence on imports more than others. But none achieved the goal of "self-sufficiency" in the defense sector. Most remained

Table 7.3   Arms Producing Countries in the Developing World by Type of Weapon Produced

Country	Small Arms & Ammunition	Ordnance, Artillery, Armored Vehicles	Aircraft & Missiles	Ships
Africa				
Algeria★	x	x		x
Burkina Faso	x			
Cameroon	x			
Egypt	x	x	x	x
Ethiopia★	x			
Ivory Coast				x
Kenya	x			
Libya	x			
Morocco★	x			
Namibia★	x			
Nigeria	x			
South Africa★	x	x	x	x
Sudan★	x			
Uganda	x			
Zimbabwe★	x			
Latin America				
Argentina	x	x	x	x
Bolivia	x			
Brazil	x	x	x	x
Chile	x	x	x	x
Colombia★	x			x
Cuba★	x			
Dominican Republic	x			
Ecuador	x			
Mexico	x	x		x
Peru★	x		x	x
Venezuela	x			x

Country	Small Arms & Ammunition	Ordnance, Artillery, Armored Vehicles	Aircraft & Missiles	Ships
West Asia				
Iran★	x	x	x	
Iraq★	x	x	x	
Israel★	x	x	x	x
Saudi Arabia	x			
Syria★	x			
East Asia				
Cambodia★	x			
Indonesia★	x	x	x	x
Korea, North	x	x	x	x
Korea, South	x	x	x	x
Malaysia★	x			x
Philippines★	x		x	x
Singapore	x	x	x	x
Taiwan	x	x	x	x
Thailand	x	x	x	x
South Asia				
Bangladesh★				x
India★	x	x	x	x
Myanmar (Burma)★	x			x
Pakistan★	x	x	x	x

Source: Michael Brzoska, "Economic Factors Shaping Arms Production in Less Industrialized Countries," *Defence and Peace Economics,* vol. 10, no. 2 (1999), table 1. , pp. 139–169; pp. 140–141. Turkey, a NATO country, is not included in the Brzoska data, nor are former Soviet or Warsaw Pact countries. Kenya's, Namibia's and Uganda's small arms and ammunition defense industries were added to the Brzoska data. Namibia's defense industry was established in late 1992. ("International Small Arms Usage and Research and Development Trends: The Executive Summary," SAWR, April 1993, p. 11.) Kenya's and Uganda's defense industrial capability was cited in "Arms Flows to Central Africa/Great Lakes," fact sheet released by the Bureau of Intelligence and Research, U.S. Department of State, November 1999. (http://www.state.gov/www/global/arms/bureau_pm/fs_9911_arms flows.html)

Note: Many of the systems "produced" by countries in the developing world may be licensed produced, kit-assembled, or simple add-ons to imported technologies. The checks above identify areas where there is some production capability but not necessarily manufacturing capability.

★Indicates governments fighting wars between 1986 and 1997.

dependent on foreign imports for a host of industrial inputs, such as manufacturing licenses, machine tools and metals, integration techniques, as well as engines, radars, and electronic components.

With the end of the Cold War and the growing threat of sanctions, domestic defense industries became an even more attractive option to combatants. Ironically, this occurred just as the global military-industrial structure was shrinking and corporations worldwide were reducing and, in some cases, divesting themselves of their military-production components. For governments facing security threats, however, as the availability of subsidized military aid fell and the likelihood of sanctions increased, indigenous production and covert imports appeared to be the most viable sources of supply.

The major changes in the size and character of the arms market have also served to inflate the value of defense industries in the eyes of combatants, while at the same time dashing any hope they might have of attaining "self-sufficiency" in modern weapons production. Since the end of the Cold War, the cost of manufacturing advanced systems and the sophisticated technical skills needed to do so have risen dramatically, along with the decline in procurement and R&D budgets and the collapse of the export market. Without significant domestic resources to spend or an export market to provide economies of scale, most governments cannot hope to competitively manufacture modern major weapons.

A new hierarchy of military-production capabilities is emerging with American and, to a lesser extent, European systems out-competing Russian and developing-world products, with the U.S. the main innovator in the system.[138] In fact, the emerging international division of labor in the military sector mimics the changing power relations among states in the post–Cold War world generally. Few states, even other industrialized powers, can compete with U.S. manufactures in the defense sector. The demonstrated military technological capability of the U.S. in the Gulf War established a hierarchy of world military and industrial power dominated by the United States which other states cannot challenge. As a result, one influential study concludes, "no nation is seeking to compete with the United States by acquiring military capabilities of equivalent magnitude across the full range of new technologies."[139] Nor is fighting a war with the U.S. any longer thought to be feasible; military effectiveness is measured against potential regional adversaries, not the United States.[140]

Accordingly, few arms producers are expected to challenge the U.S. in the production of high-end military technologies. Rather, they will focus on less advanced weapons to fulfill what many see as an increased worldwide demand for them and their own military needs.[141] Throughout the Third World and in Central and Eastern Europe, sales of domestically produced weapons are an attractive potential source of hard currency for countries that may have little else to trade. For combatants, defense industries hold the illusive promise of greater political autonomy. In sum, fear and resistance to Western, largely U.S., efforts to restrict the transfer of military technologies and manufacturing know-how, as well as the need for foreign exchange, have prompted many governments to persevere with domestic weapons manufacture in spite of a depressed world arms market and the cost of maintaining unprofitable industries. The ultimate effect has been to increase the number of suppliers in the system, creating a buyers market especially for less advanced items.

Although arms production is down in most industrialized countries, industries for low-end technologies have proliferated, particularly in the non-Western world.[142] (See Table 7.3.) As Brzoska observes, the number of Third World producers capable of manufacturing small arms, mines, mortars, ammunition, small ships, and other platforms made out of materials relatively simple to shape, without customized electronics and complicated integration skill demands, is long and growing.

By 1993, for example, more than a dozen states—all former importers of small arms—had begun manufacturing and exporting infantry weapons, some quite recently.[143] A Pakistani military analyst observed that for countries facing serious security threats and subject to embargoes—like Pakistan—reliable indigenous production capabilities combined with imported materiel, whenever possible, are the only answer for their defense needs. He argues that for Pakistan, weapon systems need not be leading-edge, only capable enough to deal with internal and regional adversaries. To achieve that, domestic production capabilities need not be sophisticated.[144]

Since the end of the Cold War, defense industries, even at the lower end of the industrial spectrum, have become important strategic assets worth fighting over. The former Yugoslavia, for example, was one of the major European producers and exporters of modern small arms and artillery.[145] When civil war broke out and the UN embargo was imposed in 1991, the factories became highly contested military targets. Rather than leave them to Bosnian separatists, Serb forces dismantled a number of plants located in Bosnia and transported them to Serbia.[146] The Bosnian government, too, moved two ammunition production lines to prevent the Croatian Defense Council from seizing them.[147] It also established small-arms factories and repair workshops in at least six centers in central Bosnia with help from other Muslim allies.[148] In Croatia, the UN sanctions prompted the creation of a small-arms industry that still manufactures and exports its products abroad.[149]

Indigenous military industries now also play a more important role in Africa. According to a State Department study, large numbers of domestically produced small arms, ammunition, and other military items are being supplied to regional combatants either from their own factories or those of their neighbors. The government-owned Zimbabwe Defense Industries, for example, provided about $250 million worth of arms to Laurent Kabila's Democratic Alliance for the Liberation of Congo (ADFL) during its 1996–97 campaign against Mobutu and supplied Kabila after he became president with more than $90 million worth when fighting began again in August 1998. Kenya, Sudan, and Uganda have indigenous defense industries, with relatively large production capacities, which reportedly transfer weapons and ammunition to combatants in the Central Africa/Great Lakes region.[150]

This, then, is the structure of the world's arms production system in which governments at war operate. A fundamental change in the level of weapons transferred to combatants in recent wars has taken place. During the Cold War, state-to-state arms transfers involved primarily high-maintenance platforms, such as helicopters, jet fighters, tanks, and aircraft. When these transfers declined with the end of the Cold War, imports of "simple," older weapons took their place. Today, government suppliers to combatants are mainly second- and third-tier producers[151] and increasingly, as the situation in Africa suggests, those in the region itself. Regional powers, with indigenous manufacturing capabilities, are placing their products at the disposal of their warring neighbors, friends, and allies. As one analyst comments: "the number of vendors of intermediate weapons and small arms has increased to the extent that it is no longer possible to monitor and control their sale."[152]

Although most non-Western governments do not anticipate ever fighting the U.S., should unforeseen circumstances lead to conflict with the U.S., these trends suggest they will "be inclined to adopt asymmetrical counters to the American style of warfare . . . [and] will try to optimize the low-technology end of the spectrum."[153]

Thus in spite of changes in the world arms market and the availability of arms from many sources, defense industries have not lost their appeal and dreams of self-sufficiency have not vanished. Only the bar has been lowered on expectations. For combatants in a world in which embargoes and sanctions are a significant threat, domestic and regional military industries have acquired increased importance as sources of supply. As long as wars are being fought and the threat of embargoes persists, defense industries in less industrialized countries will continue to proliferate and serve as major sources of supply to embattled governments.

The section below turns to nongovernmental suppliers of security assistance, tracing the changes and continuities that characterize this form of support in recent years.

Private Sources: The Privatization of Security Assistance

One of the most intriguing trends since the end of the Cold War is the growing privatization of security assistance, particularly to combatants. By privatization, we mean the provision of diplomatic, political, economic and military aid by an increasing number of nongovernmental organizations, groups, and individuals. These entities are now mimicking the activities of government suppliers by furnishing combatants with many different kinds of support. The term "privatization" also subsumes within it the many inventive ways combatants have found to finance their war efforts without recourse to the national treasury. In our survey of reported security assistance acts, we found that nongovernment sources supplied over 58 percent of the direct military aid and about one-quarter of the economic and indirect military aid to combatants between 1991 and 1997. (See Table 7.4.)

There is nothing new about this trend. Private groups and individuals have always offered support to combatants in far-off places. Anti-Fascist volunteers took up arms in the Spanish Civil War; American Jews donated monies for arms

Table 7.4.   SOURCES OF MILITARY ASSISTANCE

Types of Aid/Source	Percentage of Private vs. Government Assistance to Combatants By Type of Aid 1991–1997		
	Governments	Private★	Undetermined★★
Diplomatic/Political	93.61%	6.26%	0.13%
Economic	71.96%	26.73%	1.31%
Indirect Military	66.15%	21.68%	12.17%
Direct Military	35.84%	58.13%	6.02%

★ Private sources are individuals, groups, or nongovernment organizations.

★★ Undetermined are those cases where it was not possible to know whether the source was private or government.

and fought in Israel's various wars with the Arabs; the Irish diaspora assisted the IRA in its struggle for independence in Northern Ireland with men, materiel, and money. Today Muslim organizations and individuals are aiding Muslims in distant countries. Mercenaries have taken part in wars since organized war began.[154] What seems to have changed, however, is the growing number and geographical reach of these and other nongovernmental sources of security assistance, the magnitude of their resources, and the wide variety of their activities.

The Ethnic/Cultural Agendas of Nonstate Actors
Like governments, private organizations, groups, and individuals are offering various types of security assistance to combatants with whom they feel a cultural tie. Islamic foundations in Saudi Arabia, for example, have provided indirect military aid to embattled Muslims such as the Bosnian Muslims,[155] and Palestinian groups. Osama bin Laden, an immensely wealthy Saudi citizen, reportedly bankrolls Muslim insurgents in the far reaches of the world, including the Algerian Armed Islamic Group, the Moro Islamic Liberation Front, which is seeking an independent Islamic state in the southern Philippines, and the Chechen rebellion in Russia.[156] Individual Yemenis living in Saudi Arabia are believed to have sent large amounts of money to al-Beid's South Yemen forces to purchase weapons and military supplies when civil war erupted in Yemen in 1993.[157] Tamil groups residing in Canada, according to the Canadian government, have sent over $1 million per month to the Tamil rebels fighting the Sir Lankan government.[158] The importance of this type of funding is demonstrated by the fortunes of the IRA in 1994, whose dwindling financial support from Irish supporters in the U.S. is credited, in part, with forcing Sinn Fein (the political wing of the IRA) to agree to peace negotiations in Northern Ireland.[159]

Direct military aid in the form of foreign volunteer fighters are another form of aid to kin in recent wars, particularly from Muslims. Some six hundred Afghan Mujahideen, for example, were reported to have fought with Tajik rebels[160]; others were reported to be in Kashmir helping the separatists there.[161] Alumni of their training camps in Pakistan's North West Province are purported to have struck in such diverse places as the Philippines, Central Asia, the Middle East, North Africa, and even the World Trade Center in New York.[162]

It is unclear who is paying these fighters to conduct "holy wars" against the enemies of Islam. Some may fight with the unofficial nod of (and payment by) their own governments. Others may be employed by third parties. Yugoslavia, for example, in a communication to the Human Rights Commission, declared that Albania had secretly supported foreign mercenaries within the KLA in 1998. These fighters, according to the Yugoslavs, included not only Albanian nationals, but "so-called Mujahideens, nationals from some Arab countries, Afghanistan, Sudan, Russian Federation (Chechnya) and others"[163] who presumably were paid by Albania, as well. Yugoslavia also accused Saudi Arabia and Turkey of supporting Mujahideen units in Bosnia and Herzegovina: "Some DM 300,000 earmarked for arms purchasing and illegal transfer into Kosovo and Metohija have been provided by the 'World Office for Islamic Appeal,'" by implication a front organization for Muslim governments' contributions. It was estimated that the monthly pay of the Mujahideen recruits ranged from 3,000–5,000 Deutsche Marks.[164]

The source of funding and the role of governments may be murky but the involvement of private groups, organizations, and individuals, as proxies or independent entities providing various forms of security assistance is clearly growing. Once the domain of governments, nongovernment suppliers with huge resources and explicit cultural and political agendas are now affording combatants the wherewithal to keep fighting.

Private Military Companies.
Contrary to the eighteenth century when foreign soldiers formed a major part of regular armies, twentieth century armies were citizen armies.[165] It was only then that the term "mercenary" began to carry with it opprobrium. Mercenaries continued to operate in many parts of the world throughout the twentieth century, although reduced in number. Janice Thomson identifies two basic types of mercenary forces in use during the twentieth century: (1) foreigners employed permanently as individuals in a standing army such as the French Foreign Legion;[166] British officers in the armies of Kuwait, UAE, and Bahrain; Pakistanis in the Saudi Arabian Army; or the Nepalese Gurkhas;[167] and (2) ad hoc armies that hire foreign soldiers under contract for use in a particular conflict, such as Congo, Nigeria, Angola.[168] During the Cold War, mercenary forces were particularly active in former colonies that were transitioning violently to independence, principally in Africa, such as: the Belgian Congo (1960–1968), Nigeria (Biafra, 1967–1970); Benin (1977), Comoros Islands (1975,1978), Seychelles (1977–1981), Zaire (1977), Angola (1975), Namibia (1975), and the Ogaden region of Ethiopia (1978).

During the 1960s and 1970s, mercenaries were professional soldiers recruited by other mercenaries to fight in foreign wars for personal profit independent of cause or country.[169] Nevertheless, there is some question as to how independent from government policy these "mercenaries" actually were. Former imperial powers were the principal suppliers and in several cases clearly manipulated the conflict.[170] Cold War considerations intruded themselves as well. Certainly the presence of Cuban soldiers in Angola, Namibia, and the Horn of Africa was not unrelated to the strategic interests of the Soviet Union.[171] Nor were Korean, Philippine, and Thai troops in Vietnam fighting independent of U.S. interests. And perhaps there are other less publicized cases as well.

Writing in the late 1980s as the Cold War was winding down, Thomson argues persuasively that mercenarism was on the decline. But since then there have been official reports of more not less mercenary activity in many parts of the world: Kashmir, Afghanistan, Liberia, Democratic Republic of Congo [DRC], Angola, Congo-Brazzaville, Sierra Leone, the former Yugoslavia, Ethiopia, and Eritrea. These mercenaries come from an equally diverse list of countries: the former Soviet Union, Europe, the Middle East, the Americas, Asia, and Africa.[172] Some are simply traditional "soldiers of fortune" recently retired from downsizing armies, while others are "cultural" allies fighting for a cause, or they are neighbors throwing in their lot with local armies or regional powers.

Since the 1990s, a new form of mercenarism has appeared as well. Private military companies (PMCs) offering a full spectrum of services are now successfully hawking their wares throughout the world. One of the primary characteristics differentiating the PMCs from the ad hoc groups of private soldiers active during the 1960s and 1970s is their permanent corporate structure. David Isenberg makes an interesting distinction between traditional mercenaries and the PMCs: "Whereas paid soldiers of the previous . . . groups [of mercenaries] fall under the jurisdiction, at least in theory, of domestic or international customary law, employees of international business corporations answer only to the first. The important distinction here is that such firms are bound by the terms of a business contract and not necessarily those of international law. . . . Clearly, in the post–Cold War era an old military tradition is reemerging. Mercenaries are back and they are clearly not going away."[173] It is interesting to note that Isenberg does not claim that PMCs are outside the legal jurisdiction of their own countries (see discussion below).

Some question whether employees of these private military companies can legitimately be called "mercenaries." Even Isenberg, who views them with some skepticism, says he uses the term without value judgement.[174] The companies, understandably, reject the appellation. Ed Soyster, vice-president of international operations of MPRI, said, "We're trying very hard to eliminate the mercenary image."[175] Others ignore the issue entirely, arguing that in military and economic terms private military corporations offer a rational solution for states facing armed crises their militaries cannot handle.[176] David Shearer, for example, writes: "The United Nations and the international community might find it in their best interests to acknowledge the existence of military companies and engage them politically, rather than ignore them and hope that somehow a peace agreement will stay intact."[177] And Doug Brooks suggests: "PMCs can do the sorts of military actions that developed countries shy from due to financial cost and fear of casualties. Next time a Rwanda-style massacre breaks out the West could use the PMC option instead of simply watching the horror on our TVs."[178]

Some, however, emphatically declare that these companies are merely traditional mercenaries in another guise—wreaking long-term havoc on weak countries that hire them for short-term gain. The rapporteur to the UN Human Rights Commission, Enrique Ballesteros, forcefully expresses this view:

> Private companies offering international security represent a new operational model that is more up to date and effective and with relatively adequate legal cover, but nevertheless linked to mercenary activities, as they intervene militarily, and for pay. . . . Although mercenaries pose as technicians or military experts hired as such by private companies providing security services and military assistance and advice, or by Governments, this changes neither the nature nor the status of those who hire themselves out to meddle and cause destruction and death in foreign conflicts and countries.[179]

For our purposes, we consider "mercenaries" to be individuals that receive monetary compensation for military services rendered to a foreign country.[180] Although the term carries with it a negative image, like Isenberg we use it without prejudging the utility or morality of private military companies' activities.

The demand for these companies has grown in the 1990s, particularly from governments at war. In spite of the International Convention against the Recruitment, Use, Financing, and Training of Mercenaries adopted by the United Nations in 1989, there are, according to intelligence sources, at least ninety private military companies selling their services in Africa alone. Governments, commercial enterprises, UN agencies,[181] and even nongovernmental humanitarian organizations have availed themselves of their services.[182] As Cold War tensions fell, and the major powers grew more reluctant to commit their armies to internal conflicts in other parts of the world, foreign military companies stepped into the breach. Most are U.S. or British based. (See Table 7.5 [page 288] for a list of selected companies and the services they offer.)

For weak governments with poorly trained, undisciplined militaries, foreign military companies have become welcome sources of military assistance. No longer able to rely on their Cold War supporters for aid, these governments, with few other options, have turned to PMCs for help in defeating armed insurrections they can not suppress themselves. For these beleaguered governments, PMCs represent access to modern ways of war as well as a back door to modern military equipment.

The home countries of private military companies generally are industrialized states, and for them, too, private military companies provide important benefits at low cost. Reluctant to commit their own troops to faraway places and risk the cost in lives, resources, capital, and public opinion, the major powers use private military companies to distance themselves from politically undesirable conflicts; gain leverage over the contracting government; obtain useful intelligence; and profit from possible arms sales arranged by the company.[183] As the president of one of the PMCs remarked: "Yes. We expect to get paid, but we are a lot less expensive than a sovereign or UN force. And casualties among private military companies don't have the same emotional impact as among national forces."[184] Moreover, private military companies provide the security demanded by foreign firms with significant investments in the natural resources of the warring countries. Often the investing firms and the PMCs are based in the same home country.

Thus private military companies fulfill the needs of the home countries, the foreign investment firms in-country, and the contracting government. It is not surprising, therefore, that eleven years after its adoption, only twenty-one states are parties to the international convention prohibiting mercenary activity, and of these none are the five permanent members of the Security Council.[185]

Since the end of the Cold War, these companies have been a new and significant source of military assistance for combatants, providing everything from direct combat assistance to arms procurement, tactical and strategic advice, security protection, intelligence-gathering, aerial surveillance, and whatever else is needed to complete the job they are hired to do.

Participation in combat operations is a sensitive issue, and most private military companies claim they will not do so. Only Executive Outcomes (EO) and Sandline personnel admit to engaging in direct fighting. MPRI, for example, claims it does not participate in offensive operations. A U.S. State Department wit notes that "the only difference . . . [between EO and MPRI] is that MPRI hasn't pulled the trigger—yet."[186]

A brief description of the PMCs' activities in Angola, Sierra Leone, and Bosnia suggests the critical role they play as sources of direct and indirect military aid to combatants. Executive Outcomes was formed in 1989 and carried out operations in Angola (1993–94) and Sierra Leone (1994–95). It used, for the most part, retired personnel from elite units of the South African Defence Force, who served under the apartheid government. The majority of the troops in EO operations were black. Heavy equipment and combat aircraft were provided by the host country but were operated and serviced by EO personnel.[187] MPRI was active in Bosnia.

ANGOLA EO was called into Angola after the breakdown in the 1992 cease-fire between the Movimiento Popular para a Libertaçao de Angola (MPLA) and União Nacional para a Independência Total de Angola (UNITA). UNITA was unwilling to accept the results of an election that the MPLA had won. Fighting resumed and by 1993 UNITA controlled 80 percent of Angola, including the Soyo oil center in which several American oil companies had interests.[188] The (MPLA) Angolan government hired EO in April-May 1993 to regain the Soyo oil fields, which together EO and the Angolan army succeded in doing. Soyo was later recaptured by UNITA, and as government reversals continued in other parts of the country the MPLA again turned to EO offering it a second one-year contract in September 1993 to train five thousand troops and thirty pilots and to direct military operations against UNITA. Between September 1994 and January 1996, the government regained key strategic towns, the Cafunfo diamond fields, and Soyo. More than five hundred EO personnel were involved in training and fighting.[189] These setbacks prompted UNITA to sign a peace accord

Table 7.5   SELECTED MILITARY AND SECURITY COMPANIES & EXAMPLES OF THEIR ACTIVITIES

Type of Activity	Company[1]
Combat: Providing support for or participating in military operations[2]	Executive Outcomes (EO) (S. Africa)[3] Sandline (UK)
Military training and assistance: Providing training for state military forces, including special forces and elite groups, covering weapons, tactics, and force structures	Booz Allen Hamilton (US)[4] Braddock, Dunn, McDonald (BDM) (US) Defence Systems Limited (DSL) (UK)[5] EO Integrated Security Systems Keenie Meenie Services (KMS) (UK)[6] Military Professional Resources Incorporated (MPRI)[7] (US) Saladin Security (UK)[8] Sandline (UK) Science Applications International Corporation (SAIC)[9] (US) Vinnell (US)[10]
Procurement: Direct purchase of military equipment or advice	EO Levdan (Israel)[11] MPRI Sandline
Military analysis: Assessment of military threat to states	EO MPRI Rapport Research and Analysis Saladin Security Sandline
Logistical support: Military equipment delivery; protecting humanitarian, UN peacekeeping operations	Brown and Root (US)[12] DSL[13] DynCorp (US)[14] MPRI Pacific Architects and Engineers (PA&E) (US)[15]
Post-conflict support: Reestablishing public infrastructure; mine clearance	DSL Saladin Security Saracen Security (UK)[16]

Notes:

1. The home base of companies is included when known.

2. These are the only two companies known to have participated in military operations. It is possible that others have done so as well.

3. Executive Outcomes announced in 1999 that is was shutting down many of its operations in compliance with a new South African law restricting the activities of security companies. In 2000 it was reported to be defunct.

4. Trains the Saudi Arabian marines and maintains the Saudi Arabian Armed Forces College.

5. DSL was originally founded by former SAS soldiers. It is now part of Armor Holdings of London. DSL/Armor provides security in high-risk situations, guarding embassies and mining facilities and providing other security services. DSL is reported to be working with mercenaries to protect mining and petroleum facilities in the Democratic Republic of the Congo (DRC).

6. KMS, in the 1980s, trained the Sri Lankan Army in counterinsurgency tactics to suppress the Tamil Tigers insurrection. It is now defunct.

7. Trained the Croatian military in 1995. Currently training the armed forces of Bosnia-Herzegovina. MPRI has close ties to the U.S. Departments of Defense and State. See Table 7.6 for a selected list of MPRI's other foreign activities.

8. Trains Omani government forces.

Table 7.5 SELECTED MILITARY AND SECURITY COMPANIES & EXAMPLES OF THEIR ACTIVITIES (continued)

Type of Activity	Company[1]
Commercial security protection: Guarding property and personnel	AirScan International (US)[17] Control Risks Group (CRG) (UK) DSL Group 4 (US?) Gurkha Security Guards (UK) Integrated Security Systems (US) O'Gara Protective Services (US)[18] Rapport Research and Analysis Saladin Security
Risk analysis: Assessing insecure and unstable areas on behalf of companies evaluating investment prospects	CRG DSL Kroll Associates (US) Rapport Sandline
Investigation and intelligence-gathering: Investigation covers crimes against companies and organizations such as extortion, fraud and product contamination. Intelligence-gathering includes work on clients' potential joint-venture partners and assessment of likely political interference in commercial activities.	Argen , Inc. (US) Asmara Carratu CRG International (UK) Kroll Network Security Management (UK) Saladin Security
Kidnap response: Negotiation and advice on hostage situations	Brinks, Inc. (US) CRG EO Kroll Neil Young Associates (UK) Saladin Security

9. Advises the Saudi Arabian Navy.
10. Trains Saudi Arabian National Guard.
11. Provided arms to Congo-Brazzaville government.
12. Pimarily provides logistical assistance to the U.S. military and armies abroad.
13. Protects mining and petroleum facilities in the Democratic Republic of Congo.
14. Provided observers to Kosovo for the U.S. before the war. A number of personnel are working in Colombia with the U.S. and Colombian militaries on antidrug operations.
15. Provides primarily logistical assistance to the U.S. military and armies abroad. Maintained and operated U.S. helicopters and vehicles given by the U.S. to ECOMOG.
16. Provides protection services to mining and mineral companies in Angola.
17. AirScan offers hi-tech surveillance. It operates a mini-air force to protect oil fields in the Cabinda region of Angola. Reportedly it has also taken part in operations in Central America and Uganda.
18. Provides security for the Saudi royal family.

Sources: David Shearer, "Private Armies and Military Intervention," Adelphi Paper no. 316 (London: International Institute for Strategic Studies, 1998), table 2, "Activities of Military and Security Companies," pp. 25–26. Additional information was included from the following sources: "Report on the question of the use of mercenaries as a means of violating human rights and impeding the exercise of the right of peoples to self-determination, submitted by Mr. Enrique Bernales Ballesteros (Peru), Special Rapporteur pursuant to Commission resolution 1998/6. UN Economic and Social Council, Commission on Human Rights, 55th session [E/CN.4/1999/11, January 13, 1999], pp. 17–18; Doug Brooks, <Hoosier84@aol.com>"Private Military Companies" in H-DIPLO <H-DIPLO@H-NET.MSU.EDU>, December 15, 1999; "The Balkans-Update 6," Jane's Sentinel Security Assessment, posted February 2000. [http://www.janesonline.com]

in Lusaka in November 1994.[190] EO departed in December 1995. Since then hundreds of other private security companies have taken their place, guarding companies, embassies, and international organizations working in Angola; MPRI is now training and advising the army.[191] The Lusaka peace accord broke down at the end of 1998 and conflict resumed, but as of this writing UNITA appears to be losing the war, never having recovered from earlier losses. UNITA was routed from its strongholds in Angola's central highlands during an offensive that began October 1999. By 21 December 1999 the chief of staff of the Angolan Army, General Joao De Matos claimed that UNITA no longer had the capability to take control of the country by force. According to De Matos, UNITA had lost more than 80 percent of its fighting capacity.[192]

Curiously, shortly thereafter rumors began circulating that mercenaries were now serving with UNITA. The UN, unable to confirm these reports, did obtain direct evidence that foreign instructors (usually supplied by arms brokers) were training UNITA troops, especially those in mechanized units. The nationalities of the foreign military personnel included Russians, Ukrainians, Bulgarians, and South Africans.[193]

SIERRA LEONE   EO was also hired by the Valentin Strasser government in Sierra Leone in 1995 to help fight the Revolutionary United Front (RUF), a rebel group that emerged in 1991 with the support of Charles Taylor's rebel group in neighboring Liberia. EO, in addition to training the Sierra Leone Military Forces, played an important role in military operations against the RUF.[194] As a result of these operations, the government regained control over the Kono diamond mining area and the Sierra Rutile titanium dioxide mine. Although diamonds had constituted only a small part of government revenues prior to the war, their recapture gave the government the ability to buy political support by distributing mining concessions—a long-standing patronage system in the country. The Sierra Rutile mine and the Sierra Leone ore and metal company, on the other hand, provided around 66 percent of the government's export earnings[195] and were therefore critical to the war effort. After successive defeats, the RUF agreed to negotiate with the government for the first time and signed a peace accord in November 1996.[196] Foday Sankoh, the leader of the RUF, stated that had EO not intervened he would have won the war.[197] Observers of the war agree:

> EO was key in defeating the rebel forces in the field and setting the stage for the democratic elections which brought President Alhaji Ahmed Tejan Kabbah to power. . . . And it should be kept in mind that the period of stability that EO brought to Sierra Leone has been the only such period since Sierra Leone's war began in the early 1990s. With vastly more troops and equipment, the Nigerians and ECOMOG [peacekeepers] have not been as successful.[198]

Victory, however, had come at a price. Reportedly, EO halted RUF advances for a fee of $15 million, and a monthly stipend of $1.2 million, together with mining concessions.[199]

EO left the country in January 1997, and a hundred days later a complicated chain of events led again to government reversals. In May 1997 a military coup overthrew the Kabbah government. The army and the RUF then joined together to form a new government. Fighting resumed, prompting a number of foreign companies involved in diamond, titanium, gold, and bauxite mining to leave the country, and some stopped operating the mines. Apparently, the overthrown president Kabbah (possibly with Nigerian assistance) contracted with another private military company, Sandline International, to help him regain power.[200] A number of the foreign mining companies reportedly approved and provided partial financial backing to the contract.[201] According to Brooks, the British Foreign Office also gave its approval, informing the U.S. government of the operation.[202] Helicopters and military equipment were delivered allegedly via Bulgaria, Nigeria, and Liberia, and military experts were sent to provide tactical and operational advice "on the ground."[203] Neither the U.S. nor the British voiced concern over the violation of the 1997 Security Council arms embargo. The first weapons ordered by Sandline arrived on 22 February 1998. On March 10 a major battle, which was joined by Nigerian forces under the umbrella of ECOMOG, took place which succeeded in overthrowing the Armed Forces Revolutionary Council and the RUF.[204] Fighting continued, but in July 1999 a peace accord was again signed.[205] By October the country was engulfed in war again.

Despite the continuing instability in these countries, both EO and Sandline provided the governments of Angola and Sierra Leone with the ability to defeat their adversaries, which they were unable to do on their own, even temporarily. PMCs operating in other parts of the world were achieving similar striking results.

THE FORMER YUGOSLAVIA MPRI is perhaps best known for its controversial activities in the former Yugoslavia. An American corporation founded by retired U.S. armed forces personnel in 1987, it derives most of its contractual work from the U.S. military for ventures in the U.S. and offers a wide variety of services to foreign countries as well. In 1997 its volume of business exceeded $48 million.[206] (See Table 7.6 for a selected list of MPRI's foreign activities, 1992–c.1998).

MPRI's involvement in the former Yugoslavia began with the Democracy Transition Assistance Program (DTAP), a two-year contract (1994–95) with the Croatian government that would be extended. The full terms of the contract remain unclear. According to one source, MPRI was hired to reorganize the Croatian armed forces and help it transition to a more Western-style professional military organization and entrance to NATO's Partnership for Peace program.[207] It has also been rumored that "Washington's assistance to Croatia under the cover of MPRI was made conditional on Croatia's agreement to the creation of the Bosnian-Croat Federation, acceptance of a CIA-built base on Krk island operating 'Predator' spy-drones and support for a series of secret airdrops of supplies to the Bosnian Muslims."[208]

Two major offensives by Croatian forces, Operation Flash in May 1995 and Operation Storm in August 1995 took place a few months after MPRI arrived. The first recaptured western Slavonia. The second defeated the Serbs in the Serb-held Krajina region. Both operations demonstrated a surprisingly success-

Table 7.6   Selected MPRI Activities Worldwide, 1992–c.1998*

Country	Date	No. of Employees	Activities
Angola	1996	30 (planned)	Talks to conduct specific training to officers and NCOs. [Rumored: full-scale training of the Angolan Army and police.]
Bosnia	July 1996– September 1998	185	To equip and train the newly reconstructed Bosnian Federation Army.
Croatia	DTAP: September 1994– January 1998	DTAP:15	Instruct on civil-military relations. Develop a professional corps of NCOs. Establish the architecture, structure and organization of the MORH. Finalize Croatia's military doctrine and strategy (unconfirmed). Training of the army and development of a corp of officers (unconfirmed).
	LRMP: January 1996– January 1999	LRMP: 12	
Liberia	July 1994	2	To teach a short vehicle drivers' course on the Humvee.

ful coordination of armor, artillery, and infantry.[209] MPRI denied any link with the operation, maintaining that its involvement was limited to education on civil-military relations and did not include tactical and weapons training. But the scale and complexity of the offensives and the coordination of skills that bore little resemblance to Warsaw Pact military tactics, by an army trained in Soviet battle techniques with a dismal reputation for ineptitude on the battlefield, raised suspicion in many quarters. "That's not something you learn while being instructed about democratic values" said one military analyst.[210] The result was, according to the Croatian Chargé d'affaires in Ottawa, that Operation Storm served as the turning point of the Bosnian war, paving the way for the Dayton Accords on Bosnia and Herzegovina.[211]

A second two-year contract signed by MPRI and the Croatian government in January 1996—the Long Range Management Program (LRMP)—and then extended for another year in January 1998, called for MPRI to assist the Croats in establishing an efficient structure and organization for the Croatian Ministry of Defense. Unsubstantiated reports suggest that under this program MPRI also developed Croatia's military doctrine, although officially and publicly MPRI insists its role was limited to classroom teachings and did not involve training in tactics or weaponry.[212]

Table 7.6   Selected MPRI Activities Worldwide, 1992–c.1998★ (continued)

Country	Date	No. of Employees	Activities
Macedonia	c. 2000	?	As of November 2000, MPRI was reported to have "a consulting contract" with the government and MPRI employees were reported to be working with the military.
Serbia	1994–1995 (18 mos.)	45	To monitor military trucks and equipment crossing into Bosnia from Serbia (monitoring embargo).
Sri Lanka	early 1996– ?	1	Talks to train and assist the Sri Lankan security forces Rejected by Sri Lanka.
Sweden	early 1993	4	To teach a seminar on lessons learned during the Gulf War.
Taiwan	December 1992	4	To teach a seminar on lessons learned during the Gulf War.

Source: "MPRI: Washington's freelance advisors," *Jane's Intelligence Review*, July 1998, p. 39; "World Armies, Macedonia," *Jane's World Armies*, posted 17 November 2000; "External Affairs, Angola," *Jane's Sentinel Security Assessment*, 15 July 1998. [http://www.janesonline.com]

Key:
DTAP   Democracy Transition Assistance Program
LRMP   Long Range Management Program
MORH   Ministry of Defense, Croatia (Ministarstvo Republike Hrvatske)
NCO   Non-Commissioned Officer

★MPRI offers the following services: training; equipment procurement; force design and management; professional development; concepts and doctrine; organizational and operational requirements; simulation and war-gaming operations; humanitarian assistance; quick-reaction military contractual support; and democracy transition assistance programs. "All of these are targeted at the military forces of emerging nations favoured by the US." "The Balkans-Update 6," *Jane's Sentinel Security Assessment*, posted 25 February 2000. [http://www.janesonline.com]

As of May 2000, MPRI was still involved in the Balkans, most notably in the Train and Equip contract with the Bosnian-Croat Federation to which the U.S. contributes $103 million in military equipment; Saudi Arabia, Kuwait, the United Arab Emirates (UAE), Malaysia, and Brunei provide another $140 million in financial aid; and Egypt and the UAE donate artillery and tanks.[213] (MPRI was also active in Macedonia, helping the army restructure to NATO standards, a program also supported by U.S. foreign-assistance funding.)[214]

In all three cases described above, the presence of military companies strongly influenced the course of war and tipped the balance of power among the combatants. With relatively few personnel[215] these companies served as "force multipliers," providing training for government forces, and in some cases, working with them in the field, offering strategic advice, intelligence, and air power (usually helicopter gunships), and when necessary joining in the fighting. Multinational businesses were also furnished with the security services that allowed them to operate in a turbulent environment and to indirectly provide the host government with revenues necessary to buy loyalty and pursue the war. In countries such as Sierra Leone, Angola, and Croatia, where modern military skills are scarce, the presence of private military companies makes a difference. They constitute a potent source of military expertise that few combatants in less developed countries can successfully replicate.

PMCs can be found in almost every region of the world. The examples in Tables 7.5 and 7.6 only suggest their ubiquity. Considered "proprietary information," these relationships are rarely publicized by the PMCs or their customers. One suspects that the reported foreign activities of PMCs are but the tip of the iceberg.

During the Cold War, the affiliation of "mercenaries" was often obscure. Foreign soldiers often served in wars of only tangential interest to their home countries. In the post–Cold War, however, there seems little doubt that the loyalties of the new "mercenaries" are aligned with that of their governments. Most PMCs have close associations with the defense establishments in their base countries and, as in the case of MPRI, are often dependent upon them for domestic as well as foreign contracts. These are, after all, for-profit corporations that are not eager to alienate a major source of business. To date few have acted in ways contrary to the foreign policy of their home states. Rather they seem to be mere extensions of it.

British companies, according to Shearer, are more independent of their government than those in the U.S. If so, it is a matter of degree since they, too, have close ties with the UK's defense establishment, and have not diverged from its policy. For example, the Keenie Meenie Services (KMS) contract to train the Sri Lankan Army in counterinsurgency techniques in order to suppress the Tamil Tigers' possessive insurrection was approved by the British government.[216] So, too, apparently was the contract between Sandline and the Sierra Leone government.[217]

MPRI has worked almost exclusively as an extension of U.S. foreign policy. All PMCs are required to obtain a license from the State Department for foreign military contracts. MPRI received licenses for its work with both the Croatian and Bosnian governments, which Goulet labels "Washington's assistance under the cover of MPRI."[218] The Train and Equip program in Bosnia, for example, is believed to be a particularly clear example of MPRI's proxy role. In this case, it served to preserve the impartial image of the U.S. participation in the NATO-led Implementation Force (IFOR) and later the Stabilization Force (SFOR).[219] The U.S. State Department, in fact, runs and helps fund the program that MPRI implements.[220] A U.S. Defense Intelligence Agency official ties the knot even tighter: "The [private training] programs are designed to further our foreign policy objectives. If the government doesn't sanction it, the companies don't do it."[221]

As the above examples suggest, private military companies are playing an increasingly important role in the foreign policies of the major powers. During the Cold War foreign armies served as proxies to distance the Soviet Union and the United States from regional conflicts. Today, the PMCs are taking their place. As Shearer cynically observes, MPRI's involvement in conflict areas "allows the [U.S.] government to achieve foreign-policy goals free from the need to secure Congressional approval and safe in the knowledge that, should a situation deteriorate, official U.S. participation can be denied."[222]

Privatization of military services seems to be the trend of the future,[223] and one that will not be limited to the major powers as other governments follow suit. Pakistan has already done so. When the U.S. threatened to add Pakistan's name to a list of countries sponsoring terrorism if it continued to aid the Kashmiri rebels, Pakistan reportedly privatized its support to the insurgents through nongovernmental organizations run by retired army and intelligence officials and private organizations.[224] PMCs provide deniability to the governments of middle powers, too. Insurgents in many parts of the world also see them as useful sources of military expertise, weaponry, and other services. Because of their perceived value, private military companies will doubtless expand in number and activity in the future.

The Covert Arms Trade

For those combatants with limited military production capabilities, the covert arms market has served as an important supplementary (and sometimes sole) source of supply. A host of people and places are involved. According to R. T. Naylor, the expanded ranks of private arms dealers and go-betweens and their widely diversified backgrounds are a new development in the arms trade. He argues that traditional arms merchants—largely ex-soldiers, ex-arms company executives, former intelligence agents and government officials, and retired war correspondents—today are joined in black market sales by "everyone from oil traders to toxic waste brokers to defrocked Catholic priests," increasing the number of suppliers of arms and facilitating their purchase.[225] The most widespread trade is in nonmilitary small arms, e.g., shotguns, pistols, and hunting rifles that are for sale without restriction in numerous countries and are easy to transport. New technologies have helped create communication and transportation networks for which national borders are no longer a barrier for arms sales.

In some areas, such as Afghanistan, northwest Pakistan, and various African states, guns are a commonly traded commodity and an integral part of the local culture, as they once were in the U.S. "Wild West." In Mozambique weapons are a means of food and security. Rifles there are traded for a box or two of maize. In many parts of the world, guns are as easy to buy as eggs or cheese, and in some societies easier.[226]

Guns produced for the civilian market have found their way to local conflicts and in some instances, such as Mali, they have been adapted or upgraded to accept military ammunition. Private U.S. arms dealers are a notable channel for these and other types of small arms and ammunition. In the 1980s, items such as semiautomatic rifles were routinely bought for unlawful resale in Latin America.[227] In 1991, the U.S. government announced that over eight thousand weapons illegally exported from the U.S. had been recovered in seventeen different countries.[228] Since the disintegration of the Soviet Union, Eastern Europe too, has become a major source of illegal weapons.[229]

Governments facing international sanctions and many subnational groups have little choice but to turn to the black market for military supplies. These covert sales often travel circuitous routes generally involving many foreign nationals.[230] While these markets cannot satisfy a demand for sophisticated weapons in any number, they are able to handle sizeable orders of small arms, ammunition, and light weapons.

Other wars have also been a lucrative source of weaponry. Unless destroyed in combat, arms can be recycled from war to war and filtered out to combatants engaged in other conflicts. Weapons the U.S. military left in Vietnam in 1975 went from Vietnam to Cuba to rebels fighting the Salvadoran government. After the peace treaty was signed in El Salvador, many of the weapons ended up on the black market where they were sold to guerillas in Peru or to drug cartels.[231] Weapons used in the Afghanistan war also fueled other regional conflicts. An Iranian gunboat, for example, was caught in 1987 with sixteen Stingers whose serial numbers matched those given to the Afghan Mujahideen by the U.S.[232] Many of the small arms used in Rwanda were reported to come from Uganda.[233]

Ironically, peace initiatives in many parts of the world have loosened a flood of weapons onto the private arms market worldwide. Regional secondhand markets have emerged in Bangkok, Beirut, and in the cities (Peshawar) and small towns (Darra, Landi Kotal) of Pakistan's Northwest Frontier Province, which serve a wide variety of cash-paying customers—embargoed states, independence movements, guerilla forces, private militias, and even criminal organizations.

Since the Soviet withdrawal from Afghanistan in 1989, arms bazaars, such as Darra, have been inundated with Kalashnikov rifles, Stinger missiles, a variety of antitank launchers, mortars, and rocket launchers formerly captured by, sold, or given to the Afghan Mujahideen and now available at bargain prices.[234] Almost any type of small arm or light weapon is procurable in the various arms bazaars and gun shops that dot Pakistan's Northwest Frontier Province where the Pakistani government has little authority.[235] The *Nation,* a Pakistan newspaper, conducted a survey of the arms sold there, dividing them into four categories of weapons by source: (1) arms that leaked from the pipeline to the Afghan Mujahideen during the Afghanistan war from East Germany, Romania, Israel, Egypt, West Germany, and China; (2) Soviet weapons captured during the Afghanistan war; (3) locally made arms: copies of the AK47, standard rifles, revolvers, and pistols; (4) miscellaneous weapons from diverse places including West Germany, Iran and Saudi Arabia.[236] Many of these weapons arrived through circuitous routes from other former war-torn regions such as Vietnam and the Middle East[237] and now fuel current conflicts. The majority of weapons used by Kashmiri militants, for example, are said to have come from the Northwest Frontier Province pipeline.[238]

The settlement of Mozambique's civil war in 1992 added to the glut. In southern Africa in 1993, black market prices for an AK47–type rifle ranged from about $9 to $33 because of the huge number available.[239] In Uganda, AK47s were so plentiful they could be obtained for the price of a chicken.[240]

Peace initiatives in Latin America had a similar effect. As hostilities tapered off in Nicaragua and El Salvador, weapons from these countries migrated to other combatants in the region. The weapons released by the demobilized Contras to the United Nations Observer Group in Central America, for example, apparently were only a fraction of their total arsenal. According to some reports, the Contras sold a significant number of arms to the Farabundo Marti Front for National Liberation (FMLN) in El Salvador and other groups in Central America.[241] In turn, shipments of arms from the FMLN destined for Guatemalan National Revolutionary Unity (URNG) were intercepted in Guatemala,[242] and AK47 rifles formerly operated by the FMLN found their way to the Revolutionary Armed Forces of Colombia (FARC).[243]

Arms in the post–Cold War world glut the market. This global oversupply led the Croatian defense minister to complain during the Bosnian war that the "arms market is so saturated you would pay three times the price if you got things legally"[244]—a reversal of normal market conditions where black market prices are generally inflated well above the "manufacturer's" price. The uneasy peace in Kosovo, five year later, added to the surplus. Weapons flooding out of Kosovo turned up in Europe—many to be recycled to conflicts in other places. In Pristina, an arms agent confirmed that "There are plenty of supplies and no difficulties getting them out."[245] As wars end, the private, covert arms market offers an overflowing stream of weapons to combatants which, in the post–Cold War world, never seems to go dry. For many governments and insurgents it is an important alternate source of military assistance.

Strange and Unusual Sources of Security Assistance

Peacekeeping Forces
The peacekeeping efforts of the international community have also come to be regarded as useful, if unusual, sources of security assistance by combatants and their supporters. Persistent charges of improper aid to combatants by peacekeepers often have been accurate. Since the end of the Cold War, as international peacekeeping forces have become more active in areas of conflict, they have been accused of taking sides.

In 1984, for example, Russia angrily denounced the French intervention in Chad as anything but impartial "peacemaking." Similarly, when the Croatian government announced that it was ending the mandate for UN troops to be stationed in Croatia during the war over Bosnia, the reason given was the protection afforded the separatist Croatian Serbs by the buffer of UN troops. The Croatian prime minister, Nikica Valenic, declared: "What the United Nations is doing in Croatia is to maintain the status quo, actually providing aid to the Serbs through giving oil and food to them. Under such circumstances we cannot agree to a renewal of the mandate."[246] Perceived as potential supporters of the other side in the Bosnian conflict, UN peacekeeping forces were distrusted and unwelcome in Croatia.

A similar situation existed in Rwanda, where French peacekeeping efforts were viewed by the Tutsis as designed to halt their gains on the battlefield. Despite French assurances that their aid to Hutu refugees was not military but humanitarian in nature, the Tutsi accused the French of systematically siding with the Hutus.[247] In some cases, the peacekeeping forces themselves actually have served as important suppliers of military equipment to a combatant. Bosnia (see pp. 273–274 above) was not an isolated instance. The ECOMOG troops also sold guns to factions in the Liberian war.[248]

In Cambodia, the United Nations Transitional Authority in Cambodia's (UNTAC's) efforts to achieve a peaceful compromise among the contending factions did, in fact, change the balance of power among them by isolating the Khmer Rouge. What the other factions could not attain on the battlefield, was won by UN intervention. "The old Cold War alignment of Sihanouk, Son Sann, and the Khmer Rouge against the Vietnamese-installed government in Phnom Penh was transformed into a new coalition of everyone against the Khmer Rouge."[249]

Whether intended or not, from the combatants' point of view, peacekeeping interventions (like embargoes and sanctions) are opportunities to garner support for their war aims, and all sides strive to manipulate the peacekeepers to that end. Peacekeepers have been considered important providers of security assistance in recent wars, and in more cases than not they have supplied it. Between warring parties, impartiality is difficult if not impossible to achieve.

Humanitarian Aid

Humanitarian aid, too, is viewed by combatants as a form of security assistance. For that reason it is greeted with enthusiasm by one side in an armed conflict and with suspicion by the other. Neutrality has been a controversial issue particularly in civil wars where civilians become part of the combatants' war strategy and where it is difficult to tell one from the other. As a result, humanitarian acts by well-meaning organizations and groups have often been accused of bias.

Today, various academics, governments, and NGOs are questioning whether, in the end, humanitarian aid achieves its purpose or merely supports the war effort of intransigent belligerents.[250] Edward Luttwak argues that it is more humane in the long run to allow war to run its course. Humanitarian intervention, regardless of its original motive, prolongs war and suffering.[251] Luttwak concludes:

> An unpleasant truth often overlooked is that although war is a great evil, it does have a great virtue: it can resolve political conflicts and lead to peace. . . . Policy elites should actively resist the emotional impulse to intervene in other people's wars—not because they are indifferent to human suffering but precisely because they care about it and want to facilitate the advent of peace.[252]

In situations of armed conflict, many relief programs have benefited one side or the other and sometimes both. Adam Roberts points out that the delivery of humanitarian aid often involves compromises with belligerents, so that impartiality is hard to maintain. Convoys, aircraft, and hospitals cannot operate without consent, and so peacekeepers find themselves negotiating with one side or the other.[253] An example is the UN peacekeeping operation in Somalia in 1993–94 where the faction leaders—especially Aideed—greatly benefited from rents, security contracts, employment, currency transactions, and a variety of other fringe benefits provided by United Nations Operation in Somalia (UNO-SOM). One Somali elder remarked," UNOSOM came to save us from the warlords, and ended up aligning with them."[254]

Food, on the face of it the most neutral kind of humanitarian assistance, has been particularly problematic. In Bosnia, for instance, the humanitarian delivery of food and medicine to besieged communities, from the Serbian perspective amounted to breaking the Serbian siege,[255] and accomplished for the Bosnian Army what it could not achieve militarily itself.

The U.S. and British supply of grain in the early 1990s was meant to alleviate mass starvation in the Sudan. By the end of the decade, officials who ran the programs acknowledged it fueled the war rather than achieving its objectives. "Officials are confronting the fact that in conflict zones relief assistance is rarely neutral."[256] This has proven to be true in African wars generally. In Mozambique (1991–92) and Ethiopia (late 1980s) at least half of the food aid intended for civilians was diverted to the military.[257] And in Somalia, according to one scholar, "much of the subsequent fighting in 1992 resulted from attempts by different factions to obtain or maintain control over the posts and distribution routes through which food and other supplies passed."[258] Moreover, Somali warlords sold stolen relief supplies or "taxed" relief shipments and the NGOs to get cash for buying weapons.[259] As an African Rights report argues: "Food aid has fed wars in Africa wherever it has gone. Both sides in most conflicts feed their armies, at least in part from food aid. It allows armies to attract civilian populations to areas they control and maintain them there, under supervision and control."[260]

A government launching a counterinsurgency strategy, Keen argues, based on depopulating areas of rebel strength and using relief supplies to control the movement of civilians is often unwittingly aided by well-intended humanitarian organizations. In Sudan in the late 1980s, the famine relief concentrated "on refugee camps in neighboring Ethiopia and government garrison towns in the south" which enabled the Khartoum government to depopulate parts of the south, notably-oil rich areas. It also gave the opposition—the SPLA—reason to attack the relief shipments, which it regarded as military support for the enemy.[261]

Similarly in Uganda, rebels of the Alliance of Democratic Forces (ADF) in the west of the country threatened to attack relief convoys going to Bundibugyo, claiming that these convoys were delivering military supplies to the Ugandan army stationed there. "Any convoy of humanitarian assistance to Bundibugyo will be attacked whether escorted by uniformed or civilian personnel" stated a letter sent by the rebels to the relief organizations (ICRC and UNHCR.)[262]

Humanitarian aid in recent wars has often been diverted to other purposes. Combatants that gain control over the distribution of relief supplies not only have been able to sustain their fighting capability, but have been able to attract followers and increase them. Relief to Rwandan refugee camps in Zaire in 1994–96 allowed defeated Hutu militia to gain control over the refugees and regroup their forces in order to launch raids back across the border. Aid to Cambodian refugees in Thailand, according to Keen, helped the Khmer Rouge rebuild after its defeat in 1979–80.[263] And U.S. food aid to the SPLA rebels in southern Sudan is purposefully intended to "strengthen the military operations of the Sudan People's Liberation Army and to isolate the government."[264] Well-intended acts have had strange, unanticipated consequences in recent wars where humanitarian aid has served as security assistance.

Private Financing
During the Cold War, the superpowers' ideological and geopolitical competition penetrated regions all over the world. In the name of that competition both were willing to subsidize local forces in their disputes. Today, in the new political climate, that support has dwindled. In the U.S., foreign aid is a declining asset. Russia with its monumental economic problems can no longer afford its generosity of the past. Other states, too, have been forced to cut back. Saudi Arabia, for example, once a major source of assistance for other Muslim states, has substantially reduced its military purchases[265] and foreign aid commitments because of its own financial problems. As foreign aid has become less available, governments and insurgents have resorted to new methods of creative financing in order to support their military efforts.[266]

Countries rich in natural resources, for example, have found them to be a convenient means of funding for their war effort. In Angola, the government is reported to have mortgaged many years of oil production to pay for military services and procurements.[267] The governments of Zimbabwe and the DRC, following the lead of rebel forces, jointly set up a diamond and gold marketing venture to help finance former President Laurent Kabila's war against rebel armies in the DRC. The defense minister of Zimbabwe declared the new venture was a "noble option" that would bring millions of dollars to the two armies annually. "Instead of our army in the DRC burdening the treasury for more resources, which are not available, it embarks on viable projects for the sake of generating the necessary revenue."[268] The new marketing company will work with Comiex, a private company owned by the DRC army, which will buy the diamonds and gold from small-scale producers.[269] In West Africa, ivory has also been used to finance arms purchases.[270]

The Khmer Rouge in Southeast Asia supported their military effort by trading or selling gems and timber to "renegades" in the Thai military who controlled the border area between Thailand and Cambodia. Income from this cross-border trade was estimated to have enriched the coffers of the Khmer Rouge by $100–$250 million a year.[271] One analyst observed that "scarcely a ruby makes it to market in the West without the payment of an export tax to one or another local insurgent group."[272]

Other combatants without commercial export outlets barter rather than sell natural resources to finance their military purchases. Rwandan coffee and tea, for example, were traded for arms. In 1992 Egypt reportedly agreed to accept future Rwandan tea harvests from the then-government of Rwanda as collateral for $6 million worth of artillery, mortars, land mines, and assault rifles, and actually took delivery of $1 million in Rwandan tea before fighting damaged the tea bushes. (The deal was underwritten by a financial guarantee provided by the French state-owned bank, Credit Lyonnais.)[273] The UNITA rebels, too, funded their military effort with Angola's diamond wealth. According to one source, the revenues replaced "assistance UNITA previously received from the United States and South Africa."[274] According to the Angolan government, a well-orchestrated cross-border barter arrangement of "arms for diamonds" had been organized, and it accused South Africa, Zambia, and Congolese rebels of supplying the UNITA rebels in this way.[275]

The lucrative drug trade serves as yet another means of financing war. The relationship between the drug and arms markets apparently is uninhibited by regional or national boundaries. In most cases, the main link between combatants and drugs is via the "taxation" of the drug traffic (along with everything else) in the government- or insurgent-controlled areas. In Latin America, the drug cartels have massive financial resources and can pay large sums of money in exchange for protection from guerillas or the local army (and sometimes both)—income that allows the combatants to buy large numbers of weapons. Colombian guerillas, for example, have little need of foreign support since they have significant revenues from drug traffickers to pay for arms and materiel. In Guaviare, one of Colombia's largest coca-growing states, officials estimate that traffickers pay $5 million a year in protection money to the state's main guerilla group, the FARC.[276] As a result of steadily rising drug revenues and the surge of Eastern European weapons into the arms market, the FARC now has a secure arms pipeline. It receives "vast quantities not only of assault rifles but also heavy machine guns, hundreds of thousands of rounds of ammunition, small artillery, explosives, hand grenades and rocket propelled grenades, significantly altering the balance of power against the government in Colombia's civil war."[277] According to Colombian and U.S. intelligence analysts, the FARC has also concentrated on upgrading its communication equipment, buying Japanese and European encryption technology, voice scramblers, and other technologies that "make interception of their communications almost impossible."[278]

In Peru, the drug-arms connection appears to be less sophisticated. Nevertheless, drugs have played an important role in financing the rebels' war effort there. Before the successful government offensive in 1994, the Shining Path guerillas' earnings from the drug-protection business bought North Korean-made guns, rocket-propelled grenade (RPG) launchers and Soviet-made machine guns.[279] The Movimiento Revolucionario Túpac Amaru group in Peru also financed their operations from drug-related revenues.[280]

Similar arrangements hold in other parts of the world. The Afghan Mujahideen grew drugs during the Afghanistan war, which reportedly helped support their war against the Soviet Union.[281] The Karen ethnic minority guerillas who have fought a succession of Burmese governments for over forty years are said to obtain some of their weaponry from Cambodia in exchange for large quantities of marijuana.[282] Drugs are also reported to finance an illicit arms trade not only in Bosnia, but among Albanians in Macedonia and the Kosovo Province of Serbia.[283] When war broke out, the KLA was able to tap into a well-organized drug trade for their arms purchases. Albania, which played a key role in channeling money to the Kosovars, is reported to be at the "hub of Europe's drug trade."[284]

Private sources of financing are now supporting wars, in some cases with resources far larger than those in the public treasuries of the governments involved. Combatants and a vast network of facilitators—banks, financiers, brokers, middlemen—have created a new source of security assistance.

Security Assistance in a World in Transition

These, then, are some of the developments in security assistance taking shape in the post–Cold War world. Ethnic hostilities and unresolved border disputes largely contained during the Cold War have ruptured into violent conflict in much of the non-Western world. War, rather than becoming obsolete, continues to rage with enormous human cost and gives little sign of abating. Security assistance has continued to flow to former clients from both East and West, but reduced levels of aid, the threat of sanctions, and changed security perceptions have prompted combatants to turn to other less traditional sources of support as well. During the Cold War, these alternative sources were largely associated with insurgents, today they support governments, too.

To date, globalization—the rapid pace of technological change, the increased spread of information technologies, and the growing economic integration of the world—has increased the sources of security assistance available to all belligerents, providing them with a relative abundance of resources with which to fight wars. Governments, insurgents, and their suppliers are taking advantage of the new high-speed communication networks to access information, finances, supplies, and support thousands of miles away from the battlefield. Nonstate actors—individuals, private military companies, mercenaries, humanitarian organizations, individual arms merchants, diaspora groups, banks, financiers, and a host of other commercial and civic entities are now playing a larger and more important role in sustaining armies at war.

In many regions of the world, defense planners are revising their military doctrines to accord with local military threats and are using less advanced military systems to achieve their war aims. From their perspective, this strategy has the added advantage of reducing the influence of foreign powers on the conduct of the war and limiting the effectiveness of sanctions. In their view, it is a form of asymmetric procurement.

Globalization not only has made access to these military technologies and associated services easier for combatants, it has limited the ability of the major powers to control their flow, whether legal or illegal, across international borders. The continuing demand for arms from warring armies, the stream of older technologies into the arms market as wars end and armies modernize their inventories, the growth of low-end military industries in former nonproducing countries, the availability and ease of transportation, and the huge financial incentives to sell in a world with increasingly porous borders has made military technologies, particularly less advanced systems, more difficult to monitor and control. The same is true for other kinds of security assistance. The communication and electronic technologies that are shrinking the globe are also facilitating access to new and previously unimaginable nongovernmental and international sources of sustenance for belligerents at war.

Nevertheless, despite the complex pressures of globalization, and the contending forces of fragmentation, the United States remains the dominant power in the international system by virtue of its economic size, technological leadership, and military strength. In the military sector alone it controls the development, production, and sales of the world's most sophisticated weapons, especially precision-guided arms, information systems, and communications. The sheer weight of the U.S. in the world creates dependencies for other states and limits their ability to challenge American hegemony. As a result, combatants as well as their suppliers are forced to factor into their calculations U.S. preferences and anticipated responses before acting. When perceived U.S. interests are involved, their policy options are severely constrained, as the Gulf and Balkan wars demonstrated.

The strange blend of new and old patterns of security assistance described in this chapter reflects the global hierarchy of power during and after the Cold War but does not yet serve as a good litmus test of the future. It is unclear which of these trends are transitory and which durable and what, if anything, they augur for the unfolding world order. Ultimately, the shape and character of security assistance will be determined by the new power structure of the future and the capabilities of those that dominate it. Power politics will prove eternal and war will find a way. But whatever the ultimate shape of the international system, as it evolves, specialists in international affairs have a unique opportunity to observe and test the relevance of existing theories of war and international relations using patterns of security assistance as an empirical measure of them.

CONCLUSIONS

The Lessons of Modern Warfare

Writing from the perspective of the close of the twentieth century about the state of warfare as it appeared to evolve in that century's last few decades presents, admittedly, a picture of considerable confusion and ambiguity. Maybe more so than might have been the case at earlier junctures—1970? 1950? 1930?—there is strong ambiguity about emerging trends or about the validity of (always a dangerous temptation) extrapolations from the immediate past. One is sobered by the reminder that some writers in the early 1980s, viewing the outburst of conventional combat in Lebanon, the Falklands, Vietnam's Red River Valley, and on the Iran-Iraq border, had predicted a growing surge of Third World conventional warfare reminiscent of seventeenth- and eighteenth-century Europe; or that others writing in the 1970s saw a future dominated by Marxist insurgencies such as those that had played out in Vietnam, Algeria, Cuba et al. Those projections now seem hopelessly outdated (not precluding, however, their resurgence!) at a time when military activities and military writing seem much more focused on weapons of mass destruction and terrorism—note the dominant image of U.S. Tomahawk missiles conducting a "counter-proliferation" raid on a suspected nerve gas plant in Khartoum, Sudan (reports on that raid scarcely mentioned the more than one million persons claimed dead in the ongoing, brutal war in southern Sudan).

At the outset of this study, we described our intention to offer a corrective to what appears a considerable imbalance in the study of war in this period, specifically the absence of attention to the *conduct* of wars—war-fighting—that is, to the interface between modern security studies and traditional military history. As we had pointed out, there is a massive and growing academic literature on the causes of, patterns of, and antidotes to war or conflict. Regarding causes, most of that literature involves efforts at formal modeling intended to provide relative attributions of causation to such factors as polarity, balance of power, domestic economic factors, etc., but where the analyses are almost wholly devoted to the history of conventional interstate warfare. Regarding patterns, we have ourselves utilized the recent SIPRI data, breaking things down according to various levels of interstate and intrastate warfare, according to regional and regional-cluster patterns of warfare, wars over government versus wars over territory, etc. (This and other such data compilations utilize, in one way or another, the now classical COW project trilogy of magnitude [size of forces], severity [battle deaths], and duration.) The now burgeoning literature on war termination (the topic is now the subject of an ongoing internet debate and intellectual exchange) encompasses a major effort to understand how conflicts of various sorts, including long-term serial conflicts such as Israel-Arab, Somalia-Ethiopia, etc., might be brought to a close. We have previously noted the methodological and ideological fissions between "peace studies" and "peace science" in these regards.

As we have tried to explain, the study of the conduct of war is in a particularly confusing state of transition. Mostly, up until recently, it consisted of the study of conventional interstate war though the ages, as represented by the massive military histories provided by Liddell-Hart, Fuller, Montross, Howard, Keegan et al. True, military histories such as the classic volume on strategy edited by E. M. Earle and updated by Peter Paret, paid some heed to French colonial counterinsurgency, as well as to modern nuclear strategy and deterrence. And as we have laid it out, there was the large outpouring of writings on insurgency and counterinsurgency inspired by the West's efforts to stem the tide of Marxist- or Maoist-inspired revolutionary wars during the Cold War. By the early 1990s, the aforementioned outburst of conventional wars in the Third World produced a new vogue of "lessons learned," most notably with the publication of the three-volume series by Cordesman and Wagner which analyzed in astonishing detail the Arab-Israel (1973, 1982), Falklands, Afghanistan and Iran-Iraq Wars and the two previously cited co-edited volumes by Harkavy and Neuman. The 1990–91 Persian Gulf War likewise resulted in a massive "lessons learned" literature, much of it dwelling upon the advent of a new revolution in military affairs, a hi-tech revolution claimed to have fundamentally transformed the very nature of modern warfare. Indeed, with the Gulf War now history, the Pentagon-think tank milieu appeared, by 1995, almost wholly focused on RMA/MTR, the implications of which for conventional warfare were deemed imminently overwhelming, but with major doubts about its implications for LIC, terrorism, etc. Then by the late 1990s interest in MTR/RMA appeared to wane in the face of major power peace, U.S. budgetary restraints, etc., and it was superseded by a newly dominant emphasis on counterproliferation and the dangers of regional wars involving WMD, used either by nation-states or subnational actors.[1] Interest in "lessons learned" appeared to wane as scholars groped to make some sense of the by now major conflict phenomenon, that of ethnic warfare stretching from Kosovo to Congo to eastern Turkey to Cambodia. That indeed was a far cry from the tradition of Clausewitz, Jomini, Earle, and Fuller, but as SIPRI's and our data-sets point out unmistakably, that is now the reigning focus with regards to modern warfare. And indeed, there is no general, comparative analytical work at all when it comes to the war-fighting aspects of ethnic warfare.

Toward a Framework for the Study of Modern Warfare

We have tried here to present a general framework for the study of the conduct of modern warfare, one that would lend a more structured, conceptual cast to what is largely the domain of military history and/or certain aspects of national security policy including deterrence theory. That framework cannot easily, at this point, be fleshed out with a comprehensive data analysis or a large range of case studies—much, much more research is needed in some areas. Hence, we have presented here a heuristic analysis, but hopefully with enough data and illustrations to stand by itself as a general coverage of modern warfare. That analysis has involved a complex matrix of sorts, crossing several types or levels of analysis: a typology of warfare running from conventional to various types of LIC (but subsuming various mixes of magnitude, severity, duration, the existence or absence of "fronts," various levels of usage of weapons, various types of LIC or internal war regarding ethnic or ideological bases for conflict, etc.); a levels of analysis format running from the grand strategic to strategic to operational to tactical levels of analysis; various "functional" categories of analysis (military geography, culture, economics, outside interventions, particularly arms transfers and other forms of security assistance); the impact of the changing international system on all of the above (which changes are not easily gauged without the aid of hindsight), etc. Hence, we may then focus discussion on, for example, the role of geography (terrain, weather) in affecting the operational aspects of low-intensity warfare; or the impact of cultural factors in determining the tactics used in certain kinds of conventional wars. That is a vast and complex three-dimensional matrix, herein merely bruited, haltingly.

Conventional Wars: Main Points and Conclusions

During the past thirty to thirty-five years (the latter part of the Cold War and beyond), there have actually been a merely finite number of conventional inter-state wars, subject to the aforenoted caveats about various possible mixes of "magnitude," "severity," and "duration," and the nature of fighting in connection with "moving fronts." Indeed, the period 1945–1965 saw only the Korean War (often characterized as "limited" in the wake of World War II), the 1956 Suez Crisis, and perhaps the French struggle against the Vietminh as representative of the genre. Since 1965 we have had the three Arab-Israel wars of 1967, 1973, and 1982, the two India-Pakistan wars of 1965 and 1971, the Gulf War, Iran vs. Iraq, the Falklands, China vs. Vietnam in 1979, and Ethiopia vs. Somalia, with other conflicts—Angola, Sudan, Congo, Cambodia, Afghanistan, Chad-Libya, Yemen, Ethiopia-Eritrea—having evidenced some conventional warfare characteristics according to some of the aforenoted criteria.

Of these, the Falklands War is often treated cursorily as an odd historical echo, an anomaly, with Gilbert and Sullivan overtones, its deadly nature notwithstanding. Vietnam versus China lasted only three weeks as a very large-scale punitive raid. Somalia versus Ethiopia was, after all, mostly an extended battle over the Kara Marda Pass by relatively unsophisticated forces.

One could, of course, argue that the history of conventional warfare since the Korean War consists very largely of the serial Arab-Israel and India-Pakistan wars, plus the two Gulf wars in which Iraq first fought Iran and then the U.S.-led coalition. These are the main cases from which "lessons" or generalizations may be drawn, or questions raised leading to further research, even as the bulk of the political science profession sees the era of interstate, conventional warfare as having come to a close and with it an important component of strategic studies and military history.

In this volume we have tried to analyze these wars from various "functional" or even disciplinary perspectives: military analysis subsuming strategies, operations, tactics, and doctrines; military geography, comparative culture, and the contextual politics and diplomacy of warfare (particularly as pertains to security assistance and interventions). We eschewed the potentially important dimension of the economics of war as basically outside the scope of our study and lacking even the rudiments of a cost database for most of these conflicts. Of course, while these various domains have been studied somewhat in isolation from one another, there are important causal relationships between them, i.e., geography and culture have a major impact on strategies and tactics, as do arms transfers and other forms of military aid, and vice-versa, tactics or the expectation of them may drive decisions on procurement and resupply at the level of full systems (platforms) or just sub-systems.

This study, across some of the above categories, appears to have raised some important questions along the following lines.

- The relevance—or relative absence of same—of force balances and orders of battle, and quantitative indicators of national power (population, GNP, etc.), in relation also to more "subjective" subjects such as geography and culture;
- The importance of security assistance and the availability of arms—quantitatively and qualitatively—filtered through the problem of "absorption" (training, leadership) as critical in determining the outcome of wars, particularly protracted ones;
- The differential role of airpower and seapower in these various wars;
- The mix of experiences and "lessons" regarding wars of attrition and wars of maneuver, in turn based on extant levels of weapons technology and concomitantly alternating advantages to the offense and defense;
- The critical importance of economic, social, and cultural factors in allowing for the conduct of hi-tech, combined-arms warfare—a real dividing line in determining wars' outcomes;
- The existence or absence of decisive battles or campaigns a la Clausewitz, versus the thesis that military victories are ultimately meaningless or transitory; i.e., the contemporary ambiguity of "victory";
- "Pain thresholds" as a critical desideratum;

- Strategic depth plus terrain and weather, as a critical desideratum, modified by military effectiveness; specifically the ability to conduct long-range, decisive, combined arms offensives.

Power Indicators vs. Geography and Culture

It has become standard practice in the security literature to utilize as a point of departure in comparing the military strengths of contending regional powers, quantitative indicators of relative power: GNP, per capita GNP, population (the latter two combine for the former), military expenditures, orders of battle (numbers of army divisions and air wings, and weapons inventories). The impression is sometimes rendered that these indicators ought to predict, more or less, the outcomes of wars—who wins and loses, by how much (close struggles vs. blowouts)—and the durations of wars. Indeed, U.S. military assistance policy often is geared to such measurements, in that it is ostensibly directed at maintaining or, where necessary, rectifying such balances. Similarly, the Cold War period saw endless efforts at measuring force-on-force ratios and balances for the so-called NATO-WTO "central military balance," mostly couched in quantitative terms, somewhat modified by subjective factors such as alliance cohesion, morale, training, various ratios of "tooth to tail," etc.

The above-noted quantitative indicators have been somewhat but not entirely useful in predicting conventional war outcomes during the past thirty years, but only sometimes. At the extremes, where the balances have been highly asymmetric, as in the case of India vs. Pakistan, the factor of mass or brute numbers has been validated. That point also held for China's quick "victory" over Vietnam in 1979. But even here, much larger India, while able to conduct a successful campaign in East Bengal in 1971, was only partially successful in attempting to mount offensives against then West Pakistan. The outcomes of the Arab-Israeli wars in 1967 and 1973 confounded what would appear to have been predicted by comparisons of aggregated GNP, the size of forces, weapons inventories, etc. (The 1982 Lebanon war in this sense was far less surprising, though paradoxically the Arab side may have fared better without a huge numerical advantage.) Likewise, the outcome of the Iran-Iraq War was in contradiction to the "basic numbers." Ditto for the Libya-Chad conflict. The Gulf War's outcome, of course, validated a huge asymmetry in basic economic and other indicators.

Where the outcomes have been "surprises," the explanations have involved a mix of cultural, geographic, and politico-diplomatic factors running against the grain of standard power indicators. Cultural explanations are offered for Israel's successes on the battlefield (morale, technical capacity derived from higher educational levels, unit cohesion, training, etc.). In Iraq's case, there was a huge asymmetry involving outside support, particularly as pertains to arms resupply, in addition to the postrevolutionary chaos and disarray in Iran. And again in 1971 India displayed an organized ability to fight a major war involving combined arms operations, perhaps the only example aside from Israel. Here too, cultural factors may have been at play, as they also may have been in Chad's defeat of Libya.

But then, as we have noted, factors of strategic geography have loomed large in many of these conflicts, particularly those of strategic depth, terrain, and weather. Neither side could get close to a major victory before 1988 in the Iraq-Iran War because of this factor—even victorious Iraq in 1988 eschewed an effort at pushing its luck any further. Israel, as noted, used its interior-lines position in 1967 (the paradoxical obverse of strategic depth) to achieve a major victory; in 1973 strategic depth gave time for regrouping but was also a logistical disadvantage at the war's outset. Pakistan's absence of strategic depth was not telling in 1965 or 1971, but yet could be. Ethiopia survived a Somali onslaught in 1977 via this factor, and likewise Vietnam in 1979 was able to get away with a fairly limited defeat. Terrain and weather were major factors modifying the raw indicators of power on the Golan and Sinai, in the Punjab area, the Red River Valley, the Ahmar mountains in Ethiopia, and, of course, in Afghanistan. In short, at the margins certainly, power indicators may mean only so much.

Arms Resupply and Security Assistance: A Priori and Intrawar Supply for Conventional Wars

Most of the nations that have been involved in recent conventional warfare—Israel, all the Arab states, India, Pakistan, Vietnam, Ethiopia, Somalia—have been dependent on outside sources of arms supply and various forms of external support, to one degree or another. The exceptions: the U.S. in the Gulf War, the USSR in Afghanistan, China in Vietnam (the latter had then relied on license-built Soviet equipment, but that was irrelevant in the fighting of that war), and for the most part but not entirely (it received some U.S. assistance), Britain in the Falklands. That meant that in substantial wars, particularly those that lasted for more than a few weeks, there would be the question of external resupply of replacement (for attrited systems) equipment and spare parts, modified in some cases by indigenous capability for weapons and ammunition manufacture. That raises, in many of these cases, all manner of problems regarding the leverage of combatants over their own erstwhile suppliers and their foes' suppliers, and also the geography and logistics of resupply operations involving distance factors, overflight rights, the cargo capacity of suppliers, etc. It also raises the question of initiating arms embargoes, obtaining intelligence data, and other measures to reduce the enemy's access to military support and its combat capability. In fact, some of these wars may have been initiated because or in anticipation of arms transfer problems, i.e., when one regional power (Ethiopia in 1977, Iran in 1980) has undergone a political upheaval and lost its main arms supplier (in both of these cases, the U.S.), hence opening the possibility of a preemptive "window of opportunity" war for a temporarily advantaged regional combatant.

In very short wars, of course, even those of high intensity, security assistance and arms transfer diplomacy may not come into play. Israel in 1956 and 1967 did not require weapons transfusions, and its losses were in any case nugatory (it was in this period greatly dependent on French weaponry and had limited indigenous production capacity). The Arabs suffered huge losses of arms in these conflicts, but those losses were made up (mostly by the USSR) only gradually after the conclusion of conflict. Likewise, arms resupply was not of great moment in the 1982 war, with Syria's inventories being replaced afterwards by Moscow while Israel's losses were at any rate minimal. Neither did arms resupply diplomacy come into play much during the 1965 and 1971 India–Pakistan wars, with the U.S. and UK having embargoed both sides in 1965, a more or less meaningless gesture, though it did subsequently drive Pakistan into the arms of China. The short military phase of the 1990–91 Gulf War also saw little in the way of arms resupply to Iraq.

Among the conflicts where arms resupply was a vital matter were the 1973 Arab-Israel War, the Iran-Iraq War, the Afghanistan conflict, Ethiopia vs. Somalia, and to a lesser extent, China vs. Vietnam and the Falklands. The Angolan conflict was also marked by the vital importance of arms supplies to both sides.

Here we see a mix with regard to duration or protraction, though it is clear that long wars between contending dependent nations will magnify the importance of arms resupply and other forms of security assistance. In the 1973 war, the high intensity of the combat engendered very quickly, even in a twenty-two-day war, a competitive air and sealift effort between the U.S. and USSR. The Iran-Iraq War was largely driven by arms acquisitions by both sides, each of which had numerous suppliers (for Iraq: mostly the USSR, France, Egypt, Brazil; for Iran: Syria, Libya, China, North Korea, Israel). Iraq ended up winning the war largely because of its advantageous arms resupply diplomacy. American arms supplies to the Afghan Mujahideen—often sourced from Egypt, paid for by Saudi Arabia, and routed through Pakistan—were vital to the ultimate Soviet defeat and withdrawal after a decade of fighting. In a mixed case, Soviet arms resupply of Vietnam in 1979 may have given the Hanoi regime the backbone to combat larger China in a war of only three weeks' duration in which Vietnam's arms arsenals were not seriously diminished. During the relatively short fighting phase of the Falklands War, Argentina (whose potential resuppliers were under heavy political pressure to deny it arms) received a trickle of assistance, while the UK received some weapons and photo-reconnaissance assistance from the U.S. Future conventional-warfare scenarios in the three major cockpits of the Greater Middle East—Arab-Israel, Iraq-Iran, India-Pakistan (maybe now Iran-Pakistan)—could see some fascinating patterns of external arms resupply, particularly if the wars are protracted.

Some of the arms resupply operations underscored the critical role of en route basing and logistics access. Iraq, during its long war with Iran, relied heavily on a conduit through Jordan and its port at Aqaba. Israel in 1973 was narrowly dependent on U.S. air transit access to Portugal's Azores. The Soviets apparently had to overfly or transit India with weapons en route to Vietnam in 1979, and had to overfly several states in the Middle East to mount a resupply operation on behalf of Ethiopia in 1978.[2] Covert arms supplies to Iran by Israel and others in the mid-1980s apparently made use of Turkish airspace. This access diplomacy in relation to arms resupply has been an important desideratum in several conventional regional wars.

Naval and Airpower

For the most part, recent conventional wars have been centered on ground combat with, in many cases, a minimal role for air and sea power. Air and sea power were nugatory factors in the China-Vietnam war, also in the Chad-Libya war. The Ethiopia-Somalia conflict saw some use of tactical airpower by Cuban-flown planes in Ethiopia's successful counterattack in 1978. In the India–Pakistan wars of 1965 and 1971, particularly the latter, airpower played a somewhat significant but not dominant role, mostly involving India's interdiction of Pakistani air bases and infrastructure, with a fairly minimal ground support role. India's navy, however, played a fairly major role in 1971, blockading Pakistani ports (hence, forestalling arms resupply), particularly Karachi and Dacca, and even allowing for some amphibious operations in East Bengal. Airpower was a fairly minor factor in the Iran-Iraq War, due to the overall incapacity of air forces on either side to play a major role on the battlefield (a partial exception was the role played by air forces in the "tanker war" in the Persian Gulf). Indeed, surface-to-surface missiles supplemented aircraft for purposes of long-range strategic bombardment. In Afghanistan, the Soviets made massive efforts—with tactical aircraft and attack helicopters—to utilize aerial superiority, but were largely thwarted by the nature of the terrain and the Afghans' acquisition of Stinger SAMs from the U.S.

In a few wars, however, airpower was very significant and perhaps even decisive: the Arab-Israel wars of 1967, 1973, and 1982; the Gulf War of 1991, and perhaps to a lesser degree, the Falklands conflict. That is, the technical prowess of the American, British, and Israeli air forces allowed for airpower to be utilized as a major instrument of warfare. Numerous analysts claimed that for the first time in 1991, airpower and air superiority was the dominant factor in the war. Coalition airpower, mostly from the U.S., took down Iraq's transportation, industrial, and communications infrastructure, interdicted Iraq's efforts to resupply its forces in Kuwait, prepared the battlefield for Desert Storm with a massive onslaught against entrenched Iraqi troops, interdicted Iraq's Scud missiles, and bombarded the Iraqi army during the ground phase of the war. Israel's air force preemptively destroyed the Egyptian, Syrian, and Jordanian air forces on the ground in 1967, then gave Israel's armored forces a decisive edge with effective and unchallenged air-support missions. In 1973 newly acquired Soviet SAMs in the hands of Egypt and Syria initially thwarted the Israeli air force, but it recovered quickly with new tactics and again dominated the airspace and battlefield toward the war's end. In 1982 the Israeli air force destroyed most Syrian SAMs and shot down much of the Syrian air force, but its tactical role was perhaps less important than in 1967 and 1973 because of the more rugged and covered terrain being contested by ground forces in Lebanon. In the Falklands War, British V-bombers wrecked Argentinian air bases on the islands, while carrier-based aircraft contested the Argentinian air force and performed some combat-support roles after the invasion. The Argentinian air force came close but failed to achieve a decisive role in turning back the British invasion (if it had kept access to bases on the Falklands, it might well have succeeded).

In the Falklands War, British naval power was decisive, driving the Argentinian navy from the battle area, enabling a large-scale amphibious operation, and conducting a very lengthy logistics operation. British submarines as well as surface ships were important. In the 1973 war, Israel's small navy easily knocked out a good part of the Egyptian and Syrian navies; in 1982 it participated in some leapfrog amphibious operations up the Lebanon coast toward Beirut. The U.S. Navy played a major role in the Gulf War, logistically with sealift, with the use of carrier aircraft, and in providing the feint of a marine amphibious landing in Kuwait that tied down a part of the Iraqi army. Otherwise, Iran's fleet of small, armed patrol boats played a significant role in the 1980s in interdicting tanker and other ship traffic in the Persian Gulf, which engendered the U.S. "reflagging" operation on behalf of Kuwait. As with airpower, the same nations (U.S., UK, Israel, India) seem capable of utilizing navies for effective purposes in these recent wars.

Offense and Defense, Wars of Attrition vs. Wars of Maneuver (Conventional)

As noted, there is a (complex) tradition of military history that sees phases of warfare (at the big-power level) alternating between advantage to offense and defense, or wars of attrition and those of maneuver, driven basically by ongoing technological trends and developments. But regarding the wars of the past generation, there is a mixed bag of lessons along these lines, not easily explained or categorized.

Israel in 1967 and India in 1971 conducted classic and overwhelmingly decisive wars of offense and maneuver; so too did the U.S.-led Gulf War coalition. The grinding Iran-Iraq War of 1980–88 seemed a classic war of attrition, à la World War I. Britain's quick victory in the Falklands could probably be chalked up—in its ground phase—to a war of maneuver, albeit with limited use of mechanized forces or large-scale infantry maneuver elements. The India-Pakistan War of 1965, quickly terminated, had some of the elements of a war of attrition, as did the China-Vietnam conflict, despite the offensive progress by the People's Liberation Army (PLA) over a three-week period.

To the extent that any sense may be made of this mix, it is that where offensive operations by highly skilled forces using combined arms are involved—U.S., UK, Israel, India—successful wars of maneuver are possible, even (as was the case in East Bengal in 1971) where imposing terrain barriers are involved. Less sophisticated forces, not easily capable of coordinated combined-arms operations, will more likely be caught up in stagnant wars of attrition, as in the Iran-Iraq War where the weapons involved were altogether similar to those used by Israel and Arab armies in 1973 and 1982. But geography is a modifier—note the limited problems Israel had in conducting a rapid offensive in 1982 (relative to 1967 anyway!), or the manner in which the Indian army struggled in 1965 in the face of a short front and difficult terrain. And Chad fought a successful, quick war of maneuver against Libya.

In short, these matters are highly situational, dependent on a complex mix of mass (size of forces and their symmetries/asymmetries), terrain, weather, and, of course, weapons. As a cautionary note, initial analyses that claimed that the introduction of SAMs and anti-tank guided weapons (ATGWs) had, in 1973, fundamentally altered the nature of warfare toward defensive dominance turned out to be premature, overriden by compensatory tactics, heat balloons to counter infrared-guided SAMs, better tank armor, better use of infantry and artillery to counter hand-held ATGMs, etc.

It remains to be seen what will be wrought in this regard by the emergent MTR/RMA. It might be speculated that heretofore indicative measures of power—GNP (latent), MILEX (actual)—might become less valid relative to narrower measures of technological capacity perhaps best captured by per capita GNP or educational levels. Hence, mass and numbers might become less important. That might appear to have been the lesson of the Gulf War, the recent Arab-Israeli wars, and the Falklands War. But that is not certain and might involve an exaggerated technological determinism. Or high technology could become more "user friendly" and shift the balance back toward mass and numbers.

Decisive Battles and Campaigns, and the Meaning of Victory

Much of past military history, and related military theory, inspired by the Clausewitzian tradition, dwelled upon the importance of crucial battles and campaigns and, hence, the roots of victory. Wars were thought often to hinge on decisive "battles," or *kesselschlacten,* where superior force was brought to bear at a decisive point in a war. That was considered the hallmark of good generalship, good strategy. And there were real victories with decisive consequences. Hence, Waterloo, Königgratz, Borodino, the Marne, Gettysburg, Stalingrad, El Alamein, Midway, et al. are so familiar to readers of military history. France really lost in 1815 and 1870, Germany in 1918 and 1945, Japan in 1945, the American South in 1865, Austria in 1866. On the contrary, some would point to France being readmitted to the family of nations in 1815, to the reversal of the seeming verdict of 1870, and to the economic rise to power of defeated Japan and Germany after 1945. For the short run at least, military victories often appeared decisive and overwhelmingly consequential (ask Carthage, or Sparta, or the Byzantine Empire, or those obliterated by the Mongols).

What then can we derive from our recent wars? Have they featured decisive battles or campaigns, and have the latter lead to seemingly permanent consequences regarding victory and defeat, surrender or submission? The answer appears of mixed quality. Central here is the relationship of military victory and newly developed "norms" of the international system that may render territorial conquest "illegitimate," hence propelling a tendency for wars to end—their duration and casualties notwithstanding—at some close approximation to the status quo ante.[3]

In the Arab-Israel context, the latter won decisively in 1967 with key battles at Rafah (Gaza Strip), Abu Agheila, Jerusalem, and on the Golan Heights. The result was Israeli occupation of Sinai, Gaza, Jerusalem and the West Bank, and the Golan Heights. The more difficult (for Israel) 1973 war ended after decisive battles at the Chinese Farm (and Israel's crossing of the Suez Canal and surrounding of much of the Egyptian army) and (on the defense) on the Golan Heights. In 1982 Israel won a decisive short campaign in Lebanon, culminating at Beirut and in the Bekaa Valley, after major victories in southern Lebanon. Both wars ended in decisive victories for Israel. But ever since, Israel's hold on its "captured" territories has been pressured, and it may eventually be pressured to withdraw to the 1967 lines with only minor border adjustments. Hence, of course, pressure from the so-called "international community" has aborted Israel's military victories.

The last of the India-Pakistan wars (from the perspective of 2000) saw a decisive campaign in East Bengal culminating in the capture of Dacca (albeit little more than a stalemate in the West). But the outcome of the war was decisive and seemingly permanent, involving the dismemberment of the former Pakistan, the independence of Bangladesh, and a massive tilting of the already asymmetric power balance between the two South Asian powers. Though there may yet be more to this story, this appears one case where "victory" had a real and durable meaning, where there was no return to a status quo ante.

Britain's military victory in the Falklands, based on a successful campaign from the San Carlos landing area to Fort Stanley, restored a territorial status quo ante—whether or not that was a permanent "victory" in a larger sense may yet be determined. China's successful military victory in 1979 over Vietnam, hinged on a major breakthrough near Long San and down into the Red River Valley, ended up with withdrawal, the status quo ante, and perhaps a "lesson taught" or "lesson administered." Chad's victory over Libya, involving one major battle victory at Wadi Doum, also restored a status quo ante, perhaps resolving the issue of control of the Aouzou Strip in favor of the former. The long, brutal Iran-Iraq War ended virtually with a status quo ante, save some very minor changes in favor of victorious Iraq in the Shatt al Arab estuary area. There, Iraq's victory on the Fao Peninsula in March 1988 was probably crucial. The Gulf War ended also with a restored status quo ante in Kuwait, nothing more. Ditto the earlier Ethiopia-Somalia war, with its major turnaround victory for Ethiopia before Harar and in the Kara Marda Pass, as Ethiopia eschewed a pursuit into Somalia, in part so as not to energize political support for the latter. It is indeed noteworthy that as a result of all of these wars only India won a victory that was seemingly permanent and changed the status quo. Regarding Israel and the Arabs, the jury is still out. More recently, the wars in ex-Yugoslavia have been somewhat decisive.

Comparative Pain Thresholds: A Repressed Subject

Perhaps coincident with the rise of interest in the cultural aspects of war-fighting, but in a narrow slice of that subject, is the recognition of the importance of comparative pain thresholds (see chapter six). That refers to nations' abilities to sustain high casualties in wars, whether measured in absolute terms or relative to overall population. Few analysts wish to discuss this subject head-on because of its inherently brutal and gruesome nature and because of the extent to which it appears to dehumanize the subject of war. But one notes, for instance, John Mueller's excellent analysis of this factor as central to the U.S. conduct of the Vietnam War and its dénouement, i.e., U.S. withdrawal.[4] The matter was central to analyses—before the initiation of Desert Storm—of whether the U.S. could withstand a bloody, attrition war against Iraq; indeed, Saddam Hussein's strategy—hinged on fixed fortifications and layered barrier defenses—was based explicitly and openly on this point.

Generally speaking, numerous contemporary analysts have concluded that modern, industrialized societies can not, or will not, sustain high casualties in war, often referred to as the "Scandinavianization of warfare." This is despite the lessons of the slaughters of the two world wars. Some analysts, however, devotees of the "democratic peace" thesis, are want to claim that governments of democracies, subject to public opinion polls and elections, cannot now sustain high-attrition combat, perhaps ignoring the histories of the U.S. and UK in the world wars. (France's high casualties in World War I, however, and also Britain's, are usually cited as major reasons for the appeasement policies of the late 1930s.)

The importance of this factor does, however, appear to be borne out by our recent wars, as it ramifies into go/no go decisions on whether to enter frays, but also into tactics and strategies designed to limit casualties. Israel, of course, has an enormous sensitivity to casualties—it was traumatized by the twenty-eight hundred fatalities in 1973. Its entire conduct of the 1982 war was driven by this factor, including the decision not to enter into urban combat in Beirut (for that matter, the war was triggered in part by the limited casualties caused by Katyusha rocket attacks in northern Israel beforehand). Likewise, the withdrawal from southern Lebanon in 2000 reinforces this point in the eyes of the Arab world (as discussed in chapter six). The U.S., as noted, went beyond its pain threshold in Vietnam, even though its casualties were far fewer than its less populous foe, rendering its "body count" attrition strategy wholly misplaced. Britain worried a lot about the large-scale losses that might have been sustained by its 1982 invasion fleet by more successful Argentine air attacks, but it lucked out with very low casualties. In the period before the launching of Desert Storm, numerous political foes of an all-out attack predicted ten thousand U.S. body bags, deemed wholly unacceptable to the U.S. public. There was similar skittishness with regard to Somalia, Bosnia, and Kosovo.

On the reverse side, of course, Iraq and Iran sustained huge losses in their war, which may finally have had some impact on Iranian public morale. The Arabs have been willing to sustain highly asymmetric levels of casualties in their wars with Israel (no democratic voting there!); indeed, they are optimistic that they can ultimately prevail in a long struggle of attrition involving multiple wars. China and Vietnam sustained massive casualties in three weeks in 1979, with little evidence of stress on their nation's leaders. Ditto for Libya vs. Chad, and in Angola. Afghanistan lost a frightening proportion of its population fighting the USSR, seemingly with full public assent; indeed, that war was followed by additional very bloody internal battles among the previous winning coalition. In short, although there is some disagreement on this point, mounting evidence suggests that wealthy, consumer-society democracies cannot or will not countenance high mortality rates in war relative to nations on the lower end of the development scale, where governments may deem life cheap. This appears to have become an overwhelmingly important consideration in world security affairs.

And for nations like the U.S. and Israel, it appears to drive strategies and tactics designed to avoid casualties, i.e., extensive use of aircraft and cruise missile attacks, a reluctance to engage in meatgrinder infantry tactics. In the case of Israel, the Merkava tank was designed to protect tank crews and to carry some infantry into battle, to some extent trading off mobility for life-saving tank design.

Strategic Depth

We have previously said that the role of military geography has been seriously understated in security studies, and we have outlined a variety of subjects under that heading, for instance, the roles of terrain, weather, and seasons in determining war strategies and outcomes. But perhaps most of all the factor of strategic depth deserves to be underscored in relation to war aims and to the dearth of definitive victories in so many of the recent wars.

In recent centuries, we have had the examples of Russia's great strategic depth absorbing and defeating the offensives of Napoleon, Ludendorff, and Hitler, and of China's similar depth frustrating Japan's efforts to defeat it in World War II. In this study, we have shown how Iran's depth vis-à-vis Iraq; Ethiopia's depth vis-à-vis Somalia; the depth of the Arab confrontation states vis-à-vis Israel; Chad's depth vis-à-vis Libya, India's depth vis-à-vis Pakistan, perhaps also Vietnam's ability to absorb a strong blow from China all have illustrated this matter on a smaller scale than the historical Russian and Chinese examples. This factor has derived importance from its connection to the evolving international norms about territorial conquest and the tendency for so many recent wars to end up, ultimately, with a status quo ante. Somewhat to the contrary, in somewhat asymmetric fashion, Israel, Pakistan, and perhaps Iraq are examples of countries with limited strategic depth, and that fact has, in some cases, driven preemptive military strategies, and perhaps the acquisition and threatened use of weapons of mass destruction. Above all in these cases is the combination of strategic-depth problems and the inability of most regional powers to conduct long-range offensive operations and to hold large chunks of territory (even aside from the probable ultimate need to give them back because of the norms about territorial conquest). Israel's drive across Suez in 1973 and India's overrunning of East Bengal were the exceptions. It might even be argued that the strategic–depth problem somewhat favoring Iraq in 1991 was one reason among many that the U.S.-led coalition chose not to attempt a march on Baghdad (political pressures from Saudi Arabia, a reluctance to "pile on," and the prospect of costly urban warfare in Baghdad were others). It remains to be seen, in a general sense, whether evolving trends in military technology will alter, one way or the other, the importance of strategic depth to conventional warfare.

Unconventional or Low-Intensity Warfare—
Main Points and Conclusions

As previously discussed, the contemporary literature monolithically assumes (whether correctly or not in long-term perspective remains to be seen) that the study of low-intensity conflict, mostly ethnopolitical conflict, has become the core of contemporary security studies. That assumes that the history of large-scale conventional warfare has come to an end via obsolescence, new international norms, the democratic peace, etc. Meanwhile, recent surveys of conflict do show that most or all wars now in progress are in the low-to-mid intensity range, and that most have an ethnopolitical basis. That literature focuses mostly on the causes and potential cures of such conflicts (war termination), rarely on their conduct or on the military strategies and tactics utilized by contending sides. Regarding the latter, some of the following tentative conclusions or, more modestly, areas of inquiry needing further analysis are proffered.

- The growing irrelevance of what was (during much of the Cold War) a massive body of analysis regarding insurgency/revolutionary war doctrines and their counterparts, i.e., counterinsurgency doctrines, in an era beyond the Cold War and characterized mainly by ethnopolitical conflict.
- In military terms, the tendency for ethnopolitical conflicts to become interminable and lack definitive resolutions.
- The considerable number of ethnic conflicts characterized by asymmetric wars between incumbent regimes and insurgents or separatist minorities.
- A greater tendency toward the use of modern aircraft and armored equipment in contemporary LICs, often on an asymmetric basis in some wars, as small arms and light weapons fuel conflicts in others.
- The near absence of a decent database regarding arms transfers in LICs, particularly ethnic conflicts, rendering military analysis very difficult.
- The increased use of embargoes and sanctions rather than force to try to contain the conflicts.
- High casualties in ethnopolitical wars, combining military and civilian deaths, due to massacres, "ethnic cleansing," starvation, etc.
- A tendency for ethnopolitical conflicts to have intrastate dimensions, with military ramifications involving interventions, arms supplies, financing, and the use of mercenaries.

The Big Shift: From Marxist-Leninist Revolutionary Wars to Ethnopolitical Conflict

While during the Cold War military strategic analysis was centered on nuclear deterrence theory and conventional warfare doctrines, there was also—certainly after the ascension of the Kennedy administration in 1961—a big emphasis on insurgency and counterinsurgency warfare doctrines. That corresponded to an era when there were numerous "wars over government" pitting incumbent pro-Western regimes against Marxist-Leninist-inspired insurgents tied to and supported by the USSR and China: the Philippines, Laos, Cambodia, Vietnam, Cuba, Algeria and a variety of anticolonial revolts: Rhodesia, Namibia, Kenya, South Yemen, Guinea-Bissau. As previously noted, these revolts were often guided by the politico-military insurgency doctrines associated with T. E. Lawrence, Mao, Giap, Marighella et al., and opposed by various COIN doctrines and strategies adopted by the French, British, and Americans in Algeria, Malaya, Vietnam, etc.: oil slicks, seize and hold, fortified hamlets, search and destroy, "hearts and minds." Nowadays, very few contemporary conflicts are connected to this historical tradition—in a minor way, maybe in Colombia, Mexico, Venezuela, and Peru. Outside of Latin America, indeed, there are few pure "wars over government" (excepting conflicts such as Algeria and Egypt concerning Islamic fundamentalism). Instead there are identity conflicts—ethnic, religious, linguistic, racial, tribal, sometimes with a class or economic component. To date, few if any doctrines or general strategies have been enunciated as guides to "how to fight" these wars, unless there is an (unstated) Milosevic or Saddam Hussein "doctrine" of ethnic warfare. Hence, military analyses of these conflicts tend to have no theoretical or historical context and tend toward the random and idiosyncratic.

The Interminability and Unresolvability of Ethnopolitical Conflict

Despite the myths associated with the Mao/Giap doctrines of protracted war (assuming an Asian cultural advantage against the impatient West wedded to notions of "decisive" victories, i.e., wei-ch'i ["Go"] vs. chess or football), most of the "wars over government" pitting Marxist-Leninist revolutionary groups against incumbent "neocolonialist" regimes were indeed decisive, one way or the other, short term or long term. China, Vietnam, Algeria, Cuba, and Ethiopia saw permanent and irreversible revolutionary victories. Or there were decisive counterinsurgency wars such as in Greece, the Philippines, and Malaya. The outcomes usually also involved fatal, merciless consequences for the losers. There were a few exceptions, but not many—Cambodia, for instance, had until recently been an interminable and seemingly unresolvable ideological "war over government." That in Angola, with its ethnic component, is an only partially valid exception.

The recent ethnopolitical wars (or more broadly, identity wars), wars over territory, have been much less likely to end decisively, if for no other reason than that might entail the likelihood of genocide or something gruesome short of that. Rather, wars have stalemated, or devolved into asymmetric but continuing remnants, indeed, sometimes with de facto partitions or achievements of autonomy. To one degree or another that has been true in Iraq's and Turkey's Kurdistan, Nagorno-Karabakh, Abkhazia, Tajikistan, Kashmir, Burma, Angola, etc. But the numerous situations here almost defy generalization, so we are talking merely about tendencies. Further, we do not have sufficient perspective to judge just how interminable many of these conflicts may yet become.

Asymmetric Wars between Incumbent Regimes and Ethnic Separatists

We have noted that during the Cold War period the predominant (but by no means exclusive) "type" of LIC was a Marxist-Leninist-inspired insurgency against an incumbent, Western-backed, "comprador" regime. In the 1990s, one can probably say that the "dominant type" is an ethnic (or religious or racial or tribal) conflict featuring a central regime controlled by a majority identity type faced off against an ethnic minority (territorially based, with varying degrees of clear demarcation). The degree of asymmetry can, however, vary considerably, all the way from an overwhelming imbalance, to a roughly balanced situation (hence, symmetrical); likewise, the nature of the conflict can vary from a purely ethnic (or other identity basis) one to one evidencing a mixed ethnic and ideological basis (hence, then, a mix of war over territory and war over government). Varying too is the degree to which the insurrectionary ethnic group seeks victory and its own dominance, independence, or some degree of autonomy or a "federal" solution. In some of these conflicts, the existence of cross-border support for an ethnic insurgency further complicates the picture, adding an element of intrastate conflict to an internal war over territory.

Some examples of the dominant type may be seen in Kosovo, Turkey's and Iraq's Kurdistan, Abkhazia (more symmetry here), Moldova, Myanmar, Sri Lanka, East Timor, Sudan, Mexico's Chiapas Province (add a class or ideological element there), and Chechnya. More symmetrical situations exist in Nagorno-Karabakh, maybe Bosnia (but with outside Serbian aid intervening), and Rwanda and Burundi. But the dominant type aside, one can still point to traditional class-based insurgencies (Colombia, Venezuela, Peru, Guatemala), and those based on religion or ideology (Tajikistan, Algeria, Egypt). Regarding the "dominant type," it is here that ethnic cleansing, massacres and brutal suppressions tend to prevail, as in Kosovo, East Timor, the Sudan, and the interlocked components of Kurdistan, where heavily armed government forces have overwhelmed less well armed and less numerous insurgents. But again, in none of these cases has the asymmetry translated into final "victory," or closure, whether because of outside pressures, cross-border sanctuaries, primitive terrain allowing for retention of redoubts, or the limitations of developing-nation armies in pursuing COIN operations (note the Russians earlier fared equally poorly in Chechnya, but later had some success).

Aircraft and Armor in LICs

There is perhaps a paradox here. Mostly when we think of LICs, now predominantly ethnopolitical conflict, we think of dirty, chaotic, disorganized wars, fought mostly or even entirely with small arms, maybe some crew-served weapons such as jeep-mounted recoilless rifles or grenade launchers, but also maybe with more primitive weapons (here one thinks of the Rwandan genocide being carried out with hoes and other such implements). Many of these wars have been fought largely with such weapons whose origins, as we have noted, are often difficult to trace (it has long been a staple assumption of the arms-trade literature that small arms flows are close to unmeasurable or untraceable).

Yet a close reading of some of the battle reports from recent LICs indicates that increasingly, modern weapons platforms such as combat aircraft, tanks, armored fighting vehicles, and heavy artillery have increasingly come into play, whether or not with the decisive impact habitually ascribed to the use of Israeli airpower in 1967, 1973, and 1982, or mostly U.S. airpower in 1991.

In some cases, not unsurprisingly, the use of advanced platforms is associated with situations of high asymmetry, in which the central government or governing power alone is availed of such systems. In the Kosovo conflict, the Yugoslav army has made extensive use of helicopters, tanks, and artillery to destroy Muslim villages, while the latter's army, the KLA, has no such systems. That has also been the case with Iraq's and Turkey's suppression of the Kurds, Russia's suppression of Chechnya, and Colombia's suppression of FARC. But it is also true that relatively sophisticated regimes availed of such weapons may not use them, for fear of world opinion or because of the nature of the terrain. Hence, up to 2000 Israel had not used tactical aircraft, tanks, or artillery in the West Bank, nor have Peru or Venezuela or Mexico used such systems in COIN operations. In a relatively more symmetrical context, the Sri Lankan government has used tactical aircraft and patrol boats in battling the Tamil Tigers.

But as we have noted, the use of aircraft and tanks has begun to surface in hitherto unexpected places, including situations of greater symmetry in internal wars. Little information appears available about the sizes of aircraft and armored inventories in some of these cases, the availability of trained pilots (indigenous or external mercenary), and the state of maintenance and by whom it is performed. We have the odd paradox of, on the one hand, a "lessons learned" literature that denigrates the primitive use of airpower in the Iran-Iraq and China-Vietnam Wars, but on the other hand, more recent reports of relatively effective use of airpower around Kabul and Brazzaville; the wholly ineffective use of armor for offensive operations in the Iran-Iraq War, but its seemingly somewhat effective role in the Sudan, Chad, and the Congo. Needed here is an integration of the factors of terrain and the "absorption" of weapons of technology. The Taliban and its Islamic foes in Afghanistan both have use of tactical airpower and armor left over by long-departed Soviet forces. Armored equipment has been in evidence in Abkhazia and Nagorno-Karabakh, also with John Garang's formerly ragtag army in southern Sudan. North Yemen employed airpower and tanks in its civil war; airpower and tanks have also been used in an urban civil war in

Congo-Brazzaville and in Angola. Both Ethiopia and Eritrea have used tactical aircraft for terror bombing of civilians in their recent (interstate) conflict. Libya used some airpower in fighting Chad, albeit with minimum effect.

The Near Absence of a Database on Arms Transfers for LICs

There is now a flourishing literature on small-arms transfers and the role of arms supplies in LICs, now primarily ethnopolitical wars. There is a parallel here with the literature on conventional wars where, as we have pointed out, so much of the focus is on the origins and causes of those wars, much less on their conduct. In the conventional area, there is a very adequate data base on arms resupply during recent wars, as so well laid out in numerous case studies in previously cited works by Harkavy, Neuman, Michael Brzoska and Fred Pearson. No equivalent data exist for arms supply and resupply to the combatants in LICs for the obvious reasons, namely, the extreme difficulties encountered in tracing small-arms transfers.

In one recent paper, John Sislin and Frederic Pearson set forth a number of hypotheses intended to get at the question of arms as a precipitator or cause of ethnopolitical wars.[5] That question is come at from both sides, whether arms acquisitions by insurrectionary groups propel them into wars, or whether acquisitions by incumbent regimes with dissident minorities impel them to pursue suppression of insurrectionary groups. Hence, if we were looking at the recent situation in Kosovo, we might ask whether KLA arms acquisitions from neighboring Albania were a major cause of conflict, or (not mutually exclusive) whether Russian arms shipments to Belgrade had emboldened the Yugoslav regime to try to snuff out the Kosovar independence movement.

But generally, across the board of LICs, there is a dearth of information that would allow for an analysis of the impact of arms acquisitions on the conduct and outcome of fighting. Ethnic and other identity groups accumulate arms through various means, including foreign shipments or purchase, battlefield capture, raids on depots, and indigenous production or modification.

Further, some smaller LICs require only small amounts of arms to conduct what are mostly hit-and-run wars. That is true of Peru's Shining Path, the IRA, the Basques, all seemingly adequately armed at low levels sufficient to their own purposes. Those ethnic-war participants involved in higher level combat, such as in Sri Lanka or Iraq's and Turkey's Kurdish regions, will require larger volumes of weapons and higher levels of sophistication, acquired by some combination of the aforenoted routes of acquisition.

The evidence so far is mostly episodic, somewhat anecdotal. The various factions in the endless Afghan civil war have fought mostly with Soviet weapons captured or abandoned on the battlefields of the 1980s. Georgian and Abkhazian forces rely on ex-Soviet arms left around after the collapse of the USSR. Eritreans have fought mostly with Soviet-origin weapons captured from the Ethiopian army. At the really low end of the conflict spectrum, such as Colombia's FARC or Peru's Shining Path, arms appear either to be captured or provided by private traders, maybe sometimes related to drug transactions. In many cases, of course, arms are provided by co-ethnics or co-religionists in contiguous states. The KLA receives arms from Albania, Garang's southern Sudan forces from neighboring states, the contending forces in Nagorno-Karabakh from Armenia and Azerbaijan.

Generally, there are no longer many cases of ethnopolitical violence sustained by geopolitically inspired support from one or the other superpower. Earlier, the USSR had armed revolutionary insurgents all over the world—Algeria, Vietnam, etc.—while the U.S. Reagan Doctrine armed insurgencies of the 1980s in Nicaragua, Afghanistan, etc. Russia's recent support for the Serbs is based on traditional Slavic-Orthodox consanguinity of sorts. But military support to current ethnopolitical wars has largely been removed from big-power rivalries. But in many cases—the Kurds, the Tamil Tigers, the Islamic insurrectionists in Algeria, the several revolutionary groups in Myanmar, the sources of arms, financing, and other types of support are relatively obscure.

One other point bears mention here, and that has to do with the time-urgency (or lack of same) for military resupply in LICs. In some past conventional wars—the 1973 Middle Eastern war, and the Iran-Iraq War to a lesser degree—battlefield outcomes hinged on air- and sealifts from major powers, or the introduction of this or that weapons system (recall Iran's furious quest around 1986 for surface-to-air missiles that could deal with attack helicopters, or Argentina's desperate quest for aircraft munitions at the height of the Falklands War). In many ethnic or other LICs, rival forces often have the discretion to slow the pace of fighting, to delay actions, to withdraw into bastions or enclaves, while awaiting further arms acquisitions.

High Casualties

Based on the measurement of severity (from the widely used COW project terminology), it is clear that the mortality numbers from numerous recent LICs, again mostly ethnopolitical conflicts, are strikingly high. They are indeed high relative to many of the more recent conventional wars, only perhaps partly due to the duration variable (the Iran-Iraq War was one big exception, likewise the Iraqi side of the Gulf War). Two problems intrude here regarding measurement. One is that the measurements themselves are subject to different interpretations from different sources. SIPRI has provided such estimates for all such conflicts for many years, both with cumulative and year-to-year data. But one sees a plethora of other such measurements in various journalistic and other accounts, and for whatever reason, the SIPRI data appear to be relatively conservative, that is, on the low side. Related to this problem is that of combining or separating out mortalities due to combat, and those perhaps only indirectly related to combat, i.e., starvation, exposure to the elements, disease, etc. And even here, there may be ambiguities regarding causation, i.e., how many people might have starved or might not have starved in Ethiopia, Sudan, or Somalia if wars had not been ongoing? Or, is there any relationship between war and the AIDS epidemic?

But arguments over data at the margins—even wide margins—cannot obscure the truly grisly facts of the slaughter caused by recent LICs (we have noted before the ethnocentric, if not outright racist, ignoring of these data in the West where socially distant peoples are involved). Following (in Table 8.1) are some of the basic data provided by SIPRI, and alternatively by other sources, for some recent wars.

Intrastate Dimensions of LIC

Although we tend to think of most LICs—mostly involving ethnopolitical conflict, hence, wars over government—as primarily internal affairs (i.e., civil wars), it is noteworthy that large numbers of them have involved cross-border implications. Often, that is because of ethnic/racial/religious bonds between one or another side in an LIC, and co-ethnics or co-religionists in contiguous states and in some cases from distant places. That then will often ramify into various forms of security assistance, ranging from arms supplies to economic assistance to outright intervention to diplomatic pressures (either directly on a combatant or indirectly via other client relationships).

"Lessons Learned" Studies

In the 1980s there had arisen a virtual vogue of "lessons learned" exercises in connection with major wars. "Lessons learned" reviews of war had long been standard practice within the U.S. military services and intelligence agencies, presumably elsewhere as well, albeit with some arguments about their didactic nature. But more recently, the interest in "lessons learned" (once mostly restricted to the realm of classified studies) has expanded to the public domain.

The coauthors of this work earlier produced two edited volumes on the lessons of then (mid-1980s) recent (conventional and unconventional) wars in the

Table 8.1 Cumulative Military and Civilian War-Related Deaths

Conflict	SIPRI data	Other Sources (Maximum)*
Angola	c. 140,000 1975–1998	500,000 1975–2000
Democratic Republic of Congo (Zaire)	c. 11,000 1996–1998	1,000,000 1975–2000
Mozambique	c. 122,000 1976–1991	500,000 1976–1992
Sudan	c. 40,000 1983–1991 (military deaths only)	2,000,000 1983–2000
Sri Lanka	c. 45,000 1996–1998	800,000 1985–2000

*Data provided by relevant U.S. State Department country desk officers, November–December 2000.

Third World. They involved case studies but also some comparative coverage of "functional" areas such as military geography and military economics. A bit later on, Anthony Cordesman and Abraham Wagner produced three volumes of detailed analysis—in all areas—of the military lessons of Afghanistan, the Falklands, Iran-Iraq and several of the Arab-Israeli wars. Those lessons were devolved down to the level of small-unit tactics and various weapons systems.

The Gulf War, not unexpectedly, produced some rather formal efforts at "lessons learned." Above all, that involved the Pentagon's own massive study, *The Conduct of the Persian Gulf War,* a truly remarkable and comprehensive study of all aspects of that war. Parallel to that was the U.S. Air Force's GWAPS study in several volumes, itself a very formal and self-consciously "lessons learned" exercise. Congress and the Center for Strategic and International Studies produced others,[6] albeit less formal and less massively detailed, as did one major Israeli think tank, obviously from an Israeli perspective.[7] And also, the Los Alamos National Laboratory commissioned, after the Gulf War, a large number of "lessons learned" papers written explicitly from the perspective of most of the major and second-tier countries (France, Russia et al., plus India, Pakistan, Israel et al.).[8] Such exercises appear now to be virtually institutionalized in anticipation of future major wars. That might not be the case for less-than-major conflicts.

The institutionalization of "lessons learned" was brought home to one of the authors of this book who witnessed a detailed "lessons learned" briefing by the German navy with regard to the experiences of the one ship it sent to the Somalia imbroglio in 1993. It has begun to approximate a kind of "role expectation."

Some persons may see these exercises as having become too inflated, maybe too lacking in humility. Every war, they might say, is sui generis, unique, subject to interpretation only in its own terms and no more. For them, "lessons learned" takes on the character of something unwarrantedly didactic, verging upon hubris. They would indeed prefer a less ambitious terminology—"insights gained," "questions raised," "issues broached," and so forth. Historians tend to this more modest view, while political scientists, by their very nature, are inclined toward attempts at generalization and comparison, if not truly didactic efforts to unearth actually usable "lessons," or even theories.

Of course, even with the best of intentions, there is not necessarily an "objective" perspective on "lessons learned." Such lessons are perceived from various temporal, national, and ideological perspectives. Without resorting to outright "deconstruction" of organized "lessons learned" exercises, following are some of the "angles of vision" problems involved.

- Various time perspectives or temporal vantage points—the value of hindsight and the associated issue (never fully resolved) of revisionist writings;
- Differing national perspectives on lessons learned—that is, U.S., Soviet, British, and various less-developed countries' (LDCs) perspectives, and the perspectives of combatant and noncombatant nations;
- Differing subnational perspectives—the analytical and political context of bureaucratic rivalries and the role of intraservice disputes as applied to lessons learned;

- A spectrum running from macro- to microlevel approaches to lessons learned—grand strategy, grand tactics, operational levels, small-unit tactics, and so on;
- Disciplinary perspectives on lessons learned (anthropology, political science, and so on) as they correlate with the aforementioned spectrum of macro- to microlevels;
- Ideological perspectives—Marxist, liberal, conservative, developed and underdeveloped "world";
- The uses of lessons learned for strictly analytical purposes versus as a propaganda vehicle (which may involve the issue of conscious versus subconscious uses);
- Losers' perspectives and winners' perspectives—either way, they both fight the last war;
- Negative versus positive lessons—what not to do again, what to do again;
- The direction of inferences—lessons applicable to a potential big-power war in Central Europe, to other Third World wars, and lessons applicable to the conduct of war versus those applicable merely to the diplomacy of warfare;
- The role of leadership and the depersonalization or bureaucratization of warfare as a historical datum;
- The application of "time-tested principles"—for instance, the use of Clausewitz's dicta as a checklist of sorts.

The problem of time lags or the amount of hindsight required for validly ascertaining lessons is a daunting one that may ultimately be unresolvable. One is reminded of the common claim, not entirely facetious, that a Metternich or a Bismarck could be adjudged "good" or "bad" (successful or unsuccessful) diplomats depending on which later—even *much* later—retrospective vantage points are used. The 1967 Arab-Israeli war offers an excellent example of this problem. Widely considered an unambiguous triumph for Israel until well after 1967, it is now viewed—even by strong Israeli supporters—as a mixed blessing, to the extent that it exacerbated Arab feelings of humiliation and produced additional irredentist claims and political problems.

Regarding such time perspectives, there might be a division between general perspectives or general trends, but then also the specific lessons attributed to a given war. In the former category, it is now apparent that the end of the Cold War and the coming to primacy of LIC in the 1990s has provided a wholly different perspective on warfare than existed a decade ago. Regarding specific wars, however, the nature of lessons—ranging from tactical to operational to strategic—may shift as time passes and the impact of early assumptions recede. The assumptions about the advent of PGMs, which were rife after the 1973 war, changed after a few years. So too, the nature of the 1967 Israeli victory. For that matter what had appeared an unalloyed victory for the U.S. and its allies in the immediate aftermath of the Gulf War in 1991 appeared much different ten years later, as military victory transmuted into political defeat. All kinds of general assumptions may be made subject to revisionist views. Early contrasts between

World War I as a war of attrition compared to World War II as a war of maneuver now give way to a new view that both were fundamentally wars of attrition.

Sometimes the significance of certain aspects of warfare only much later come to be recognized. Only much later was it recognized that some aspects of the Boer War and the Russo-Japanese war of 1905 were important indicators of what would be the nature of World War I, likewise the Japan-Japanese 1939 war in Mongolia as well as the Spanish Civil War as a precursor to World War II. Maybe only by the late 1990s was it becoming evident that terrorism against the U.S., as a form of "asymmetric strategy," was one of the most vital results and "lessons" of the Gulf War.[9]

Until recently, in terms of lessons learned, the problem of vantage point had been particularly acute. But by 1990, the now vaunted "peace epidemic" seems to have produced conclusions of sorts to the wars in the Persian Gulf, Afghanistan, Central America, Western Sahara and Chad, among others, allowing at least for a first post hoc cut at "lessons." Whether those lessons would, historically, prove durable and the extent to which historians would agree over them remained to be seen.

In some cases, of course, cessation of hostilities may or may not be "permanent." In some cases, the end of hostilities may later be perceived as a breathing spell; that is, there may yet be additional rounds whose conduct and outcomes may greatly alter perceptions of the lessons of earlier rounds that have been the subjects of numerous instant histories (Lebanon, the Horn of Africa, and perhaps China-Vietnam or the Falklands).

The uncertainties apply not only to predominantly politico-military lessons but perhaps also to strictly military ones (that is, tactical or doctrinal). If Argentina were to be more successful with submarines or air-to-ship missiles in a new round, or if Syrian surface-to-air missiles (SAMs) were to be more effective in a new Lebanon round—particularly if such wars were to take place soon—perceptions of the first rounds' lessons would surely be altered or at least rendered very ephemeral. Certainly from the vantage point of the 1980s, the lessons of 1973 had been modified by the broader perspective provided by the lessons of 1982—perhaps with a natural overall centripetal tendency toward perception of more even, incremental change.

There are numerous external vantage points, of course, from which lessons may be read from Third World wars. There is an American view, a French view, a Soviet view, a Chinese view, and many others, including those of numerous watchful smaller powers that are themselves in situations of potential conflict. The Falklands War, for instance, may have been read by U.S. naval experts primarily in the context of the ongoing debate between respective advocates of large and small carriers (which also illustrates the role of "lessons" in interservice and even intraservice doctrinal and budgetary battles). In the USSR, however, the ease with which British nuclear-attack submarines rendered the Argentine surface fleet useless may have been seen as the most instructive lesson.[10] There is also the rather murky, not easily answered question of what lessons are read into war outcomes by the relevant Third World military planners themselves and how such lessons are then applied. Just such a division of perspectives would, for instance, impel one to question whether Egyptian military leaders' evaluations of the 1967 war were congruent with those of Western military historians and, if not, whether the differences would involve essentially "nonrational" factors—that is, a lack of sufficient detachment.[11]

Sometimes one regional power will read lessons from a conflict in a neighboring region, in a seemingly related but distinct context. Pakistani military planners are claimed (ironically, in view of their long-time hostility to Israel) to have thought in terms of imitating the 1967 Israeli blitzkrieg to achieve a quick thrust into the Indian heartland, the facts of strategic depth notwithstanding. Thanks to the Los Alamos lab's near-global study of how various nations perceived the lessons of the Gulf War, we have for the first time a comprehensive coverage of such diverse perceptions. India, for instance, was seen recognizing that even a nation of its power and size could not match a Desert Storm-type onslaught, but that it might develop some niche technologies in some areas of the MTR (such as more effective SAMs) so as to provide some deterrence against such an onslaught.[12] Others obviously (as inferred from subsequent history) drew more pessimistic conclusions about their ability to meet the U.S. head-on, and strove to achieve deterrence via "asymmetric strategies" such as terrorism or the ability to launch "triangular" strikes against nearby U.S. allies and friends.[13]

The facts of who has won or lost wars may have an important bearing on how those wars are adjudged regarding "lessons." The claim is sometimes made that a loss in one war, if not fatal, can prove an advantage in planning for the next one. The losers rethink tactics and strategies; also they replace failed leaders and elevate those who performed well in a losing cause. Meanwhile, the winners tend to be locked into "proven" strategies, perhaps even to the point of intensifying or concentrating on previously successful tactics, even as the context defined by new weapons developments is altered, perhaps crucially. Hence, van Creveld notes Israel's increasing reliance on "King Tank" and its armored shock effect after 1967, even as new developments in antitank weapons were creating the need for a shift toward a more balanced arms approach.[14] (This view was subject, again, to new interpretation after 1982.) Pakistan's misreading of the approximate standoff it achieved against larger India in 1965 may have had a major influence on its disaster in 1971; in addition, Pakistan appeared, as noted, prone to misapplying lessons it apparently thought it could apply from the intervening Israeli victory in 1967. Jordan was apparently so overawed by the Israeli performance in 1967 and so dismayed by its own blunder in getting involved that it stayed out of the initial phases of the 1973 war, which may well have cost the Arabs a possible victory.

The winners of wars often are misled into thinking themselves omnipotent, or into applying successful lessons in subsequent wars, maybe even against different opponents. Iraq had success against Iran with massive, layered fixed defenses, backed by a road system that allowed for rapid redeployment of mobile reserves—a "mobile defense." It banked on causing massive attrition to its enemies. The same strategy applied against the U.S.-led coalition in 1991 was a total failure, given the U.S. control of the air, superior battlefield surveillance provided by satellites, and technological prowess in combined arms operations, or even offensives against layered fixed defenses. The basic strategy of deterrence via anticipated high attrition was theoretically correct, but impossible to execute against an enemy far more capable than Iran.

Sometimes the winner of a war may conclude that, victory notwithstanding, its basic strategy or force postures need wholesale change. China "won" the brief war in 1979 against Vietnam, but its leadership then concluded that the PLA was too manpower intensive, too backwards technologically, and particularly lacking in tactical airpower. The result was a massive restructuring of the PLA.

Roger Beaumont has pointed out, with considerable cogency, that the lessons of war (and, presumably other categories of lessons) might be further divided into positive and negative lessons—that is, what to do again because it worked and what not to do again.[15] This distinction involves more than a clever verbal trick; indeed, it may provide fertile ground for theorizing in the context of the extensive literature on the psychological dimensions of decision making. For instance, it may alert us to examine the concept of satisficing (satisfactory decisions short of maximizing) and to generalizations about why decision makers instinctively concentrate on avoiding mistakes at the expense of more positive, risky, and aggressive aims. That is, it is possible that a negative lesson ("Let's not repeat that blunder") may be more salient and may receive more attention than a positive one, even to the point of weighting overall analysis.

A football analogy may be pertinent here. Penn State's football coach Joe Paterno was once quoted to the effect that "you are never as bad as you seem when you lose, never as good as you appear when you win." That may be peculiarly apt with regard to the serial Arab-Israel wars. Egyptian troops fought hard on the defensive at the beginning of the war, in the Gaza Strip at Rafah, and at Abu Agheila. But the Egyptians cracked, were routed by armored "shock," and the outcome seemed to indicate a truly vast disparity between Israel and its foe. For that reason, the outset of the 1973 war came as a surprise. But then, the stunning initial reversals suffered by the Israelis in 1973 seemed to presage, particularly for their air force, a permanently rough time, a prediction not borne out at the outset of the 1982 war.

"Paterno's dictum" could indeed be applicable elsewhere. It is not clear that the Argentinian forces are as bad—or the British as good—as the Falklands War appeared to indicate. The Iranians may not be as inept as they appeared, particularly in 1988—what they could do under effective military leadership appears yet to be learned.

The U.S. Army seems to have benefited from some of the negative lessons of Vietnam, notwithstanding the fact that in a narrow sense it never really suffered military defeats there. The lessons had to do with the need for public support back home and—strategically—the need to use overwhelming force to achieve a quick, decisive victory in lieu of the "ratchet" escalations of the Vietnam War. These were translated through the so-called Powell Doctrine, which eventuated in the overwhelming and virtually costless victory in Desert Storm. Kosovo has, of course, provided still newer lessons of a perhaps more ambiguous sort.

The role of leadership, whether at the level of supreme commanders, or involving layers of military elites, is a subject that remains highly obscured in contemporary military analysis, all the more curious as it was such a centerpiece of traditional military histories. Those histories focused on the theories, foibles, and battlefield execution of all of the great captains from Scipio Africanus to Frederick to Napoleon, and many more. Even after World War II, the roles of Montgomery, Bradley, MacArthur, Patton, Rommel, Guderian et al., were closely studied, it being assumed that that leadership, good or bad, was an important variable in analyzing the course of warfare and ultimate victory and defeat. Some of these leaders' names are emblematic of certain strategies or patterns of warfare: Guderian for blitzkrieg armored warfare, Rommel for desert warfare, Patton also for rapid armored warfare, MacArthur in connection with daring leapfrog amphibious warfare during World War II and at Inchon in Korea.

Somehow that tradition of military history has largely been lost in the post–World War II period. True, there have been analyses of the generalship of Ridgway in Korea, Westmoreland in Vietnam, and Schwarzkopf in Desert Storm (the latter and his aides given credit for the famous left hook/Hail Mary offensive against Iraq in 1990). During the Falklands War, victorious British admiral Sandy Woodward and General Jeremy Moore were acclaimed for a near textbook-perfect victorious strategy. During India's also near perfect military operation in 1971, General Manekshaw became very visible in the West.

During the Iran-Iraq War, almost nothing emerged about the military leadership on either side. The focus of the press was entirely on the political leadership, pitting Saddam Hussein and his surrounding entourage from Tikrit against Khomeini and the mullahs. To his credit, however, Edgar O'Ballance provides some detail on the changing military leadership on both sides, pointing to the crucial roles of several Iraqi generals—Abdul Jawad Zanoun, Hisham Sabah al-Fakhri, and Saadi Tuma Abbas—in explaining the important Iraqi victories after 1985.[16]

Regarding many of the LICs, however, very little is available on the roles of key generals or smaller-unit commanders in explaining victory or defeat, save perhaps in such cases as Bosnia, where some leaders became notorious for massacres and war crimes. There is little regarding strategic debates between contending military commanders. One exception: the role of General Garang in southern Sudan in conducting a seemingly successful, long-term insurgency against the central Khartoum regime, moving from guerilla warfare to something approximating limited conventional warfare. It is a vast gulf in the literature of modern warfare.

A few other leaders have gained some attention with respect to regional conventional wars. Numerous Israeli generals became famous because of the exploits in 1956, 1967, and 1973: Dayan and Rabin for overall leadership; Joffe, Tal, Sharon, and Gavish in connection with rapid armored warfare; Eitan in connection with the defense of Golan in 1973; Hod for the successful preemptive air attacks at the outset of the 1967 war. Likewise, several of the high-level Indian commanders in the speedy 1971 blitzkrieg into East Bengal became the subjects of military analysis, particularly General Manekshaw. General Giap's leadership in Vietnam (he was a leading theorist of insurgency warfare) drew accolades. But even in many large-scale conventional wars (China/Vietnam, Ethiopia/Somalia), the names and the roles—good or bad—of military leadership have been totally obscured.

Summary: Warfare at the Turn of the Century

As previously stated, there is always a great risk in predicting the future on the basis of extrapolation from the past. Therefore, it is not easy to say whether in the first couple of decades of the twenty-first century warfare will continue to be defined mostly by the examples recently set in Sierra Leone, the Congo, Kosovo, Chechnya, Bougainville, Timor, Colombia et al, and by the absence of major interstate conventional warfare. The nature of ethnopolitical warfare, featuring contests over territory, partition, and devolution, is not likely to change from its present basis in massacres, ethnic cleansing, small-unit operations, roadblocks manned by drunken or drugged teenagers, the covert small-arms trade, the use of mercenaries, and the role of co-ethnic external security assistance. Some increase in the use of major weapons platforms might also be anticipated. At stake here, presumably, is the question of the frequency, duration, and lethality of such conflicts, and their geographic distribution, as well as the response by the so-called international community as regards peacemaking and peacekeeping. If present trends predict the future, then instruments short of armed force increasingly will be used by the international community to intervene.

Major conventional interstate warfare is harder to predict. Although dormant for the past decade, the continuing threat of war between the Arabs and Israel, India and Pakistan, and across the Taiwan Straits raises the question of what will happen if the balloon should go up in one or more of these cases. That, to a large degree, involves questions concerning modernization à la Military Technical Revolution, and how that in turn might affect the equation between wars of attrition and of maneuver. Could Israel again conduct a lightning preemptive offensive against an Arab coalition including Egypt? Could India do better in launching a successful offensive in the Punjab region than it did in 1965 and 1971? Could China launch a successful amphibious operation against Taiwan? With no major wars having been fought since 1990–91, there is little to go by in assessing the pace of modern military technological development. Now, of course, in each of these cases there is the looming prospect of use of weapons of mass destruction (nuclear, chemical, biological), most likely by a side fearing collapse and defeat on the conventional battlefield. One has the sense that the "obsolescence of war" thesis is yet to be tested fully. With it might be tested some of the war-fighting issues raised in this book, after a decade or so of very relative quiescence.

APPENDIX 1

Distribution of Major (Ongoing) Armed Conflicts 1986–98

NOTE: Miscellaneous information post–1998 has been included when significant.

SOURCE: Data unless otherwise noted is drawn from SIPRI YEARBOOK 1987–1998.

Key to Appendix 1 Symbols

mil.	Military battle-related deaths; where there is no indication of mil. or civ. (below), the figure refers to total military and civilian battle-related deaths in the specified period or year given.
civ.	Civilian battle-related deaths; where there is no indication of mil. or civ., the figure refers to total military and civilian battle-related deaths in the specified period or year given.
(★[date])	Figure includes deaths in that year.
. . .	Information unknown.
Combatant ([date]/[date])	Year armed conflict began or recommenced/Year of peace treaty, military victory, or cessation of hostilities when known.

Distribution of Major (Ongoing) Armed Conflicts 1986–98

REGION/ State	COMBATANT	COMBATANT	COMBATANT	COMBATANT	COMBATANT	COMBATANT	TOTAL DEATHS[1]
AFRICA							
Algeria (Govt)[2]	vs. FIS:Front Islamic du Salut, Jibhat al-Inqath (Islamic Salvation Front)[3] 1992[4]	vs. GIA:Groupe Islamique Armé (Armed Islamic Group) 1993					40,000–100,000 (*1998)
Angola (Govt)	SWAPO: South West African People's Organization, Namibia 1975/1988	Cuba (Govt) 1975/1988	vs. S. Africa (Govt) 1987/1988	vs. UNITA: União Nacional para a Independência Total de Angola (National Union for the Total Independence of Angola)[6] 1975/1996[5] 1998/	vs. FNLA: Frente Naciona oara a Libertação de Angola (Angolan National Liberation Front)[6] 1975/1990(?)	vs. FLEC Frente da Libertação do Enclave de Cabinda (Front for the Liberation of the Enclave of Cabinda) 1975/1991[7]	>40,000 (mil.) >100,000 (civ.)[8] (*1996) >1000 (*1998)
Burundi (Govt)	vs. CNDD: Conseil National pour la Défense de la Démocratie (National Council for the Defense of Democracy)[9] 1994						>2000[10] (*1998)

1. Total death figures refer to total battle-related deaths during the conflict. (Mil.) and (Civ.) refer, where figures are available, to military and civilian deaths respectively; where there is no such indication, the figure refers to total military and civilian battle-related deaths during the conflict. Dates enclosed in parentheses indicate deaths in the period or year given. Dates enclosed in parentheses with an asterisk (*date) indicate that the figure includes deaths in that year.

Distribution of Major (Ongoing) Armed Conflicts 1986–98 (continued)

REGION/ State	COMBATANT	COMBATANT	COMBATANT	COMBATANT	COMBATANT	COMBATANT	TOTAL COMBATANT DEATHS[1]
Chad (Govt)[11]	vs. MDD Mouvement pour la Démocratie et le Developpement (Movement for Democracy and Development)[12]	vs. CSNPD: Committeo of National Revival for Peace and Democracy	vs. Forces of Koti	vs. FNT: Front Nationale du Tchad (Chadian National Front)	vs. FAO: Forces Armées Occidentales (Western Armed Forces)	vs. Libyan Govt (Aozou Strip)	1992: 300–600
	1989	1992	1992	1992	1992?	1979/1990	

2. Algeria witnessed the rise of Islamic militancy after the government's cancellation of the 1991 elections which would have brought Islamic parties to power.

3. The Islamic Salvation Army (Armé Islamique du Salut–AIS) is considered to be the armed wing of FIS. There are several other armed Islamic groups under the FIS.

4. See Key, p. 333. Date=year armed conflict began or recommenced; /Date=year of peace treaty or military victory when known. It is often difficult to know when various combatants are no longer participants in a conflict. Absent a formal peace treaty or cease-fire, groups listed may no longer be active or may simply disappear for many reasons: defeat, exhaustion, mergers among combatants or coalitions, unpublicized deals with the government. Others may simply disband and disappear. Even when peace treaty and/or cease-fire dates are available, it may not mean that all factions and parties accept the terms of the agreement or that violence might not again erupt. Many of the conflicts in this table are serial conflicts that may go into remission for periods of time but erupt again at a later date.

5. In 1997 the peace process ran into renewed trouble, and armed conflict broke out anew in 1998. The Angolan government's involvement in the war in Congo (Brazzaville) and its support for the ADFL in Zaire were related to the conflict with its opponent, UNITA, which in turn was associated with the Mobutu regime in Zaire.

6. FNLA was a reported faction of FLEC. According to the government 1,003 former resistance movement UPA/FNLA (Union of Angolan People/Angolan National Liberation Front) troops surrendered in January 1990.

7. The conflict between the government and FLEC concerned the oil-rich Cabinda enclave. The government agreed in October 1991 to negotiate autonomy and a greater share of oil revenues for Cabinda and requested the Portuguese government's assistance in negotiating a resolution to the conflict.

8. An estimated 1.5 million war-related deaths (military and civilian) from 1975, of which approximately 50 percent occurred since the war restarted in October 1992.

9. The Hutu-based opposition to the Tutsi government of Pierre Buyoya was formed in 1994, led by Leonard Nyangoma.

10. Political violence in Burundi since 1993, involving groups other than the CNDD, has claimed a total of at least a hundred thousand lives.

11. Numerous factions in Chad in changing alliances have fought for control since the mid-1960s. Hissene Habre seized *defacto* power in 1982 and became President that year. In December 1990 Idriss Déby seized power. The 1996 and 2001 presidential elections returned him to power.

12. A coalition of former President Habré loyalists and remnants of FANT.

Distribution of Major (Ongoing) Armed Conflicts 1986–98 (continued)

REGION/State	COMBATANT	COMBATANT	COMBATANT	COMBATANT	COMBATANT	COMBATANT	COMBATANT	COMBATANT	TOTAL COMBATANT DEATHS[1]
Congo (Govt) Brazzaville	vs. FDU: Forces Démocratiques Unies (United Democratic Forces)[13] 1997/1997	vs. Govt. of Angola 1997/1997							4000–7000 (*1997)
Democratic Republic of Congo (Govt)	Angola 1998/	Namibia 1998/	Zimbabwe 1998/	vs. RCD: Reassemblement Congolais pour la Démocratie (Congolese Democratic Rally) 1998/	vs. MLC: Mouvement de libération Congolais (Congolese Liberation Movement) 1998/	vs. Rwanda 1998/	vs. Uganda 1998/		>2000 (*1998)
Ethiopia (Govt)	Cuba (Govt) 1977/1988	vs. Somalia (Govt) 1977/1988							Ethiopia: 1964–86: 38,000 Cuba: 1980–88: 2,000
Ethiopia	vs. EPRP: Ethiopian People's Revolutionary Party 1975/1991[14]	TPLF:Tigray People's Liberation Front 1976/(1989)	vs.OLF: Oromo Liberation Front 1977/1991	vs. AFL.Afar Liberation Front 1975/1991	vs.EPRDF: Ethiopian People's Revolutionary Democratic Front[15] 1989/1991				1962–91: 150,000–200,000 (mil.)
Ethiopia (Govt)	vs. Eritrea (Govt) 1998/								>1000 (1998)

Distribution of Major (Ongoing) Armed Conflicts 1986–98 (continued)

REGION/ State	COMBATANT	COMBATANT	COMBATANT	COMBATANT	COMBATANT	COMBATANT	COMBATANT	TOTAL DEATHS[1]
Guinea–Bissau	Senegal (Govt)	Guinea (Govt)	vs. Military Faction					>1000 (1998)
Liberia (Govt)	vs. ECOMOG: The ECOWAS [Economic Community of West African States] Monitor- ing Group. 1989/1996	vs. NPFL: National Patriotic Front of Liberia[16] 1989/1996[17]						1989–1992: 20,000[18]
Morocco (Govt)	vs. Polisario: People's Front for the Liberation of Saguiet El Hamra and Rio DE Oro 1976/1991[19]							10,000–13,000 (*1989)[20]

13. A short but severe civil war erupted in 1997 resulting in the victory of Denis Sassou-Nguesso. Armed action was primarily carried out by the Cobras, the private militia of FDU leader Sassou-Nguesso. This conflict had been successfully contained by international mediation since 1993.

14. The EPRP was the first major force to oppose Mengistu Haile Mariam. A faction of EPRP members formed a movement in 1991 called Forum 84, which rallied behind the new Ethiopian regime.

15. In 1989 the TPLF and a newly organized party, the EPDM (Ethiopian People's Democratic Movement) merged as the EPRDF.

16. Maintains close ties with RUF in Sierra Leone.

17. In August 1995, seven armed factions in Liberia (including the NPFL) signed a peace agreement, and their leaders formed a transitional Council of State. Implementation of the 1995 peace treaty was disrupted by fighting in 1996 between two new conflicting parties, the Ulimo-J (Roosevelt-Johnson faction) fighting both the government and ECOMOG, following the suspension of Johnson from the cabinet.

18. Note that this figure includes the fighting in 1990–91 (incurring fifteen thousand deaths) in which more than the two parties listed above participated.

19. UN-monitored cease-fire came into effect at the end of 1991.

20. Figures for up to 1989. Military activity during 1990 was low.

Distribution of Major (Ongoing) Armed Conflicts 1986–98 (continued)

REGION/ State	COMBATANT	COMBATANT	COMBATANT	COMBATANT	COMBATANT	COMBATANT	TOTAL COMBATANT DEATHS[1]
Mozambique (Govt)	Govt of Zimbabwe 1976/1992	vs. RENAMO: Resistência Nacional Moçambicana (Mozambican National Resistance, MNR or RENAMO) 1976/1992[21]					10,000 – 12,000 (mil.) 110,000 (civ.) (*1991)
Namibia (Govt) (So. West Africa)	S. Africa (Govt) 1967/1988	SWAPO: South West African People's Organization (based in Angola) 1967/1988					1967–84: >10,000 1985–87:1,500 1988: 1,000
Rwanda	vs. RPF: Front Patriotique Rwandais (Rwandan Patriotic Front) 1990/1994[22]	vs. Opposition Alliance: Forces Armées Rwandaises (Rwandan Armed Forces) and the Interahamwé militia 1998/					1990–93: 5500 1998: >1500

Distribution of Major (Ongoing) Armed Conflicts 1986–98 (continued)

REGION/State	COMBATANT	COMBATANT	COMBATANT	COMBATANT	COMBATANT	COMBATANT	TOTAL COMBATANT DEATHS[1]
Senegal (Govt)	vs. MFDC: Mouvement des Forces Démocratiques de la Casamance (Movement of Democratic Forces of Casamance) 1982						>1000[23] (*1998)
Sierra Leone (Govt)	vs. RUF: Revolutionary United Front[24] 1991/1996[25] 1998/						>5000[26] (*1998)
Somalia (Govt)	vs. SNM: Somali National Movement 1981/	DFSS: Democratic Front for the Salvation of Somalia 1981/	SPM: Somali Patriotic Movement 1989/				1988–89: >700,000

21. A mediated peace accord, signed in October 1992, brought the civil war to an uneasy peace, which was supported by UN peacekeeping operations.

22. RPF took control of most of the country by July 1994. The previous government fled with its troops to neighboring Tanzania and Zaire.

23. The protracted conflict over the territory of Casamance, which began in 1982, reached the threshold of a thousand deaths in 1997, and there were no signs of an early end to this conflict.

24. Maintains close ties with NPFL in Liberia.

25. A peace agreement in 1996 led to a reduction of fighting among previous combatants, but led to the formation of a new alliance after a military coup in May 1997 when the former opposition organization, RUF, and the army joined together in the new government. The conflict was further complicated as Nigerian forces, under the umbrella of ECOMOG, confronted the new government on the side of the overthrown civilian government. ECOMOG, established in 1990, is the monitoring group of the Economic Community of West African States (ECOWAS). Fighting resumed with over fifteen hundred deaths in 1998.

26. Includes approximately three thousand war-related deaths since 1991.

Distribution of Major (Ongoing) Armed Conflicts 1986–98 (continued)

REGION/ State	COMBATANT	COMBATANT	COMBATANT	COMBATANT	TOTAL DEATHS[1]
Somalia (Govt) (Taken to be the USC (United Somali Congress faction [Mahdi])	vs. USC faction (Aideed) 1991/1997[27]				. .[28]
South Africa	vs. ANC: African National Congress; armed wing: MK, Umkhonto we Sizwe 1961/1993–94[29]	vs. PAC: Pan Africanist Congress; armed wing: APLA, Azanian People's Liberation Army 1992/1993–94	vs. AZAPO: Azanian People's Organization; armed wing: AZANLA, Azanian National Liberation Army 1992/1993–94	vs. FA: Freedom Alliance (Conservative Party, Inkatha Freedom Party, Afrikaner VolksFront, and the leaders of the homeland governments of Bophuthatswana and Ciskei) 1993/1993–94	1984–93: 18,900
Sudan (Govt)	vs. NDA: National Democratic Alliance[30] 1983				37,000–40,000 (mil.)[31]
Uganda (Govt)[32]	vs. LRA: Lord's Resistance Army 1994	vs. ADF: Alliance of Democratic Forces 1996			1986–90: >12,000 >2000 (*1998)

Distribution of Major (Ongoing) Armed Conflicts 1986–98 (continued)

REGION/ State	COMBATANT	COMBATANT	COMBATANT	COMBATANT	COMBATANT	COMBATANT	TOTAL COMBATANT DEATHS[1]
Zaire (Govt)[33]	vs. ADFL: Alliance des Forces Democratiques pour la Libération du Congo– Kinshasa (Alliance of Democratic Forces for the Liberation of Congo-Kinshasa) 1996/1997	vs. Rwanda[34] 1996/1997					4000–9000 (★1997)

27. In 1997, large scale fighting abated among the combatants. The Ethiopian-backed Sodere Declarations of January 1997, uniting twenty-six Somali factions in the National Salvation Council, changed the political situation toward a climate of negotiation. The Hussein Aideed faction, which did not join the negotiations initially, did become involved in subsequent negotiations in Cairo in November 1997. The only major faction rejecting all negotiations was the Somali National Movement of Somaliland, because it considers Somaliland to be independent and no longer part of Somalia.

28. Total deaths unknown. The following yearly figures are recorded by SIPRI: 1996: 300–600; 1995:200–500; 1992:3000–4000; 1991:10,000–25,000; 1988–1991: 60,000 (civ. and mil.).

29. Long-running conflict between the antiapartheid opposition and the white minority government ended in late 1993, and the peace settlement was ratified by the elections in May 1994.

30. In 1996, the Sudanese People's Liberation Army (SPLA), which had been fighting the Sudanese government for secession of the south, was reported to have bases in Uganda and to be receiving support from the Ugandan government. (The SPLA is the military wing of the SPLM [Sudan People's Liberation Movement].)

Fighting between Sudanese and Ugandan opposition organizations complicated the situation. The prospects for more neighboring countries becoming involved was high, with Ethiopia and Eritrea supporting a more united opposition against the regime in Khartoum. In late 1996, the SPLM entered into an alliance with leaders from the north in the hope of overthrowing the National Islamic Front government in Khartoum. The NDA is an alliance of several southern and northern opposition organizations, of which the SPLM is the largest. SPLM leader John Garang is also the leader of the NDA. By the end of 1997, the military situation on the ground had not changed significantly.

31. Figure for up to 1991.

32. Several armed resistance groups confronted the NRM (National Resistance Movement) government after it seized power in January 1986. The number of these groups decreased during the following years.

33. The conflict began late 1996 and ended 16 May 1997 with the victory of the ADFL, led by Laurent Kabila. After the ADFL victory, the name of the country was changed to the Democratic Republic of Congo.

34. The ADFL received support from Rwanda and indirect support from Angola, Burundi, and Uganda.

Distribution of Major (Ongoing) Armed Conflicts 1986–98 (continued)

REGION/ State	COMBATANT	COMBATANT	COMBATANT	COMBATANT	COMBATANT	COMBATANT	TOTAL COMBATANT DEATHS[1]
Zimbabwe (Mugabe Govt)	vs. ZAPU: Zimbabwe African National Union 1980/1986	Other Dissidents 1980/					1979–87: >1,500
ASIA							
Afghanistan (Govt)	USSR 1978/1988	vs. Jamiat-e-Islami 1978	vs. Hezb-e-Wahdat 1990	vs. Uzbek militia (Dostum) 1992	vs. Taliban 1994/1996[35]	vs. Jumbish-i-Milli-ye Islami (National Islamic Movement [NIM]) 1992	>20,000[36] (*1997)
Bangladesh (Govt)	vs. JSS/SB: Parbatya Chattagram Jana Sanghati Samiti (Chittagong Hill Tracts People's Co-ordination Association/ Shanti Bahini [Peace Force]) 1982/1997[37]						1975–: 3000–3500 (*1997)
Cambodia (Kampuchea) (Govt)	vs. PDK: Party of Democratic Kampuchea (Khmer Rouge) 1979/1992–3						>25,500 (*1997)

Distribution of Major (Ongoing) Armed Conflicts 1986–98 (continued)

REGION/ State	COMBATANT	COMBATANT	COMBATANT	COMBATANT	COMBATANT	COMBATANT	COMBATANT	TOTAL DEATHS[1]
China[38]	vs. Vietnam 1979/1979							1979: 21,000 (mil) 9,000 (civ) 1980–87: 1,000 1988: <100
India (Govt)[39]	vs. Kashmir insurgents[40] 1989	vs. ATTF: All Tripura Tribal Force 1992	vs. ULFA: United Liberation Front of Assam 1988	vs. Sikh insurgents 1981/1995[41]	vs. PLA: People's Liberation Army 1991	vs. NSCN: National Socialist Council of Nagaland . . ./	vs. BdSF: Bodo Security Force 1992	>20,000 (Kashmir conflict only) (*1997) 25,000 (Sikh conflict only) (*1995)
India (Govt)	vs. Pakistan (Govt) 1947, 1965, 1971, 1984, 1992, 1996/							1971: 11,000 (mil) . . .

35. In late 1996, the Taliban took control of large parts of Afghanistan, including the capital. Other groups united against them. (By 1999, the Taliban controlled almost all of Afghanistan.) The new government had not won recognition from countries other than Pakistan, Saudi Arabia and the UAE. Other countries with diplomatic relations with Afghanistan recognized the deposed government, which had the country's seat in the UN General Assembly. [Economist, 6–12 February 1999, p. 41])

36. This figures includes deaths in fighting since 1992 in which parties other than those listed above participated.

37. The Chittagong Hill Tracts dispute in Bangladesh ended in 1997, but some instances of internal rioting and unrest occurred as a result.

38. Although China withdrew from Vietnam in 1979, border skirmishes continued.

39. In 1992, in addition to the above combatants, there were the JMM (Jharkand Multi Morcha), MCC (Maoist Communist Centre), and the People's War Group fighting the Indian government. These groups do not appear in the SIPRI data after 1992.

40. According to the Indian government, approximately 180 groups of Kashmiri insurgents existed in 1992, 140 in 1991, and 60 in 1990. By 1997, SIPRI reports that "several" groups are active; some of the most important are the Jammu and Kashmir Liberation Front (JKLF), the Hizb-e-Mujahideen, and the Harkat-ul-Ansar.

41. Several Sikh groups exist. There were also reportedly over twenty-four Sikh organizations and splinter groups in existence in 1992. However, by 1995, few Sikh insurgents were active. In 1996, it was reported that Sikh groups were aligning themselves with Kashmiri factions rather than giving up the armed struggle.

Distribution of Major (Ongoing) Armed Conflicts 1986–98 (continued)

REGION/ State	COMBATANT	COMBATANT	COMBATANT	COMBATANT	COMBATANT	COMBATANT	TOTAL COMBATANT DEATHS[1]
Indonesia (Govt)	vs. Fretilin: Frente Revolucionária Timorense de Libertação e Independência (Revolutionary Front for an Independent East Timor) 1975/	vs. OPM: Organisasi Papua Merdeka (Free Papua Movement) 1984/	vs. Aceh Merdeka (Sumatra) 1989/1991[42]	vs. National Liberation Front of Aceh (Sumatra) 1989/1991			15,000– 16,000 (mil.)[43] (*1998)
Laos (Govt)	vs. opposition groups (probably ULNLF: United Lao National Liberation Front) 1975/	vs. Free Democratic Lao National Salvation Force 1992/					...
Laos (Pathet Lao Govt)	Vietnam 1976/1988	vs. Thailand 1976/1988					1975–88: 10,000 (mil.) 30,000 (civ.)
Malaysia (Govt)	Thailand (Govt)	vs. CPM and CPT: Communist Party of Malaysia[44] and Communist Party of Thailand					

REGION/State	COMBATANT	COMBATANT	COMBATANT	COMBATANT	COMBATANT	COMBATANT	COMBATANT	TOTAL DEATHS[1]
Myanmar (Govt)	vs. KNU: Karen National Union (KNLA: Karen National Liberation Army: armed wing of KNU) 1948	vs. MTA Mong Tai Aung[45] 1993[46]/1996[47]	vs. ABSDF: All Burma Student's Democratic Front 1991/	vs. Arakan insurgents 1991/	vs. KIO/KIA: Kachin Independence Organization/Army .../	vs. KNPP: Karenni National Progressive Party 1992/	vs. Naga insurgents (probably NSCN: National Socialist Council of Nagaland) 1992	1948–50 8,000 1981–88 5000–8500 1993–94 >1000[48]
Pakistan (Govt)	vs. Pathan/Baluchi separatists 1972/1987							1973–77: 3,000 (mil.) 6,000 (civ.)
Philippines (Govt)	vs. NPA: New People's Army 1968	vs. MNLF: Moro National Liberation Front (armed wing–Bangsa Moro Army) 1986/1990(?)						21,000–25,000[49] (*1998)

42. Government subdued the secessionist Aceh movement in the northern tip of Sumatra.

43. Only the conflict between the government and Fretilin.

44. CPM guerillas were mainly based in Thailand and in border areas (as were some of the CPT). Since amnesty was offered and some members of the CPM surrendered to the Thai government in 1988, no activity was reported in the SIPRI YEARBOOK.

45. Fighting for the independence of the Shan state.

46. The Mong Tai Army was formed in 1987, but it is unclear when the demand for independence of the Shan state was declared. Armed conflict with the government broke out in December 1993.

47. Peace was achieved by the victory of the Myanmar government, but splinter groups vowed to keep up the struggle after the surrender in early January 1996 of the MTA leader, Khun Sa, which observers considered resulted from a deal with the government connected to the heroin trade.

48. This figure includes deaths only in the Shan conflict. (SIPRI YEARBOOK, 1996)

49. Official military sources claim that sixty-five hundred civilians were killed during 1985–91.

Distribution of Major (Ongoing) Armed Conflicts 1986–98 (continued)

REGION/ State	COMBATANT	COMBATANT	COMBATANT	COMBATANT	COMBATANT	COMBATANT	COMBATANT	TOTAL DEATHS[1]
Sri Lanka (Govt)	Indian Govt (IPKF:Indian Peace Keeping Forces) Dec. 1987/ Mar. 1990	vs. LTTE: Liberation Tigers of Tamil Eelam 1983/	vs. JVP: Sinhalese People's Liberation Front 1987/1990					>45,000 (*1998)
Tajikistan (Govt)	CIS Collective Peace Keeping Force in Tajikistan/ CIS Border Troops[50] 1992/1996	vs. United Tajik Opposition[51] 1992/1996[52]						20,000–50,000 (*1996)
CENTRAL AND SOUTH AMERICA								
Colombia (Govt)	vs. FARC: Fuerzas Armadas Revolucionarias Colombianas (Revolutionary Armed Forces of Colombia) 1978	vs. ELN: Ejército de Liberación Nacional (National Liberation Army) 1978	vs. EPL: Ejército Popular de Liberación 1977/1991(?)					...[53]
El Salvador (Govt)	vs. FMLN: Farabundo Marti Front for National Liberation[54] 1979/1991[55]							1979–91: 77,000– 82,000

Distribution of Major (Ongoing) Armed Conflicts 1986–98 (continued)

REGION/ State	COMBATANT	COMBATANT	COMBATANT	COMBATANT	COMBATANT	COMBATANT	TOTAL COMBATANT DEATHS[1]
Guatemala (Govt)	vs. URNG: Unidad Revolucionaria Nacional Guatemalteca (Guatemalan National Revolutionary Unity)[56] 1968/1996						<2800 (mil.) <43500 (civ.) (*1996)
Nicaragua (Govt)	vs. Contras: Counter- revolutionaries[57] 1981/1990						1981–90: >30,000 (mil.)

50. The CIS operation included Russian border guards and peacekeeping troops with minor reinforcements from Kazakhstan, Kyrgystan, and Uzbekistan.

51. The major groups constituting the United Tajik Opposition (formerly the Popular Democratic Army) are the Islamic Resistance Movement, the Democratic Party of Tajikistan, and the Rastokhez People's Movement.

52. Although a comprehensive peace agreement in late 1996 ended the conflict, some factions from both sides, led by warlords, were involved in sporadic violence in 1997.

53. In the past three decades the civil wars of Colombia have claimed a total of some thirty thousand lives. (SIPRI YEARBOOK 1998)

54. FMLN is a coalition of five armed opposition groups (People's Revolutionary Army, ERP; Popular Liberation Forces, FPL; Armed Forces of National Resistance, FARN; Revolutionary Party of Central American Workers, PRTC; and Armed Forces of Liberation, FAL) formed in 1980.

55. Parties agreed on a peace accord December 1991, mediated with the help of the UN.

56. URNG is a coalition of three main groups: Ejército Guerillero de los Pobres, Fuerzas Armadas Rebelde, and Organización del Pueblo en Armas.

57. U.S.-supported Contras were founded in 1981 in the wake of the Sandinista revolution against the Somoza regime in 1979.

Distribution of Major (Ongoing) Armed Conflicts 1986–98 (continued)

REGION/ State	COMBATANT	COMBATANT	COMBATANT	COMBATANT	COMBATANT	COMBATANT	TOTAL COMBATANT DEATHS[1]
Peru (Govt)	vs. Sendero Luminoso (Shining Path) 1981	vs. MRTA: Movimiento Revolucionario Túpac Amaru (Túpac Amaru Revolutionary Movement) 1986/?					>28,000 (*1998)
EUROPE							
Azerbaijan (Govt)	vs. Republic of Nagorno–Karabakh 1990/1994[58]	vs. Armenia (Govt) 1992/					>10,000 (*1994)
Bosnia & Herzegovina (Govt)[59]	Govt of Croatia 1993/1994	vs. Serbian Republic of Bosnia & Herzegovina 1992/1996[60]	vs. Serbian irregulars 1992/1996	vs. Govt of Yugoslavia 1992	vs. Republic of Herzeg-Bosnia 1993/1994[61]		25,000–55,000 (*1995)
Croatia (Govt)	vs. Serbian Republic of Krajina 1990/1996[62]	vs. Serbian irregulars 1990/1996					6000–10,000[63] (*1995)
Georgia[64]	vs. Republic of Abkhazia 1992/1994[65]						>2500 (*1994)

Distribution of Major (Ongoing) Armed Conflicts 1986–98 (continued)

REGION/ State	COMBATANT	COMBATANT	COMBATANT	COMBATANT	COMBATANT	COMBATANT	COMBATANT	TOTAL COMBATANT DEATHS[1]
Russia (Govt)	vs. Republic of Chechnya 1994[66]/1997							10,000–40,000 (*1996)
United Kingdom (Govt)	vs. Provisional IRA: Provisional Irish Republican Army 1969/1998	vs. INLA: Irish National Liberation Army 1992/						1500[67] (*1997)
Yugoslavia (Govt)	vs. Slovenia 1991/1992	vs. Croatia 1990/1992						…

58. A cease-fire was negotiated through the auspices of the Conference on Security and Cooperation in Europe (CSCE) in May 1994.

59. Fighting between the army of the Serbian Republic of Bosnia and Herzegovina and the Bosnian Croat Defense Council (or Bosnian HVO, the armed forces of the Croat Republic of Herzeg-Bosnia) is not included as a conflict since neither of these parties is the government of an internationally recognized state.

60. The General Framework Agreement was reached in Dayton,. Ohio, in November and signed in Paris on 14 December 1995.

61. A cease-fire between the Bosnian government and the Bosnian Croat forces in Bosnia and Herzegovina was agreed in February 1994 and a federation established in March between them.

62. The conflict between the Croatian government and the Croatian Serbs reignited in May and August 1995 over the Krajina and ended with the Croatian government's military victories and a peace agreement in 1995. The Croatian government recaptured Western Slavonia and Krajina, after which an agreement was reached for the return of Eastern Slavonia to Croatian government control: The Basic Agreement on the Region of Eastern Slavonia, Baranja, and Western Sirmium, 12 November 1995.

63. This figure includes the fighting during 1991 where not only the two parties participated.

64. In Georgia, troops fighting for the independence of Abkhazia evicted government soldiers from the region.

65. Abkhaz forces have controlled most of the territory of Abkhazia since September 1993. A Russian–Georgian–Abkhaz cease-fire agreement was reached in May 1994, resulting in the deployment of a Russian peacekeeping force.

66. Armed conflict broke out in December 1994 between the unilaterally declared independent Republic of Chechnya, led by General Dzhokhar Duydayev, and the Russian government.

67. The total number of deaths in political violence in Northern Ireland is approximately 3,200. The figure given here is an estimate of the deaths incurred between the government of the UK and the Provisional IRA; the remaining deaths were mainly caused by other paramilitary organizations such as the Ulster Volunteer Forces and the Ulster Freedom Fighters.

Distribution of Major (Ongoing) Armed Conflicts 1986–98 (continued)

REGION/ State	COMBATANT	COMBATANT	COMBATANT	COMBATANT	COMBATANT	COMBATANT	TOTAL COMBATANT DEATHS[1]
Yugoslavia (Serbia and Montenegro)	vs. Albanian Kosovo Liberation Army (KLA) or Ushtria Clirimjatare e Kosoves, (UCK) 1998/						1000–2000 (1998)
MIDDLE EAST							
Iran (Govt)	vs. Mujahideen e-Khalq (NLA: National Liberation Army- military wing) 1991	vs. KDPI: Kurdish Democratic Party of Iran 1979/1996[68]					…
Iran (Govt)	vs. Iraq (Govt) 1980/1988						1980–82: 27,000 (mil.) 1982–88: 500,000 1988: >5000 (mil)
Iraq (Govt)	vs. Kurds 1974/88[69]	vs. Communists (ICP) 1980/					Communists: <5,000 (*1988)
Iraq (Govt)	vs. SAIRI: Supreme AssemblyPatriotic Union for the Islamic Revolution in Iraq[70] 1991	vs. PUK: of Kurdistan[71] 1990/1996	vs. DPK: Democratic Party of Kurdistan 1974/? 1980/1996	(United States)[72] 1996	vs. Kuwait (Govt)[73] 1990/1991[74]	vs. multi-national force[75] 1991/1991	…

Distribution of Major (Ongoing) Armed Conflicts 1986–98 (continued)

REGION/ State	COMBATANT	COMBATANT	COMBATANT	COMBATANT	COMBATANT	COMBATANT	TOTAL DEATHS[1]
Israel (Govt)	vs. Non-PLO groups[76] 1964	vs. PLO groups[77] 1964					1948–: >13,000 (*1997)
Lebanon (Civil War)	Christians 1975/1990	Muslims 1975/1990	Druse 1975/1990	Palestinians 1975/1990	Israel (Govt) 1978 &1982/	Syria (Govt) 1976/	1975–89: 131,000
Syria (Govt)	vs. Sunni 1976/1987	vs. Other opposition 1976/1987					1976–87: 15,000

68. The Kurdish Democratic Party was largely suppressed by 1997 but bases remain in Iraqi Kurdistan. There were also indications of possible activity in the Kurdish–Iranian conflict, but the reports could not be verified.

69. After the cease-fire in the Iran–Iraq War, Iraq moved against the Kurds and drove DPK and PUK members out of nearly all of Iraq.

70. Most of the Shi'a rebels belong to this group.

71. By 1996 in Iraqi Kurdistan there was no fighting between the Iraqi government and Kurdish groups. The U.S. responded militarily to the Iraqi invasion of Iraqi Kurdistan in 1996, when Iraq supported one group against the other. Following this, the government was forced to leave rival Kurdish groups to fight among themselves.

72. Air strikes against Iraq in 1996 in connection with Kurdish conflict in the north. Casualties unknown.

73. Iraq invaded Kuwait in August 1990.

74. The Iraq-Kuwait conflict concerning the status of Kuwait was regulated by UN Security Council Resolution 687 of 3 April 1997.

75. On 17 January 1991 a multinational force (Argentina, Australia, Bahrain, Bangladesh, Belgium, Canada, Czechoslovakia, Denmark, Egypt, France, Greece, Honduras, Italy, Kuwait, Morocco, Netherlands, Niger, Norway, Oman, Pakistan, Portugal, Qatar, Saudi Arabia, Senegal, Spain, Syria, United Arab Emirates, the UK, and the U.S.) launched an offensive, Operation Desert Storm. In February 1991 Iraq accepted all UNSC resolutions on the conflict and military operations ceased. U.S. and Saudi forces reportedly buried 16,000–17,000 Iraqi soldiers. The multinational force lost 216 soldiers.

76. Examples of these groups are: Hamas, PFLP-GC (Popular Front for the Liberation of Palestine–General Command), Islamic Jihad, Hizbollah, and Amal.

77. The Palestine Liberation Organization (PLO) is an umbrella organization; armed action is carried out by member organizations. The main groups represented on the executive committee are Al-Fatah, PFLP (Popular Front for the Liberation of Palestine; George Habash), DFLP (Democratic Front for the Liberation of Palestine; branch of Nayef Hawatmeh), DFLP (Democratic Front for the Liberation of Palestine; branch of Yasser Abed Rabbo), ALF (Arab Liberation Front), PPSF (Palestine Popular Struggle Front; Samir Ghosheh), PLP (Palestinian Liberation Front; Mahmoud Abul Abbas), and PPP (Palestinian People's Party [formerly PCP Palestinian Communist Party]). Apart from these groups, ten other members of the executive committee are not affiliated with any particular political party, ideology, or organization. Although Al-Fatah, the largest group within the PLO, did not use armed force in 1996, other groups (e.g. PFLP) that reject the 1993 Declaration of Principles on Interim Self-Government Arrangements (Oslo agreement) did. These groups opposed the PLO leadership but were still part of the PLO in 1996. By 1997, the process of implementing the Oslo peace accord proceeded in spite of damaging sporadic violence and disagreements between the PLO and Israel.

Distribution of Major (Ongoing) Armed Conflicts 1986–98 (continued)

REGION/ State	COMBATANT	COMBATANT	COMBATANT	COMBATANT	COMBATANT	COMBATANT	TOTAL COMBATANT DEATHS[1]
Turkey (Govt)	vs. PKK: Partiya Karkeren Kurdistan (Kurdish Worker's Party, or Apocus) 1984						>30,000 (*1997)
Yemen (Govt)	vs. Democratic Republic of Yemen 1994 /1994[78]						1500–7000 (*1994)

* Data unless otherwise noted is drawn from SIPRI YEARBOOK 1987–1998.

78. The war in Yemen broke out in July when the self-declared Democratic Republic of Yemen was decisively defeated by the forces of the Republic of Yemen (Govt.).

APPENDIX 2

Arms Deliveries to
Combatants, 1991-1996
(in millions of current US)
by Major Supplier (% Total Delivered)

SOURCE: These figures are derived from Table III in *WMEAT* 1997 (for 1994–1996) and *WMEAT* 1993–1994 (for 1991–1993). The 1997 edition of *WMEAT* substantially revises upward U.S. arms export figures using a new interim method to calculate U.S. commercial exports by assuming that "deliveries constitute a medial 50 percent of total [commercial] authorizations by country." See the article, "Revision of U.S. Arms Exports Data Series," on the U.S. Department of State website under *WMEAT* 1997 [http://www.state.gov/www/global/arms/bureauvc.html] The then Arms Control and Disarmament Agency (ACDA) provided us with revised U.S. commercial export figures for 1991–1993 which have been incorporated into table 7.2. The 1993–1994 edition of *WMEAT* does not have the revised figures. (Since the 1998 edition, *WMEAT* has been published by the U.S. Department of State Bureau of Verification and Compliance.)

ARMS DELIVERIES TO COMBATANTS, 1991-1996 (in millions of current US$) BY MAJOR SUPPLIER (% Total Delivered)

Suppliers (%)/ Combatants	Arms Deliveries Total $ value	US[1]	UK	Russia	France	Germany	China	Other NATO	Other West European	Other East European	Other East Asia	Others	Undistributed by supplier
WORLD TOTAL (of combatants)	37,463	45.27	2.1	21.28	1.57	4.83	7.66	3.05	1.09	4.4	1.24	5.76	1.69
WORLD TOTAL (all countries)	218,768	60.6	12.36	9.13	4.42	3.34	2.33	2.17	1.48	1.41	.38	2.32	NA
AFRICA Combatant Total	3,973	15.42	.12	29.44	2.13	0	3.52	4.9	5.03	8.55	.25	23.53	7.04
AFRICA All Countries Total	5,858	16.95	5.2	27.31	6.14	.34	8.53	4.6	3.84	8.79	.42	17.83	
ASIA Combatant Total	9,215	18.66	8.51	40.64	1.13	3.03	12.64	2.76	.21	4.72	.92	4.39	2.33
ASIA All Countries Total	53,935	58.91	4.57	18.16	3.36	3.94	4.95	1.72	.55	1.41	.42	1.97	NA
CENTRAL & SOUTH AMERICA Combatant Total	1,590	38.67	0	8.8	0	10.06	1.25	3.14	0	22.01	1.25	13.2	1.57

ARMS DELIVERIES TO COMBATANTS, 1991-1996 (in millions of current US$) BY MAJOR SUPPLIER (% Total Delivered) (continued)

Suppliers (%)/ Combatants	Arms Deliveries Total $ value	US[1]	UK	Russia	France	Germany	China	Other NATO	Other West European	Other East European	Other East Asia	Others	Undis- tributed by supplier
CENTRAL & SOUTH AMERICA All Countries Total	7,015	44.04	4.34	13.32	7.76	4.77	.99	4.77	.42	5.77	.92	12.82	NA
EUROPE Combatant Total	800	13.12	0	0	0	0	0	11.25	3.75	13.75	6.25	50.62	1.25
EUROPE, All Countries Total	51,335	78.62	1.49	4.09	3.63	5.47	0	2.25	1.85	.47	.09	2.04	NA
MIDDLE EAST Combatant Total	21,885	63.55	0	13.34	1.82	6.25	7.05	2.53	.73	1.89	1.37	.93	.47
MIDDLE EAST All Countries Total	97,235	54.47	23.85	5.7	5.25	2.07	1.92	2.12	1.79	1.2	.49	1.04	NA

1. The sum of regional totals will not equal WORLD TOTAL (all countries) because of (1) rounding and (2) omission of transfers to NATO agencies, other inter-national agencies, and classified transfers, which are not attributed to individual recip-ient countries or regions. (See *WMEAT* 97, Table III, footnote c.)

NOTES

Chapter 1

1. See, among numerous examples, Dennis Meadows and Donella Meadows, *The Limits to Growth* (New York: Universe Books, 1972); and Dennis Pirages, *The New Context for International Relations: Global Ecopolitics* (N. Scituate, MA: Duxbury Press, 1978).
2. Samuel Huntington places this in the context of what he perceives as five waves of "declinist" anxiety in the U.S., one of which was in the late 1970s and early 1980s in connection with Soviet military power. See his "The U.S.—Decline or Renewal?" *Foreign Affairs,* vol. 67, no. 2 (winter 1998/99), pp. 76–96.
   The scenarios are in Tom Clancy, *Red Storm Rising* (New York: Putnam, 1986); and Sir John W. Hackett, *The Third World War: The Untold Story* (New York: Macmillan, 1982).
3. Perhaps the best examples of this genre are the three-volume series by Anthony Cordesman and Abraham Wagner, *The Lessons of Modern War* (Boulder, CO: Westview Press, 1990), pertaining to the Arab-Israeli conflicts, the Iran-Iraq War, and the Afghanistan and Falklands wars.
4. See Michael Howard, "The Use and Abuse of Military History," *Parameters,* vol. 6, no. 1 (March 1981), pp. 9–14.
5. This theme was developed by Eliot Cohen, "Distant Battles," in Stephanie G. Neuman and Robert Harkavy, *The Lessons of Recent Wars in the Third World* (Lexington, MA: D. C. Heath, 1987), pp. 7–32. The thesis that the frequency of interstate conventional wars should be tamped down by the regional proliferation of nuclear weapons is in Martin van Creveld, *The Transformation of War* (New York: Free Press, 1991), chapters 1 and 7.
6. Otto Chaney, *Zhukov* (Norman: University of Oklahoma Press, 1971), chapter 4, under "Khalkhin-Gol"; Richard Whymant, *Stalin's Spy: Richard Sorge and the Tokyo Espionage Ring* (New York: Thomas Dunne, 1998), p. 109; and Viktor Anfilov, "Zhukov," in Harold Shukman, ed., *Stalin's Generals* (London: Weidenfeld and Nicolson, 1993), chapter 26.
7. This is pointed out in Jack Snyder, *The Ideology of the Offensive: Military Decision Making and the Disasters of 1914* (Ithaca, NY: Cornell University Press, 1984), chapter 1, esp. p. 21.
8. See Edward Luttwak, *The Pentagon and the Art of War* (New York: Simon and Schuster, 1984), pp. 98–107.
9. See General Wesley K. Clark (ret.), "How to Fight an Asymmetric War," *Time,* 23 October 2000, p. 40, in connection with Israel and the West Bank Palestinians.
10. See Harlan Jencks, "Lessons of a 'Lesson': China-Vietnam, 1979," in Robert E. Harkavy and Stephanie G. Neuman, *The Lessons of Recent Wars in the Third World,* vol. 1 (Lexington, MA: D. C. Heath, 1985), pp. 139–160.
11. Among the efforts at organized and formal "lessons learned" analyses of the Gulf War are Department of Defense, *Conduct of the Persian Gulf War,* Final Report to Congress, Pursuant to Title V of the Persian Gulf Conflict Supplemental Authorization and Personnel Benefits Act of

1991 (Public Law 102–25, Washington, DC, April 1992) [hereinafter, The Pentagon Report]; and James F. Dunnigan and Austin Bay, *From Shield to Storm* (New York: William Morrow, 1992).

12. This is argued, pro and con, in Edward Luttwak, "The Gulf War in its Purely Military Dimensions," in John O'Loughlin, Tom Mayer, and Edward S. Greenberg, eds., *War and Its Consequences: Lessons from the Persian Gulf Conflict* (New York: HarperCollins, 1994), pp. 33–50.

13. In a broader historical sense, this is discussed in Frank Kendall, "Exploiting the Military Technical Revolution: A Concept for Joint Warfare," *Strategic Review,* vol. 20, no. 2 (spring 1992), pp. 23–30; and Michael J. Mazaar, *The Revolution in Military Affairs: A Framework for Defense Planning* (Carlisle, PA: U.S. Army War College, Strategic Studies Institute, June 1994).

14. The possible threat of a rising, "hegemonic China" has been bruited and popularized in Richard Bernstein and Ross Munro, *The Coming Conflict with China* (New York: Alfred Knopf, 1997).

15. For various schemes outlining possible "images" or structures of an emerging international system around the turn of the century, see Robert E. Harkavy, "Images of the Coming International System," *Orbis,* vol. 41, no. 4 (fall 1997), pp. 568– 590. See also Alexander Nacht, "U.S. Foreign Policy Strategies," *The Washington Quarterly,* vol. 18, no. 3 (summer 1995), pp. 195–210, and Samuel Huntington, *The Clash of Civilizations and the Remaking of World Order* (New York: Simon and Schuster, 1996), pp. 21–35.

16. This gap or barrier between military history and the related social sciences, particularly as it pertains to how the former might inform questions about the causes of war, is discussed in Walter Emil Kaegi, Jr., "The Crisis in Military Historiography," *Armed Forces and Society,* vol. 7, no. 2 (winter 1980), pp. 299–316. See also, regarding the linkage-or lack of same-between military history and modern strategic studies, Harry L. Coles, "Strategic Studies since 1945: The Era of Overthink," *Military Review,* vol. 53, no. 4 (April 1973), pp. 3–15.

17. Cordesman and Wagner, *The Lessons of Modern War.*

18. See among others, Keith Krause, *Arms and the State: Patterns of Military Production and Trade* (Cambridge: Cambridge University Press, 1992); and Robert E. Harkavy and Stephanie G. Neuman, special ed., "The Arms Trade: Problems and Prospects in the Post–Cold War World," *The Annals,* American Academy of Political and Social Science, vol. 535, September 1994.

19. In addition to the works of Keegan, van Creveld, and Kennedy cited elsewhere in this chapter, see Brian Bond, *The Pursuit of Victory: From Napoleon to Saddam Hussein* (New York: Oxford University Press, 1996).

20. See, in particular, Colin Gray, *The Leverage of Sea Power: The Strategic Advantage of Navies in War* (New York: Maxwell Macmillan, 1982); and George Modelski and William R. Thompson, *Seapower in Global Politics, 1494–1993* (Seattle: University of Washington Press, 1988).

21. Harry Summers, *On Strategy: A Critical Analysis of the Vietnam War* (Novato, CA: Presidio Press, 1982).

22. Eliot Cohen, "Distant Battles."

23. John Mueller, *Retreat from Doomsday: The Obsolescence of Major War* (New York: Basic Books, 1989).

24. See Kenneth Waltz, "The Spread of Nuclear Weapons: More May be Better," Adelphi Paper no. 171 (London: Brassey's for the IISS, 1987); Kenneth Waltz and Scott Sagan, *The Spread of Nuclear Weapons: A Debate* (New York: Norton, 1995); and Martin van Creveld, *Nuclear Proliferation and the Future of Conflict* (New York: Free Press, 1983).

25. Mueller, *Retreat from Doomsday,* p. 4.

26. Ibid., p. 5. This point is also made in John Keegan, with reference to Mueller's work, *A History of Warfare* (New York: Alfred Knopf, 1993), pp. 58–59. Hence, according to Keegan, "Despite confusion and uncertainty, it seems just possible to glimpse the emerging outline of a world without war."

27. Mueller, *Retreat from Doomsday,* p. 11.

28. This term is drawn from and has been popularized by, John Lewis Gaddis, *The Long Peace: Inquiries into the History of the Cold War* (New York: Oxford University Press, 1987).

29. Mueller, *Retreat from Doomsday,* p. 6.

30. This is discussed in V. V. Aspaturian, "Russia: A Threat of Tomorrow," in Werner Kaltefleiter and Ulrike Schumacher, *Conflicts, Options, Strategies in a Threatened World* (Kiel: Christian-Albrechts-University, 1995), pp. 39–66.

31. See Samuel Huntington, "No Exit: The Errors of Endism," *The National Interest* (fall 1989), pp. 3–11.

32. Francis Fukuyama, *The End of History and the Last Man* (New York: Free Press, 1992).

33. John Keegan, *A History of Warfare* (New York: Alfred Knopf, 1993); and Brian Bond, *The Pursuit of Victory.*

34. Max Singer and Aaron Wildavsky, *The Real World Order: Zones of Peace, Zones of Turmoil* (Chatham, NJ: Chatham House, 1993).

35. Amidst a near blizzard of contemporary analysis of the "democratic peace," see in particular Bruce M. Russett, *Grasping the Democratic Peace* (Princeton: Princeton University Press, 1993).

36. Paul Kennedy, *Preparing for the Twenty-First Century* (New York: Random House, 1993); and Robert Kaplan, *The Ends of the Earth: A Journey at the Dawn of the Twenty-First Century* (New York: Random House, 1996).

37. Martin van Creveld, *The Transformation of Warfare* (New York: Free Press, 1991).

38. Ibid., chapters 1 and 7.

39. John Keegan, *A History of Warfare,* esp. chapter 1 and the conclusion, pp. 386–392.

40. Ibid., p. 391.

41. Ibid.

42. Ibid., p. 392.

43. This was primarily exemplified in the geopolitical formulations of Nicholas Spykman. See his later summary work, *The Geography of the Peace* (New York: Harcourt Brace, 1944).

44. Fukuyama, *The End of History and the Last Man,* esp. chapter 28, discusses this and other aspects of historical pessimism in questioning whether the era of warfare is truly ended. In his initial article on this subject, "The End of History?" *The National Interest,* no. 16 (summer 1989), pp. 3–18 (18), he refers to the role of "nostalgia" which "will continue to fuel competition and conflict even in the post-historical world for some time to come."

45. Bernstein and Munro, *The Coming Conflict with China.*

46. William J. Perry, "Desert Storm and Deterrence," *Foreign Affairs,* vol. 70, no. 4 (fall 1991), pp. 65–82.

47. Admiral William A. Owens, "Introduction," in Stuart E. Johnson and Martin C. Libicki, eds., *Dominant Battlespace Knowledge* (Washington, DC: National Defense University, 1996), pp. 1–14.

48. Douglas A. MacGregor, "A Future Battle: The Merging Levels of War," *Parameters,* vol. 22, no. 4 (winter 1992–93), pp. 33–47.

49. Alvin H. Bernstein, "Conflict and Technology, The Next Generation," in Werner Kaltefleiter and Ulrike Schumacher, *Conflicts, Options, Strategies in a Threatened World* (Kiel: Christian Albrechts University Press, 1995), pp. 145–157; and Martin Libicki, *The Mesh and the Net: Speculations on Armed Conflict in a Time of Free Silicon* (Washington, DC: National Defense University, 1994), McNair Paper no. 28.

50. Andrew Krepinevich, "Cavalry to Computer," *The National Interest,* no. 37 (fall 1994), pp. 30–42.

51. See "The Revolution in Military Affairs," *Strategic Forum,* no. 11 (Washington, DC: Institute for National Strategic Studies, November 1994), which provides a taxonomy of future threats to the United States in classifying potential MTR competitors as "peer," "niche," and "regional."

52. See Robert D. Kaplan, "The Coming Anarchy," *Atlantic Monthly,* February 1994, pp. 44–76.

53. Such scenarios are laid out by Casper Weinberger and Peter Schweizer, *The Next War* (Washington, DC: Regency Press, 1996).

54. Generally, regarding asymmetric strategies, see Patrick J. Garrity, *Why the Gulf War Still Matters: Foreign Perspectives on the War and the Future of International Security* (Los Alamos, NM: Center for National Security Studies), report no. 16, July 1993, pp. 87–90.

55. Sundarji is quoted in George Quester and Victor Utgoff, "No-First-Use and Non-Proliferation: Redefining Extended Deterrence," *Washington Quarterly,* vol. 17, no. 2 (spring 1994), pp. 103–14 (107).

56. Trend data for the numbers of ongoing conflicts in the world are presented annually (or can be analyzed serially from year to year) in *The SIPRI Yearbook* (Oxford: Oxford University Press), under "Major Armed Conflicts."

57. In addition to the aforementioned annual chapter in SIPRI's Yearbooks, see also the several reviews by John Laffin, *The World in Conflict* (London: Brassey's, 1986–1993); and the also annual *Strategic Survey* by the International Institute for Strategic Studies, London.

58. For a review and classification of many of these conflicts, see Geoffrey Kemp and Robert E. Harkavy, *Strategic Geography and the Changing Middle East* (Washington, DC: Brookings Institution, 1997), chapter 3, under "The Contemporary Middle East: The End of the Cold War and Continuing Regional Conflict."

59. See the much discussed article by John Mearsheimer, "Back to the Future: Instability in Europe after the Cold War," *International Security,* vol. 15, no. 1 (summer 1990), pp. 5–56.

60. Keegan, *A History of Warfare,* esp. chapters 1 and 5.

61. Keegan, ibid., discusses this more broadly in the context of a "Western," Clausewitzian cultural tradition as applied to warfare. A putative "American way of war," said to stress total victory, was earlier noted in Lincoln Bloomfield, "American Approaches to Military Strategy, Arms Control, and Disarmament: A Critique of the Postwar Experience," in Robert Harkavy and Edward Kolodziej, eds., *American Security Policy and Policy-Making* (Lexington, MA: D. C. Heath, 1980), Chapter 14, pp. 225–226.

62. "The Low Intensity Conflict Environment of the 1990s," *The Annals,* AAPSS, 517, September 1991, pp. 127–132 under "variations."

63. Ernest Evans, *War Without Splendor: The U.S. Military and Low Level Conflict* (New York: Greenwood Press, 1987). See also Lincoln Bloomfield and Amelia Leiss, *Controlling Small Wars: A Strategy for the 1990s* (New York: Knopf, 1969).

64. Sam Sarkesian, *The New Battlefield* (New York: Greenwood Press, 1986), p. 110.

65. Richard Shultz, "The Low Intensity Conflict Environment of the 1990s," *The Annals,* The American Academy of Political and Social Science, 517 September 1991, pp. 127–132.

66. This is defined and discussed in Ramses Amer et al., "Major Armed Conflicts," in *SIPRI Yearbook 1993* (Oxford: Oxford University Press, 1993), pp. 80–130, quote on p. 87.

67. See note 88.

68. J. David Singer, "The Level of Analysis Problem in International Relations," in Klaus Knorr and Sidney Verba, eds., *The International System* (Princeton: Princeton University Press, 1961), pp. 77–92.

69. Patrick Morgan, *Theories and Approaches to International Politics,* 4 ed. (New Brunswick, NJ: Transaction Books, 1987), pp. 10–11.

70. Paul Viotti and Mark Kauppi, *International Relations Theory: Realism, Pluralism, and Globalism,* 2 ed. (New York: Macmillan, 1993).

71. Edward Luttwak, *Strategy: The Logic of War and Peace* (Cambridge, MA: Belknap Press of Harvard University Press, 1987), chapter 5.

72. The realm of "grand tactics" apparently derives from the military historian Jomini, as discussed in David M. Glantz, "The Nature of Soviet Operational Art," *Parameters,* vol. 15, no. 1 (spring 1985), pp. 1–12 (3). See also U.S. Army War College, *Military Strategy: Theory and Application,* glossary, p. A5, wherein, "Grand" or "Higher" tactics is defined as "the employment of major units in combat supporting a military strategy executed at unified or combined command level."

73. Allan R. Millett and Williamson Murray, eds., *Military Effectiveness,* 3 vols. (London: Allen and Unwin, 1988), esp. p. 4 of vol. 1.

74. Luttwak, *Strategy,* p. 70, and p. 179.

75. John Collins, "The Essence of Strategy," in *Military Strategy: Theory and Application,* reference text for the Department of Military Strategy, Planning, and Operations, 1983–1984 (Carlisle, PA: U.S. Army War College, 1983), p. 3–1.

76. Millett and Murray, *Military Effectiveness,* vol. 1, p.4.

77. Luttwak, *Strategy,* p. 113.

78. Collins, "The Essence of Strategy," p. 3–1.

79. Ibid., pp. 3–2.

80. Millett and Murray, *Military Effectiveness,* p. 7.

81. According to Luttwak, *Strategy,* p. 91, "In the modern tradition of continental European military thought, by contrast there is an adjectival term in common use directly translatable as 'operational' and this level is indeed salient in German and Soviet professional military literature, whose primary concern is with *operational art,* as opposed to tactics narrowly applicable to specific types of forces (infantry tactics, air-combat tactics, antisubmarine tactics)."

82. Ibid., pp. 69–70.

83. Ibid., pp. 92–97. See also Martin van Creveld, *Military Lessons of the Yom Kippur War: Historical Perspectives* (Washington, DC: Georgetown CSIS, 1975), Washington Papers no. 24.

84. Millett and Murray, *Military Effectiveness,* p. 50.

85. Ronald M. D'Amura, "Campaigns: The Essence of Operational Warfare," *Parameters,* vol. 17, no. 2 (summer 1987), pp. 42–67 (44).

86. Dwight L. Adams and Clayton R. Newell, "Operational Art in the Joint and Combined Arenas," *Parameters,* vol. 18, no. 2 (June 1988), pp. 33–39 (35). See also David Jablonsky, Strategy and the

Operational Level of War," part 1, *Parameters,* vol. 17, no. 1 (spring 1987), pp. 67–76; John Turlington, "Truly Learning the Operational Art," *Parameters,* vol. 17, no. 1 (spring 1987),, pp. 51–64; Jay Luvaas, "Thinking at the Operational Level," *Parameters,* vol. 16, no. 1 (spring 1986), pp. 2–6; and John F. Meechan III, "The Operational Trilogy," *Parameters,* vol. 16, no. 3 (autumn 1986), pp. 9–18.

87. Millett and Murray, *Military Effectiveness,* p. 19.

88. Luttwak, *Strategy,* p. 84.

89. Ibid., chapter 5.

90. The Pentagon Report has a lengthy appendix in which the performance of virtually all of the U.S. weapons systems utilized in that war are evaluated in detail.

91. Douglas A. MacGregor, "Future Battle: The Merging Levels of War," *Parameters,* vol. 22, no. 4 (winter 1992–93), pp. 33–47 (38).

92. Ibid., p. 38. The previously cited works of Alvin Bernstein and Martin Libicki are also germane here.

93. Ibid.

94. Quincy Wright, *A Study of War,* 2d ed. (Chicago: University of Chicago Press, 1965), pp. 701–716.

95. Ibid., p. 42.

96. See John Keegan, *The Face of Battle* (New York: Pentium Books, 1978); and Paul Fussell, *Wartime, Understanding and Behavior in the Second World War* (New York: Oxford University Press, 1989); *Doing Battle: The Making of a Skeptic* (Boston: Little, Brown, 1996); and "My War," *Harper's,* vol. 264, no. 1580 (January 1982), pp. 40–48.

97. Nick Vaux, *Take That Hill!: Royal Marines in the Falklands War* (Washington, DC: Pergamon-Brassey's, 1986); and Max Hastings and Simon Jenkins, *The Battle for the Falklands* (New York: Norton, 1984).

98. Avidgor Kahalani, *The Heights of Courage: A Tank Leader's War on the Golan* (Westport, CT: Greenwood Press, 1984).

99. Rick Atkinson, *Crusade, The Untold Story of the Persian Gulf War* (Boston: Houghton Mifflin, 1993); and Michael Gordon and Bernard Trainor, *The General's War: The Inside Story of the Conflict in the Gulf* (Boston: Little, Brown, 1995).

100. Edgar O'Ballance, *The Gulf War* (London: Brassey's, 1988); Randolph S. Churchill and Winston S. Churchill, *The Six Day War* (Boston: Houghton Mifflin, 1967).

101. S. L. A. Marshall, *Sinai Victory* (New York: William Morrow, 1967).

102. Ze'ev Schiff and Ehud Ya'ari, *Israel's Lebanon War* (New York: Simon and Schuster, 1984).

103. Itamar Rabinovich, *The War for Lebanon, 1970–1983* (Ithaca, NY: Cornell University Press, 1984); and Walter Laqueur, *Confrontation: The Middle East and World Politics* (New York: Quadrangle/New York Times, 1974).

104. J. Bruce Amstutz, *Afghanistan: The First Five Years of Soviet Occupation* (Washington, DC: National Defense University, 1986); and Rosanne Klass, ed., *Afghanistan: The Great Game Revisited* (New York: Freedom House, 1987).

105. Nayan Chanda, *Brother Enemy: The War after the War* (San Diego: Harcourt, Brace, Jovanovich, 1986).

106. Millett and Murray, *Military Effectiveness.*

107. See Trevor Dupuy, "Measuring Combat Effectiveness: Historical Quantitative Analysis," in Robert E. Harkavy and Stephanie G. Neuman, *The Lessons of Recent Wars in the Third World,* vol. 1, pp. 73–96.

108. Robert E. Harkavy and Stephanie G. Neuman, *The Lessons of Recent Wars in the Third World,* vols. 1 and 2.

109. Robert Taber, *The War of the Flea: A Study of Guerilla Warfare Theory and Practice* (New York: Lyle Stuart, 1965).

110. David Charters and Maurice Tugwell, eds., *Armies in Low-Intensity Conflict* (London: Brassey's, 1989). See also Michael T. Klare and Peter Kornbluh, eds., *Low Intensity Warfare* (New York: Pantheon, 1988).

111. Hew Strachan, *European Armies and the Conduct of War* (London: Allen and Unwin, 1983). See also Colin McInnes and G. D. Sheffield, *Warfare in the Twentieth Century* (London: Unwin Hyman, 1988).

112. Edward Mead Earle, *Makers of Modern Strategy: Military Thought From Machiavelli to Hitler* (Princeton: Princeton University Press, 1943), updated by a new edition in 1986 edited by Peter Paret.

113. J. F. C. Fuller, *A Military History of the Western World,* 3 vols. (New York: Funk and Wagnalls, 1954–56).

114. John Laffin, *The World in Conflict* (London: Brassey's), annual beginning in 1986.

115. Patrick Brogan, *The Fighting Never Stopped: A Comprehensive Guide to World Conflict Since 1945* (New York: Vintage Books, 1990).

116. James F. Dunnigan and Austin Bay, *A Quick and Dirty Guide to War* (New York: William Morrow, 1986).

117. Richard Ned Lebow, *Between Peace and War* (Baltimore: Johns Hopkins University Press, 1981); Francis A. Beer, *Peace against War: The Ecology of International Violence* (San Francisco: W. H. Freeman, 1981); and Robert L. Butterworth, *Managing Interstate Conflict, 1945–74* (Pittsburgh: University of Pittsburgh Center for International Studies, 1976).

118. Martin van Creveld, *Supplying War: Logistics from Wallerstein to Patton* (Cambridge, U.K.: Cambridge University Press, 1977); Patrick O'Sullivan, *Terrain and Tactics* (New York: Greenwood Press, 1991); and O'Sullivan and Jesse W. Miller, *The Geography of Warfare* (London: Croom Helm, 1983).

119. Nicholas Bethell, "The Forgotten War," *Harper's,* vol. 263, no. 1574 (July 1981), pp. 8–11; Francisco Goldman, "Guatemalan Death Masque," *Harper's,* vol. 272, no. 1628 (January 1986), pp. 56–60; Maria Thomas, "A State of Permanent Revolution," *Harper's,* vol. 274, no. 1640 (January 1987), pp. 53–59; Denis Johnson, "The Small Boys' Unit," *Harper's,* vol. 301, no. 1805 (October 2000), pp. 41–60; and Patrick Symmes, "Miraculous Fishing: Lost in the Swamps of Colombia's Drug War," *Harper's,* vol. 301, no. 1807, (December 2000), pp. 61–71.

Chapter 2

1. Quincy Wright, *A Study of War,* 2d ed. (Chicago: University of Chicago Press, 1965).

2. Geoffrey Blainey, *The Causes of War* (New York: Free Press, 1988), first American edition of work originally published in 1973; and Stephen Van Evera, *Causes of War* (Ithaca, NY: Cornell University Press, 1999).

3. Numerous such "microlevel" explanations are discussed in James E. Dougherty and Robert W. Pfaltzgraff, *Contending Theories of International Relations* (New York: Harper and Row, 1981), chapter 7.

4. Kenneth Waltz, *Man, the State, and War: A Theoretical Analysis* (New York: Columbia University Press, 1959).

5. A variety of such "macrolevel" explanations are discussed in Dougherty and Pfaltzgraff, *Contending Theories,* chapters 8 and 9.

6. See L. L. Farrar, *The Short-War Illusion* (Santa Barbara, CA: ABC-Clio, 1973). See also Van Evera, *Causes of War,* chapter 2, under "False Optimism: Illusions of Coming War."

7. Blainey, *The Causes of War,* chapter 5.

8. Ibid., chapter 5. Regarding the "displacement" phenomenon, see Dougherty and Pfaltzgraff, *Contending Theories.,* pp. 271–273.

9. Blainey, *The Causes of War,* chapter 6.

10. Joshua Goldstein, "Kondratieff Waves as War Cycles," *International Studies Quarterly* 29 (December 1985), pp. 411–444. See also the discussion in Richard Rosecrance, "Long Cycle Theory and International Relations," *International Organization,* vol. 41, no. 2, pp. 283–301.

11. Blainey, *The Causes of War,* chapter 7.

12. Ibid., chapter 8. For an earlier formulation, see A. F. K. Organski, *World Politics* (New York: Alfred Knopf, 1958), chapter 11.

13. Blainey, *The Causes of War,* chapter 9.

14. Van Evera, *Causes of War,* p. 105.

15. The concept of "lateral pressures" is ably summarized in Nazli Choucri and Robert C. North, "Lateral Pressure in International Relations: Concept and Theory," in Manus I. Midlarsky, ed., *Handbook of War Studies* (Ann Arbor: University of Michigan Press, 1993), chapter 12.

16. The recent works of Mueller, van Creveld, and Keegan were discussed and cited in chapter 1.

17. K. J. Holsti, *The State, War and the State of War* (New York: Cambridge University Press, 1996), esp. chapter 2.

18. Ibid., chapters 5 and 6.

19. Ibid., pp. 136–137.

20. The concept of a "pluralistic security community" was developed by Karl Deutsch et al. in *Political Community and the North Atlantic Area* (Princeton: Princeton University Press, 1957), esp. pp. 5–7.

21. This thesis was originally proffered in Robert E. Harkavy, *Spectre of a Middle Eastern Holocaust: The Strategic and Diplomatic Implications of the Israeli Nuclear Weapons Program* (Denver: University of Denver Graduate School of International Studies, 1977).

22. Fritz Fischer, *Germany's Aims in the First World War* (New York: W.W. Norton, 1967), translation of *Griff Nach der Weltmacht;* and Hugh R. Trevor-Roper, "History and Imagination: A Valedictory Lecture" (Oxford: Clarendon Press, 1980), which emphasizes "historical free will," including what easily might have happened, rather than "explanations."

23. Arthur Goldschmidt, *A Concise History of the Middle East,* 2d ed. (Boulder, CO: Westview Press, 1983), p. 49.

24. Arms resupply during conflict is discussed, in a general way, in Robert E. Harkavy, "Arms Resupply during Conflict: A Framework for Analysis," *Jerusalem Journal of International Relations,* vol. 7, no. 3 (1985), pp. 5–41; and in Stephanie G. Neuman, *Military Assistance in Recent Wars: The Dominance of the Superpowers* (New York: Praeger, 1986); Michael Brzoska and Frederic S. Pearson, *Arms and Warfare: Escalation, De-Escalation and Negotiation* (Columbia: University of South Carolina Press, 1994).

25. Brian Bond, *The Pursuit of Victory from Napoleon to Saddam Hussein* (Oxford: Oxford University Press, 1996). See also Michael Howard, "When Are Wars Decisive?" *Survival,* vol. 41, no. 1 (spring 1999), pp. 126–135.

26. Though the concept of "lateral pressure" was unknown to earlier scholars dealing with "theories of imperialism," there were assertions of the thesis that competitive imperialist expansion in Africa and elsewhere was impelled by the pressures of political rivalries within Europe, i.e., that imperialism was a "safety valve" for European problems. See, for instance, Nicholas Mansergh, "Diplomatic Reasons for Expansion," in Harrison M. Wright, ed., *The New Imperialism* (Lexington, MA: D. C. Heath, 1961), pp. 89–95.

27. Robert D. Kaplan, *The Ends of the Earth: A Journey at the Dawn of the Twenty-First Century* (New York: Random House, 1996); and Mary Kaldor, *New and Old Wars* (Cambridge, U.K.: Polity Press, 1999).

28. See Edward Mueller and Mitchell Seligson, "Inequality and Insurgency," *American Political Science Review,* vol. 81, no. 2, pp. 425–451, which looks at the question of whether land inequality or income inequality is a more determining factor in the occurrence of political insurgency.

29. Klaus Knorr, *Power and Wealth: The Political Economy of International Power* (New York: Basic Books, 1973); and Ray S. Cline, *World Power Trends and U.S. Foreign Policy for the 1980s* (Boulder, CO: Westview Press, 1980).

30. A more elaborate method of measuring power is in J. David Singer, Stuart Bremer, and John Stuckey, "Capability Distribution, Uncertainty, and Major Power War 1820–1965," in Bruce Russett, ed., *Peace, War and Numbers* (Beverly Hills, CA: Sage, 1972). They begin with six indicators, combine them into three, and then combine these into a single power base: demographics (total population and number of people in cities of twenty thousand or more), an industrial dimension (energy consumption and steel production), and military expenditures and armed forces size.

31. See Geoffrey Kemp, "Arms Transfers and the 'Back-End' Problem in Developing Countries," in Stephanie Neuman and Robert Harkavy, eds., *Arms Transfers in the Modern World* (New York: Praeger, 1979), chapter 15.

32. Anthony Cordesman, *After the Storm: The Changing Military Balance in the Middle East* (Boulder, CO: Westview Press, 1993).

33. U.S. Arms Control and Disarmament Agency, *World Military Expenditures and Arms Transfers,* annual (Washington, DC: U.S. Government Printing Office); International Institute for Strategic Studies, *The Military Balance,* annual (London: Brassey's); and *SIPRI Yearbook,* annual (Oxford: Oxford University Press).

34. Cline, *World Power Trends and U.S. Foreign Policy for the 1980s.*

35. For an assessment of the geographical components of national power, see A. F. K. Organski, *World Politics* (New York: Alfred Knopf, 1958), esp. pp. 118–131.

36. Hans Morgenthau, *Politics Among Nations,* 5th ed. (New York: Alfred Knopf, 1973), pp. 140–144.

37. Fischer, *Griff Nach der Weltmacht.*

38. See John Toland, *The Rising Sun: The Decline and Fall of the Japanese Empire, 1936–1945* (New York: Random House, 1970).

39. The traditional but long dormant concept of "revisionism" (and the opposite status quo orientation) has been revived of late. See, for instance, Randall Schweller, "Tripolarity and the Second World War," *International Studies Quarterly*, vol. 37, no. 1 (March 1993), pp. 73–103.

40. Harlan Jencks, "Lessons of a 'Lesson': China-Vietnam, 1979," in Robert E. Harkavy and Stephanie G. Neuman, *The Lessons of Recent Wars in the Third World* (Lexington, MA: D. C. Heath, 1985), chapter 7.

41. Sylvia K. Crosbie, *A Tacit Alliance: France and Israel from Suez to the Six Day War* (Princeton: Princeton University Press, 1974).

42. See Harkavy, *Spectre of a Middle Eastern Holocaust*.

43. Chaim Herzog, *The War of Atonement, October 1973* (Boston: Little, Brown, 1973), opening chapters.

44. Barbara Tuchman, *The Guns of August* (New York: Macmillan, 1962), chapters 1–6.

45. This analogy in the minds of the Pakistani military hierarchy is pointed out in D. K. Palit, *The Lightning Campaign* (New Delhi: Thomson Press, 1972), p. 77, wherein: "The Pakistani high command has for a number of years nursed a pipedream about launching a massive surprise offensive deep into Indian territory—spearheaded by armoured formations, a la Moshe Dayan."

46. Van Evera, *Causes of War*, chapter 6.

Chapter 3

1. See *Geography 89/90*, 4th ed., ed. Gerald R. Pitzl (Guildford, CT: Dushkin, 1989).

2. John M. Collins, *Military Geography for Professionals and the Public* (Washington: Brassey's, 1998).

3. United States Military Academy, *A Bibliography of Military Geography*, vols. 1–4 (West Point, NY: U.S. Military Academy, circa 1990).

4. Hugh Faringdon, *Confrontation: The Strategic Geography of NATO and the Warsaw Pact* (New York: Routledge and Kegan Paul, 1986).

5. Patrick O'Sullivan, *Terrain and Tactics* (New York: Greenwood Press, 1991); Patrick O'Sullivan and Jesse W. Miller, *The Geography of Warfare* (London: Croom Helm, 1983); and O'Sullivan, "A Geographical Analysis of Guerilla Warfare," *Political Geography Quarterly*, vol. 2, no. 2 (1983), pp. 139–150. See also earlier, Louis C. Peltier and E. Etzel Pearcy, *Military Geography* (Princeton: Van Nostrand, 1966).

6. Roger E. Kasperson and Julian Minghi, eds., *The Structure of Political Geography* (Chicago: Aldine, 1969); Dennis Rumley and Julian Minghi, *The Geography of Border Landscapes* (New York: Routledge and Keegan Paul, 1991); and Arnon Sofer and Y. Bar Gal, *Geographical Changes in the Traditional Arab Villages in Northern Israel* (Durham, U.K.: University of Durham, Center for Middle Eastern and Islamic Studies, 1981).

7. Anthony Cordesman and Abraham Wagner, *The Lessons of Modern War*, vol. 3 (Boulder, CO: Westview Press, 1990), pp. 1–237.

8. John Keegan and Andrew Wheatcroft, *Zones of Conflict: An Atlas of Future Wars* (London: Jonathan Cape, 1986).

9. Patrick O'Sullivan, "The Geography of Wars in the Third World," in Stephanie G. Neuman and Robert E. Harkavy, *The Lessons of Recent Wars in the Third World: Comparative Dimensions*, vol. 2 (Lexington, MA: D. C. Heath, 1987), p. 51.

10. Ibid.

11. Ibid., p. 38.

12. Collins, *Military Geography*, pp. 27–32.

13. Harold M. Forde, "An Introduction to Military Geography," *Military Review*, vol. 28, no. 11 (February 1949), pp. 26–36 and (March 1949), pp. 52–62.

14. O'Sullivan, "The Geography of Wars in the Third World," p. 46.

15. OCOKA: observation and fields of fire, cover and concealment, obstacles, key terrain, and avenues of approach, as noted in Kemp and Harkavy, *Strategic Geography and the Changing Middle East, op cit.,* p. 158.

16. Maj. James E. Wilson, Jr., "The Fourth Dimension of Terrain," *Military Review*, vol. 26, no. 6 (September 1946), pp. 49–55 (49).

17. André Gimond, "Desert Warfare," *Military Review*, vol. 28, no. 5 (August 1948), pp. 73–83 (73).

18. See Department of Defense, *Conduct of the Persian Gulf War*, Final Report to Congress, Pursuant to Title V of the Persian Gulf Conflict Supplemental Authorization and Personnel Benefits Act of

1991 (Public Law 102–25), Washington, D.C., April 1992 (hereinafter, The Pentagon Report), p. 138.

19. Collins, *Military Geography,* pp. 34–36.

20. Ibid., pp. 17–18.

21. General D. Palit, *The Lightning Campaign,* p. 77. See also Shirin Tahir-Kheli, "Defense Planning in Pakistan," in Stephanie G. Neuman, ed., *Defense Planning in Less-Industrialized States* (Lexington, MA: D. C. Heath, 1984), chapter 7.

22. The military aspects of Israel's strategic depth problem on the Golan Heights is illustrated, in an analysis of the tank warfare in 1973, in Avigdor Kahalani, *The Heights of Courage: A Tank Leader's War on the Golan* (Westport, CT: Greenwood Press, 1984).

23. Strategic depth in the Arab-Israeli context is discussed in Geoffrey Kemp and Robert E. Harkavy, *Strategic Geography and the Changing Middle East* (Washington, DC: Brookings Institution, 1997), pp. 163–164.

24. For a general treatment, see Stephanie G. Neuman, *Military Assistance in Recent Wars: The Dominance of the Superpowers* (New York: Praeger, 1986); and Michael Brzoska and Frederic Pearson, *Arms and Warfare: Escalation, De-Escalation and Negotiation* (Columbia, SC: University of South Carolina Press, 1994).

25. O'Sullivan, "The Geography of Wars in the Third World," p. 40.

26. Such natural barriers as an element of power are discussed in A. F. K. Organski, *World Politics* (New York: Alfred Knopf, 1958), pp. 126–127.

27. See, in particular, Anthony H. Cordesman and Abraham Wagner, *The Lessons of Modern War: The Iran-Iraq War,* vol. II (Boulder, CO: Westview Press, 1990), esp. pp. 70–74.

28. Anthony H. Cordesman and Abraham Wagner, *The Lessons of Modern War,* vol. I (Boulder, CO: Westview Press, 1990), esp. pp. 122–125.

29. Palit, *The Lightning Campaign,* chapter 7 and appendix B; "Indian Army Seeks to Tighten Ring around Isolated Pakistani Forces in East," *New York Times,* 7 December 1971, p. A1; and "Indians Cross Wide River and Drive on Dacca," *New York Times,* 11 December 1971, p. A1.

30. Cordesman and Wagner, *The Lessons of Modern War,* vol. II, pp. 71–74.

31. See Robert Harkavy, *Preemption and Two-Front Conventional Warfare: A Comparison of 1967 Israeli Strategy with the Pre-World War I German Schlieffen Plan,* Leonard Davis Institute, Hebrew University, Jerusalem Papers on Peace Problems, no. 23 (1978).

32. The basics of the Schlieffen Plan are rendered in Barbara Tuchman, *The Guns of August* (New York: Dell, 1962), esp. chapters 2–7; and Gerhard Ritter, *The Schlieffen Plan* (London: Oswald Wolff, 1958). See also Jack Snyder, *The Ideology of the Offensive* (Ithaca, NY: Cornell University Press, 1984).

33. See "Eritrea Rebels Besiege Massawa: Defenders Yield in Street Fighting," *New York Times,* 28 December 1977, p. A10.

34. In addition to previously cited sources, i.e., O'Sullivan, see also John M. Collins, *Military Geography, op cit.,* chapters 3, 5, and 6.

35. The Pentagon Report, p. 256.

36. Cordesman and Wagner, *The Lessons of Modern War,* vol. 2, *The Iran-Iraq War,* pp. 72 and 97.

37. "Ethiopia Reports Recapture of Key Ogaden Town," *New York Times,* 6 March 1978, p. A3.

38. This thesis is propounded in G. D. Sheffield, *Blitzkrieg and Attrition: Land Operations in Europe, 1914–1945,* in Colin McInnes and G. D. Sheffield, eds., *Warfare in the Twentieth Century: Theory and Practice* (London: Unwin, Hyman, 1988), chapter 3. Hence, on p. 51: "So deeply rooted is this belief that the world wars represent two distinct types of war and areas of generalship that the official biographer of Field-Marshal Montgomery regarded it as a slur upon his subject that the undeniably attritional battle of Alamein should be seen as being 'in the mold of World War I.' This chapter argues that this interpretation is misguided and that continuity, not change, was the hallmark of warfare at the tactical and operational levels during the period under examination, and further that it was the First World War, not the Second, that was the main period of innovation."

39. Van Creveld, *Military Lessons of the Yom Kippur War,* and for a later interpretation, Edward Luttwak and Dan Horowitz, *The Israeli Army* (Harper and Row, 1975), chapter 10.

40. Ibid.

41. Overall, the role of U.S. airpower in the Gulf War and the question of its decisiveness is discussed in Edward Luttwak, "The Gulf War in its Purely Military Dimension," in John O'Loughlin, Tom Mayer, and Edward S. Greenberg, eds., *War and Its Consequences: Lessons from the Persian Gulf Conflict* (New York: HarperCollins, 1994), pp. 33–50. In greater, indeed massive, detail, see also

the Pentagon's *Gulf War Airpower Survey,* directed by Eliot A. Cohen (Washington, DC: U.S. Government Printing Office, 1993), six volumes (hereinafter called GWAPS).

42. Palit, *The Lightning War,* chapter 6 and 7.

43. Cordesman and Wagner, *The Lessons of Modern War,* vol. 3, p. 52.

44. The Pentagon Report, p. XXIV and pp. 354–356; and James F. Dunnigan and Austin Bay, *From Shield to Storm* (New York: William Morrow, 1992), pp. 306 and 445.

45. Molly Moore, "Desert Defies Machine Age: Saudi Sun, Sand Hobble Weaponry," *Washington Post,* 3 September 1990, p. A1. See also "In the Table-Flat Land, Sand, Wind, and Flies," *New York Times,* 6 February 1991, p. A7.

46. "Chadians Describe Victory in Desert," *New York Times,* 14 August 1987, p. A1, wherein quoting a Chadian official, "we know it's better to have a good Toyota than a T-55."

47. Refer to Luttwak chapter and GWAPS volumes cites in note 40, this chapter.

48. For the role of Ascension and Britain's V-bomber attacks therefrom, see Cordesman and Wagner, *The Lessons of Modern War,* vol. 3, pp. 247 and 262. On p. 278, there is also discussion of British basing of Nimrod long-range maritime surveillance aircraft on Ascension during this war.

49. The point is made in Robert Taber, *The War of the Flea: A Study of Guerrilla Warfare* (New York: Lyle Stuart, 1965), pp. 129–130.

50. *Hammond Atlas of the World* (New York, 1999), p. 32.

51. "Sudan air force bombs refugee camp, killing 6," Associated Press dispatch, 25 July 1997, *Center Daily Times,* p. 9A.

52. "Afghanistan's capital region again surrounded by combat," Associated Press dispatch, 28 July 1997, *Center Daily Times,* p. 6A.

53. The Pentagon Report, pp. XVII and XXII-XXIII.

Chapter 4

1. See Douglas A. MacGregor, "Future Battle: The Merging Levels of War," *Parameters,* vol. 22, no. 4 (winter 1992–93), pp. 33–47.

2. Paul Kennedy, "Grand Strategy in War and Peace: Toward a Broader Definition," in Kennedy, ed., *Grand Strategies in War and Peace* (New Haven, CT: Yale University Press, 1991), p. 2.

3. Ibid., pp. 2–3. This is taken from Basil H. Liddell Hart, *Strategy* (New York: McGregor, 1967), pp. 335–336.

4. Kennedy, *Grand Strategies,* p. 5.

5. Edward Luttwak, *Strategy: The Logic of War and Peace* (Cambridge, MA: Belknap Press of Harvard University Press, 1987), esp. chapter 12. See also John M. Collins, "The Essence of Strategy," *Military Strategy: Theory and Application,* reference text for the Department of Military Strategy, Planning and Operations, U.S. Army War College, Carlisle Barracks, PA, 1983–1984, pp. 3–1 to 3–5, which differentiates between "national," "grand," and "military" strategies. For a "case study" of sorts centered on the U.S. at the close of the Cold War, see Edward Luttwak, "Do We Need a New Grand Strategy?" *The National Interest,* no. 15 (spring 1989), pp. 3–14.

6. Allan R. Millett, Williamson Murray, and Kenneth H. Watman, "The Effectiveness of Military Organizations," in Millett and Murray, eds., *Military Effectiveness,* vol. I (Boston: Allen and Unwin, 1988), esp. pp. 2–12.

7. A variation of this is in Samuel Huntington, "The Clash of Civilizations," *Foreign Affairs,* vol. 72, no. 3 (summer 1993), pp. 22–49 (22–23), looking at phases of the evolution of conflict in the modern world from a clash between monarchs to a clash between nation states to a clash of ideologies and then a clash of civilizations. These themes are also bruited in Richard Rosecrance, *The Rise of the Trading State* (New York: Basic Books, 1986).

8. Francis Fukuyama, *The End of History and the Last Man* (New York: Free Press, 1992).

9. The concept of "imperial overstretch" is associated with Paul Kennedy, *The Rise and Fall of the Great Powers* (New York: Random House, 1987).

10. Steven R. David, "Explaining Third World Alignment," *World Politics,* vol. 43, no. 2 (January 1991), pp. 253–256. This latter point is amplified in a related context, i.e., arms acquisitions and military expenditures, by Keith Krause, "Middle East Arms Recipients in the Post–Cold War World," *The Annals,* vol. 535 (September 1994), pp. 75–80.

11. George Modelski, "The Theory of Long Cycles and U.S. Strategic Policy," in Robert Harkavy and Edward A. Kolodziej, *American Security Policy and Policy-Making* (Lexington, MA: D.C. Heath, 1980), chapter 1.

12. Edward Milenky, "Argentina," in Edward A. Kolodziej and Robert E. Harkavy, eds., *Security Policies of Developing Countries* (Lexington, MA: D.C. Heath, 1982), chapter 2.

13. The "strategy" level of this conflict (encompassing "grand strategy") is covered in Harlan K. Ullman, "Profound or Perfunctory: Observations on the South Atlantic Conflict," in Harkavy and Neuman, eds., *The Lessons of Recent Wars in the Third World,* vol. 1, chapter 11. See also, among others, the *Sunday Times* of London, Insight Team, *War in the Falklands* (New York: Harper and Row, 1982), part 1; Lawrence Freedman and Virginia Gamba-Stonehouse, *Signals of War: The Falklands Conflict of 1982* (Princeton: Princeton University Press, 1991); and John Laffin, *Fight for the Falklands* (New York: St. Martin's Press, 1982). The Argentine "geopolitical perspective" is discussed in Ruben O. Moro, *The History of the South Atlantic Conflict* (New York: Praeger, 1989), esp. chapters 1–3.

14. The a priori grand strategic aspects of the Iran-Iraq War, albeit with other terminology, is discussed in Edgar O'Ballance, *The Gulf War* (London: Brassey's, 1988), chapters 1 and 3. Summarized in one sentence, Iraq's war aims were: "Fearing the Iranian Shi'a Revolution might over-spill into Iraq, President Saddam Hussein intended to cut Ayatollah Khomeini down to size, weaken his personal influence in the region, and perhaps topple him from absolute power in his own country." See also Cordesman and Wagner, *The Lessons of Modern War,* vol. 2, chapter 2, esp. pp. 21–36, under "The Struggle for Regional Influence," "The Question of Iraqi Objectives," and "The Question of Iranian Objectives," and Efraim Karsh, ed., *The Iran-Iraq War: Impact and Implications* (Basingstoke, U.K.: Macmillan, 1989).

15. The earlier phases of Iraqi "grand strategy," which focused on a desire for a leadership role in the Arab world vis-à-vis Egypt, are discussed in George Lenczowski, *The Middle East in World Affairs* (Ithaca, NY: Cornell University Press, 1962), chapter 7.

16. Amidst a blizzard of writings on Israeli security problems, elements of its putative (and evolving) grand strategy, absent explicit analysis of this concept, can be found in Edward Luttwak and Dan Horowitz, *The Israeli Army* (New York: Harper and Row, 1975); and in various selections in Efraim Karsh, ed., *Between War and Peace: Dilemmas of Israeli Security* (London: Frank Cass, 1996), esp. the piece by Efraim Inbar, "Israel's Security in a New International Environment," pp. 32–45. See also Karsh and Gregory Mahler, eds., *Israel at the Crossroads* (London: British Academic Press, 1994); and Bernard Reich and Gershon R. Kieval, eds., *Israeli National Security Policy* (New York: Greenwood Press, 1988). On a less comprehensively political basis than what is conveyed by the term "grand strategy," Michael Handel earlier provided an analysis of Israel's overall military doctrine, hinged on the preemptive offensive, in *Israel's Political-Military Doctrine* (Cambridge, MA: Harvard Center for International Affairs, 1973).

17. Martin van Creveld, *Military Lessons of the Yom Kippur War: Historical Perspectives* (Washington: Georgetown CSIS, 1975), Washington Papers no. 24.

18. This was discussed, regarding the earlier period preceding the 1967 war, in Robert E. Harkavy, *Spectre of a Middle Eastern Holocaust: The Strategic and Diplomatic Implications of the Israeli Nuclear Weapons Program* (Denver: University of Denver, 1977), Monograph Series in World Affairs, pp. 13 and 68.

19. Israel's "strategy of the peripheries" is discussed in Aharon Kleiman, *Statecraft in the Dark: Israel's Practice of Quiet Diplomacy* (Boulder, CO: Westview Press, 1988), for the Jaffee Center for Strategic Studies, pp. 76–77.

20. Among the works covering the "grand strategic" aspects of Israel's venture into Lebanon in 1982, see Ze'ev Schiff and Ehud Ya'ari, *Israel's Lebanon War* (New York: Simon and Schuster, 1984); and Richard Gabriel, *Operation Peace for Galilee: The Israeli-PLO War in Lebanon* (New York: Hill and Wang, 1984).

21. These pressures on U.S. foreign policy are discussed, among many sources (and for the progression of American presidential administrations from Truman to Reagan), in Steven L. Spiegel, *The Other Arab-Israeli Conflict* (Chicago: University of Chicago Press, 1985).

22. Michael Handel, *Israel's Political-Military Doctrine.* The failure of Israel's preemptive doctrine in 1973 is discussed in Chaim Herzog, *War of Atonement* (London: Weidenfeld and Nicolson, 1975), chapter 1, under "The New Strategic Concept."

23. From an earlier, and more narrowly Egyptian, perspective, see Ibrahim A. Karawan, "Egypt's Defense Policy," in Neuman, *Defense Planning in Less Industrialized States,* chapter 5; and Mohammed Heikal, *The Road to Ramadan* (New York: Quadrangle/New York Times, 1975).

24. For the politics of grand strategy encompassing this war and its historical background, see Nayan Chanda, *Brother Enemy: The War after the War* (New York: Harcourt, Brace, Jovanovich, 1986), esp. chapter 10, under "A Red Christmas." See also William Duiker, *China and Vietnam: The Roots of Conflict* (Berkeley, CA: University of California, Institute of East Asian Studies, 1986), esp. chapter 4.

25. Ibid., p. 361, wherein: "Whether the Chinese taught a lesson or the Vietnamese learned one, this was one war that nobody won." See also Harlan Jencks, "Lessons of a 'Lesson:' China-Vietnam 1979," in Harkavy and Neuman, eds., *The Lessons of Recent Wars in the Third World,* vol. 1, chapter 7.

26. The basics for an analysis of Ethiopian and Somalian grand strategies before, during, and after the Horn war can be gleaned from (for an earlier period) J. Bowyer Bell, *The Horn of Africa: Strategic Magnet in the Seventies* (New York: Crane, Russak, 1973), for the National Strategy Information Center; Colin Legum and Bill Lee, *The Horn of Africa in Continuing Crisis* (New York and London: Africana Publishing, 1979); and Paul B. Henze, *The Horn of Africa: From War to Peace* (London: Macmillan, 1991), esp. part 1.

27. Elements of a Pakistani grand strategy, during the era of the major wars with India, can be gleaned from Stephen P. Cohen, *The Pakistan Army* (Berkeley, CA: University of California Press, 1984), esp. chapters 1, 5, and 6; and Shirin Tahir-Kheli, "Defense Planning in Pakistan," in Stephanie G. Neuman, ed., *Defense Planning in Less-Industrialized States* (Lexington, MA: D.C. Heath, 1984), chapter 7.

28. A good review of the 1965 Indo-Pakistani war is Russell Brines, *The Indo-Pakistani Conflict* (London: Pall Mall, 1968).

29. See the introductory sections of Palit, *The Lightning Campaign,* Raju G. C. Thomas, "Defense Planning in India," in Neuman, *Defense Planning in Less-Industrialized States,* chapter 8; and Raju G. C. Thomas, *Indian Security Policy* (Princeton: Princeton University Press, 1986), esp. chapters 1, 2, and 8.

30. The lack of warm winter clothes (bootees, long underwear), is noted in Freedman and Gamba-Stonehouse, *Signals of War,* p. 390.

31. See Lawrence Freedman, *Britain and the Falklands War* (Oxford: Basil Blackwell, 1988), chapter 3; and Freedman and Gamba-Stonehouse, *Signals of War,* chapters 2 and 3.

32. Department of the Army, *Field Manual no. 100–5* (hereinafter *FM 100–5*), *Operations,* Washington, DC, 5 May 1986.

33. Luttwak, *Strategy: The Logic of War and Peace.*

34. Dwight L. Adams and Clayton R. Newell, "Operational Art in the Joint and Combined Arenas," *Parameters,* vol. 18, no. 2 (June 1988), pp. 33–39 (35). See also David Jablonsky, "Strategy and the Operational Level of War," part 1, *Parameters,* vol.. 17, no. 1 (spring 1987), pp. 67–76; John Turlington, "Truly Learning the Operational Art," ibid., pp. 51–64; Jay Luvaas, "Thinking at the Operational Level," *Parameters,* vol. 16, no. 1 (spring 1986), pp. 2–6; and John F. Meechan III, "The Operational Trilogy," *Parameters,* vol. 16, no. 3 (autumn 1986), pp. 9–18.

35. *FM 100–5,* p. 9.

36. Ibid.

37. Luttwak, *The Israeli Army,* p. 113.

38. Ibid.

39. *FM 100–5,* p. 10.

40. Ibid.

41. Ibid.

42. Luttwak, *The Israeli Army,* p. 91.

43. Basil H. Liddell Hart, *Strategy,* 2d rev. ed. (New York: Praeger, 1967).

44. Luttwak, p. 92.

45. Ibid., p. 93.

46. *FM 100–5,* pp. 11–13.

47. Luttwak, pp. 92–97, and van Creveld, *Military Lessons of the Yom Kippur War.*

48. *FM 100–5,* pp. 14–18.

49. *FM 100–5,* pp. 101–106.

50. David G. Chandler, *Atlas of Military Strategy* (New York: Free Press, 1980), under "Classical Maneuvers of War," pp. 12–13.

51. *FM 100–5,* pp. 101–105.

52. Chandler, *Atlas,* p. 12.

53. *FM 100–5,* appendix B, p. 180. The concept of "interior lines" is also discussed in Hart, *Strategy,* p. 108, wherein the strategy of interior lines is defined as "striking outwards from his central pivot against one of the forces on the circumference, and utilizing the shorter distance he had thus to travel to concentrate against one of the enemy forces before it could be supported by the others." This may be referenced to our discussion in chapter 3 about fighting two-front wars, as did Israel in 1967 and 1973.

54. Chandler, *Atlas.*

55. *FM 100–5,* pp. 134–135.

56. Ibid., p. 134.

57. Ibid.

58. Ibid., pp. 145–146. Again, it is noted that many of these concepts are discussed, with historical examples, in Hart, *Strategy.*

59. *FM 100–5,* appendix A, pp. 173–178.

60. Ibid., appendix B, pp. 179–182.

61. Ibid., p. 179.

62. Ibid., p. 181.

63. Ibid., p. 182.

64. See "U.S. and Soviet Bid India Avoid War," *New York Times,* 22 October 1971, p. A1, wherein: "The monsoons are ending and there are about four to five weeks before snow fills the passes in the Himalayas and hampers movement." But, according to Palit, *The Lightning Campaign,* pp. 65–67, there were other reasons why India calculated that the threat from China might have been neutralized: its debut in the U.N. and growing rapprochement with the U.S., and the tying down of more than five hundred thousand troops along the border with the USSR in connection with the boundary dispute along the Ussuri River. Ironically, many of the Indian Army units moved to the eastern fronts were mountain divisions, lightly armed, previously stationed near the Himalayas.

65. Palit, *The Lightning Campaign,* pp. 69–75. See also "New Delhi Sources Admit Troops Entered Pakistan," *New York Times,* 8 November 1971, p. A1; "Pakistan Reports Repulsing a Major Indian Offensive," *New York Times,* 11 November 1971, p. 12; "India Approaches War Footing as Frontier Fighting Intensifies," *New York Times,* 21 November 1971, p. A1; "A Major Attack in East Pakistan Reported Begun," *New York Times,* 23 November 1971, p. A1; "India Admits an Incursion, Says It Was Self-Defense," *New York Times,* 25 November 1971, p. A1; and "India Says Force Entered Pakistan for Second Time," *New York Times,* 27 November 1971, p. A1. The three-day long skirmish around Hilli is discussed in Palit, *The Lightning Campaign,* pp. 74–75.

66. "India and Pakistan Prepare for Possibility of Full War," *New York Times,* 3 December 1971, p. A1, which provides extensive prewar order of battle data. More such data are provided in "War! The Bitter Neighbors Take Up Arms Again," *New York Times,* 5 December 1971, p. 10, Week in Review section.

67. Pakistan's defensive plan is analyzed in Palit, *The Lightning Campaign,* pp. 94–98. Here, actually, Pakistani General Niazi is seen as having two broad choices for a defensive posture: "to resist the enemy with all his strength and to aim to stop him at the border; or to fight a flexible battle on the border and, if unsuccessful, to conduct an organized withdrawal back to ground of his own choosing where he could offer protracted resistance. The former has the advantage, if it succeeds in not giving up any great extent of territory to the enemy, but carries the risk of being defeated in detail at the border. The latter, though it is likely to result in early loss of territory, gives the defender an opportunity of fighting a mobile battle and making the best use of ground" (p. 95). Pakistan first chose the first operational strategy, then fell back on the latter.

68. Palit, *The Lightning Campaign.,* chapter 5 under "Pakistan Attacks in the West." See also "India and Pakistan Jets Clash; Both Sides Claim Ground Gain." *New York Times,* 5 December 1971, p. A1.

69. "Indians Report More Advances; Pakistan Cites Gain in Kashmir; Peace Moves Are Stalled in U.N.," *New York Times,* 6 December 1971, p. A1. See also Palit's analysis of the Indian offensive plan in his chapter 6, under "The Lightning Concept." See also "India vs. Pakistan," *New York Times,* 12 December 1971, Week in Review section, IV, p. 1, wherein India's "strategy of stand-off pending victory in the east" is discussed.

70. Palit, chapter 7, under "Twelve Days to Dacca."

71. "Indians Cross Wide River and Drive on Dacca; Pakistanis Find Outlook Grave," *New York Times,* 11 December 1971, p. A1; and regarding helicopter air-bridging and bridge-building operations, see Palit, *The Lightning Campaign,* p. 125. Pakistan's failed offensive in the western Rajasthan Desert is reported on in "Indian Army Seeks to Tighten Ring around Isolated Pakistani Forces in East," *New York Times,* 7 December 1991, p. 16. See also "India Says Her Troops from the North, Are within Six Miles of Dacca," *New York Times,* 1 December 1971, p. 18. Palit, *The Lightning Campaign,* p. 95, reports that "In general it can be said that Bangla Desh is perhaps the most river-crossed terrain in the world—a land indeed for defensive tactics. Not only do two of the world's great rivers flow through it, quadri-secting the country into four geographically isolated sections, a complex criss-cross of minor rivers and rivulets obstruct land movement."

72. Palit, *The Lightning Campaign,* chapter 5, describes the failed Pakistani offensive in the West, and the Indian counteroffensive. See also "Battle at Kashmir River Said to Leave 900 Dead," *New York Times,* 12 December 1971, p. 26. The latter describes the Pakistani assault across the shallow, sandy Munnawar Tawi River in an attempt to interdict the strategic Indian highway used to supply Indian troops in western Kashmir, near the village of Chhamb.

73. Palit, *The Lightning Campaign,* pp. 88–93.

74. Among the several book-length treatments of the Horn war, there is little in the way of analysis of the purely military aspects of the war. Operational and tactical considerations must, therefore, be gleaned from, or inferred from, the largely descriptive, factual reportage in the press, particularly *New York Times.*

75. The early phase of the war, fought in the Ogaden, is detailed in "Ethiopia and Pro-Somali Rebels Claim Success in Border Conflict," *New York Times,* 22 July 1977, p. 3; "Ethiopia Says it Shot Down 2 Jets," *New York Times,* 26 July 1977, p. 3; "Four Ethiopian Craft Downed," *New York Times,* 29 July 1977, p. A4; "Somalia Reports Gains By Rebels in Ethiopia," *New York Times,* 31 July 1977, p. 7; "Somali Insurgents Say They Seized Ethiopian Town," 3 August 1977, p. 4; and "Heavy Casualties are Reported in Month of Ethiopia-Somali Conflict," *New York Times,* 12 August 1977, p. A4.

76. "Africa's Horn Has Plenty of Trouble," *New York Times,* 7 August 1977, IV, p. 5.

77. "Secession Wars Push Ethiopia to the Brink," *New York Times,* 7 August 1977, p. 5, which also reports on support for the Eritrean guerillas by Arab states. See also "Eritrea Rebels Besiege Massawa; Defenders Yield in Street Fighting," *New York Times,* 28 December 1977, p. A10.

78. The Somali assault on Dire Dawa is reported in "Somali Mortars Pound Key City in Intensive Warfare in Ethiopia," *New York Times,* 18 August 1977, p. A2; "Ethiopia Said to Have Repelled Fierce Somali Attack," *New York Times,* 23 August 1977, p. 8; "Ethiopia Concedes It is Losing Ground on Two War Fronts," *New York Times,* 26 August 1977, p. 3.

79. The Ethiopian counterattack is reported in "Ethiopia Drives Somalia's Forces from Key Areas," *New York Times,* 13 February 1978, p. A1.

80. The Ethiopian recapture of Jijiga, supported by Soviet advisors and Cuban troops, is reported in "Ethiopia Reports Recapture of Key Ogaden Town," *New York Times,* 6 March 1978, p. A3; and "Ethiopia Says it Now Holds Entire Ogaden Region," *New York Times,* 25 March 1978, p. 4.

81. In an ironic twist, in 1999 Ethiopia fought a very stationery war of attrition against now independent Eritrea, one in which Ethiopia appears to have taken massive casualties in frontal assaults against Eritrean positions. The difference from 1978 appears to have resulted largely from the terrain (hard desert), the much greater frontal width of the battle area and absence of mountains, and also the absence of Cubans and Russians who had engineered Ethiopia's earlier mobile offensive. See Karl Vick, "Modern Weapons, Old-Style Tactics," *Washington Post* 5 April 1999, p. 14, National Weekly Edition, in which it is stated that, quoting Richard Cromwell, "mobile warfare, combined arms warfare is not easily waged—it has to be very finely tuned to go forward without suffering huge casualties."

82. For basic order of battle data, including the diversion of Vietnamese troops to Cambodia, see Duiker, *China and Vietnam: The Roots of Conflict,* pp. 84–89, who reports (p. 85) that "the cream of the PAVN was operating in Cambodia." For further analysis of the situation preceding the war, see Edward Friedman, "The Risk China Faces," *New York Times,* 4 February 1979, p. E19. For additional order of battle information, see "'Friendship Pass' No Longer Links Peking to Hanoi," *New York Times,* 5 February 1979, p. A3. Operational considerations are discussed in "Scholars Interpret Invasion in Two Ways," *New York Times,* 19 February 1979, p. A11.

83. Drew Middleton, "Chinese Options for Any Move on Vietnam."

84. Drew Middleton, "A Classic Military Operation," *New York Times,* 18 February 1979, p. A1. See also Nayan Chanda, *Brother Enemy: The War after the War* (New York: Harcourt, Brace, Jovanovich, 1986), esp. pp. 356–358. Herein it is reported that China first attempted human-wave tactics utilizing some eighty-five thousand troops streaming into Vietnam through twenty six points along the border, but after suffering massive casualties, switched to a "more discriminating attack in coordination with artillery and tank support" (p. 357).

85. Ibid.

86. "China Pauses in Vietnam Attack for Reinforcement." *New York Times,* 19 February 1979, p. A6.

87. The battle of Lang Son is described in Chanda, *Brother Enemy,* p. 357, with the border town laying in rubble, littered with corpses. See also "Chinese Decreasing Pressure on Town in Vietnam Attack," *New York Times,* 24 February 1979, p. A1; "The Chinese Push: Waiting for the Climax," *New York Times,* 27 February 1979, p. A10.

88. "China's Options for the Invasion's Last Act," *New York Times,* 3 March 1979, p. A3.

89. Ibid.

90. Ibid.

91. Chanda, *Brother Enemy,* p. 357, refers to a "sixteen-day pedagogical war" which left a swathe of devastation along the China-Vietnam border. Most towns occupied by the Chinese in this war were "objects of systematic destruction; some of it after the Chinese announced their impending withdrawal (p. 358).

92. Ze'ev Schiff and Ehud Ya'ari, *Israel's Lebanon War* (New York: Simon and Schuster, 1984), chapters 2 and 3; and more specifically, Richard Gabriel, *Operation Peace for Galilee* (New York: Hill and Wang, 1984), chapter 3.

93. Gabriel, *Operation Peace,* p. 61, mentions the precedent of Operation Litani.

94. Ibid.

95. Ibid.

96. Ibid., pp. 67–68.

97. Ibid., p. 81, claims that the Israeli forces failed to take sufficient account of the terrain, i.e., were not adequately prepared to fight a mountain campaign. Hence, "the IDF had no experience in mountain warfare, and the tactics they brought to bear on this war—rapid advance, heavy-armor formations, and mounted infantry—were more suitable for open terrain and desert warfare."

98. Schiff and Ya'ari, *Israel's Lebanon War,* p. 108.

99. Ibid., chapters 7 and 8, and Gabriel, *Operation Peace,* chapter 3, esp. pp. 75–82, under "Order of Battle and Tactical Plan."

100. Schiff and Ya'ari, *Israel's Lebanon War,* p. 132.

101. Ibid., pp. 142–150.

102. Ibid., chapter 9; and Gabriel, *Operation Peace,* pp. 92–95.

103. Gabriel, *Operation Peace,* p. 97.

104. The air operation against the Syrian SAMs is discussed in Gabriel, *Operation Peace,* pp. 97–99; and Schiff and Ya'ari, *Israel's Lebanon War,* pp. 166–168.

105. See Gabriel, *Operation Peace,* map on p. 101.

106. The Israeli dilemma regarding the investiture of Beirut is discussed in Gabriel, *Operation Peace,* chapter 4; and Schiff and Ya'ari, *Israel's Lebanon War,* chapter 11.

107. See Nick Vaux, *Take That Hill! Royal Marines in the Falklands War* (McLean, VA: Pergamon-Brassey's, 1986), esp. chapter 4; and the *Sunday Times* of London Insight Team (hereinafter Insight Team), *War in the Falklands* (New York: Harper and Row, 1982), esp. pp. 103–104 , and 158–161. Actually, Wideawake Field had been leased to the U.S., so the U.K. needed permission to use a base on its own territory. Additionally, Freedman and Gamba-Stonehouse, *Signals of War,* p. 86, point to the importance of a SIGINT station on Ascension deemed critical for listening to Argentinian naval communications.

108. Insight Team, pp. 164–167; Harlan Ullman, "Observations on the South Atlantic Conflict," p. 242; and Freedman and Gamba-Stonehouse, *Signals of War,* pp. 260–269, 286–294.

109. See Insight Team, esp. pp. 205–207. Therein it is pointed out that without a base on the Falklands themselves, the nearest Argentinian air base at Rio Gallegos was four hundred miles away, making the Argentinian pilots fly close to the limits of their range and leaving them little loiter

time to find a target or to engage in a dogfight. See also Freedman and Gamba-Stonehouse, pp. 326–327 for an analysis of the inability of the Argentine Air Force to utilize the airbase at Stanley for operations with aircraft larger than the Pucara.

110. Ibid., pp. 206–207. See also Freedman and Gamba-Stonehouse, *Signals of War*, pp. 255–259.

111. Ibid., pp. 114–118; and Ullman, "Observations in the South African Conflict," p. 256.

112. Insight Team, p. 185.

113. Freedman and Gamba-Stonehouse, *Signals of War*, chapters 19 and 20.

114. Ibid., p. 235.

115. Anthony Cordesman and Abraham R. Wagner, *The Lessons of Modern War*, vol. 2 (Boulder, CO: Westview Press, 1990).

116. Cordesman and Wagner, *The Lessons of Modern War*, pp. 31–33, discuss Iraq's war objectives, including the objective of seizing and holding oil-rich Khuzistan Province.

117. See ibid., chapter 10, for an analysis of Iran's near-collapse in 1988.

118. Ibid., p. 79.

119. Ibid., pp. 79–85.

120. Iraq's land invasion of Iran in 1980 is covered in detail in ibid., pp. 84–90.

121. Ibid., pp. 89–90.

122. Ibid. See also ibid., chapter 12, under "Combined Arms and the Land War."

123. Ibid., pp. 479–483, under "Close Air Support."

124. Ibid., chapter 5, under "Phase Two: Iran Regains Its Territory, 1981–1982."

125. Ibid., chapter 6, under "Phase Three: Iran Invades Iraq, June 1982–March 1984."

126. Ibid., pp. 178–183.

127. This phase is covered in ibid., chapter 7, under "Phase Four: The War of Attrition and the War in the Gulf, April 1984 to 1986."

128. Ibid., pp. 219–225.

129. Ibid., chapter 8, under "Phase Five: Iran's 'Final Offensives,' 1986–1987."

130. Ibid., pp. 257–262.

131. Ibid., p. 261.

132. Ibid., pp. 363–368 covers "the war of the cities."

133. Ibid., pp. 307–317.

134. Ibid., pp. 318–319.

135. Ibid., p. 353.

136. Ibid., chapter 10, under "Iraqi Offensives and Western Intervention Force a Cease-Fire, September 1987–March 1989," esp. pp. 353–357.

137. Ibid., pp. 363–368, under "The War of the Cities Turns into a Missile War."

138. Ibid., pp. 370–372.

139. Ibid., pp. 373–375.

140. Ibid., pp. 395–403.

141. B.H. Liddell Hart, *Strategy*.

142. Those serial objectives are reviewed in Geoffrey Kemp and Robert E. Harkavy, *Strategic Geography and the Changing Middle East* (Washington, D.C.: Brookings Institution, 1997), p. 300. The air operations are covered in greater detail in the Pentagon Report, *Conduct of the Persian Gulf War*, chapter 6; and James F. Dunnigan and Austin Bay, *From Shield to Storm* (New York: William Morrow, 1992), chapters 6 and 7.

143. See again Edward Luttwak, "The Gulf War in its Purely Military Dimensions," in O'Loughlin, Mayer, and Greenberg, eds., *War and Its Consequences*, pp. 33–50.

144. The Pentagon Report, p. 248. This report also notes, p. 142, nearly a hundred thousand total combat and support sorties flown throughout the war.

145. The Pentagon Report, pp. 170–173 and 413–415; Dunnigan and Bay, pp. 200–202.

146. The Pentagon Report, p. 227. See also Dunnigan and Bay, p. 271, for expansion on the "Hail Mary" concept, said to reflect AirLand 2000 Battle's concepts of initiative and agility.

147. Deception operations are discussed in the Pentagon Report, pp. 247–248.

148. Ibid., p. 294.

149. The Pentagon Report, p. 238.

150. Accounts of the battlefield fighting and tactics of this war appeared in the following *International Herald Tribune* articles: "Fighting Again Heavy along Eritrean Front," 25 May 2000, p. 4; "Ethiopia Claims Capture of Another Key Town," 22 May 2000, p. 4; "Ethiopian Troops Cele-

brate a Victory," 20–21 May, p. 4; "Ethiopians Bomb Airstrip in Eritrea as Talks Begin," 30 May 2000, p. 6; "War in Eritrea: Withdrawal or Rout?" 26 May 2000, p. 1.

151. Lynn Montross, *War through the Ages,* 3d ed. (New York: Harper and Row, 1960); and J. F. C. Fuller, *A Military History of the Western World,* 3 Vols. (New York: Funk and Wagnalls, 1954–1956). See also, among other such analytical histories of weapons and tactics, Richard A. Gabriel and Karen S. Metz, *A Short History of War: The Evolution of Warfare and Weapons* (Carlisle, PA: U.S. Army War College, Strategic Studies Institute), Professional Readings in Military Strategy, no. 5, 30 June 1992; and Tom Wintringham, *The Story of Weapons and Tactics from Troy to Stalingrad* (Boston: Houghton Mifflin, 1943).

152. Montross, *War through the Ages,* p. 6.

153. See ibid., p. 44 (Macedonia siege technology), p. 95 (invention of the stirrup, allowing for cavalry shock tactics, deemed "the foremost contribution of the Dark Ages to the science of war), pp. 167–172 (the longbow at Crecy), pp. 398–399 (the Prussian development of heavy artillery), p. 450 (the cannonade at Valmy in 1792), and pp. 735–739 (the introduction of massed tank formations at Cambrai).

154. As previously noted, this common theme is contested in G. D. Sheffield, "Blitzkrieg and Attrition: Land Operations in Europe 1914–1945," in Colin McInnes and G. D. Sheffield, eds., *Warfare in the Twentieth Century,* chapter 3.

155. The later contested thesis was laid out in Martin van Creveld, *The Military Lessons of the Yom Kippur War.*

156. Montross, *War through the Ages,* p. 39.

157. Ibid., p. 60.

158. Ibid., p. 7.

159. Ibid., p. 8.

160. Ibid., pp. 85–86 in the context of the Roman army, but also of Masada. Or, p. 27, in the context of Macedonia's defeat of Persia: "An orderly retreat was rare except among the most disciplined troops; and the pursuit of broken foemen almost invariably turned into a massacre lasting for miles and for hours."

161. John Keegan, *A History of Warfare,* pp. 169–177.

162. Ibid., p. 176.

163. Ibid., p. 177.

164. Ibid., p. 259.

165. Montross, *War through the Ages,* pp. 152–153.

166. Keegan, *A History of Warfare,* pp. 191–200. See also Montross, *War through the Ages,* pp. 120–122.

167. Montross, *War through the Ages,* pp. 168–172.

168. See among others, Hew Strachan, *European Armies and the Conduct of War* (London: Allen and Unwin, 1983), chapter 9.

169. G. D. Sheffield, "Blitzkrieg and Attrition 1914–1945," in Colin McInnes and G. D. Sheffield, eds., *Warfare in the Twentieth Century,* pp. 58–60.

170. See Randolph S. Churchill and Winston S. Churchill, *The Six Day War* (London: Heinemann, 1970), pp. 180–191; and Eric Hammel, *Six Days in June* (New York: Charles Scribner's Sons, 1992), part 7.

171. Churchill and Churchill, *The Six Day War,* chapter 6; and Hammel, *Six Days,* part 4.

172. Chaim Herzog, *War of Atonement,* chapters 12 and 13; and Van Creveld, *The Military Lessons of the Yom Kippur War.* See also Cordesman and Wagner, vol. 1, esp. pp. 53–67, for an analysis of Israel's failure at the outset of the 1973 war, in part because of underutilization of infantry and artillery.

173. Avigdor Kahalani, *The Heights of Courage* (Westport, CT: Greenwood Press, 1984), esp. p. 41. See also Cordesman and Wagner, *The Lessons of Modern War,* vol. 1, p. 70, regarding Israeli use of a large tank ditch on the perimeter of the Golan.

174. Kahalani, *The Heights,* pp. 48–50. See also Cordesman and Wagner, vol. 1, pp. 57–64, for an analysis of the use of armored equipment on both sides during the 1973 war.

175. Gabriel, *Operation Peace,* p. 74. See also Cordesman and Wagner, *The Lessons of Modern War,* vol. 1, pp. 168–169, which refers to "the continued Israeli stress on armor and use of armor-heavy combat teams" being evident throughout the Lebanon war, reporting that "in many instances, tanks proceeded with very little infantry support."

176. Gabriel, *Operation Peace,* p. 81. See Cordesman and Wagner, *The Lessons of Modern War,* vol. 1, pp. 122–125, for an analysis of the terrain in Lebanon. See also their pp. 213–215, regarding Israel's use of combined-arms operations.

177. Gabriel, *Operation Peace,* pp. 197–200. See also Cordesman and Wagner, *The Lessons of Modern War,* vol. 1, pp. 172–173, for a discussion of the tactical implications of the Merkava tank in Lebanon.

178. Ibid., pp. 98–99. The successful Israeli campaign against Syrian SAM batteries and in air-to-air combat is covered in Cordesman and Wagner, *The Lessons of Modern War,* vol. 1, pp. 74–98.

179. Drew Middleton, "A Classic Military Operation," *New York Times,* 18 February 1979, p. A1.

180. Fox Butterfield, "Incursion by China Placed at 10 Miles after New Fighting," *New York Times,* 21 February 1979, p. A1.

181. See also Drew Middleton, "Pause in the Vietnam Battle," *New York Times,* 19 February 1979, p. A1.

182. Drew Middleton, "China's Soldier is Put to the Test," *New York Times,* 25 February 1979, p. A1. See also "Vietnamese Are Locked in Battle with Chinese at 3 Frontier Towns," *New York Times,* 26 February 1979, p. A1, and "China Renews Push; Hanoi Said to Move Up Regulars," *New York Times,* February 23, 1979, p. A1, which states that "Peking's commanders are believed to be having some trouble maneuvering large forces, perhaps because they have had no battle experience since the Korean War, 25 years ago."

183. Drew Middleton, "China's Options for the Invasion's Last Act," *New York Times,* 3 March 1979, p. A3.

184. Ibid.

185. "Chinese, after New Fighting, Are Reported 10 Miles inside Vietnam," *New York Times,* 21 February 1979, p. A1.

186. "Vietnamese and Chinese Locked in Battle at 3 Towns," *New York Times,* 26 February 1979, p. A8.

187. Ibid.

188. "Chinese After New Fighting, Are Reported 10 Miles inside Vietnam," *New York Times,* 21 February 1979, p. A1, and Drew Middleton, "China's Last Chance: No Quick, Easy Victory in Vietnam," *New York Times,* 27 February 1979, p. A10.

189. India's use of mixed armor and infantry units, i.e., reinforced infantry brigades, in East Pakistan is discussed in "Indian Force in Pakistan for the 4th Day, *New York Times,* 1 December 1971, p A3.

190. Comparative Indian and Pakistani doctrines and tactics for tank warfare are discussed in "India and Pakistan Prepare for the Possibility of a General War," *New York Times,* 3 December 1971, p. A10. See also Palit, *The Lightning Campaign,* op cit., pp. 83–84; and "Battle at Kashmir River said to Leave 900 Dead," *New York Times,* 12 December 1971, p. A26.

191. Regarding tank warfare in the Rajasthan Desert, see "Indian Army Seeks to Tighten Ring around Isolated Pakistani Forces in East," *New York Times,* 7 December 1971, p. A16, and Palit, *The Lightning Campaign,* p. 89.

192. Palit, *The Lightning Campaign,* pp. 146–150. See also "Indians Said to Mine Port," *New York Times,* 27 November 1971, p. A12.

193. Palit, *The Lightning Campaign,* pp. 141–145.

194. See also "Somali Mortars Pound Key City in Intensive Warfare in Ethiopia," *New York Times,* 18 August 1977, p. A2.

195. "Somalis Found in Control of Ethiopian Town and Key Mountain Pass," *New York Times,* 29 September 1977, p. A10. This article gives detailed account of the tactics and weapons (mortars, tanks, antitank weapons, etc.) used by both sides. Also, Ethiopia's counterattack resulting in extensive captures of Somali tanks and armored personnel carriers is reported in "A Jubilant Ethiopian Capital Hears Its Army Has Routed Somali Force," *New York Times,* 7 September 1977, p. A2.

196. "Ethiopians Say They Strafed Somali Foe," *New York Times,* 17 August 1977, p. A10; "Ethiopia Said to Have Repelled Fierce Somali Attack," *New York Times,* 23 August 1977, p. A8; and "Somalis Found in Control of Ethiopian Town and Key Mountain Pass," *New York Times,* 29 September 1977, p. A10, which reports on Somali use of F-5 fighter aircraft in the battle for Jijiga.

197. "Heavy Fighting Reported in Harar, fall of Ethiopian City Held Likely," *New York Times,* 27 November 1977, p. A15.

198. "Somalis Say Ethiopians Are Preparing Big Attack," *New York Times,* 7 February 1978, p. A3;"Pitfalls for a Soviet-Backed Ethiopian Offensive," *New York Times,* 9 February 1978, p. A6.

199. "Ethiopia Drives Somalia's Forces from Key Areas," *New York Times,* 13 February 1978, p. A1, which reports on the critical importance of Soviet-supplied MIGs flying out of a base at Dire Dawa. See also "A Visit to the Ogaden Front Finds Somali Rebels Holding On Grimly," *New York Times,* 20 February 1978, p. A8.

200. "Ethiopia Reports Recapture of Key Ogaden Town," *New York Times,* 6 March 1978, pp. A3 and A4, and "Somali Forces Have Abandoned Positions in Ogaden," *New York Times,* 9 March 1978, p. A4.

201. Anthony Cordesman and Abraham Wagner, *The Lessons of Modern War,* volume 2, p. 423.

202. Ibid., p. 425.

203. Ibid., pp. 424 and 435–436.

204. Ibid., p. 424.

205. Ibid.

206. Ibid., p. 425.

207. Ibid., p. 437.

208. Ibid., pp. 431–432.

209. Ibid., p. 427.

210. Ibid.

211. Ibid., p. 432.

212. Ibid., p. 437.

213. Ibid.

214. Ibid., pp. 435–436.

215. Ibid., pp. 113–114.

216. Ibid., p. 439.

217. Ibid., p. 449.

218. Ibid.

219. Ibid., p. 450.

220. Ibid.

221. Ibid.

222. Ibid., p. 440.

223. Ibid., pp. 442–443.

224. Ibid.

225. Ibid., p. 446.

226. The Pentagon Report.

227. See, for example, Michael J. Mazaar, Jeffrey Shaffer, and Benjamin Ederington, *The Military Technical Revolution: A Structural Framework* (Washington, DC: Center for Strategic and International Studies, 1993); William A. Owens, "Introduction," in Stuart E. Johnson and Martin C. Libicki, eds., *Dominant Battlespace Knowledge* (Washington, DC: National Defense University, 1996), pp. 1–14; William J. Perry, "Desert Storm and Deterrence," *Foreign Affairs,* vol. 70, no. 4 (fall 1991), pp. 65–82; and Martin C. Libicki, *The Mesh and the Net: Speculations on Armed Conflict in a Time of Free Silicon* (Washington, DC: National Defense University, March 1994), McNair Paper no. 28.

228. The Pentagon Report, *op cit.,* pp. 251–252.

229. Ibid., pp. 264–268.

230. Those tactics are covered in *The Pentagon Report,* pp. 270–283.

231. James F. Dunnigan, and Austin Bay, *From Shield to Storm,* (New York: William Morrow, 1992), p. 214.

232. Ibid., p. 294.

233. Ibid., pp. 192–193, 352, and 392.

234. Ibid., pp. 196–197.

235. Ibid., p. 276.

236. Ibid., pp. 259–260.

237. Ibid., p. 284.

238. Cordesman and Wagner, *The Lessons of Modern War,* vol. 1, pp. 185–203.

239. The subsequent analysis is drawn from Palit, *The Lightning Campaign,* chapter 9, under "The War in the Air and at Sea," and chapter 5, under "Pakistan Attacks in the West."

240. Cordesman and Wagner, *The Lessons of Modern War,* vol. 2, p. 456.

241. Ibid., vol. 3, pp. 169–219.

242. Ibid.

243. Ibid., pp. 180–191.

244. Pentagon's *Gulf War Airpower Survey,* directed by Eliot A. Cohen (Washington, D.C.: U.S. Government Printing Office, 1993), six volumes (hereinafter called GWAPS), vol.2, p. 110.

245. The Pentagon Report, chapter VI, under "The Air Campaign."

246. Dunnigan and Bay, *From Shield to Storm,* p. 207.

247. Dunnigan and Bay, p. 182.

248. The Pentagon Report, pp. 674–675.

249. GWAPS, vol. 4, pp. 222, 356.

250. The Pentagon Report, pp. 166–168; and Dunnigan and Bay, *From Shield to Storm,* pp. 183–190, review the "Great Scud Hunt"; see also Anthony Cordesman, *After the Storm,* esp. pp. 410–412, 491–493.

251. Palit, *The Lightning Campaign,* chapter 9.

252. Ibid., p. 149.

253. A more detailed analysis of these issues is in Kemp and Harkavy, *Strategic Geography and the Changing Middle East,* pp. 185–187.

Chapter 5

1. Steven R. David, "Internal War: Causes and Cures," *World Politics,* vol. 49 (July 1997), pp. 552–576.

2. Ibid., p. 554.

3. Michael Klare, "The New Arms Race: Light Weapons and International Security," *Current History* vol. 96, no. 609, pp. 173–178; Aaron Karp, "Arming Ethnic Conflict," *Arms Control Today,* vol. 23, pp. 8–13; and John Sislin, "Arms and Escalation in Ethnopolitical Conflicts," paper presented at meeting of International Studies Association, Washington, D.C., 16–20 February 1999.

4. A representative publication is J. David Singer and Melvin Small, *Resort to Arms: International and Civil Wars, 1816–1980,* 2d ed. (Beverly Hills, CA: Sage, 1982).

5. Holsti, *The State, War, and the State of War.*

6. Discussed in S. David, "Internal War," pp. 562–567, based on a review of Michael E. Brown, "The Causes and Regional Dimensions of Internal Conflict," in Brown, ed., *The International Dimension of Internal Conflict* (Cambridge, MA: MIT Press, 1996), chapter 17, pp. 571–601.

7. Chaim Kaufmann, "Possible and Impossible Solutions to Ethnic Civil Wars," *International Security,* vol. 20, no. 4 (spring 1996), pp. 136–175.

8. Kaufmann, "Possible and Impossible," pp. 146–147.

9. Kaldor, *New and Old Wars,* p. 8.

10. Ibid., Then, Ibid., p. 9, in commenting on the economics of these new wars, states that "the fighting units finance themselves through external assistance. The latter can take the following forms: remittances from the diaspora, 'taxation' of humanitarian assistance, support from neighboring governments or illegal trade in arms, drugs, or valuable commodities such as oil or diamonds."

11. Lt. Col. George Stetser, "Concepts of Guerilla Warfare and Insurgent War," in *Military Strategy: Theory and Application,* a reference text (Carlisle, PA: U.S. Army War College, 1983), p. 13–1. Generally, regarding guerilla, revolutionary, and insurgency warfare (however defined and mutually distinguished), see Frank Kitson, *Low Intensity Operations: Subversion, Insurgency, Peacekeeping* (Hamden, CT: Archon Books, 1974); Nathan C. Leites. *Rebellion and Authority: An Analytical Essay on Insurgent Conflicts* (Santa Monica, CA: RAND Corp., 1970); and Andrew Mackey, *Insurgency* (Chapel Hill: University of North Carolina Press, 1970).

12. Lt. Col. George R. Stetser, "Concepts," chapter 13. See also Gerard Chaliand, ed., *Guerilla Strategies: An Historical Anthology from the Long March to Afghanistan* (Berkeley, CA: University of California Press, 1982).

13. Jean Gottmann, "Bugeaud, Gallieni, Lyautey: The Development of French Colonial Warfare," in Edward M. Earle, ed., *Makers of Modern Strategy* (Princeton: Princeton University Press, 1948), pp. 206–238.

14. Stetser, "Concepts," p. 13–1.

15. Ibid., p. 13–4.

16. Ibid., p. 13–5.
17. Ibid., pp. 13–6, 13–7.
18. Ibid., p. 13–7.
19. Ibid., pp. 13–7, 13–8.
20. Ibid., p. 13–8.
21. Ibid., pp. 13–8, 13–9.
22. Ibid., p. 13–9.
23. Ibid., p. 13–9.
24. Ibid.
25. Ibid., p. 13–10. See also George K. Tanham, *Communist Revolutionary Warfare from the Vietminh to the Vietcong* (New York: Praeger, 1967).
26. Stetser, p. 13–11.
27. Ibid.
28. Ibid., pp. 13–11, 13–12.
29. Ibid., p. 13–12.
30. Ibid.
31. Ibid., p. 13–13.
32. Ibid.
33. Ibid.
34. Ibid.
35. Ibid.
36. Ibid., p. 13–14.
37. Ibid., p. 13–15.
38. Ibid.
39. Ibid.
40. The basics of the Reagan Doctrine are discussed in Mark P. Lagon, *The Reagan Doctrine: Sources of American Conduct in the Cold War's Last Chapter* (Westport, CT: Praeger, 1994); Fareed Zakaria, "The Reagan Doctrine of Containment," *Political Science Quarterly,* vol. 105 (fall 1990), pp. 373–395; Christopher DeMuth et al., *The Reagan Doctrine and Beyond* (Washington, DC: American Enterprise Institute for Public Policy Research, 1987); Charles Krauthammer, "Morality and the Reagan Doctrine: The Rights and Wrongs of Guerilla Warfare," *New Republic,* 8 September 1986, pp. 17–24 and "The Poverty of Realism," 17 February 1986, pp. 14–22; and Robert A. Johnson, *Rollback Revisited: A Reagan Doctrine for Insurgent Wars?* (Washington, DC: Overseas Development Council, 1986).
41. See in particular, Douglas S. Blaufarb, *The Counterinsurgency Era: U.S. Doctrine and Performance, 1950 to the Present* (New York: Free Press, 1977); D. Michael Shafer, *Deadly Paradigms: The Failure of U.S. Counterinsurgency Policy* (Princeton: Princeton University Press, 1988); Nathan Leites and Charles Wolf, Jr., *Rebellion and Authority: An Analytic Essay on Insurgent Conflicts* (Chicago: Markham, 1970); John Maynard Dow, *National Building in Southeast Asia,* rev. ed. (Boulder, CO: Pruett Press, 1966); Andrew Scott et al, *Insurgency* (Chapel Hill: University of North Carolina Press, 1970); and Rod Paschall, *LIC 2010* (Washington, DC: Brassey's, 1990).
42. Shafer, *Deadly Paradigms,* p. 4 and pp. 18–19 provides commentary on the relationship between U.S. nuclear doctrines and the emerging emphasis on counterinsurgency.
43. Jean Gottmann, "Bugeaud, Gallieni, Lyautey: The Development of French Colonial Warfare," pp. 206–233.
44. Ibid., p. 211.
45. Blaufarb, *The Counterinsurgency Era,* chapter 4. Generally, regarding counterinsurgency, see also John J. McCuen, *The Art of Counter-Revolutionary War: The Strategy of Counter Insurgency* (Harrisburg, PA: Stackpole Books, 1966); and Richard Shultz, ed., *Guerilla Warfare and Counterinsurgency* (Lexington, MA: D.C. Heath, 1989).
46. Charles Maechling, Jr., "Counterinsurgency: The First Ordeal By Fire," in Michael T. Klare and Peter Kornbluh, eds., *Low-Intensity Warfare* (New York: Pantheon Books, 1988), p. 40.
47. Britain's ultimately futile conduct of a string of colonial wars in the 1950s and 1960s is related in Gregory Blaxland, *The Regiments Depart* (London: William Klimber, 1971).
48. Blaufarb, *The Counterinsurgency Era,* pp. 103–106; Shafer, *Deadly Paradigms,* pp. 266–268.
49. Charles Maechling, Jr., "Counterinsurgency: The First Ordeal By Fire," p. 39.
50. Ibid.
51. Blaufarb, *The Counterinsurgency Era,* chapter 8.

52. See Anthony Cordesman, *The Lessons of Modern War,* vol. 3, pp. 3–237, for a detailed analysis of Soviet counterinsurgency operations.

53. Departments of the U.S. Army and the U.S. Air Force, *Military Operations in Low Intensity Conflict, FM 100–20* and *Air Force Pamphlet 3–20,* Washington, D.C., 5 December 1990; and U.S. Department of the Army, *Operations in a Low-Intensity Conflict,* Washington, D.C., 17 October 1992.

54. *FM 100–20,* p. 2–6.

55. Ibid.

56. Ibid., p. 2–5.

57. Ibid., pp. 2–7 and 2–14.

58. Victor T. LeVine, "Conceptualizing 'Ethnicity' and 'Ethnic Conflict': A Controversy Revisited," *Studies in Comparative International Development,* vol. 32, no. 2 (summer 1997), pp. 45–75. See also various contributions to Donald L. Horowitz, ed., *Ethnic Groups in Conflict* (Berkeley: University of California Press, 1985); Ted Gurr and Barbara Harff, *Ethnic Conflict in World Politics* (Boulder, CO: Westview Press, 1994); Raymond C. Taras and Rajat Ganguly, *Understanding Ethnic Conflict: The International Dimension* (New York: Longman, 1998); and David Corment and Patrick James, eds., *Wars in the Midst of Peace: The International Politics of Ethnic Conflict* (Pittsburgh: University of Pittsburgh Press, 1987).

59. LeVine, "Conceptualizing," p. 47.

60. Ibid.

61. Ibid.

62. Ibid., p. 48.

63. Ibid., p. 51.

64. Ibid., pp. 56–62.

65. Ibid., p. 59.

66. According to Kaufmann's "Possible and Impossible," note 42, p. 147, the political restraints on the use of firepower in ideological disputes do not apply in ethnic wars. Accidentally inflicting collateral damage on enemy civilians does little harm since there was never any chance of gaining their support. Even accidentally hitting friendly civilians, while awkward, will not cause them to defect.

67. Kaufmann, "Possible and Impossible," pp. 146–147.

68. Susan Jacoby, *Wild Justice: The Evolution of Revenge* (New York: Harper and Row, 1983); Thomas Schiff, *Bloody Revenge* (Boulder, CO: Westview Press, 1994); Donald Kagan, "Our Interests and Our Honor," *Commentary,* vol. 103, no. 4 (April 1997), pp. 42–50; and Jonathan Mercer, "Approaching Emotions in International Politics," paper presented at meeting of International Studies Association, San Diego, April 1996. For a recent overall review of these issues, see Robert E. Harkavy, "Defeat, National Humiliation, and the Revenge Motif in International Politics," *International Politics,* vol. 37, no. 3 (15 September 2000), pp. 345–68.

69. See, among others, Heinz Kohut, "Narcissism and Narcissistic Rage," *The Psychological Study of the Child,* vol. 27 (1992), pp. 360–400; and Sidney Levin, "The Psychoanalysis of Shame," *International Journal of Psychoanalysis* vol. 52, no. 4(1971), pp. 355–361.

70. This dilemma is analyzed in detail in William Bloom, *Personal Identity, National Identity, and International Relations* (Cambridge, U.K.: Cambridge University Press, 1990). See also S. E. Perry, "Notes on the Role of National: A Social-Psychological Concept for the Study of International Relations," *Journal of Conflict Resolution,* vol. 1 (1957), pp. 346–363; and Harold Lasswell, "The Climate of International Action," in Herbert Kelman, ed., *International Behavior* (New York: Holt, Rinehart, and Winston, 1965), pp. 344–346, under "Theory of a Collective Mood."

71. Regarding the Arabs vis-à-vis Israel, see Harold W. Glidden, "The Arab World," *American Journal of Psychiatry,* vol. 128, no.8 (February 1992), pp. 98–100. A good case study of the Cyprus situation by a psychiatrist is Vamik D. Volkan, *Cyprus—War and Adaptation: A Psychoanalytical History of Two Ethnic Groups in Conflict* (Charlottesville: University of Virginia Press, 1979).

72. John W. Dower, *War without Mercy: Race and Power in the Pacific War* (New York: Pantheon Books, 1986).

73. Kaufmann, "Possible and Impossible," esp. pp. 161–175.

74. The nature of the war during the period of India's intervention is conveyed in "India Bogged Down in Sri Lanka's Ethnic Conflict, *New York Times,* 31 July 1988, p. A14; "Sri Lanka Bombing Kills 38 in Market," *New York Times,* 14 April 1989, p. A1; "India Reports Gain in Sri Lanka Drive," *New York Times,* 20 October 1987, p. A8; "Tamil Snipers Slowing Indian Advance," *New*

York Times, 13 October 1987, p. A3; and "Goodbye—and Good Riddance," *Time,* 2 April 1990, p. 32.

75. "Sri Lanka Concedes a Town to Tamil Rebels," *New York Times,* 2 October 1994, p. A6.

76. "Sri Lanka: On the Trail of the Tigers," *Jane's Defense Weekly,* 15 November 1995, p. 27.

77. Actually, some estimates run as high as eighty thousand dead on both sides. See "Sri Lankans Hear Details of Decade of Slaughter," *New York Times,* 21 May 1995, p. A10.

78. The Sri Lankan Army's counterinsurgency operations in 1995–96 are covered in "Interview," *Jane's Defense Weekly,* 31 July 1996, p. 32. See also "Sri Lankan Army Seeks to Expand Strength," *Jane's Defense Weekly,* 12 June 1996, p. 20. The tactical aspects of later fighting in 1997–98 are covered in "War without End," *Washington Post,* 11 August 1997, p. 18 national weekly edition; "Unable to Beat Rebels, Sri Lanka Eases Stance," *New York Times,* 5 November 1997, p. A3.

79. See "Tamil Tigers Admit Heavy Losses But Fight On," *Jane's Defense Weekly,* 12 August 1995, p. 6. For reports on some of the more recent fighting in Sri Lanka, see "Bombing in Sri Lanka Kills 21," *International Herald Tribune,* 8 June 2000, p. 1; "The Tamil Tigers Prove Ferocious, with Help from Abroad," *International Herald Tribune,* 19 June 2000, p. 8; "Sri Lankan Military Base Captured, Tigers Claim," *International Herald Tribune,* 19 May 2000, p. 6; and "Sri Lanka Struggles to Block Offensive," *International Herald Tribune,* 6–7 November 1999, p. 5.

80. "Afghanistan, Always Riven, Is Breaking into Ethnic Parts," *New York Times,* 14 January 1995, p. A1.

81. The tactical aspects of the main part of the Taliban takeover of Afghanistan around 1995 are covered in "Afghanistan's Neighbors Carry On Playing the Great Game," *Jane's Defense Weekly,* 9 December 1995, p. 14; "Afghan Force's Victories Overtake UN Peace Effort," *New York Times,* 19 February 1995, p. A1; "An Afghan Leader is Warily Hopeful About Peace," *New York Times,* 5 March 1995, p. A1; and numerous other *New York Times* articles in, particularly, the period 1995–1997. See also "Considering Ceasing Fire in Afghanistan," *Jane's Defense Weekly,* 10 January 1996, p. 19.

82. "Still a Killing Field," *Time,* 30 April 1990, pp. 26–29.

83. The Khmer Rouge was still a viable fighting force as recently as April 1998, as reported in "Khmer Rouge Are Victors in a Fierce Battle," *New York Times,* 22 April 1998, p. A9. But by February 1999 they were a spent force, as reported by "Khmer Guerillas Yield Guns amidst Peace Hopes," Associated Press Dispatch, 10 February 1999; and "A Final, Bloody Chapter," *Time,* 20 April 1998, p. 41. For a portrayal of an earlier phase of conflict at and beyond the point of Vietnam's military withdrawal, see "Still a Killing Field," *Time,* 30 April 1989, pp. 26–29. Some of the fighting in this three-sided war involved large-unit formations, artillery, and light armor, shading into conventional operations.

84. For the early 1983 phase of the war, in addition to extensive *New York Times* coverage, see "Kaddafi: On the Move Again," *Newsweek,* 15 August 1983, pp. 24–25.

85. "France to Arm Chad against Libya Threat," *International Herald Tribune,* 2 August 1983, p. 1; "Chad Reports New Air Raids by Libyan Jets," *International Herald Tribune,* 5 August 1983, p. 1.

86. "Big Libyan Losses Claimed by Chad," *New York Times,* 9 September 1987, p. A11; "Chad's Leader, in an Interview, Predicts Long War," *New York Times,* 16 August 1987, p. A9; "Chadians Describe Victory in Desert," *New York Times,* 14 August 1987, p. A1; and "Gaddafi on the Run," *Near East Report,* 2 February 1987, p. 19.

87. The earlier "hot" phase of the Sudan war in the late 1980s is covered in "Less Sting to Sudan's Rain-and-War," *New York Times,* 19 July 1989, p. A3, wherein PLA forces are described attacking grain-laden trains. See also "Sudan Rebels Say They Are Victims of Poison Gas," *New York Times,* 10 January 1989, p. A12. The murderous government tactics are described in "For Sudanese Youths Seared by War and Starvation, a Refuge in Ethiopia," *New York Times,* 18 February 1988, p. A3; "Of Sudan's Woes, War's the Worst," *New York Times,* 19 October 1988, p. A10; and "Disaster in Sudan," *New York Times,* 12 February 1983, p. A35.

88. "Sudanese Rebels United in Latest Drive for Power," *Jane's Defense Weekly,* 22 January 1997, p. 15; "Sudan PLA Repels Major Government Assault," *Jane's Defense Weekly,* 5 April 1996, p. 14; "Sudan, Why is this Happening Again," *Time,* 27 July 1998, pp. 29–32. See also "Hospitals No Haven from Sudan War," AP Dispatch, 20 November 1998. See also numerous *New York Times* articles in the period 1997–98. The diplomacy surrounding the war is discussed in Alexis Heraclides, "Janus or Sisyphus? The Southern Problem of the Sudan," *The Journal of Modern African Studies,* vol. 25, no. 2 (1987), pp. 213–231.

89. "Many in Sudan Tired of Unending War," *New York Times,* 3 March 1998, p. A1, wherein "Once a ragtag force of irregular soldiers with light arms, the rebels mounted a formidable attack on Juba with tanks, anti-aircraft, and artillery."

90. "Sudan—Why Is This Happening Again?, *Time,* 27 July 1998, p. 32.

91. "Ending Years of Stalemate Eritrean Rebels Drive Ethiopians into Retreat," *New York Times,* 23 August 1988, p. A10, wherein it is said this was "The world's longest guerilla war"; and "Ethiopia Base and 2 Towns Said to fall to Rebels," *New York Times,* 28 December 1989, p. A8. Later, after Eritrean independence in 1998–99, a newer, interstate war between Ethiopia and Eritrea would take on the character of a more conventional war. See "Eritrea Says It Killed Hundreds in Routing Ethiopians on Border," *New York Times,* 18 March 1999, p. A5.

92. Soviet Arms Aid Is Seen As Pivotal to Ethiopia," *New York Times,* 30 April 1988, p. A5.

93. The battle of Afabet, a major Eritrean victory, is described in "Eritrea: A Crucible of Misery," *Time,* 1 August 1998, pp. 32–35.

94. "On the Ethiopian Front, Rebel Confidence Rises," *New York Times,* 14 February 1990, p. A15; and "Ethiopian Government Seen as Fighting to Survive," *New York Times,* 17 April 1990, p. A5.

95. The battle of Cuito Cuanavale, involving Cuban and South Africans utilizing attack aircraft and tanks, is portrayed in "Angolans Besting South Africa in a Remote Battle," *New York Times,* 18 May 1988, p. A1. See also "Cuba's Wider Role Cheers Angolan," *New York Times,* 17 May 1988, p. A3; "Outsiders Stoke Angola Civil War with Men, Weapons, and Bases," *New York Times,* 31 May 1988, p. A9; and Angola Truce Is as Deadly as Civil War," *New York Times,* 27 August 1989, p. A6; and "Angola: No Respite," *Economist,* 10 March 1990, pp. 48–49.

96. "Angola Rebel Chief Breaks Off Europe Tour," *New York Times,* 31 January 1990, p. A8.

97. "Railroad in Angola to Be Revived," *New York Times,* 13 November 1989, p. D12. As this manuscript approached completion, the war in Angola had resumed, featuring an MPLA sustained offensive that resulted in the capture of the UNITA stronghold at Jamba in December 1999.

98. The nature of the Congo fighting in 1998, over a wide swathe of territory and involving air and armored equipment, is captured in "Tides Shift in Congo's Growing Conflict," Associated Press dispatch, 24 August 1998; "Threat Eased, Congo Leader Arrives Back in his Capital," *New York Times,* 26 August 1998, p. A5; "Congolese Troops Battle Rebels on Kinshasa's Outskirts," *New York Times,* 27 August 1998, p. A6; "Congo's War Turns to Brutal Killings on City's Streets," *New York Times,* 28 August 1998, p. A3; and "Zimbabwe Troops Might go to Congo to Fight Rebels," *New York Times,* 15 October 1998, p. A12.

99. "Rebels Backed by Angola Take Brazzaville and Oil Port," *New York Times,* 16 October 1997, p. A10.

100. "Congo's Struggle May Unleash Broad Strife to Redraw Africa," *New York Times,* 12 January 1999, p. A1; and "3 Kabila Allies Agree to Attack Rebel Strongholds," *New York Times,* 22 October 1998, p. A7.

101. "Fighting Breaks Out in Georgia Buffer Region," *New York Times,* 27 May 1998, p. A3. For a broader analysis of conflict in the Caucasus, see Fiona Hill, "War in the Caucasus?" *New York Times,* 30 January 1996, p. A15.

102. "In Caucasus, Separatist Struggle Is Pursued as a Pogrom," *New York Times,* 5 February, p. A1.

103. "Armenia Runs Show in Disputed Enclave," *New York Times,* 27 November 1995, p. A9; and Ramses Amer et al., "Azerbaijan: Nagorno-Karabakh," under "Major Armed Conflicts, 1992," *SIPRI Yearbook 1993,* pp. 95–96.

104. "Ukraine Helps Azeris Build-Up, Says Armenia," *Jane's Defense Weekly,* 12 March 1997, p. 3. See also "2 Caucasus Regions Sinking Deeper into Civil War," *New York Times,* 6 July 1993, p. A3. See also Ramses Amer et al., "Georgia: Three Civil Wars," under "Major Armed Conflicts," *SIPRI Yearbook 1993* (Oxford: Oxford University Press, 1991), pp. 98–99; and "Fighting Breaks Out in Georgia Buffer Region," *New York Times,* 27 May 1998, p. A3.

105. "Tajik Rebels Said to Kill UN Aide in Hostage Deal Gone Awry," *New York Times,* 14 February 1997, p. A11.

106. "Hopes for Peace in Tajikistan are Fading," *Jane's Defense Weekly,* 4 September 1996, p. 29. A later estimate of fifty thousand dead is in "Tajik Leader, in Vienna, Appeals for Aid," *New York Times,* 25 November 1997, p. A10. In "Tajikistan: Rebels Withdraw to Mountains," *New York Times,* 10 November 1998, p. A6 it is reported that government troops, after five days of fighting, chased the last large group of rebel fighters into the mountains. See also Ramses Amer, et al, "Tajikistan," under "Major Armed Conflicts," *SIPRI Yearbook 1993,* pp. 104–107. See also, "Tajik Tangle: Odd Alliances Worry Neighbors," *New York Times,* 20 October 2000, p. A3, discussing Islamic-led warlord armies operating outside the capital of Dushanbe. See also "Sur-

prised by Islamic Insurgents, Kyrgyzstan Is Walking a Fine Line," *International Herald Tribune*, 19 October 1999, p. 4.

107. The character of the fighting in Somalia during and after the ill-fated American intervention is described in "In an Armed Land, Somalis Live and Prosper by the Gun," *New York Times*, 4 January 1995, p. A5. "Nearly Everything in Somalia is Now Up for Grabs," *New York Times*, 28 February 1995, p. A1; and "U.S. Force Ready to Take Last Aides from Somalia," *New York Times*, 29 June 1994, p. A10.

108. Amidst the massive day-to-day press coverage see, for details of military tactics, "Serb Police Endure Siege in Kosovo City," *Pittsburgh Post-Gazette*, 20 July 1998, p. A1.

109. Ibid.

110. Ibid. See also "In Kosovo, the Rebels Rally," *Washington Post National Weekly Edition*, 23 November 1998, pp. 16–17; "Serbs Try to Empty Kosovo of Albanians, NATO Aides Say," *New York Times*, 29 March 1999, p. A9; "Tit for Tat in the Balkans," *U.S. News and World Report*, 20 July 1998, pp. 30–34; and "Pentagon Admits Errors in Kosovo but Calls War a Triumph," *International Herald Tribune*, 16–17 October 1999, p. 3; and "How Fear of Losses Kept Super-Copters from Kosovo Action," *International Herald Tribune*, 30 December 1999, p. 1.

111. Among numerous press commentaries on the fighting in Chechnya, see "Russian Scout Units Repelled from Grozny," *International Herald Tribune*, 21 December 1999, p. 6; "This Time in Chechnya, Massive Firepower is Russia's Strategy," *International Herald Tribune*, 9 December 1999, p. 5; "Russian Tanks Probe Grozny Defenses," *International Herald Tribune*, 18–19 December 1999, p. 1; and "Hard Lessons," *Time*, 27 December 1999, pp. 124–125.

112. "Thousands Flee Paramilitary Violence in East Timor," *New York Times*, 1 February 1999, p. A6; "With Peace Accord at Hand, East Timor's War Deepens," *New York Times*, 26 April 1999, p. A3; "Indonesia Panel to Study Reports of Army Slayings in East Timor," *New York Times*, 25 November 1998, p. A10, "Army Pullback in East Timor Disputed by Leaked Reports," *New York Times*, 30 October 1998, p. A6; "Joy in the Jungle, at Last," *U.S. News and World Report*, 9 November 1998, pp. 39–40; and "Hiding in the Hills of East Timor," *Washington Post National Weekly Edition*, 27 September 1999, p. 15; and "Timor: Militias Attack near UN Office," *International Herald Tribune*, 2 September 1999, p. 1.

113. "Shining Path Rebels Step Up Terror Campaign in Peru," *New York Times*, 20 March 1985, p. A9. See also "Failed Economy and Resolute Tactics Have Rebels Tightening Grip in Peru," *New York Times*, 12 June 1984, p. A1; "Pope Begins Visit to Peru; Guerillas Stage Offensive," *New York Times*, 15 May 1988, p. A3; "Peruvian Guerillas Emerge As an Urban Political Force," *New York Times*, 17 July 1988, p. A1; "Elusive Rebels are Spreading Fear across Peru," *New York Times*, 11 November 1987, p. A1; and "Peru's Rebels Expand Attacks to Border Area," *Christian Science Monitor*, 16 May 1986, p. 9.

114. "Speedy Gonzalez Lives," *U.S. News and World Report*, 3 August 1998, pp. 41–42; and "Feuding Indians Bring Mexican Region to Brink of War," *New York Times*, 2 February 1998, p. A6.

115. One earlier estimate in 1995 was thirty to forty thousand deaths in Algeria by 1995. See "Mitterand's Call for Europe Talks on Algeria Stirs Paris Split," *New York Times*, 7 February 1995, p. A6. Later estimates by 1998–99 were about double those.

116. The nature of the war is captured in "In 6–Day Offensive, Algerians Step Up War on the Rebels," *New York Times*, 28 March 1995, p. A1. Herein it is reported that in their search for a pure Islamic state, militants had been systematically killing intellectuals, writers, artists, and journalists, and that the Algerian government special forces were reacting by launching ambushes using helicopters and artillery.

117. The brutality of the Sierra Leone conflict is discussed in "UN Seeks Way to Bring Rebel Leader to Trial," *International Herald Tribune*, 19 May 2000, p. 8.

118. The nature of the internal war in Sierra Leone, mostly featuring urban massacres and some artillery bombardments, is captured in "January Toll in Sierra Leone Is Put at 2,700," *New York Times*, 28 January 1999, p. A4; "A Brutal War's Machetes Maim Sierra Leone," *New York Times*, 26 January 1999, p. A1; "Sierra Leone Rebels Start Truce with a Warning," *New York Times*, 19 January 1999, p. A7; and "Fighting Over, Sierra Leone Now Faces Other Woes," *New York Times*, 17 February 1998, p. A9, wherein it is stated that "Much of Freetown's infrastructure was damaged by the fighting. Sections of the city are bullet-riddled or blackened and scarred by artillery blasts."

119. Ramses Amer, et al., "Moldova: The Trans-Dniester Region," under "Major Armed Conflicts," *SIPRI Yearbook 1993*, pp. 101–102.

120. "Burmese Rebels Press Government Attacks," *New York Times,* 27 October 1988, p. A15. See also "Uprising in Burma: The Old Regime under Siege," *New York Times,* 12 August 1988, p. A1; and "Burma Rebels Find a Cause in Autonomy," *New York Times,* 14 March 1988, p. A9. See also "Rebel Camp on Thai Border Captured by Burmese Troops," *New York Times,* 20 January 1989, p. A6; and "Leading God's Army," *Time,* 7 February 2000, pp. 60–61, concerning the Karens' childrens' army.

121. "A Silent Revolution, Fought by Unsung Warriors," *New York Times,* 30 June 1987, p. A4.

122. "After 20 Years, Philippines Insurgency Falters," *New York Times,* 21 October 1989, p. A1.

123. "Turkish Commandos Capture a Kurdish Leader in Raid Into Iraq," *New York Times,* 15 April 1998, p. A5.

124. David Keen, *The Economic Functions of Violence in Civil Wars* (Oxford: International Institute for Strategic Studies (IISS), 1998), Adelphi Paper no. 320. See in particular Keen's excellent appendix (pp. 75–79) rendering basic information on all internal conflicts, 1994–1998. Most of the materials pertaining to the small wars in this section—Mozambique, Papua New Guinea, Mali, Niger, Senegal, Central African Republic—were obtained via telephone interviews with the relevant U.S. State Department desk officers in the summer of 1998.

125. The nature of the recent fighting in Colombia, centered on a FARC force of about two thousand, is covered in "Key Roads Taken from Rebels, Colombia Says," *New York Times,* 14 November 2000, p. A10. See also "Raising the Stakes in Colombia," *The Washington Post,* 30 August 1999, p. 15, national weekly edition. See also Patrick Symmes, "Miraculous Fishing: Lost in the Swamps of Colombia's Drug War," *Harper's,* December 2000, pp. 61–71; and "King of the Jungle," *Time,* 27 November 2000, pp. 62–64. The latter portray a complex four-way war involving FARC and ELN, the government, the United Self-Defense Forces of Colombia (right-wing death squads), and the drug lords. Units of FARC and the USDFC sized in the several hundreds are portrayed battling in the rainforests with mortars, rockets, grenades and Israeli-origin Galil assault rifles. Otherwise, random kidnappings, assassinations, and roadside ambushes are combat modus operandi.

126. "Bangladesh Insurgents Kill 13 Bengali Settlers," *New York Times,* 14 May 1988, p. A17; and "Bangladesh Turns to Dampen Ethnic Insurgency with Ballots," *New York Times,* 26 June 1989, p. A12.

127. The main phase of the Polisario guerilla war in Western Sahara is analyzed in William H. Lewis, "War in the Western Sahara," in Robert E. Harkavy and Stephanie G. Neuman, eds., *The Lessons of Recent Wars in the Third World,* vol. 1, pp. 117–137.

128. In addition to the State Department desk officer input, see Ramses Amer et al., "Mozambique," under "Major Armed Conflicts," *SIPRI Yearbook 1993,* pp. 115–118, and "War 12 Years Long with No End in Sight, Strangles Mozambique," *New York Times,* 25 January 1988, p. A1. Therein, "In ambushes and hit-and-run attacks, rebels have cut food supply lines, isolated districts, disrupted economic and social activity and destroyed bridges, rail lines and hundreds of schools and health centers." See also "22 Are Killed in Raid on Mozambique Train," *New York Times,* 3 January 1988, p. A1; "Mozambique Says Rightist Guerillas Massacred 380 Civilians," *New York Times,* 22 July 1987, p. A3; "American Tells of Mozambique Raid," *New York Times,* 25 July 1987, p. A11; and "Road to Prosperity Has a Special Hazard: Rebels," *New York Times,* 21 February 1989, p. A4; and "Mozambique: Few Escape Fury of War," 12 February 1988, p. A10.

129. "Fiji Coup Leader Forges Deal with Military Rulers," *International Herald Tribune,* 2 June 2000, p. 5.

130. See "Solomon Islands Capital Seized by Rebels in Coup," *International Herald Tribune,* 6 June 2000, p. 1.

131. "Uganda: After the Terror," *New York Times,* 12 March 1989, p. 38, portrays the terror, ambushes, and massacres throughout the Ugandan countryside, perhaps similar to the later situation in Rwanda and the then concurrent situation in Mozambique. For an earlier phase of this conflict, see "Uganda Signs Pact with rebels, but No One Seems Happy," *Christian Science Monitor,* 18 December 1985, p. 1; and "Museveni's Task: Bridging Uganda's Historical Divisions," *Christian Science Monitor,* 26 February 1986, p. 11. Herein is portrayed a congeries of conflicts within and between the Bantu and Nilotic-speaking communities, with the Achali and Langi peoples in the former, and several subsets of the Baganda people in the latter. See also "201 Rebels in Uganda Said to Die in Assault," *New York Times,* 7 August 1987, p. A2.

Chapter 6

1. "In the Desert, Chad Exhibits Spoils of War," *New York Times,* 13 April 1987, pp. A1, A12.
2. Exceptions include a group of security-policy analysts and Soviet area specialists who used the concept of "strategic culture" to explain why the two superpowers allegedly held dissimilar views on the use of nuclear weapons, e.g.: Jack Snyder, *The Soviet Strategic Culture: Implications for Nuclear Options* (Santa Monica, CA: RAND R-2154-AF, 1977); Colin Gray, "National Styles in Strategy: The American Example," *International Security,* vol. 6, no. 2 (1981), pp. 21–47; Carnes Lord, "American Strategic Culture," *Comparative Strategy,* vol. 5, no. 3 (1985), pp. 269–293. Other than a few isolated works, little attention was paid to different countries or regions of the world: see Ken Booth, *Strategy and Ethnocentrism* (New York: Holmes and Meier, 1979); Joel Larus, *Culture and Political-Military Behavior: The Hindus in pre-Modern India* (Calcutta, India: Minerva Associates, 1979).
3. Examples include Jongsuk Chay, ed., *Culture and International Relations* (New York: Praeger, 1990); Samuel P. Huntington, "A Clash of Civilizations?" *Foreign Affairs,* vol. 72, no. 3 (summer 1993), pp. 22–49; Alastair Iain Johnston, *Cultural Realism: Strategic Culture and Grand Strategy in Chinese History* (Princeton: Princeton University Press, 1995); Peter Katzenstein, ed., *The Culture of National Security: Norms and Identity in World Politics* (New York: Columbia University Press, 1996); Yosef Lapid and Friedrich Kratochwil, eds., *The Return of Culture and Identity in IR Theory* (Boulder, CO: Lynne Rienner, 1996); Kevin Avruch, *Culture and Conflict Resolution* (Washington, DC: United States Institute of Peace, 1998); Dominique Jacquin-Berdal, Andrew Oros, and Marco Verqeij, eds., *Culture in World Politics* (New York: St. Martin's Press, 1998); Keith Krause, ed., *Culture and Security: Multilateralism, Arms Control and Security Building* (Portland, OR: Frank Cass, 1999).
4. See Avruch, *Culture and Conflict Resolution;* Alexander Wendt, "Anarchy Is What States Make of It: The Social Construction of Power Politics," *International Organization,* vol. 46 (1992), pp. 391–425; Thomas U. Berger, *Cultures of Antimilitarism: National Security in Germany and Japan* (Baltimore, MD: Johns Hopkins University Press, 1998). Martha Finnemore and Kathryn Sikkink, "International Norm Dynamics and Political Change," *International Organization,* vol. 52, no. 4 (autumn 1998), pp. 887–917. For a nuanced discussion of this debate, see Jack Snyder, "Anarchy and Culture: Insights from the Anthropology of War," paper presented to the working group on Political Violence, War and Peace in the Contemporary World, Center for Global Change and Governance, Rutgers University, Newark, NJ, 19 October 2000.
5. Exceptions include: Berger's *Cultures of Antimilitarism;* Elizabeth Kier's work on the organizational cultures of the British and French militaries between the two world wars, *Imagining War: French and British Military Doctrine between the Wars* (Princeton: Princeton University Press, 1997); Johnston, *Cultural Realism* on China; and Kenneth M. Pollack, "The Influence of Arab Culture on Arab Military Effectiveness," (Ph.D. diss., Massachusetts Institute of Technology, 1996).
6. William C. Wohlforth, "Reality Check: Revising Theories of International Relations in Response to the End of the Cold War," *World Politics,* vol. 50 (July 1998), p. 651.
7. Michael Vlahos, "Culture and Foreign Policy," *Foreign Policy,* vol. 82 (spring 1991), p. 63.
8. Howard J. Wiarda, "Political Culture and National Development," *The Fletcher Forum of World Affairs,* vol. 13, no. 2 (summer 1989), p. 197.
9. Daniel Lerner, *The Passing of Traditional Society* (New York: Free Press, 1964).
10. Howard J. Wiarda, *Ethnocentrism in Foreign Policy: Can We Understand the Third World?* (Washington, DC: American Enterprise Institute, 1985).
11. Anthony Pascal, *Are Third World Armies Third Rate? Human Capital and Organizational Impediments to Military Effectiveness,* RAND Paper Series P-6433 (January 1980), p. 1.
12. W. Seth Carus, "Defense Planning in Iraq," in *Defense Planning in Less-Industrialized States,* ed. Stephanie Neuman (Lexington, MA: Lexington Books, 1984), pp. 42–43. This point is also made repeatedly in connection with Iraq's ability to conduct combined-arms operations in Anthony Cordesman and Abraham R. Wagner, *The Lessons of Modern War: The Iran-Iraq War,* vol. 2 (Boulder, CO: Westview Press, 1991).
13. Quoted in *New York Times,* 19 February 1989, pp. 1, 34.
14. Anthony Cordesman, *The Gulf and the Search for Strategic Stability* (Boulder, CO.: Westview Press, 1984), pp. 652–655; Edgar O'Ballance, *The Gulf War* (London: Brassey's, 1988), p. 48; Shahram Chubin and Charles Tripp, *Iran and Iraq at War* (London: I.B. Tauris, 1989), p. 59.

15. Niccolo Machiavelli, *The Art of War* (Indianapolis, IN: Bobbs-Merrill, 1965), pp. 25, 61, 169, 202, quoted in Joseph Rothschild, "Culture and War," in *The Lessons of Recent Wars in the Third World: Comparative Dimensions,* vol. 2, ed. Stephanie G. Neuman and Robert Harkavy (Lexington, MA: Lexington Books, 1987), p. 54.

16. See for example, Pascal, *Are Third World Armies Third Rate?,* pp. 1–23.

17. Joseph D. Douglass, Jr., "Critical Questions Loom in Assessing the Gulf War," *Armed Forces Journal International* (April 1991), p. 46.

18. "Gulf War Analysis Slows Canadian Look at Defense Changes," *Defense News,* 25 March 1991, p. 4.

19. Patrick Garrity summarizes the findings of this study in "Why the Gulf War Still Matters: Foreign Perspectives on the War and the Future of International Security," Los Alamos National Laboratory, Center for National Security Studies, report no. 16, 1993.

20. Sigmund Freud, *Beyond the Pleasure Principle,* vol. 18 of the *Standard Edition of the Complete Psychological Works of Sigmund Freud* (London: Hogarth Press and the Institute of Psycho-Analysis, 1995, c 1966, 1957), p. 93.

21. Norman F. Dixon, *On the Psychology of Military Incompetence* (London: Jonathan Cape, 1976), pp. 4, 278, 381, cited in Eliot A. Cohen and John Gooch, *Military Misfortunes: The Anatomy of Failure in War* (New York: Free Press, 1990), pp. 8–10.

22. Robert Ardrey, *The Territorial Imperative* (New York: Atheneum, 1966); Konrad Lorenz, *On Aggression* (New York: Harcourt, Brace and World, 1966).

23. William McDougal, "The Instinct of Pugnacity," in *An Introduction to Social Psychology* (London: Methuen, 1915), ch. 11; William James, "The Moral Equivalent to War," in *Memories and Studies* (New York: Longman's Green, 1910), pp. 267–296; Thomas Hobbes, *Leviathan* (New York: Penguin Books, 1986; originally published in 1651).

24. R. Paul Shaw and Yuwa Wong, *Genetic Seeds of Warfare: Evolution, Nationalism and Patriotism* (Boston: Unwin Hyman, 1989), pp. 23–42.

25. Gene Bulinsky, "New Clues to the Causes of Violence," *Fortune,* (January 1973), pp. 134–146; Sandra Blakeslee, "Study Links Antisocial Behavior to Early Brain Injury That Bars Learning," *New York Times,* 19 October 1999.

26. See also D. G. Meyers, *Psychology,* 5th ed. (New York: Worth, 1998), pp. 56–57.

27. Douglas Pasternak, "Wonder Weapons," *U.S. News Online,* July 1997, <http://www.usnews.com/usnews/issue970707/7weir.html>; Nick Lewer, "Nonlethal Weapons," *Forum,* summer 1999, <http://forum.ra.utk.edu/summer99/nonlethal.html>.

28. Charles Burgess, "Superbugs," *Jane's Defence Weekly,* 25 October 2000, p. 23.

29. Lucian W. Pye, *Asian Power and Politics: The Cultural Dimensions of Authority* (Cambridge, MA: Belknap Press of Harvard University Press, 1985), p. 9.

30. This is particularly true for political culture since. Some of the publications include: Samuel P. Huntington, "Will More Countries Become Democratic?" *Political Science Quarterly,* vol. 99 (1984), pp. 193–214; Aaron Wildavsky, "Choosing Preferences by Constructing Institutions: A Cultural Theory of Preference Formation," *American Political Science Review,* vol. 81 (March 1987); Harry Eckstein, "A Culturalist Theory of Political Change," *American Political Science Review,* vol. 82 (September 1988), pp. 789–804; Herbert Werlin, "Political Culture and Political Change," *American Political Science Review,* vol. 84, no. 1 (March 1990), pp. 249–253.

31. Paul B. Pedersen, Juris Draguns, Walter J. Conner, and Joseph E. Trimble, *Counseling across Cultures* (Honolulu: University of Hawaii Press, 1989); Alan Roland, *In Search of Self in India and Japan: Toward a Cross-Cultural Psychology* (Princeton: Princeton University Press, 1988); Daniel Goleman, "Making Room on the Couch for Culture," *New York Times,* 5 December 1995, pp. C1 and C3.

32. Quoted in Daniel Goleman, "The Self: From Tokyo to Topeka, It Changes," *New York Times,* 7 March 1989, pp. C1, C6; see also, Fred Rothbaum et al., "Attachment and Culture: Security in the United States and Japan," *American Psychologist,* (October 2000), pp. 1093–1104.

33. Roger D. Masters," Evolutionary Biology and Political Theory," *American Political Science Review,* vol. 84, no. 1 (March 1990), p. 198; See also Albert Somit and Steven A Peterson, *Darwinism, Dominance, and Democracy* (Westport, CT: Praeger, 1997).

34. Wiarda, "Political Culture and National Development," p. 197.

35. Over the years, "national character" became a "loaded" term thought to have racist connotations. Beginning in the 1970s, authors started using the more neutral term "national styles"— defining it more probabalistically as the tendency of a particular cultural group to exhibit a

particular type of behavior. See Snyder, *Soviet Strategic Culture;* Gray, "National Styles in Strategy." A closely related theoretical school focuses on national images—how a people sees itself—as a determinant of conflict behavior: see Nathan Leites, *The Operational Code of the Politburo* (New York: McGraw Hill, 1951); Alexander L. George, "The 'Operational Code': A Neglected Approach to the Study of Political Leaders and Decision-Making," *International Studies Quarterly,* vol. 13 (June 1969), pp. 190–222; Noel Kaplowitz, "National Self-Images, Perception of Enemies and Conflict Strategies: Psychopolitical Dimensions of International Relations," *Political Psychology,* vol. 11, no. 1 (1990), pp. 39–82.

36. Pye, *Asian Power and Politics,* p. 20.
37. Robert E. Harkavy, "Recent Wars in the Arc of Crisis," in *Defense Planning in Less-Industrialized States,* p. 282.
38. See discussion below, p. 249.
39. Raymond L. Garthoff, *Soviet Military Doctrine* (Glencoe, IL: Free Press, 1953), pp. 236–237, cited in Booth, *Strategy and Ethnocentrism,* p. 9.
40. Ze'ev Schiff, "The Palestinian Surprise," *Armed Forces Journal International* (February 1984), p. 42.
41. Ibid., pp. 42–43
42. Benjamin Schwartz, *Casualties, Public Opinion, and U.S. Military Intervention* (Santa Monica,CA: RAND Corp., 1994).
43. Harrison Salisbury, *Behind the Lines: Hanoi* (New York: Harper and Row, 1967), cited in Miroslav Nincic, "Casualties, Military Intervention, and the RMA," paper presented at the conference on the Revolution in Military Affairs, Monterey, August 1995, <http://ps.ucdavis.edu/JCISS/cmi.html>. On the role of U.S. public opinion see also John Mueller, *War, Presidents, and Public Opinion* (New York: John Wiley, 1973).
44. Nincic, "Casualties, Military Intervention, and the RMA."
45. Commentary by Talal Awkal, *Ramallah Al-Ayyam,* 25 May 2000, Information Service Foreign Broadcast (FBIS) Translated Text (FBIS-NES-0525); Interview with former Iranian foreign affairs minister 'Ali Akbar Velayati by unidentified correspondent, date and place not given: "Future Belongs to Palestinians," *Teheran Resalat,* FBIS Translated Excerpt (FBIS-NES-2000–1122); Interview with Hezbollah secretary-general Hassan Hasrallah, Al Jazira TV (Doha), 27 May 2000, cited in Eyal Zisser, "Israeli Policy after the Withdrawal from South Lebanon: New Realities, Old Dilemmas," *Middle East Intelligence Bulletin,* vol. 2, no. 10 (November 2000).
46. Commentary by Awkal, *Ramallah Al-Ayyam.*
47. Interview with former Iranian foreign affairs minister Velayati.
48. Zisser, "Israeli Policy after the Withdrawal from South Lebanon."
49. "Editorial: Is Military Action in Palestine Feasible?" *Free Arab Voice,* 30 October 2000, <http://www.fav.net>; Yossi Olmert, "Arabs Read Prudence As Weakness," *Jerusalem Post,* 19 October 2000; see also Anthony H. Cordesman, "Israel and Lebanon: The Risk of New Conflicts," August 2000 p. 68, unpublished work.
50. See, for example: Norville de Atkine, "Why Arabs Lose Wars," *MERIA Journal,* vol. 4, (March 2000); Yehoshofat Harkabi, "Basic Factors in the Arab Collapse during the Six Day War," *Orbis,* vol. 11 (fall 1967), pp. 677–691; Pollack, "The Influence of Arab Culture"; William O. Staudenmaier, "Commentary: Defense Planning in Iraq: An Alternative Perspective," in *Defense Planning in Less-Industrialized States.*
51. Staudenmaier, "Commentary," p. 55.
52. Ibid. These cultural characteristics are also discussed by Y. Harkabi in connection with Egyptian and Syrian performances in the 1967 war. He focuses on the authority relationship between officers and enlisted men in the Egyptian and Syrian armies, the absence of initiative on the part of small unit commanders, and the lack of unit cohesion. See Harkabi, "Basic Factors in the Arab Collapse," pp. 677–691.
53. Pollack, "Influence of Arab Culture," p. 759.
54. Ibid.
55. Ibid., p. 760.
56. Johnston, "Cultural Realism," pp. 1, 37. The term remains remarkably undefined. Among those who use it, there is little consensus on what is meant by "strategic culture," who its carriers are (elites, institutions, or mass society), or how it influences military behavior.
57. Hew Strachan, "The Battle of the Somme and British Strategy," *The Journal of Strategic Studies,* vol. 21 (March 1998), pp. 79–95, cited in Colin S. Gray, "Strategic Culture as Context: The First Generation Strikes Back," *Review of International Studies,* vol. 25 (1999), p. 59.

58. Gray, "Strategic Culture," p. 59.

59. Richard Pipes, "Why the Soviet Union Thinks It Could Fight and Win a Nuclear War," *Commentary*, vol. 64, no. 7 (1977), pp. 21–34.

60. Lincoln P. Bloomfield, "American Approaches to Military Strategy, Arms Control, and Disarmament: A Critique of the Postwar Experience," in Edward Kolodziej and Robert E. Harkavy, eds., *American Security Policy and Policy-Making* (Lexington, MA: D.C. Heath, 1980), chapter 14, esp. 225–226.

61. Scott A. Boorman, *The Protracted Game* (New York: Oxford University Press, 1969). Developed in China between three thousand and four thousand years ago, "Go" (called Wei Ch'i in China) is played with black and white stones on a board marked by nineteen intersecting lines into 361 crosses. It has as its object the possession of the larger part of the board and the capturing of the opponent's stones.

62. Steven Stinemetz, "Clausewitz or Khan? The Mongol Method of Military Success," *Parameters*, vol. 14, no. 1 (spring 1984), pp. 71–80.

63. De Atkine, "Why Arabs Lose Wars"; see also Pollack, "The Influence of Arab Culture."

64. Lynn Montross, *War through the Ages*, 3d ed. (New York: Harper and Row, 1960).

65. Larus, "Culture and Political-Military Behavior."

66. Carlo M. Cipolla, *Guns, Sails, and Empires: Technological Innovation and the Early Phases Of European Expansion, 1400–1700* (New York: Pantheon Books, 1965), chapter 2.

67. Examples include Charles A. Kupchan, *The Vulnerability of Empire* (Ithaca, New York: Cornell University Press, 1994); Johnston, "Cultural Realism"; Berger, "Cultures of Antimilitarism." To date, however, as Gray observes, rigorous empirical and theoretical scholarship on strategic culture remains limited. (Gray, "Strategic Culture as Context," p. 50.)

68. See note 2.

69. Adda Bozeman, writing somewhat later, declared that the early religious and quasireligious texts or oral tradition of non-Western cultures are "indisputably at one in hallowing war, whether fought in open pitched battles, covertly in devious protracted style, or permanently as low-intensity conflict and cold war of nerves. In short, we need not go on wondering just why violence and war were and continue to be endemic throughout Asia and Africa. Peace, by contrast, does not emerge from the culture histories of non-Western societies as either norm, superior value, or actual condition. Indeed, reflections on the records cannot bypass the well documented reality that peace is not conceived as the opposite of war or as different from war. What one learns instead is that war and peace interpenetrate in thought and in behavior on the levels of both internal and external statecraft. An Islamic definition of *peace as dormant war* and a Hindu view of peace as *ruse of war* may thus tell it like it is in most of the world." Adda B. Bozeman, "Non-Western Orientations to Strategic Intelligence and Their Relevance for American National Interests," *Comparative Strategy*, vol. 10, no. 1 (1991), pp. 67–68.

70. Joseph Rothschild, "Culture and War," in *The Lessons of Recent Wars in the Third World: Comparative Dimensions,* 59.

71. Ibid.

72. Ibid.

73. Edward S. Boylan, " The Chinese Cultural Style of Warfare," *Comparative Strategy*, vol. 3, no. 4 (1982), pp. 341–363.

74. Adda Bozeman also notes the "uncompromising" hostility the Chinese directed at all non-Chinese who were considered, among other things, "barbarians." (Bozeman, "Non-Western Orientations to Strategic Intelligence," p. 66.)

75. Harlan W. Jencks, "China-Vietnam, 1979," in *The Lessons of Recent Wars: Approaches and Case Studies*, ed. Robert E. Harkavy and Stephanie G. Neuman (Lexington, MA: Lexington Books, 1985), p. 145.

76. Johnston, "Cultural Realism," p. 249.

77. Ibid., pp. 250 and 256–257. Johnston cites a study by Wilkenfeld, Brecher, and Moser showing that the PRC was involved in eleven foreign-policy crises between 1950 and 1985, and resorted to violence in eight (72 percent)—proportionately far more than any other twentieth-century major power.

78. Michael I. Handel, *Masters of War: Classical Strategic Thought,* 2d rev. ed. (London: Frank Cass, 1996), p. 33.

79. Ibid., p. 24.

80. Ibid., xiii.

81. Rothschild, "Culture and War," p. 65; See also R. A. D. Applegate and J. R. Moore, "The Nature of Military Culture," *Defense Analysis*, vol. 6, no. 3 (September 1990), pp. 302–305.

82. Yitzhak Klein, "A Theory of Strategic Culture," *Comparative Strategy*, vol. 10, no. 1 (1991), p. 5.

83. Elizabeth Kier, *Imagining War*.

84. See also Jeffrey Legro, "Which Norms Matter? Revisiting the 'Failure' of Internationalism," *International Organization*, vol. 5, no. 1 (winter 1997), p. 57.

85. Niccolo Machiavelli, *Discourses on the First Ten Books of Titus Livius* (New York: Random House, 1950), book 2; *The Prince* (New York: Random House, 1950), chapters 12, 13, 24, cited in Joseph Rothschild, "Culture and War," p. 54.

86. The bulk of the literature on ethnicity and the military is devoted to describing the ethnic composition of armies, primarily in the Third World. Only random attention has been given to the implications of ethnicity for military performance.

87. Quoted in Joseph J. Collins, "The Soviet-Afghan War," in *The Lessons of Recent Wars in the Third World: Approaches and Case Studies*, p. 198.

88. *Washington Post*, 18 January 1990, p. 1.

89. "From Afghanistan to Azerbaijan, Discord Undermines the Red Army," *New York Times*, 28 January 1990, p. E3.

90. Efraim Karsh, *The Iran-Iraq War: A Military Analysis*, Adelphi Paper no. 220, International Institute for Strategic Studies (spring 1987), p. 15.

91. W. G. Sumner, *Folkways* (Boston: Ginn, 1906), p. 13, quoted in Booth, "*Strategy and Ethnocentrism*, p.15.

92. C. W. S. Brodsky, "India and Pakistan," in *Fighting Armies, Nonaligned, Third World, and Other Ground Armies: A Combat Assessment*, ed. Richard A. Gabriel (Westport, CT: Greenwood Press, 1983); see also discussion below.

93. Dewitt C. Ellinwood, "Ethnicity in a Colonial Asian Army: British Policy, War, and the Indian Army, 1914–1918," in *Ethnicity and the Military in Asia*, ed. Dewitt C. Ellinwood and Cynthia H. Enloe (New Brunswick, NJ: Transaction Books, 1981), p. 91.

94. Ibid., p. 93.

95. Donald L. Horowitz, *Ethnic Groups in Conflict* (Berkeley: University of California Press, 1985), pp. 447–448.

96. "The Psychological Geography of War," extracts from Ewald Banse, *Raum Und Volk Im Weltkriege*, published in *Pakistan Army Journal* (March 1984), p. 66.

97. Ralph Bolton, "The Hypoglycemia-Aggression Hypothesis: Debate versus Research," *Current Anthropology*, vol. 25 (1984), pp. 1–53, cited by James M. Wallace, "Is War a Cultural Universal? Anthropological Perspectives on the Causes of Warfare in Human Societies," in *Culture and International Relations*, p. 25.

98. For a discussion of the transformation in the Jewish self-image, see Paul Breines, *Tough Jews: Political Fantasies and the Moral Dilemma of American Jewry* (New York, Basic Books, 1990).

99. Larus, *Culture and Political-Military Behavior.*

100. Neville Maxwell, *India's China War* (New York: Doubleday, 1972).

101. Keith F. Otterbein, *The Evolution of War: A Cross-Cultural Study* (New Haven, CT: HRAF Press, 1970), p. 104, cited by Wallace, "Is War a Cultural Universal?" p. 25.

102. Berger, *Cultures of Antimilitarism*, p. 6.

103. Hedley Bull, *The Anarchical Society* (New York: Columbia University Press, 1977), p. 39.

104. I. W. Zartman and M. R. Berman, *The Practical Negotiator* (New Haven, CT: Yale University Press, 1982), p. 226.

105. Peter Young, *The Israeli Campaign 1967* (London: William Kimber, 1967), chapter 7; Cordesman and Wagner, *The Lessons of Modern War: The Iran-Iraq War*, pp. 437–440.

106. Wallace, "Is War a Cultural Universal?" p. 25.

107. Jeffrey Herbst, "War and the State in Africa," *International Security*, vol. 14, no. 4 (spring 1990), p. 118.

108. John Mueller, *Retreat from Doomsday: The Obsolescence of Major War* (New York: Basic Books, 1989), p. 240. The author argues that the experience of past wars have had an effect on the mental habits and values of Western states so that war has now become "subrationally unthinkable" to them.

109. Klein, "A Theory of Strategic Culture," pp. 14–15.

110. Harry Eckstein, "Political Culture and Political Change," in *American Political Science Review*, vol. 84. no. 1 (March 1990), p. 256.

111. Harry Eckstein has argued that German culture, because it has been subject to large-scale shock after shock—including war and its devastating aftermath, should be regarded as extremely weak and thus unable "to provide much friction against either raw political power (the Nazis) or reconstruction through rationally devised law (the Federal Republic)." War, like other disorienting experiences, has contributed to culture change in Germany. (Eckstein, "Political Culture and Political Change," p. 256.)

112. "The Concept of Culture in the Theory of International Relations," in *Culture and International Relations,* p. 8.

Chapter 7

1. U.S. Department of State, *World Military Expenditures and Arms Transfers* (Washington, DC: Department of State Publications, 1969–1978, 1990). (Hereafter referred to as *WMEAT.*)

2. See, for example, David Louscher and Michael Salamone, *Marketing Security Assistance: New Perspectives on Arms Sales* (Lexington, MA: Lexington Books, 1987); Stephanie Neuman, *Military Assistance in Recent Wars: The Dominance of the Superpowers,* Washington Papers/122 (New York: Praeger, 1986); Donald Sylvan, "Consequences of Sharp Military Assistance Increases for International Conflict and Cooperation," *Journal of Conflict Resolution,* vol. 20 (1976), pp. 609–636; Philippe C. Schmitter, "Foreign Military Assistance, National Military Spending and Military Rule in Latin America: Function, Consequences and Perspectives," in *Military Role in Latin America,* ed. Philippe C. Schmitter (Beverly Hills, CA: Sage, 1973), pp. 117–187. Schmitter includes training in his operational definition of military assistance.

3. Coerced domestic security assistance can take many forms. For example, LRA rebels in Uganda reportedly have abducted young children and turned them into soldiers, porters, and concubines. It is estimated that over 70 percent of the LRA forces are composed of these children.("Uganda: A Dirty War That Can't Be Won," *The Economist,* 4 October 1997, p. 52.) Another example is hostage-taking in order to trade men for weapons, financial assets, and other forms of diplomatic, military, and economic aid. Armenian nationalists, for example, exchanged Russian army officers for weapons, and in Tajikistan, UN hostages were traded for various diplomatic concessions. (Steve LeVine, "Tajik Gunmen Seize 23 Hostages, Including 8 UN Observers," *New York Times,* 21 December 1996, p. 3.) In Peru, the hostages held in the Japanese Embassy by MRTA rebels were to be ransomed for diplomatic, financial, or military assistance and the kidnapping of Bolivian tycoon Samuel Doria furnished MRTA with $1.2 million in ransom monies for its operations. ("MRTA Said to Have Transferred Funds for Operation via Panama," *British Broadcasting Corporation (BBC) Summary of World Broadcasts,* 1 January 1997 Foreign Broadcast Information Service [FBIS].)

4. African Rights, "Somalia: Operation Restore Hope: A Preliminary Assessment," *Situation Report* (London: African Rights, 1993), pp. 2, 4. See also Richard Betts, "The Delusion of Impartial Intervention," *Foreign Affairs,* vol. 73 (1994), pp. 20–33, for a trenchant analysis of why, in practice, intervention during wartime often makes matters worse.

5. Jane Perlez, "U.S. Weighs Using Food as Support for Sudan Rebels," *New York Times,* 29 November 1999, pp. A1, A10.

6. Ivo Skoric, writing about the Kosovo war, believes that anti-Milosevic opinions expressed by the leading U.S. media, nongovernmental organizations and nonprofit foundations encouraged the U.S. to go ahead with the bombing since public opinion would not be a collateral cost. He argues that the U.S. was able to effectively ostracize Serbia because unlike their opponents, the Serbs did not recognize the power of the electronic media or the internet. "Croatia, Bosnia, and Kosovar Albanians all hired a U.S. public relations firm to represent their cause to the global media. In 1991, when the war in Croatia started, Croatia immediately formed the Foreign Press Bureau staffed with American-born, college-educated youth of Croatian ancestry to address the needs and whims of American prima-donna journalists. . . . Albanian internet activists, for example, engaged in cyberwar by organizing a consumer boycott against the products of companies that advertised with beograd.com, a pro-Serbian site managed from Toronto, Canada. . . . The consumer threat was ultimately successful, forcing advertisers to withdraw their support and starve the Serb website of funds." Serbia, on the other hand, concentrated its propaganda efforts on the domestic public, never seriously addressing the foreign public, and treated foreign journalists and human rights observers as unwelcome intruders with reverberations that were

felt long after the end of hostilities. (Ivo Skoric <ivo@reporters.net> 19 November 1999, personal email [19 November 1999]; see also, Mary Kaldor, *New and Old Wars: Organized Violence in a Global Era* [Stanford, CA: Stanford University Press, 1999], pp. 39–40, on Milosevic's domestic use of the electronic media.)

7. Carl Bernstein and Marco Politi, *His Holiness* (New York: Doubleday, 1996), pp. 257–264.

8. Harry Dunphy, "U.S. will aid opposition efforts in Iraq, Albright tells leaders," *Associated Press News,* 25 May 1999; Christopher S. Wren, "U.S. Gives Its Backing, and Cash, to Anti-Hussein Groups," *New York Times,* 2 November 1999.

9. "ANC Against Sale of Printing Press to SADF," *Xinhua General Overseas News Service,* 14 January 1993 (Lexis-Nexis).

10. Paradoxically, the absence of foreign assistance programs is sometimes blamed for the inability of the U.S. to influence war outcomes. In August 1999, for example, U.S. diplomats repeatedly warned North Korea of serious consequences should North Korea proceed with an anticipated second missile test. But rather than acceding to U.S. admonitions, North Korea responded with a warning of its own that any attempt to pressure it into abandoning launch plans would trigger "unpredictable consequences." Speculating on why North Korea responded belligerently, one analyst opined: "Our problem is we've got no carrots to take away." Isolated economically, politically, and militarily, North Korea didn't have many tangible benefits to lose by ignoring U.S. threats until desirable economic carrots were offered. (Robert Manning, quoted in *China Times,* 8 August 1999. <http://www.freerepublic.com/forum/a37ac85b941e1.htm>. See also Howard W. French, "North Korea Says It Will Halt Missile Tests during U.S. Talks," *New York Times,* 25 September 1999, p. A5.)

11. The far-reaching sensitivity of combatants to this form of assistance is illustrated by Angola's accusation that France was supporting the UNITA rebel movement by allowing the "growing presence of Savimbi supporters in Paris which, the government claimed, was in contravention of the sanctions imposed by the United Nations on UNITA." ("Angola: State media criticise France," *UN IRIN Southern Africa: IRIN-SA Weekly Round-up 45,* 12 November 1999, <IRIN-SA@irin.org.za> [12 November 1999].)

12. We are indebted to Bertil Dunér's work on intervention for this conceptual breakdown. He distinguishes between high-level and low-level intervention based on the "closeness or immediacy of acts of intervention to a battle situation." Arms transfers, for example, because of their remoteness from the physical battlefield, are a low-level or indirect intervention, whereas the provision of troops for combat is a high-level or direct intervention. His typology and criteria for inclusion, however, are more restrictive than ours. Dunér's analysis, for example, is limited to twelve civil wars that fall completely within the 1970–1980 time period. He does not include what he calls indirect supporting activities, i.e., different types of humanitarian aid, or a government allowing its territory to be used for the storage of supplies, for troops passage, or the transit of aid from other donors. (Bertil Dunér, *Military Intervention in Civil Wars: The 1970s,* The Swedish Institute of International Affairs [Aldershot, UK: Gower, 1985], pp. 14–15.)

13. Conceptual clarity has been elusive when it comes to these terms. "Peace-enforcement," "peacekeeping" and "peacemaking" traditionally have been vaguely defined and inconsistently implemented. In the 1990s, UN Secretary-General Boutros Boutros-Ghali and others attempted to establish some conceptual order by linking the definition of these terms largely to the various activities prescribed in the Charter of the United Nations.

    It is generally accepted that "peace-enforcement" refers to Chapter VII in the Charter, empowering the Security Council to use necessary measures, including the use of force, to maintain or restore international peace and security without the consent of the belligerents. Examples of peace-enforcement cited by Boutros Boutros-Ghali include the 1950 Security Council authorization to undertake enforcement action in the Korean peninsula, the 1990 authorization to enforce peace in Kuwait, the authorization of member states to create conditions for humanitarian relief operations in Somalia and Rwanda, and the authorization of the use of force to restore democracy to Haiti. (Boutros Boutros-Ghali, "Supplement to an Agenda for Peace," 3 January 1995, reference to UN Document A/50/60–S/1995/1 in *An Agenda for Peace* (New York: United Nations, 1995), p.28, paragraph 78. The U.S. Department of Defense defines "peace enforcement" as a coercive measure "to compel compliance with resolutions or sanctions designed to maintain or restore peace and order" that do not require the consent of the belligerents. (Department of Defense, *DOD Dictionary of Terms* definition accessed at <http://www.dtic.mil/doctrine/jel/doddict/data/p/04676.html> [12 November 1999].)

There is less definitional consensus regarding "peacekeeping" and "peacemaking." Peacekeeping activities, often referred to as "Chapter VI 1/2" because they are not explicitly stipulated in the Charter, involve military deployment and operations that are intended to implement or monitor a settlement *agreed to* by the major belligerents under the provisions of Chapter VI of the Charter "and/or to protect the delivery of humanitarian relief." However the issue of the belligerents' consent remains ambiguous, since peacekeepers may have to act unilaterally to protect humanitarian relief supplies. (UN Department of Peacekeeping Operations [DPKO], <http://www.un.org/Depts/dpko/glossary/p.htm> [15 November 1999].) The U.S. Department of Defense asserts that the consent of all parties is a precondition for peacekeeping activities: "Military operations undertaken with the consent of all major parties to a dispute, designed to monitor and facilitate implementation of an agreement (cease-fire, truce, or other such agreement) and support diplomatic efforts to reach a long-term political settlement." Department of Defense definition accessed at <http://www.dtic.mil/doctrine/jel/doddict/data/p/04677.html> (12 November 1999). In practice, consent has proven elusive in many cases and UN peacekeeping troops, in Somalia and the former Yugoslavia for example, have been involved in military operations to impose peace on dissenting forces. In fact, as Shashi Tharoor observes, in the post–Cold War world "peacekeeping" has become a catch-all term for a variety of behaviors.(See Shashi Tharoor, "Should UN Peacekeeping Go 'Back to Basics'?" *Survival,* vol. 37, no. 4 (winter 1995–96), p. 54.) On this question, see also I. William Zartman, "Preventing and Reducing Conflict: Goals All Nations Share," *USIA,* December 1996, <http://www.arc.arg.tw/USIA/www.usia.gov/topical/pol/conres/zartman.htm12> (November 1999).

"Peacemaking," too, theoretically involves the consent of the disputants and refers to the process of mediating an end to conflict using peaceful rather than military measures "to bring hostile parties to agreement, through such peaceful means as outlined in Chapter VI of the Charter of the United Nations." (Boutros Boutros-Ghali, *An Agenda for Peace* [reference to UN Document A/47/277–S/24111, 17 June 1992] [New York: United Nations, 1995], p. 45, paragraph 20.) I. William Zartman cites the Lusaka agreement of 1994 (to end the Angolan civil war) as an example. (Zartman, "Preventing and Reducing Conflict.") However, even here there is some vagueness about what consent really means. The UN Department of Peacekeeping Operations (DPKO) glossary of terms suggests that peacemaking entails: "a diplomatic process of brokering an end to conflict, *principally* through mediation and negotiation, as foreseen under Chapter VI of the UN Charter; military activities contributing to peacemaking include military-to-military contacts, security assistance, shows of force and preventive deployments"(italics mine). (UN Department of Peacekeeping Operations [DPKO], <http://www.un.org/Depts/dpko/glossary/p.htm> [15 November 1999].)

A new term, designed to deal with some of these ambiguities appears in the DPKO glossary of terms: "peace-restoration and conflict mitigation operation." It is defined as a "new and tentative concept applying to the multidimensional operations which, while originally mandated under Chapter VI, are forced by realities in the field to turn into Chapter VII operations, as when humanitarian convoys need to be defended by force of arms, or exclusion zones enforced by air strikes." (UN Department of Peacekeeping Operations [DPKO], <http://www.un.org/Depts/dpko/glossary/p.htm> [15 November 1999].)

14. See M.V. Naidu, "The origins of UN peace enforcement and peacekeeping: re-examination of the crises in Korea (1950), Kashmir (1948) and the Suez (1956)," February 1995, (Lexis-Nexis); Karl Maier, "Hunted Warlord Spits Defiance," *Independent,* 23 June 1993, p. 12 (Somalia); Seidi Mulero, "Zimbabwe: Shut Up!" *Africa News,* 10 November 1999 (Democratic Republic of Congo)(Lexis-Nexis);Yuri Rogov, "Chad Conflict: Western Support for Habre Hinders Settlement" (Lexis-Nexis). Rogov argues that: "In their attempts to conceal the real state of affairs in Chad, the Western media have had to pile up lie upon lie, claiming that the interference in the Chad events by France and then by the U.S.A. was a peace-making effort."

15. During the Cold War the concept of sovereignty and the closely associated principle of "consent," especially in civil wars, had been at the root of the conceptual disarray. But in the post–Cold War world these concepts have come under increasing attack. In a path-breaking statement, Secretary-General Kofi Annan addressed the opening session of the General Assembly in September 1999 declaring that "national borders would no longer protect leaders who abuse people under their control." This statement was followed by his November 1999 report on the UN's performance in Srebrenica (July 1995) which condemned the organization for trying to

remain neutral in a civil conflict. (Barbara Crossette, "UN Details Its Failure to Stop '95 Bosnia Massacre," *New York Times,* 16 November 1999, p. 3.) It is, as of this writing, unclear whether these statements will be endorsed by the UN membership and whether they will lead to greater consensus on the role of military interventions in the cause of "peace."

16. "Total War," is "a theoretical concept implying the use of all available resources and weapons in war and the elimination of all distinctions between military and civilian targets." (Edward Luttwak and Stuart L. Koehl, *The Dictionary of Modern War* [New York: HarperCollins], p. 625.)

17. Two bizarre incidents reported in the media illustrate the murkiness surrounding many alleged acts of security assistance and the difficulty of corroborating them. U.S. aircraft using "highly sensitive missiles" and bypassing the normal NATO command structure, are accused by China of deliberately bombing the Chinese Embassy in Belgrade during the war in Kosovo. NATO's official explanation was that the bombing was a tragic mistake. "One of our planes attacked the wrong target because the bombing instructions were based on an outdated map." This version was subsequently rejected by sources at the U.S. National Imagery and Mapping Agency, the Defense Intelligence Agency, and by other senior U.S. and European officials.(John Sweeney, Jens Holsoe, and Ed Vulliamy, "Revealed NATO Bombed Chinese Deliberately," *Observer,* 17 October 1999, p. 1.) According to other senior U.S. and European sources, the air attack was launched because the Chinese embassy was assisting Milosevic by sending electronic signals to the Yugoslav army in the field, after NATO had succeeded in silencing all of Milosevic's transmitters. China, on the other hand, denied the embassy in Yugoslavia served as an intelligence-gathering center for the Serbs. ("China Denies That Reporters Killed in NATO Bombing Were Spies," *Associated Press,* 29 June 1999, (Lexis-Nexis).

A second incident involves a private British security company, Aims Ltd, which "has close links to British intelligence and the SAS (Special Air Service)." It is alleged to have offered to help the Turkish military in its ongoing conflict with the Kurds by arranging the covert irradiation of Kurdish rebels held by the Turks in northern Iraq in order to track their activities after their release and later kill them. Confidential company documents, reportedly written for the Turkish military, state that radiation detection "is a method in which a radioactive source is placed in the target and the source is then monitored. This can be done by aircraft or satellite. The downside is that the target succumbs to radiation poisoning in approximately 21 days. This has been used by certain nations when they have released POWS." (David Leppard, Paul Nuki, and Gareth Walsh, "British Firm Told Turkey How to Irradiate Kurds," *Sunday Times* [London], 31 October 1999.) The truth of these allegations may never be known. They illustrate the strange forms security assistance assumes as reported in the media, and the difficulties an analyst might have in even imagining them, much less determining their authenticity.

18. Government analysts, with access to classified material, have a substantial research advantage in this regard. Open-source information (publicly available information) is collected by many government agencies to supplement classified data. Reportedly, over 80 percent of the information collected, analyzed, and disseminated by the U.S. Central Intelligence Agency (CIA) is derived from open sources. Government officials, however, can use classified information as a cross-check to winnow out useful additional material from open sources and discard what is inaccurate. But for nongovernment analysts without security clearances, assessing the credibility of the public record is a major problem. Open sources often contain inaccuracies, biased perspectives, irrelevant data, or disinformation that is difficult to detect and usually impossible to verify. See Wyn Bowen, "Open-Source Intel: A Valuable National Security Resource," *Jane's Intelligence Review,* November 1999, pp. 50–54, for a discussion of how intelligence organizations can and do utilize open-source data.

19. Our research on the type and frequency of security assistance furnished combatants is ongoing. The percentages in Table 7.1, which covers the period 1991 through 1997, are preliminary findings. We are in the process of analyzing trends for the years 1989–1999 and for several wars fought during the Cold War period for comparative purposes. Thus far, the data for the expanded post–Cold War period support the general trends found for 1991–1997.

20. This finding is similar to Dunér's for civil wars fought between 1970 and 1980. He found that the majority of military interventions did not involve the commitment of combat forces or foreign military personnel, but rather a preponderance of "lower level" forms of assistance, such as advisory functions, arms supply, military training, armed blockade, financial support, threats, transport, and base functions. (Dunér, "Military Intervention in Civil Wars," p. 65.)

21. For a discussion of some of the methodological and data problems facing arms trade specialists, see Michael Brzoska and Frederic S. Pearson, *Arms and Warfare: Escalation, De-Escalation, and Negotiation* (Columbia: University of South Carolina Press, 1994), pp. 18–22.

22. There is no universally accepted definition of small arms. Weapons used in today's conflicts include virtually any instrument of lethality ranging from sticks, stones, and machetes to shoulder-fired missiles. According to the UN Development Programme, the mandate of the United Nations in this field focuses on the following three categories of weapons: *Small Arms:* revolvers and self-loading pistols; assault rifles, rifles and carbines; submachine-guns and light machine-guns; *Light Weapons:* heavy machine-guns; handheld and mounted grenade launchers; portable antiaircraft guns; portable antitank guns; recoilless rifles; portable launchers of antitank and anti-aircraft missile systems; mortars of calibers of less than 100 mm; *Ammunition & Explosives:* cartridges (rounds) for small arms; shells and missiles for light weapons; mobile containers with missiles or shells for single-action; antiaircraft and antitank systems; antipersonnel and antitank hand grenades; and mines and explosives.<http://www.undp.org/erd/archives/brochures/small_arms/sa8.htm>.

23. For a comprehensive description of the historical development of weapons and their impact on strategy and tactics, see R. Ernest Dupuy and Trevor N. Dupuy, *The Harper Encyclopedia of Military History: From 3500 B.C. to the Present* (New York: HarperCollins, 1993), esp. pp. 1005–1008, 1113–1123, 1316–1321 for the twentieth century.

24. Aaron Karp, "The Arms Trade Revolution: The Major Impact of Small Arms," *Washington Quarterly,* vol. 17, no. 4 (autumn 1994), pp. 65–77. See also Michael Klare, "Who's Arming Who? The Arms Trade in the 1990s," *Technology Review,* vol. 93, no. 4 (May 1990), p. 42.

25. Richard Norton-Taylor, "Small Arms under Fire," *Guardian* (UK), 24 September 1999, <http://www.newsunlimited.co.uk/analysis/story/0,3604,85296,00.html>. Aaron Karp, too, noted the ubiquity of small arms in recent wars. He found that of the thirty major conflicts in progress in 1992, all but four were fought almost entirely with small and light armaments, "mostly the cheapest and least advanced kinds." "Arming Ethnic Conflicts," *Arms Control Today,* vol. 23, no. 7 (September 1993).

26. Bureau of Intelligence and Research, U.S. Department of State, "Arms and Conflict in Africa" (Washington, DC: U.S. State Department, July 1999).

27. Bureau of Intelligence and Research, "Arms and Conflict in Africa"; Bureau of Intelligence and Research, U.S. Department of State, "Africa/U.S.: Fact Sheet on Arms Flows to Central Africa/Great Lakes" (Washington, DC: U.S. State Department, November 1999). Rwanda and Uganda reportedly can only use the tanks they bought as "fixed or modestly mobile gun emplacements." (p. 3).

28. Neither the UN Register of Conventional Arms nor SIPRI—primary sources of statistics on the arms trade—include these weapons in their databases.

29. "Africa/U.S.: Fact Sheet on Arms Flows to Central Africa/Great Lakes," p. 2.

30. *WMEAT,* prior to the 1998 edition, was issued by the former U.S. Arms Control and Disarmament Agency (ACDA). *WMEAT* is now published by the U.S. Department of State's Bureau of Verification and Compliance. We have continued to refer to ACDA as the issuing agency for editions published prior to the 1998 edition.

31. For a detailed list of the items included in the dollar value of *WMEAT*'s arms import and export tables, see *WMEAT,* 1998, p. 205.

32. *The Military Balance* published by the International Institute for Strategic Studies (IISS), London, uses U.S. data among other sources and so includes small arms and light weapons in its aggregate dollar values. But like U.S. data, the value of small arms and light weapons are not presented separately. (IISS analyst, telephone interview by author, 13 May 1999.)

33. See Richard F. Grimmett, *CRS Report for Congress: Conventional Arms Transfers to the Third World* (Washington, DC: Congressional Research Service, Library of Congress, series) and Department of Defense, Defense Security Assistance Agency, *Foreign Military Sales, Foreign Military Construction Sales and Military Assistance Facts* (Washington, DC: Department of Defense, annual series). Other U.S. government documents are not more enlightening. Section 36 of the Arms Export Control Act requires the president to report exports to Congress of major defense equipment valued at $1 million or more. Rarely are small arms, light weapons, or support services bought in sufficient quantity to qualify, and so the number and value of these transfers are not identified in U.S. congressional publications either.

34. "Revision of U.S. Arms Export Data Series," *WMEAT* (1997), p. 2.

35. U.S. government official, interview with author, 9 January 1995.

36. Testimony by Joel L. Johnson, vice president, International Aerospace Industries Association to the U.S. House Foreign Affairs Subcommittees on International Organizations and Human Rights and International Operations Hearing on U.S. Policy on Conventional Arms Transfers, 9 November 1993; See also Martin L. van Creveld's discussion of the relative impact and effectiveness of weapon technologies used in major wars and low-intensity conflict in *The Transformation of War* (New York: Free Press, 1991), chapter 20.

37. *WMEAT* (1997), table V, "Number of Major Weapons Delivered" and Table II, "Arms Transfer Deliveries and Total Trade, 1986–1996."

38. See, for example, Martin L. van Creveld, *Supplying War: Logistics from Wallenstein to Patton* (Cambridge, UK: Cambridge University Press, 1977) and Geoffrey Kemp, "Arms Transfers and the 'Back-End' Problem in Developing Countries," in *Arms Transfers in the Modern World,* ed. Stephanie G. Neuman and Robert E. Harkavy (New York: Praeger, 1979), pp. 264–274.

39. U.S. government official, telephone interview with author, November 1998.

40. A State Department analyst insisted that transfers to subnational groups are not included in U.S. published data. *WMEAT,* he observed, clearly states that "Both deliveries and agreements data represent arms transfers to governments and do not include the value of arms obtained by subnational groups." (*WMEAT* [1996], p. 190 and Department of State official, interview with author, 3 May 1999.)

41. Covert transfers to Iran during the Iran-Iraq War were perhaps the best publicized, but there is evidence to suggest that this type of assistance has played a role in most regional wars. See note 45 below, for various estimates of its size.

42. U.S. government official, interview with author in Washington, D.C., 3 May 1999.

43. The use of telephone and computer encryption is expanding and expected to grow sharply in the coming years as the U.S. releases for export advanced encryption software. Seymour Hersh writes that these technologies already cripple the U.S. National Security Agency's collection ability. Seymour Hersh, "The Intelligence Gap," *New Yorker,* 6 December 1999, pp. 58–76.

44. One analyst, when asked whether it was possible to hide events or locations in the age of reconnaissance satellites, responded: "The answer is clearly 'yes.' In fact in 1999 it is easier than in 1989, as in the 1980s the intelligence services were focused on a small number of players, in well-known geographical locations. Today the same, or reduced, resources are tasked with tracking a multitude of bit players, spread around the world, mobile and without a clearly defined organizational structure. If you are looking in the wrong direction, anticipating an event, you may be blind-sided by other more public events. Consider the total lack of NSA and CIA anticipation of the Indian nuclear tests. . . . Daily we see examples of deception, from governments down to private individuals. In the Information Age, collecting information is easy; analyzing it and making sense of that analysis is getting increasingly difficult. Hence it becomes much easier to practice deception."(Alan Simpson <news@comlinks.com> "Re: Deception," 3 December 1999, <intelforum@his.com> [3 December 1999].)

45. *The Economist* writes: "Guesses range from $1 billion–$2 billion for the average year's skulduggery (mostly by governments that do not want their neighbors to know what weapons they are buying or selling), to $5 billion–10 billion if there is a good war or two to drive demand."("The Covert Arms Trade," *The Economist,* 12 February 1994, pp. 19–21.) Michael Klare, a veteran analyst of the covert arms trade, estimates it amounts to "several billion dollars per year." ("The Subterranean Arms Trade: Black-Market Sales, Covert Operations, and Ethnic/Insurgent Warfare," [unpublished paper, c. 1993], p. 13.)

46. Patrick J. Garrity, *Why the Gulf War Still Matters: Foreign Perspectives on the War and the Future of International Security* (Center for National Security Studies, Los Alamos National Laboratory, report no. 16, July 1993).

47. "Malaysia's Defense: Long on Borders but Short on Funds," *International Defense Review,* (February 1994), p. 60.

48. Sales to developing countries have been in decline since 1991. Although the United States remains the largest supplier to developed countries, it provides only 40 percent of their arms imports, in contrast to 74 percent of the developed world's, see *WMEAT,* 1998, p. 165. A similar trend holds for arms deliveries to combatants. Whereas the United States supplied 61 percent of the world's arms between 1991 and 1996, it delivered only 45.3 percent of weapons (known to have been) transferred to combatants (see Table 7.2).

49. An example is Osama bin Laden, sought for the bombings of two U.S. embassies in East Africa, who was reported by Russia to be helping to finance the Muslim insurgency in northern Cau-

casus by sending $30 million to two Chechen warlords involved in the incursion into the Russian autonomous republic of Dagestan. "Russia: Bin Laden Financing Chechens," *United Press International,* 22 September 1999 (Lexis-Nexis).

50. The number of IGOs and NGOs operating in the international system has increased tremendously. In 1909 there were 37 IGOs and 176 international NGOs in comparison to 1996 when there were nearly 260 IGOs and 5,472 NGOs. (David Held, Anthony McGrew, David Goldblatt, Jonathon Perraton, *Global Transformations: Politics, Economics and Culture* [Stanford, CA: Stanford University Press, 1999], p. 53.)

51. Mary Kaldor observes that although there were always expatriate nationalist groups plotting their country's liberation in cafés in Paris and London, such groups have grown much larger and more significant because of the scale of emigration, the ease of travel and the spread of telephones, faxes and electronic mail." (Kaldor, *New and Old Wars,* p. 85.)

52. These data, drawn from *WMEAT,* for all the reasons discussed above are incomplete, reflecting only what is published (not necessarily known) about official government imports and exports.

53. SIPRI estimates a decline of 34 percent between 1988 and 1998. *SIPRI YEARBOOK* 1998, p. 192; *SIPRI YEARBOOK* 1999, p. 270.

54. Sean DiGiovanna and Ann Markusen, "From Defense to Development in the 1990s: Evidence from Eight Countries on Four Continents," paper presented at the Study Group on Arms Exports and Transnationalization of the Defense Industry, Council on Foreign Relations, New York, 10 December 1999, p. 1.

55. Michael Brzoska, "Economic Factors Shaping Arms Production in Less Industrialized Countries," *Defence and Peace Economics,* vol. 10, no. 2 (1999), table 4, pp. 139–169; 151.

56. During the Cold War, the Soviet Union was estimated to spend within the range of one-third and two-fifths of the world's military R&D total. (Mary Acland-Hood, "Statistics on Military Research and Development Expenditure," *SIPRI YEARBOOK* 1984, pp. 165–174. Since then there has been a precipitous decline in Russian military R&D expenditures. (*SIPRI YEARBOOK* 1999, pp. 204–206,211.)

57. David R. Stone, "*Roosvooruzhenie* and Russia's Return to the World Arms Market," *Columbia International Affairs Online,* March 1997, p. 2, <http://wwwc.cc.columbia.edu/sec/dlc/ciao/conf/ece01/ece01std.html>.

58. Ibid., p. 2.

59. Ibid., p. 10.

60. Steven Erlanger, "Moscow Insists It Must Sell the Instruments of War to Pay the Costs of Peace," *New York Times,* 3 February 1993, p. A6.

61. BBC Summary of World Broadcasts, "Angola is the 'Spearhead' of Soviet Expansionism," 20 September 1986 (Lexis-Nexis). For a discussion of indirect sources of supply to combatants during the Cold War, see Neuman, *Military Assistance in Recent Wars,* chapter 3.,

62. *SIPRI YEARBOOK* 1999, p. 16.

63. See Neuman, *Military Assistance in Recent Wars,* pp. 35–37.

64. *WMEAT* 1997, table III (revised 29 January 1999). China also has signed a military cooperation agreement with Myanmar, which will include training, the exchange of intelligence, and arms shipments at "friendship prices." "China, Burma Said to Sign Military Cooperation Accord," *FBIS-CHI-97–014,* 22 January 1997.

65. It is unclear whether the facility is controlled by Myanmar or China. *International Security Digest,* vol. 1, no. 4 (February 1994), p. 3. See also Bertil Lintner, "Myanmar's Chinese Connection," *International Defense Review* (November 1994), p. 24.

66. *International Security Digest,* vol. 2, no. 2 (November 1994), p. 2.

67. "PRC: 'Roundup' Considers Sino-Sri Lankan Relations," *FBIS-CHI-96–078,* 19 April 1996.

68. On Taiwan, Tibet, and human rights issues, the government of Sri Lanka regularly supports China's position in the UN and other public fora. Chinese cargo vessels were attacked by Tamil Tiger dissidents in 1997 and again in 1999 because their activities were said to be "associated with the Sri Lankan military." ("LTTE Rebels Attack Chinese Ship off Sri Lanka," *FBIS-NES-1999–0926,* 27 September 1999.) Sri Lanka also provides China with a strategically positioned ally, close to the southern tip of India, should Indo-Chinese relations again erupt into war.

69. "Info Bites," *Small Arms World Report,* vol. 4, no. 4 (December 1993), p. 18. (Hereafter cited as *SAWR.*)

70. *SAWR,* vol. 4, no. 2 (April 1993), p. 35.

71. Ibid., p. 40.

72. Ibid., p. 44.

73. *Daily Telegraph,* November 1994, cited in *International Security Digest,* vol. 2, no.2 (November 1994), p. 3; Andrew Hull and David Markov, "Trends in the Arms Market" part 2, *Jane's Intelligence Review,* 1 May 1997, p. 232.

74. *SAWR,* vol. 5, no.2 (summer 1994), p. 29.

75. "A Network of Islamic Terrorism Traced to a Pakistan University," *New York Times,* 20 March 1995, p. A1, A4.

76. "Israeli Weapons Find Way to Bosnia's Serbs," *Xinhua News Agency,* 21 January 1995 (Lexis-Nexis).

77. Israel sold thirty thousand rounds of mortar ammunition to India to replenish stocks used fighting Islamic dissidents in Kashmir. (Rahul Bedi, "India Finalising $50m Contract for Ammunition," *Jane's Defence Weekly,* 9 June 1999, p. 8.)

78. "Israel to Allow Arms Sales to Jordan, Newspaper Says," *Deutsche Presse-Agentur,* 18 October 1999 (Lexis-Nexis).

79. Kurds speak an Indo-European language and, although Muslim, are not considered Arabs.

80. Steve Rodan, "Israeli Firms Sold Arms to Iran till '93," *Jerusalem Post,* 12 September 1997, p. 1.

81. "Israeli Firm to Sell Arms to Jordan," *Xinhua News Agency,* 18 October 1999 (Lexis-Nexis).

82. Raymond Bonner, "Despite Cutoff by U.S., Ethiopia and Eritrea Easily Buy Weapons," *New York Times,* 23 July 1995, p. A10.

83. In the late 1970s, during the war between Ethiopia and Somalia, Israel's assistance to Ethiopia was funneled through a trading company based in Ethiopia headed by an Israeli ex-colonel. "Ethiopia 'Relies on Israel for Arms,'" *Jane's Defence Weekly,* 26 January 1985, p. 124; in 1999, aid was reported to be directly related to an agreement between the two governments to exchange arms for the release of a small community of Jews from Kuwara in northern Ethiopia. Israel agreed to provide ammunition, missiles, and to upgrade Ethiopia's old Russian MiG fighters. ("Strange Swap in Ethiopia," *Foreign Report,* no. 2549 [June 24, 1999], pp. 1–2.)

84. "Strange Swap in Ethiopia," pp. 1–2; "Iran Advances Pawns in Red Sea," *Middle East Data Project, Inc., The Iran Brief,* 6 May 1996 (Lexis-Nexis).

85. Aaron Karp defines the gray market as "those officially approved arms exports from governments which do not want to be associated with their actions. Grey deals need not be illegal, only covert or unacknowledged." In contrast he defines the black market as secret deals "consisting mostly of small transactions that violate the laws of the nation from which they originate." [*SIPRI Yearbook* 1988, pp. 190–192.]

86. *SAWR,* vol. 6, no. 4 (winter 1995–1996), p. 34.

87. "Israeli Weapons Find Way to Bosnia's Serbs," *Xinhua News Agency,* 21 January 1995 (Lexis-Nexis).

88. *SAWR* (summer 1994), p. 26.

89. "Some Hamas Money Comes from U.S., But Its Importance Questioned," *Associated Press,* 20 October 1994 (Lexis-Nexis).

90. Perlez, "U.S. Weighs Using Food as Support," pp. A1 and A10; Jane Perlez, "In a War, Even Food Aid Can Kill," *New York Times,* 4 December 1999, section 4, p. 3.

91. Robert A. Pape, "Why Economic Sanctions Still Don't Work," *International Security,* vol. 22, no. 2 (fall 1997), p. 90.

92. Richard N. Haass, *Economic Sanctions and American Diplomacy* (New York: Council on Foreign Relations, 1998.) See also Margaret Doxey, "United Nations Sanctions: Lessons of Experience," paper presented at the International Studies Association annual convention, Washington, D.C., February 1999.

93. Gary Hufbauer and Jeffrey Schott, "Economic Sanctions: A Volatile Foreign Policy Tool," *Transatlantic Perspectives,* no. 8, (May 1983), p. 7.

94. Gary Clyde Hufbauer, Jeffrey J. Schott, and Kimberley Ann Elliot, *Economic Sanctions Reconsidered,* 2d ed. (Washington, DC, Institute for International Economics, 1990), pp. xii-xvi.

95. See, for example, Pape, "Why Economic Sanctions Still Don't Work"; Doxey, "United Nations Sanctions"; Haass, *Economic Sanctions and American Diplomacy;* Dianne E. Rennack and Robert D. Shuey, "Economic Sanctions to Achieve U.S. Foreign Policy Goals: Discussion and Guide to Current Law," Foreign Affairs and National Defense Division, Congressional Research Service, 20 October 1997, <http://205.177.54.21/Sanction.htm>; and Manfred Kulessa and Dorothee

Starck, "Peace through Sanctions?" BICC (Bonn International Center for Conversion) Policy Paper no. 7, Development and Peace Foundation/Stiftung Entwicklung und Frieden (SEF), December 1997, <http://bicc.uni-bonn.de/sef/events/1998/sanct/epd.html>.

96. Richard N. Haass believes that the increased strength of single-issue constituencies in American politics is also responsible for the popularity of sanctions in U.S. government circles. (Haass, *Economic Sanctions and American Diplomacy,* p. 2.)

97. Doxey, *United Nations Sanctions,* p. 3.

98. The following mix of sanctions were applied to: Iraq, Haiti, and Serbia Montenegro (Yugoslavia)—comprehensive trade, financial, and transportation restrictions; Libya—arms embargo, a limited assets freeze and a ban on air links; Sudan—diplomatic sanctions; the UNITA movement in Angola—arms embargo, travel restrictions, freeze of funds affecting senior officials and their families, limited import and export bans on territory under its control; Rwanda–arms embargo; Somalia—arms embargo; Liberia—arms embargo; Sierra Leone—arms embargo, oil embargo, and travel restrictions. (As of 1999, sanctions had been lifted against Kuwait, Haiti, and the government of Sierra Leone. All others were still in force.) Doxey, *United Nations Sanctions,* pp. 3–4.

99. *SIPRI YEARBOOK* 1999, table 11.5: "International Arms Embargoes in Effect, 1994–98," p. 437.

100. Libya, for example, was subjected to a UN arms embargo in 1992 because of its refusal to extradite suspects accused of destroying the Pan Am flight 103 plane over Lockerbie, Scotland. In addition to Libya, full or partial arms embargoes were applied to: Afghanistan, Angola (UNITA), Armenia, Azerbaijan, Bosnia and Herzegovina, Burundi, China, Croatia, Haiti (lifted 1994), Iraq, Liberia, Myanmar, Nigeria, Rwanda (lifted 1995), Rwanda rebels, Sierra Leone, Sierra Leone rebels, Slovenia (lifted 1998), Somalia, South Africa, Sudan, Yugoslavia, and Zaire. (*SIPRI YEARBOOK* [1999], table 11.5, p. 437.)

101. Cited in Rennack and Shuey, *Economic Sanctions to Achieving U.S. Foreign Policy Goals.*

102. The President's Export Council, "Unilateral Economic Sanctions: A Review of Existing Sanctions and Their Impacts on U.S. Economic Interests with Recommendations for Policy and Process Improvement," June 1997, pp. 12–13 and appendix I. <http://www.usaengage.org/studies/unilat1.html> (16 February 2000).

103. Cited in James A. Paul and Senwan Akhtar, "Sanctions: An Analysis," *Global Policy Forum paper,* 13 August 1998, <http://globalpolicy.org/security/sanction/analysis2.htm> (16 September 1999).

104. See Pape, "Why Economic Sanctions Still Don't Work," pp. 90–92, for an excellent discussion of the arguments and their advocates.

105. Questions about the utility of sanctions were also raised during the Cold War when U.S. arms sales to Latin America were restricted by the Carter administration's policy of linking human rights to U.S. military and economic aid. A RAND study maintained that the policy invoked a "double standard" since important recipients, such as Iran, were treated to "undue consideration" despite human rights violations, while several Latin America governments had their U.S. security assistance cut off on these grounds. (Lewis H. Diuguid, "U.S. Arms Aid, Rights Link Called Uneven," *Washington Post,* 18 December 1977, p. A13.)

106. See Paul and Akhtar, "Sanctions: An Analysis"; Doxey, "United Nations Sanctions"; Haass, *Economic Sanctions and American Diplomacy";* Kulessa and Starck; Richard Garfield, "The Impact of Economic Sanctions on Health and Well-being," Relief and Rehabilitation Network, Overseas Development Institute, November 1999, <http://www. oneworld.org/odi>.

107. Until 1996, the Bosnian Serbs had many more tanks, armored vehicles, and guns than those of the army of Bosnia-Herzegovina and the Croatian Defense Council together. (Fran Visnar, "After Large Deliveries of U.S. Weapons, Bosniaks Are Becoming the Dominant Military Power in Bosnia-Herzegovina," *Zagreb Vjesnik* [in Serbo-Croatian], 5 November 1997, p. 3 (FBIS-EEU-97–314).

108. "Iranian radio: OIC contact group final declaration says arms embargo 'invalid,'" Voice of Islamic Republic of Iran Network 1 (Teheran, in Persian), 22 July 1995 in BBC Summary of World Broadcasts, 24 July 1995 (Lexis-Nexis).

109. "Foreign Ministry Opposes Yugoslavia Embargo Violations," *Moscow INTERFAX* (in English), 5 July 1994 (FBIS-SOV-94–129).

110. "UNPROFOR Sells Weapons," *Defense and Foreign Affairs Strategic Policy,* vol. 22, no. 11–12 (November-December 1994), p. 1.

111. Ibid., p. 5.
112. Ibid. "Arms allegedly sold illegally to Republic of Herzegovina," BBC Summary of World Broadcasts (Source: 'Clarin' web site, Buenos Aires, in Spanish, 2 October 1998), 7 October 1998 (Lexis-Nexis).
113. "UNPROFOR Sells Weapons," p. 5.
114. Ibid.
115. "Croatia's Arms Revealed," *Jane's Defence Weekly,* 5 October 1991, p. 599; *SIPRI YEARBOOK* 1999, pp. 438, 497–314
116. "U.S. Ends Arms Embargo," *Facts on File World News Digest,* 1 March 1975 (Lexis-Nexis).
117. "ANC Radio on de Klerk's U.S. Visit, 'Sanctions Must Remain,'" Radio Freedom (Dar es Salaam, in English), 25 September 1990, in BBC Summary of World Broadcasts, 27 September 1990 (Lexis-Nexis).
118. "Sudan: Rebel Leaders Call for Economic Sanctions Against Khartoum," Inter Press Service, 21 September 1994 (Lexis-Nexis).
119. "EU Lifts Ban on Arms to Syria, Irking Israel," *Christian Science Monitor,* 1 December 1994.
120. Farhan Haq, "Rwanda: UN Ambassador Decries Arms Embargo," Inter Press Service, 2 August 1995 (Lexis-Nexis). Raymond Bonner, "How Minority Tutsi Won the War," *New York Times,* 6 September 1994, p. 6.
121. Edward J. Lawrence, "Light Weapons and Intrastate Conflict," Carnegie Commission on Preventing Deadly Conflict, 1998, p. 20. <http://www.ccpdc.org/pubs/weapons/weapons.htm>.
122. "Security Council Terminates Arms Embargo against Sierra Leone," *Africa News,* 8 June 1998 (Lexis-Nexis); Jerome Hule, "Nigerian Envoy Seeks UN Support for Sierra Leone," *Africa News,* 31 December 1998 (Lexis-Nexis).
123. "Liberia Says Guinea Provides Artillery Shielding for Rebels," Xinhua News Agency, 17 August 1999 (Lexis-Nexis); Desmond Davies, "Liberia Launches Offensive against UN Arms Embargo," Pan-African News Agency, 23 August 1999, <http://www.africanews.org/PANA/index.html>.
124. Hule, "Nigerian Envoy Seeks UN Support."
125. Davies, "Liberia Launches Offensive."
126. Visnar, "After Large Deliveries of U.S. Weapons," p. 3.
127. For a detailed analysis of the constraints facing small and medium-size arms producers, see Richard Bitzinger, "Problems and Prospects Facing Second-Tier Arms-Producing States in the Post–Cold War Era: A Comparative Assessment," paper presented to the Study Group on the Arms Trade and the Transnationalization of the Defense Industry: Economic versus Security Drivers, Council on Foreign Relations, New York, 15 December 2000.
128. Arms embargoes were imposed on Israel many times: after the 1948 war by the U.S., Britain, and France; during the 1967 war by France. During the 1973 war the threat of sanctions by the U.S., upon whom Israel was dependent for resupply, forced the Israeli government to change its war strategy and later increase its arms production capability. "The result was disastrous for the IDF (Israel Defense Forces)." ("Coping with Supplier Control: The Israeli Experience," in *The Dilemma of Third World Defense Industries: Supplier Control or Recipient Autonomy?* ed. Kwang-il Baek, Ronald D. McLaurin, and Chung-in Moon, Pacific and World Studies Series, no. 3 [Republic of Korea: Inha University, Center for International Studies, 1989], pp. 137–151.) For a history of these and other embargoes and restrictions, see pp. 138–141.
129. Drew Middleton, "Israeli Arms: A Top Expert [sic] Military Analysis," *New York Times,* 15 March 1981, pp. A1, 9.
130. Quoted in Scott B. Lasensky, "Friendly Restraint: U.S.-Israel Relations during the Gulf Crisis of 1990–1991," *MERIA Journal,* vol. 3, no, 2 (June 1999), p. 24. In this article Lasensky provides a detailed analysis of U.S.-Israeli interaction and the positive and coercive measures used by the United States to achieve its goals during the Gulf War (pp. 24–35).
131. Thomas W. Graham, "India," in *Arms Production in Developing Countries: An Analysis of Decision Making,* ed. James Everett Katz (Lexington, MA: Lexington Books, 1984), p. 157; Raju G. C. Thomas, "Strategies of Recipient Autonomy: The Case of India," in *The Dilemma of Third World Defense Industries,* pp. 186., 191–199
132. Sanders, *Arms Industries: New Suppliers and Regional Security* (Washington, DC: National Defense University, 1990), p. 20.
133. "New 'Source' for Defence Supplies Lauded," *The Nation* (Islamabad), 22 April 1995, p. 6 (FBIS-NES-95–078).

134. The main products include: automatic rifles; light, medium and heavy machine guns; a complete range of mortar and tank ammunition and antitank ammunition; bombs; grenades; land mines; pyrotechnics and signal stores. "New 'Source' for Defence Supplies Lauded," p. 6; Shahwar Junaid, "Defence Equipment in 'Buyer's Market' Viewed," *The Nation* (Islamabad), 15 May 1996, p. 6 (FBIS-NES-96–096); "Pakistan Ordnance Factories," *The News* (Islamabad), 24 November 1999, p. 17 (FBIS-NES-1999–1125).

135. "Self-sufficiency" was defined as: "The local ability to conceptualize products and systems in order to satisfy local requirements, and then to develop and produce these without direct assistance from abroad." (Republic of South Africa, Department of Defense, *White Paper on Defense and Armaments Supply* [1982], p. 26, quoted in Ewan Anderson, "South Africa," in *Arms Production in Developing Countries*, p. 334.)

136. Sanders, *Arms Industries,* p. 70. The oil embargo apparently had a similar effect on the South African government's policy. It stimulated a major domestic synthetic fuels program as well as the construction of additional nuclear power plants. Economist David Gold observes, "As with the arms embargo, it stimulated some technical advances but also raised domestic energy costs and, in my view, contributed to a weakening of the economy," private communication, 30 January 2001.

137. "Iran Boosts Domestic Arms Industry," *International Defense Review,* (April 1994), p. 72.

138. Di Giovanna and Markusen, "From Defense to Development in the 1990s," p. 10.

139. Garrity, "Why the Gulf War Still Matters," p. 10.

140. Ibid., p. 10.

141. Ammunition-manufacturing facilities are being closed down, phased out, or merged in many developed countries. If this continues, the foreign market for these items will expand beyond the demand created by local wars. Advanced industrial countries reportedly intend to acquire ammunition from cheaper foreign sources and by so doing eliminate the expense of maintaining factories that never run to capacity in peacetime anyway." Munitions Firms Remain under Fire," *Jane's Defence Weekly,* 17 December 1994, pp. 27–28.

142. Brzoska, "Economic Factors Shaping Arms Production," p. 143.

143. "International Small Arms Usage and Research and Development Trends: The Executive Summary," *SAWR* (April 1993), p. 11. Namibia's first arms and ammunition plant, for example, began operating in late 1992.

144. Junaid, "Defense Equipment," p. 6.

145. *SIPRI YEARBOOK* 1994, p. 497; *International Security Digest,* vol. 1, no.2 (December 1993), p. 2.

146. John Pomfret, "Serbia Seeks to Rebuild Yugoslav Arms Industry," *Washington Post,* 18 September 1993, p. A15.

147. SAWR (fall 1994–winter 1995), p. 38.

148. Robert Fox, "Iran And Sudan Sending Weapons to Bosnian Army," *Daily Telegraph,* 16 November 1994, p. 13.

149. "Global Industry: Counterfeit Armaments," *The Economist,* 30 June 1997, <htttp://viewswire/display_article.asp?doc_id=E110768>.

150. "Africa/U.S.: Fact Sheet on Arms Flows to Central Africa/Great Lakes." Kenya's Eldoret ammunition factory has an annual production capability of 20 million 7.62 NATO-standard rounds of ammunition. Sudan's Military Industry Corporation manufactures ammunition, land mines, and small arms. Uganda's National Enterprise in Nakasongola makes ammunition, small arms, and, possibly, landmines.

151. Second-tier producers manufacture a range of advanced weapons at or near the "technological frontier" and are able to adapt them to market needs but rarely are able to innovate themselves. These are largely European states that remain dependent on the R&D and innovations of first-tier producers for state-of-the-art technologies. Third-tier producers, found in some parts of Eastern Europe and the Third World, copy and reproduce existing military systems through the transfer of design and technological know-how, often through licenses. Arms production is confined to a few weapon systems, rather than spread across-the-board, and the ability to innovate or adapt them is very limited. First-tier producers are able to innovate at the technological frontier and have an across-the-board research, design, and manufacturing capability. (Keith Krause, *Arms and the State: Patterns of Military Production and Trade* [Cambridge, UK: Cambridge University Press, 1992], pp. 31, 82.) During the Cold War, this tier was limited to the U.S. and the Soviet Union. Today, only the U.S. has that capability.

152. Junaid, "Defense Equipment," p. 6.

153. Garrity, "Why the Gulf War Still Matters," pp. 9–11.

154. We use the traditional definition of "mercenary": "one that serves merely for wages; especially a soldier hired into foreign service." (Merriam-Webster Collegiate Dictionary, 10th edition [1993]; Oxford English Dictionary, 2nd edition [1989].) Although other motivations may be involved, the receipt of pay is generally regarded as a prerequisite for the appellation "mercenary." Blackburn, for example, argues that Korean, Philippine, and Thai troops qualify as mercenaries because they fought in South Vietnam based on an agreement that they and their governments were to be remunerated by the U.S. for their services. Robert M. Blackburn, *Mercenaries and Lyndon Johnson's "More Flags": The Hiring of Korean, Filipino and Thai Soldiers in the Vietnam War* (Jefferson, NC: McFarland, 1994), p. 145ff.

155. *Daily Telegraph,* November 1994, cited in *International Security Digest,* vol. 2, no.2 (November 1994), p. 3.

156. "Philippine newspaper says Bin Laden continues to support rebel group," *Deutsche Presse-Agentur,* 13 February 1999; "Algeria accuses bin Laden of financing Islamic terrorists," *Deutsche Presse-Agentur,* 8 October 1999 (Lexis-Nexis). See note 49.

157. *SAWR,* (summer 1994), p. 26.

158. "Tamils in Canada fund Sri Lanka's rebels," *Xinhua News Agency,* 18 June 1998 (Lexis-Nexis).

159. *SAWR* (summer 1994), p. 33.

160. *SAWR* (April 1993), p. 41.

161. *SAWR* (December 1993), p. 27. Other sources report that the government of Afghan prime minister Gulbuddin Hekmatyar in 1993 supplied men and weapons to Muslim separatists fighting India. ("The Military-Industrial Complex Strikes Back," *Baltimore Sun,* 26 August 1993, p. 21.)

162. John F. Burns, "A Network of Islamic Terrorism Traced to a Pakistan University," *New York Times,* 20 March 1995, p. A8.

163. "Report on the question of the use of mercenaries as a means of violating human rights and impeding the exercise of the right of peoples to self-determination, submitted by Mr. Enrique Bernales Ballesteros, Special Rapporteur, pursuant to Commission resolution 1998/6" (New York: UN Economic and Social Council, Commission on Human Rights, 55th session, E/CN.4/1999/11, 13 January 1999), p. 4.

164. Ibid., p. 5.

165. The eighteenth century army was multinational. Foreigners comprised at least 25 percent and as much as 60 percent of these regular standing armies. Switzerland was a regular supplier of mercenary soldiers but was the only state not to employ them. In Europe, the last state to raise an army of foreigners was Britain in 1854 when it hired German, Italian, and Swiss mercenaries to fight in the Crimean War. Janice E. Thomson, "State Practices, International Norms, and the Decline of Mercenarism," *International Studies Quarterly,* vol. 34 (1990), pp. 24–25.

166. The French Foreign Legion was created in 1831 after instability in Europe brought refugees, revolutionaries, and army deserters flooding into France. A Foreign Legion recruited from this group was organized to fight with the French army in distant places. Recruits were promised French citizenship after five years service—a reward that still exists today. Numbering thirty-six thousand in the early 1960s, the Legion was composed of men from a hundred different countries. After World War II, 60 percent were Germans. With the end of the Cold War, Eastern Europeans became the majority. Around 5 percent of Legionnaires are British. During the 1970s, the Legion was most active in former French protectorates. In the 1980s, the Legion saw service in Lebanon and Afghanistan. A slimmed down Legion, downsized to eighty-five hundred in the 1990s, has seen action in Rwanda, Somalia, Bosnia, and the Central African Republic.

167. The Gurkhas, recruited from Nepal, have served with the British Army since 1814. Once numbering sixteen thousand, they were downsized to thirty-eight hundred by 1999. Since the end of World War II, the Gurkhas have served for Britain in Malaya, Brunei, Belize, the Falklands, the 1990–1991 Gulf War, Hong Kong, and Kosovo.

168. Thomson, "State Practices, International Norms," p. 27. Thomson includes here the U.S. allies during the Vietnam War who were paid "a per capita fee" for the use of their troops: Thailand, the Philippines, Korea. See also Blackburn, note. 154, above.

169. "Report on the question," p. 8.

170. Thomson, "State Practices, International Norms," p. 29.

171. More than four hundred thousand Cuban soldiers and technical advisers were stationed in Angola and Namibia between 1975 and 1991. The last Cuban soldier returned from Angola on 25 May 1991. ("Last Cuban Ships Return from Angola," Associated Press, 13 June 1991 [Lexis-Nexis].)

172. "Report on the question," pp. 3–7; "An Assessment of the Mercenary Issue at the Fifty-Fifth Session of the UN Commission on Human Rights: Executive Summary and Main Recommendations," *International Alert,* May 1999, <dilly@international-alert.org> (16 June 1999).

173. David Isenberg, "Soldiers of Fortune Ltd: Profile of Today's Private Sector Corporate Mercenary Firms" (Washington, DC: Center for Defense Information, Summer 1997), p. 4.

174. Ibid., p. 5.

175. Colin Nickerson, "Dogs of War: Different Breed of Mercenaries Let Loose on Africa," *Gazette* (Montreal), 6 November 1999 (Lexis-Nexis).

176. Governments hiring private military corporations also reject the term "mercenary as irrelevant." Prime Minister Sir Julius Chan of Papua New Guinea responding to outside pressures to abandon his plan to hire Executive Outcomes complained: "Why . . . do we have to contend with international scrutiny of a training operation?" ("Australia Toughens Line against Papua New Guinea Mercenary Plans," *Deutsche Presse-Agentur,* 25 February 1997 [Lexus-Nexis].) A former paratrooper, now employed by one of the companies, said: "We're politically correct alternatives to the old-style mercenaries. We don't overthrow governments. We don't do combat operations. We do training and security." (Nickerson, "Dogs of War".)

177. David Shearer, "Outsourcing War," *Foreign Policy* (fall 1998), p. 5.<http://www.csulb.edu/~bbruins/shearer1.html>.

178. Doug Brooks, <Hoosier84@aol.com> "Private Military Companies," <H-DIPLO@H-NET.MSU.EDU> (15 December 1999).

179. "Report on the question," pp. 17–19, 20.

180. See note 154, above.

181. Doug Brooks believes that the UN High Commission for Refugees used private security companies to protect their staff and to provide security in refugee camps, specifically the camps bordering Rwanda. (Brooks, "Private Military Companies.")

182. Nickerson, "Dogs of War."

183. David Shearer, "Private Armies and Military Intervention," Adelphi Paper no. 316 (London: International Institute for Strategic Studies, 1998), p. 37. According to a UN report, Executive Outcomes used equipment purchased from companies in South Africa and various European countries. It included airplanes, helicopters, and aerial photography aircraft. ("Report on the question," p. 21).

184. Tim Spicer, an ex-British Army colonel who heads Sandline is quoted in Nickerson, "Dogs of War."

185. For the Convention to enter into force, twenty-two parties to it are necessary. As of January 2000, the twenty-one parties to the International Convention against the Recruitment, Use, Financing, and Training of Mercenaries, adopted 4 December 1989, are: Azerbaijan, Barbados, Belarus, Cameroon, Croatia, Cyprus, Georgia, Italy, Libya, Maldives, Mauritania, Qatar, Saudi Arabia, Senegal, Seychelles, Suriname, Togo, Turkemenistan, Ukraine, Uruguay, Uzbekistan. (*Commission on Human Rights,* <http://www.un.org/ENGLISH/bible/englishinternetbible/part1/chapter XVIII/treaty6.asp>.

186. Quoted in Shearer, "Private Armies," p. 39.

187. Brooks, "Private Military Companies."

188. Shearer, "Private Armies," p. 46.

189. Ibid.

190. Al J. Ventner, "Mercenaries Fuel Next Round in Angolan Civil War," *Jane's International Defence Review,* March 1996, cited in Isenberg, "Soldiers of Fortune, Ltd," p. 6; Shearer, "Private Armies," p. 65.

191. Shearer, pp. 46–48; "Army, Angola," *Jane's Sentinel Security Assessment,* posted 5 September 2000. <http://www.janesonline.com>.

192. "Angola: Government Pushes UNITA to Edge of Country," *Africa News,* 21 December 1999 (Lexis-Nexis).

193. UN Document S/2000/203, "Letter Dated 10 March 2000 from the Chairman of the Security Council Committee Established Pursuant to Resolution 864 (1993) Concerning the Situation

in Angola Addressed to the President of the Security Council," 10 March 2000, <http://www.un.org/News/dh/latest/angolareport_eng.htm>.

194. EO was supported by Nigerian aircraft and artillery present in the country as part of the ECO-MOG force. (Shearer, "Private Armies," p. 54.)

195. Shearer, "Private Armies," p. 49.

196. "Report on the question," p. 8.

197. Shearer, "Private Armies," p.51.

198. Brooks, "Private Military Companies."

199. "The Future Role of Private Military Companies in Africa," *Oxford Analytica,* 4 October 1999, cited in Tom Kamara, "Sierra Leone: A Search for Peace Against Odds," WriteNet Paper no. 21/1999 (January 2000), <http://www.unchr.ch/refworld/country/wn21_99.htm>.

200. Unlike EO, Sandline claims it only contracts with governments. (Brooks, "Private Military Companies.")

201. "Report on the question," p. 9.

202. Brooks, "Private Military Companies."

203. Ibid.

204. *SIPRI YEARBOOK* 1998, p. 19."Report on the question," p. 9.

205. "Irin-WA update 605," *UN IRIN-West Africa,* 30 November 1999, <irin-wa@irin.ci>.

206. See www.mpri.com.

207. Shearer, "Private Armies," p.58.

208. Yves Goulet, "MPRI: Washington's Freelance Advisors," *Jane's Intelligence Review,* July 1998, p. 38.

209. Ibid., p. 39.

210. Roger Charles, a retired marine lieutenant colonel and military researcher, quoted in Ken Silverstein, "Privatizing War," *The Nation,* 28 July–4 August 1997, <http://www.thenation.com> (16 February 1999).

211. Kolinda Graba, "Serbs' Departure from Croatia Cannot Be Compared to Kosovo," *The Ottawa Citizen,* 9 August 1999 (Lexis-Nexis).

212. Goulet, "MPRI," p. 39.

213. Ibid., p. 40.

214. Statement by Assistant Secretary Marc Grossman, "The U.S. Stake in Europe," Congressional Budget Justification for Foreign Operations, Fiscal Year 2001, released by the Office of the Secretary of State, Resources, Plans, and Policy, Department of State, 15 March 2000.

215. EO is believed not to have fielded more than four hundred men at any given time (Brooks, "Private Military Companies"). MPRI allegedly had a maximum of fifteen instructors in Croatia at any one time. (See table 7.6.)

216. Shearer, "Private Armies," p. 36.

217. Brooks, "Private Military Companies."

218. Goulet, "MPRI," p. 38.

219. Ibid., p. 40.

220. See page 293, above.

221. Silverstein, "Privatizing War."

222. Ibid., p. 63.

223. See Thomas K. Adams, "The New Mercenaries and the Privatization of Conflict," *Parameters* (summer 1999), pp. 103–116.

224. *SAWR* (summer 1994), p. 29.

225. R. T. Naylor, "The Structure and Operation of the Modern Arms Black Market," in *Lethal Commerce: The Global Trade in Small Arms and Light Weapons* (Cambridge, MA: Committee on International Studies, American Academy of Arts and Sciences, 1995), p. 48.

226. Greg Mills, "Small Arms Control and Southern Africa," *Defence Analysis,* vol. 9, no. 3 (1993), p. 348; Swadesh Rana, "Small Arms and Intra-State Conflicts," unpublished paper, Centre for Disarmament Affairs, United Nations, New York, January 1995), p. 7.

227. Aaron Karp, "The Rise of the Black and Gray Market," in Robert E. Harkavy and Stephanie G. Neuman, special eds., *The Arms Trade: Problems and Prospects in the Post–Cold War World,* The Annals of the American Academy of Political and Social Science, vol. 535, September 1994, p. 184.

228. *SAWR* (April 1993), p. 45.

229. Karp, "The Rise of the Black and Gray Market," p. 184. "Arms Flows to Central Africa/Great Lakes," Bureau of Intelligence and Research, November 1999.

230. For example, middlemen from Singapore arranged for the shipment to Yangon (Rangoon) of $1.5 million (U.S.) worth of 120mm and 81mm mortars manufactured in Portugal, thus evading and violating the European Community's arms embargo on Myanmar. ("Myanmar's Chinese Connection," p. 25.)

231. "The Primary Tools of Violence," *Japan Times,* 25 November 1999 (Lexis-Nexis).

232. M. Urban, *War in Afghanistan* (Basingstoke, UK: Macmillan, 1990), p. 187, cited by Chris Smith, "Light Weapons and Ethnic Conflict in South Asia," in *Lethal Commerce,* p. 66.

233. Rana, "Small Arms and Intra-State Conflicts," p. 7.

234. *SAWR* (April 1993), p. 41. See also Smith," Light Weapons and Ethnic Conflict," pp. 64–65.

235. Smith, "Light Weapons and Ethnic Conflict," p. 66.

236. "Article Surveys Market for Light Weapons," *Nation,* 13 September 1994, pp. 1,6 (FBIS-NES-94–178).

237. Rana, "Small Arms and Intra-State Conflicts," p. 8.

238. Smith, "Light Weapons and Ethnic Conflict," p. 71. Jasjit Singh, director of the Institute for Defense Studies and Analyses in New Delhi, India, estimates that thousands of weapons were recovered in the Kashmir Valley between 1990 and 1994, including fifteen thousand Kalashnikov rifles and fifteen hundred machine guns. (Personal communication to author, 29 March 1995).

239. *SAWR* (April 1993), p. 37.

240. Rana, "Small Arms and Intra-State Conflicts," p. 7.

241. Ibid., p. 21.

242. *SAWR* (December 1993): 22.

243. Ibid., p. 23.

244. Roger Cohen, "Arms Trafficking to Bosnia Goes On Despite Embargo," *New York Times,* 5 November 1994, p. A1.

245. Steve Gboggan and Kim Sengupta, "KLA Weapons on Sale in Britain, *Independent* (London), 16 August 1999 (Nexis-Lexis).

246. "Croatia Tells UN Troop Accord Ends," *New York Times,* 13 January 1995, p. A3; "Croatia Is Set to End Mandate of UN Force on Its Territory," *New York Times,* 12 January 1995, p. A4.

247. "France Presses Plan for Rwanda Mission," *Washington Post,* 20 June 1994, p. 9.

248. "ECOMOG Sold Weapons to Rebels—Arnold Quainoo," *Africa News Service,* 20 January 1999 (Lexis-Nexis).

249. Betts, "The Delusion of Impartial Intervention," p. 30.

250. See, for example, Adam Roberts, "Humanitarian Action in War," Adelphi Paper no. 305 (London: International Institute for Strategic Studies, 1996).

251. The empirical evidence gives some support for this argument, particularly for civil wars where compromise between the belligerents has proven almost impossible to reach. Most have been resolved by force. Barbara Walter finds that while 66 percent of international wars since 1800 ended in negotiation, only 24 percent of civil wars ended with a compromise settlement. "Instead, most civil wars ended with the extermination, expulsion or capitulation of the losing party." Barbara F. Walter, *The Resolution of Civil Wars: Why Negotiations Fail"* (Ph.D. diss., University of Chicago, December 1994), p. 1. See also Paul Pillar, *Negotiating Peace: War Termination as a Bargaining Process* (Princeton: Princeton University Press, c.1983); Stephen John Stedman, *Peacemaking in Civil Wars: International Mediation in Zimbabwe, 1974–1980* (Boulder, CO: Lynne Rienner, 1991); Roy Licklider, *Stopping the Killing: How Civil Wars End* (New York: New York University Press, 1993.)

252. Edward N. Luttwak, "Give War a Chance," *Foreign Affairs,* vol. 78, no. 4 (July/August 1999), pp. 36, 44.

253. Roberts, "Humanitarian Action in War," p. 37.

254. Ken Menkaus and John Prendergast, "Political Economy of Post-Intervention Somalia," Somalia Task Force Issue Paper no. 3, April 1995), p. 15, quoted in David Keen, "The Economic Functions of Violence in Civil Wars," Adelphi Paper, no. 320 (London: International Institute for Strategic Studies, 1998), p. 61.

255. Betts, "The Delusion of Impartial Imperialism," p. 24.

256. Perlez, "In a War, Even Food Aid Can Kill," section 4. p. 3.

257. African Rights, "Somalia: Operation Restore Hope," p. 3.

258. Joan M. Lewis, "Making History in Somalia: Humanitarian Intervention in a Stateless Society," *Horn of Africa,* vol. 15 (December 1997), p. 15.

259. "The Gun Running Sequel in Africa," *Times of Zambia,* distributed by Africa News Online, 21 August 1999 <http://www.africanews.org>.

260. African Rights, "Somalia: Operation Restore Hope," pp. 49–50.

261. David Keen, "The Economic Functions of Violence in Civil War," Adelphi Paper, no. 320 (London: International Institute for Strategic Studies, 1998), p. 59.

262. "Uganda: ADF Threaten To Attack Aid Convoys," in IRIN-CEA Update 826 for the Great Lakes, United Nations Office for the Coordination of Humanitarian Affairs, Integrated Regional Information Network for Central and Eastern Africa, 20 December 1999, <irin@ocha.unon.org>.

263. Keen, "The Economic Functions of Violence," p. 59.

264. Perlez, "U.S. Weighs Using Food as Support," p. 10.

265. "Saudi Arms Market Wanes," *Defense News,* 10–16 January 1994, p. 1.

266. David Keen ("The Economic Functions of Violence") argues that as a war progresses, often economic motives take precedence over political/military goals and war itself becomes an activity that benefits both sides in a conflict.

267. *Angola: Arms Trade and Violations of the Laws of War Since the 1992 Elections* (Leverett, MA: Rector Press, 1994), p. 39.

268. "Zimbabwe: Soldier to Market Diamonds, Gold," *Southern Africa: IRIN News Briefs,* 23 September 1999, <IRIN-SA@irin.org.za>.

269. Ibid.

270. Naylor, "The Structure and Operation," p. 53.

271. Bertil Lintner, "Cambodia—A Political and Military Overview," *Jane's Intelligence Review,* October 1994, p. 470.

272. Naylor, "The Structure and Operation," p. 53.

273. "Foreign Arms Sales To Rwanda Made Slaughter Easier," *Washington Times,* 21 April 1994, p. 13.

274. U.S. covert aid to UNITA during the Cold War totaled about $250 million between 1986–1991. *Angola: Arms Trade and Violations,* pp. 3–4, 59.

275. "UNITA makes full use of the 'arms-for-diamonds' trade," *Saferworld Arms Bulletin,* no. 13, 18 June 1999, <sworld2@gnapc.org>.

276. "Traffickers in Colombia Stalking U.S. Copters," *New York Times,* 27 March 1993, p. A5.

277. Douglas Farah, "Colombia Rebels Tap E. Europe for Arms; Guerillas Fire Power Superior to Army's," *Washington Post,* 4 November 1999 (Lexis-Nexis).

278. Ibid.

279. *Christian Science Monitor,* cited in *SAWR* (summer 1994), p. 31.

280. Keen, "The Economic Functions of Violence," p. 42.

281. Ibid., p. 41.

282. *SAWR* (April 1993), p. 43.

283. *SAWR* (summer 1994), pp. 34–5.

284. Roger Boyes, "Drug Money Linked to KLA," *Gazette* (Montreal), 24 March 1999 (Lexis-Nexis).

Conclusions

1. For an updated discussion of MTR/RMA at the end of the 1990s, in the context of American defense budget allocations, see Cindy Williams and Jennifer M. Lind, "Can We Afford a Revolution in Military Affairs?" *Breakthroughs,* vol. 8, no.1 (spring 1997), pp. 3–8.

2. Robert E. Harkavy, "Arms Resupply *During* Conflict: A Framework for Analysis," *Jerusalem Journal of International Relations,* vol. 7, no.3 (1985), pp. 5–41.

3. These matters are discussed in historical context in Brian Bond, *The Pursuit of Victory from Napoleon to Saddam Hussein* (Oxford: Oxford University Press, 1996).

4. John Mueller, "The Search for the 'Breaking Point' in Vietnam: The Statistics of a Deadly Quarrel," *International Studies Quarterly,* vol. 24, no. 4 (December 1980), pp. 497–579.

5. John Sislin and Frederic Pearson, "Arms and the Outbreak of Ethnopolitical Violence," paper delivered at the meeting of International Studies Association, 17–21 March 1998, Minneapolis, Minnesota.

6. Michael J. Mazaar, Don M. Snider, and James A. Blackwell, Jr., *Desert Storm: The Cold War and What We Learned* (Boulder, CO: Westview Press, 1993).

7. Joseph Alpher, ed., *War in the Gulf: Implications for Israel* (Boulder CO: Westview Press, 1992), report of a Jaffee Center Study Group.

8. A summary of the conclusions of these studies is in Patrick J. Garrity, "Why the Gulf War Still Matters: Foreign Perspectives on the War and the Future of International Security," Center for National Security Studies, Los Alamos National Laboratory, New Mexico, report no. 16, July 1993.

9. Ibid., pp. 87–90, under "The Outlines of an Asymmetric Strategy."

10. Schuyler Foerster, "Clients and Conflicts: Soviet Perspectives on the Limited Wars of 1982," in James Brown and William P. Snyder, eds., *The Regionalization of Warfare* (New Brunswick, NJ: Transaction Books, 1985), chapter 10, pp. 229–230.

11. This question arises from a reading of Saad el Shazly, *The Crossing of the Suez* (San Francisco: American Mideast Research, 1980).

12. James P. Thomas, "Indian Military Lessons Learned from the Gulf War," unpublished report for the Center for National Security Studies, Los Alamos National Laboratory, New Mexico, 1993.

13. This concept of "triangular" deterrence is developed in Robert E. Harkavy, "Triangular or Indirect Deterrence/Compellence," *Comparative Strategy*, vol.17.1 (January-March 1998), pp. 63–81.

14. Martin van Creveld, *Military Lessons of the Yom Kippur War: Historical Perspectives* (Beverly Hills, CA: Sage, 1975), Washington Papers no. 3.

15. Roger A. Beaumont, "Guideposts or Guesses? Is the 'Lessons of War' Concept Valid?" in James Brown and William P. Snyder, eds., *The Regionalization of Warfare* (New Brunswick, NJ: Transaction Books, 1985), chapter 11 (p. 250).

16. Edgar O'Ballance, *The Gulf War* (London: Brassey's, 1988), esp. pp. 162–163.

INDEX